The fifteen years of the GATT between the conclusion of the Tokyo Round in 1979 and the finalization of the Uruguay Round in 1994 witnessed a sea-change in attitudes toward the role of international trade in developing countries. Encouraged by the manifest success of the outward-oriented economies of East Asia, many developing countries began to undertake radical liberalizations of their trade regimes. The shift in orientation toward relatively open trading systems was reflected in the attitudes and participation of developing countries in the Uruguay Round. They involved themselves fully in formulating the rules of the new trading system, and also made significant offers both in the conventional area of reducing tariff protection on manufactures trade, and in the "new" areas, such as trade in services, trade in agriculture, and trade-related intellectual property.

This volume provides an assessment of the economic impact of the Uruguay Round of the GATT on the developing countries. The authors, all leading international trade economists, examine all aspects of the agreement and conclude that the cuts in protection should strengthen the world trading system and result in increases in real incomes in developing countries.

The Uruguay Round and
the developing countries

The Uruguay Round and the developing countries

Edited by

WILL MARTIN
The World Bank

and

L. ALAN WINTERS
The World Bank

Published by the Press Syndicate of the University of Cambridge
The Pitt Building, Trumpington Street, Cambridge CB2 1RP
40 West 20th Street, New York, NY 10011–4211, USA
10 Stamford Road, Oakleigh, Melbourne 3166, Australia

First published 1996

Printed in Great Britain at the University Press, Cambridge

A catalogue record for this book is available from the British Library

Library of Congress cataloguing in publication data

The Uruguay Round and the developing countries / edited by Will Martin
and L. Alan Winters.
    p.   cm.
  ISBN 0 521 57235 5 (hardcover)
  1. Free trade – Developing countries. 2. Developing countries –
Commercial policy. 3. Uruguay Round (1987–1994) I. Martin, Will.
II. Winters, L. Alan.
HF1717.D44U78 1996
382′.71′091724–dc20 96-10872 CIP

ISBN 0 521 57235 5 hardback
ISBN 0 521 58601 1 paperback

Contents

Contributors

Marcelo de Paiva Abreu
Catholic University, Rio de
Janeiro, Brazil

Kym Anderson
University of Adelaide, Australia

Richard Blackhurst
World Trade Organization and
Graduate Institute of International
Studies, Geneva

Drusilla K. Brown
Tufts University

Alan V. Deardorff
University of Michigan

Betina Dimaranan
Purdue University

Alice Enders
World Trade Organization

J. Michael Finger
The World Bank

Alan K. Fox
University of Michigan

Joseph F. Francois
World Trade Organization

Ian Goldin
The World Bank and European
Bank for Reconstruction and
Development

Glenn W. Harrison
University of South Carolina

Dale E. Hathaway
National Center for Food and
Agricultural Policy

Thomas Hertel
Purdue University

Bernard Hoekman
The World Bank

Merlinda D. Ingco
The World Bank

Patrick Low
The World Bank and World Trade
Organization

Bradley McDonald
World Trade Organization

Will Martin
The World Bank

Håkan Nordström
World Trade Organization

Carlos A. Primo Braga
The World Bank

Thomas F. Rutherford
University of Colorado

Robert M. Stern
University of Michigan

Arvind Subramanian
International Monetary Fund

David G. Tarr
The World Bank

Dominique van der Mensbrugghe
Organization for Economic
Cooperation and Development

L. Alan Winters
The World Bank

John Whalley
University of Western Ontario,
Canada

Koji Yanagishima
The World Bank and University of
Missouri

Foreword

For much of the post-war era most developing countries have excluded themselves from full participation in the global economy. Gradually, this situation has been changing, with developing countries becoming increasingly integrated into world commerce. The Uruguay Round was a milestone on this journey. In fact, its completion marks the end of the beginning of this critical process: as a result of the Round, developing countries will now operate in the world economy on more or less the same terms as industrial countries.

Developing countries as a group have shown much higher growth rates of output, employment, and trade than industrial countries in recent years, and have become increasingly important markets both for industrial countries and for each other. In multilateral trade rounds prior to the Uruguay Round, they focused their attention on obtaining preferential access to industrial country markets; few of them participated actively in the core business of the negotiations – the exchange of market access concessions.

The fifteen years between the conclusion of the Tokyo Round in 1979 and the finalization of the Uruguay Round in 1994 saw a dramatic change in attitudes towards the role of international trade in developing countries. Encouraged by the manifest success of the outward-oriented economies of East Asia, many developing countries turned away from earlier views about the necessity for import substitution. Slowly at first, but rapidly by the late 1980s, developing countries began to undertake radical liberalizations of their trade regimes.

This change of heart was also reflected in the attitudes and participation of developing countries in the Uruguay Round. Many of them were active participants throughout the Round, while others increased their participation as the Round evolved. A World Bank publication, *The Uruguay Round: A Handbook for the Multilateral Trade Negotiations*, designed as a guide to developing countries participating in the Round, became a best seller. Not only did developing countries participate in formulating the rules of the new trading system; they also made offers both in the conventional area of reducing tariff protection on manufactures trade, and in the "new" areas, such as services, agriculture, and trade-related intellectual property rights (TRIPS).

The number of signatories to the GATT has expanded dramatically – from 91 in 1986 to 128 in April 1996, with a further 28 countries formally seeking accession to the World Trade Organization (WTO). The developing countries are much more heavily represented in the WTO, created as a consequence of the Round, than they were in the GATT, which initiated the Round.

Given the importance of the Uruguay Round for developing countries, the World Bank organized a conference on "The Uruguay Round and the Developing Economies" in Washington DC, January 26–27, 1995. It was attended by 350 economists from thirty-nine countries and included papers by authors from the World Bank, the World Trade Organization, the International Monetary Fund, and universities worldwide. This volume contains revised and updated versions of the papers presented at the conference.

The Bank's conference was the first featuring analyses based entirely on the actual commitments recorded in the country schedules appended to the Uruguay Round agreement, rather than on general statements of intent to liberalize. It also featured an unusually large number of papers quantifying the implications of the Round agreement based on these analyses. While no numerical estimates can be expected to be precisely right, the combination of quantitative and qualitative analysis contained in this volume offers a thorough assessment of the implications of the Round for developing countries.

The next fifteen years promises to be at least as dramatic as the past fifteen for the developing countries and for the world trading system with which their fortunes are now so closely intertwined. The papers in this volume are intended both for policy makers and the analysts on whom they rely. These papers will provide them with valuable insights into the trading system and perspectives on the new and interesting problems which are certain to emerge.

Michael Bruno
Senior Vice President and Chief Economist
The World Bank

Acknowledgments

This book could not have been prepared without the assistance of a large number of friends and colleagues. We and the authors benefited substantially from the insightful comments made by the participants at the conference on "The Uruguay Round and the Developing Economies" held at the World Bank, January 26–27, 1995. We would particularly like to thank the Discussants at the conference: Louis Emerij, J. Michael Finger, Brian Hindley, Robert Hudec, Ravi Kanbur, Anne Krueger, Michael Leidy, Alex McCalla, Arvind Panagariya, David Richardson, David Robertson, Sherman Robinson, Jeffrey Schott, and Alberto Valdés. Thanks are due to the staff of the International Trade Division of the World Bank, all of whom contributed very substantially and enthusiastically, either directly as participants or in myriad other ways. Many people also contributed by providing comments on drafts of the introductory chapter, including: Masood Ahmed, Christian Bach, Jagdish Bhagwati, Michael Bruno, Hugh Corbet, Alice Enders, J. M. Finger, Naheed Kirmani, Sarwar Lateef, Peter Lloyd, Patrick Low, Alex McCalla, Costas Michalopoulos, Håkan Nordström, Sheila Page, Sarath Rajapatirana, David Robertson, Marcelo Selowsky, Richard Snape, and T. N. Srinivasan. We thank them all.

We would also like to express our gratitude to the Research Advisory Staff of the World Bank who provided many suggestions that contributed to the success of this program of research, and the financial support that made it possible.

We are extremely grateful for the exceptional job done by Nellie Artis in ensuring that the conference went off smoothly, and to her colleagues in the International Trade Division who helped with various aspects of the conference and preparing typescripts: Aban Daruwala, K. Anna Kim, Audrey Kitson-Walters, Sarah Lipscomb, Leo Oteyza, and Minerva Pateña. Particular thanks go to Jeff Hayden for managing the editorial process from initial rough typescripts through to the complete final document. Thanks also to Bruce Ross-Larson for the challenging production editing task and to Linda Randall of Cambridge University Press for the final copy edit.

Abbreviations

ACP	Africa, Caribbean, and Pacific
APEC	Asia-Pacific Economic Cooperation
ASEAN	Association of Southeast Asian Nations
ATC	Agreement on Textiles and Clothing of the WTO
CCCN	Customs Cooperation Council Nomenclature
CES	constant elasticity of substition
CFCs	chlorofluorocarbons
CGE	computable general equilibrium
CITES	Convention on International Trade in Endangered Species
CRTS	constant returns to scale
DFI	Direct Foreign Investment
EFTA	European Free Trade Association
FDI	foreign direct investment
GATS	General Agreement on Trade in Services
GATT	General Agreement on Tariffs and Trade
GDP	gross domestic product
GNP	gross national product
GPA	Government Procurement Agreement
GTAP	Global Trade Analysis Project
HS	Harmonized System
IDB	Integrated Database
IPRs	intellectual property rights
IRTS	increasing returns to scale
ISIC	International Standard Industrial Classification
MFA	Multifibre Arrangement
MFN	most-favored nation
NAFTA	North American Free Trade Agreement
OECD	Organization for Economic Cooperation and Development
OEEC	Organization for European Economic Cooperation
PSE	producer subsidy equivalent

RCA	revealed comparative advantage
RUNS	Rural–Urban North–South model
TFP	total factor productivity
TPRM	Trade Policy Review Mechanism
TRIMs	trade-related investment measures
TRIPS	trade-related intellectual property rights
UNCED	United Nations Conference on Environment and Development
UNCTAD	United Nations Conference on Trade and Development
UPOV	Union for the Protection of Plant Varieties
VERs	voluntary export restraints
WIPO	World Intellectual Property Organization
WTO	World Trade Organization

1 The Uruguay Round: a milestone for the developing countries

Will Martin and L. Alan Winters

The Uruguay Round was an important milestone for developing countries in their integration into the global economy. As a group, developing countries have shown much higher growth rates of output, employment, and trade than industrial countries in recent years, and have become increasingly important markets for industrial countries and for each other. There has also been a sea-change in attitudes towards trade and investment in many developing countries, with the success of a number of outward-oriented economies in East Asia leading to much greater interest in trade liberalization and export expansion.

In the seven previous GATT rounds of multilateral trade negotiations, developing countries focused most of their attention on obtaining preferential access to industrial country markets; few of them participated actively in the core business of the negotiations – the exchange of market access concessions. By contrast, many developing countries were very active participants in the Uruguay Round both individually and in coalitions with industrial countries. Not only did they participate in formulating new rules for the world trading system, but they also made important market access offers in the conventional area of reducing tariff protection on manufactures trade and in areas, such as trade in services and trade in agricultural products, that were new to the trade liberalizing process. Many developing countries had undertaken substantial liberalization outside the Round after the mid-1980s, and their commitments at the end of the Round allowed them to lock-in at least part of their gains from this liberalization.

This book presents the outcome of a major program of research on the implications of the Round, culminating in a conference in January 1995. This chapter presents a brief overview of the research and an introduction to the chapters that follow. Among the chapter's key conclusions are:

The agriculture agreement was important for developing a set of rules as a basis for future liberalization, but actual liberalization was limited by the way that nontariff barriers were converted into tariffs.

1

This slippage, however, reduces the risk of adverse effects on net food-importing countries.

Substantial liberalization was achieved in manufactures trade, both in the area of tariffs and through the phaseout of nontariff barriers such as VERs and the quotas imposed under the MFA.

Cuts in protection on merchandise trade are estimated to increase real incomes in developing countries by between US $60 and 100 billion at 1992 prices despite the cautious commitments made by many developing countries.

GATS is a landmark in terms of creating trade disciplines in virgin territory, but achieved little in terms of immediate liberalization.

The TRIPS agreement will increase the protection of IPRs worldwide – but may entail short-term costs for developing countries.

The establishment of the WTO, with its responsibilities for goods, services and intellectual property, stronger dispute settlement procedures, permanent policy review mechanism, and greater ministerial involvement, is necessary for the successful implementation of the Round, and seems likely to contribute to a much-needed strengthening of the trading system.

In terms of policy implications for developing countries we find that:

The countries that liberalize their own trade policies are predicted to be the greatest gainers.

The WTO agreement provides legally binding minimum standards for reform and liberalization, not economically optimal ones. Weak disciplines on antidumping, and the high tariff bindings chosen by many countries, allow very costly protection measures to be maintained or introduced.

There remain substantial gains from liberalization beyond that undertaken in the Round – particularly in areas such as agriculture and services, where multilateral disciplines are new.

Over the next few years, developing country members of the WTO will need to participate in critical decisions on the future of the trading system, including whether or not to include labor and environmental standards, and investment and competition policies.

Agricultural liberalization

Prior to the Round, the multilateral trading rules for agriculture were largely ineffective, with a plethora of nontariff barriers providing high and variable rates of protection, both in industrial and in developing countries. Export subsidies were a particular source of discord, with competitive export subsidies by the European Union and the United States depressing and destabilizing world prices. Farmers in developing countries have been adversely affected by depressed and highly variable world prices, and the disposal of surpluses by industrial countries.

New rules for agricultural trade

A major achievement was the agreement to convert virtually all agricultural nontariff barriers into tariffs subject to agreed maximum rates (so-called tariff bindings). This important advance provides transparency and stability in protection rates which were previously opaque and highly volatile. At one stroke, the agreement on agriculture leapt beyond what had been achieved in forty-five years of negotiations in manufactures: bindings were introduced immediately on almost 100 percent of agricultural tariff lines.

In some cases, tariff bindings were set below the rate of protection previously applied, and hence will require tariff reductions. Unfortunately, however, many others were set above the previously applied tariff equivalents, as discussed by Dale Hathaway and Merlinda Ingco in chapter 2 and documented by Ingco (forthcoming). By reducing the very high rates of protection that occur from time to time, even these bindings reduce average levels of protection, and they reduce the average cost of protection even more sharply because the high rates of protection ruled out by bindings are the most costly. Francois and Martin (1995) provide a number of examples where tariff bindings set above the prevailing average rate of protection substantially reduce the expected costs of protection to the importing country.

While not outlawing export subsidies, the export subsidy rules introduce some disciplines into an area where the general GATT principle of banning these subsidies had not been applied. The new rules prohibit the introduction of new export subsidies and require that industrial countries reduce their existing export subsidies.

The new rules on total agricultural support go beyond the general GATT rules by imposing some restraint on domestic support, with the total value of internal and border support to be reduced by 20 percent from its level in the 1986–88 base period. However, the disciplines on domestic support are weakened by the exemption of many important forms of support, such as the direct payments linked to land retirement programs in industrial countries and general programs of assistance to encourage rural development in developing countries. There is no requirement to make reductions in support for individual commodities, so assistance to some commodities may increase if reductions occur elsewhere.

Minimum market access conditions were introduced in addition to disciplines on border and domestic protection. These provide specified levels of access at favorable tariff rates (tariff quotas) to ensure that market access will not be reduced even if the tariffs introduced following the Round are more restrictive than the measures previously applying. There is, of course, a risk that such measures might generate a constituency in support of the agricultural protection which makes the tariff quotas valuable. Many of these tariff quotas have been used to replace the market access which was previously provided under preference schemes such as the European Union's arrangements for ACP countries; in only a few cases, such as Japanese rice, do these arrangements provide additional market access opportunities.

Liberalization will be less than the tariff cuts

As Dale Hathaway and Merlinda Ingco demonstrate in chapter 2, the agreement on agriculture involved substantial cuts in import tariffs on agricultural products. In industrial countries, protection is to be cut by an average of 36 percent over six years. Developing countries committed themselves to reductions of 24 percent over a ten-year period, and only least-developed countries were exempted from reduction commitments. The effectiveness of the agriculture agreement in cutting protection was less impressive than these cuts would suggest, however, because the cuts took place from base levels that were frequently inflated. Increases in the base level of protection occurred in three ways: through the choice of base period, the methods used to measure the protection existing prior to the Round, and the use of "ceiling" bindings in developing countries.

Where nontariff barriers were used previously, the amount of assistance provided by the pre-Round protection regime typically varied from year to year and it was necessary to calculate the tariff which would have had the same effects as the actual protection provided in some base period. The base period chosen was 1986–88, a period of very low world prices and generally high rates of agricultural protection. The use of these years permitted a significant increase in protection relative to actual levels either in recent years or over the longer run. Moreover, in many industrial countries, a process of "dirty tariffication" occurred, whereby the tariff bindings agreed between the negotiating parties permit substantially higher rates of protection than those in the base period.

For industrial countries, the agreed tariff rates frequently incorporate two steps up from average rates prevailing before the Round: one from the choice of the 1986–88 base year, and one from the way the tariff equivalents of nontariff barriers were calculated. The agreed reductions in protection take place from the resulting high levels. Figure 1.1 illustrates this pattern of "two steps up and one step down" for wheat import protection in the European Union.

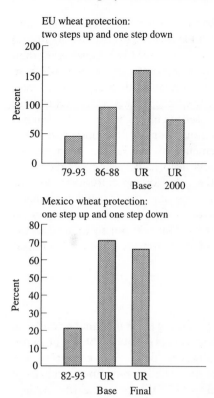

Figure 1.1   Two examples of Uruguay Round agricultural protection settings
Source: Ingco forthcoming.

Developing countries were allowed to convert unbound tariffs into "ceiling bindings" unrelated to previous rates of protection, and many countries chose to use this freedom to set rates well above those that previously applied. In developing countries utilizing the ceiling binding option, a pattern of "one step up and one step down" is evident, with final tariff bindings frequently above the average rates of protection prevailing prior to the Round. In the lower part of figure 1.1, this pattern is illustrated for Mexican wheat imports.

The effect for industrial and developing countries is broadly the same: the tariff bindings resulting from the Round are frequently now higher than the average rates of protection prior to the implementation of the Round. If countries choose to use their freedom to set high tariffs, the costs to their economies could be very large.

The "slippage" in the agriculture agreement resulting from the setting of high tariff rates and from weak disciplines on domestic support greatly restricts the gains generated by the Round. In chapter 6, Ian Goldin and Dominique van der Mensbrugghe conclude that the gains from the Round would have been over two and a half times greater ($137 billion, rather than $48 billion) had the agreed cuts in agricultural protection been made from the levels prevailing prior to the Round, rather than from inflated levels, and had the cuts in domestic support not been weakened by exemptions. Further, the wide discretion allowed for setting tariffs below the tariff bindings reduces the gains from increased transparency of the trade regime.

The disappointing overall achievements of the Round in increasing market access for agricultural products need to be weighed against the major progress made in improving the rules for agricultural trade. The introduction of virtually universal tariff bindings is a signal achievement. Much of the slippage during the Round occurred during the one-off process of converting nontariff barriers to tariffs. This will not recur, and so the Uruguay Round has provided the foundation for more extensive liberalization in future rounds.

Manufactures trade liberalization

A comprehensive framework of rules governing trade in manufactures had been developed in earlier rounds of negotiations. Two key items of unfinished business were extending disciplines to developing countries, and dealing with the "gray area" measures which had sprung up as a means of circumventing the disciplines imposed by GATT rules and tariff bindings. These measures included VERs imposed on a wide range of industrial products from developing countries, and the export quotas imposed on textiles and clothing under the MFA.

Significant tariff reductions

In chapter 5, Richard Blackhurst, Alice Enders, and Joseph Francois estimate that tariffs on manufactures imports into industrial countries were reduced by an average of around 40 percent, from a trade-weighted average of 6.3 percent to 3.8 percent, with the reductions to be phased in over a five-year period. Tariff reductions under the Round were not uniform across commodities, but were the outcome of a series of bilateral negotiations whose results were subsequently extended to all Round participants.

The proportion of industrial countries' imports of industrial products subject to bindings rose from 94 to 99 percent; in developing countries, it rose from 13 to 61 percent. Clearly, developing countries made very substantial progress with their tariff bindings and reductions, but a great deal more remains to be done.

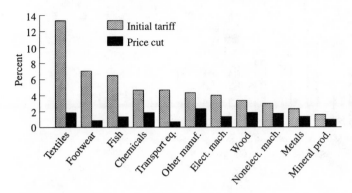

Figure 1.2   Initial tariffs and price reductions for industrial countries' imports from developing countries
Source: chapter 3.

Because of differences in the mix of products supplied, the magnitude of the tariff cuts varied considerably between suppliers. In chapter 3, Marcelo Abreu estimates that in industrial countries tariffs on imports from other industrial countries were reduced by an average of 40 percent, while those on imports from developing countries were reduced by only 28 percent. In developing countries, he estimates that the reductions in tariff rates on manufactures averaged 25 percent on products imported from industrial countries, and 21 percent on products imported from developing countries.

If the average cut in tariff rates achieved in the Uruguay Round had been applied uniformly, it would have had the economically desirable feature of implying a larger reduction in the tariff-inclusive price of more highly protected goods. In figure 1.2, we compare such price declines on industrial countries' imports of manufactures from developing countries against the initial tariff rates applying to these goods. It appears that there was only a very weak relationship between the initial rate of protection and the price reduction achieved. Importantly for developing countries, the two sectors with the highest tariffs (textiles and clothing, and footwear) experienced smaller price reductions than those achieved in other sectors.

The relationship between the initial tariff and the depth of the resulting price cut is presented for developing country imports from industrial countries in figure 1.3. Here, there is little evidence of a consistent relationship between the initial tariff level and the reduction in the price of imported goods. Comparing figures 1.2 and 1.3, however, makes it clear that the average depth of the tariff-induced price cuts resulting from the Round was greater in developing countries than in the industrial countries. While the

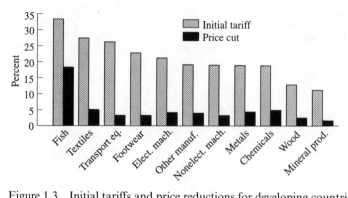

Figure 1.3   Initial tariffs and price reductions for developing countries' imports from industrial countries
Source: chapter 3.

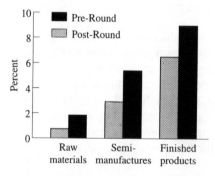

Figure 1.4   Tariff escalation in industrial countries remains, but at lower levels
Source: GATT 1994.

proportional tariff cuts were smaller in developing countries, the price cuts are larger because they were applied to higher initial tariffs.

Tariff escalation in industrial country markets, where tariff rates increase with the stage of processing, is a long-standing concern of developing countries because it discourages processing of raw material exports. Tariff cuts under the Round reduced the absolute degree of tariff escalation on imports of manufactures, although some escalation clearly remains in the post-Round tariff.

Nontariff barriers

A key feature of the Round was the substantial progress made in dealing with the nontariff barriers that have proliferated in recent decades. Perhaps the most important nontariff barriers affecting developing countries have been VERs, which are prohibited and must be phased out within four years, and the MFA, which is to be phased out over a ten-year period.

The abolition of the MFA can be expected to generate considerable benefits not just to exporting countries but, perhaps foremost, to the importing countries that imposed this peculiar and perverse form of protection. The MFA imposes three sets of costs on the importing economies by: introducing inefficiencies into production and consumption patterns; distorting the pattern of import sourcing; and creating quota rents that importers must pay in order to obtain supplies from developing country producers. Developing countries as a whole can also be expected to gain from the abolition of the MFA, as they increase their exports into the major industrial country markets, benefit from increased prices in other markets, and eliminate the distortions associated with quota allocation and administration.

Continuing industrial restructuring is inevitable in a dynamic world economy, with particular sectors rising and falling in response to changes in factor endowments and the pattern of consumer demand. The MFA has retarded the movement of the clothing sector from industrial to developing countries by imposing increasing burdens on the latter's exports of textiles and clothing. In recent years, it has also delayed the relocation of the industry between developing country suppliers, as economies such as those of Hong Kong, Taiwan (China), and the Republic of Korea lose their competitive edge in labor-intensive products to lower-wage countries.

VERs, like the MFA, violated the spirit of two of the most fundamental principles of the GATT, the prohibition on quantitative restrictions and the MFN principle. To operate, these protection measures obtained the compliance of exporters by giving them the opportunity to retain some of the artificial scarcity rents they created. These measures were of doubtful legality under the GATT. The Uruguay Round agreement removes any ambiguity, prohibiting VERs and measures with a similar effect. Since the protectionist pressures that gave rise to these measures will remain strong, however, outlawing them is likely to increase the pressures for other forms of contingent protection, such as antidumping and safeguards.

Abolition of the MFA will require particular attention, since the quotas will be phased out progressively according to schedules determined by the importers, with virtually half of the quotas, and typically the quotas on the most sensitive items, remaining in place (albeit growing at accelerated rates) until the tenth year. Strong political pressures for delay are likely to emerge, which are unlikely to be successfully resisted unless they are met by determined governments bolstered by a strong World Trade Organization (WTO).

Table 1.1 *Estimates of the annual benefits of Uruguay Round trade liberalization*

		Increase in real income[a]		
Model/variant	Year	World	Industrial[b]	Developing[b]
WTO (Francois, McDonald, Nordström)				
Static, perfect competition	1992	40	27	13
		(0.17)	(0.16)	(0.30)
Static, imperfect competition	1992	99	40	59
		(0.44)	(0.23)	(1.23)
Induced investment, imperfect condition	1992	214	90	125
		(0.94)	(0.5)	(2.6)
BANK (Harrison, Rutherford, Tarr)				
Static, perfect competition	1992	93	75	18
		(0.40)	(0.41)	(0.38)
Static, imperfect competition	1992	96	77	19
		(0.42)	(0.42)	(0.42)
Induced investment, imperfect competition	1992	171	115	55
		(0.74)	(0.61)	(1.20)
GTAP (Hertel, Martin, Yanagishima, and Dimaranan)				
Liberalization in projection to 2005, perfect competition	2005	258	172	86
		(0.89)	(0.72)	(1.56)

[a] Billions of US dollars at 1992 prices (percentages of GDP in parentheses).
[b] Definitions of developing countries differ slightly between models.

Gains from goods market liberalization

The Uruguay Round agreements on merchandise trade are expected to generate substantial welfare gains because they result in sizable reductions in protection on manufactures, and because the relatively small reductions in agricultural protection occur in a highly protected sector where there is potential for very sizable efficiency gains. The evaluation of these gains is a complex task and we have approached it by drawing on three independently conducted studies. Summary results from these studies are presented in table 1.1.

The results in table 1.1 focus purely on the trade liberalization brought about under the Round, without attempting to evaluate the benefits from improvements in the rules governing merchandise trade, or of earlier uni-lateral liberalizations. Because data are not available, none of these studies takes into account the impact of Uruguay Round tariff cuts on the value of tariff preferences extended to developing countries. This omission seems unlikely to have a major impact on the results since, in most cases, the preference margins on manufactured goods and on resource-based products were typically very small even prior to the Uruguay Round (see Page and Davenport 1995; and Harrold 1995). In agriculture, the preference margins provided by the European Union under the Lomé Convention were frequently larger, but erosion of these preferences will be limited because of the very limited extent of agricultural liberalization under the Round. Further, as Blackhurst, Enders, and Francois point out, the volumes of many of the imports subject to preferential access were expanded and made more secure as a result of the Round.

In their initial base run, where they assumed a perfectly competitive world economy, the WTO modeling team (Joseph Francois, Brad McDonald, and Håkan Nordström, chapter 9) estimated the gains from merchandise trade liberalization to be $40 billion per year if implemented in the world economy in 1992. Where products were differentiated by firm and production was subject to imperfect competition, the estimated welfare gains more than doubled, to $99 billion. When induced increases in the capital stock were also incorporated, the gains rose to $214 billion, or 0.94 percent of global income. A striking feature of their results is that the gains accruing to the developing economies, particularly as a share of GDP, exceed those to industrial countries.

The analysis provided by Glenn Harrison, Thomas Rutherford, and David Tarr in chapter 8 uses the same data on manufactures tariff cuts as Francois, McDonald, and Nordström, but, in agriculture, uses price-based measures of liberalization provided by Ingco (forthcoming) rather than focusing on the effects of the market access guarantees provided under the Round. This difference, together with an assumption that the products of different countries are closer substitutes than assumed by the WTO team, contributes to a considerably higher estimate of the welfare gains – $93 billion in the static, perfect competition case. Allowing for increasing returns to scale at the level of the firm, via rationalization of firm costs rather than changes in variety, resulted in virtually no increase in the estimated income gains. Moving to their preferred steady-state version of the model, in which the capital stock adjusts to keep the return on capital constant, causes the estimated income gains to rise to $171 billion, or 0.74 percent of global GDP. Roughly one third of this gain accrues to countries classified by the World Bank as developing.

A third set of estimates is provided in chapter 7 by Thomas Hertel, Will Martin, Koji Yanagishima, and Betina Dimaranan. Their study focuses on the structure of the world economy at the end of the implementation period, which tends to increase the estimated gains because the world economy is larger and, in the absence of the Round, more distorted in 2005 than in 1992. Average global distortions rise because the baseline projection involves both more rapid growth in developing countries, where current average protection rates are higher, and increased restrictiveness of the MFA because export quota growth fails to keep up with the growth and international relocation of demand and supply. In this context, the estimated welfare gain resulting from the Round is $258 billion in 1992 prices (or 0.9 percent of GDP in 2005), even in the absence of economies of scale or Round-induced capital accumulation. The gains to the developing countries are much larger as a share of GDP (1.6 percent) than in industrial countries (0.7 percent).

The distribution of gains by region

While international trade negotiations typically emphasize the exchange of concessions, and market liberalization is frequently viewed as a cost to be incurred in order to gain market access, most of the gains from trade liberalization arise as a consequence of countries' own liberalization. In particular, the efficiency gains resulting from market opening are a benefit that accrues directly to the country undertaking liberalization. There may be benefits to the country's trading partners if its import expansion is large enough to improve the exporter's terms of trade. However, terms-of-trade changes are inherently a zero-sum game, while efficiency gains are a positive-sum game where all countries can potentially gain.

All of the models provide estimates of the gains from trade liberalization by region. All suggest that the largest gains accrue to the countries/regions that committed themselves to relatively rigorous liberalization, especially under the MFA. Abolition of the MFA also clearly benefits the relatively efficient textile and clothing exporters.

The most regionally disaggregated results are provided by Harrison, Rutherford, and Tarr (chapter 8, table 8.7). They suggest that East Asian WTO members such as Indonesia, Malaysia, Korea, and Thailand will be proportionately among the largest gainers from the Round. These countries have committed themselves to relatively rigorous liberalization in both agriculture and in manufactures, and tend to be relatively competitive and highly restricted exporters of textiles and clothing. The South Asia region is also estimated to benefit substantially, for much the same reasons. China, Hong Kong, and Taiwan (China) have in common the fact that they undertook essentially no liberalization. China and Taiwan (China) are not yet WTO members, while Hong Kong had essentially no protection to remove. The small benefits that accrue to this non-liberalizing region arise from the abolition of the MFA,[1] and from improved market access.

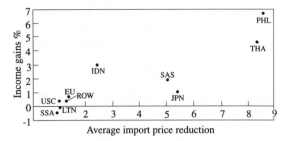

Figure 1.5   Cuts in border protection and welfare gains from
the Uruguay Round[2]
Source: chapter 7.

Most other developing countries are estimated to experience worthwhile welfare gains from the Round. Significant gains are estimated for the Latin American countries, primarily from their liberalization of manufactures and agriculture. This region tends to be less competitive in the production of textiles and apparel, and hence to gain less from the abolition of the MFA. The Middle East and North Africa, and the economies in transition, seem likely to experience small gains relative to GDP, primarily because they undertook very few commitments to liberalize under the Round; indeed, many of these countries are not yet members of the WTO.

The estimated loss to Sub-Saharan Africa reflects a number of factors, including: the region's lack of liberalization; increases in world prices for some foods; and increases in the prices of imported textile and apparel products, which highly efficient MFA-restricted exporters currently divert away from the MFA import markets and are forced to sell at low prices. An offsetting long-run advantage to Africa, not captured in these welfare estimates, is that the abolition of the MFA takes away the sword of Damocles hanging over any efficient new exporter of textiles and clothing.

Among the industrial countries, the largest percentage gains in welfare and in real wages occurred in New Zealand and Australia, which took greater advantage of the opportunity provided by the Round to lock-in their reductions in protection. The gains to Japan and to the European Union were larger as a share of GDP than in the United States and Canada because Japan and the European Union had much higher levels of agricultural protection and, despite their initial reluctance, began the process of liberalizing this protection. The European Union and the United States also benefit greatly from the abolition of the MFA.

The relationship between the depth of a region's cuts in protection and its percentage gains in welfare is shown in figure 1.5. The measure of liberalization is very crude – a simple average of the reduction in the post-tariff prices of agricultural and manufactures imports – and does not account for vitally important features of the Uruguay Round agreement such as the abolition of the MFA. Further, the simple partial relationship depicted here omits other important features such as the height of the remaining tariff, and the importance of trade in the economy. Despite this, it is clear that the regions with the larger reductions in import prices are generally predicted to achieve larger welfare gains.

Terms-of-trade effects of agricultural liberalization

A particular concern raised by some developing countries was the possibility of adverse terms-of-trade effects resulting from agricultural trade liberalization. The high agricultural protection provided by many industrial countries was depressing world prices of many temperate agricultural products both by restricting access to importing markets, and by generating surpluses that had to be disposed of on world markets with the help of export subsidies. Reductions in agricultural support will benefit countries that reduce their own distortions and those that are net exporters of the products whose world prices rise. However, net importers of goods whose prices rise may be hurt.[3]

The very limited degree of agricultural liberalization reached under the Uruguay Round has one fortunate side effect – it implies that the adverse terms-of-trade effects imposed by the Uruguay Round are much smaller than had previously been expected. Goldin and van der Mensbrugghe conclude that the Round will cause the world prices of most major agricultural commodities to rise by less than 2 percent, and some actually to fall, relative to the average price of OECD exports of manufactures. While the prices of commodities such as sugar and beef are projected to increase substantially from 1993 levels, it is clear from figure 1.6 that the Uruguay Round is only a very small contributing factor.

Gains and losses from abolishing the MFA

The largest gains from the abolition of the MFA accrue to the industrial country importers who created it. These countries will benefit for three reasons: sourcing their imports more efficiently, rationalizing their own production and consumption decisions, and ceasing to pay the cost of MFA quotas in their import prices.

Harrison, Rutherford, and Tarr estimate the long-run gains of abolishing the MFA at $8 billion per year for the European Union and $9 billion for the United States, while Francois, McDonald, and Nordström estimate the joint effects of abolishing the MFA and of reducing tariffs on textiles and

Price changes 1993–2002, with and without the Round

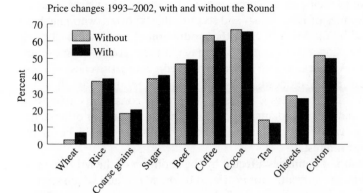

Figure 1.6   The Uruguay Round is projected to have only minor impacts on world food prices
Sources: chapter 6; World Bank 1995.

clothing to be $18 billion and $23 billion respectively. After allowing for worsening of the MFA distortions up to 2005, Hertel, Martin, Yanagishima, and Dimaranan estimate the gains to the European Union at $28 billion (in 1992 prices) and to the United States and Canada at $29 billion, even without allowing for scale effects or investment of the gains from the Round.

Whether developing country exporters gain or lose from the MFA is a more complex question. Exporters who are severely restricted by quotas clearly stand to gain. Under the MFA, they must dispose of their overquota exports on unrestricted third markets where prices are lower, and divert some of their productive resources into other activities where returns are lower. The MFA imposes a range of additional costs on exporters, many of which are difficult to quantify; a good deal of the value of the quota rents is probably lost because the systems for quota allocation create incentives for rent seeking, or because the rent is shared with importers (Trela and Whalley 1995; Krishna, Erzan, and Tan 1994).

Relatively new, and tightly restricted, exporters of textiles and clothing such as China, the Southeast Asian exporters, and the more competitive South Asian exporters, also seem likely to gain from the abolition of the MFA – for example, $2 billion per year for each of China and ASEAN (see chapter 4). These gains reflect their ability to expand exports strongly when markets are freed, and would be even larger if the hard-to-measure costs of quota allocation and rent sharing were taken into account.

Two groups of exporters are likely to suffer losses from the abolition of the MFA. First, those countries whose historically determined quotas are large relative to their current comparative advantage – the newly industrializing economies of East Asia – and second, the exporters who may have been induced by the MFA to enter the production of textiles and clothing without possessing a comparative advantage in these goods – some countries in Latin America. Where the constraints on competitiveness of these industries are policy-induced, sustained domestic reform may allow the development of a competitive industry. Where the constraints arise from the country having a fundamental comparative advantage in other activities, then a transfer of resources to other industries would be in the country's best interest.

A final group of countries affected by the abolition of the MFA is those whose imports are currently not restricted by the MFA, and which serve as the residual market for constrained developing country exporters. These regions, including Japan in apparel and Sub-Saharan Africa in textiles, currently gain from the availability of low-cost exports diverted from the restricted markets. When the restrictions are eliminated, they will face higher import prices. While able to gain in the short run from continuation of the MFA, the developing countries in this group need to weigh these gains against the negative implications of the MFA-distorted market structure for the longer-term development of a competitive and efficient industry of their own.

Contingent protection and trade-related investment measures

The GATT includes several mechanisms through which a country can suspend the market access it has previously granted. As discussed by Michael Finger in chapter 11, these discretionary measures include safeguards, antidumping, and countervailing actions, and balance-of-payments actions. These measures are inter-related, as protectionist pressures will flow to the relief valve that most readily allows the erection of trade barriers.

TRIMs distort trade by imposing a range of performance requirements on multinational enterprises. As emphasized by Patrick Low and Arvind Subramanian in chapter 13, the TRIMs discussions covered a wide range of measures to deal with these policies, including a perceived need for competition policies to regulate the behavior of multinational firms, but yielded an agreement focused narrowly on the trade effects of TRIMs.

Safeguard actions

The key achievement of the safeguards agreement was its requirement to notify and abolish VERs and similar mechanisms. These managed-trade measures adversely affected the expansion of developing country exports and undermined the overall credibility of the trading system.

Prior to the Round, GATT safeguards could only be applied on an MFN basis and were subject to a range of conditions including a requirement to notify the GATT Secretariat, and to consult with principal suppliers. When safeguards were introduced, the principal suppliers had a right to retaliate if they felt they had not been adequately compensated. These conditions proved to be more stringent than those applying to other forms of discretionary protection, and particularly antidumping measures.

A conscious effort was made in the Round to make safeguards more usable in the hope that this would reduce the use of alternative discretionary protection measures such as antidumping. Two major changes were made to this end: to allow discriminatory application of safeguards, and to remove the exporting country's right to compensation during the first three years. While countries are encouraged to use nondiscriminatory and price-based measures, quantitative restrictions are allowed and may be administered by the exporting member. In return, a number of constraints were introduced. The administrative procedures to be followed are specified in detail. A time limit of four years was introduced, with only one extension of four years allowed; except for discriminatory measures where no extensions are allowed. Safeguards cannot be reintroduced within two years, or the life of the previous measure, whichever is longer. Given the increase in protectionist pressure created by the abolition of VERs, there is a danger that the new safeguards provisions could be used to replace them by a web of similar measures that will enjoy the haven of unquestioned GATT legality.

Antidumping, subsidies, and countervailing duties

The agreement defines dumping to occur when goods are exported at a price below their selling price in the home country. When a large producer uses discriminatory pricing to drive competitors out of the market, there are clearly grounds for concern. In practice, however, such predatory dumping is extremely rare. Antidumping actions themselves have become a problem because, as Finger points out, the procedures used to determine antidumping duties usually tend to overstate dumping margins, to define normal business practices as dumping, and to create trade-inhibiting uncertainty.

Antidumping has become a much more serious problem since the mid-1970s. In mid-1992, the GATT Secretariat estimated that there were 546 antidumping orders in place in GATT contracting parties, thirty-six times as many as safeguard actions.[4] Further, in an unfortunate example of technology transfer, this form of protection is spreading from industrial to developing countries. Finger offers four reasons for the popularity of anti-dumping actions: they allow discriminatory action; the injury test tends to be weaker than that applied in safeguard actions; the rhetoric of foreign unfairness helps build a case for protection; and the threat of antidumping action has frequently helped importers gain exporter acquiescence to VERs.

The Uruguay Round agreement specifies the general principles to be followed in antidumping actions and requires countries to publish the details of the procedures to be followed. These procedures must be transparent and interested parties must be given the opportunity to present their views. Exhortations are provided against statistically invalid procedures such as the exclusion of sales at below estimated average costs in the home market, and the practice of comparing the average price in the home market with individual sales in the export market. However, these biased procedures may still be used as long as they are explained in the final report. On the basis of past experience, Finger concludes that these procedural requirements will not significantly restrain the biases inherent in current antidumping practice.

Moreover, appeal to the dispute settlement procedures provides little comfort. Dispute settlement panels can only decide whether the actions of the antidumping authorities were consistent with the procedures laid down in the agreement, not whether the finding is economically justifiable. A five-year sunset clause is incorporated, but extensions are permitted subject to a review to determine whether dumping would occur in the absence of the duty.

Prior to the Uruguay Round, the GATT provisions on subsidies and countervailing duties contained many inconsistencies. Export subsidies were not explicitly defined, and there was no consistency between the definitions of subsidies and measures that could be subject to countervailing duties. Export subsidies on agricultural goods were banned only if they led to achieving "more than an equitable market share."

The Uruguay Round agreement explicitly defines export subsidies, and categorizes them as prohibited, actionable, and nonactionable. Prohibited subsidies are those contingent on export performance or on using domestic rather than imported inputs. Actionable subsidies are those that cause adverse effects on other countries. Nonactionable subsidies include a range of subsidies for research, for developing disadvantaged regions, and for meeting environmental requirements. This traffic-light approach clarifies the rules on subsidies.

WTO members may take action against other countries' prohibited or actionable subsidies either through the consultation-dispute settlement procedures or, after an investigation, through the imposition of countervailing duties. While both avenues can be followed, only one form of relief may be introduced.

In industrial countries, currently existing prohibited subsidies are to be phased out over a three-year period. In developing countries, longer phase-out periods are allowed. Subsidies conditional on use of domestic inputs have a five-year grace period in developing countries and an eight-year grace period in least-developed countries. Subsidies conditional on exports have a grace period of eight years in developing countries except for the least-developed countries and countries with GNP per capita of less than $1,000, where no reduction is required. Developing countries which reach export competitiveness, defined as a share of 3.25 percent in world trade of that product, must phase out their export subsidies within two years.

Clearly, the enhancements to the rules on export subsidies and counter-vailing duties for merchandise trade are an improvement. Agricultural subsidies are now subject to at least some discipline. The procedures for dealing with subsidies on industrial products have been clarified in a way which makes it much more likely that they will be effectively disciplined. The restrictions on the use of subsidies by developing countries are an important innovation, even though they are subject to a long phase-in period. However, the rules still provide considerable latitude for the provision of subsidies that are economically damaging, and economically efficient policy is likely to make considerably less use of subsidies than is allowed under the rules.

Many countries supported the introduction of an overall agreement on investment policy within the Uruguay Round. Other countries, and particularly many developing countries, felt that measures to regulate the activities of foreign firms were needed as a counter to the potential monopoly power of multinational firms. As a consequence of these concerns, the final TRIMs agreement deals only with a relatively narrow set of TRIMs measures that directly affect trade in goods, rather than with investment policies generally.

As Low and Subramanian note, the TRIMs agreement outlaws local content requirements, trade- and/or foreign-exchange-balancing requirements and domestic sales requirements on the grounds that they are inconsistent with the national treatment principle of the GATT or are quantitative restrictions. The agreement allows industrial countries two years to comply, developing countries five years, and least-developed countries seven years. On one level, the agreement is very weak, since it, in fact, attempts no more than to enforce existing GATT disciplines. However, if it does so successfully, it must be counted as a significant improvement.

The TRIMs agreement is far from a comprehensive investment agreement, but may provide the basis for negotiating such an agreement. Low and Subramanian conclude that an investment agreement would be desirable for a number of reasons, including locking in the advantages of the widespread liberalization of investment regimes undertaken in recent years, and restraining the potentially costly international competition in investment incentives such as tax holidays. Inclusion of an agreement on investment would remove the current asymmetry whereby the WTO agreement provides rules for trade in both goods and services, but for investment only in services. The TRIMs agreement is to be reviewed within five years, to consider, *inter alia,* the possible addition of investment and competition policy.

GATS

As Bernard Hoekman points out in chapter 4, the GATS establishes a framework for trade in services which, in many respects, parallels that provided by the GATT for trade in goods. Its architecture differs from the GATT, however, because trade in services is different and because of the particular approach adopted in the negotiations.

The basic principles

The basic principles of the GATS are similar to those of the GATT: national treatment (treating imports and domestic supplies equally in a national market) and most-favored-nation treatment (nondiscrimination between supplies from different exporters). In addition, both prohibit the use of quantitative restrictions.

The GATS breaks new ground by including market access commitments that extend beyond border restrictions on trade. While trade in goods involves physical movement of the goods across borders, this is only one of four ways in which service trade can occur: cross-border supply not requiring the movement of the provider or the consumer; trade involving international movement of the consumer (for example, tourism); trade involving temporary international movement of suppliers (for example, consultancy services); and trade involving provision of services through the commercial presence.

Because services trade is typically restricted by regulations rather than tariffs, negotiators proceeded on the basis of all-or-nothing commitments to liberalize each services trade for particular sectors, modes of supply, and protective instrument. Negotiations revolved around which sectors were included in the liberalized set. In contrast to merchandise trade, no quantitative measure of trade restrictiveness comparable to a tariff rate has been developed to allow bargaining over degrees of liberalization for services sectors.

Each country's GATS schedule gives a positive list specifying the sectors and modes of delivery in which the national treatment and market access principles will be applied. Within the sectors and modes of supply so listed, a negative list specifies particular types of trade-restricting measures in violation of national treatment and market access that may be maintained – unless a measure is listed, it may not be used. A negative list approach is also used for the MFN principle; that is, the MFN principle applies to all services except those specifically exempted. The MFN principle was intended to be a general commitment but, in the end, over sixty countries listed exemptions.

Market access commitments apply only to listed services, and market access is not even explicitly defined. Instead, six types of market access restrictions on the size and structure of service providers are prohibited. Unfortunately, measures that are equivalent in effect to the listed measures are not proscribed; experience with the GATT has highlighted the risk that measures with the same effect, but a different name, will emerge in this situation.

The national treatment condition is designed to ensure that foreign suppliers are treated no less favorably than domestic suppliers, except in ways specified in the schedules.

The GATS includes a number of other provisions designed to facilitate trade in services, for at least the sectors listed in the agreement. All members must establish inquiry points for information on laws, regulations, and administrative practices. Qualification requirements, technical standards, and licensing procedures must be based on objective and transparent criteria, and not constitute a restriction on supply. Procedures for recognition of licenses, education, and experience must be transparent and reasonable. Members are also required to refrain from applying restrictions on international payments relating to their specific services commitments.

The GATS also contains a number of "safeguard" provisions which roughly parallel those provided under the GATT. No provision is made for antidumping or countervailing duties. The Dispute Settlement Body of the WTO is responsible for dispute resolution under the GATS as well as GATT and TRIPS.

Services liberalization

The GATS approach of listing sectors and measures does not allow calculation of a simple summary measure of liberalization corresponding to an average tariff rate. In chapter 4, Bernard Hoekman provides estimates of the extent to which the Uruguay Round offers cover trade in services.

From his results, it is clear that the high-income countries listed just under half of their services trade categories, with just under a quarter having market access subject to no policy exemptions. When market access subject to policy exemptions is included with a weight of one half, the share listed rises to 36 percent. Fortunately, the sectors listed are relatively large; using GDP weights, this latter index is 45 percent.

Developing countries were more reluctant to make offers, with only 16.2 percent of sectors in developing countries listed in any fashion, and 6.9 percent listed with no policy exemptions. Using Hoekman's policy weights, the developing countries listed 10.3 percent of their sectors; with GDP weights to allow for the importance of different sectors, this share rises to 12.2. Many developing countries made virtually no use of the opportunity to commit themselves to an open trading regime for services: four countries listed only one of the 155 service sectors (the minimum required for membership of the WTO) and five others listed only two sectors. Importantly, the relatively large developing countries, defined by Hoekman as countries with GDP above $40 billion, proved more willing to make GATS commitments. These countries listed almost 40 percent of total sectors, including 14 percent with no policy restrictions.

A major weakness of the initial GATS outcome was that it resulted in very few commitments that require the elimination of current restrictive measures. That is, countries generally listed their current regulations and restrictions, committing, at best, only to a "standstill" in which the introduction of a wide range of some new measures has been ruled out. While this has value, given the likelihood that some of the proscribed measures would have been introduced in the absence of the GATS, that value is limited, and the beneficial effect is further reduced by the restricted range of sectors and modes of supply offered by many members.

The future of GATS

The current structure of GATS has a number of deficiencies that appear to require attention before substantial further progress can be achieved. One problem is that GATS, as it stands, does little to promote transparency – no information is provided on the policy measures applying in the sectors in which no commitments are scheduled. This is a particularly serious problem in developing countries, which have listed only a small fraction of their trade in services. Even where sectors have been listed, however, the information provided on the trade restrictions that continue to apply is frequently very limited.

The positive-list approach used for the inclusion of sectors and modes of supply may make it politically more difficult for a government to add sectors to its schedule. In this situation, a government must be prepared to confront each industry that it seeks to subject to multilateral disciplines.

Under a negative-list approach, by contrast, each industry that seeks to be exempted from disciplines must explain why the general principles for trade liberalization should not apply to it. This is particularly important for future negotiations since it is likely that the industries currently listed are considerably less sensitive than those not yet listed. Relatedly, the use of a positive list allows restrictions to be introduced in any unlisted sector.

The ability to specify different restrictions for different modes of supply raises the risk that incentives will be created for services sectors to relocate in order to avoid restrictions. If, for instance, national treatment is allowed for the supply of a service through establishment of a local entity, but not for cross-border supply from a foreign establishment, then powerful incentives may be created for trade barrier-hopping investment.

In future negotiations, it would be desirable for the architecture of the GATS to be altered to an approach involving more generally applicable rules and disciplines rather than the sector-based approach that now prevails. This change would bring the GATS more into line with the GATT approach. One key change would involve a move to a negative-list approach for sectoral coverage. Another would be to harmonize commitments across all modes of supply for each sector so as to avoid creating artificial incentives for movement of industries. Drawing on experience with the GATT, it would also seem desirable to move away from the current sector-by-sector approach to the use of a formula-based negotiating approach.

The stakes involved in undertaking a comprehensive liberalization of trade in services are very high. A pathbreaking analysis presented by Drusilla Brown, Alan Deardorff, Alan Fox, and Robert Stern in chapter 10 concludes that the gains from liberalization of services trade are potentially of the same order of magnitude as the gains from liberalizing merchandise trade. With services trade growing considerably more rapidly, and with the remaining protection in the manufactures sector coming down substantially, it is likely that the gains from liberalizing services trade will become even more important in the future.

TRIPS

The TRIPS agreement is, with the GATT 1994 and the GATS, one of the three fundamental pillars of the WTO. The TRIPS agreement applies the basic principles of national treatment and MFN treatment to IPRs. However, as Carlos Braga points out in chapter 12, it goes far beyond border issues, and hence needs a considerably different architecture from either the GATT or the GATS. The fact that it goes so far was the source of considerable controversy between developing and industrial countries during the negotiations, and agreement was reached only with great difficulty. However, the outcome is a substantial one with wide-ranging implications.

The TRIPS agreement covers IPRs such as patents, copyright, industrial designs, geographical indications, and trademarks. In the past, international protection of these rights was provided under agreements such as the Berne and Paris Conventions administered by WIPO. TRIPS provides for minimum standards of IPR protection, in contrast with the WIPO conventions that tended to focus on ensuring the implementation of national legislation. Braga points out that the TRIPS agreement increases the country coverage of such arrangements from around ninety countries to all 123 signatories of the Uruguay Round's Final Act. While many of the additional signatories were small, important economies such as Hong Kong, Indonesia, Singapore, and Thailand are now under multilateral disciplines, and TRIPS will ensure the addition of other major economies such as China and Russia as they join the WTO.

In some areas, such as copyright, TRIPS broadly applies the principles of the relevant agreement, in this case the Berne Convention. In other areas, the agreement provides for higher standards than were previously required; in the area of patents, for example, the agreement goes well beyond the Paris Convention by extending patent protection to all areas of technology, including pharmaceuticals, requiring a life of at least twenty years for patents, restricting the scope for compulsory licensing of patent rights, and strengthening the protection of patent rights. The standards of IPR protection required by the TRIPS agreement will frequently require substantial changes in the laws granting intellectual property protection and in the effectiveness of their enforcement, particularly in developing countries.

An important factor in obtaining the agreement of developing countries to the TRIPS agreement was the inclusion of transitional arrangements. While industrial countries have only one year to implement the agreement, developing countries have an additional four years during which only the basic requirements of MFN and national treatment must be provided. Further, developing countries are allowed an additional five-year delay in introducing product patents in areas not protected at the date of application of the agreement. Least-developed countries are allowed a total of eleven years before being required to provide full protection of IPRs.

A major concern in recent years has been the frequency of disputes on IPR issues. In the absence of agreed rights, these have tended to be resolved by bilateral confrontations between developing countries and the major industrial countries. A major outcome of the Uruguay Round is the integrated dispute settlement mechanism with automatic procedures and strict timetables. With the new agreement on property rights, this new dispute settlement mechanism is expected to play a major role in the operation of the new intellectual property rights system. Cross-sectoral retaliation may be authorized under this dispute settlement system, so the stakes will be high in securing agreement. This will particularly be the case at the end of the ten-year phase-in period for the Round, when the industrial countries are dismantling the MFA, and developing countries are simultaneously bringing their IPR systems into full compliance with the TRIPS agreement.

The economic effects of IPRs involve a tradeoff between the incentives they create for innovation and the inefficiencies that arise from granting a monopoly over the use of the patented good/technique. IPRs have become increasingly important with the growth in production and trade of high-technology goods, and protection standards for IPRs have progressively become stronger in all currently industrial countries, suggesting a widespread assessment that higher standards are economically desirable.

At the international level, patents involve transfers between countries, as well as between consumers and producers of IPRs. In 1982, almost 90 percent of the 200,000 patents awarded by developing countries were to patent holders in other countries. Where countries have the ability to free-ride on intellectual property, by consuming the good without paying any fee to developers in other countries, it is in their immediate interest to do so, just as it is in the interests of users in the originating country to free-ride on the invention if the institutional arrangements allow them to do so. In the longer term, however, IPRs protection is important for a country seeking to develop its own knowledge-based industries. Further, the provision of IPRs can be expected to encourage the development, inside or outside the particular developing country, of technologies that are of particular interest to it, such as medical or agricultural techniques relevant to its specific needs.

Institutional reforms and the agenda for the future

The Uruguay Round resulted in the most profound institutional reform of the multilateral trading system since the establishment of the GATT in 1947. The trading rules were reformed across the whole spectrum, and the new rules were brought under the aegis of the newly created WTO. The WTO is an apex organization whose function is to oversee three subsidiary international agreements – GATT 1994, GATS, and TRIPS. The WTO is ultimately responsible for implementing the reforms in all of these areas, and for further development of the global trading system.

The impact of the Round on the overall strength of the trading system is, however, difficult to gauge. Since international law is inherently limited by the willingness of sovereign nations to submit to its disciplines, a working set of international laws must walk a fine line between being too restrictive to be accepted and too lenient to be effective.

John Whalley's analysis in chapter 14 points to a range of areas in which these reforms can be expected to strengthen the trading system overall. The agreement overturns a number of derogations that had previously weakened the integrity of the trading system – such as agriculture, VERs and the MFA. The dramatic increase in the scope of tariff bindings increases the importance of the trading system in regulating trade policy. The incorporation of services and TRIPS expands the scope of the system, and hence the scope for gains from negotiation, although the architecture of the GATS may cause difficulties both in enforcing it and extending it into new areas. The fact that the Round was introduced as a single undertaking – whereby virtually all of its disciplines apply to all members – represents a big advance on the Tokyo Codes approach, where many disciplines were optional, and were not widely accepted by developing countries.

The dispute settlement procedures of the WTO are substantially stronger than those of the GATT. In the past, dispute settlement procedures could be blocked either at the formation of a panel, or the adoption of its report, and the procedures could be delayed interminably. Under the new system, the right to a panel is virtually automatic, the panel's report may be rejected only if there is a consensus among WTO members to reject it, and all procedures must adhere to a strict timetable. Some concerns have been expressed about the potentially enormous workload generated by this system, the pressure on panels to mitigate their recommendations (because their reports will almost certainly be adopted), and the difficulties involved in maintaining credibility if some of the major trading countries refuse to comply with panel findings. The estimated gains from the Uruguay Round depend upon the implementation of the agreement during its ten-year phase-in period. Unless this proceeds as agreed, despite the inevitable pressures for delay and diversion, many of the gains discussed above from measures such as abolition of the MFA will be in jeopardy. The dispute settlement process could prove to be a vital link in this chain.

Agreement was reached to establish the TPRM on a permanent basis following its successful provisional introduction after the mid-term review of the Uruguay Round. With a broad mandate to review the trade policies of member countries in goods and services, the TPRM should help to improve the operation of the trading system by increasing the transparency of countries' trade policies. While the interest groups benefiting from protection are typically very well informed about the measures that affect them directly, the opacity of many forms of protection and the complexity of their effects make it difficult to build opposition to even very costly trade distortions.

A key challenge for the WTO is to manage its work program on trade and the environment. This work program has extremely broad terms of reference, including: the relationship between trade and environmental measures in promoting sustainable development; the relationship between the multilateral trading system and trade measures used for environmental purposes; the environmental effects of trade liberalization; and the relationship between the dispute settlement mechanisms of the WTO and those in multilateral environmental agreements.

As environmental issues have become increasingly important in the public perception, developing an effective agreement on trade and the environment poses extremely difficult challenges. It is clear that significant environmental externalities arise from phenomena such as the greenhouse effect, and that, consequently, markets fail to deliver first-best outcomes. The key question for the WTO is thus whether the benefits of intervening through the multilateral trade system will exceed the costs.

In chapter 15, Kym Anderson notes that in any policy framework for trade and the environment, it is crucial that the directly favorable implications of trade liberalization be recognized. Trade liberalization promotes efficient resource allocation that inherently reduces the strain placed on natural resources and the environment. It also increases living standards, which increases communities' willingness to pay for environmental quality, increases levels of education, and reduces rates of population growth.

The risks to the global trading system from ill-considered incorporation of environmental measures are extreme. Proposals to harmonize national environmental standards ignore the differences in ability to pay for environmental goods between countries. Despite this, protectionist interests will press for harmonized standards as a means to reduce competition from emerging competitors. If such standards were introduced, and some developing countries were unable to comply, then they would be exposed to trade retaliation that could have disastrous impacts on their development, and their progress in achieving environmental goals. The ultimate impact of such policies could be to damage, or even destroy, the multilateral trading system.

As long as these difficulties are carefully avoided, there might be gains from the careful inclusion of provisions dealing with the evident problems of the current system. The relationship between WTO provisions and those of multilateral environmental agreements is one area in which clarification of the rules for interaction seems to be needed.

The rapid growth of regional trade agreements in recent years seems set to continue. During the Uruguay Round, an agreement was reached on the interpretation of the GATT procedures for dealing with discriminatory regional arrangements, but it did not result in fundamental changes. Thus, some degree of continuing tension between regional and multilateral liberalization is expected. Recent manifestations of regionalism seem to pay tribute to the goal of trade liberalization that they share with the multilateral trading system. Vigilance will be required, however, to ensure that regional blocs do not undermine the operation and evolution of the multilateral system.

Negotiations on sensitive areas of services trade are continuing. The near-collapse of the negotiations on financial services in mid-1995 highlighted the difficulties involved in obtaining substantial progress on a sector-by-sector basis, but, for the first time, demonstrated the possibility of making significant progress without the involvement of the United States.

The Uruguay Round agreement calls for new negotiations to begin within five years on agriculture and on services, and for consideration of negotiations on investment and competition policy. There will be pressure to develop new rules in areas such as trade and the environment and for a social clause covering labor standards and human rights. Given the extremely high stakes for developing countries in these issues, and in the continuation of negotiations in merchandise trade and services, active and creative involvement by developing countries in the new world trading system will be vitally important.

The chapters of this book make clear the substantial gains that will accrue from the Uruguay Round to developing countries as a group, and the very large gains anticipated for those countries that participated most actively in the main process of trade liberalization. While an important step forward, this is surely only an early milestone on the developing countries' journey to full participation in the global economy. Much remains to be done to reduce protection in developing countries, and to improve the rules-oriented trading system in ways that better protect the interests of smaller players in the world trading system.

Notes

This chapter draws heavily on the contributions of the authors, discussants, and participants at the World Bank conference on the Uruguay Round. We are grateful to the many friends and colleagues who provided detailed comments on an earlier version, including: Marcelo Abreu, Christian Bach, Hugh Corbet, Alice Enders, J. Michael Finger, Bernard Hoekman, Naheed Kirmani, Michael Leidy, Patrick Low, Peter Lloyd, Alex McCalla, Costas Michalopolous, Håkan Nordström, Sheila Page, Sarath Rajapatirana, David Robertson, Richard Snape, T. N. Srinivasan, and Arvind Subramanian. Any remaining errors are entirely our responsibility.

1. Here it is assumed that China will become a WTO member during the phase-out period of the MFA quotas, and hence benefit from their abolition.

2. Key for figure 1.5. PHL Philippines; THA Thailand; SAS South Asia; JPN Japan; IDN Indonesia; EU European Union; ROW rest of world; USC United States/ Canada; SSA Sub-Saharan Africa; LTN Latin America.
3. This statement is slightly oversimplified. If countries' trade patterns are due to distortionary policies, the result that exporters gain and importers lose may be reversed. If a country explicitly or implicitly subsidizes imports, a rise in world prices which causes imports to fall may reduce expenditure on import subsidies sufficiently to increase overall welfare.
4. This comparison perhaps overstates the relative impact of antidumping measures since safeguard actions apply uniformly to all imports while antidumping duties apply only to particular suppliers.

References

Francois, J. F., and W. Martin 1995. "Multilateral Trade Rules and the Expected Cost of Protection." CEPR Discussion Paper 1214. London: Centre for Economic Policy Research.

GATT 1994. *The Results of the Uruguay Round of Multilateral Trade Negotiations. Market Access for Goods and Services: Overview of the Results.* Geneva: GATT, November.

Harrold, P. 1995. *The Impact of the Uruguay Round on Africa: Much Ado About Nothing?* World Bank Discussion Paper 311. Washington DC: World Bank.

Ingco, M. forthcoming. "Agricultural Trade Liberalization in the Uruguay Round: One Step Forward, One Step Back?" *The World Economy.*

Krishna, K., R. Erzan, and L. Tan 1994. "Rent Sharing in the Multifibre Arrangement: Theory and Evidence from US Apparel Imports from Hong Kong." *Review of International Economics* 2(1): 62–73.

Page, S., and M. Davenport 1995. *World Trade Reform: Do Developing Countries Gain or Lose?* ODI Special Report. London: Overseas Development Institute.

Trela, I., and J. Whalley 1995. "Internal Quota-Allocation Schemes and the Costs of the MFA." *Review of International Economics* 3(3): 284–306.

World Bank 1995. *Commodity Markets and the Developing Countries.* Washington, DC: World Bank.

2 Agricultural liberalization and the Uruguay Round

Dale E. Hathaway and Merlinda D. Ingco

For many countries, especially low-cost agricultural exporters, agriculture was a crucial element of the Uruguay Round negotiations. The agricultural objectives were sweeping and impressive: "[to] bring all measures affecting import access and export competition under strengthened and more operationally effective GATT rules and disciplines . . . through, *inter alia*, the reduction of import barriers . . . [and] by increasing discipline on the use of all direct and indirect subsidies" (GATT 1986). Disagreement over these objectives blocked completion of the mid-term review in December 1988, and the absence of an agricultural agreement was the primary reason that the Uruguay Round was not concluded at the Brussels ministerial meeting in December 1990. Moreover, agricultural issues were largely responsible for the negotiations dragging on three full years beyond the scheduled completion date.

It is useful to remember where the agricultural trading system was at the start of the Uruguay Round. From the beginning, agriculture was treated differently than other sectors under GATT rules. Whereas nontariff barriers are prohibited for nonagricultural goods, in agriculture quantitative restrictions were permitted under certain circumstances. Over time these circumstances were broadened, limiting agricultural imports by quotas, variable levies, VERs, minimum import prices, and other protective measures in virtually every country in the world. Many agricultural products were protected by ordinary tariffs, but these were bound for only 55 percent of the products in developed countries and only 18 percent in developing countries.

In the area of export competition, agriculture was also given special treatment under GATT rules. Whereas export subsidies are prohibited for industrial products, in agriculture they were allowed as long as the country using them did not gain more than an equitable share of the world market (Article XVI:3). Over the years the equitable-share concept had proven useless in practice, and thus there was no effective GATT discipline over the

30

use of export subsidies for agricultural products. In the 1980s, as world markets softened and world trade in key products stagnated or declined, more and more countries resorted to the use of export subsidies to maintain market share or to dispose of surplus domestic production, driving world prices for several commodities to post-World War II lows in real terms. Farmers in countries that did not provide them with income protection saw their incomes plummet as a result of export competition.

GATT has never had a prohibition or limit on domestic subsidies to industries. In this regard agriculture's treatment was no different, and most of the trade-distorting border measures were obviously designed to protect domestic policies that supported internal prices for agricultural products. These policies distorted trade by encouraging high-cost domestic output, discouraged domestic consumption, and protected domestic farmers from changes in the world market. Border protection was needed to sustain the policies, protection that often took the form of quantitative import controls and other nontariff measures. If the country in question produced a supply exceeding domestic consumption, export subsidies were used to bridge the gap between high internal prices and world market prices. Most countries in the OECD followed such policies on almost all agricultural products.

At the same time, many other countries followed policies that effectively transferred income from the agricultural producer to the consumer, among them overvalued exchange rates, state buying agencies that paid producers less than world prices, export taxes in countries with exportable surpluses, and import subsidies in importing countries. Because these policies tend to inhibit output expansion and lessen producer income, they are often offset, in part at least, by extensive subsidies on agricultural inputs such as credit, fertilizer, and water. Almost without exception, it has been developing countries that have followed such policies.

Political forces made it difficult to change the situation. Even though the number of farm producers has fallen so sharply in OECD countries that now they make up just a small fraction of the population, they are still a powerful political force in most industrial countries. Conversely, in developing countries the political power of urban consumers and civil servants tends to outweigh the power of farm producers, even when farmers are a large fraction of the population.

Much of the background work for the Uruguay Round agricultural negotiations was done in the OECD, which performed pioneering analysis of the huge income transfers and market distortions arising from the agricultural support and protection policies so common in its member countries. In GATT's Committee on Agriculture, which helped frame the terms of reference for agricultural negotiations, and in the ministerial meeting launching the Uruguay Round, discussion focused on reducing or removing the trade-distorting policies of developed countries. Thus the issues that drove the negotiations were primarily of interest to developed countries and those developing countries directly affected by the policies of developed countries, mainly developing country exporters that were denied access to lucrative markets in developed countries or that faced competition in third-country markets from subsidized exports from developed countries. Once the framework for the agricultural negotiations was set, then, the issues were relevant to only a limited number of countries. However, many developing countries with a keen interest in the agricultural negotiations were also critical to the success of negotiations in other sectors, especially services and intellectual property. Most developing countries paid more attention to the negotiations on textile quotas, services, and intellectual property than to the agricultural negotiations.

From the beginning, countries with a vested interest in the agricultural negotiations divided into two opposing camps. On one side were those who insisted on significant reform of agricultural trade rules and on effective liberalization of agricultural trade through reductions in border protection and the removal of other trade-distorting policies. On the other side were those who argued that agriculture is a special case, and that all countries should not be required to adopt the same policies for internal support and border protection regardless of farm structure or level of self-sufficiency. Several participants took the position that reforming certain trade rules would be acceptable to reduce some of the worst market distortions, but they were opposed to significant liberalization of border protection because of the economic burden on and political pressure from farmers at home.

From the outset, the United States carried the banner for advocates of reform and liberalization. It was strongly backed by the Cairns Group, fourteen countries named after the Australian city where they first met, a mix of developed and developing country exporters comprising Argentina, Australia, Brazil, Canada, Chile, Colombia, Fiji, Hungary, Indonesia, Malaysia, New Zealand, the Philippines, Uruguay, and Venezuela. These countries had few if any domestic or export subsides and wanted to end subsidies in both their prospective foreign markets and by competing exporters. While their major focus was on eliminating export subsidies, they recognized that domestic policy was what primarily motivated export subsidies and stringent border protection. Thus they pushed for the reduction or elimination of domestic trade-distorting subsidies.

The European Community (EC) led the forces opposed to liberalization. The European Community was supported by EFTA countries, Japan and Korea, and some developing countries. Most of them were willing to entertain limited reform of GATT's agriculture rules, but they differed on which reforms were acceptable. For instance, the European Community would accept some reform to limit the types of import protection but was opposed to reform of the rules governing export subsidies. The European Community's priority was to protect their members' ability to compete in international markets without lowering internal prices to match world prices. Even though the European Community was willing to accept some limits to the form of border protection that could be used for agricultural products, it fought against liberalization achieved through reduced protection and increased access.

Conversely Japan, which has no appreciable export activity in agricultural products, supported the prohibition of export subsidies but vigorously opposed the abolition of quantitative import controls and the reduction of tariffs. The Japanese adamantly opposed the idea of relinquishing quantitative import controls for rice.

As the lines were drawn, the negotiation came down to a tug of war between the European Community and the United States over changes in the rules as well as the framework for liberalization. There were also some bilaterals between the United States and Japan and Korea on rice and one or two other specific products.

An overview of the agreement

The final agreement can be best understood by looking at the steps leading up to it. The initial position of the United States and its Cairns Group allies was that all trade-distorting domestic and export subsidies should be phased out, and that all import protection should be converted to tariffs, which would be sharply reduced. The initial position of the European Community and its allies was that there should be an agreement to reduce aggregate spending on domestic and export subsidies and some limits on border protection. These were the positions as negotiations entered what was intended to be their concluding phase in late 1990.

A ministerial meeting was scheduled in Brussels in December 1990 to complete the Uruguay Round. The European Community entered the meeting confident that the United States and its supporters would abandon their position on agricultural reform and liberalization, as they had in previous trade negotiations, in hopes of not jeopardizing the nonagricultural negotiations. Thus the European Community was shocked when developing country members of the Cairns Group rejected the EC position on agriculture and forced a continuation of negotiations beyond their scheduled conclusion.

After the Brussels ministerial meeting, the European Community realized just how adamant the countries demanding reform were. At this point,

EC officials concluded that achieving an international agreement would require substantial reform of the European Community's so-called Common Agricultural Policy, either in advance of the agreement or in response to it. Other participants also recognized that it would not be politically possible to complete the Uruguay Round without such reform before or after the agreement. EC officials insisted that it was politically more feasible to make reforms first and fit an international agreement to the reforms than to win approval by member countries of a Uruguay Round agreement, which would force major reforms on the Common Agricultural Policy. Thus the European Community embarked on a major reform of its agricultural policy in early 1991. The initial phases were completed late that year, leading many to hope the Uruguay Round would be completed before the end of 1991.

Reform was driven by more than the issues of the Uruguay Round. The United States had obtained a GATT ruling that found the European Community's oilseed policy to be in violation of GATT obligations. Thus the European Community was pushed to reform its grain and oilseed as well as its dairy and livestock policies. Essentially, the changes lowered the internal support for grain and oilseed, and compensated farmers by direct payment for crops. The amount of the payment was based on regional crop yield and the difference between the internal support price and a target price. Lower internal grain prices allowed internal support for livestock to be reduced with compensation to producers. Lower grain and livestock prices reduced internal support but did not close the gap between internal prices and the expected world price. Thus even with the reformed regime, the European Community needed export subsidies to remain competitive in world markets for many products.

Serious negotiations on agricultural reform did not resume until the fall of 1991. As the year approached its end, discussions were still stalled on key issues in agriculture and other sectors. The Director-General of GATT decided that the only way to move the negotiation to a conclusion was to produce a draft text, including possible compromises in a number of areas in agriculture and other sectors. The draft, issued in late December 1991 and known as the Dunkel Text, became the benchmark for remaining negotiations. It called for immediate "tariffication," that is, conversion of all nontariff agricultural import barriers to ordinary tariffs. Tariffs resulting from tariffication, and tariffs on products already subject to tariff protection, were to be reduced by a minimum of 15 percent. The arithmetic (unweighted) average of tariff cuts was to be 36 percent. Where nontariff barriers were converted to tariffs, a minimum access level was to be established of 3 percent of domestic consumption in a base period of 1986–88, or of imports in those years (current access), whichever was higher.

Minimum access would be increased to 5 percent of base-period consumption. Tariff quotas at reasonable levels were to facilitate access, which would be established on a tariff-line-by-tariff-line basis. All tariffs were to be bound at the end of the implementation period.

The Dunkel Text called for a phased reduction of 36 percent in spending on export subsidies, and a reduction of 24 percent in the volume of subsidized exports. These were to apply on a product-by-product basis, and at the end of the first year of implementation levels were to be set below the 1986–90 base level. However, because in 1992 both the EC and the United States had export subsidy levels for some products that were well above the base level in either volume or value, the Dunkel approach required a drastic reduction in subsidized exports of such products in the first year of implementation. For instance, the Dunkel formula would have required the United States to reduce outlays on export subsidies of soybean oil by 89 percent in the first year.

The Dunkel Text called for a 20 percent reduction in all trade-distorting domestic subsidies on a commodity-by-commodity basis, and it was fairly rigorous in its definition of such subsidies. For instance, it classified both US deficiency payments and the new EC compensation payments as trade-distorting subsidies and thus would have required that they be scaled back.

The Dunkel Text contained a so-called modalities for specific binding commitments (Draft Final Act, pp. L19 to L34). These spelled out commitments to be undertaken in the agreement and how they were to be expressed. Articles 13 through 20 (Special and Differential Treatment) became the governing portion of the agreement for developing countries. Several provisions of these articles are crucial. Article 14 states, "In the case of products subject to unbound custom duties developing countries shall have the flexibility to offer ceiling bindings on these products." Article 15 says developing countries can apply lower rates of reduction in the areas of market access, domestic support, and export competition provided the rate of reduction is no less than two-thirds of that applying to industrial countries. Developing countries are also given ten years to implement commitments, four more years than industrial countries. Article 16 exempts least-developed countries from reduction commitments. Article 18 specifically exempts government assistance to encourage agriculture and rural development from inclusion in the base calculations of the total measure of support. Finally, Article 20 exempts developing countries from commitments on export subsidies during the implementation period.

Thus the Dunkel Text established substantially different treatment for developing countries. They could entirely avoid commitments in many areas, and where commitments were required they were lower and phased in over a longer period.

As soon as the Dunkel Text was published, the focus of agricultural groups shifted to what the proposed agreement would require in terms of changes in policy and levels of protection. Japan and Korea vigorously protested the requirement of universal tariffication in the Dunkel Text, insisting they could not drop their ban on rice imports. France rejected the draft before it was officially published and threatened to block EU approval of the Uruguay Round if changes were not made in the agricultural agreement to make it more consistent with the European Community's reformed Common Agricultural Policy. France was joined by Germany, which had approved the European Community's reform for grains and livestock only after receiving a commitment from the European Commission that the new compensatory payments would not be subject to reductions or limitations under a GATT agreement.

Specifically, the French objected to the Dunkel Text's rollback in export subsidies, especially the commitment to reduce the volume of subsidized exports by 24 percent. The European Community's agricultural policy reform, which lowered internal prices, would have made expenditure reductions on export subsidies less likely to be binding for most products. Even so, the French argued that proposed reductions in the volume of subsidized exports would force further changes in internal prices or force the European Community to adopt policies to curtail output of key commodities. The French and several other European Community members also objected to product-by-product requirements for minimum access, insisting that the European Community be allowed to aggregate individual products into broad categories such as meat and dairy products, to measure access. In addition, because the United States had successfully challenged the European Community's domestic oilseed policy and was challenging other aspects of the Common Agricultural Policy, the French wanted an agreement that would sharply curtail the ability of other countries to challenge that policy through GATT channels.

The United States and the Cairns Group, having already retreated from earlier demands for greater liberalization, especially in export subsidies and domestic policy reforms, both endorsed the Dunkel Text and intimated that this was their final compromise. In early 1992 a second GATT panel ruling found that the European Community's reformed oilseed policy still violated GATT. The United States threatened to retaliate against EC products unless the latter's oilseed policy was altered.

Months of high-level negotiations finally came to an end on November 20, 1992, in Washington, DC. The result was dubbed the Blair House agreement because it was negotiated in Blair House, the official residence of visitors hosted by the US government. The Blair House agreement dealt with all of the outstanding issues between the European Community and the

United States in the Dunkel Text, and it contained an agreement to end the US–EC impasse over oilseed policy. It was mute on all of the issues directly affecting developing countries.

The major elements of the Blair House agreement moved in the direction of the European Community. First, the reduction in the volume of subsidized exports was scaled down from 24 to 21 percent. Second, it was agreed that commodities could be aggregated to meet minimum-access requirements. Third, it was agreed that domestic subsidy cuts be required not on a commodity-by-commodity basis, but rather for all commodities as an aggregate (a cut of 20 percent). On domestic subsidies, the important element was that EC compensation payments and US deficiency payments would be exempt from reduction.

Finally, the Blair House agreement included a cease fire: GATT complaints on certain issues could not be filed for the duration of the six-year implementation period if the country in question was complying with its Uruguay Round commitments. The European Community had pushed this because of the series of GATT complaints that had been brought by the United States against the European Community's internal policy.

The Blair House agreement left many advocates of major reform unhappy, and US oilseed producers were especially unhappy at the modest adjustments in EC oilseed policy made after they had won two GATT cases. The Cairns Group reluctantly agreed to an arrangement which fell far short of their demands. But despite their successes the French remained dissatisfied. They still objected to the export subsidy limitations, and they still wanted permanent immunity from GATT challenge for the European Community's revised Common Agricultural Policy.

In January 1993 a new US administration took office and raised issues about other parts of the Blair House agreement. After much posturing and many high-level negotiations, an agreement was finally reached in December 1993 that involved two modifications of the Blair House agreement. First, in implementing reductions in export subsidies countries would have a choice: they could start either from the 1986–90 level and move in even reductions to the end, or from the 1991–92 level and move in even reductions to the same end. This eliminated the front-loading of reductions contained in the Blair House agreement for commodities, for which recent subsidies were well above base-year subsidies. It had the practical effect of allowing the European Community – by now called the European Union – and the United States to subsidize significantly more products during the implementation period than otherwise would have been the case. For instance, the European Union could now subsidize an additional 8 million tons of exported wheat during the implementation period, and the United States could subsidize an additional 7.5 million tons. It allowed the European Union an additional 363,000 tons of subsidized beef exports and the United States an additional 1.2 million tons of subsidized soybean oil exports.

The final agricultural agreement (annex 5) also allowed a few countries to postpone tariffication of some products by agreeing to minimum import levels higher than those required under tariffication. This provision was negotiated to allow Japan and Korea to postpone tariffication of their rice import regime.

The final Uruguay Round agreement consists of two parts. One is a set of general commitments spelling out the new GATT rules. The second is a series of schedules setting out individual nations' commitments in terms of the level of tariffs declared when nontariff import controls are converted to tariffs; tariff reductions on a line-by-line basis; minimum access concessions and related details; the level of base-year spending, the volume of export subsidies, and the schedule of reductions on a yearly basis; the aggregate level of trade-distorting domestic supports in the base period; and the level of final commitments for reduction. The modalities for specific, binding commitments, revised to reflect the negotiations between December 1991 and December 1993, were published as a separate note by the chairman of the market access group. However, they are not part of the final agreement, and they are not to "be used as a basis for dispute settlement proceedings under the WTO agreement" (GATT 1993, p. 1).

The formula for minimum tariff cuts was in the original modalities. However, specific tariff cuts were in many cases negotiated on a bilateral basis, as were many specific access provisions. Thus after seven years of negotiation over reform and a framework for implementing it, much of the liberalization achieved was realized as part of a request-offer procedure in the final hours.

While many aspects of the modalities in the original Dunkel Text were the subject of keen attention and negotiation that led to changes, the portions relating to differential treatment for developing countries remained largely undiscussed and untouched. The framework that guided developing countries in the preparation of their country schedules was that laid out in the Dunkel Text. It was not until country schedules were tabled in the final days of 1993 and early 1994 that it was generally recognized that developing countries could choose to escape the disciplines, and that many had done so.

Despite the substantial retreat by the advocates of liberalization, the Uruguay Round agreement on agriculture appears to hold great promise. It requires that all nontariff barriers be converted to ordinary tariffs, which are to be cut along with other tariffs by an average of 36 percent. At the end of the implementation period all tariffs on agricultural products will be bound. It requires that countries either continue current access levels or establish new minimum access levels. It establishes firm product-by-product limits on export subsidies, rolling them back to levels below those of 1986–90.

Developing countries won differential treatment in several regards. Their obligations for tariff reductions could be as low as two-thirds those of industrial countries. Many programs counted as export subsidies for industrial countries are not counted for developing countries. Domestic subsidies that are part of economic development are exempt from cutbacks or controls. Developing countries are given ten years instead of six to implement all changes. And these nations can escape tariff reductions on a large number of products if they choose to do so.

Did tariffication, tariff cuts, and bindings produce liberalization?

To what extent has the Uruguay Round brought liberalization to the highly protected agricultural markets of the world? Estimates of liberalization are surprising in several regards (tables 2.1a and 2.1b). There is markedly little liberalization for most products in most countries. The major exception is Japan and other high-income Asian countries, where there is a consistent pattern of liberalization. Apart from Japan, the highly protected markets in OECD countries were liberalized little if at all. The pattern for developing countries is not markedly different. Most show little or no liberalization for most products. It is instructive to look at the commodity distribution of liberalization that did occur. Highly protected commodities – sugar, meat, and milk – show little or no liberalization. Oilseeds, which were already less protected, were further liberalized, as were fruits and vegetables.

The obvious question is this: How can a trade agreement with such major reforms result in so little liberalization? The devil is in the details, which are spelled out in country schedules. These indicate how different nations interpreted rules and guidelines in such crucial matters as tariffication, access, and tariff cuts.

Prior to the implementation of the Uruguay Round, border protection could take one of several forms. There were ordinary bound tariffs, which some countries used for some products. A large number of countries, especially developing, used tariffs to provide border protection, but the upper limit of these tariffs was not bound and thus they were subject to change at will. Many countries, both industrial and developing, employed any one of a number of nontariff barriers – sometimes in conjunction with tariffs – to limit or control imports. And many countries gave state trading entities exclusive rights to control imports.

There are four important elements of the agreement designed to bring

Table 2.1a *Estimates of average import price changes from baseline, 1982–93 (percent)*

Country/region	Wheat	Rice	Coarse grains	Sugar	Meat	Other meat	Coffee	Cocoa	Tea	Oil-seeds	Dairy	Fruits & veg.	Wool	Cotton	Other nonfood
European Union	0	0	0	0	-9	0	-6	-4	-2	0	0	-4	0	-1	-13
United States	-9	0	0	0	0	0	0	0	-1	0	-8	-4	-4	-9	0
Japan	-47	n.a.	-55	-35	-6	0	-4	-2	-3	0	0	-3	0	0	0
Australia	-1	-9	0	0	0	-8	-1	0	0	-1	-16	0	-1	-1	-4
Canada	0	0	0	0	0	0	0	0	-5	0	0	0	0	0	-1
EFTA	0	-8	0	-11	0	0	-2	0	-1	0	0	0	0	-1	-3
Upper-income Asia	-109	0	-78	-7	-33	-20	0	0	0	-3	0	0	-2	-2	-20
Indonesia	0	0	0	0	0	0	0	0	0	-33	0	0	0	0	0
India	0	0	0	0	0	0	0	0	0	-18	0	0	0	0	0
Low-income Asia	0	0	0	0	0	0	0	0	0	0	0	0	0	0	0
Brazil	-7	0	0	0	0	0	0	0	0	0	0	0	0	0	0
Mexico	0	0	0	0	0	0	0	0	0	0	0	0	0	0	0
Other Latin America	0	0	0	0	0	0	0	0	0	0	0	0	0	0	0
Nigeria	-15	0	-75	0	0	0	0	0	0	0	0	0	0	0	0
Mediterranean	0	0	0	0	0	0	0	0	0	0	0	0	0	0	0
Other Africa	0	0	0	0	0	0	0	0	0	0	0	0	0	0	0
South Africa	0	0	0	0	0	0	0	0	0	0	0	0	-26	0	0
Maghreb	0	0	0	0	0	0	0	0	0	0	0	0	0	-50	0

Note: average price reductions estimated as $(t(f)-t(b))/(1+0.5((t(f)+t(b))$ where $t(f)$ is the final tariff and $t(b)$ is the baseline tariff. Where $t(f)>t(b)$, an import price change of zero is recorded.

Table 2.1b *Estimates of average import price changes from baseline, 1989–93 (percent)*

Country/region	Wheat	Rice	Coarse grains	Sugar	Meat	Other meat	Coffee	Cocoa	Tea	Oil seeds	Dairy	Fruits & veg.	Wool	Cotton	Other nonfood
European Union	0	0	0	0	-12	0	-6	-4	2	0	0	-4	0	1	-13
United States	-15	0	0	0	0	0	0	0	-1	0	-8	-4	0	0	0
Japan	-81	n.a.	-91	-47	-1	-9	0	0	0	0	-14	0	0	0	0
Australia	0	-4	0	0	0	-5	-1	0	0	-1	-19	0	-1	-1	-4
Canada	0	0	0	0	0	0	0	0	-5	0	0	0	0	0	-1
EFTA	0	0	-1	-14	0	0	-2	0	0	-18	0	0	0	0	-3
Upper-income Asia	0	0	0	0	0	0	0	0	0	-33	0	0	0	0	0
Indonesia	0	0	0	0	0	0	0	0	0	0	0	0	0	0	0
India	0	0	0	0	0	0	0	0	0	0	0	0	0	0	0
Low-income Asia	0	0	0	0	0	0	0	0	0	0	0	0	0	0	0
Brazil	-31	0	0	0	0	0	0	0	0	0	0	0	0	0	0
Mexico	0	0	0	0	0	0	0	0	0	-1	0	0	0	0	0
Other Latin America	0	0	0	0	0	0	0	0	0	0	0	0	0	0	0
Nigeria	-12	0	-16	0	0	0	0	0	0	0	0	0	0	0	0
Mediterranean	0	0	0	0	0	0	0	0	0	0	0	0	0	0	0
Other Africa	0	0	0	0	0	0	0	0	0	0	0	0	0	0	0
South Africa	0	0	0	0	0	0	0	0	0	0	0	0	-26	0	0
Maghreb	0	0	0	0	0	0	0	0	0	0	0	0	0	-51	0

Note: average tariff reductions estimated as $(t(f)-t(b))/(1+0.5((t(f)+t(b)))$ where $t(f)$ is the final tariff and $t(b)$ is the baseline tariff. Where $t(f)>t(b)$, an import price change of zero is recorded.

order to border protection. One is the conversion of all nontariff barriers to tariffs, effective immediately – in other words, tariffication. The second is the cutting of existing bound tariffs, previously unbound tariffs, and new tariffs resulting from tariffication. The third is the binding of all tariffs at the end of the implementation period. Finally, there is a minimum access commitment for all products where nontariff barriers have been in place. No minimum access provision was made for products with previous tariffs set at prohibitive levels.

In addition, to protect against import surges of products previously protected by nontariff barriers, there is a special safeguard that allows additional tariffs above the scheduled levels if imports surge or their border prices fall too low during the implementation period. This was a feature demanded from the beginning by the European Union as another way of protecting their internal markets, in this case especially against exchange rate fluctuations.

Without question, the prohibition and tariffication of nontariff barriers represent a major change in the trade rules relating to agriculture. First, it makes transparent a series of barriers that have been hidden from view and exposes the strong protection that many countries give to their farmers. Will the process result in less protection now, and if not, why? Second, though an average tariff reduction of 36 percent sounds like a significant loosening of protection, is that the case when the resulting final bound tariffs are tabled? Third, in theory the binding of unbound tariffs is liberalizing because it prevents countries from raising tariffs above bound levels (Martin and Francois 1994). At what levels did bindings occur, and what do those levels imply for trade purposes?

The years 1986–88 were chosen as the base for tariffication because world prices for many agricultural commodities were the lowest in decades. Thus when the world price in the base period is compared with protected and supported internal prices, the gap – the measure of the tariff equivalent – is unusually wide. The unusual situation in the base period made it clear that the new tariffs would provide high levels of protection in normal times. In addition, however, many countries used prices to calculate their tariff equivalents, which resulted in higher initial tariffs than more objective calculations might have produced and gave rise to so-called dirty tariffication.

For many products in many countries, tariff equivalents tabled as part of a country schedule were appreciably higher than tariff equivalents during the base period (tables 2.2a and 2.2b). Of course, the new tariffs are almost always appreciably higher than the tariff equivalent calculated for more recent years when world prices were higher. In other words, the base period used for tariffication gave unusually high protection, and many countries

Table 2.2a *Comparison of estimated* ad valorem *tariff equivalent, 1986–88, and tariffs declared in country schedules (percent)*

	Rice			Wheat			Coarse grains			Sugar		
	Estimate 1986–88	UR base	Difference	Estimate 1986–88	UR base	Difference	Estimate 1986–88	UR base	Difference	Estimate 1986–88	UR base	Difference
	(1)	(2)	(2)–(1)	(3)	(4)	(4)–(3)	(5)	(6)	(6)–(5)	(7)	(8)	(8)–(7)
Industrial countries												
Australia	13.5	0.0	−13.5	0.7	0.0	−0.7	0.0	0.4	0.4	11.8	52.4	40.6
Canada	n.a.	0.9	n.a.	30.0	57.7	27.7	39.0	34.7	−4.3	39.0	34.7	−4.3
United States	1.0	5.0	4.0	20.0	6.0	−14.0	4.0	8.0	4.0	131.0	197.0	66.0
European Union	153.0	360.5	207.5	103.0	155.6	52.6	133.0	134.4	1.4	234.0	297.0	63.0
Japan	500.0	n.a.[a]	n.a.	651.0	239.6	−411.4	679.0	233.1	−445.9	184.0	126.1	−57.9
New Zealand	0.0	0.0	0.0	0.0	0.0	0.0	0.0	7.2	7.2	0.0	2.9	2.9
Austria	0.0	0.0	0.0	188.0	400.0	212.0	108.0	241.0	133.0	183.0	178.0	−5.0
Finland	n.a.	10.0	n.a.	239.0	352.0	113.0	342.0	204.0	−138.0	265.0	493.0	228.0
Norway	n.a.	454.0	n.a.	266.0	495.0	229.0	361.0	394.0	33.0	0.0	n.a.	n.a.
Switzerland	0.0	67.0	n.a.	245.0	179.0	−66.0	226.0	242.0	16.0	277.0	273.0	−4.0
Turkey	n.a.	50.0	n.a.	36.0	200.0	164.0	35.0	200.0	165.0	12.0	150.0	138.0
Developing countries												
Mexico	6.8	50.0	43.2	−1.0	74.0	75.0	73.0	174.0	101.0	−57.7	173.0	230.7
Colombia	4.0	210.0	206.0	20.0	138.0	118.0	14.0	221.0	207.0	25.3	130.0	104.7
Venezuela	174.9	135.0	−39.9	n.a.	130.0	n.a.	293.0	123.0	−170.0	47.0	100.0	53.0
Thailand	1.0	58.0	57.0	n.a.	64.0	n.a.	n.a.	81.0	n.a.	n.a.	104.0	n.a.
South Africa	n.a.	5.0	n.a.	10.3	74.5	64.2	47.8	68.0	20.2	98.0	124.0	26.0
Indonesia	8.8	180.0[b]	171.2	n.a.	30.0	n.a.	6.0	70.0[b]	64.0	87.0	110.0[b]	23.0
Rep. of Korea	213.8	n.a.[a]	n.a.	n.a.	10.9	n.a.	421.3	450.0	28.7	n.a.	23.7	n.a.
Mexico	6.8	50.0	43.2	−1.0	74.0	75.0	73.0	174.0	101.0	−57.7	173.0	230.7
Morocco	n.a.	233.5	n.a.	14.0	224.0	210.0	8.0	150.0	142.0	58.3	221.0	162.7
Czech Republic	14.0	70.0	56.0	−38.0	16.0	54.0	−8.0	20.0	28.0	14.0	70.0	56.0

[a] Delayed tariffication.
[b] Ceiling binding.
Note: selected commodities to which tariffication was applied and which are subject to safeguards.

Table 2.2b Comparison of estimated ad valorem tariff equivalents, 1986–88, and tariffs declared in country schedules (percent)

	Beef & veal			Pork			Poultry			Dairy		
	Estimate 1986–88	UR base 1995	Difference	Estimate 1986–88	UR base 1995	Difference	Estimate 1986–88	UR base 1995	Difference	Estimate 1986–88	UR base 1995	Difference
	(1)	(2)	(2)–(1)	(3)	(4)	(4)–(3)	(5)	(6)	(6)–(5)	(7)	(8)	(8)–(7)
Industrial countries												
Australia	0.0	0.0	0.0	0.0	0.0	0.0	0.0	0.0	0.0	49.3	6.7	−42.6
Canada	2.0	38.0	36.0	0.0	0.0	0.0	19.0	226.0	207.0	187.0	288.4	101.4
United States	3.0	31.0	28.0	0.0	0.0	0.0	15.0	7.0	−8.0	132.0	144.0	12.0
European Union	83.0	125.4	42.4	40.0	51.7	11.7	51.0	44.5	−6.5	177.0	288.5	111.5
Japan	87.0	38.5	−48.5	99.0	87.3	−11.7	13.0	14.0	1.0	501.0	489.4	−11.6
New Zealand	0.0	0.0	0.0	1.7	20.0	18.3	100.7	28.5	−72.2	0.0	19.6	19.6
Austria	79.0	239.0	160.0	72.0	178.0	106.0	41.0	38.0	−3.0	196.0	463.0	267.0
Finland	193.3	394.0	200.07	227.0	320.0	93.0	206.6	264.0	57.4	387.0	389.0	2.0
Norway	145.0	405.0	260.0	255.0	428.0	173.0	614.0	379.0	−235.0	148.0	435.0	287.0
Switzerland	236.0	479.0	243.0	157.0	227.0	70.0	585.0	767.0	182.0	321.0	795.0	474.0
Turkey	−4.4	250.0	254.4	n.a.	250.0	n.a.	11.5	30.0	n.a.	35.0	200.0	165.0
Developing countries												
Mexico	41.6	50.0	8.4	n.a.	50.0	n.a.	n.a.	217.7	n.a.	−3.0	75.0	78.0
Colombia	n.a.	120.0	n.a.	n.a.	120.0	n.a.	n.a.	126.0	n.a.	n.a.	150.0	n.a.
Venezuela	n.a.	50.0	n.a.	n.a.	53.0	n.a.	n.a.	150.0	n.a.	n.a.	96.0	n.a.
Thailand	n.a.	60.0	n.a.	n.a.	60.0	n.a.	n.a.	60.0	n.a.	n.a.	63.0	n.a.
South Africa	n.a.	210.0	n.a.	n.a.	50.0	n.a.	30.0	116.7	86.7	30.0	189.0	159.0
Indonesia	n.a.	70.0	n.a.	n.a.	70.0	n.a.	n.a.	70.0	n.a.	n.a.	154.0	n.a.
Rep. of Korea	95.5	44.5	−51.0	38.7	33.3	−5.4	2.2	26.3	24.1	103.4	220.0	116.6
Mexico	41.6	50.0	8.4	n.a.	50.0	n.a.	n.a.	217.7	n.a.	−3.0	75.0	78.0
Morocco	n.a.	315.0	n.a.	n.a.	45.0	n.a.	n.a.	132.5	n.a.	n.a.	115.0	n.a.
Czech Republic	134.0	43.0	−91.0	15.0	46.0	31.0	n.a.	36.0	n.a.	−20.0	64.0	84.0

Note: selected commodities to which tariffication was applied and which are subject to safeguards.

made matters worse with dirty tariffication. The tariffication process resulted in levels of protection for many products in many countries as high as or higher than under the old system of variable levies or quotas, even after subsequent tariff cuts.

An examination of base-level tariffs and reductions for nine major products shows that most OECD countries used tariffication procedures which resulted in base tariffs appreciably above the estimated tariff equivalents in 1986–88. The European Union declared base tariffs, which were higher than in 1986–88 for eight of the nine products, and for all but two the final bound tariffs ended up exceeding levels in 1986–88 (already a period of high protection). The United States also practiced dirty tariffication, but for only three products were the final bound tariffs above base-year levels of protection. Japan, often accused of being highly protectionist, declared base tariffs below estimated protection levels in 1986–88, and its final bound rates were almost always below the estimated border protection in 1986–88.

An examination of the schedules for developing countries where tariffication occurred shows a similar pattern. However, for many products developing countries took the opportunity to declare bound tariffs where there had been unbound tariffs, bypassing the issue of previous nontariff barriers and the level of unbound tariffs at the beginning of the Round. Because most newly declared bound tariffs are well above previous levels of protection calculated for individual countries – or above applied levels of unbound tariffs in effect on September 1, 1986 – they do not represent liberalization.

Developing country schedules show a varied pattern of protection. Some countries went through tariffication and some practiced dirty tariffication to maintain strong protection. However, many developing countries, notably in Africa and South Asia, took advantage of the opportunity apparently provided by section 14 of the modalities relating to unbound tariffs to declare new base and bound tariffs, which were set at very high levels and appear completely unrelated to previous levels of protection (table 2.3). The same countries did not use tariffication, nor did they table tariff cuts in the bound tariffs they declared. Such special treatment was never challenged. These nations declared a uniform pattern of tariffs of 100, 150, or 200 percent for all products. One notable exception was Egypt, which had relatively low or negative levels of protection for most products in the base period and declared very low base and final bound tariffs.

Some countries in Latin America did not follow the practice of using a fixed common tariff rate. In general, tariffs in Latin America tend to be lower than in other parts of the developing world, a reflection of the changes in economic policy that have been occurring in that region over the past decade or so.

Table 2.3 Border protection for selected agricultural goods, 1986–88, 1995, and 2000 (percent)

	Wheat			Sugar			Dairy			Meat		
	Actual protection	As bound in Uruguay Round		Actual protection	As bound in Uruguay Round		Actual protection	As bound in Uruguay Round		Actual protection	As bound in Uruguay Round	
	1986–88	1995	2000	1986–88	1995	2000	1986–88	1995	2000	1986–88	1995	2000
European Union	106	170	82	234	297	152	177	289	178	96	96	76
United States	20	6	4	131	197	91	132	144	93	3	31	26
Japan	651[a]	240	152	184	126	58	501	489	326	87	93	50
Brazil	98	45	45	n.a.	55	35	-21	53	46	-52	25	25
Mexico	-1	74	67	-58	173	156	-3	66	54	42	50	45
Other Latin America	-17	34	34	41	85	80	n.a.	75	69	n.a.	51	47
Nigeria	249	..	150	32	..	150	n.a.	..	150	n.a.	..	150
South Africa	10	75	47	98	124	105	30	189	89	40	150	81
Sub-Saharan Africa	10	..	133	44	..	100	n.a.	..	100	n.a.	..	100
Maghreb[b]	36	196	151	64	220	165	50	113	87	n.a.	303	213
Mediterranean[c]	25	169	152	-13	107	93	n.a.	166	150	n.a.	166	149

[a] Figure based on reference prices reported by OECD. If based on government resale prices, pre-Uruguay Round protection is 279 percent.

[b] Includes Algeria, Morocco, and Tunisia.

[c] Includes Cyprus, Egypt, Israel, Jordan, Lebanon, Libya, Malta, Syria, and Turkey.

Note: .. indicates no tariff bindings for the period in question.

The pattern of tariff cuts for products after tariffication shows a common approach that further limits liberalization. In general, for sensitive products that had been protected by nontariff barriers, there was a minimum reduction of 15 percent. To offset minimum cuts, tariffs on little-protected products were cut by a substantially greater percentage. Thus, a 100 percent cut in a 2 percent tariff could offset 15 percent cuts in three highly protected products.

The combination of dirty tariffication and uneven distribution of tariff cuts means that for many products protected by nontariff barriers prior to the negotiations, the bindings at the end of implementation will provide as much protection as the system did before the Uruguay Round began. Overall, the tariff-cutting exercise will probably increase the gap between highly protected and little-protected items. For instance, commodity patterns around the world suggest that border protection for sugar and dairy products was maintained or even increased by the changes, whereas protection on products such as soybean meal was generally reduced from an already low level.

This does not take into account the special safeguard clause that can be invoked for products subject to tariffication if imports rise too rapidly or import prices fall too low. The Blair House agreement changed the Dunkel Text to make safeguards easier to apply by lowering the trigger levels needed to invoke them. The price-triggered safeguard can be invoked if the import price in local currency falls below a trigger price based on the 1986–88 average import price. The additional duty that can be levied is a function of how far the import price falls below the trigger price. Many observers have viewed this particular safeguard as a disguised variable levy. The trigger has a variable element related to the access level for the product in question, in this case, the average level of imports in the last three years compared with total consumption. The higher the access level the lower the trigger level, so that if imports amount to over 30 percent of consumption a surge over 105 percent of base imports allows the safeguard to be used. The safeguard clause does not require proof of injury to domestic producers. While safeguards are limited in duration and in the levels of protection they afford, countries will be tempted to invoke them if world prices decline or there are wide currency fluctuations. If the binding of all tariffs is an important element of liberalization, then the safeguard clause could represent a major move away from liberalization.

The impact of minimum access commitments

From the outset it was recognized that tariffs resulting from tariffication would often be high, although no doubt many participants did not anticipate the outcome. Minimum access provisions were designed to deal with continued strong border protection by ensuring access for a minimum quantity of imports, defined as either existing levels or higher levels if current imports did not equal 5 percent of consumption. Tariff quotas would make access possible; that is, countries would establish lower tariffs for quantities of imports up to minimum access commitments. Minimum access commitments were to be established on a most-favored nation basis (GATT 1993, annex 3, C.14).

There are several remarks to be made about the minimum access commitments as tabled. Countries aggregated individual tariff lines into product groups. As a result, in most cases access provides for no more than base-period imports of given products. Despite the MFN requirement, countries are also allowed to count special arrangements as part of their minimum access commitments and to allocate their minimum access to exporters that have special arrangements. Thus current sugar imports from the Lomé countries meet the European Union's access requirements, and the European Union can continue allocating all its sugar imports as it did formerly. The United States did the same for its sugar and beef imports, both of which were allocated as under the previous quota system.

With a few notable exceptions, the minimum access commitments will provide relatively little additional access and even less additional trade. Access is allowed, but there is no guarantee that products will be imported. For example, minimum access for maize in low-cost net-exporting countries like Hungry and Thailand would seem unlikely to produce more trade. However, there will be new trade created in rice. Applied to the Japanese and Korean markets, minimum access will result in nearly a million tons of new imports by the turn of the century. Trade expansion compared to 1992 levels appears to have been modest for most products except rice (see table 2.4). In the case of rice, new trade opportunities come almost entirely from the access commitments made by Japan and Korea.

The tariff quotas will create quota rents or continue existing rents, which in most cases will accrue to exporters. Thus a considerable constituency will grow for continuation of quotas. Quota holders will oppose moves toward a more liberal, competitive trading system. A substantial expansion of tariff quotas or a significant reduction in the overquota tariffs will reduce the value of quota rents along with the income of both domestic producers of the products involved and exporters earning quota rents. This may well establish a strong constituency that opposes future reforms.

The Uruguay Round agreement does nothing to remove one of the most serious barriers to trade in agricultural products, the use of government or government-controlled monopoly importing agencies. Even if tariffs are lowered, consumers may not see lower prices, and suppliers may not be able

Table 2.4 *Estimated trade expansion from the Uruguay Round's access provision*

	World trade 1992 (million metric tons)	Declared minimum access (million metric tons)	Access as a percentage of trade	Final access compared with 1992 imports (million metric tons)	New access compared with 1992 world trade (percent)
Sugar	30.4	3.6	11.8	+0.112	0.4
Wheat	108.3	13.8	14.6	+0.512	0.5
Beef	3.1	1.2	38.7	+0.088	2.8
Rice	14.1	1.8	12.9	+1.040	7.5
Maize	63.7	13.1	20.6	+1.400	2.2
Poultry	2.1	0.25	12.0	+0.053	2.5

Note: from country schedules of forty-three major trading countries, including the European Union as a single country.

to compete for the market. For instance, the Japanese food agency, which controls all wheat imports into Japan, can designate the amount imported from each supplier without regard to price, and it can establish Japanese trading companies as the only buying agents. Japan can, and probably will, do the same thing for its new rice imports. No restrictions apply on the resale price of imports, and thus the Japanese government can use low-cost imports as a way to finance domestic subsidy programs. In some countries, especially developing ones, state buying agencies resell imports at prices that are below world prices, thus distorting their internal markets in another way.

Article XVII of GATT sets certain rules for state trading agencies, including a provision calling for nondiscriminatory treatment and treatment in accordance with commercial practices, but the rules have never been enforced and are probably unenforceable anyway. Article XVII also contains a requirement that countries using state trading entities report on their operations. This has never been adequately enforced. The Uruguay Round agreement contains a new explanatory note on state trading, but all it does is require that the use of such agencies be reported; it does nothing to curb their restrictive practices. It remains to be seen whether a successful complaint can be brought in the WTO against the practices of state trading entities that violate tariff bindings by maintaining internal prices above levels implied by the bindings.

Overall, then, the access negotiations resulted in major reform of the rules but limited trade liberalization. The elimination of all nontariff barriers and the binding of all tariffs on agricultural products are sweeping new rules that move toward liberalization but do not appreciably reduce border protection from previous levels. In the long run, the increased transparency of continuing intense protection should increase pressure for liberalization in future trade negotiations. For now, though, low-cost exporters still face major barriers in most foreign markets.

Export subsidy reforms

In the case of export competition, changes in the rules are less sweeping but may have a more significant effect on trade. Though nontariff barriers were eliminated, it proved politically impossible to completely phase out export subsidies. Instead, the agreement defines upper limits for export subsidies by country and commodity and incorporates the limits in country schedules. Countries that had no export subsidies in the base period are prohibited from using them now, and countries that have them now cannot use them on any products to which they were not applied in the base period.

The definition of export subsidies contained in Article 9 of the agriculture agreement is fairly rigorous. As is the case for other commitments, developing countries are only required to reduce two-thirds as much (14 percent in volume, 24 percent in spending) as industrial countries, and they have ten years to implement the reductions instead of six. Developing countries are also exempt, during the implementation period, from commitments on subsidies to reduce the cost of marketing exports or internal freight subsidies.

While the definition of export subsidies is fairly rigorous, the definition of commodities is not. Countries declared commodity aggregates instead of individual tariff lines. For instance wheat, wheat flour, and some derivatives of wheat are included as a single group. The European Union included some forty products as coarse grains. Aggregations give exporting countries a flexibility in export competition that line-by-line commitments would not allow. For instance, a country with a subsidy for wheat during the base period will be able to continue subsidizing all of its flour exports by merely substituting flour exports for wheat in the reporting. Aggregation appears likely to shift export subsidy competition to products with greater value added.

The world's top five users of export subsidies for any given major product account for virtually all such subsidies applied worldwide and for virtually all commitments for reduction (table 2.5). For product after product, the European Union is the largest user of export subsidies. With a few notable exceptions, among them Brazil, there are relatively few developing countries with export subsidy commitments. In the case of some commodities the reduction in subsidized exports will be significant, but it is difficult to judge exactly what the market impact will be.

Table 2.5 *Base and final subsidy commitments for selected commodities in major subsidizing countries (metric tons)*

	1986–90	1995	2000
Wheat			
United States	18,382.4	20,238.3	14,522.1
European Union	17,008.1	19,118.6	13,436.4
Canada	11,204.8	13,590.3	8,851.8
Turkey	2,306.0	2,600.2	1,461.2
Hungary	1,444.0	1,393.0	1,141.0
Total (top 5 countries)	50,345.3	56,940.3	39,412.4
Total[a]	53,018.3	—	—
World trade 1991–92	108,289.0	—	—
Top 5 countries' % of total export subsidies	95.0	—	—
Top 5 countries' % of world trade in 1991–92	46.5	—	—
Rice			
Indonesia	299.8	295,553.0	257,785.0
European Union	183.7	177,300.0	145,100.0
Uruguay	53.2	—	45,712.0
United States	48.8	271,660.0	38,554.0
Colombia	18.9	—	16,263.0
Total (top 5 countries)	604.3	744,513.0	503,414.0
Total [a]	604.5	—	—
World trade	14,080.0	—	—
Top 5 countries' % of total export subsidies	100.0	—	—
Top 5 countries' % of world trade in 1991–92	4.3	—	—
Vegetable oil			
Brazil	552.1	544.3	474.7
Hungary	185.0	179.0	146.0
United States	178.9	587.5	141.3
Canada	117.4	113.3	92.8
Turkey	72.2	94.5	76.5
Total (top 5 countries)	1,105.6	1,518.7	931.3
Total [a]	1,197.2	—	—
World trade	21,470.0	—	—
Top 5 countries' % of total export subsidies	92.4	—	—
Top 5 countries % of world trade in 1991–92	5.1	—	—

Table 2.5 (*cont.*)

	1986–90	1995	2000
Coarse grains			
European Union	12,624.5	12,182.6	9,973.4
Canada	4,392.0	4,418.9	3,617.6
Mexico[b]	3,577.8	3,513.1	2,951.0
United States	1,975.4	1,906.3	1,560.6
Rep. of South Africa[c]	1,893.5	1,827.3	1,495.9
Total (top 5 countries)	24,463.2	23,848.2	19,598.5
Total[a]	28,328.6	—	—
World trade	91,680.0	—	—
Top 5 countries' % of total export subsidies	86.4	—	—
Top 5 countries' % of world trade in 1991–92	26.7	—	—
Beef & veal			
European Union	1,034.3	1,118.7	817.1
Brazil	106.7	105.2	91.8
Austria	80.9	90.1	63.9
Poland[d]	51.7	49.9	40.9
Hungary	36.0	35.0	28.0
Total (top 5 countries)	1,309.6	1,398.9	1,041.7
Total[a]	1,372.4		
Top 5 countries' % of total export subsidies	95.4	—	—
Top 5 countries' % of world trade in 1991–92	27.0	—	—
Pigmeat			
European Union	508.6	490.8	401.8
Hungary	115.0	111.0	91.0
Poland[d]	51.7	49.9	40.9
Sweden	47.0	45.4	37.1
Finland	8.1	11.3	6.4
Total (top 5 countries)	730.4	708.4	577.2
Total[a]	741.0		
World trade	2,441.0	—	—
Top 5 countries' % of total export subsidies	98.6	—	—
Top 5 countries' % of world trade in 1991–92	29.9	—	—

Table 2.5 (*cont.*)

	1986–90	1995	2000
Poultry			
European Union	367.8	440.1	290.6
Hungary	141.0	136.0	111.0
Brazil	97.9	96.7	84.2
United States	35.4	34.2	28.0
Poland	16.4	15.8	13.1
Total (top 5 countries)	658.6	722.7	526.9
Total[a]	663.7	—	—
World trade	2,074.0	—	—
Top 5 countries' % of total export subsidies	1.0	—	—
Top 5 countries' % of world trade in 1991–92	31.7	—	—

[a] Total export subsidies.
[b] Corn and sorghum subsidy volumes have been added.
[c] Barley, maize and maize products, oats, and grain sorghum subsidy volumes have been added together.
[d] The volume of export subsidy for Poland includes all meats except for poultry.

Generally speaking, countries use export subsidies to compensate for policies that maintain domestic prices above world prices and thus prohibit or limit the ability to export given products. Policies that affect domestic prices include support prices and tariff protection. The impact of the new limits on subsidized exports will depend on the quantity of the product affected, the significance of the reduction relative to the total volume of trade, and policy adjustments the subsidizing country makes. For instance, because the European Union lowered internal prices through agricultural policy reform, the binding constraint for most EU products will be on volume, which will require a 21 percent reduction below the volume in the base period 1986–90. For most US products, spending could be the binding constraint because during the base period the United States had lower subsidies and therefore spent much less per unit of product exported than did the European Union. Unless world prices appreciably exceed prices in the base years 1986–90, the constraint for the United States will be the 36 percent reduction in expenditure. In the case of Canada, the export subsidy on wheat is primarily a rail subsidy paid on all grain leaving the country. There will be substantial incentive for the Canadians to replace their rail subsidy with some type of assistance to producers, which would be classified as a domestic subsidy and would not be trade distorting.

Policy shifts could also remove the export subsidy constraints in the United States and the European Union. Export subsidies are only required when domestic prices are maintained above world prices. If internal prices in the European Union and the United States were allowed to drop to world levels, exports would occur without subsidies, and farmers could be compensated with higher direct payments, which are exempt from reductions.

These illustrations merely indicate the difficulty of predicting exactly what will happen to export volumes in individual countries or to commodity prices. For wheat, beef, and some dairy products, the rollback in subsidized exports will be considerable relative to the volume of trade in those products. For most other products, the effect is likely to be minimal. The export subsidy agreement does not restrict how remaining allowable export subsidies can be used or the markets to which they can be directed.

Developing countries, in addition to being granted a longer adjustment period and smaller rollbacks in subsidy levels, are also exempt from reductions in some export subsidies during the ten-year transition period. These subsidies are related to the marketing of exports, for example, handling, upgrading and processing costs, and to the internal transport of exports.

While the export subsidy arrangement is not a tidy one and will be difficult to monitor because of the detailed reports involved, it is a significant improvement on the old GATT rules, which defined limits on export subsidies so loosely as to be unworkable. Moreover, as the world market grows trade will expand without the distortions of direct export subsidies. This means that future market growth should benefit low-cost producers, including those countries that lack the fiscal resources to subsidize their agricultural exports.

Though the export subsidy commitments have been cited as one of the major achievements of the Uruguay Round, it should be noted that trade in many products will still be subjected to significant distortions at the end of the adjustment period. With trade at current levels, subsidized exports can account for a third or more of trade for beef and veal, wheat, pigmeat, and vegetable oil. Over one fifth of the trade in poultry and coarse grains can still be subsidized. This still is a long way from an undistorted trading regime.

As in the case of imports, the negotiations did not address the issue of monopoly exporting entities under a single-seller system. The single-seller system allows the exporting entity to discriminate between markets and, in the view of many, amounts to unfair competition in the same way that targeted export subsidies do. Nor did the negotiations address the issue of differential export taxes. Some exporters have argued that differential export taxes are an implicit subsidy for the export of products taxed at a lower level. In recent years there has been criticism of some Latin American exporters for using differential export taxes to encourage the export of soy meal and oil over unprocessed soybeans.

Domestic policy reform

Initial proposals for domestic policy reform included bold GATT rules to limit or prohibit trade-distorting domestic subsidies. This would have pushed GATT rules for agriculture well beyond those for other products, which have no limit on domestic subsidies. Initially, the United States and the Cairns Group pushed for drastic reform by suggesting the complete phaseout of trade-distorting domestic subsidy programs, but the proposal ran into a wall of opposition from every country with significant domestic subsidies. Many producers and legislators viewed the idea of international controls over domestic policy as an infringement of national sovereignty. At first, there was support for the idea of a balanced approach, with the reduction in trade-distorting domestic subsidies aligned with reductions in tariffs and export subsidies.

The Dunkel Text had a fairly strict definition of trade-distorting domestic subsidies, and it called for their reduction by 20 percent on a commodity-specific basis. However, EU farmers had been promised that if they accepted Common Agricultural Policy reform their subsidy levels would not be cut. Therefore they were strongly opposed to the Dunkel Text, which would have classified their new subsidies as subject to cuts and individual limits. In some cases such as sugar, reform has not occurred, and thus the Dunkel Text would have required a reduction in the EU internal support level for sugar. Similar political problems existed in the United States as well. Despite reductions in support for many commodities in the 1985 and 1990 farm bills, some heavily subsidized commodities such as peanuts, rice, and sugar faced the possibility of reduced domestic subsidies or a switch to a nondistorting policy. The switch to nondistorting or decoupled polices was anathema to producers of these crops because it would have exposed the extent of income transfers and the distribution of benefits, neither of which would be politically popular.

Thus there was support on both sides of the table at Blair House to back away from the strict disciplines and commodity-by-commodity cutbacks of domestic support as laid out in the Dunkel Text. The concept of an international agreement that would force reductions in trade-distorting domestic subsidies was abandoned. First, the United States and the European Union agreed to move to an aggregate measure of support for all products and to reduce the aggregate level without reference to a specific commodity. This brought them back to the initial position of the European Union.

Second, they agreed to exempt the major support policies of both the European Union and the United States, even though neither met the strict nondistorting criteria.

These two changes removed most of the political opposition to reduction in domestic support by eliminating the need for a country to cut subsidies for any specific commodity. There is little question that countries will resist reducing internal supports for politically sensitive commodities such as rice in Japan, sugar in the United States and the European Union, and dairy products in most OECD countries. No doubt there will be few policy changes that would reduce the incentive to produce in high-cost areas. Thus hoped-for cutbacks in subsidized output are unlikely to be realized.

This does not mean that the new GATT provisions will not have any impact. For the first time there is official recognition of the fact that domestic subsidies can and do distort trade, and policies considered trade distorting have been classified as such. As countries consider ways to assist their agricultural producers, they will probably drift toward those policies not subject to challenge as trade distorting. Moreover, since the cap on spending for trade-distorting subsidies is fixed in nominal values, it will erode with inflation and increase the incentive to move to nondistorting policies.

For developing countries this could be especially important. Most of the countries with large expenditure bases for distorting programs are OECD countries, whereas few developing countries have high domestic subsidy levels in the base period. If they wish to subsidize their agriculture as part of economic development, they will have to use nondistorting policies, which will be beneficial to both them and the rest of the world.

The global impact of the agricultural agreement

Much has been written and said about the agricultural agreement, some of which is either misleading or plain wrong. Certain negotiators, supporters, and officials have portrayed the agreement as a sweeping reform of world agricultural trade and a significant move toward liberalization. Scrutiny of the details suggests it is something considerably less. While the agreement may involve a major change in the rules for border protection, it does not represent a significant reduction in border protection or a major increase in access to protected markets. It appears that the protection afforded the most protected commodities, such as sugar and dairy products, was reduced the least. As a result, distortions among commodities probably intensified.

Critics of the agreement have made three points. First, they claim, it will require poor developing countries to throw their markets open to uncontrolled imports from developed countries that have large-scale industrialized farms, pushing peasants from their farms into urban slums. While it is true that some developing countries have chosen to open their internal markets to outside competition, as Mexico did in the NAFTA, the Uruguay Round did not require this of developing countries. Indeed, a quick look at tariff levels established by the poorest countries suggests that they will maintain strong border protection. Of course, it is well documented that the biggest problem of peasants in many developing countries is the policy their own governments follow of holding internal prices below world prices to maintain the political support of urban consumers. The Uruguay Round did nothing to stop this practice or to encourage countries to phase it out.

Second, critics maintain, the agreement will increase the world prices for major agricultural commodities, thus adversely affecting the situation of food-importing developing countries. Given the modest policy adjustments that will result from the round, it appears that at most the supply of commodities will be affected only slightly. If that is the case, it is difficult to see what would cause a significant increase in prices. Most efforts to measure the probable price impact of the Uruguay Round imply that the impact would be minimal (chapter 6).

Third, critics of the agreement assert that the reduction in domestic subsidies in industrial countries will reduce the quantity of food aid available. This view assumes that the quantity of aid is primarily a function of the need for surplus disposal: if surpluses disappear, the quantity of aid will drop. However, as discussed earlier, there is nothing in the agreement that will appreciably reduce domestic subsidies and the incentives to produce, and so the surplus-disposal problem will not be changed as a result of the Uruguay Round. Moreover, since the agreement puts specific limits on the use of export subsidies as a method of moving surpluses into world markets, food aid will remain the one legitimate method of moving excess supplies into world markets. If countries continue the use of output-expanding subsidies in the face of the limits on export subsidies, the agreement may encourage rather than curb food aid.

The most likely constraint on both domestic agricultural subsidies and food aid is the budget cost of programs. Widespread publicity for these policies arising from the Uruguay Round has focused attention on their costs. Though the poorest countries were not instrumental in the agricultural negotiations, it does not appear that they are worse off for the agreement. Nor will they be appreciably better off. Exporting developing countries will find few new market openings for their products, but they will face less subsidized competition for existing markets and they will not be elbowed out of growing markets by export subsidies from industrial countries.

Conclusion

The final agricultural agreement that emerged from the Uruguay Round was shaped largely by the fact that the European Union and the United States were the chief negotiators. Despite rhetoric about ridding the world of trade-distorting subsidies, the United States had as its ultimate objective effective international control over the European Union's ever-expanding export subsidies. The Cairns Group hoped to control or eliminate export subsidies used by the European Union and the United States. The European Union and Japan had as their prime objective the continuation of their strong protection and their isolation from world market forces. Theirs was a defensive strategy, and to a large extent it worked. Despite the political furor the agreement created in those countries, their farmers will still be heavily shielded from international competition.

Developing countries outside the Cairns Group had a limited impact on the agenda for the agricultural negotiations and the outcome. Provisions in the Dunkel Text allowed many to escape tariffication and to maintain high levels of protection. Thus most of the distortions that a developing country imposes on its economy through agricultural policy will remain largely untouched if the country chooses.

The revised rules for agriculture, which clarify the limits on export subsidies and provide uniform methods of border protection, should soothe tension in GATT over agricultural trade issues. This, together with the cease fire, should remove agriculture as one of the major questions about the way the trading system functions. If countries fail to comply with their commitments, the system's functioning will resurface as an issue.

The promise of the Uruguay Round agreement really lies in the future it makes possible. The groundwork has been laid for serious trade liberalization in the next round of negotiations. The agricultural agreement calls for discussions at the end of five years on the need for further reform. It remains to be seen whether the major stakeholders in world agricultural trade want to pursue real liberalization.

References

GATT 1986. *Uruguay Declaration*. Geneva: GATT.
   1993. *Modalities for the Establishment of Specific Binding Commitments under the Reform Program*. MTN.GNG/MA/W/24. Geneva: GATT Goods Negotiating Group, December 20.
Martin, W., and J. Francois 1994. "Bindings and Rules as Trade Liberalization." Paper presented at the Festschrift Conference, "Quiet Pioneering: Robert M. Stern and his International Economic Legacy," University of Michigan, Ann Arbor, November 18–20.

3 Trade in manufactures: the outcome of the Uruguay Round and developing country interests

Marcelo de Paiva Abreu

Evaluating the impact of the Uruguay Round's multilateral negotiations on trade in industrial products entails broad-ranging comparison of this sector before and after the negotiations. With respect to developing economies in particular, the key questions are: Will the Uruguay Round provide developing economies that export industrial goods with more markets in both industrial and developing countries? [1] Will liberalization in developing countries significantly increase exports by industrial countries? Which categories of products are likely to be most affected?

Results of the Uruguay Round: an overview

Before evaluating the gains from the Uruguay Round, it is important to examine the general structure of world industrial trade (table 3.1). Today there is a substantial market in industrial economies for the industrial goods of developing countries, about US $171 billion a year.[2] Developing economies offer a slightly smaller market for the exports of industrial countries, about US $161 billion. However, the market in developing countries for industrial imports from other developing countries is rather small, about US $21 billion, in the data base used, where coverage is less comprehensive for developing than for industrial economies.[3] Developing Asia exports account for almost 60 percent of total developing country industrial exports, while developing America exports account for slightly more than 30 percent. Industrial exports from Africa (low level) and from developing Europe (modest) are overwhelmingly directed to the European Union. About 57 percent of industrial exports from industrial economies are directed to developing Asia and 23 percent to developing America. Africa and developing Europe import mostly from the European Union.[4]

Evaluating the gains from the Uruguay Round is a complex task. There is uncertainty about when liberalization schedules and rules will be implemented. No detailed information on restrictive measures exists, nor is there

Table 3.1 *World trade in industrial products by region of origin and destination (US $billion)*

	Industrial economies						Developing economies					All economies
	United States	European Union	Japan	Other industrial Asia^a	Other industrial	Total	Developing America	Developing Asia	Africa	Developing Europe	Total	
United States	0	54.3	32.2	15.9	82.5	184.9	18.7	22.2	0.2	2.4	43.5	228.5
European Union	68.4	0	21.4	15.8	117.6	223.1	10.9	19.4	3.1	17.0	50.4	273.6
Japan	91.0	45.2	0	32.8	25.2	194.1	3.6	33.8	0.1	1.3	38.8	232.9
Other industrial Asia	17.6	9.9	3.0	3.6	4.6	38.8	0.4	7.4	0	0.2	8.0	46.8
Other industrial	90.6	105.6	22.5	6.9	30.9	256.3	3.6	9.2	0.3	7.0	20.0	276.4
Total industrial economies	267.6	215.0	79.1	74.7	260.8	897.3	37.2	92.0	3.8	27.9	160.8	1,058.1
Developing America	29.2	11.6	5.0	1.2	3.4	50.3	6.0	2.3	0	0.6	8.9	59.2
Developing Asia	35.7	19.1	25.8	18.6	7.2	106.2	0.4	7.2	0	0.7	8.4	114.6
Africa	0.1	1.9	0.2	0	0.1	2.2	0	0.1	0.1	0	0.2	2.4
Developing Europe	1.3	8.9	0.5	0.2	2.0	12.9	0.2	0.5	0.1	2.5	3.3	16.2
Total developing economies	66.2	41.4	31.4	19.9	12.6	171.5	6.6	10.1	0.2	3.9	20.9	192.4
Total	333.9	256.4	110.6	94.6	273.4	1,068.8	43.8	102.1	4.0	31.8	181.7	1,250.5

^a "Other industrial Asia" refer to Hong Kong and Singapore. "Other industrial" are Australia, Austria, Canada, Finland, Iceland, New Zealand, Norway, Sweden, and Switzerland.

Note: data refer to imports only to countries for which there is information in GATT's IDB. Year of trade data varies in IDB from 1986 to 1991. Data cover MFN trade, trade conducted under free-trade arrangements, which is not affected by tariff reduction, and trade under other preferential arrangements. Of the US $1,251 billion total trade in industrial products, about $168 billion corresponds to trade under free-trade arrangement area agreements. Columns indicate destination regions; rows, origin regions.

Source: IDB GATT/World Bank data base.

consensus about how to gauge liberalization. Commitments cannot be easily translated into a measure of liberalization.[5] These difficulties are reflected in the evaluation of tariff bindings in the Uruguay Round.[6] A country binds the tariff on a product when it commits itself multilaterally not to increase the tariff above a specific level, except by negotiation with affected trading partners. In the case of a previously bound tariff, the rate of tariff reduction is a reasonable indication of improved market access. Before the Uruguay Round, bindings were heavily concentrated in the tariff lines of industrial economies and the actual level of duties generally corresponded to bound levels. However, it is much more difficult to gauge improvements in market access for previously unbound tariffs – the case of most tariff lines in developing countries. Martin and Francois (1994) proposed a methodology to prevent extreme distortions in simultaneously evaluating tariff reduction and bindings, the approach adopted here. When comparing an unbound pre-Uruguay Round duty with a higher bound post-Round duty, tariff liberalization is approximated as zero and not as a negative value, which would imply an increase in protection.[7]

In most cases, tariff reduction resulting from the Uruguay Round was scheduled to be evenly distributed over a five-year period after January 1, 1995, when the WTO agreement entered into force. Market access for industrial products of developing countries in both industrial and developing countries has improved. The coverage of tariff bindings was expanded. In computing average duties, to take into account the impact of increased bindings, pre-Uruguay Round duties were considered to be the lesser of pre-Round bound tariffs and pre-Round applied tariffs, while post-Round tariffs were considered to be the lesser of pre-Round tariffs and new tariff bindings resulting from the Round.

The proportion of bound tariffs has increased as a result of the Uruguay Round, especially in developing countries. (Even before the Round, 94 percent of imports to industrial countries were traded under bound rates [table 3.2].) Many developing countries, mainly in Latin America, agreed to bind 100 percent of tariff lines, while Indonesia agreed to bind 90 percent; India, the Republic of Korea, Malaysia, the Philippines, Singapore, and Thailand to between 60 and 89 percent; and Hong Kong, Macau, and Sri Lanka to between 10 and 25 percent. The overall percentage of bound tariff lines on industrial products in Asia is 70 percent, compared with 100 percent in Latin America.[8]

Average duties have been reduced for all countries or groups of countries in all markets (table 3.3). In industrial countries, average tariffs remained higher on imports from developing countries, 3.9 percent, than on imports from other industrial countries, 2.3 percent. The Uruguay Round widened this gap, setting higher tariff cuts for trade between industrial countries

Table 3.2 *Percentage of total imports of industrial products under bound rates and of trade affected by bindings and tariff reduction in the Uruguay Round*

	Industrial economies	Developing economies	Transition economies
Imports under bound rates pre-Round	94	13	74
Imports under bound rates post-Round	99	61	96
Outcome of the Round:			
Already bound duty free	18	1	12
Bindings with reductions	64	32	76
Bindings without reductions	3	26	1
No offer	16	42	10

Source: GATT 1994b, pp. 9 and 26.

than for trade between industrial and developing countries. Average tariffs in the developing countries remained significantly higher than those in the industrial world, and higher for imports originating in industrial than in developing countries.[9]

Improved market access is not the only area in which the Uruguay Round stands to liberalize industrial trade. Liberalization will also result from the abolition of the MFA, better rules on safeguards, new antidumping and subsidy countervailing measures, and a more effective GATT. Moreover, nontariff protection will probably be significantly reduced in most developing countries as a result of improved rules on and surveillance and enforcement of balance-of-payments provisions, import licensing, and preshipment inspection.

Industrial exports from developing countries, and access to industrial country markets

Industrial exports are of crucial importance for most developing countries. For forty-four of the eighty-seven such countries participating in the Uruguay Round, industrial exports exceed 70 percent of total exports, excluding fuel.[10]

Textiles and clothing, fish products, metals, and mineral products represent major export interests for many developing countries participating in the Uruguay Round. The interest of the main developing country exporters is concentrated on textiles and clothing (China, Hong Kong, India, Korea, Macao, Pakistan, the Philippines, Egypt, Morocco, and Tunisia),

Table 3.3 Pre-and post-Uruguay Round average tariffs and tariff cuts for industrial products by region of origin and destination (percent)

	Industrial economies			Developing economies			All economies		
	Pre-Round	Post-Round	Reduction (percent)	Pre-Round	Post-Round	Reduction (percent)	Pre-Round	Post-Round	Reduction (percent)
United States	2.1	1.1	50	16.1	12.5	23	4.8	3.2	32
European Union	5.1	3.1	39	20.8	16.2	22	8.0	5.5	31
Japan	4.9	3.3	33	24.1	16.9	30	8.1	5.6	32
Other industrial Asia	7.3	5.3	28	22.1	16.3	26	9.9	7.2	27
Other industrial	2.7	1.4	50	14.3	10.9	24	3.6	2.1	43
Total industrial economies	3.9	2.3	40	19.6	14.7	25	6.3	4.2	33
Developing America	4.2	2.8	34	6.5	5.2	20	4.5	3.1	31
Developing Asia	5.9	4.3	26	20.1	15.5	23	6.9	5.2	20
Africa	7.9	6.4	20	10.4	7.7	25	8.2	6.5	26
Developing Europe	7.2	4.9	31	12.6	10.9	14	8.3	6.1	26
Total developing economies	5.5	3.9	28	13.0	10.3	21	6.3	4.6	27
All economies	4.1	2.6	38	18.8	14.2	25	6.3	4.3	32

Note: trade-weighted tariffs. Tariff cuts are based on average tariffs before rounding off. Columns indicate destination regions; rows, origin regions.
Source: computed from IDB GATT/World Bank data base using World Bank country classifications and GATT product classifications.

metals (Argentina, Brazil, and Egypt), mineral products (Algeria, Colombia, India, Indonesia, and Morocco), electric and nonelectric machinery (Malaysia, Mexico, and Singapore), and wood and pulp (Indonesia and Malaysia).[11] No main developing country has a major export interest in the other industrial groups: leather, rubber, footwear, and travel goods; fish and fish products; chemicals and photographic supplies; transport equipment and other manufactured articles.[12]

Tariff cuts in the Uruguay Round did not radically alter tariff structures in industrial economies (table 3.4). Tariffs faced by developing economies in industrial economies will remain higher in the European Union than in other industrial economies or the US. Tariffs in Japan and particularly in other Asian industrial economies were generally lowered from already very low levels. For all imports from developing countries the tariff cut in industrial economies was 28 percent, compared with 40 percent for imports from other industrial economies. The implied import price reduction is 1.5 percent in both cases as tariffs are higher on imports from developing economies than on imports from other industrial economies. The United States and the European Union cut tariffs by 25 percent; more significant cuts were made by Japan and other industrial economies, which slashed tariffs by 36 and 38 percent respectively. Because pre-Uruguay Round tariffs in industrial Asian economies other than Japan were near zero, their tariff cuts were negligible.

Tariff rates in industrial countries tend to be higher on imports from developing Asia than on imports from developing America. This is a result of both the different composition of total exports – more textiles and clothing from Asia, for instance – and the concentration of Asian exports either in high-tariff markets or in high-tariff products within industrial categories. Industrial country tariffs are still higher on imports from developing Europe and Africa.

Cuts were not homogeneously distributed by sector (table 3.5). They were below average for textiles and clothing, transport equipment, leather products, and fish products. For most other products, tariff cuts were above 40 percent. Data suggest a close relationship between the level of pre-Uruguay Round industrial product sectoral tariffs and the average tariff cuts in the Uruguay Round: high-tariff sectors had smaller cuts than low-tariff sectors.[13] This pattern of liberalization is unfortunate, especially for least-developed countries whose exports are concentrated in some of these sectors, such as textiles and clothing.[14] Exports by least-developed countries amount to a modest proportion of total developing country exports to industrial economies – only 2.3 percent of GATT's integrated data base trade – and total exports of industrial products by least-developed countries are in the region of US $2 billion.[15]

Table 3.4 *Average pre- and post-Uruguay Round tariff rates on imports by industrial economies from developing economies, by region of origin and destination (percent)*

	United States		European Union		Japan		Other industrial Asia		Other industrial		Total	
	Before	After	Before	After	Before	After	Before	After	Before	After	Before	After
Developing America	4.9	3.3	3.5	2.5	1.8	0.7	0.2	0.1	5.7	3.4	4.2	2.8
Developing Asia	7.4	5.8	8.4	6.4	3.9	2.7	0.1	0.1	13.6	8.5	5.9	4.3
Africa	3.4	2.7	8.6	7.0	4.4	2.9	0.0	0.0	5.8	4.1	7.9	6.4
Developing Europe	9.2	7.4	7.4	5.1	4.2	1.4	0.1	0.0	6.7	4.1	7.2	4.9
Total developing economies	6.3	4.7	6.8	5.1	3.6	2.3	0.1	0.1	10.3	6.4	5.5	3.9
All economies	3.7	2.4	6.0	3.6	2.6	1.4	0.1	0.1	5.0	3.2	4.1	2.6

Note: trade-weighted tariffs. Columns indicate destination countries; rows, origin countries.
Source: computed from IDB GATT/World Bank data base using World Bank country classifications and GATT product classifications.

Table 3.5 *Pre- and post-Uruguay Round average tariffs and tariff cuts on imports by industrial economies from developing economies*

	Trade (US $billion)	Average tariff (percent)		Tariff reduction (percent)
		Pre-Round	Post-Round	
Fish and fish products	7.7	6.5	5.0	22
Wood, pulp, paper, and furniture	11.5	3.5	1.5	59
Textiles and clothing	30.0	13.2	11.1	16
Leather, rubber, footwear, and travel goods	16.9	7.1	6.1	13
Metals	23.8	2.3	0.8	66
Chemicals and photographic supplies	7.1	4.6	2.7	41
Transport equipment	7.9	4.6	3.9	15
Nonelectric machinery	11.6	3.0	1.2	59
Electric machinery	25.7	3.9	2.4	39
Mineral products	17.9	1.6	1.0	38
Other manufactured articles	11.3	4.5	2.0	57
Industrial products (excluding petroleum)	171.5	5.5	3.9	28

Note: trade-weighted tariffs. Tariff cuts are based on average tariffs before rounding off.
Source: computed from IDB GATT/World Bank data base using World Bank country classifications and GATT commodity classifications.

Through "zero for zero" tariff commitments, industrial countries totally eliminated tariffs on a few specific product categories in pharmaceuticals, construction equipment, distilled spirits, beer, furniture, steel, medical equipment, agricultural equipment, toys, and paper. Some of these commitments are immediate, while others will be phased in over periods of up to ten years. Developing countries significantly reduced tariffs in these products.[16]

Evidence on tariff profiles for industrial products in industrial countries shows that the share of products with duty-free treatment rose considerably, from 20 percent to 43 percent. Progress on tariff peaks – tariffs above 15 percent – was modest, as the percentage of affected trade decreased only from 7 to 5 percent (table 3.6). Tariff peaks remain important for textiles and clothing and to a lesser extent for hides and leather, transport equipment, and fish products. For these industrial groups the increase in the share of duty-free trade was rather small.

Table 3.6 *Percentage of value of imports by industrial economies by tariff brackets before and after the Uruguay Round*

	Duty free		0.1–15.0%		15.1–35.0%		Over 35%	
	Before	After	Before	After	Before	After	Before	After
Fish and fish products	21	24	78	73	7	3	0	0
Wood, pulp, paper, and furniture	50	84	46	15	4	0	1	0
Textiles and clothing	2	4	63	68	33	27	2	1
Leather, rubber, footwear, and travel goods	16	19	71	70	11	9	3	2
Metals	36	70	62	29	2	1	1	0
Chemicals and photographic supplies	14	34	81	66	5	1	1	0
Transport equipment	16	21	75	71	5	4	4	3
Nonelectric machinery	11	48	86	50	2	2	1	0
Electric machinery	5	30	91	68	3	2	1	0
Mineral products	59	81	41	19	2	1	0	0
Manufactured articles	15	49	83	50	2	1	0	0
Industrial products (excluding petroleum)	20	43	72	53	6	4	1	1

Note: GATT's definition of industrial economies excludes Hong Kong and Singapore.
Source: adapted from GATT 1994a, p. 12.

Nontariff barriers are relevant for a range of manufactured products. Information from GATT's trade policy review reports until early 1993 indicated seventy-five voluntary export restraints, covering travel goods (fourteen cases), electrical equipment and appliances (eleven), footwear (eight), television and television tubes (five), machine tools (four) and other products (thirty-three). Estimates of the *ad valorem* tariff equivalents of these measures, however, are notoriously fragile and incomplete because of methodological problems or lack of information.[17]

The agreement on safeguards negotiated in the Uruguay Round will close some loopholes that allowed the circumvention of GATT rules. Such gray-area measures as VERs and orderly market arrangements are now prohibited. Article XIX stipulates that emergency action on import surges should be introduced without discrimination, that is, on an MFN basis. Safeguards should be applied only following an investigation that establishes injury or threat of serious injury, and only to the extent necessary to prevent or remedy injury. Safeguards apply for no more than four years – renewable to eight years in industrial countries and ten years in developing countries – and provisional safeguards for no more than 200 days. After the cutoff no safeguard can be applied again before a minimum period of two years or a period equal to the period of previous application. Countries whose market access is restricted by safeguards are allowed to retaliate after three years. The possibility of negotiated quota sharing introduces selectivity (discrimination) to the agreement making it possible to target suppliers whose imports have increased in "disproportionate percentage." Many analysts believe that the prohibition of voluntary export restraints and the legalization of discriminatory safeguards will benefit the world trading system. Gray-area measures are to be phased out over a period not exceeding four years after the date of entry into force of the agreement establishing the WTO, with one possible exception for each importing country until the end of 1999.[18] Safeguards cannot be applied to a developing country member whose share in the market of the importing country is less than 3 percent.[19]

The antidumping agreement states that, if the facts have been adequately established and the investigative evaluation has been objective, decisions by national authorities cannot be overturned. It improves the process of determining injury and the method of calculating the margin of dumping, and sets deadlines for the investigation, for refunds, and for the application of measures. It also establishes a *de minimis* margin of dumping below which proceedings are terminated. Measures cannot be extended beyond five years unless persistent injury is likely. Attention has been drawn to the dangers of the remaining scope for picking and choosing in the computation of average prices. Such bias will continue to generate dumping findings where dumping does not exist, and, more generally, will tend to exaggerate the magnitude of dumping margins.[20]

In the application of countervailing measures, subsidies are divided into two types, specific and general, of which only the former are subject to disciplines. Specific subsidies are prohibited, actionable, or nonactionable. The nonactionable include those subsidies related to research and development and regional development. Prohibited subsidies are those contingent upon export performance or the use of domestic inputs. The Uruguay Round improved methods of subsidy calculation and determination of injury, conditions of application of minimal criteria for the level of subsidization and of "negligibility" for subsidized volumes, and investigation procedures, as well as strengthened measures to counter circumvention and provisions concerning time limits for the imposition of countervailing measures and their review.

In view of GATT's notorious failure to bring discipline to antidumping and subsidy/countervailing measures, and the fact that many countries, particularly the United States, take antidumping rules as "a statement of the right of the government to take action to protect its industries from certain forms of import competition," the changed rules provide grounds only for measured optimism.[21]

In principle, the establishment of the WTO and in particular the improved rules and procedures for dispute settlement are a significant liberalization. But much hinges on the WTO's capacity to create a level playing field among contracting parties of different sizes and heterogeneous bargaining power. The WTO allows suspension of concessions across sectors – goods, services, and trade-related investment procedures – as a last resort. The asymmetrical interests of industrial and developing countries in these three sectors are well known: industrial economies have clearly been *demandeurs* with respect to services and trade-related investment procedures. In complaints related to these sectors, cross-sectoral retaliation on the part of industrial economies against developing economies is likely to be concentrated in market access for goods.[22] Conversely, if industrial countries show reluctance to dismantle protection in sectors such as textiles and clothing that are critical to developing countries, they may, at least in principle, reevaluate their commitment in sectors such as services and especially trade-related investment issues.

Textiles and clothing

Liberalization of trade in textiles and clothing is significantly understated if the implications of progressive dismantlement of the MFA over the next ten years are not taken into account.[23] The arrangement, in place since

1974 but with roots going back to the late 1950s, allows most industrial countries to impose restraints on textile and clothing exports from developing countries. It is to be phased out in three stages. Special transitional safeguards can be applied to products not yet integrated into GATT and not already under constraint, import surges of which could seriously damage or threaten domestic industry.

Three paths to the liberalization of trade in textiles and clothing were considered possible before 1990: liberalization within the framework of the MFA; restructuring the arrangement with new instruments such as tariff quotas and quota auctions; or an instantaneous fall back on the GATT with adjusted levels of protection.[24] The most conservative format, liberalization of the MFA, prevailed in the end.

The MFA will be phased out over ten years from the entry into force of the WTO agreement (1995), at which time no less than 16 percent of the total volume of imports covered, but not necessarily restricted by, the arrangement will be integrated into WTO. A further 17 percent will be integrated in 1998, 18 percent in 2002, and the remaining 49 percent in 2005. For the first three years (stage 1) remaining restrictions should be increased by 16 percent above the yearly growth rate established under the arrangement. For example, a 2 percent rate of growth will be increased to 2.32 percent. For the next four years (stage 2) rates will be increased 25 percent above the new rates of stage 1, and for the last three years (stage 3) 27 percent above the new rates of stage 2. For countries whose exports are subject to restriction and whose restrictions represented less than 1.2 percent of the total volume of restrictions on December 31, 1991, the rules concerning increased rates of quantitative restrictions mentioned above should be advanced one stage.[25]

Abolition of the MFA will be a major achievement of the Uruguay Round. During the transition period, however, expansion rules will increase quotas for textiles and clothing only modestly: their aggregate levels after ten years will be 16.6 percent higher in the European Union and 22.6 percent higher in the United States than under the arrangement. For countries in the standard category that are important suppliers, application of these rules will increase quotas only modestly. By the end of the ten-year period, quotas on exports from Hong Kong will have increased only 6.3 percent to the US market and 6.2 percent to the European Union, compared with their levels under the MFA.[26] At the other extreme, end-of-period quotas on exports will have increased by more than 50 percent in the European Union (for Sri Lanka), and more than 40 percent in the United States (for Colombia, Costa Rica, and Macau).[27]

Taking into account both the arrangement's expansion rates and quota expansion rules, however, the aggregate of quotas for all countries in the ten-year period will increase 62.4 percent in the European Union and 85 percent in the United States in relation to levels in the beginning of the period. For Hong Kong, quotas after ten years will be 20.4–20.7 percent higher in these markets. In contrast, such quotas will increase by 204.2 percent for Sri Lanka in the European Union and by 167.7 percent for Bangladesh in the United States.

Special transitional safeguards can be applied to products that are not integrated into the GATT and that face serious damage or threat of damage as a result of an import surge. In this situation, least developed, small suppliers and exporters, and those with a high proportion of outward processing trade are to be given preferential treatment. Such safeguards, which are not allowed to reduce trade below the average volume in the recent past, must provide for yearly quota growth of at least 6 percent.

The complete removal of MFA quotas will be favorable to developing countries that export textiles and clothing and will add to the benefit of tariff cuts on textiles and clothing in industrial economies. Estimates of the impact of the arrangement's dismantlement, based on assumptions that the *ad valorem* equivalent of binding quotas is 30 percent, and that 50 percent of developing country exports are bound by the arrangement, suggest that total tariff and nontariff barrier protection reduction should be in the region of 61 percent rather than the 21 percent estimated by GATT/WTO as resulting from tariff reduction alone.[28]

Estimates of the net impact of textile and clothing liberalization indicate that in general the effect of trade expansion greatly outweighs the loss of quota rents. But such estimates vary widely. Partial equilibrium estimates by Kirmani, Molajoni, and Mayer (1984) of the effect of removing MFA quotas and eliminating of tariffs showed the imports of major members of the OECD expanding by 81.8 percent for textiles and 92.6 percent for clothing. UNCTAD (1986) estimates are in the same range for textiles (78 percent) but differ for clothing (135 percent). Using a CGE model, Trela and Whalley (1990) found that textile and clothing imports to the European Union, Canada, and the United States would increase by 190.2 to 305.5 percent in the event of total liberalization. Elimination only of quotas would expand imports by 115.7 to 235.8 percent.[29] Such estimates crucially depend on data on Hong Kong quota auctions and methodologies used to adjust such data for costs in other countries.[30] Alternative CGE work by Goto (1990) results in much lower estimates because of the adoption of different price elasticity values and hypotheses about how binding underutilized quotas are.[31] Yang, Martin, and Yanagishima (forthcoming) have called attention to the fact that the countries most likely to gain from MFA liberalization are those that are relatively more constrained by quotas and thus have a large share of total exports directed to unrestricted markets.

Recent estimates suggest that welfare gains from trade liberalization in textiles and clothing and from abolition of the arrangement are concentrated in industrial countries and a few developing countries, especially China, Indonesia (about 3 percent of GDP), and in South Asia. Latin America and Sub-Saharan Africa in fact are likely to lose 0.08 percent and 0.51 percent of their GDP respectively.[32]

None of these studies takes into account the dynamics of the MFA abolition. The liberalization format for textiles and clothing that emerged from the Uruguay Round will induce industries that want to restrict imports to integrate first into WTO those products on which initial quantitative restrictions are relatively less binding. Liberalization will be concentrated toward the end of the period. There are still no quantitative estimates to indicate how uneven liberalization will be as it unfolds. Transitional safeguards could further decrease the mid-term trade gains realized from dismantling the MFA. Even if liberalization were uniformly distributed over the transition period, the integration of 49 percent of total trade in textiles and clothing on the last day raises doubt about the credibility of liberalization after the transition. It is feared that the use or misuse of safeguards and other protectionist instruments may *de facto* prolong the life of the MFA. In fact, restraining countries may be able to carry out integration all the way to the beginning of the third stage without liberalizing existing restrictions, as the agreement on textiles and clothing includes in its annex many products that are presently unrestricted – nearly 35 percent of total imports to the European Union and the United States according to the International Textiles and Clothing Bureau.[33]

Trade regimes in developing countries

Unlike previous GATT rounds, the Uruguay Round was a genuinely reciprocal negotiation that resulted in the exchange of concessions between industrial and developing economies, for example, in the areas of tariff cuts, tariff bindings, and improved disciplines on such issues as the balance of payments. The former discretionary use of nontariff barriers insulated markets in developing economies, providing producers there with absolute protection. However, in the mid-to late 1980s there were comprehensive policy shifts toward liberalization even in the more interventionist of developing countries, and this trend made the exchange of concessions easier.

Uruguay Round tariff cuts in developing economies on the whole preserve the relative rank of average tariffs, according to suppliers (table 3.7). Tariffs on products from the European Union, Japan, and other Asian countries, all slightly above 16 percent, are generally higher than tariffs on

Table 3.7 Pre- and post-Uruguay Round average tariff rates on imports by developing economies from industrial economies by region of origin and destination (percent)

| | Developing economies | | | | | | | | | | | | | | All economies | |
| | America | | Asia | | Africa | | Europe | | Total | | | | | | | |
	Before	After	Before	After	Before	After	Before	After	Before	After					Before	After
United States	16.2	14.0	16.0	10.9	12.0	11.9	17.0	14.3	16.1	12.5					4.8	3.2
European Union	21.2	17.0	24.4	16.8	23.6	23.6	15.9	13.6	20.8	16.2					8.0	5.5
Japan	28.5	22.1	23.9	16.4	17.5	17.5	18.0	16.1	24.1	16.9					8.1	5.6
Other industrial Asia	26.0	22.1	22.0	15.9	23.0	22.1	18.1	16.2	22.1	16.3					9.9	7.2
Other industrial	16.1	13.3	16.0	11.1	16.5	16.5	11.1	9.3	14.3	10.9					3.6	2.1
Total industrial economies	18.9	15.7	21.2	14.6	22.1	22.1	14.9	12.7	19.6	14.7					6.3	4.2
All economies	16.8	13.9	20.9	14.6	21.6	21.6	14.4	12.3	18.8	14.2					6.3	4.3

Note: trade-weighted tariffs. Columns indicate destination countries; rows, origin countries.
Source: computed from IDB GATT/World Bank data base using World Bank country classifications and GATT product classifications.

imports from the United States (12.5 percent) and other industrial countries (10.9 percent). Average cuts were higher on imports from Japan (29 percent) than on those from other industrial economies (22 to 26 percent). Because tariff levels in developing economies are much higher than in industrial economies, the same degree of tariff cuts across the board implies much deeper cuts in import prices in those countries, and consequently more trade expansion there. Average post-Round tariffs in developing America and in developing Asia countries other than Japan are very similar, around 15 percent, slightly lower in developing Europe, and higher in Africa. Tariff cuts were deeper in developing Asia, about 31 percent, compared with 17 percent in developing America, 15 percent in developing Europe, and 0 percent in Africa.

There was much variation in tariff levels among industrial groups in developing countries before the Uruguay Round, a situation that continues. In industrial economies, one sector, textiles and clothing, tends to have a tariff way above the average. In developing economies, above-average protection for transport equipment and textiles and clothing, and below-average protection for fish products explain most tariff variance (table 3.8).[34]

There is no suggestion in developing economies of a relationship between deeper tariff cuts and less protected products, as there is in industrial economies. The acceptance of blanket bindings by many developing economies was made easier by the fact that they are now imposing tariffs well below their post-Round bound levels. There are also no industrial sectors with a position symmetrical to that of the ailing sectors in the industrial economies, such as textiles and clothing, whose level of protection is out of step with those in other products.

As mentioned, similar tariff cuts may imply quite different rates of reduction in import prices. For the aggregate of industrial products, the average price reduction in developing countries on imports from industrial economies would be 4.1 percent, substantially higher than an import price reduction of 1.5 percent in industrial economies on imports from developing economies. With the exception of outliers such as fish products (a deep cut) and mineral products (a rather small cut), implied price reductions in industrial sectors vary between 2.8 percent for wood products and 4.8 percent for textiles and clothing.

Data on tariff profiles in developing economies show a modest increase in duty-free trade (from 39 to 42 percent) and a modest decrease in trade affected by tariffs above 15 percent (from 43 to 38 percent, in contrast to only 5 percent in industrial economies). The share of trade affected by tariffs above 35 percent, however, fell from 15 to 8 percent.[35]

Nontariff liberalization induced by the Uruguay Round is also significant

Table 3.8 *Pre- and post-Uruguay Round average tariffs and tariff cuts on imports by developing economies from industrial economies, by sector*

	Trade (US $billion)	Average-tariff (percent)		Tariff reduction (percent)
		Before	After	
Fish and fish products	0.8	33.4	8.7	74
Wood, pulp, paper, and furniture	6.6	12.8	9.6	49
Textiles and clothing	7.8	26.8	20.7	23
Leather, rubber, footwear, and travel goods	2.9	22.9	18.5	19
Metals	18.1	18.8	13.5	28
Chemicals and photographic supplies	27.7	18.6	13.0	30
Transport equipment	13.0	26.1	21.8	17
Nonelectric machinery	36.8	18.9	14.4	24
Electric machinery	23.3	21.2	16.0	25
Mineral products	9.9	11.4	9.4	17
Other manufactured articles	13.9	19.0	13.9	27
All industrial products (excluding petroleum)	160.8	19.6	14.7	25

Note: trade-weighted tariffs. Tariff cuts are based on average tariffs before rounding off.
Source: computed from IDB GATT/World Bank data base using World Bank country classifications and GATT product classifications.

in developing countries, but in many cases, as with tariff liberalization, important policy shifts toward liberalization have already occurred. There are now more restrictive rules on balance-of-payments provisions, which for many years were the basis for introducing quantitative import restrictions in developing countries. More important, preference for less distortive price-based measures has been clearly established. The use of quantitative controls – limited to cases where "price-based measures are not an adequate instrument to deal with the balance of payments situation" – will have to be justified. They should be short-lived, and should attempt to restrict imports on a nondiscriminatory basis. Exemptions and limitations are restricted to essential products for direct consumption, capital goods, and inputs. The process of notification has been tightened with respect to timetable, conditions of review, and amount of information required to assure transparency in the implementation of such measures.

The scope for import licensing as an instrument of protection was reduced by tightening the criteria for automatic and nonautomatic licenses. Provisions were also improved for increasing transparency and predictability in allocating nonautomatic licenses. The basic objective is still to limit the protectionist impact of licensing. As before, the effectiveness of the new agreements, on both balance of payments and import licensing, depends to a large extent on implementation. Preshipment inspection, practiced by developing countries only, is the object of a specific agreement ensuring that such activity is nondiscriminatory and transparent. The universal coverage of such agreements, which former GATT codes lacked, is a significant step toward liberalization.

Special provisions apply to the use of safeguards by developing countries. The maximum period of safeguard application can be extended from eight to ten years if compared to industrial economies, with reimposition of measures allowed only after half the initial application period has elapsed. It is not easy to see safeguards as the main source of increased protection in developing countries in the future. This is partly because of the restrictions imposed by the new rules, which, by forcing the intermittent use of such instruments and limiting the period without compensation to three years, would seem to deter their use for fostering strategic industrial policies. It is also because of the relatively small size and bargaining power of developing economies – the reason VERs were exclusively adopted by industrial countries in the past. The rules on antidumping seem to pose more serious risk of misuse to selectively increase protection in developing economies.

As liberalization through tariff reduction and the removal of nontariff barriers proceeds in developing countries, governments, following the lead of industrial economies, will probably lean more on antidumping and subsidy countervailing to restore selective protection. Hindley (1994) stresses the point that the ban on VERs may force contracting parties faced with a choice between Article XIX of GATT and no protection at all to apply antidumping measures. Data for 1980–89 indicate the beginning of such a trend in developing economies. Post-1990 data hint at a similar trend in subsidy/countervailing measures.[36] The improvements introduced in the agreements on antidumping and subsidy countervailing, however, make their adoption more technically demanding and consequently harder for developing countries to use.

It is in the agreement on subsidy countervailing that the concept of graduation of developing economies is more explicit as a result of the Round. One group of developing countries, including the least-developed countries and twenty countries with incomes below $1,000 per year, is exempted from the prohibition of export subsidies. In 1992, total manufactured exports thus exempted amounted to US $54.8 billion, of which no less than 78.8 percent originated in Indonesia, India, the Philippines, and Pakistan.[37]

Other developing countries must phase out any export subsidies over eight years, unless they are deemed to have reached export competitiveness (defined as a 3.25 percent share of the world market), in which case the phase-out period is two years. Under the agreement, developing countries cannot increase the level of subsidies and must eliminate any that are inconsistent with "development needs."

Inter-developing country trade in industrial products

Inter-developing country trade in industrial products is a small share of world trade. Most such trade is between countries in developing Asia or those in developing America trade (see table 3.1). Intra-regional trade is a higher proportion of total trade with developing economies in developing Asia than in developing America. Developing America has in fact a favorable trade balance with developing Asia.

Because of the Uruguay Round, in developing economies the average tariff rate on imports from other developing economies will be about 30 percent lower than the average tariff rate on imports from industrial economies. In developing America, however, the average tariff will be particularly low on imports from developing countries, mostly because of the low tariff on inter-developing America trade. In fact, the developing America average tariff on imports from developing Asia will be almost as high as that on imports from Japan, and above tariffs on imports from the United States and the European Union. The reverse is not true: in developing Asia, the average tariff on developing America products will remain lower than that on inter-developing Asia products. The very small flow of exports from developing Europe to developing Asia face high tariffs. Sectoral average tariffs for imports from developing economies will be below those for imports from industrial economies (table 3.9, and see also table 3.7).

In developing countries, the average tariff cut of 21 percent on imports from other developing economies is smaller than the cut on imports from industrial economies. Because the initial tariff level on imports from industrial economies was higher, discrepancies in import price reduction are still deeper: 2.6 percent for imports from other developing economies, in contrast to 4.9 percent for imports from industrial economies. Only for tariffs on nonelectric machinery and leather goods imported from developing economies were the reductions deeper than those on imports from industrial economies (table 3.10, and see also table 3.8).

Exports from developing economies to other developing economies will

Table 3.9 *Pre- and post-Uruguay Round average tariff rates on imports by developing economies from developing economies, by region of origin and destination (percent)*

	Developing America		Developing Asia		Africa		Developing Europe		Total developing		All economies	
	Before	After	Before	After	Before	After	Before	After	Before	After	Before	After
Developing America	3.4	3.0	13.3	9.8	16.6	16.5	9.5	8.6	6.5	5.2	4.5	3.1
Developing Asia	25.8	20.5	20.4	15.5	18.2	18.1	14.8	13.2	20.1	15.5	6.9	5.2
Africa	7.8	7.8	15.7	10.9	0.9	0.9	14.2	12.9	10.4	7.7	8.2	6.5
Developing Europe	9.0	8.0	27.1	22.4	20.1	20.1	10.1	8.7	12.6	10.9	8.3	6.2
Total developing	4.9	4.2	19.0	14.4	13.5	13.5	10.9	9.5	13.0	10.3	6.3	4.6
All economies	16.8	13.9	20.9	14.6	21.6	21.6	14.4	12.3	18.8	14.2	6.3	4.3

Note: trade-weighted tariffs. Columns indicate destination countries; rows, origin countries.
Source: computed from IDB GATT/World Bank data base using World Bank country classifications and GATT product classifications.

Table 3.10 *Pre- and post-Uruguay Round average tariffs and tariff cuts on imports by developing economies from developing economies, by sector*

	Trade (US $billion)	Average-tariff (percent)		Reduction (percent)
		Before	After	
Fish and fish products	0.3	30.9	15.9	49
Wood, pulp, paper and furniture	1.7	8.8	7.3	17
Textiles and clothing	1.6	26.6	21.1	21
Leather, rubber, footwear, and travel goods	1.2	12.0	8.2	31
Metals	5.4	10.1	8.5	16
Chemicals and photographic supplies	2.9	12.4	9.2	25
Transport equipment	0.9	11.7	10.6	9
Nonelectric machinery	1.9	13.8	10.2	26
Electric machinery	1.7	17.6	14.0	21
Mineral products	2.1	9.4	8.1	14
Other manufactured articles	1.0	10.5	8.8	16
All industrial products (excluding petroleum)	20.9	13.0	10.3	21

Note: trade-weighted tariffs. Tariff cuts are based on average tariffs before rounding off.
Source: computed from IDB GATT/World Bank data base.

also benefit from the liberalization of nontariff barriers. Provisions making it more difficult to use balance-of-payments problems to justify protection were an important advance. Still, exports from developing economies face measures such as antidumping and subsidy/countervailing taken by other developing countries in the absence of alternative forms of protection. It is possible that, owing to unequal bargaining power between developing and industrial nations, developing countries will take antidumping and subsidy countervailing actions more often against imports from other developing countries than against imports from industrial countries. There are already signs of such a trend in the commercial policy of some developing countries.

Conclusion

It may be argued that developing countries obtained less than was envis-aged before the Round on such issues as speed of dismantlement of the

MFA and tariff reduction in industrial countries. But overall, the Round's liberalization of trade in industrial products is clearly favorable to developing countries.

Any evaluation of the Uruguay Round must consider what concessions countries obtained from their trade partners, but it is also crucial to gauge what countries did to help themselves by liberalizing access to their own markets. A comparison of tariff cuts shows that on average they were larger in industrial economies for imports from developing economies than in developing economies for imports from industrial economies, 28 percent compared with 25 percent (see tables 3.2, 3.8, and 3.10). Tariff cuts in developing economies on imports from industrial economies (28 percent) were deeper than those on imports from other developing economies (25 percent), while cuts in industrial economies were considerably higher on imports from other industrial economies (40 percent), than on imports from developing economies (28 percent).

For the aggregate of industrial products, import price reductions implied by tariff cuts would be on average 1.5 percent in industrial economies for imports from both developing and other industrial economies; 2.4 percent for inter-developing country trade; and 4.1 percent in developing economies for imports from industrial economies. Even in developing America, where the average tariff cut was smaller than in developing Asia, it implied import price reduction exceeding the average price reduction in industrial economies: 2.5 percent compared with 1.5 percent. Africa is an altogether different case. Perhaps the most disappointing outcome of the Uruguay Round is the lack of trade liberalization on that continent.

The more comprehensive analyses of the Round concentrate on its impact on welfare. Despite criticism of simulations based on CGE models,[38] their results are generally accepted as fairly assessing the welfare gains realized by the Uruguay Round. There are many alternative estimates available.[39] Assumptions of IRTS and, in particular, of monopolistic competition through product differentiation significantly increase estimates of welfare gains related to industrial tariff cuts and the removal of nontariff barriers on industrial products.[40] Developing countries reap important benefits from the round mainly because of trade liberalization affecting industrial products.

In some instances, assessment hinges on how agreements are to be implemented. Industrial products, safeguards, antidumping and subsidy countervailing measures, and the functioning of the GATT system are all issues whose evaluation depends on the enforcement of agreements. Liberalization involving developing country concessions – import licensing and nontariff barriers justified by balance of payments – would appear less vulnerable to national prevarication owing to better multilateral disciplines, less obvious loopholes, extended coverage, and a general commitment to sounder macro-economic policies.

To a large extent, results of the Round reflect the leverage of the main contracting parties, particularly the European Union and the United States. Given the modest importance of even big developing countries as global trading partners, it has long been recognized that to influence the outcome of the Round, developing countries would have to enter into coalitions. However, the only significant coalition of developing countries during the negotiations was the Cairns Group of agricultural "fair traders," which also included industrial countries and benefited from the sympathy of the United States.[41] Even then, the final outcome was to a great extent undermined by the European Union, which resisted modest liberalization in agriculture.

Coalitions of developing countries addressing issues of trade in manufactures were much less effective. Sectoral interests that could have provided a basis for convergence of positions were obscured by the focus on improved standards of surveillance, enforcement, and dispute settlement through specific instruments such as safeguards and antidumping or subsidy countervailing measures. Even in the case of textiles, the desire for liberalization varied considerably among developing countries, which had reaped uneven advantages from the series of market-sharing arrangements starting in the early 1960s. Depending on their relative advantages, individual exporters, and perhaps even some export-restricted contracting parties, were reluctant to see the MFA dismantled.[42]

Pre- and post-Round comparisons are not necessarily the most realistic method of assessing the advantages of the Round. It is unlikely that the status quo would have been maintained had the GATT negotiations failed. A better indication of the relative success of the negotiations would be to compare their actual results with what would have happened had they failed (most likely, increased protection in a wave of cross-retaliation). It is of course difficult to model a scenario of Uruguay Round failure. It must at least be kept in mind that an evaluation of liberalization's benefits is likely to produce lower-bound estimates of gains.

Developing countries entered into important commitments to liberalize their economies, participating in the Uruguay Round much more actively than in previous rounds. In the case of agriculture-trade liberalization, their role was critical. Even more important, their diplomatic activity, especially since 1986, has been motivated by a changed concept of special and differential treatment. The notion of permanent nonreciprocity of concessions was abandoned in favor of phasing in universally applied rules. Trade liberalization in developing economies is clearly an ongoing process whose true significance is not reflected in the evaluations mentioned above. In many developing countries applied duties are considerably lower than bound duties, and applied duties and nontariff barriers are being further reduced. The argument that in the Uruguay Round industrial countries did not fully reciprocate concessions made by developing countries, particularly in agricultural trade, but perhaps also with respect to selected tariff cuts and conditions of dismantlement of the MFA, misses the essential point. Most developing countries, because of their modest economic size and the difficulty of entering into effective coalitions with other developing countries, are genuinely interested in a WTO that is effective. The fate of many of the Uruguay Round results relevant to trade in industrial products – notably, safeguards, antidumping provisions, and subsidy countervailing measures – depends on how the agreements are implemented. Political will in industrial countries, crucial yesterday to the conclusion of the Uruguay Round, even if it did produce a somewhat disappointing liberalization package, remains crucial today if the WTO and a truly multilateral trade system are going to work.

Notes

The author thanks Sanjoy Bagchi, Afonso Bevilaqua, Thomas W. Hertel, Luiz Magalhães, Will Martin, Mário Marconini, Arvind Panagariya, Shane Streifel, and L. Alan Winters for their help and comments. Ulrich Reincke provided country data on trade and average tariffs from the GATT data base, and Guilherme Ribenboim performed competent research assistance.

1. Industrial products as defined by GATT include certain unprocessed products, especially in the following categories: fish and fish products; wood, pulp, paper, and furniture; leather, rubber, and footwear; and mineral products and precious stones. (See table 3.5 for categories of industrial products.) Some petroleum products are not included as industrial products.

2. Other industrial Asia economies in table 3.1 are Hong Kong and Singapore. Other industrial economies are Australia, Austria, Canada, Finland, Iceland, New Zealand, Norway, Sweden, and Switzerland.

3. GATT's IDB, used here for all computations of tariff reductions, includes forty contracting parties, with the European Union's twelve members counted as one. Only imports by countries in the data base from countries in the data base were used in the analysis. The data base is estimated to cover about 90 percent of world trade and 98 percent of trade by contracting parties, excluding petroleum. It includes data on twenty-four of the ninety-three developing countries participating in the Round; this accounts for more than 80 percent of total merchandise exports of developing countries. GATT's definition of a developing country includes Singapore and Hong Kong. In this chapter developing economies are those classified by the World Bank as low- and middle-income economies.

4. Developing America countries in table 3.1 are Argentina, Brazil, Chile, Colombia, El Salvador, Jamaica, Mexico, Peru, Uruguay, and Venezuela. Developing Asia economies are Korea (Republic of), India, Indonesia, Macau, Malaysia, the Phillipines, Sri Lanka, and Thailand. In Africa, only Senegal, Tunisia, and Zimbabwe are included. Developing Europe consists of the Czech Republic, Hungary, Poland, Romania, and Turkey. Estimates based on GATT (1993b, appendix, table 2), and trade data from GATT (1995) suggests that IDB coverage of exports as defined here is around 80 percent. China is the most important exclusion.

5. See Anderson and Neary (1994) for a criticism of the use of trade-weighted average tariffs and tariff equivalents of quotas in the assessment of trade liberalization.

6. All computations of average tariffs unless otherwise stated refer to total integrated data base trade, that is, including free-trade-area trade, which is considered to be conducted at zero tariff before and after the Uruguay Round. As it is not possible to exclude preferential trade, this is a source of distortion. Trade conducted under initiatives such as the Andean Pact, the ACP preferential arrangements with the European Union, and the Generalized System of Preferences was not excluded from the data here. But trade in manufactures affected by the Lomé Convention – which will be diverted by tariff reduction in the European Union – is relatively limited. Tariff reductions related to the Generalized System of Preferences are intrinsically uncertain, depending entirely on the policies of preference-giving countries. It is an open question how Uruguay Round results are likely to affect the proportion of eligible developing country exports favored by lower tariffs under the Generalized System of Preferences. Davenport (1994) presents data for preferential trade in industrial products in the European Union and United States. The main beneficiaries in the European Union – China, India, Brazil, and Thailand – exported almost 60 percent of total preferential exports. The main beneficiaries in the United States – Mexico, Malaysia, Thailand, and Brazil – exported more than 70 percent of their total preferential exports.

7. This is relevant for many developing economies. GATT (1994b, p. 70) lists Indonesia, Jamaica, Romania, Senegal, Tunisia, and Uruguay as countries in this position. This was also the case for many tariff lines in Chile and Mexico.

8. See GATT (1994b, pp. 25–26). In these comments on bindings, developing economies, following GATT's taxonomy, include Hong Kong and Singapore. Transition economies are the Czech Republic, Hungary, Poland, and Romania.

9. Throughout this chapter reference is made to comparative tariff cuts. While such cuts are relevant to assess the impact of the Round on trade flow, this does not imply that the standard exchange of concessions view in trade negotiations is a useful way of analyzing trade liberalization. Different average tariffs may of course reflect different combinations of nominal tariff levels and trade structures.

10. See GATT (1993b, appendix, table 2). The GATT definition of industrial products used in this chapter includes mineral products but not fuels.

11. Major export interests are defined as sectors corresponding to more than 20 percent of industrial exports and more than 5 percent of total exports. Mention has been limited to countries exporting more than US $1 billion of industrial products annually.
12. The many fish product exporters are not listed because of the limited value of their total exports.
13. A simple measure of rank correlation for industrial product sectors disproves the hypothesis of no relation between tariff cuts and pre-Uruguay Round tariff levels at a level of significance of 1 percent.
14. Dismantlement of the MFA is an important additional source of reduced protection affecting textiles and clothing exports by developing economies.
15. GATT (1993b, p. 31).
16. See Schott and Buurman (1994, p. 62).
17. See GATT (1994b, pp. 17–18) for data on voluntary export restraints. See Laird and Yeats (1990) for a survey of tariff equivalent estimates for nontariff barriers, and Haaland and Tollefsen (1994) for recent estimates for the European Union, the United States, and Japan. See Anderson and Neary (1994) for a critical view of the use of such equivalents.
18. Such measures had to be agreed to by importer and exporter and notified within ninety days of the entry into force of the WTO. The only such exception that has been agreed limits Japanese exports of motor vehicles to the European Union until 1999.
19. Where such developing country members do not account for more than 9 percent of the import market.
20. See Schott and Buurman (1994, pp. 156–57), Hindley (1994, pp. 97–98), and chapter 11.
21. See Finger (1994, p. 107).
22. It is expected that the use of instruments such as section 301 of the US Trade Act of 1974, as amended, will be curtailed, as it can be applied unilaterally only if the issue is not covered by WTO obligations.
23. GATT (1994c).
24. See Wolf (1990, pp. 225ff).
25. The following countries would qualify as small suppliers: Peru and Sri Lanka in the European Union; Colombia, Costa Rica, Jamaica, Macau, Mexico, and Uruguay in the United States; South Korea and Sri Lanka in Finland; and Costa Rica, Macau, and Uruguay in Canada. See International Textiles and Clothing Bureau (1994a, p. 3).
26. In all cases such computations exclude China. Quotas affecting Chinese exports will remain constant while China is not a WTO member. Information on quotas under the MFA and after its enlargement was supplied by the International Textiles and Clothing Bureau through the World Bank.
27. Data provided by Sanjoy Bagchi of the International Textiles and Clothing Bureau.
28. See GATT (1994a, p. 15). Table 7.2 in chapter 7 presents detailed data on tax equivalents associated with the MFA by supplier and main export market.

29. See Trela and Whalley (1990, pp. 1199 and 1201).
30. See Whalley (1994, pp. 74–75) for a short survey of the values of quota premiums.
31. See Goto (1990, pp. 19ff), but also Anderson and Neary (1994) for criticism of standard evaluation methodologies. Trela and Whalley's estimates (1990, p. 1199) of the general equilibrium effect of removing MFA quotas as well as tariffs on textiles and clothing exports from developing economies suggest that the major disadvantage is likely to be felt by Hong Kong and Macau and some of the small economies in the Caribbean, such as the Dominican Republic and Haiti.
32. See Hertel, Martin, Yanagishima, and Dimaranan (1995, table 13).
33. See International Textiles and Clothing Bureau (1994b, p. 3).
34. Tariff variance computed for the very aggregate eleven GATT-defined industrial groups of products.
35. See GATT (1994b, p. 11). Following GATT's taxonomy, developing countries in this paragraph include Hong Kong and Singapore.
36. For data on antidumping and subsidy countervailing measures, see Finger (1993, p. 4) and GATT (1991, pp. 113–18; 1992, pp. 81–85; and 1993a, pp. 65–70).
37. GATT's trade policy review evaluations suggest that for most of the more advanced developing countries these limitations are unlikely to be significant.
38. See in particular two newspaper articles by Maurice Allais (1993a and 1993b) and the answer by Jean Waelbroeck (1993).
39. See Schott and Buurman (1994, pp. 17–19 and 199–208), and GATT (1994b, pp. 27–38 and 59–64).
40. To mention just one such estimate, in the dynamic scenario including increasing returns and monopolistic competition, estimated total welfare gains are equivalent to 1.36 percent of world GDP. Industrial tariff cuts account for 25.9 percent of the total gain and removal of nontariff barriers for 63.6 percent. See GATT (1994b).
41. The Cairns Group of agricultural "fair traders" was composed of Argentina, Australia, Brazil, Canada, Chile, Colombia, Fiji, Hungary, Indonesia, Malaysia, New Zealand, the Phillipines, Thailand, and Uruguay.
42. For a view on developing country expectations from the Uruguay Round and of the difficulties of coalition formation, see Abreu (1989).

References

Abreu, M. de P. 1989. "Developing Countries and the Uruguay Round of Trade Negotiations." *Proceedings of the World Bank Annual Conference on Development Economics.* Washington, DC: World Bank.

Allais, M. 1993a. "Une gigantesque mystification." *Le Figaro*, November 15. Paris. 1993b. "Une erreur fondamentale." *Le Figaro*, November 16. Paris.

Anderson, J., and J. P. Neary 1994. "The Trade Restrictiveness of the Multi-Fibre Arrangement." *The World Bank Economic Review* 8 (2): 171–90.

Davenport, M. 1994. "Possible Improvements to the Generalized System of Preferences." United Nations Conference on Trade and Development, ITD/8, April 18.

Finger, M., ed. 1993. *Antidumping: How It Works and Who Gets Hurt.* Ann Arbor: University of Michigan Press.

1994. "Subsidies and Countervailing Measures and Anti-Dumping Agreements." In *The New Trading System: Readings.* Paris: OECD.

GATT 1991. *Activities 1990.* Geneva: GATT.

1992. *Activities 1991.* Geneva: GATT.

1993a. *Activities 1992.* Geneva: GATT.

1993b. "An Analysis of the Proposed Uruguay Round Agreement, with Particular Emphasis on Aspects to Developing Countries." MTN.TNC/W/122 MTN.GNG/W/30. Geneva: GATT, November 29.

1994a. "Increases in Market Access Resulting from the Uruguay Round." In *News of the Uruguay Round.* Geneva: GATT.

1994b. "The Results of the Uruguay Round of Multilateral Trade Negotiations: Market Access for Goods and Services: Overview of the Results." Mimeo. Geneva: GATT.

1994c. *The Results of the Uruguay Round of Trade Negotiations: The Legal Texts.* Geneva: GATT.

1995. *International Trade: Trends and Statistics, 1994.* Geneva: GATT.

Goto, J. 1990. "A Formal Estimation of the Effect of the MFA on Clothing Exports from LDCs." Working Paper, WPS 445. Washington, DC: World Bank, International Trade.

Haaland, J. I., and T. C. Tollefsen 1994. "The Uruguay Round and Trade in Manufactures and Services: General Equilibrium Simulations of Production, Trade, and Welfare Effects of Liberalization." Discussion Paper 1008. London: Centre for Economic Policy Research.

Hertel, T., W. Martin, K. Yanagishima, and B. Dimaranan 1995. "Liberalizing Manufactures Trade in a Changing World Economy." In W. Martin and L. A. Winters, eds., *The Uruguay Round and the Developing Economies.* World Bank Discussion Paper 307. Washington, DC: World Bank.

Hindley, B. 1994. "Safeguards, VERs and Anti-Dumping Action." In *The New Trading System: Readings.* Paris: OECD.

International Textiles and Clothing Bureau 1994a. "The Implementation of the Agreement on Textiles and Clothing." Council of Representatives, XIX Session, Arequipa, Peru, June 27–July 1.

1994b. "Agreement on Textiles and Clothing: An Evaluation." Council of Representatives, XIX Session, Arequipa, Peru, June 27–July 1.

Kirmani, N., P. Molajoni, and T. Mayer 1984. "Effects of Increased Market Access on Exports of Developing Countries." *IMF Staff Papers* 31 (4): 661–84.

Laird, S., and A. Yeats 1990. *Quantitative Methods for Trade Barrier Analysis.* New York: New York University Press.

Martin, W., and J. Francois 1994. "Bindings and Rules as Trade Liberalization." Paper presented at the Festschrift Conference, "Quiet Pioneering: Robert M. Stern and his International Economic Legacy," University of Michigan, Ann Arbor, November 18–20.

Schott, J., and J. W. Buurman 1994. *The Uruguay Round: An Assessment.* Washington, DC: Institute of International Economics.

Trela, I., and J. Whalley 1990. "Global Effects of Developed Country Trade Restrictions on Textiles and Apparel." *Economic Journal* 100 (403): 1190–205.

UNCTAD 1986. "Protectionism and Structural Adjustment." Report by the UNCTAD Secretariat, Restrictions on Trade and Structural Adjustment, TD/B/1081, part 1. Geneva.

Waelbroek, J. 1993. "Le coût mondial du protectionnisme agricole." *Le Figaro*, December 17. Paris.

Whalley, J. 1994. "Agreement on Textiles and Clothing in OECD." In *The New Trading System: Readings.* Paris: OECD.

Wolf, Martin 1990. "How to Cut the Textile Knot: Alternative Modalities for Integration into GATT." In Carl Hamilton, ed., *Textiles Trade and the Developing Countries: Eliminating the Multi-Fibre Arrangement in the 1990s.* Washington, DC: World Bank.

Yang, Y., W. Martin, and K. Yanagishima forthcoming. "Evaluating the Benefits of Abolishing the MFA in the Uruguay Round Package." In T. W. Hertel, ed., *Global Trade Analysis Using the GTAP Model.* New York: Cambridge University Press.

4   Assessing the General Agreement on Trade in Services

Bernard Hoekman

One of the major results of the Uruguay Round was the creation of a General Agreement on Trade in Services. GATS establishes rules and disciplines for policies affecting access to service markets, greatly extending the coverage of the multilateral trading system. In some respects it is a landmark achievement. In other respects it can be considered a failure. It is a landmark in terms of creating multilateral disciplines in virgin territory; a failure in terms of generating liberalization. Commitments made in the Uruguay Round on services are best described as bound standstill agreements for policies pertaining to specific sectors. Abstracting from ongoing talks on financial services, liberalization awaits future rounds of negotiations. This suggests there are two key issues that must be addressed in evaluating GATS. First, what does it do to bind current policies? Second, has it established a mechanism that is likely to induce significant liberalization in the future? The primary objective of this chapter is to provide answers to these questions.

The chapter begins with a brief overview of global trade flows in services and a discussion of the implications of the lack of information on trade barriers for multilateral negotiations. Next, it provides a summary of the main elements of GATS and analyzes the sectoral coverage of the commitments made by the ninety-seven members that had presented their services schedules to the GATT Secretariat as of mid-1994.[1] The chapter discusses possible implications of the scheduling approach that was chosen, and asks whether future negotiations in the GATS context are likely to lead toward a fully nondiscriminatory trade regime (as opposed to managed trade). The final section of the chapter examines options for addressing the architectural weaknesses of GATS.

Trade flows, market access barriers, and data issues

Driven by innovations in information technology, increasing specialization, and product differentiation, as well as government policies such as

Table 4.1 *Global services trade flows, 1980 and 1992*

Services	1980	1992	Average annual change
Total trade in services (US$ billion)	358	931	8.3
OECD	283	765	8.6
Rest of world	75	166	6.8
Services as share of goods and services (percent)	17.0	22.0	2.2
OECD	18.8	22.7	1.6
Rest of world	12.7	19.2	3.5

Note: data pertain only to countries reporting to the International Monetary Fund.
Source: World Bank.

deregulation and liberalization, trade in services grew faster than trade in merchandise throughout the last decade. In 1992 global-services trade (nonfactor services in the balance of payments, minus government transactions) stood at some US $930 billion (table 4.1). This was equal to 22.7 percent of global trade (goods plus services), compared with 18.8 percent in 1980. Such trade occurs across borders by way of telecommunications, travel abroad by consumers (for example, tourism), or temporary entry of service providers into the territory of a consumer (for example, consulting). Over the last decade, the average annual growth rate of services trade was 8.3 percent. Both industrialized and developing countries have seen the relative importance of trade in services increase, although services account for a larger share of the total trade of OECD countries. In 1992 OECD countries accounted for 82 percent of global exports of commercial services, up from 79 percent in 1982.

Many services are not tradable, in the sense that cross-border interaction through telecommunication networks or temporary physical movement of providers and consumers is not enough to make an exchange feasible (Bhagwati 1984). Producers of such services can contest foreign markets only by establishing a long-term physical presence in them, that is, engaging in FDI. Not surprisingly, such investment in services accounts for a large share of the total stock of inward FDI in most host countries. As of the early 1990s, some 50 percent of the global stock of FDI was in service activities. The share of the annual flow to many countries has been over 60 percent in recent years.[2] The relative importance of trade in services (registered in a country's balance of payments) as opposed to sales of services by affiliates is not known. Conventional wisdom holds that FDI is the dominant "mode of supply" for many services, but that it is being eroded by technological developments. Data compiled by the United States – the only country that currently collects detailed data on both trade in services and sales of services by firms active in its market – suggest that trade and sales are of roughly the same importance.[3] Not too much can be inferred from this, however, as both trade and sales via FDI will in part reflect barriers to the provision of services imposed by partner countries. Quantitative measures of these barriers do not exist.

Available data on trade in services are weak compared with those on merchandise (box 4.1). Only a limited number of industrialized countries collect and report statistics on trade in services at a relatively disaggregated level (ten categories or more). Most non-OECD countries only report data on trade in commercial services, broken down into transport (largely freight and passenger transport by sea and air), travel (expenditures by nonresidents, mostly tourists, while staying in a foreign country),[4] and "other services." The last category includes items such as brokerage, insurance, communications, leasing and rental of equipment, technical and professional services, income generated by the temporary movement of labor, as well as property income (royalties).

In aggregate value, the OECD dominates global trade in services (table 4.2). This does not imply that developing countries have little interest in services trade. To the contrary, many developing countries are relatively specialized in exporting services, especially tourism. As RCA indices suggest,[5] small countries (defined as those with less than 1 million people) are the most specialized in this area. Moreover, their relative specialization increased significantly during the last decade. These countries have higher-than-average export intensities for all three services categories but are clearly most specialized in tourism. The relative importance of tourism receipts was about twice the world average in 1980, rising to over three times in 1992.

Cross-country data on the magnitude of barriers to trade in services do not exist. Because services tend to be intangible, barriers to trade do not take the form of import tariffs. Instead, trade barriers take the form of prohibitions, quantitative restrictions, and government regulation. Quantitative restrictions may limit the quantity or value of imports of specific products for a given time, or the number or market share of foreign service providers. Such discriminatory restrictions go hand in hand with measures that apply to both foreign and domestic service providers, usually limitations on the number of firms allowed to contest a market or on the nature of their operations. Frequently, this involves either a monopoly such as basic telecommunications services or an oligopolistic market structure (often the case in financial services or self-regulating professional services).

Box 4.1 *Services data needs and weaknesses*

The main source of data on trade in services is the balance of payments. Balance-of-payments data have many weaknesses:

Consistency and coverage. For example, a user of such statistics cannot be certain that reported exports of port services by country A consist of the same items as reported exports of port services by country B. Moreover, at virtually any level of aggregation, some nations may not report information on a certain item. Examples include maritime shipment exports and air transport services as well as many business and professional services. The result is biased figures when data are added across countries to arrive at regional totals, and discrepancies when comparing world imports and exports for a given category.

Trade by origin and destination. This information is not available on a comparable and detailed basis. While some countries report information on the direction of trade by geographic region or by major trading partner, most do not.

Disaggregation. The amount of detail or disaggregation of data on trade in services is limited.

Data on trade by volume. Balance-of-payments data on services trade refer only to value, not volume or quality. This makes it difficult to determine what proportion of growth in a given category in a given year is due to inflation as opposed to improvements in quality.

Comparability across time. Another problem when comparing developments in trade in services over time at both the country and global level, is that methodologies and definitions may vary from year to year. When countries improve the sectoral coverage of their data collection, it can be difficult to determine how much of an increase in recorded trade in services for a specific period is "real," as opposed to deriving from improvements in data collection.

Concordances. It is difficult, if not impossible, to relate services-trade statistics to domestic production and employment data. This is partly because different countries include different items in various components of the current account. More important is that trade data are too aggregated, so that concordances have little meaning. Even if there were consistent disaggregated trade data across countries, trade statistics would include items that do not appear in national accounts. An example is expenditure by travelers.

Data on sales by foreign affiliates. Balance-of-payments conventions imply that if factors of production move to another country for more than one year, a change in residency status has occured. The output generated by such factors and sold in the host market will no longer be registered as trade in the balance of payments. Data are rarely collected on the magnitude of sales by affiliates and natural persons who have established themselves in a host country. The United States is a notable exception.

Note: for a more detailed discussion of the shortcomings of services data, see Hoekman and Stern 1991.

Table 4.2 *Shares in global service exports and revealed comparative advantage, 1980 and 1992*

	Tourism		Transport		All other	
	1980	1992	1980	1992	1980	1992
Share in global trade (percent)						
OECD member countries	75.0	79.1	79.8	80.5	81.4	85.2
Developing countries	25.0	20.9	20.2	19.5	18.6	14.8
RCA						
OECD member countries	1.01	0.96	1.10	1.02	1.13	1.06
Developing countries	0.93	1.12	0.65	0.82	0.65	0.74
Small developing countries						
(1 million people or less)	2.19	3.45	1.19	1.85	0.39	1.11

Source: World Bank.

Often such market structures are tolerated because of the information problems involved in the exchange of services. Considerations relating to consumer protection, prudential supervision, and regulatory oversight often induce governments to require establishment by foreign providers, such as financial or professional services, or to reserve activities for government-owned or -regulated entities.

The nonexistence of tariffs as a restraint to trade greatly complicates analysis of or negotiations on incremental reductions in barriers to services trade. Analysis requires an estimation of the tariff equivalent of a given set of measures and regulations pertaining to a service activity. Little work has been done in this connection.[6] Negotiators require a focal point, some tangible variable enabling parties to set objectives, evaluate the position of others, and assess negotiating progress. In past merchandise-trade negotiations, the focus of negotiators was on the value of bilateral trade flows and the matching vector of applied tariffs. It was a measure that took into account the relative size of different countries (trade volume) and was simple to calculate. The complexity of identifying and quantifying barriers to trade in services focused the attention of negotiators on rules. Thus, a substantial amount of time and resources was devoted to determining whether and how GATT-like concepts such as national treatment and the MFN principle could be applied to service sectors. Indeed, discussions rapidly became sector-specific. But rather than focusing on the identification, quantification, and reduction of barriers, absolute sectoral reciprocity was emphasized. This contrasts with the "first-difference" approach to reciprocity used in GATT tariff negotiations (Bhagwati 1988).[7]

A synopsis of GATS disciplines

GATS consists of two main elements: general concepts, principles, and rules that apply across the board to measures affecting trade in services; and specific commitments on national treatment and market access.[8] The agreement includes a provision for periodic negotiations that will progressively liberalize trade in services. It also carries a set of attachments and annexes that take into account sectoral specificities and ministerial decisions relating to implementation.

GATS applies to "measures by Members affecting trade in services" (Article I) and covers four modes of supply: cross-border supply of a service (that is, not requiring the physical movement of supplier or consumer); provision involving movement of the consumer to the country of the supplier; services sold in the territory of a member by (legal) entities that have established a commercial presence there but originate in the territory of another member; and provision of services requiring the temporary movement of natural persons.[9] The agreement does not apply to services supplied in the exercise of governmental functions.

Nondiscrimination and market access

GATT's core principle is nondiscrimination, as reflected in the MFN and national treatment rules. These apply generally to all trade flows except where explicit allowance is made for their violation, for instance, in the context of regional integration. MFN and national treatment are also key provisions of GATS, albeit less all-encompassing than in the GATT. MFN coverage for each GATS member is subject to a negative list – it applies to all services except those listed by each member. The coverage of national treatment is determined by a "conditional" positive-list approach – it only applies to sectors listed in a country's schedule, and then only to measures not exempted. In addition to MFN and national treatment rules, GATS introduces a commitment not found in GATT: a market access obligation. Its reach is also determined by a positive listing of sectors by each GATS member.

Although MFN is a general obligation, GATS contains an annex allowing countries to invoke an exemption to it. MFN exemptions may only be made upon the agreement's entry into force. Once a country becomes a member, further exemptions can only be sought by requesting the Ministerial Conference of the WTO for a waiver, which must be approved by three-quarters of the members. MFN exemptions are in principle to last no longer than ten years and are subject to negotiation in future trade-liberalization rounds, the first of which must take place within five years of the agreement's entry into force. The need for an annex on MFN exemptions largely reflects a concern on the part of some industries that MFN may allow competitors located in countries with relatively restrictive policies to benefit from their sheltered markets while enjoying a free ride in less restrictive export markets. This concern was expressed vividly in GATS discussions on financial services and telecommunications, prompting industry representatives in relatively open countries to lobby for exemptions as a way to force sectoral reciprocity.[10] In the closing days of the Uruguay Round, it became clear that a number of participants were ready to invoke the annex on MFN exemptions for financial services, basic telecommunications, maritime transport, or audiovisual services. Rather than allowing countries to withdraw commitments in these areas or to exempt them from the MFN obligation, a compromise solution was reached under which negotiations on a number of these sectors were to continue without endangering the establishment of GATS (and the WTO).

Negotiations on financial services, basic telecommunications, and maritime transport were restarted in the spring of 1994. Those on financial services were concluded in July 1995. Negotiations on basic telecommunications and maritime transport are to be concluded by the end of April and the end of June 1996, respectively. Until then, neither the MFN requirement nor the possibility of invoking an exemption will enter into force unless a member has made a specific commitment for a sector.

More than sixty GATS members had submitted MFN exemptions as of mid-1994. Three sectors in particular are affected: audiovisual services, transportation (road, air, and maritime), and financial services. Exemptions in the audiovisual area tend to be justified on the basis of cultural objectives, allowing for preferential coproduction or distribution arrangements with a limited number of countries. Exemptions in the transport area often are motivated by the Liner Code of UNCTAD, a concern for many African countries in particular, or the existence of bilateral or regional agreements. Exemptions for financial services were usually made by countries seeking the flexibility to retaliate against members that did not offer reciprocal access to financial-service markets.[11] In the end, most governments decided not to invoke these exemptions for a two-year period (until November 1, 1997). The exception to this was the United States, which concluded in June 1995 that the offers made by a number of countries were inadaquate in terms of guaranteeing access to financial services markets, and therefore took an MFN exemption for the whole financial services sector. It is noteworthy – and cause for some optimism – that the US decision did not cause a domino effect. Instead, all other countries will apply their commitments on financial services, many of which had been improved during the six-month additional negotiation period, on an MFN basis. The question of modifying commitments in this area and taking MFN exemptions will be addressed again in November 1997.

Many MFN exemptions relate to existing regional-integration agreements, even though GATS makes explicit allowance for economic-integration agreements involving members. Such preferential arrangements are subject to three conditions. First, they must have "substantial sectoral coverage." Second, they must either eliminate existing discriminatory measures or prohibit the introduction of new ones. Third, the overall level of barriers to trade in services against other GATS members within the respective sectors or subsectors must not rise above the level previously applicable. There is no requirement that integration agreements be open in principle to the accession of third countries.[12] These three conditions are weaker than those applying in the GATT context (Hoekman and Sauvé 1994), the second in particular (a mere standstill agreement may be sufficient). The weakness of the disciplines on regional economic integration imply only a limited constraint on strategic violations of the MFN obligation. Many countries have nonetheless felt the need to invoke MFN exemptions for existing integration agreements.

As mentioned earlier, market access and national treatment are specific commitments. These obligations apply only to services included in the members' schedules and then are only subject to listed qualifications or conditions. In principle, six types of market access restrictions are prohibited: limitations on the number of service suppliers allowed, on the value of transactions or assets, on the total quantity of service output, on the number of employees, on the type of legal entity through which a service supplier is permitted to operate (for example, branches vs. subsidiaries for banking), and on the participation of foreign capital (a limit on the percentage of foreign shareholding or on the absolute value of foreign investment). *National treatment* is defined as treatment no less favorable than that accorded to like domestic services and service providers. However, such treatment may not be identical to that applying to domestic firms, because identical treatment could actually worsen the conditions of competition for foreign-based firms (for example, a requirement for insurance firms that reserves be held locally).

The introduction of a market access commitment reflects one of the distinguishing characteristics of service markets: their contestability is frequently restricted by nondiscriminatory measures. The market access article explicitly covers six such measures that were felt to be of particular importance. However, it overlaps with the national treatment requirement, for prohibited market access measures may be discriminatory as well as nondiscriminatory. The overlap creates the potential for confusion and disputes. Because national treatment and market access are not general obligations, in the GATS context the schedules of commitments are crucial to determining the extent of market access opportunities resulting from the agreement. As discussed below, schedules are constructed in such a manner that the liberalization dynamics of GATS may turn out to be weaker than those of GATT.

Other obligations and disciplines

Other GATS obligations address issues such as transparency, recognition of licenses and certification, payments and transfers, domestic regulation, and the behavior of public monopolies. Article III (Transparency) requires that all members establish inquiry points to provide specific information on any laws, regulations, and administrative practices affecting services covered by the agreement. Article VI (Domestic Regulation) requires members to establish disciplines guaranteeing that qualification requirements, technical standards, and licensing procedures are based on objective and transparent criteria, are no more burdensome than necessary, and do not constitute a restriction on supply (thereby possibly circumventing a specific commitment). Article XI (Transfers and Payments) prohibits members from applying restrictions on international transfers and payments for current transactions relating to activities for which specific commitments have been made. Article VII (Recognition) allows the establishment of procedures for (mutual) recognition of licenses, education, or experience granted by a particular member. It is noteworthy in requiring members to "afford adequate opportunity" for other members to negotiate their accession to an existing bilateral or plurilateral recognition agreement. Monopoly or oligopoly supply of services is allowed under GATS, but governments must ensure that firms do not abuse their market power to nullify specific commitments relating to activities that fall outside the scope of their exclusive rights (Article VIII).

As mentioned earlier, many of the framework's rules and disciplines apply only where specific commitments are made. This serious shortcoming is a consequence of the positive-list approach taken for scheduling commitments. Clearly one would want – and expect – disciplines regarding payments and transfers to be general. To the extent that other parties are willing to allow a country to maintain restrictions, a negative-list approach would allow for exemptions. But at least the principle would be general, not specific. Similarly, the requirement in Article VI (Domestic Regulation) that "all measures of *general application affecting trade in services*" be "administered in a reasonable, objective and impartial manner" applies only "in sectors where specific commitments are undertaken" (GATT 1994, p. 333, emphasis added).

GATS' MFN, national treatment, and market access obligations do not extend to government procurement of services. Negotiations on this issue are to be initiated within two years of the WTO's entry into force.[13] This greatly reduces the coverage of GATS, as procurement typically represents a significant share of total demand for many services, for instance, consulting engineering and construction. GATS does not impose general disciplines on subsidies either, only subjecting them to general obligations (transparency, MFN, and dispute settlement). The time frame for negotiations on this topic will be determined by a future work program. Article IX (Business Practices) recognizes that business practices of service suppliers that have *not* been granted monopoly or exclusive rights may restrain competition and thus trade in services, but no obligations are imposed regarding the scope and enforcement of competition policy. Members are only obliged to supply nonconfidential information of relevance to a competition-related matter if so requested by another member.

GATS has a number of safeguards, including Article X (Emergency Safeguard Measures), Article XII (Restrictions to Safeguard the Balance of Payments), Article XIV (Exceptions), and Article XXI (Modification of Schedules). Article X, which allows for possible industry-specific safeguard actions, is largely a shell calling for further negotiations on this topic within three years of the WTO's entry into force. The balance-of-payments provision only applies to those services for which specific commitments have been made. It requires that such measures be nondiscriminatory and phased out progressively as the invoking member's balance of payments improves.[14] Article XIV on exceptions is similar to what is found in GATT, providing members with the legal cover to take measures safeguarding public morals, order, health, security, consumer protection, and privacy. It also allows measures that violate national treatment if they are used to ensure equitable or effective collection of direct taxes, or that violate MFN if they result from a bilateral double-taxation agreement.[15] Article XXI on modification of schedules allows concessions (specific commitments) to be withdrawn subject to negotiation and compensation. Arbitration is anticipated in the event that bilateral negotiations on compensation are unsuccessful. Retaliation will only be authorized when a member does not comply with arbitration. Finally, the WTO's Dispute Settlement Body will be responsible for addressing disputes relating to GATS, as well as those pertaining to GATT and the agreement on TRIPS. Retaliation from goods to services and vice versa is possible.

Developing country-specific provisions

GATS Article XIX allows developing countries to make fewer specific commitments than industrialized nations. Other provisions addressing developing country concerns include Articles IV (Increasing Participation of Developing Countries), III (Transparency), and XV (Subsidies).[16] Article IV states that increased participation of developing countries in world trade in services is to be encouraged through negotiated specific commitments relating to: access to technology on a commercial basis; improved access to distribution channels and information networks; and the liberalization of market access in sectors of export interest to developing countries. On transparency, industrialized nations are to establish contact points to give developing country service suppliers more information on the commercial and technical aspects of specific services; requirements for registration, recognition, and obtaining professional qualifications; and the availability of services technology.[17] Although the negotiation of substantive disciplines on subsidies was left open (see above), Article XV recognizes the role of subsidies in the development programs of developing countries.

Specific commitments under GATS

The specific commitments are the core of GATS. To a large extent its impact depends on the commitments made by members. Negotiators chose to pursue a hybrid positive–negative list for scheduling specific commitments. It is positive in determining sectoral coverage of market access and national treatment commitments, negative with regard to identifying measures that violate either national treatment or market access disciplines. Each member first decides (negotiates) which service sectors will be subject to these disciplines. It then decides, for each such sector, what measures will be kept in place that violate market access or national treatment. Limitations and exceptions must be specified by mode of supply. With four modes of supply, there are eight opportunities for GATS members to avoid full application of market access or national treatment. In addition to specific commitments, countries also make horizontal commitments. These are usually laws and policies that restrict the use of a mode of supply by foreign suppliers, independently of the sector involved. A policy that is often scheduled is an "economic needs" test, that is, laws or regulations stipulating that foreign service providers may contest a market only if domestic providers do not exist, or are unable to satisfy demand. Another example is a general licensing or approval requirement. In many instances such horizontal "headnotes" involve a restriction on the inward movement of natural persons. The format of a schedule of specific commitments is illustrated in table 4.3. An entry of "none" means that a member binds itself to not having any measures that violate market access or national treatment for a specific sector–mode of supply combination; "unbound" implies that no commitments are made for a particular mode of supply.[18]

Table 4.3 *Example of a schedule of specific commitments*

	Mode of supply	Conditions and limitations on market access	Conditions and qualifications on national treatment
Horizontal commitments (across all sectors)	Cross-border supply	None	None other than tax measures that result in differences in treatment with respect to R&D services
	Consumption abroad	None	Unbound for subsidies, tax incentives, and tax credits.
	Commercial presence (FDI)	Maximum foreign equity stake is 49 percent	Unbound for subsidies, under law x, approval is required for equity stakes over 25 percent; new investment that exceeds y million
	Temporary entry of natural persons	Unbound except for the following: intra-corporate transferees of executives and senior managers; specialist personnel for up to one year; specialist personnel subject to economic-needs test for stays longer than one year; service sellers (sales people) for up to three months	Unbound except for categories of natural persons mentioned referred to in the market-access column
Specific commitments (e.g. legal services)	Cross-border supply	Commercial presence required	Unbound
	Consumption abroad	None	None
	Commercial presence (FDI)	25 percent of senior management should be nationals	Unbound
	Temporary entry of natural persons	Unbound, except as indicated in horizontal commitments	Unbound, except as indicated in horizontal commitments

Source: GATS schedules of commitments.

Quantifying the specific commitments: conceptual issues

Assessing the contents of country schedules requires a quantitative measure that allows for cross-country comparisons. Ideally, one would have information on the size (total output) of service activities across countries and would determine the level of restrictions facing foreign suppliers (a tariff-equivalent analogue of some kind) before and after negotiations. Unfortunately, although a common list of services has been used by members in scheduling commitments, inadequate information exists on the economic variables of interest. With the exception of communication and financial services, to which a GATS-specific breakdown of activities is applied (see Hoekman 1995), the list derives from the United Nations' Central Product Classification. No countries collect or report disaggregated data on the basis of this classification system, as it was only developed in the early 1990s. Obtaining output data for all GATS members, even for the eleven major service categories distinguished in the GATS list, would be a major endeavor. It has not been undertaken here, in large part because sector-specific information does not exist on the restrictiveness of measures relating to national treatment and market access.

The absence of such data is a major problem in evaluating GATS. To compare schedules, commitments listing measures that violate national treatment and market access obligations must be somehow discounted. In most cases there is no information regarding the restrictiveness of policies maintained or the relative importance of modes of supply on a sector-by-sector basis. Some modes may be irrelevant because of technological factors. For example, there is little value in offering zero restrictions on cross-border delivery or consumer movement in the context of retail banking services, as selling such products usually requires a commercial presence. A commercial presence in retail banking in turn requires some movement of personnel (management, technical support staff for data processing and information technology, for example). If there are no limitations on commercial presence, but if there are restrictions on the movement of personnel, market access may be severely limited. Similarly, there may be restrictions on an activity (for example, no deposit taking allowed) but no limitations on movement of personnel. Establishing mode-of-supply weights on a sector-by-sector basis is another monumental task.[19] A final problem concerns quantifying the restrictiveness of horizontal commitments, which though they apply to particular modes of supply across all sectors will affect particular sectors differently.

Clearly, a significant amount of conceptual and empirical work remains to be done. No attempt is made here to determine the change in restrictiveness of policies affecting either scheduled or nonscheduled services.[20]

Instead, the focus is on scaling the sectoral commitments of GATS members and thereby "quantifying" two things: the extent to which policy measures have been bound; and the share of sectors where such binding relates to the absence of any policy violating market access or national treatment. Lack of information on the economic impact of policies applied to services makes it impossible to have even a qualitative assessment of the liberalization implied by specific commitments. Unfortunately, schedules do not reveal to what extent they imply liberalization, if at all. It *appears* that virtually all commitments are standstill, that is, a binding of (part of) the status quo. This is the perception of negotiators, and in what follows it is assumed.[21] Because liberalization in the sense of reducing discrimination and enhancing market access did not occur, the relevance of weighted sectoral-coverage indicators increased; the key issue became one of determining the extent to which members were willing to bind the status quo.

For purposes of evaluation, each member's specific commitments were entered into a spreadsheet (commitments made as of April 1994 were considered in this exercise). With 155 nonoverlaping service sectors in the GATS classification list and four modes of supply, there is a maximum of 620 possible commitments (table 4.4).[22] As commitments apply to national treatment and market access separately, there are 1,240 data cells for each member. Schedules were submitted by ninety-seven members. Two country groups were created for comparison, one for low- and middle-income countries, one for high-income countries. Country groups follow World Bank classifications. The high-income group includes all OECD member countries except Mexico and Turkey, as well as Brunei, Cyprus, Hong Kong, Israel, Kuwait, and Singapore. The European Union is counted as one member. The low- and middle-income group includes countries with a wide range of per capita income and substantial variation in service-market size (GDP).

Commitments were classified as "none" (no restrictions applied on either market access or national treatment for a given mode of supply or sector), "unbound" (no policies bound for a given mode of supply or sector), and "other" (restrictions are listed and thus bound for a mode of supply or sector). These limitations (policies) are bound. To calculate the sectoral coverage of commitments, one of three numerical indicators (weights) was allocated to each element of a member's schedule: a 1 in all instances where "none" was stated for a sector–mode of supply; a 0 in all instances where members list "unbound" for a sector–mode of supply; and 0.5 in all instances where specific restrictions or limitations are listed for a sector–mode of supply.[23] These values were chosen to allow aggregation across sectors and countries. The higher the number, the greater the implied extent of openness-cum-binding.[24] Assigning 0 to unbound commitments

Table 4.4 *GATS members: number of commitments scheduled*

Developing countries

Algeria	4	Nicaragua	196
Antigua and Barbuda	68	Niger	20
Antilles (Netherlands)	144	Nigeria	96
Argentina	208	Pakistan	108
Aruba	140	Paraguay	36
Bahrain	16	Peru	96
Bangladesh	4	Philippines	160
Barbados	24	Poland	212
Belize	8	Romania	176
Benin	44	St. Lucia	32
Bolivia	24	St. Vincent and	
Brazil	156	the Grenadines	32
Burkina Faso	8	Senegal	104
Cameroon	12	Slovak Republic	308
Chile	140	South Africa	288
China	196	Sri Lanka	8
Colombia	164	Suriname	16
Congo	16	Swaziland	36
Costa Rica	52	Tanzania	4
Côte d'Ivoire	56	Thailand	260
Cuba	120	Trinidad and	
Czech Republic	304	Tobago	68
Dominica	20	Tunisia	52
Dominican Republic	264	Turkey	276
Egypt	104	Uganda	8
El Salvador	92	Uruguay	96
Fiji Islands	4	Venezuela	156
Gabon	44	Zambia	64
Ghana	100	Zimbabwe	72
Grenada	20		
Guatemala	40	*High-income countries*	
Guyana	72	Australia	360
Honduras	64	Austria	412
Hungary	336	Brunei	76
India	132	Canada	352
Indonesia	140	Cyprus	36
Jamaica	128	European Union	392
Kenya	84	Finland	328
Korea	311	Hong Kong	200
Macao	76	Iceland	372
Madagascar	8	Israel	180
Malaysia	256	Japan	408
Malta	28	Kuwait	176
Mauritius	43	New Zealand	276
Mexico	252	Norway	360
Morocco	144	Singapore	232
Mozambique	48	Sweden	320
Myanmar	12	Switzerland	400
Namibia	12	Liechtenstein	312
New Caledonia	24	United States	384

Note: the maximum number of commitments is 620 – 155 activities multiplied by 4 modes of supply.

and 0.5 to commitments implying maintenance of measures violating national treatment or market access reflects the perception that scheduling and binding have value, no matter how restrictive the policies being maintained.

Tariff bindings (schedules) are critical to the functioning of GATT because they establish a benchmark for the conditions of market access to which a country commits itself. Any measure taken or supported by a government that nullifies or impairs the "concession" implied by the tariff binding may give rise to a complaint to GATT. That is, the binding limits the possibility not only of raising tariffs but also of using measures that have an equivalent effect. However, this constraint only bites if tariffs are bound at applied rates. In practice, many developing countries have bound their tariffs at levels substantially higher than currently applied rates. This greatly reduces the relevance of binding but does not reduce it to 0. Martin and Francois (1995) argue that a binding above the applied rate is valuable because it reduces the expected mean tariff.

Under GATS, services policy bindings are less powerful than GATT tariff bindings because the market access article applies only to some policy measures. Some market access barriers are not "caught" by the scheduling exercise. Examples include labor legislation, tax regimes, restrictions on land availability, ownership or use, licensing and related fees, the existence and reach of competition policies, regulation of monopolies, and judicial enforceability of contracts. Such measures can satisfy national treatment and are not captured by the market access article, but they can restrict the contestability of markets. Nonetheless, binding policies that violate national treatment or market access has value because the introduction of new measures violating these commitments is no longer possible. Moreover, if a member schedules a sector and later introduces policies that are not prohibited but have the effect of nullifying its specific commitments, it can face a nonviolation complaint. If the measure is determined by the Dispute Settlement Body to have nullified or impaired a specific commitment, the affected member is entitled to compensation, and if agreement cannot be reached, to retaliation (Article XXIII, GATS).[25]

Sectoral shares can be used as an indicator of the openness of countries if attention is limited to those sectors where GATS members offer free market access and full national treatment. The sectoral coverage of such no-restriction commitments in the country schedules is perhaps the most obvious quantifiable focal point available to negotiators. It also lends itself to a formula-type approach. Negotiators might have agreed that all offers should include at least x percent of their service sector (weighted by output) for which no restrictions on market access or national treatment would be maintained. This would have provided a clear benchmark and a minimum threshold against which country offers could be objectively compared. Adoption of such a criterion, while still allowing countries substantial flexibility in their choice of sectors, would have ensured that the minimum acceptable offer was proportional to country size. In the event, quantitative targets were not used in the scheduling exercise, leaving it to bilateral negotiations to determine the minimum acceptable level of participation. Thus, instead of pursuing a formula-based approach, service negotiators resorted to the classic bid-offer approach to liberalization.

Measures of sectoral coverage of specific commitments

For both market access and national treatment, three indicators were calculated (table 4.5): the number of sector–mode of supply combinations (cells) where a commitment was made relative to the maximum possible; the "average coverage" of the schedule defined as the arithmetic weighted mean of the scale factors allocated to each cell (0 for unbound, 0.5 for bound restrictions, and 1 for no restrictions); and the share of no-restriction commitments in a member's total commitments, and relative to the 155 possible sectors of the GATS classification list. The higher the number, the more liberal the country. The first of these ratios is conceptually similar to nontariff-barrier-frequency ratios, the second to a nontariff-barrier coverage ratio (see, for example, Nogues, Olechowski, and Winters 1986).

High-income members made commitments of some kind for 47 percent of the GATS list, compared with 16 percent for developing countries. Commitments made by large developing countries, arbitrarily defined as those with GDPs of US $40 billion or more, were substantially higher than the low- and middle-income country average, accounting for 38.6 percent of the GATS list. Generally, this reflects the fact that many developing countries made very limited commitments. One quarter of the low- and middle-income group scheduled less than 3 percent of the GATS list. Four countries scheduled only 1 of the 155 service sectors; five others made commitments on only 2 subsectors. Countries in the low- and middle-income group with the highest number of specific commitments include the Czech Republic, Hungary, Korea, and the Slovak Republic, each with more than 300 sectors/modes of supply scheduled (Hoekman 1995, p. 344).

The weighted average coverage of market access commitments is 35.9 percent for high-income countries, 10 percent for low- and middle-income countries, and 22.9 percent for large developing countries. If these figures are related to the simple count of the number of sectors where commitments were made, high-income countries appear to be more liberal, since the proportion of commitments registering a 1 or a 0.5 is higher than for low- and middle-income countries (table 4.5). The ratio achieved by dividing the average coverage of commitments by the count is some 15 percentage points lower for low- and middle-income countries than for high-income countries. Almost 60 percent of commitments for the high-income group imply no restrictions, as compared to 45 percent for low- and middle-income countries. Thus, although many developing countries made only a few specific commitments, many of them involve free access. Relative to the GATS list, no-restriction commitments account for 27 percent of the maximum possible for high-income members, 7 percent for low- and middle-income countries, and 15 percent for the large developing country group.

Identical ratios were calculated for national treatment commitments. A comparison of commitments on national treatment and market access reveals that all countries tend to be more liberal with regard to the former, and that the difference between country groups narrows somewhat. There is a high correlation between commitments in these two areas. The proportion of commitments where the value of a market access cell is equal to the corresponding national treatment cell exceeds 90 percent for both groups (Hoekman 1995). What about the magnitude of commitments where no restrictions apply to both market access and national treatment for a given sector–mode of supply? The figure for high-income countries is 25 percent, for low- and middle-income countries 7 percent. These numbers vividly illustrate how far away GATS members are from attaining free trade in services, and the magnitude of the task that remains.

The data reported in table 4.5 do not take into account the relative importance of different service activities in GDP (that is, the size of the various service markets), or the relative importance of countries in the world economy (that is, the size of the different GATS members). Table 4.6 reports coverage indicators that incorporate an attempt to take these factors into account. Table 4.6 pertains to market access commitments only, given that these tend to be more restrictive than those on national treatment. For ease of comparison, the first row repeats the unweighted average sectoral coverage ratios reported in table 4.5. The second row illustrates the importance of taking into account the relative importance (size) of individual service activities (see Hoekman 1995, pp. 352–33 for the output weights used; the same weights were employed for all countries). Sectoral coverage indicators rise substantially for high-income countries: increasing by 10 percentage points to 45 percent. The coverage ratio for low- and middle-income countries rises by 2 percentage points. This indicates that commitments were made in activities that are of above average importance in GDP terms. The third row in table 4.6 relates the specific commitments, weighted by sectoral contributions to GDP, to the global market for services, as measured by country shares in global GDP.

Table 4.5 *Sectoral coverage of specific commitments (percent)*

	High-income countries	Low- and middle-income countries	Large developing nations
Market access			
Unweighted average count (sectors–modes listed as a share of maximum possible)	47.3	16.2	38.6
Average coverage (sectors–modes listed as a share of maximum possible, weighted by openness or binding factors)	35.9	10.3	22.9
Coverage/count (average coverage as a share of the average count)	75.9	63.6	59.3
No restrictions as a share of total offer (unweighted count)	57.3	45.5	38.7
No restrictions as a share of maximum possible	27.1	7.3	14.9
National treatment			
Unweighted average count (sectors–modes listed as a share of maximum possible)	47.3	16.2	38.8
Average coverage (sectors–modes listed as a share of maximum possible, weighted by openness or binding factors)	37.2	11.2	25.5
Coverage/count (average coverage as a share of average count)	78.6	69.1	66.1
No restrictions as a share of total offer (unweighted count)	65.1	58.0	52.3
No restrictions as a share of maximum possible	30.8	9.4	20.2
Memo item			
No restrictions on market access and national treatment as a share of maximum possible	24.8	6.9	14.3

Source: author's calculations based on WTO and World Bank data.

Table 4.6 *Sectoral coverage of specific commitments on market access, weighted by sectoral contributions to GDP and country shares in global GDP*

	High-income countries	Low- and middle-income countries
Weighted by restrictiveness	35.9	10.3
Weighted by restrictiveness and GDP	45.4	12.2
Weighted by restrictiveness, sectoral contributions to GDP, and country share in world GDP	48.4	5.2
GDP weight in world	78.9	16.4

Note: weights do not add to 1, as GATS members do not include all countries in the world.
Source: author's calculations based on GATS schedules and World Bank data.

Commitments for high-income countries cover about half of the global services market. Those by low- and middle-income countries represent only 5 percent of the world market, reflecting their much smaller share in global GDP (estimated at 16.4 percent).[26] Adjusting for the relative importance of modes of supply across service sectors suggests that this has little impact on the magnitude of coverage ratios (Hoekman 1995).

Again, sectoral coverage indices are of limited use from an economic perspective, as no account can be taken of the actual restrictiveness of policy stances maintained by different countries by sector–mode of supply. The least ambiguous measure in this respect is the no-restrictions coverage ratio.[27] This is 25 percent on average for the high-income group, 7 percent on average for other GATS members. Because it is reasonable to assume that countries scheduled the "easiest" sectors, these relatively low coverage indicators suggest that in the foreseeable future most trade in services will remain subject to market access or national treatment restrictions. Of course, the average coverage of sectoral commitments is greater than the no-restriction measure. Weighted by sectoral contributions to GDP, it is about 45 percent for high-income countries and 12 percent for low- and middle-income countries. The average sectoral-coverage ratio of the bottom fifty developing countries (which account for over 60 percent of the group in number) falls substantially below the group average, only 3 percent. Many of these countries are small and have very low per capita incomes, reducing pressure from trading partners to schedule more sectors. However, this by no means justifies such a passive stance.

Although a number of poor countries scheduled a significant number of

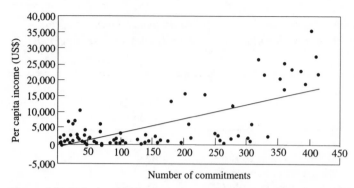

Figure 4.1   Relationship between per capita income and specific commitments

sectors, many did not (figure 4.1). It is unclear why coverage ratios (unweighted) are not close to 100 percent for all members. The mere fact that so much of the service sector was not scheduled must be counted against GATS. The cost of making specific commitments is, after all, modest, even for those countries that do not favor liberalization, for any measure violating national treatment or market access may be scheduled. This argument applies *a fortiori* to those countries that either desire to liberalize access to their service markets or that already maintain a liberal policy stance.

There is a fair amount of variance in the sectoral coverage of specific commitments (table 4.7). The fewest commitments were made by high-income countries in sectors such as land, water and air transport, postal services, basic telecoms, research and development, education, health, and recreation and social services. Of these "sensitive" sectors, developing countries have a potential export interest in the last three. But the coverage of business services, computer-related services, and construction is quite high. These sectors cover many activities where developing countries have an export potential.

Although market access commitments by high-income countries tend to be restrictive with respect to activities where developing countries have a comparative advantage – both low- and high-skill labor-intensive activities that require either temporary entry or establishment or work permits – nothing is to be gained from a retaliatory policy. Most countries are too small to influence the market access policies of large traders. Nonliberalization by trading partners restricts the potential gains from liberalization but by no means eliminates them. The annex on the movement of natural persons – currently the only mode-of-supply-specific part of GATS – requires simply that natural persons who are service suppliers or employed by the service supplier of a member be allowed to provide services in accordance with the terms of specific commitments relating to their entry and

Table 4.7 *Commitments by sector*

ISIC	Numbers of GATS sectors and modes of supply	Average number of commitments		Commitments/GATS items (percent)	
		High-income countries	Low- and middle-income countries	High-income countries	Low- and middle-income countries
Construction	20	11.2	3.3	56.0	16.5
Motor vehicle repair	4	1.8	0.3	45.0	7.5
Wholesale trade	8	4.6	0.5	57.5	6.3
Retail trade	8	4.4	0.8	55.0	10.0
Hotels, restaurants	4	2.8	2.8	70.0	70.0
Land transport	40	9.4	2.3	23.5	5.8
Water transport	48	4.4	3.0	9.2	6.3
Air transport	20	3.7	1.5	18.5	7.5
Auxiliary transport	20	5.1	1.3	25.5	6.5
Postal	4	1.3	0.6	32.5	15.0
Basic telecom	28	1.5	1.3	5.4	4.6
Value-added telecom	28	18.7	5.0	66.8	17.8
Financial	60	31.3	12.4	52.2	20.6
Real estate	8	3.5	0.3	43.8	3.8
Rental activities	20	9.5	1.3	47.5	6.5
Computer-related	20	15.5	4.2	77.5	21.0
Research and development	12	4.1	1.0	34.2	8.3
Business	108	56.5	12.2	47.9	11.3
Refuse disposal	16	8.8	1.0	55.0	6.3
Education	20	4.7	1.3	23.5	6.5
Health and social	24	5.0	1.9	20.8	7.9
Recreation, culture	48	13.3	4.6	27.9	9.6

temporary stay. The extent to which labor movement is allowed is therefore completely dependent on what is specified in the schedules. Specific restrictions on labor movement may be horizontal or sector-specific. Most members only allow for entry of specialists and higher-level management staff, significantly curtailing the scope for cross-border (nonestablishment related) trade in services. Similarly, a lack of general disciplines on discriminatory licensing practices involving citizenship or permanent residency requirements can be expected to weaken the impact of GATS on trade in professional services.[28]

For developing countries the potential gains of GATS membership will result primarily from liberalizing access to their own markets. There is substantial evidence that many constraints reducing the economic efficiency of service industries are home grown (UNCTAD and World Bank 1994). Government policy measures should focus on such concerns as augmenting domestic productive capacity, increasing the quality of services and establishing a reputation for reliable supply. The availability of higher-quality or lower-cost services will often increase the output of goods and make them more competitive on world markets. The level of specific commitments under GATS suggests that governments did not grasp the opportunity to bind the status quo, let alone liberalize access to service markets.

The framework's possible incentive effects

Progressive liberalization is a central objective of GATS. How successful will the current structure be in expanding the coverage of bindings and inducing substantial liberalization of access to service markets? Concerns can be expressed regarding both dimensions. Problems include the lack of transparency, sector-specificity, the modalities of scheduling, and the limited number of generic rules. All of these reflect the structural weaknesses of GATS.

GATS does not do nearly enough to further the goal of transparency, which should be a fundamental objective of any multilateral agreement. No information is generated on sectors, subsectors, and activities for which no commitments are scheduled – most often sensitive areas where restrictions and discriminatory practices abound. A commitment consisting of the single word "unbound" conveys nothing but the government's unwillingness to have its hands tied, in which case the regulatory stance is likely to be restrictive. Lack of transparency is a serious shortcoming considering the nature of impediments to trade in services (regulatory barriers at both the national and subnational levels). A negative list would have significantly enhanced transparency, even if it did result in country-specific "phone books" of nonconforming measures. Service providers have no comprehensive cross-country source of information on regulatory regimes. If members remain firmly committed to the positive-list approach, all should agree to compile and publish this information on a sector-by-sector basis within a given time. Article III (Transparency) may provide the justification for such a compilation. Without such transparency, negotiations will remain difficult, driven primarily by powerful export interests.

There is also a great deal of variance across countries regarding the transparency of the commitments themselves. Some members have invested substantial effort in listing all relevant laws and regulations that may limit access. Others simply make reference to a limitation, without specifying applicable laws. Limitations mentioned in a schedule may be vague and therefore open to interpretation (indeed, require it).[29] Dispute settlement in GATS is likely to revolve around interpretation of country schedules. Because of the ambiguity of the schedules, disputes may be frequent. Overlap and inconsistency between national treatment and market access obligations may prove particularly problematic, as any market access restriction will violate national treatment if it applies only to foreign service providers. For example, a member may have made a no-restriction commitment under national treatment but scheduled a limitation on the maximum equity share held by an established foreign supplier. Greater care should have been taken to ensure that the two commitments are distinct.

GATS' structure reflects the fact that negotiations in the services area were (and will be) sectoral. They can be expected to be driven by the concerns of major players in each industry. At some level a sectoral approach is probably unavoidable, given the widely differing regulatory regimes across countries and sectors. But to foster MFN-based liberalization, sectoral agreements should be firmly embedded in a framework of general rules and disciplines. GATS' emphasis on sectoral reciprocity may prove especially troublesome if incremental liberalization becomes less feasible and the scope for cross-issue tradeoffs is reduced. Turf fights between regulatory agencies might ensue, curbing chances for an economy-wide perspective and tradeoffs across issues. The positive-list approach may also make it more difficult for a government to add sectors to its schedule. Those industries affected could argue against their inclusion. With a negative list, each industry seeking special treatment has to justify why the rules should not apply to it, even though they apply to everyone else; with a positive list the government must be ready to confront each industry that it seeks to subject to multilateral disciplines. As mentioned, the "easy" sectors will probably be included first, leaving the more sensitive sectors to be dealt with in the future.

The scheduling of commitments by modes of supply may further distort incentives and resource allocation by creating the opportunity for biasing incentives toward a particular mode of supply. Ironically, given the early resistance of many developing countries to discussing establishment-related matters in the negotiations, their commitments lodged under the commercial-presence supply mode tend to be the least restrictive. But this is perhaps not surprising, commercial presence being the mode that appears to generate the most in terms of local content-domestic value added. However, more stringent controls on other modes may give firms an incentive to engage in tariff-hopping investment. Indeed, commitments on commercial presence may amount to disguised trade-related investment measures, insofar as foreign service providers are compelled to use this mode and, in the process, are subjected to measures that violate either market access or national treatment. At the same time, commitments relating to commercial presence may be subject to the right to maintain or impose authorization or screening procedures (horizontal restrictions), and the criteria or measures underpinning such procedures may not be clearly defined in the schedule.

There is another potentially perverse incentive created by the combination of specific commitments and the positive-list approach: members may be induced to adopt policies that are in principle prohibited, then seek to negotiate these away over time. Policies in many countries may be consistent with market access and national treatment obligations. Rather than locking this in, GATS allows for the future imposition of restrictions. GATS' impact would have been substantially greater if the status quo had been bound for all sectors. The market access article is a step in the right direction, but it should have been a general obligation subject to a negative list of exemptions. Moreover, it is too weak. Instead of defining market access, GATS includes a finite list of measures prohibited in principle, leaving others that have similar effects untouched. The article would have been strengthened, and dispute settlement facilitated, if the words "or measures with equivalent effect" had been added. Such language would have allowed violation complaints; its absence puts all the weight on nonviolation, a much weaker mechanism.

To the extent that market access restrictions are maintained, their impact on the MFN obligation must be considered. With the market access restrictions being quantitative in nature – limits on the number of firms, their assets, or their turnover – there appears to be a natural incentive to negotiate quantitative increases in market access as well. Suppose that currently there are only three foreign firms established, and that they are restricted to four lines of activity. Trade negotiators might seek to increase the number of firms or lines of permitted activity. That is, GATS' approach to liberalization has a built-in incentive for the reciprocal negotiation of voluntary import–investment expansion. If a country permits a few additional firms into a sector, incentives may exist to ensure that firms from certain countries obtain access. Market access/share criteria could result in managed trade, as voluntary import–investment expansion agreements can easily be inconsistent with MFN.

Implications for developing countries

GATS imposes few limitations on national policy, only requiring that no discrimination occurs across alternative sources of supply. It allows members to implement policies that are detrimental to – or inconsistent with – economic efficiency. A good example is the article specifying the conditions under which measures to safeguard balance of payments may be taken, such measures rarely being efficient. Furthermore, GATS does not require a participating country to alter regulatory structures or to pursue an active antitrust or competition policy. Liberalization of trade and investment may need to be augmented by regulatory change (frequently deregulation) and an effective competition policy to increase the efficiency of service sectors such as finance, transportation, and telecommunications. If simply equated with increased market access for (certain) foreign suppliers, liberalization may have little effect in noncompetitive markets. The main result will be to redistribute rents across firms.

Many developing countries were able to accede to GATS with minimal commitments. The adoption of a positive-list approach was partly due to arguments by developing countries that a negative list was too resource intensive to be feasible within the time frame originally envisaged (completion of the round by the end of 1990). Acceptance of this argument, willingness to accept little in the way of scheduled specific commitments, and the fact that a number of the framework's rules apply only if specific commitments are made, mean that GATS will have little impact on most developing countries. Indeed, the impact may be negative. Nongenerality of national treatment and sector-specific market access commitments limit the value of GATS to governments seeking to liberalize. Lobbies that oppose liberalization cannot be told that GATS membership requires national treatment for all sectors. Instead, the government must explicitly list each and every sector to guarantee that national treatment and market access obligations will apply.

GATS does not emulate GATT by embodying special and differential treatment provisions, but it continues the GATT tradition of putting little pressure on small and poor developing countries to participate fully, as these have little to offer in the multilateral mercantile game of give and take. However, these countries, largely left to pursue liberalization unilaterally, are arguably the ones for which a liberal policy stance is crucial. GATS allows them to lock in liberalization if so desired, but does not do much to nourish a liberal policy environment.

Options for fixing the framework

There are many challenges that negotiators need to address if GATS is to become an effective and therefore credible instrument of multilateral liberalization. Agreement on disciplines in the areas of subsidies, procurement, and safeguards must be reached. Sectoral coverage of GATS must be greatly extended through binding all measures violating national treatment and market access. The set of generally applicable rules and disciplines must be expanded, and the weight of specific commitments reduced. And the approach taken toward scheduling commitments in the Uruguay Round needs to be critically assessed to determine whether it will encourage significant liberalization of service markets.

The first order of business should be to explore whether a more general approach – similar to that of the European Union, NAFTA, or the Australia–New Zealand Closer Economic Relations Trade Agreement – might be feasible.[30] Given that negotiators were well aware of the approaches taken toward liberalizing service markets in regional contexts, presumably this is not an option. But it should be possible to come closer to this model. Deardorff (1994) and Snape (1994) have argued that the key requirement is to make national treatment a general obligation, the former proposing a *quid pro quo* whereby each country would be allowed to levy taxes, perhaps prohibitive, on foreign providers. Scheduled, these taxes would become the focal point for future liberalization efforts. Snape (1994) proposes the adoption of general obligations prohibiting all forms of discrimination against foreign suppliers, but rather than tariffication suggests a negotiated set of legitimized measures to reduce the contestablity of any service market for foreign suppliers. Future negotiations could focus on these measures.

The current wording of GATS implies that tariffication would have to pertain to existing market access restrictions as well as limitations on national treatment. Both Deardorff and Snape focus on classic national treatment, that is, discrimination against *foreign* suppliers. In principle, tariffication of discriminatory measures appears straightforward, because each government can simply set a tax rate. In practice, however, it may be difficult to determine the nationality of firms and to curb opportunistic behavior. Member schedules suggest that tariffs are likely to be lower on establishment than on cross-border trade, thus fostering establishment. Because origin rules will invariably exempt ventures with some degree of local ownership, policies can be expected to favor joint venture-based establishment. This is not much of a problem; the current incentive structure does it already. However, it is important that tariffication not make the policy stance more restrictive. This may easily happen, as no one knows what the tariff equivalent of the status quo is. In many instances current policy toward foreign providers is consistent with national treatment, but countries have avoided scheduling (binding) this state of affairs. To the extent that entry is in principle free (the applied policy is liberal), this should not be supplanted by discriminatory taxation of foreign providers. A relatively liberal status quo should be reflected in tax rates that are imposed. Thus, established foreign firms should be grandfathered from tariffication if they are presently granted national treatment, and no tariffication should be permitted in such sectors. Otherwise, the argument for tariffication is greatly weakened. The main rationale is harnessing the mercantilist approaches developed in GATT to liberalizing service markets. If conditions are already liberal, tariffication is counterproductive and may be captured by – or create – vested interests that will oppose future reductions.[31] Therefore it may be preferable to pursue Snape's proposal (1994) to seek a limited set of policies that could be applied by GATS members to discriminate against foreign suppliers. What those measures might be is unclear, however, as lengthy discussions during the Uruguay Round indicated.

The tariffication proposal might be more readily applied to nondiscriminatory market access restrictions. There is no reason potential domestic entrants would not be willing to pay an entry fee to contest a market currently subject to quota restrictions. One tariffication option could be to periodically auction off such restrictions. This would appear most appropriate for regulated monopolies and for self-regulated industries where there is a *numerus fixus* constraint on new entry. Determining origin is not a problem if the measures are applied on a nondiscriminatory basis and the focus can be on all potential entrants. Another possibility for regulated activities is to exchange price-reduction commitments based on price comparisons of several of the lowest-cost suppliers of a service. This would require substantial information and may not be feasible for some sectors. However, if there were multilateral scrutiny of pricing policies, and if the WTO's dispute-settlement mechanism were extended to cover the pricing practices of monopolies, it could help GATS get around existing legal constraints on competition in many jurisdictions.

Realistically, proposals for improving GATS should build upon the existing structure and involve the following steps: adopting a negative-list approach to scheduling for the purpose of transparency, with a transition period that gives members sufficient time to do this;[32] eliminating all overlap between national treatment and market access, ensuring that the latter applies only to nondiscriminatory measures; agreeing to horizontal disciplines on modes of supply, and eliminating mode-of-supply-specific limitations in schedules; expanding the reach of the market access article by including the term "or measures with equivalent effect"; exploring the feasibility of converting quota-like market access restrictions to price-based equivalent measures by auctioning them off, guaranteeing that MFN and national treatment are satisfied; making all framework disciplines generally applicable by eliminating all instances where rules are conditional upon the scheduling of specific commitments; and agreeing to a formula-based approach for future liberalization and expansion of the sectoral coverage of GATS. GATT experience suggests that progress is made when negotiators use a quantifiable focal point. A formula approach could help negotiations on services by establishing a target for the share of each member's service sector that should be scheduled with no restrictions, and for the share of the GATS list of services that should be bound.

So far, many GATS discussions have tended to be sector-specific. In principle, it makes sense to take into account the idiosyncrasies of particular sectors. But the current format of the schedules allows for too much discretion. Sectoral agreements should be annexes that extend or complement generally applicable rules. Such general disciplines should also pertain to modes of supply. Elimination of the mode-of-supply criterion in specific commitments may be relatively straightforward. Nothing in GATS compels members to schedule commitments by mode of supply.[33] Horizontal commitments already pertain to the four modes of supply, independent of sector. What is required is that horizontal commitments no longer consist of a positive list of bound policies, but that they be transformed into a negative list of policies that are inconsistent with generally applicable rules and disciplines. A model that could be emulated in this connection is NAFTA's, where generic disciplines were negotiated for modes of supply. This is ambitious, of course, and may be feasible only if goods and services are treated symmetrically (as they are in NAFTA). Developing common WTO disciplines on investment in goods and services should therefore be a matter of some urgency.

Outstanding issues: subsidies, safeguards, and procurement

Space constraints prohibit a detailed discussion of subsidies, safeguards, and procurement, the outstanding issues that remain on the immediate negotiating agenda.[34] All three are important, and the disciplines that emerge will influence the effectiveness of GATS as an instrument for binding policies and promoting liberalization. Without subsidy disciplines, the scope for contesting scheduled markets may be limited. Similarly, if safeguard actions are relatively easy to implement, specific commitments may lose much of their impact. Expanding the reach of GATS to government procurement is critical, as the rules and procedures that are established will help determine the potential for developing countries to expand exports of services. A key issue here will be to ensure consistency with the GPA, which was extended to services in the Uruguay Round. Noteworthy in this regard is that the GPA makes no distinctions between modes of supply. Indeed, it requires signatories not to discriminate on the basis of mode of supply. This is one more reason to eliminate the mode-of-supply distinction in specific commitments.

Conclusion

GATS is the first multilateral agreement on policies affecting trade in services. As such, it is not surprising that minimal liberalization was achieved. More worrisome is that GATS' structure allows members not to bind the status quo in many sectors. Much work remains if GATS' coverage is ever to be universal. The fundamental question is whether GATS will induce members to go further in future negotiating rounds. Although doubts have been expressed in this connection, many structural shortcomings can be addressed relatively easily, while others are probably best handled by expanding disciplines to apply to both goods and services. Priorities were argued to be the scheduling, or binding, of all sectors – preferably as part of the shift to a negative-list approach – and the elimination of modes of supply in schedules. The credibility of GATS as a multilateral instrument of liberalization greatly depends on the political will of members to open their markets in the future and to make changes to GATS' structure (Sauvé 1995).

The need for greater transparency cannot be overemphasized. Reference to the GATT experience in agreeing to the TPRM is appropriate here. Although most countries did not have much desire to subject themselves to a transparency-based review of their trade policies, the benefit of obtaining information on trading partners outweighed the perceived cost of being subjected to review. The agreement to create a mechanism for trade policy review has given domestic groups (and the Ministry of Finance) access to a substantial amount of information regarding trade policies applied by various countries. Better information will help analysts determine the costs and benefits of current policy in service sectors. A dearth of objective data impedes analysis and the formation of interest groups favoring liberalization.[35] Tariffication and calculation of price-cost margins, even if not used as explicit focal points for negotiations, can do much to expand information on market opportunities and the relative restrictiveness of regulatory regimes. The WTO Secretariat or the OECD could undertake efforts to calculate price-cost margins and tariff equivalents of services policies.

It is important to recognize that the problems involved in fixing GATS extend beyond services. Future multilateral efforts must center on eliminating the artificial goods–services distinction and on developing generic disciplines for foreign direct investment and labor movement. In this context, attention could also be given to whether and how market access commitments might be replaced with competition disciplines. Market access restrictions as defined in GATS are, of course, not limited to services, although competition is often more restricted in these industries than in goods-producing sectors. The subject of competition policy has been actively discussed as a likely topic for future multilateral negotiations under WTO auspices. The same applies to policies affecting investment. Attention should be devoted to both goods and services in this connection, and the same rules should apply to both. The probable expansion of the multilateral trading system to include rules on policies affecting investment is another important reason for developing horizontal, generally applicable disciplines on mode of supply. It would be most unfortunate if, in investment-related matters, GATS' approach of scheduling by mode of supply and with a positive list were extended to GATT.

Notes

The views expressed in this chapter are the author's and should not be attributed to the World Bank. I am grateful to Julian Arkell, Carlos Braga, Alan Deardorff, Brian Hindley, Guy Karsenty, Patrick Low, Will Martin, Petros Mavroidis, Pierre Sauvé, Richard Snape, and Alan Winters for helpful comments and discussions. My thanks as well to Faten Hatab and Ying Lin for computational assistance, and to David Hartridge for providing the GATS schedules.

1. The term "member" denotes that signatories of GATS are members of the WTO and not simply contracting parties (signatories) to a treaty.
2. See UNCTAD and World Bank (1994) for data on foreign direct investment in services.
3. In 1987 foreign sales by US majority-owned affiliates were 15 percent lower than service exports; in 1992 they had grown to be 20 percent larger (World Bank 1995).
4. Note that part of tourist expenditures will be on goods such as souvenirs or artifacts.
5. These are defined as the ratio of exports of a given product to a country's total exports of goods and services, divided by the same ratio for the world: RCA = $[X_{ij}/Y_j]/[X_{iw}/Y_w]$, where X_{ij} are exports of product i by country j, Y_j are total exports of goods and services by country j, and w stands for the world. The

value of this index may range from zero to a very large number. If the index is greater than one, it implies that the country is relatively specialized in that product.

6. As discussed in greater detail in Hoekman (1994), research has focused on theoretical issues, not empirical analyses. While perhaps not surprising given the difficulty of generating data on barriers to trade, this has left negotiators without much guidance regarding the costs and benefits of alternative negotiating strategies/policy stances. It is beyond the scope of this chapter to discuss the myriad issues that complicate estimation of tariff equivalents or price-cost margins in the services context. In addition to standard problems that arise in modeling the effect of nontariff measures (see, for example, Deardorff and Stern 1985), analysts must take account of nondiscriminatory market access restrictions; the importance of natural barriers to trade (distance, language, climate, etc.); the fact that establishment is often required; complementarities between modes of supply; the prevalence of joint production (such as the need for the consumer/provider to cooperate); and the role of reputation and nonprice competition in many service industries. See, for example, Hindley (1988), Messerlin and Sauvant (1990), Sapir (1993), Sapir and Winter (1994), and UNCTAD and World Bank (1994).

7. See, for example, Brock (1982), Bhagwati (1987a,b), Drake and Nicolaidis (1992), Feketekuty (1988), Giersch (1989), Grey (1985), Helleiner (1988), Hindley (1990), Richardson (1987), Sampson and Snape (1985), Sapir (1985), and Snape (1990).

8. For the complete text, see GATT (1994).

9. This follows the typology suggested in the academic literature, especially Bhagwati (1984) and Sampson and Snape (1985). "Trade in Services" in the GATS context therefore covers both trade in the balance-of-payments sense and local sales by foreign affiliates.

10. The issue mainly concerned industries in relatively open markets seeking to obtain access to more closed markets. It was not that the *demandeur* industries feared cross-subsidized competition. This implied that the carrot being offered – MFN – was unlikely to induce much pressure on countries being asked to open up.

11. Interestingly, the European Union made an exemption for distribution of audiovisual works and audiovisual services more generally, allowing it to impose "redressive duties . . . to respond to unfair pricing practices" by third-country distributors, and to "prevent, correct or counterbalance adverse, unfair, or unreasonable conditions or actions affecting EC [European Community] audiovisual services, products, or service providers, in response to corresponding or comparable actions taken by other members."

12. In contrast to Article VII on recognition (see below).

13. The GATT GPA was revised to include services. However, this is a plurilateral agreement that binds only signatories. The new agreement has eleven members, mostly OECD countries (Israel and Korea are the only non OECD parties). Coverage of procurement of services is subject to a double positive list: only the

procurement by covered entities of services explicitly scheduled in annexes are subject to the agreement's rules, and then only insofar as no qualifications or limitations are maintained in the relevant annexes. A number of countries made derogations to commitments on services specifying that offered services are covered only if other parties to the agreement provide reciprocal access to those services. The approach taken in GATS regarding sectoral reciprocity was therefore also pursued in the procurement context. The new GPA is discussed in Hoekman and Mavroidis (1995).

14. As in the GATT context, import restrictions are not recognized to be second-best instruments to deal with balance-of-payments difficulties.

15. A ministerial decision included in the Final Act states that "since measures necessary to protect the environment typically have as their objective the protection of human, animal, or plant life or health, it is not clear that there is a need to provide for" an explicit "environmental" exception. The Committee on Trade and Environment is given the tasks of determining whether there is such a need and of examining the relationship between trade in services and the environment.

16. For a more detailed discussion, see UNCTAD and World Bank (1994, pp. 144–46).

17. This provision goes beyond the requirement to establish inquiry points contained in Article III (transparency), which simply relate to laws, regulations, decisions, etc., that affect the supply of services. The contact points for developing countries also cover technical matters.

18. Most members do not list horizontal restrictions on cross-border supply or consumer movement. It is not clear whether this implies that they have bound themselves. GATS allows additional commitments to be made going beyond national treatment/market access. Virtually no use has been made of this option.

19. Hoekman (1995) uses a subjective weighing scheme to determine the possible impact of (sensitivity to) incorporating this into the analysis.

20. The GATS schedules can be used to generate some information on the *relative* restrictiveness of the policy regimes maintained by members (see Hoekman 1995, annex 2; and Brown, Deardorff, Fox, and Stern, chapter 10 in this volume).

21. The only area where some liberalization occurred is in financial services, where a number of countries improved market access conditions.

22. The GATS list has four levels of aggregation. This chapter uses the 155 "three-digit" level of aggregation. The 155 activities include various categories of other services that are not strictly comparable across countries. There is little difference between the three- and four-digit levels – the latter only differs from the former in that item 7.B.f. of the list (trading in financial instruments) is disaggregated into six types of instruments.

23. If countries made commitments on sectors not individually mentioned in the GATS classification list, only one sector is recorded. The economic significance of the activities mentioned in such cases tend to be minor. Members sometimes specify that a commitment applies only to a subset of a disaggregated item. A

common example is under legal services, where foreign providers are often limited to the practice of – advice on – home country law. In these cases, it is assumed that the commitment applies to the whole subsector, biasing sectoral coverage indicators upward. Some GATS members may schedule commitments for an aggregated item instead of all five of the relevant subsectors. In such cases it is assumed that the commitment applies to all respective subsectors. In a number of cases a mode of supply is not technically feasible. A good example is cross-border provision of building assembly and installation services. Most schedules note this fact, stating that the mode of supply is "unbound due to lack of technical feasibility." Such cases are allocated the value 1 for coverage calculation purposes, if other modes of supply are unrestricted. In the case of nations with a federal structure, a limitation on a mode of supply may only apply for one of the subfederal entities. No account of this is taken in the calculations here; it is assumed that the limitation applies to the whole nation. This results in a downward bias of coverage. Affected members include Canada, the European Union, and the United States.

24. A value of 1 for a sector/mode of supply does not necessarily imply that foreign service providers can freely contest a specific market through a given mode of supply. This depends on applicable horizontal commitments, which tend to focus on labor mobility. In all cases where a reference is made under the temporary entry mode of supply to a horizontal commitment (restriction), a value of 0.5 is entered.

25. See Hoekman and Mavroidis (1994) for a discussion of the nonviolation option.

26. Sources for GDP data are the World Development Report and the World Bank STARS data base.

27. The complement of the no-restrictions ratio – with services weighted by shares in GDP – is an indicator of the extent to which policy affects access to service markets. This indicator can be seen as a direct analogue of the standard nontariff barrier frequency indicator if unweighted by GDP shares, and of the nontariff barrier coverage ratio if weighted.

28. A ministerial decision taken in Marrakesh established a negotiating group to pursue talks on further liberalization of the movement of natural persons for the purpose of supplying services. This group was to conclude its talks within six months of the WTO's entry into force. The developing country objective to improve access to markets for independent professionals was met to only a limited extent.

29. Sometimes it is not even clear what limitations apply to what sector or subsector. Some schedules fail to mention a specific mode of supply for a given sector. Members at times also diverge from the positive-negative-list approach to scheduling, instead opting for a positive-positive-list approach. That is, the sectors to which the market access article and national treatment principle apply are listed, and then what is offered for each mode of supply is specified (as opposed to listing the limitations on national treatment or market access). This reduces transparency further, by not identifying all the

policies that conflict with market access and/or national treatment. As noted previously, it is also not clear whether nonlisting of horizontal measures on modes of supply implies a binding of no restrictions.

30. See Hoekman and Sauvé (1994) for a description of these arrangements.
31. Thus the difference with agriculture, where stratospheric bindings were considered an acceptable price to pay to get this sector back into the GATT, is that the current policy regime in many service sectors may be much less distorted.
32. The offer of official grant-based financial assistance for low-income countries would be a great boost.
33. Article XX of GATS (Schedules of Specific Commitments) states that separate commitments must be made for national treatment and for market access, but does not require that this be by mode of supply.
34. See Hoekman (1993) and Hoekman and Mavroidis (1995) for discussions on safeguards and government procurement.
35. A negative-list approach to scheduling, while important and necessary, is not sufficient to allow analysis. An additional requirement is that comparable production, consumption and trade data are available. Members should be required to report such data for at least the eleven major GATS service sectors, and preferably on a "2-digit" basis.

References

Bhagwati, J. 1984. "Splintering and Disembodiment of Services and Developing Nations." *The World Economy* 7: 133–44.
———. 1987a. "Trade in Services and Developing Countries." In O. Giarini, ed., *The Emerging Service Economy*. New York: Praeger.
———. 1987b. "Trade in Services and the Multilateral Trade Negotiations." *The World Bank Economic Review* 1: 549–69.
Brock, W. 1982. "A Simple Plan for Negotiating on Trade in Services." *The World Economy* 5: 229–40.
Deardoff, A. 1994. "Market Access." In *The New World Trading System: Readings*. Paris: OECD.
Deardorff, A., and R. Stern 1985. *Methods of Measurement of Non-Tariff Barriers*. Geneva: UNCTAD.
Drake, W., and K. Nicolaidis 1992. "Ideas, Interests, and Institutions: Trade in Services and the Uruguay Round." *International Organization* 46: 37–100.
Feketekuty, G. 1988. *International Trade in Services: An Overview and Blueprint for Negotiations*. Cambridge, Mass.: Ballinger.
GATT 1994. *The Results of the Uruguay Round of Multilateral Negotiations: The Legal Texts*. Geneva: GATT, Secretariat.
Giersch, H., ed. 1989. *Services in World Economic Growth*. Tubingen: J. C. B. Mohr.
Grey, R. 1985. "Negotiating about Trade and Investment in Services." In R. Stern, ed., *Trade and Investment in Services: Canada/U.S. Perspectives*. Toronto: Ontario Economic Council.

Helleiner, G. 1988. "Trade in Services and the Developing Countries: Negotiating Approaches." In K. Haq, ed., *Linking the World: Trade Policies for the Future.* Islamabad: North–South Roundtable.

Hindley, B. 1988. "Service Sector Protection: Considerations for Developing Countries." *World Bank Economic Review* 2: 205–24.

———. 1990. "Services." In Jeffrey Schott, ed., *Completing the Uruguay Round.* Washington DC: Institute for International Economics.

Hoekman, B. 1993. "Safeguard Provisions and International Agreements Involving Trade in Services." *The World Economy* 16: 29–49.

———. 1994. "Conceptual and Political Economy Issues in Liberalizing International Transactions in Services." In A. Deardorff and R. Stern, eds., *Analytical and Negotiating Issues in the Global Trading System.* Ann Arbor: University of Michigan Press.

———. 1995. "Tentative First Steps: An Assessment of the Uruguay Round Agreement on Services." In W. Martin and L. A. Winters, eds., *The Uruguay Round and the Developing Economies.* World Bank Discussion Paper 307. Washington, DC: World Bank.

Hoekman, B., and P. C. Mavroidis 1994. "Competition, Competition Policy, and the GATT." *The World Economy* 17: 121–50.

———. 1995. "The WTO's Agreement on Government Procurement: Expanding Disciplines, Declining Membership?" *Public Procurement Law Review* 4: 63–79.

Hoekman, B., and P. Sauvé 1994. *Liberalizing Trade in Services.* World Bank Discussion Paper 243. Washington DC: World Bank.

Hoekman, B., and R. Stern 1991. "Evolving Patterns of Trade and Investment in Services." In P. Hooper and J. D. Richardson, eds., *International Economic Transactions: Issues in Measurement and Empirical Research.* Chicago: University of Chicago Press.

Martin, W., and J. Francois 1995. "Bindings and Rules as Trade Liberalization." In K. Maskus *et al., Quiet Pioneering: Robert M. Stern and his International Legacy.* Ann Arbor: University of Michigan Press.

Messerlin, P., and K. Sauvant 1990. *The Uruguay Round: Services in the World Economy.* Washington, DC: World Bank.

Nogues, J., A. Olechowski, and A. Winters 1986. "The Extent of Nontariff Barriers to Industrial Countries Exports." *World Bank Economic Review* 1: 181–99.

Richardson, J. 1987. "A Subsectoral Approach to Services Trade Theory." In O. Giarini, ed., *The Emerging Service Economy.* New York: Praeger.

Sampson, G., and R. Snape 1985. "Identifying the Issues in Trade in Services." *The World Economy* 8: 171–81.

Sapir, A. 1985. "North–South Issues in Trade in Services." *The World Economy* 8: 27–42.

———. 1993. "The Structure of Services in Europe: A Conceptual Framework." *European Economy* 3: 83–99.

Sapir, A., and C. Winter 1994. "Services Trade." In D. Greenaway and L. A. Winters, eds., *Surveys in International Trade.* Oxford: Basil Blackwell.

Sauvé, P. 1995. "The General Agreement on Trade in Services: Much Ado about What?" In D. Schwanen, ed., *Trains, Grains and Automobiles: Canada and the Uruguay Round*. Toronto: C. D. Howe Institute.

Snape, R. 1990. "Principles in Trade in Services." In P. Messerlin and K. Sauvant, eds., *The Uruguay Round: Services in the World Economy*. Washington, DC: World Bank.

1994. "Services and the Uruguay Round." In *The New World Trading System: Readings*. Paris: OECD.

UNCTAD and World Bank 1994. *Liberalizing International Transactions in Services: A Handbook*. Geneva: United Nations.

World Bank 1995. *Global Economic Prospects*. Washington DC: World Bank.

5   The Uruguay Round and market access: opportunities and challenges for developing countries

Richard Blackhurst, Alice Enders, and
Joseph F. Francois

Traditionally, market access has referred to the tariff treatment govern-ments give to industrial (nonagricultural) products imported from trading partners. Aside from the fact that the framework of the multilateral trading system has been extended to include trade in services, and that agriculture has been integrated into the system, there are several reasons why this definition is not appropriate to the results of the Uruguay Round. The rights and obligations embodied in the WTO are not limited to tariffs. They include the phaseout of VER agreements on textile and clothing products applied under the MFA, the removal of similar measures in other sectors, and a more extensive set of agreements specifying the scope of actions on nontariff measures to be applied by all WTO members. Amended pro-cedures for the settlement of disputes and for the regular monitoring of the policies of WTO members will strengthen adherence to new and existing obligations. Progress in these and other "systemic" parts of the Uruguay Round will enhance security for negotiated increases in market access.

Implementation of the market access results of the Uruguay Round will offer significant opportunities for the expansion of developing country trade in products of both current and potential export interest. On the demand side, new opportunities are available to the developing world through the principle of nondiscrimination. As in the past, however, they will be more easily exploited by countries that have removed or are poised to remove domestic economic policies inhibiting a market-oriented domes-tic supply response. Thus one of the more significant benefits of the Uruguay Round for developing countries is the greater predictability of their own trade policy regimes with respect to bindings on tariffs and the acceptance of obligations on nontariff measures. This will limit the scope for arbitrary increases in protection and, more broadly, enhance the domes-tic and foreign credibility of trade reform, helping to stimulate badly needed domestic and foreign direct investment.

The view that countries benefit from reducing and binding their own

125

tariffs, and from subjecting themselves to tighter trade rules and disciplines, is part of a broader criticism of the common mercantilist approach to trade negotiations. Negotiators speak of "concessions," which increase international access to their domestic market, as being the "price" they pay to obtain better access abroad for their own exports. And they often seek to maximize the extent to which other countries are bound by rules and disciplines, while at the same time trying to minimize the extent to which their own policy discretion is reduced. In fact, in tallying the income gains from a trade negotiation such as the Uruguay Round, it becomes clear that much of the gain a country receives is the result of its own liberalization (GATT 1994a). Similarly, there are good political economy reasons for believing that there are further gains from accepting additional rules and disciplines on the country's "room for maneuver" in the trade policy area.

Tariff reductions and other commitments by industrial countries

Two aspects of the commitments made in GATT 1994 schedules are important. The first is the binding of protective measures. Through bindings, governments make a commitment not to increase protection above the level specified in schedules (except by negotiation with affected trading partners). Second is the reduction of trade barriers, which together with binding assures more open and secure markets for goods.

Petroleum products

The overall change in the tariff treatment of crude and refined products once Uruguay Round results are implemented is difficult to ascertain because many countries maintain specific as opposed to *ad valorem* duties on these products (table 5.1).[1] The virtual absence of major exporter interests from GATT tariff negotiating rounds means that crude petroleum will continue to be bound at a low level in major markets (only the European Union has bound HS 2709), although applied tariffs for crude petroleum are generally low or nonexistent. Bindings for refined products are substantially higher than for crude petroleum, but average tariffs (where available) are also generally higher.

Industrial products

Under the Uruguay Round agreements, the share of imports of industrial products subject to tariff bindings rises from 94 to 99 percent (table 5.2, and see appendix A). Bearing in mind that trade-weighted tariff averages mask significant disparities in the treatment of products of current export interest to individual developing countries, the new tariff commitments

Table 5.1 *Post-Uruguay Round tariff treatment of crude and refined petroleum products in major markets*

Importer	Crude petroleum		Refined petroleum	
	Percentage of lines bound	Post-UR simple average *ad valorem* tariff	Percentage of lines bound	Post-UR simple average *ad valorem* tariff
European Union	100	0.0	100	2.6
United States	0	n.a.	100	n.a.
Japan	0	n.a.	35	n.a.

n.a. Not available in percentage terms; specific duties apply.
Note: specific duties apply on one quarter of imports of refined petroleum products.

Table 5.2 *Tariff bindings on industrial products (percent)*

	Tariff lines		Imports	
	Pre-Uruguay Round	Post-Uruguay Round	Pre-Uruguay Round	Post-Uruguay Round
Industrial economies	78	99	94	99
Developing economies	21	73	13	61
Transition economies	73	98	74	96
Total	43	83	68	87

made by industrial countries represent a 40 percent reduction in the average tariff on imports of industrial products (from 6.3 percent to 3.8 percent). The proportion of imports subject to bound, MFN zero duties rises from 20 to 44 percent. The reduction in the average tariff applied by industrial countries is below the 40 percent overall cut in four categories – fish and fish products; textiles and clothing; leather, rubber, and footwear; and transport equipment;[2] – and 60 percent or more in three categories – wood, pulp, paper, and furniture; metals; and nonelectric machinery (table 5.3). The overall reduction in the average tariff applied to imports from developing countries is lower than on imports from all sources (37 percent compared with 40 percent for industrial countries), owing to the below-average tariff cuts applied to textiles and clothing, which are relatively more important as developing country exports.

Table 5.3 *Industrial country reductions in bound tariff rates, by major industrial product group (US $billion)*

Product category	Import value (US $billions)		Tariff averages weighted by: (percent)					
			Imports from all sources			Imports from developing economies		
	All sources	Developing economies	Pre-Uruguay Round	Post-Uruguay Round	% reduced	Pre-Uruguay Round	Post-Uruguay Round	% reduced
Fish and fish products	18.5	10.6	6.1	4.5	26	6.6	4.8	27
Wood, pulp, paper, and furniture	40.6	11.5	3.5	1.1	69	4.6	1.7	63
Textiles and clothing	66.4	33.2	15.5	12.1	22	14.6	11.3	23
Leather, rubber, and footwear	31.7	12.2	8.9	7.3	18	8.1	6.6	19
Metals	69.4	24.4	3.7	1.4	62	2.7	0.9	67
Chemicals and photographic supplies	61.0	8.2	6.7	3.7	45	7.2	3.8	47
Transport equipment	96.3	7.6	7.5	5.8	23	3.8	3.1	18
Nonelectric machinery	118.1	9.8	4.8	1.9	60	4.7	1.6	66
Electric machinery	86.0	19.2	6.6	3.5	47	6.3	3.3	48
Mineral products and precious stones	73.0	22.2	2.3	1.1	52	2.6	0.8	69
Manufactured articles (n.e.s.)	76.1	10.9	5.5	2.4	56	6.5	3.1	52
Total industrial products	736.9	169.7	6.3	3.8	40	6.8	4.3	37

Table 5.4 *Changes in tariff escalation on industrial products imported by industrial countries from developing economies, based on bound tariff rates*

			Tariff (percent)		
Product category	Imports (US $billion)	Share of each stage	Pre-Uruguay Round	Post-Uruguay Round	Absolute reduction
All industrial products					
Raw materials	36.7	22	2.1	0.8	1.3
Semimanufactures	36.5	21	5.4	2.8	2.6
Finished products	96.5	57	9.1	6.2	2.9
All tropical industrial products					
Raw materials	5.1	35	0.1	0.0	0.1
Semimanufactures	4.3	30	6.3	3.4	2.9
Finished products	4.9	34	6.6	2.4	4.2
Natural resource-based products					
Raw materials	14.6	44	3.1	2.0	1.1
Semimanufactures	13.3	40	3.5	2.0	1.5
Finished products	5.5	17	7.9	5.9	2.0

In the case of textiles and clothing, tariff concessions must be viewed in the context of the phaseout by 2005 of restraints applied under the MFA. As of 1994 Austria, Canada, the European Union, Finland, Norway, and the United States had amassed 145 bilaterally agreed or unilaterally imposed restraints on developing country and transition economy exporters of textile and clothing products.[3] Where a quota under the MFA is the binding restraint, the tariff equivalent of the quota will obviously exceed the ordinary tariff, often by a sizable amount. In such cases, percentage reductions in import barriers calculated on the basis of ordinary tariffs can greatly understate the full degree of liberalization.

Reducing tariff escalation in industrial country markets was a major objective of developing countries in the Uruguay Round. Escalation occurs when the tariff applied on a product "chain" rises as the level of processing increases, which may inhibit the development of processing industries in developing countries. Industrial country tariffs, averaged over all industrial products, were subject to escalation before the Uruguay Round tariff cuts and in most instances will remain so after the cuts (table 5.4).[4] However, there have been greater absolute reductions in average tariffs at more advanced stages of production than at earlier stages of production, for all industrial products as well as for natural resource-based and tropical industrial products. This suggests that, overall, escalation has been reduced. For natural resource-based products, for example, the average tariff applied to semimanufactures has come down to the same level as that applied to raw materials (2 percent). While the new average tariff on finished natural resource-based products remains above that on semimanufactures (5.9 compared with 2 percent), the tariff wedge is smaller (3.9 percent compared with 4.4 percent).

One feature of the tariff commitments made by the United States, the European Union, and Japan, whose markets together account for 85 percent of industrial country imports, is a substantial rise in duty-free treatment (table 5.5). Duty-free treatment will cover almost 40 percent of imports into the United States, compared with just over 10 percent before the Uruguay Round; almost 38 percent of imports into the European Union, compared with almost 24 percent before the Uruguay Round; and 71 percent of Japan's imports, compared with 35 percent before the Uruguay Round. In each market, this change has been accomplished primarily by increasing the duty-free treatment of industrial products that are not considered "sensitive."

At the same time, departure from the Tokyo Round's formula and harmonization approach has enabled governments to concentrate tariff reduction or elimination on products for which there is less domestic opposition to trade liberalization. This has perpetuated the pattern of "peak" tariffs (over 15 percent) on sensitive products and disparity in tariffs across product groups. The tariff treatment of textiles and clothing is a case in point. For example, the average tariff on US imports of textiles and clothing will decline from 16.7 to 14.6 percent (down 13 percent compared with an average reduction of 35 percent on all industrial products), with more than half of textile and clothing imports remaining subject to peak tariffs. While average tariffs applied to this product group are lower in the European Union and Japan than in the United States, these will remain above the average for other product categories in those two markets, with the exception of fish products in the European Union and leather, rubber, footwear, and travel goods in Japan.

Africa and preference erosion

During the Uruguay Round, one issue that was of particular interest was the market access opportunity of African countries. Virtually all these countries have entered into contractual preference arrangements with the European Union and obtain preferential treatment for certain exports in

Table 5.5 *Bound tariff treatment of imports of industrial products of three major industrial country markets, by product category (percent)*

A. United States

| Product category | Average tariff | | Distribution of imports | | | | | | | | | | | | |
| | | | Duty free | | 0.1–5.0 | | 5.1–10.0 | | 10.1–15.0 | | 15.1–35.0 | | Over 35 | |
	Pre-UR	Post-UR	Pre-UR	Post-UR	Pre-UR	Post-UR	Pre-UR	Post-UR	Pre-UR	Post-UR	Pre-UR	Post-UR	Pre-UR	Post-UR
Fish and fish products	1.4	1.2	78.3	87.5	8.8	1.9	5.7	4.0	7.0	6.4	0.2	0.2	0.0	0.0
Wood products	2.9	0.5	27.0	89.5	50.4	5.6	22.4	4.8	0.0	0.1	0.2	0.0	0.0	0.0
Textiles and clothing	16.7	14.6	0.7	4.9	6.6	9.2	27.9	25.9	6.6	8.0	57.7	52.0	0.5	0.0
Leather, rubber, and footwear	7.6	7.1	9.0	12.7	24.3	33.2	59.6	47.3	3.1	2.9	1.6	1.5	2.4	2.4
Metals	3.9	1.5	13.1	59.7	48.0	30.8	35.8	8.9	2.6	0.6	0.5	0.0	0.0	0.0
Chemicals and photographic supplies	5.3	2.8	16.5	31.5	43.4	49.1	28.1	19.4	7.9	0.0	4.1	0.0	0.0	0.0
Transport equipment	3.7	3.5	6.7	8.7	86.8	85.2	0.7	0.3	0.7	0.7	5.1	5.1	0.0	0.0
Nonelectric machinery	3.6	1.0	5.7	62.8	90.0	35.0	3.4	2.2	0.9	0.0	0.0	0.0	0.0	0.0
Electric machinery	4.6	2.0	1.4	35.9	72.4	61.1	26.0	2.8	0.1	0.2	0.1	0.0	0.0	0.0
Minerals, precious stones and metals	3.7	2.5	52.0	59.8	12.5	14.3	26.1	23.5	5.1	1.3	4.3	1.1	0.0	0.0
Manufactures n.e.s.	4.7	1.5	7.6	59.4	59.8	31.3	30.2	8.8	2.1	0.4	0.3	0.1	0.0	0.0
Total	5.4	3.5	10.4	39.5	59.6	42.9	20.4	10.2	2.4	1.3	7.0	6.0	0.2	0.1

Table 5.5 (cont.)

B. European Union

| Product category | Average tariff | | Distribution of imports | | | | | | | | | | | |
| | | | Duty free | | 0.1–5.0 | | 5.1–10.0 | | 10.1–15.0 | | 15.1–35.0 | | Over 35 | |
	Pre-UR	Post-UR	Pre-UR	Post-UR	Pre-UR	Post-UR	Pre-UR	Post-UR	Pre UR	Post-UR	Pre-UR	Post-UR	Pre-UR	Post-UR
Fish and fish products	12.3	10.2	6.2	6.9	15.2	14.5	20.7	29.6	19.9	31.2	38.0	17.8	0.0	0.0
Wood products	3.0	0.7	60.3	88.5	3.3	3.0	34.8	8.5	1.6	0.0	0.0	0.0	0.0	0.0
Textiles and clothing	11.0	9.1	0.6	1.3	5.3	19.1	29.7	25.5	64.3	54.1	0.1	0.0	0.0	0.0
Leather, rubber, and footwear	6.5	5.1	23.3	24.5	12.1	40.7	52.8	23.0	0.0	0.0	11.8	11.8	0.0	0.0
Metals	2.3	1.1	60.8	73.7	18.7	19.6	19.4	6.7	0.0	0.0	1.1	0.0	0.0	0.0
Chemicals and photographic supplies	7.3	4.5	2.7	27.2	11.2	4.0	70.3	68.8	15.6	0.0	0.2	0.0	0.0	0.0
Transport equipment	7.2	6.5	22.0	23.4	6.9	15.7	65.5	59.9	4.4	0.8	1.2	0.2	0.0	0.0
Nonelectric machinery	4.4	1.4	6.0	33.9	84.1	63.1	8.8	3.0	1.1	0.0	0.0	0.0	0.0	0.0
Electric machinery	8.6	5.2	2.2	3.9	25.9	69.9	37.0	8.3	34.9	17.9	0.0	0.0	0.0	0.0
Minerals, precious stones, and metals	0.9	0.6	68.2	85.2	24.3	10.4	6.1	3.3	1.4	1.1	0.0	0.0	0.0	0.0
Manufactures n.e.s.	6.4	3.5	8.4	24.2	13.0	58.9	70.7	12.0	7.3	4.3	0.6	0.6	0.0	0.0
Total	5.7	3.6	23.6	37.7	26.3	34.2	35.5	19.0	13.2	8.2	1.4	0.9	0.0	0.0

Table 5.5 (*cont.*)

C. Japan

Product category	Average tariff		Distribution of imports											
			Duty free		0.1–5.0		5.1–10.0		10.1–15.0		15.1–35.0		Over 35	
	Pre-UR	Post-UR	Pre-UR	Post-UR	Pre-UR	Post-UR	Pre-UR	Post-UR	Pre-UR	Post-UR	Pre-UR	Post-UR	Pre-UR	Post-UR
Fish and fish products	6.1	4.0	1.9	1.9	64.4	70.7	22.8	25.7	10.8	1.7	0.1	0.0	0.0	0.0
Wood products	2.2	0.7	61.3	89.2	26.5	4.3	7.1	6.5	0.8	0.0	4.3	0.0	0.0	0.0
Textiles and clothing	11.3	7.6	3.0	4.5	3.3	19.1	33.7	54.7	44.4	21.5	15.6	0.2	0.0	0.0
Leather, rubber, and footwear	9.7	8.3	34.7	40.6	6.4	0.9	20.4	34.0	16.2	2.9	22.1	21.5	0.2	0.1
Metals	2.2	0.5	40.1	84.2	43.9	14.0	15.7	1.8	0.3	0.0	0.0	0.0	0.0	0.0
Chemicals and photographic supplies	4.9	1.9	11.3	47.2	44.3	49.7	42.0	3.1	1.6	0.0	0.8	0.0	0.0	0.0
Transport equipment	2.1	0.0	54.5	100.0	44.3	0.0	1.2	0.0	0.0	0.0	0.0	0.0	0.0	0.0
Nonelectric machinery	3.8	0.0	22.9	100.0	61.8	0.0	15.3	0.0	0.0	0.0	0.0	0.0	0.0	0.0
Electric machinery	2.9	0.1	33.4	97.3	61.1	2.7	5.5	0.0	0.0	0.0	0.0	0.0	0.0	0.0
Minerals, precious stones and metals	1.8	0.2	51.9	94.5	43.7	3.1	4.4	2.4	0.0	0.0	0.0	0.0	0.0	0.0
Manufactures n.e.s.	2.7	0.6	46.8	86.9	31.9	9.1	19.3	4.0	2.0	0.0	0.0	0.0	0.0	0.0
Total	3.9	1.7	34.8	71.0	40.5	16.6	16.7	9.7	5.5	2.0	2.5	0.7	0.0	0.0

Note: figures refer to tariff lines that were duty free prior to the Uruguay Round, including the fully bound, partially bound, and unbound.

Table 5.6 *Bound tariff treatment of imports from African countries by major industrial country markets*

	Value (US $billion)	Percentage distribution of imports					
		Pre-UR			Post-UR		
		0	0.1–3.0	Over 3	0	0.1–3.0	Over 3
European Union's imports from							
South Africa	13,058.9	86	5	9	93	2	5
Other Africa	13,056.3	43	13	44	49	15	36
Total Africa	26,115.2	65	9	26	71	9	20
Japan's imports from							
South Africa	1,737.6	69	9	22	83	5	11
Other Africa	1,364.9	18	7	75	24	40	35
Total Africa	3,102.5	47	8	45	57	21	22
US imports from							
South Africa	1,501.9	71	17	11	75	15	10
Other Africa	1,374.7	62	12	26	69	9	22
Total Africa	2,876.5	67	15	18	72	13	15

the United States, Japan, and other industrial country markets under the Generalized System of Preferences.[5] Consequently there has been concern that implementation of the Uruguay Round market access results would diminish African trade and economic prospects.

Roughly half of the European Union's imports from African countries is petroleum and other fuels, already bound duty free; the other half is divided between agricultural and industrial products. In its Uruguay Round schedule the European Union has expanded market access for agricultural products, only partly covered by preferential treatment.[6] Industrial products is the main area where the European Union's MFN tariff reductions will have an impact. Almost three-quarters of African exports to the European Union already enter at rates of less than 3 percent and this will rise to 80 percent (table 5.6). For these products, the margin of preference afforded under the Fourth Lomé Convention is likely to be consumed in large part by associated administrative costs.[7]

Exports of African countries, both individual and collective, are concentrated in primary product categories such as metals, minerals, precious stones, and wood products. Even at MFN rates, and before Uruguay Round reductions, these products are dutied at only 0.4 percent (table 5.7). Other sectors of export interest for some individual countries are fish and

Table 5.7 Reductions of bound tariffs on imports of industrial products from African countries by major industrial country markets

	Value (US $million)	Average tariff (percent)		(%) Reduced
		Pre-UR	Post-UR	
European Union				
All industrial products	26,115,170	2.8	2.0	29
Wood, pulp, paper, and furniture	1,379,856	1.6	0.5	69
Textiles and clothing[a]	2,222,510	11.8	10.0	15
Leather, rubber, footwear, and travel goods	516,146	3.0	2.3	23
Metals	4,044,224	1.9	1.3	32
Chemicals and photographic supplies	1,047,613	6.9	2.1	70
Transport equipment	510,327	1.0	0.8	20
Nonelectric machinery	156,302	3.7	1.1	70
Electric machinery	179,378	8.0	4.3	46
Mineral products, precious stones, and metals	14,829,442	0.4	0.2	50
Manufactured articles, n.e.s.	100,185	5.3	2.7	49
Fish and fish products	1,129,187	17.3	14.8	14
Japan				
All industrial products	3,095,216	3.4	1.8	47
Wood, pulp, paper, and furniture	145,134	1.2	0.1	92
Textiles and clothing[a]	82,121	1.5	1.0	33
Leather, rubber, footwear, and travel goods	10,437	7.8	6.0	23
Metals	1,302,820	4.2	2.1	50
Chemicals and photographic supplies	71,654	2.5	0.5	80
Transport equipment	41,318	0.1	0.0	100

Table 5.7 (cont.)

	Value (US $million)	Average tariff (percent)		(%) Reduced
		Pre-UR	Post-UR	
Nonelectric machinery	513	3.7	0.0	100
Electric machinery	564	0.6	0.0	100
Mineral products, precious stones, and metals	903,394	0.3	0.0	100
Manufactured articles, n.e.s.	4,491	1.3	0.8	38
Fish and fish products	532,770	7.6	5.2	32
United States				
All industrial products	2,876,509	2.3	1.9	17
Wood, pulp, paper, and furniture	102,393	0.7	0.1	86
Textiles and clothing[a]	255,054	16.4	14.9	9
Leather, rubber, footwear, and travel goods	108,080	1.0	0.8	20
Metals	892,190	1.5	1.4	7
Chemicals and photographic supplies	48,577	4.8	2.6	46
Transport equipment	8,011	2.7	1.7	37
Nonelectric machinery	47,081	3.1	0.7	77
Electric machinery	17,348	4.6	0.9	80
Mineral products, precious stones, and metals	1,316,854	0.2	0.1	50
Manufactured articles, n.e.s.	37,406	5.1	1.4	73
Fish and fish products	43,515	0.9	0.4	56

[a] Figures understate the increase in market access because they do not take into account the phaseout of bilateral quotas imposed under the MFA.

fish products, which do not figure in preference programs, and textiles and clothing, generally under MFA quotas or similar restraints.

At the same time, market access for Africa's exports has improved in Japan and the United States. The share of Africa's exports benefiting from duty-free or low-tariff MFN treatment has risen from 55 to 78 percent in Japan, and from 82 to 85 percent in the United States. Low or duty-free access applies to most products of current export interest such as metals and mineral products. While it could be argued that price advantages to African exporters granted under the Generalized System of Preferences will dissipate, preference erosion is not likely to have a significant impact on the market access opportunities of African countries because of the low level of tariff rates on products that generally figure in this system.

Claims that many low-income countries, in particular African countries, will lose from the Uruguay Round take into account only projected reductions in margins of preference and higher prices for imported food. Although such effects are likely to be pronounced, they should not overshadow other results of the negotiations. In any event, one of the chief factors limiting the gains of African countries in the Uruguay Round was their reluctance to bind more of their own tariffs and to make larger cuts in their tariffs and other trade barriers.

The pattern of applied protection

The regional pattern of developed country protection for industrial products, including both MFN tariffs from the WTO's IDB and supplemental estimates of nontariff protection, is illustrated in figure 5.1.[8] Reductions in MFN tariffs are based on a comparison of offered rates to current applied rates; where applied rates are above offered rates, a tariff cut to the new offered rate is assumed. These are combined with estimates of the protection afforded by nontariff barriers (mainly MFA) and other measures of protection, such as antidumping and countervailing measures. Calculations of the reduction in these overall rates of import protection are presented in table 5.8 based on data on regional export patterns for 1992 and *including* imports from free-trade area partners.[9] In comparing post-Uruguay Round levels of protection with base levels in 1992, it is assumed that no change in antidumping and countervailing measures occurs.

In 1992, industrial countries had low rates of protection in wood and wood products, mineral products, and metals; higher rates on other industrial products, in particular, chemicals and machinery;[10] and on textile and clothing products, relatively high rates through tariffs and the MFA. As a result of the Uruguay Round, the pattern of industrial country protection

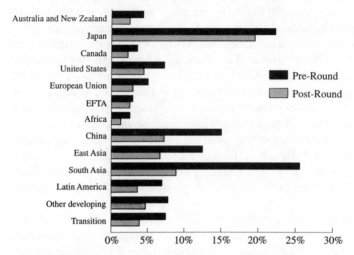

Figure 5.1   OECD protection by exporter, tariff equivalent
Includes bound MFN tariffs, MFA quotas, and other non-MFN barriers;
excludes protection in agriculture. See Francois, McDonald, and Nordström
1995, Technical Annex, for a description of data. Regions are based on GATT
classifications.

(applied tariffs and nontariff barriers) should change dramatically, primarily because of MFN tariff reductions and the elimination of the MFA
(table 5.8).

In the developing world, the implications of changes in market access for
exports vary by region and country. For some regions, the phaseout of the
MFA is likely to be the single most important result of the Uruguay Round.
For others, the Round's significance may instead relate to tariff concessions
for industrial products besides textiles and clothing. For textile and clothing exporters alone, though, the phaseout carries different implications.
Elimination of quotas in this sector should significantly expand export
opportunities for the most constrained suppliers. However, less constrained
suppliers, forced to compete more directly with what had been more heavily
restricted suppliers, may see their preferences erode. At the same time, as
more constrained suppliers shift resources into textiles and clothing and
out of other sectors, the competitive position of producers in the latter
sectors in other countries should improve.

Before the Uruguay Round, countries with the greatest concentration of
exports subject to MFA constraints faced the highest weighted-average
trade barriers in industrial country markets. Because over 40 percent of
South Asian merchandise exports (valued free on board) consist of textiles
and clothing, this region faced the highest import barriers in industrial

Table 5.8 *Import protection, based on applied MFN rates and tariff equivalents of nontariff barriers (proportion)*

Import source	Industrial countries	Africa[a]	East Asia	South Asia	Latin America	Other developing	Transition economies
Pre-Uruguay Round							
All sources	0.07	0.18	0.09	0.46	0.24	0.19	0.10
Developing countries							
Africa[b]	0.03	0.16	0.06	0.35	0.16	0.22	0.04
China	0.15	0.25	0.02	0.49	0.26	0.16	0.11
East Asia	0.12	0.23	0.09	0.51	0.27	0.18	0.12
South Asia	0.25	0.26	0.08	0.52	0.29	0.17	0.13
Latin America	0.07	0.17	0.08	0.55	0.22	0.21	0.10
Other	0.08	0.12	0.13	0.59	0.16	0.24	0.05
Transition economies	0.07	0.17	0.11	0.45	0.22	0.17	0.06
Post-Uruguay Round							
All sources	0.05	0.18	0.06	0.33	0.18	0.15	0.08
Developing countries							
Africa[b]	0.01	0.16	0.04	0.25	0.12	0.16	0.03
China	0.07	0.25	0.01	0.34	0.19	0.13	0.09
East Asia	0.07	0.23	0.06	0.38	0.20	0.14	0.10
South Asia	0.09	0.26	0.05	0.40	0.21	0.13	0.10
Latin America	0.04	0.17	0.05	0.35	0.17	0.16	0.08
Other	0.04	0.12	0.09	0.54	0.12	0.18	0.04
Transition economies	0.05	0.17	0.07	0.30	0.16	0.13	0.05

Importing region

Table 5.8 (*cont.*)

| | Importing region | | | | | |
Import source	Industrial countries	Africa[a]	East Asia	South Asia	Latin America	Other developing	Transition economies
Relative change							
All sources	−0.29	0.00	−0.27	−0.30	−0.27	−0.23	−0.18
Developing countries							
Africa[b]	−0.43	0.00	−0.30	−0.30	−0.23	−0.26	−0.18
China	−0.51	0.00	−0.30	−0.30	−0.26	−0.22	−0.20
East Asia	−0.47	0.00	−0.29	−0.26	−0.27	−0.23	−0.17
South Asia	−0.65	0.00	−0.31	−0.22	−0.27	−0.23	−0.21
Latin America	−0.45	0.00	−0.35	−0.36	−0.26	−0.26	−0.18
Other	−0.50	0.00	−0.28	−0.08	−0.22	−0.23	−0.20
Transition economies	−0.37	0.00	−0.41	−0.34	−0.26	−0.25	−0.17

[a] Excludes South Africa.
[b] Import weights exclude South Africa and include the Middle East. Tariffs in the Middle East are not included in the integrated data base.

country markets. While East Asia faces similar barriers for textile and clothing exports, these products account for "only" 15.8 percent of total merchandise exports. China, with 26.2 percent of its merchandise exports in textiles and clothing, faces weighted-average trade barriers at levels somewhere between those of East Asia and South Asia.[11] Because other developing country regions are much less dependent on textile and clothing exports, the impact on them of removing the MFA is much more limited. Countries in Africa, which have the lowest export share for textiles and clothing in the developing world and the highest for raw materials, also face the lowest rate of aggregate protection in industrial country markets.

Of developing regions, Africa and the Middle East have faced the least protection in industrial markets and will continue to, because of preferential access in the European Union and the heavy concentration of Africa's exports on primary commodities, which generally face the lowest tariffs. Asia faces the highest average tariffs because of the importance of its export manufactures, including consumer electronics, textiles, and apparel. The largest expansion of market access is therefore enjoyed by developing economies in Asia, primarily owing to the elimination of the MFA. The greatest absolute reduction in barriers faced is realized by the economies of South Asia, where the average tariff faced falls from 25 percent to 9 percent on a weighted-average basis. Absolute reduction in protection is smaller for Latin America and Africa than for Asia, although in both cases the actual rate of protection faced has been much lower, both before and after the Uruguay Round.

Recent numerical studies point to significant new export opportunities for developing countries (Francois, McDonald, and Nordström 1995). Of course, estimates of the magnitude of export effects should not be treated as forecasts. However, while particular estimates are sensitive to the model structure adopted, studies have generally produced a consistent set of qualitative results.[12] For developing countries the most important effects are related to the elimination of the MFA. This is especially notable in China, East Asia, and South Asia. South Asian exports were among the most concentrated in products constrained by the arrangement. For developing countries outside Asia, the implications of the phaseout are more indirect and interact with tariff reductions in other sectors. In particular, while producers in Asia may be expected to shift resources into the production of textiles and clothing for export, this means that they must also reduce production and exports in other sectors as resources are shifted out of those sectors. This process simply reflects the economywide constraint on employment of domestic resources. For regions outside of Asia, improved market conditions in these other sectors suggest opportunity, reinforced by industrial country tariff concessions, for a broad expansion in exports.

Tariff reductions and other commitments by developing countries

Industrial countries constitute the most important merchandise export markets for developing countries (63 percent in 1992). In part, this is because industrial countries account for the bulk of global income and expenditure. At the same time, market access opportunities for developing countries in other developing country markets have long been affected by protection in their own markets. In many instances these markets are heavily protected. Because import protection ultimately acts as a tax on exports, protection in developing economies also hinders integration not just between developing countries but also with the larger global trading system.

Industrial products

Under the Uruguay Round agreement, the share of developing country imports of industrial products subject to bindings rises from 13 to 61 percent (see table 5.2). This rise is mainly due to commitments made by Latin American countries and Asian developing economies to apply ceiling bindings on 100 percent of tariff lines. Chile was the only developing country offering to bind 100 percent of its tariff lines in the context of the Tokyo Round, while Costa Rica, El Salvador, Mexico, and Venezuela bound 100 percent of tariff lines upon their accession to GATT between 1986 and 1991 (table 5.9). During the Uruguay Round, all other Latin American countries committed to bind 100 percent of tariff lines. Among Asian developing economies, Indonesia has bound more than 90 percent of tariff lines; India, the Republic of Korea, Malaysia, the Philippines, Singapore, and Thailand have bound between 60 and 89 percent; and Hong Kong, Macau, and Sri Lanka have bound between 8 and 25 percent. The figures for developing countries are influenced by the fact that Hong Kong, which accounts for one third of total imports of developing countries, did not make an offer on a substantial number of tariff lines for which the unbound applied tariff is zero.

Assessing the scope of bindings among African countries is problematic, as the WTO's IDB covers only 30 percent of total imports into the region (Egypt, Senegal, Tunisia, and Zimbabwe; South Africa is considered an industrial country). Compounding the problem, least-developed countries were granted an additional year from April 15, 1994 to submit their GATT 1994 schedules for verification.

The reductions in bound tariffs by developing economies are difficult to assess for two reasons. First, in many cases comprehensive information on base-period tariffs (1986) is unavailable as a result of the low level of bindings among developing countries. In these cases, the post-Uruguay

Table 5.9 *Bindings on industrial products of developing economies*

		Percentage bound			
	Imports from MFN origins (US $million)	Pre-Uruguay Round		Post-Uruguay Round	
Participant		Share of lines	Share of imports	Share of lines	Share of imports
Argentina	2,981	5	21	100	100
Brazil	11,409	6	23	100	100
Chile	1,838	100	100	100	100
Colombia	3,530	1	3	100	100
Costa Rica	840	100	100	100	100
El Salvador	557	100	100	100	100
Hong Kong	115,549	1	1	24	23
India	10,179	4	12	62	68
Indonesia	12,603	10	30	93	92
Jamaica	1,111	0	0	100	100
Korea, Rep. of	40,610	10	24	90	89
Macau	1,542	0	0	10	10
Malaysia	11,270	0	2	62	79
Mexico	10,988	100	100	100	100
Peru	1,399	7	20	100	100
Philippines	9,189	6	9	59	67
Romania	3,456	21	10	100	100
Senegal	613	29	40	32	41
Singapore	32,860	0	0	65	73
Sri Lanka	2,357	4	7	8	11
Thailand	14,555	2	12	68	70
Tunisia	2,976	0	0	46	68
Turkey	5,832	34	38	37	39
Uruguay	508	3	11	100	100
Venezuela	5,097	100	100	100	100
Zimbabwe	631	8	11	9	13

Round average bound tariff usually involves a decrease in the ceiling bind-ings applied to items already bound, combined with ceiling bindings above currently applied rates for previously unbound items. Second, for those developing economies that bound all or a significant portion of tariffs before the Uruguay Round ended (Chile, Costa Rica, El Salvador, Mexico, and Venezuela), the Uruguay Round tariff commitments often reflect a decline in ceiling (rather than applied) rates. Thus it is generally presumed that the implementation of Uruguay Round tariff commitments by developing countries will involve virtually no declines in currently applied tariffs.

At the same time, current tariff levels already reflect often substantial reductions undertaken autonomously in the course of the Uruguay Round. Though many developing countries may not be required to introduce further cuts, previous liberalization has been at least partially locked in through new commitments on bindings. Ceiling bindings are considered so important that countries agreeing to bind previously unbound tariffs are given "negotiating credit," even if the tariff is bound at a level *above* the currently applied level (the case for many developing countries that participated in the Round). Bindings have also played a key role in establishing the domestic and international credibility of domestic reform programs in many countries. Although an integral part of the tariff negotiations, bindings, by making market access more predictable, are more akin to rules and procedures than to direct increases in market access. However, even ceiling bindings yield benefits related to liberalization when they reduce the expected value and variance of protection.[13]

Following implementation of the Uruguay Round, the best external conditions for developing country exports – based on applied rather than bound rates – will generally be offered by industrial countries (see table 5.8). A pattern of protection comparable to that in industrial countries can be found in East Asia's developing economies, although opportunities vary widely by country.[14] Substantial liberalization was undertaken during the Round by Latin American and South Asian participants, though import protection in these countries remains relatively high, particularly in South Asia. Regarding rationalization of developing country trade regimes, less has been accomplished in Africa. The average tariff for African IDB members is 18 percent and will remain effectively unchanged.[15]

Systemic changes: GATT 1994 and the WTO

The WTO is a single institutional framework comprising commitments on a wide array of policy instruments affecting trade in goods and services, and providing for protection of IPRs. These commitments provide for dispute settlement procedures to interpret and enforce those obligations, the monitoring of trade policies to provide for transparency and improved adherence to obligations, and an institutional setting for WTO members to oversee the functioning of the multilateral trading system. This institutional setting also provides a forum for negotiations to improve and extend the rules-based framework for the conduct of trade relations. This section outlines in greater detail the elements of the WTO framework relevant to market access for goods.

GATT 1994

The cornerstone of the multilateral rules on trade in goods is the General Agreement on Tariffs and Trade (now known as GATT 1947), as subsequently amended, modified or rectified.[16] Main elements of the GATT include the MFN principle, a prohibition on quantitative restrictions, and the "national" treatment of imported products, so that once imported products are inside the border, they face the same conditions of competition as domestically produced products. Exceptions to these obligations may be invoked under certain conditions, including for the purpose of establishing free-trade areas or customs unions, to protect the balance of payments, for health and safety reasons, or for national security.

GATT 1994 includes two understandings on the interpretation of GATT provisions of particular importance to trade regimes of developing countries: on schedules of concessions (Article II:1(b)), and balance-of-payments provisions (XII and XVIII:B). The understanding on Article II:1(b) provides for the binding of all duties or charges other than tariffs in schedules of concessions. The understanding on the balance-of-payments provisions strengthens the disciplines regarding the application of such measures by requiring (i) the public announcement of time schedules for the removal of restrictive import measures; (ii) a preference for price-based measures over quantitative measures; (iii) the need for justification when quantitative measures are applied, and the need to administer them in a transparent manner.

Although GATT 1994 applies in principle to all trade in goods, measures affecting sensitive sectors are to be phased in. For example, the ATC provides for the phaseout of MFA restraints in four stages, starting on January 1, 1995 and ending in 2005. The Agreement on Safeguards requires that gray-area measures not in conformity with Article XIX be either brought into conformity or phased out within four years after the entry into force of the agreement establishing the WTO.[17] The agreement on TRIMs provides that GATT-inconsistent performance requirements are to be notified and eliminated within a transition period of two years (industrial countries), five years (developing countries), or seven years (least-developed countries).

Agreements on nontariff measures

Agreements on nontariff measures clarify the administration of anti-dumping and countervailing measures, safeguards, customs valuation, and import licensing procedures. They also extend the rules to sanitary and phytosanitary measures, technical barriers to trade, preshipment inspection, subsidies, and issues of origin (the Agreement on Rules of Origin contains a commitment to agree on guidelines within three years). Nontariff measures were not originally, or were inadequately, covered by GATT 1947. Now a WTO member applying such a measure is required to follow precise guidelines, including transparency, predictability (including specified criteria for decisions), and procedural guarantees for exporters.

While the WTO agreement does not require its members to adopt anti-dumping legislation, for example, if they do they must abide by the minimum standards of treatment in the antidumping agreement. The purpose of these agreements is to ensure that if such legislation is implemented, exporter interests are respected according to the rules established by negotiators rather than left vulnerable to arbitrary action by importing country governments, the case under the original GATT.

Several of the agreements are more extensive versions of those concluded on these trade policy matters in the Tokyo Round. These had failed to acquire a multilateral status because many developing countries chose not to accept any, and others only some, of the agreements. This left many key aspects of trade policy in developing countries subject to a substantial degree of uncertainty, and undermined the functioning of the agreements themselves (Enders and Seade 1994). In contrast, under the single undertaking, all WTO members agree to respect the agreements on nontariff measures concluded in the Uruguay Round.[18]

Most of the agreements establish special treatment for developing countries, in particular least-developed countries. This includes longer transition periods for the implementation of most obligations, lesser obligations for developing countries, and exemptions for least-developed countries; technical assistance; and more favorable treatment to developing country exporters in the application of nontariff measures. For example, developing countries are not expected to use international standards inappropriate to their situation as a basis for technical regulations or standards. With regard to export subsidies on industrial products, least-developed countries and low-income developing countries are not subject to the prohibition on export subsidies applicable to WTO members, and other developing country members have a transition period of at least eight years (with further extension possible) to phase out such measures. With respect to customs valuation, developing country members that are not signatories to the Tokyo Round Agreement may delay the application of provisions for five years and request a further extension.

Table 5.10 *Number of requests for consultations in the GATT system, 1989–94*

	Applicant				Respondent			
		Subsidies/				Subsidies/		
	GA	AD	CVD	GP	GA	AD	CVD	GP
Industrial economies	38	12	13	3	39	21	14	3
Developing economies	32	9	1	0	31	3	0	0
Transition economies	1	0	0	0	1	0	0	0
Total	71	21	14	3	71	24	14	3

GA: general agreement.
AD: antidumping agreement.
Subsidies/CVD: subsidies and countervailing measures agreement.
GP: government procurement.
Note: The data comprise formal notifications of requests for consultations received by the Secretariat, known to be comprehensive only for the general agreement.

Enforcement of obligations

A key objective of the negotiations, and one of particular interest to developing countries, was to make the multilateral rules more enforceable. Developing countries increased their use of the rules during the Uruguay Round, not only as applicants but also as respondents (table 5.10). However, the overall effectiveness of dispute settlement in the GATT system was adversely affected by (i) the nonadoption of reports submitted by panels to the GATT Council in certain highly politicized cases and concerns over the implementation of adopted panel reports; and (ii) the low proportion of panel reports adopted by the Committees of the Tokyo Round Agreements on antidumping, and subsidies and countervailing measures.

A major change introduced under the WTO is the integration of all dispute settlement procedures established under individual agreements (goods, services, trade-related investment procedures, and plurilateral agreements) into a single system operating under the Dispute Settlement Body. In addition, the WTO dispute settlement system provides claimants with "automaticity" for the establishment of a panel, adoption of the panel ruling, and authorization of countermeasures in the event where an adopted panel ruling is not implemented. This is made possible by the Dispute Settlement Body's negative consensus approach to decisions.

Consensus is needed to halt formal dispute settlement proceedings. To ensure greater confidence, legal findings are subject to review by the Appellate Body. If an appeal is not made, the panel report is adopted; if an appeal is made, the report of the Appellate Body is unconditionally accepted by the parties unless the Dispute Settlement Body decides by consensus against its adoption.

Following adoption, the party concerned must notify its intentions to implement the recommendations. Under GATT, panels have generally recommended that an inconsistent measure be brought into conformity with the rules. If such a step is not taken within a reasonable period of time, compensation or the suspension of concessions or other obligations is available as a temporary measure. If compensation is not agreed on, the claimant, using the negative consensus approach, may request authorization from the Dispute Settlement Body to retaliate. The general principle is that suspension of concessions should take place within the same sector of trade. If this is not feasible or effective, and if the circumstances are serious enough, the suspension of concessions may be made under another agreement. For instance, retaliation over a violation of commitments made in the area of trade-related investment procedures may involve goods.

Regular monitoring of trade policies

The TPRM, in place since 1989 on a provisional basis, will now have a permanent place in the world trading system, and all aspects of WTO commitments will be covered. In examining a country's trade policies and practices from an economic perspective, regular periodic TPRM reviews highlight the significant domestic resource costs associated with protection, and are helpful to governments in maintaining pressure for trade liberalization. This should help to ensure that WTO principles are observed, and may help governments to resist pressure from domestic groups to introduce new protective measures or use existing trade policy instruments in a discretionary and protectionist fashion. As part of their monitoring activities, WTO members will also continue to annually appraise developments which are having an impact on the multilateral trading system, assisted by an annual report by the Director-General.

Avoiding the mercantilist trap

One of the goals of this chapter is to clarify and expand the definition of "market access," as that term is used in descriptions of the Uruguay Round results. Too often, the term is defined – implicitly or explicitly – in a way that is both too narrow and, even worse, mercantilist. The narrowness results from limiting the analysis of changes in market access to changes in tariffs and quotas. As has been stressed above, this overlooks three other key aspects of market access, namely the binding of tariffs, the rules and disciplines on the use of other trade-related government interventions, and the institutional arrangements for monitoring and enforcing compliance with those disciplines. It is progress in these latter three areas that determines the security of increases in market access from reductions in tariffs and the elimination of quantitative restrictions. Since the gains from trade liberalization depend heavily on the stimulus it provides to trade-related investment, the security aspect is crucial. Thus virtually the entire Uruguay Round agenda was about market access, and any analysis that purports to cover the negotiated changes in market access, but which is limited to tariffs and quotas, is seriously deficient.[19]

A mercantilist definition of market access is implicit in any analysis of the Uruguay Round results that focuses exclusively on changes in access abroad for the exports of a particular country or group of countries. Increased access to trading partners' markets is part of the picture, of course, but only a part. Properly defined, the negotiated changes in market access must also include the increases in foreigners' access to a country's own domestic market – if for no other reason than the fact that it is this "own liberalization" that often proves to be the most important determinant of the welfare (income) gains which the country gets from the trade negotiation.

Mercantilist thinking can also infect the analysis of those parts of the Uruguay Round that influence the degree of security of increased market access from tariff reductions and quota elimination. This is evident, for example, when bindings and the requirement to adhere to stronger rules and disciplines are viewed as burdens on a country that agrees to them.[20] While the binding of tariffs and the willingness to submit the country's trade regime to multilateral rules and disciplines benefit trading partners, they benefit even more the country itself because such actions enhance the security of access to the country's own domestic market. The government gains because the reduced discretion over trade policy reduces the political cost of saying no to the constant special interest demands for protection. Domestic consumers of course gain, but so do domestic firms that use tradable inputs, as well as domestic firms more generally because they can plan their new investments on a more secure basis. And, by "locking in" reforms of the trade regime, bindings and the acceptance of multilateral rules and disciplines enhance the credibility of the reforms among domestic and foreign investors.[21]

It follows that one of the most important sources of gains for developing countries in the Uruguay Round is the "single undertaking" nature of the final package. As was noted above, WTO members are required to accept the entire package, including the new and strengthened rules and disciplines covering the invocation of balance-of-payments provisions, the use of non-tariff import charges, and nontariff measures. It is no longer possible to evade certain rules and disciplines, as many developing countries did by not signing the Tokyo Round Codes. And every WTO member must submit a schedule of "concessions" for goods and a schedule of commitments for services. In contrast, prior to the Uruguay Round, less than one third of GATT's developing contracting parties had submitted a schedule of tariff "concessions."[22] When considering the potential gains from the increased stability and transparency of the trade regime under WTO rules, it is helpful to recall that for much of the period since World War II a common characteristic of most developing country trade regimes was their instability coupled with opacity.

The various considerations outlined above explain why it is difficult not to be impatient with claims that many low-income countries, and in particular African countries, will "lose from the Uruguay Round," when those claims take into account only the projected reductions in margins of preference and higher prices for imported food. Quite aside from the likely magnitude of those two effects (the former of which was discussed above), such claims suffer from a neglect of other results of the negotiations, in particular the gains to developing WTO members from the increased transparency and stability of their own trade regimes.[23]

Conclusion

In this chapter we have explored the principal market access results of the Uruguay Round for trade in nonagricultural products, with a particular emphasis on the implications for developing countries and regions. Among industrial products, the phaseout of the MFA is the largest single liberalization affecting access for developing countries in developed country markets, and is therefore also the major source of identifiable trade effects in studies of the Uruguay Round based on computable general equilibrium models.

The focus on market access emphasizes the change in the external trading conditions facing developing countries. However, the implications for development depend not on external conditions of trade alone, but on the interaction of external conditions with internal conditions. In the end, external conditions are opportunities, but whether or not such opportunities are realized will depend on the mix of internal policies that are pursued, including reductions in the country's own trade barriers, and its acceptance of stronger multilateral rules and disciplines on its own trade-related policies.

For this reason, nonquantifiable aspects of the Uruguay Round are likely to prove at least as important to developing countries as the quantifiable aspects of market access.

Appendix A   Methods and sources

The main source of data on tariff reductions and bindings realized in the Uruguay Round is the WTO Secretariat's IDB. The data bases' forty-four participants include all industrial countries (Australia, Canada, Japan, New Zealand, the United States, the twelve states of the European Union counting as one, the EFTA states, and South Africa), four transition economies (the Czech Republic, Hungary, Poland, and the Slovak Republic), and twenty-seven of ninety-four developing countries as self-selected in the Uruguay Round (countries in Latin America and the Caribbean, Africa, the Middle East, and Asia, as well as Romania).

The IDB comprises data on commitments made by participants on all tariff lines in their schedules before and after the Uruguay Round, and data on imports by origin denominated in US dollars on a tariff-line basis. The base year for the data on tariffs is 1986, when the Uruguay Round was launched, except for countries that acceded to GATT in the course of the Uruguay Round. Regarding the data on imports, most countries submitted data in 1990 on the latest available year (1988 or 1989); countries that acceded to GATT thereafter submitted data for later years. Because trade has continued to expand in the interim, import data generally underestimate the current value of trade.

Industrial product categories are defined in terms of the six-digit HS codes or the four-digit CCCN headings. For textiles and clothing, they reflect the product coverage specified in the relevant sections of the Uruguay Round Final Act. The eleven product groups for industry comprehensively cover this sector.

Unless otherwise stated, the trade values reported in tables and used for the purpose of computing average trade-weighted tariffs are imports *only* from origins-assessed MFN tariffs, or imports subject to preferential treatment under the Generalized System of Preferences (developing countries) as of 1993. This excludes imports from free-trade partners and imports under the following contractual preferential arrangements: the Australia–New Zealand Closer Economic Relations Trade Agreement; the Australia–Papua New Guinea Agreement; the South Pacific Regional Trade Cooperation Agreement; the Canada–United States Free Trade Agreement; the Israel–United States Free-Trade Agreement; the EFTA; European Economic Community free-trade agreements with EFTA member states; EEC association agreements with Bulgaria, Cyprus, the Czech Republic, Hungary, Malta, Poland, Romania, the Slovak Republic, and Turkey; EEC cooperation agreements with Algeria, Egypt, Jordan, Lebanon, Morocco, Syria, and Tunisia; the ACP–EEC Fourth Lomé Convention; and EFTA free-trade agreements with Bulgaria, the Czech Republic, Hungary, Israel, Poland, Romania, the Slovak Republic, and Turkey.

Unless otherwise stated, reductions in average trade-weighted MFN tariffs are computed by comparing pre- and post-Uruguay Round commitments made by participants on all tariff lines in their schedules. They are not based on a comparison of currently applied and offered rates.

Notes

The views expressed here are strictly those of the authors and do not necessarily represent those of the Secretariat of the WTO, or of its members.

1. The United States, for example, applies an unbound specific duty of $0.0525 per barrel of crude petroleum testing under 25 degrees API (the American Petroleum Institute's measurement of density), and an unbound specific duty of $0.105 per barrel of crude petroleum testing over 25 degrees API.
2. The below-average reduction for transportation equipment is largely explained by the smaller tariff reductions in the major markets on motor vehicles, which account for the bulk of this product category.
3. An agreement is defined as a restraint involving an importer government and an exporter government covering MFA products. See "Report of the Textiles Surveillance Body to the Textiles Committee, Addendum, Status of Restrictions and Arrangements maintained by Participants on 14 October 1994" (COM.TEX/SB/1975/Add.1).
4. The indicator is the change in the tariff wedge or the absolute difference between tariffs at the higher and lower stages of processing. See annex II of GATT (1994a) for a discussion why the change in the tariff wedge is generally a good indicator of the direction of change in tariff escalation.
5. The ACP–EC Fourth Lomé Convention covers all Sub-Saharan African countries except for South Africa, and free-trade agreements cover North African countries. In 1993, about two-thirds of Africa's exports were shipped to the European Union.
6. The European Union has preserved the access for bananas and raised the allocation of ACP states on sugar by 6 percent to 1,294,700 tons. The post-Uruguay Round EU regime for agriculture is likely to raise the income of preferential suppliers for any given level of access owing to the tariffication of variable levies, which were previously not included in the definition of free-trade-area treatment.
7. The Uruguay Round negotiating group on market access considered that tariffs at or below 3 percent were "nuisance" tariffs. Herin (1986) found that the costs associated with meeting the origin requirements for EFTA exports to the European Union led to payment of MFN duties on one quarter of these exports.
8. For more detailed information on nonMFN protection data, see Francois, McDonald, and Nordström (1995 and the technical annex). For a broader discussion of alternative approaches to estimating nontariff barriers, see Laird (1995).
9. The data on export shares are based on 1992 UN trade data. Data include both UN trade statistics reported by COMTRADE as reconciled for the GTAP data set (see Chyc et al., 1994), and UN trade statistics reported by TARS.

10. The chemicals sector has been heavily protected by a mix of tariffs, anti-dumping duties, and nontariff measures. For example, Japan maintains import quotas for a broad range of chemical products (GATT 1992, table AIV.3), and the European Union relies on a mix of antidumping duties and price under-takings (Chyc *et al.*, 1996; GATT 1993a, 76–91). Industrial countries have also protected the production of other machinery through a mix of tariff and non-tariff measures (see GATT 1993a on gray-area measures in the European Union, GATT 1994b on similar measures applied in the United States and UNCTAD 1994).

11. In GTAP-concorded export data, reexports of textiles and clothing originating from China, mostly through Hong Kong, have been assigned to the country of origin.

12. It is important to keep in mind that, while export effects carry policy signifi-cance, they are not necessarily welfare effects. In part, this is because exports require resources that might otherwise support domestic consumption. Depending on the resource cost of exports and shifts in the terms of trade, increased exports could accompany a fall in real income.

13. Simply by truncating the range of protection, bindings and related rules and obligations can lead to significant improvements in market access (Francois and Martin 1995).

14. Comparisons based on regional averages can be misleading. Within regions, there are substantial variations in pre- and post-Uruguay Round average tariffs on goods. Within East Asia, for example, the post-Uruguay Round average rate for the Republic of Korea is 7.2 percent (excluding food), for Thailand, 23.6 percent.

15. Of course, given the small number of African participants in the IDB (five including South Africa), these rates may not indicate the average level of pro-tection in the region. In developing countries, such tariffs are often supple-mented by other restrictions such as customs surcharges. For example, see the GATT TPRM report on Zimbabwe (forthcoming) and on India (1993b). In Zimbabwe, tariffs have averaged 17 percent and surcharges around 15 percent.

16. GATT 1994 also contains the provisions of the legal instruments that entered into force under GATT 1947 before the date of entry into force of the WTO. These include protocols and certifications relating to tariff concessions, proto-cols of accessions, waivers granted under Article XXV, and other decisions of the contracting parties to GATT 1947. The decision on Differential and More Favorable Treatment, Reciprocity, and Fuller Participation of Developing Countries (Basic Instruments and Selected Documents, 26th supplement, 203) or the enabling clause provides a permanent legal cover for tariff preferences granted under the Generalized System of Preferences by developed countries on imports from developing countries, and special provisions for preferential trade arrangements concluded among developing countries.

17. These are VERs, orderly marketing arrangements, or any similar measures on the export or the import side. Each importing member of the WTO is per-mitted to keep one specific measure in force until the end of 1999, subject to

the agreement of the exporting country, and subject to review and acceptance by the Committee on Safeguards.

18. However, the Tokyo Round agreement on government procurement (which will be superseded by a new agreement), the civil aircraft agreement (where negotiations on a new agreement are continuing), and the arrangements on dairy and bovine meat will retain their plurilateral status. The new agreement on government procurement, coming into force on January 1, 1996, will expand the existing agreement by requiring bid-challenge procedures and by increasing the coverage of procurement subject to the rules. The increase, by a factor of about ten, will amount to several hundred billion dollars.

19. The effort to broaden the definition of market access is not helped by CGE modelers who fail to stress clearly that their efforts cover only a part – and perhaps a less significant part – of the Uruguay Round results.

20. It is important to distinguish between such changes being viewed as a burden *per se*, and a situation in which the need to bring domestic laws, practices, and institutions into conformity with the new rules within a short time is considered a burden. The latter can be a legitimate basis for a developing country to demand a longer implementation period.

21. In the past decade or two, a large number of developing countries have autonomously liberalized their trade regimes, often with encouragement by the World Bank and the International Monetary Fund. However, there are few if any instances in which such liberalization was then autonomously bound in GATT. When the countries concerned agreed in the Uruguay Round to bind the liberalization and to accept multilateral disciplines on other trade interventions, it enhanced the credibility of the liberalization and thus its "value" to the private sector.

22. Under the terms of GATT Article XXIV, dependent territories that acquire autonomy in the conduct of external commercial relations may become members of GATT without undergoing the process of accession under Article XXXIII.

23. The credibility of claims that the results of the Uruguay Round are disappointing for African countries would also be enhanced if the commentators recognized that one of the chief factors limiting the gains of African countries in the Uruguay Round was the African countries' reluctance to bind more of their own tariffs and to make larger cuts in their tariffs and other trade barriers. This point is seldom, if ever, made by the "Africa loses" advocates.

References

Enders, A., and J. Seade 1994. "Developing Countries and the Uruguay Round." *Informacion Comercial Espanola* 734: 23–44.

Francois, J., and W. Martin 1995. "Multilateral Trade Rules and the Expected Cost of Protection." CEPR Discussion Paper 1214. London: Centre for Economic Policy Research.

Francois, J., B. McDonald, and H. Nordström 1995. "Assessing the Uruguay Round." In W. Martin and L. A. Winters, eds., *The Uruguay Round and the Developing Economies*. World Bank Discussion Paper 307. Washington, DC: World Bank.

GATT 1992. *Trade Policy Review: Japan*, vol. I. Geneva: GATT.

1993a. *Trade Policy Review: European Communities*, vol. II. Geneva: GATT.

1993b. *Trade Policy Review: India*, vol. I. Geneva: GATT.

1994a. *The Results of the Uruguay Round of Multilateral Trade Negotiations: Market Access for Goods and Services: Overview of the Results*. Geneva: GATT.

1994b. *Trade Policy Review: United States*, vol. I. Geneva: GATT.

forthcoming. *Trade Policy Review: Zimbabwe*, vol. I. Geneva: GATT.

Herin, J. 1986. "Rules of Origin and Differences between Tariff Levels in EFTA and in the EC." Occasional Paper 13. Geneva: EFTA.

Laird, S. 1995. "Measuring Tariff and Non-Tariff Barriers." In J. Francois and K. Reinert, eds., *Applied Methods for Trade Policy Analysis*. Cambridge: Cambridge University Press.

UNCTAD 1994. *The Outcome of the Uruguay Round: An Initial Assessment*. Geneva: UNCTAD.

6 Assessing agricultural tariffication under the Uruguay Round

Ian Goldin and Dominique van der Mensbrugghe

Arduous negotiations separated the 1986 Punta del Este declaration to "halt and reverse protectionism and to remove distortions to trade" and the Marrakesh signature that concluded the Uruguay Round. Initial optimism that the Uruguay Round could overcome the hurdles that bogged down the less ambitious Tokyo Round for six years soon evaporated. As the breadth and scope of the negotiations widened with the active participation of 108 countries, the Uruguay Round soon became the most complex multilateral negotiation ever attempted. Initiated before the fall of communism, the Uruguay Round crowns the end of the Cold War with a global commitment to a world economy.

For this reason alone, the Marrakesh agreement is a significant milestone. Had it failed, world trade would have collapsed into conflicting trade blocks, presaging growing economic and political strife that would have fanned political nationalism, with adverse effects on disadvantaged developing and formerly centrally planned countries that are seeking to enter established markets. For countries excluded from the primary trading blocks – especially Sub-Saharan Africa, which is not envisaged as a part of the emerging EU, US, or ASEAN trade regions – the downside consequences of a failed Uruguay Round would be particularly severe. For the world economy, and not least for developing countries, the conclusion of the Uruguay Round offers benefits that go well beyond those captured in modeling exercises.

By pulling virtually all trade within its orbit, GATT has laid a comprehensive foundation for future trade negotiations. Viewed in a longer-term perspective, the inclusion of all agricultural trade under the GATT umbrella is especially significant. Even if liberalization is less substantial than anticipated, the decision to convert agricultural nontariff barriers into tariff barriers will ensure transparency and provide a universal standard for future reductions. The impact of the Uruguay Round on any country will depend primarily on its domestic economic environment, rather than on changes in external prices or markets. The extent to which governments facilitate a flexible and transparent trade environment and minimize the transactions costs involved in pursuing existing trade opportunities or establishing new ones will be critical to whether the Uruguay Round will expand trade and promote economic growth. The benefits of the Uruguay Round must accrue to domestic producers, consumers, and investors as incentives in the form of higher and more stable world prices, improved transparency, and greater market access. In conjunction with other economywide reforms to enhance the efficiency of scarce natural, human, and financial resources, trade reforms provide an historic opportunity to contribute to sustainable growth.

Negotiations in the Uruguay Round offered a fertile ground for economic analysis. Benefiting from advances in computer modeling and forecasting, economists from various institutions or governments prepared projections of various tariff proposals to inform the process of negotiations.[1] But with the Marrakesh signatures and its 22,000 pages of submissions, a quantitative analysis may now be undertaken of the actual tariffication process and tariff reductions.[2] This chapter draws on the available evidence from the Uruguay Round to quantify its projected impact. However, at best, it captures only one aspect of the Uruguay Round. It does not evaluate the long-term gains associated with establishing a comprehensive rule-based trading system. It is also confined to an analysis of tariffication of agriculture and, in an aggregated manner, manufacturing. It does not account for the major achievements of the Uruguay Round in embracing the previously neglected, but increasingly significant, trade in services, investment, and intellectual property. In addition, in contrast with GATT's own assessment of the Uruguay Round, it does not assume economies of scale or imperfect competition.

From Punta del Este to Marrakesh

A comparison of the difference between current levels of protection with what countries have agreed to implement suggests that, to the extent that the Uruguay Round does not live up to the most optimistic range of anticipated outcomes, it is for two primary reasons. First, using 1986–88 as the base period for projections undercuts the reductions in protection associated with the Uruguay Round because many of the countries whose agricultural protection was particularly high during that period have since reduced their protection levels to the point at which they conform more closely to their commitments in the Uruguay Round.

Second, developing countries, and to a lesser extent OECD countries, have established their offers at levels that are well above current tariff levels to insure against the risk of collapse in world prices, and as a bargaining chip for future negotiations. Although the tariffication of all nontariff barriers and the establishment of tariff binding ceilings remove uncertainty in the trade regime, they might not lead to the anticipated quantitative gains in the short term because many developing countries currently apply tariffs unilaterally below the new bindings. In such cases, these countries could increase protection legally, since the current tariff levels will be allowed to increase to the new bindings under the final Uruguay Round agreement. Yet this scenario is unlikely, since most of the countries that have liberalized unilaterally have done so for solid economic reasons and are benefiting from a more open and competitive trade environment.

Agricultural offers by region and commodity

The basis of the analysis in this chapter is a set of five simulations of the RUNS model that compare the actual commitments of countries to reducing tariffs and export subsidies with benchmark levels of protection in the absence of the Uruguay Round commitments.[3] But what were the actual offers made by the Uruguay Round commitments?

Asia

Significant agricultural liberalization is not envisaged in low-income Asia, China, and India (table 6.1), because China is not a GATT member (despite participating in the Uruguay Round) and because the countries of low-income Asia generally tax their agriculture. The only significant commitment in these three regions is the complete removal of the food oils tariff in India.

Upper-income Asia has committed to significant changes in a variety of commodities. These countries will almost eliminate barriers on wheat (from 272 percent to 13 percent) and will significantly reduce barriers on coarse grains (from 316 percent to 95 percent). But they have committed to smaller reductions in rice protection, and although they will substantially reduce protection on meats, they will maintain their protection on food oils. The end result will still be a comparatively protected agricultural sector in upper-income Asia, with tariff equivalents in the 40 to 100 percent range. The average PSE will drop from 49 percent to 31 percent.

The only apparent significant commitment in Indonesia is a reduction in the protection on oils, from 77 percent to 28 percent.

Africa, the Maghreb, and the Middle East

Sub-Saharan Africa taxes virtually all commodities; the GATT submissions indicate that this region will keep this policy intact. Nigeria

Table 6.1 *Average agricultural tariff equivalents (percent)*

Region/country	Former[a]	Current[b]	Current (base)[c] 2002	Current (liberalization)[d] 2002	Difference 2002[e]	Percentage difference 2002[f]
Low-income Asia	10.5	15.7	17.9	17.9	0.0	-0.1
China	0.0	0.0	0.0	0.0	0.0	0.0
India	0.0	-13.1	-2.4	-3.2	-0.9	35.5
Upper-income Asia	94.5	52.3	49.4	31.4	-18.0	-36.4
Indonesia	14.3	9.3	9.2	8.1	-1.1	-12.3
Other Africa	22.4	-18.5	-4.7	-4.7	0.0	0.6
Nigeria	44.7	14.6	77.9	72.0	-5.9	-7.6
South Africa	25.9	7.8	12.9	12.8	0.0	-0.2
Maghreb	21.8	13.1	14.0	14.0	0.0	0.3
Mediterranean	57.1	2.1	2.3	0.9	-1.4	-59.6
Gulf Region	107.6	117.7	111.1	113.2	2.1	1.9
Other Latin America	21.8	3.3	3.5	3.5	0.0	0.4
Brazil	17.2	3.9	4.1	2.2	-1.8	-45.0
Mexico	14.8	3.6	3.8	3.8	0.0	0.6
United States	47.6	18.2	35.5	35.5	0.0	0.1
Canada	38.4	41.6	42.9	42.5	-0.4	-0.9
Australia, New Zealand	8.6	14.0	14.4	4.9	-9.6	-66.2
Japan	132.5	108.6	97.4	79.0	-18.5	-18.9
EEC	68.6	43.7	42.4	38.1	-4.3	-10.1
EFTA	144.9	124.7	124.2	94.6	-29.6	-23.8

Table 6.1 (*cont.*)

Region/country	Former[a]	Current[b]	Current (base)[c] 2002	Current (liberalization)[d] 2002	Difference 2002[e]	Percentage difference 2002[f]
European economies in transition	29.4	3.5	7.1	6.7	−0.4	−5.9
Former Soviet Union	−1.1	0.3	0.0	0.0	0.0	−28.1

[a] Average tariff equivalents from the previous base simulations of RUNS. They were assumed to be constant through the year 2002; previous Uruguay Round scenarios involved a 30 percent across-the-board reduction in their levels (including negative tariff equivalents).

[b] Average tariff equivalents in the new base (derived for this chapter) in 1993.

[c] Average tariff equivalents in the new base in 2002.

[d] Average tariff equivalents under the new liberalization scenario in 2002. Because liberalization will be phased in for some commodities and in some regions, the full impact of liberalization does not necessarily start in 1996.

[e] Differences between "current 2002 base" and "current 2002 liberalization."

[f] Percentage differences between "current 2002 base" and "current 2002 liberalization"

Note: the numbers in the first four columns represent tariff equivalents for different years and different simulations. These numbers represent the average tariff equivalent only on protected commodities in each region in the base year (1985). If a commodity was not protected in 1985, then it is omitted from the aggregation. Household consumption was used as the weight in computing the averages. Production weights provide similar results.

Source: authors' calculations based on World Bank data.

strongly protects grain production and will lower rates on wheat from 182 percent to 150 percent, and on sugar from 50 percent to 29 percent. Tariff rates are low in South Africa compared with other middle-income countries, and it is committed to further reductions. Its most significant commitment will be in wool, which it will liberalize completely.

Analyzing the situation in the Maghreb and the Middle Eastern regions is more difficult. Although much of this region has lowered its tariff ceilings and made them binding, many of the current levels of protection are also well below the binding ceilings. We have thus assumed virtually no liberalization in the Maghreb and the Gulf regions, and only significant commitments in the Mediterranean region for grains and sugar.

Latin America

In the Latin America region, the only commitment is in cocoa. The only significant commitment in Brazil is in wheat (a reduction from 98 percent to 45 percent). We assume no changes in Mexico.

The OECD

Previous simulations with the RUNS model highlighted the importance of changes in the trade regime of OECD countries. The modesty of the proposed reforms now accounts largely for the smaller than anticipated impact of the Uruguay Round. The United States will lower its tariff equivalent on wheat from 20 percent to 4 percent, and on wool from 8 percent to 5 percent. But beyond these sectors, it is committed to little modification – particularly in the heavily protected sugar and dairy sectors.

Canada is committed to few modifications, although Canada is already relatively open. The strongly protected dairy sector will remain a bastion of protection.

Australia and New Zealand – the OECD regions with the lowest tariff levels – will lower tariffs on rice, other meats, and dairy. Virtually the only protected sectors remaining will be sugar at 10 percent and dairy at 7 percent.

Japan has committed to large reductions – particularly in grains, although the final tariff levels for grains will remain prohibitively high. It will drop its rate on wheat from 492 percent to 193 percent, on coarse grains from 566 percent to 180 percent, and on dairy from 389 percent to 207 percent. It has not committed to reductions in protection on other commodities. In the rice market, improved market access, rather than tariff reductions, is expected to lead to significant liberalization.

The European Union has agreed to modest changes. The average PSE will fall from 42 percent to 38 percent. The EFTA has been slightly more forthcoming, with a commitment to reduce the average PSE from 124

Table 6.2a *Manufacturing tariffs (percent)*

Region/country	Former 1986	Current 1986	Current 1996	Difference (former −current 1986)	Current liberalization
Low-income Asia	76.0	23.4	23.2	−52.6	−0.2
China	51.0	0.0	0.0	−51.0	0.0
India	106.0	72.2	32.0	−33.8	−40.2
Upper-income Asia	6.0	11.2	6.8	5.2	−4.4
Indonesia	27.0	11.9	11.3	−15.1	−0.6
Other Africa	22.0	10.6	10.4	−11.5	−0.2
Nigeria	29.0	0.0	0.0	−29.0	0.0
South Africa	21.1	0.0	0.0	−21.1	0.0
Maghreb	31.0	27.8	27.5	−3.3	−0.2
Mediterranean	17.0	28.3	24.9	11.3	−3.4
Gulf Region	8.0	0.0	0.0	−8.0	0.0
Other Latin America	29.0	28.2	20.1	−0.8	−8.1
Brazil	68.0	41.4	23.5	−26.6	−17.9
Mexico	16.7	10.8	10.7	−6.0	0.0
United States	3.8	4.6	3.1	0.9	−1.5
Canada	4.7	8.3	4.6	3.6	−3.8
Australia, New Zealand	12.0	17.2	10.5	5.2	−6.7
Japan	1.8	3.8	1.6	2.0	−2.2
EEC	4.2	6.3	3.5	2.2	−2.8
EFTA	1.0	6.0	3.9	5.0	−2.1
European economies in transition	15.0	10.6	7.8	−4.4	−2.8
Former Soviet Union	0.0	0.0	0.0	0.0	0.0

Source: authors' calculations based on World Bank data.

percent to 95 percent. It will significantly reduce its protection on wheat, coarse grains, sugar, oils, and dairy.

Eastern Europe and the former Soviet Union
Changes in Eastern Europe are modest and no changes have been agreed to by the former Soviet Union.

Reductions in "other" manufacturing protection by region

Only India and Brazil are committed to substantial tariff reductions in light manufacturing, from 72 percent to 32 percent and from 41 percent to 24 percent, respectively (table 6.2a). Upper-income Asia, and other

Table 6.2b *Energy tariffs (percent)*

Region/country	Former 1986	Current 1986	Current 1996	Difference (former −current 1986)	Current liberalization
Low-income Asia	31.0	24.8	24.8	−6.3	0.0
China	8.0	0.0	0.0	−8.0	0.0
India	54.0	55.5	51.0	1.5	−4.4
Upper-income Asia	3.0	7.4	6.4	4.4	−1.0
Indonesia	3.0	2.9	2.9	−0.1	0.0
Other Africa	13.0	5.7	5.7	−7.3	0.0
Nigeria	10.0	0.0	0.0	−10.0	0.0
South Africa	0.0	0.0	0.0	0.0	0.0
Maghreb	7.0	10.7	10.7	3.7	0.0
Mediterranean	3.0	23.8	22.9	20.8	−0.8
Gulf Region	6.0	0.0	0.0	−6.0	0.0
Other Latin America	14.0	19.4	18.3	5.4	−1.1
Brazil	23.0	8.8	7.1	−14.2	−1.7
Mexico	2.4	3.8	3.8	1.3	0.0
United States	0.6	0.6	0.6	0.0	0.0
Canada	3.5	0.9	0.7	−2.6	−0.2
Australia, New Zealand	1.0	1.1	0.7	0.1	−0.4
Japan	3.0	2.7	0.5	−0.3	−2.2
EEC	0.4	1.9	1.2	1.4	−0.7
EFTA	0.0	4.2	4.1	4.2	−0.1
European economies in transition	5.0	5.0	4.8	0.0	−0.2
Former Soviet Union	0.0	0.0	0.0	0.0	0.0

Source: authors' calculations based on World Bank data.

Latin America have made comparatively substantial commitments, but started from a lower base. The OECD regions have committed to roughly a one third reduction in tariff rates, also starting from already very low levels. There are virtually no changes in the energy sector (table 6.2b). The equipment goods sector (table 6.2c) is very similar to light manufacturing. India and Brazil have made major commitments to reductions but other regions and countries are committed only to minor changes. Given the small anticipated changes, except for India and Brazil, we would not expect manufacturing liberalization to generate significant structural changes or any significant increase in real world income.

Table 6.2c *Equipment tariffs (percent)*

Region/country	Former 1986	Current 1986	Current 1996	Difference (former −current 1986)	Current liberalization
Low-income Asia	46.0	11.8	11.8	−34.2	0.0
China	29.0	0.0	0.0	−29.0	0.0
India	86.0	74.9	28.7	−11.1	−46.2
Upper-income Asia	6.0	11.8	8.0	5.8	−3.8
Indonesia	24.0	14.2	13.6	−9.8	−0.6
Other Africa	17.0	5.7	5.7	−11.3	0.0
Nigeria	20.0	0.0	0.0	−20.0	0.0
South Africa	8.1	0.0	0.0	−8.1	0.0
Maghreb	14.0	23.2	23.2	9.2	0.0
Mediterranean	23.0	24.0	21.0	1.0	−3.0
Gulf Region	8.0	0.0	0.0	−8.0	0.0
Other Latin America	18.0	21.8	17.7	3.8	−4.1
Brazil	53.0	44.3	27.4	−8.7	−16.9
Mexico	17.0	11.9	11.9	−5.1	0.0
United States	2.2	2.8	1.6	0.6	−1.2
Canada	4.1	4.4	2.4	0.3	−2.0
Australia, New Zealand	7.0	13.4	8.0	6.4	−5.4
Japan	0.9	2.7	0.0	1.8	−2.7
EEC	5.1	4.1	2.2	−0.9	−2.0
EFTA	1.0	3.0	1.8	2.0	−1.2
European economies in transition	13.0	10.5	8.0	−2.5	−2.5
Former Soviet Union	0.0	0.0	0.0	0.0	0.0

Source: authors' calculations based on World Bank data.

The RUNS model and the simulations

The RUNS model consists of three dimensions: regions, commodities, and time. The twenty-two regions of the model are essentially divided by geographical area and reflect regional groupings and the relative weight of countries (see appendix A). Commodities consist of twenty sectors, fifteen of which are agricultural (table 6.3). Many of the agricultural commodities are highly homogeneous, including wheat, rice, coarse grains, sugar, coffee, cocoa, and tea. Two large aggregates are referred to as "other food" and "other nonfood." Other food includes fruits, vegetables, and beverages. Livestock is dispersed across four sectors – three food categories (beef, veal,

Table 6.2d *Fertilizer tariffs (percent)*

Region/country	Former 1986	Current 1986	Current 1996	Difference (former −current 1986)	Current liberalization
Low-income Asia	0.0	1.6	1.6	1.6	0.0
China	6.0	0.0	0.0	−6.0	0.0
India	51.0	58.5	44.6	7.5	−13.9
Upper-income Asia	5.0	15.7	14.2	10.7	−1.4
Indonesia	0.0	4.3	4.3	4.3	0.0
Other Africa	6.0	7.2	7.2	1.2	0.0
Nigeria	5.0	0.0	0.0	−5.0	0.0
South Africa	15.0	0.0	0.0	−15.0	0.0
Maghreb	2.0	13.5	13.5	11.5	0.0
Mediterranean	2.0	24.9	19.4	22.9	−5.6
Gulf Region	0.0	0.0	0.0	0.0	0.0
Other Latin America	7.0	16.6	15.2	9.6	−1.4
Brazil	10.0	4.0	3.2	−6.0	−0.8
Mexico	4.5	9.1	9.1	4.7	0.0
United States	0.0	1.4	0.5	1.4	−0.8
Canada	0.0	0.1	0.1	0.1	0.0
Australia, New Zealand	0.0	6.7	4.9	6.7	−1.8
Japan	0.0	1.2	0.8	1.2	−0.4
EEC	2.9	4.3	3.8	1.5	−0.5
EFTA	0.0	3.3	2.2	3.3	−1.1
European economies in transition	5.0	7.4	6.0	2.4	−1.4
Former Soviet Union	0.0	0.0	0.0	0.0	0.0

Source: authors' calculations based on World Bank data.

and sheep; other meats, largely poultry and pork; and dairy) and one nonfood category (wool). The time range covers the 1985–2002 period for a total of seventeen years – each year from 1985 to 1987, and each three years from 1987 to 2002. All the factor accumulation functions and growth parameters reflect the three-year gap. The period 1985–93 is used to validate the model to observable data.

The key feature of the RUNS model is that it captures the links between the agricultural and urban sectors and between world markets and domestic markets. This is one of the mechanisms that explains the winners and losers under trade liberalization. If trade liberalization increases food prices worldwide, countries that import food will have to pay more – in other

Table 6.3 *Commodities captured by RUNS*

Agriculture		Nonagriculture
Food	Nonfood	
Wheat	Wool	Other manufacturing
Rice (paddy)	Cotton	Energy
Coarse grains[a]	Other nonfood[b]	Services
Sugar (refined)		Equipment goods
Beef, veal, and sheep		Fertilizers
Other meats[c]		
Coffee		
Cocoa		
Tea		
Vegetable oils[d]		
Dairy and dairy products		
Other food[e]		

[a]Maize, rye, barley, oats, sorghum, millet, and other grains.
[b]Tobacco, sisal, jute, and so on.
[c]Pork, poultry, eggs, and other meats.
[d]Oil seeds, oils, and oil cakes.
[e]Fruits, vegetables, beverages, and so on.

words, they will suffer from a reduction in their terms of trade, and hence a reduction in real income.

The RUNS model also consists of two components – a static model and a dynamic model. In the static model, supply and demand relations are specified for each good and for each region, which in turn define trade relations across countries. Supply is driven by underlying technology and resource endowments: labor, land, and capital. In addition, government policies on input subsidies, export subsidies, and taxes affect supply directly. Demand is driven primarily by household income. Government policy on import tariffs or subsidies also plays a role in demand because it affects the relative price of goods. The dynamic model captures some of the growth processes that are inherent in the world economy. The key factors are factor accumulation (labor force growth and capital growth with savings and investment) and productivity improvements. Productivity gains are exogenous (although they vary over time). Changes in trade policies thus affect growth primarily by affecting savings, investment, and government revenue. For example, agricultural protectionism in the OECD countries may be inducing greater investment in the rural sectors than necessary, despite the fact that certain OECD countries may have a comparative

advantage in industry in the absence of protection. This inefficient allocation of investment reduces the long-term growth rate. (Appendix B provides
more detailed specifications of the RUNS model.)

The simulation models

The five simulations used in our quantitative analysis of the Uruguay
Round differ according to their assumptions about the underlying reference period that provides the benchmark against which the effects of the
trade reforms are measured. Because we cannot predict what world trade
would be in the absence of the Uruguay Round, we provide alternative
assessments based on whether the reference period for the future should
represent the recent past (1989–93) or a longer-run average of previous
trade patterns (1982–93). The argument for using the recent past is the
rapid structural shift in trade policies in the past decade; many developing
countries and some OECD countries (for example, New Zealand) have
engaged in fundamental trade reforms, while others, primarily OECD
regions (including the European Union, the EFTA, the United States, and
Japan) have displayed the reverse tendency by increasing protectionism.
The argument for a using longer-run average is that tariffs are inherently
unstable, reflecting world prices and domestic politics, with the assumption
that tariff levels have not been a function of any underlying trend.

The different simulations also capture diverse perceptions about the
extent to which the signatories of the GATT agreement will undertake
reforms in the coming years. In many cases, the commitments entered into
in the Uruguay Round agreement diverge from observed behavior. The
simulations assume that developing countries will not raise their tariffs,
despite the fact that many of the new tariff bindings are above previously
applied tariff rates. But the extent of "dirty tariffication" – the setting of
tariff bindings above the rate suggested by the agreement – may be approximated from a comparison of our simulations.

Simulation 1
    The first simulation is based on a reference-period scenario which
assumes that the future (1994–2002) benchmark levels of protection are the
longer-run (1982–93) average levels of protection, and that the Uruguay
Round submissions of the countries for tariff and export subsidy reductions
are offered against this. In simulation 1 input subsidies remain the same,
depicting an interpretation of the Uruguay Round that the reforms will
affect only the relationship between border and domestic producer prices.
For developing countries whose binding tariff offers are above their
observed levels, simulation 1 assumes that tariffs do not change, implying

the presumption that countries will not exercise the option to increase protection under the Uruguay Round agreement. (All other simulations also make this assumption.)

Simulation 2

The second simulation is identical to the first, except that the most recent (1989–93) estimates of average protection are used as the benchmark against which future reforms are evaluated. Simulation 2 is based on the hypothesis that the 1994–2002 levels of protection would reflect the recent past, rather than a long-run average, in the absence of liberalization.

Simulation 3

The third simulation is similar to simulation 2, with the 1989–93 benchmark protection levels for the 1994–2002 period. But, in addition to applying tariff reductions as the actual Uruguay Round submissions, simulation 3 examines the effect of "formula" reductions in input subsidies. Input subsidies for agriculture are not inconsequential, and reducing them was a key objective of the Uruguay Round, although largely unattained. In order to measure the welfare effects, we assumed that OECD countries reduce input subsidies by 36 percent, and that nonOECD countries reduce their subsidies by 24 percent to reflect an overall commitment of these countries towards reducing the aggregate level of support for agriculture.

Simulation 4

The fourth simulation examines what was expected on the basis of the Dunkel Draft Final Act, rather than what was achieved in the Uruguay Round. This simulation is comparable to our previous work with the RUNS model, in that it analyzes the effects of broad formula cuts in tariffs, rather than the specific changes that were eventually agreed upon. The reference period is the same as in simulation 3 (1989–93), but rather than applying the individual submissions we examine the consequences of tariff reductions of 36 percent in OECD countries and 24 percent in nonOECD countries. Where agricultural protection is negative, implying that agricultural production is taxed, we assumed no changes in protection rates or no increase in taxation.

Simulation 5

Whereas the previous simulations were based on our full-employment version of the model, simulation 5 offers perspectives about the implications of assumptions about unemployment. Simulation 5 is comparable to simulation 3. In simulation 5, the effects of tariff reductions under the Uruguay Round and across-the-board reductions in input subsidies are

Table 6.4 *Change in world agricultural prices (percentage deviations from benchmark levels in 2002) (measured relative to OECD manufactured export prices)*

Commodity	Simulation 1	Simulation 2	Simulation 3	Simulation 4	Simulation 5
Wheat	1.2	3.8	6.3	10.3	6.6
Rice	−1.5	−0.9	0.8	3.6	1.3
Coarse grains	0.1	2.3	3.2	5.4	3.3
Sugar	−1.0	1.8	2.5	11.4	3.0
Beef, veal, and sheep	0.2	0.6	1.4	6.0	2.3
Other meats	−0.9	−0.6	−0.1	2.3	0.6
Coffee	−1.7	−1.5	−1.4	−0.7	−0.7
Cocoa	−1.3	−0.7	−0.6	0.3	−0.1
Tea	−1.6	−1.4	−1.2	0.9	−0.7
Oils	−0.6	−0.3	3.9	5.4	4.6
Dairy	−1.3	1.2	2.3	12.1	2.5
Other food products	−1.3	−1.4	−1.5	−0.7	−1.1
Wool	−1.1	−0.9	0.5	1.2	0.2
Cotton	−1.3	−1.2	−0.3	1.1	0.2
Other agriculture	−0.5	0.8	0.9	2.9	1.4

Source: RUNS model.

evaluated against a benchmark in which the 1989–93 level of protection continues throughout 1994–2002.

Simulation results: changes in world prices and welfare

Changes in world agricultural prices that are generated by the five simulations are specified as percentage deviations from the benchmark levels in the year 2002 (table 6.4). Changes in welfare are specified as the percentage of benchmark GDP in the year 2002 (table 6.5).

Simulation 1

Under simulation 1, changes in world prices would be modest, and never greater than 1.7 percent. Viewed in the context of the instability and secular decline in world commodity prices, the predicted changes would barely be

Table 6.5 *Change in real income (percent of benchmark GDP in the year 2002)*

Country/region	Simulation 1	Simulation 2	Simulation 3	Simulation 4	Simulation 5
Low-income Asia	0.2	0.1	0.0	0.4	0.0
China	−0.1	−0.1	−0.2	−0.2	−0.2
India	0.4	0.5	0.7	0.8	0.0
Upper-income Asia	0.8	1.3	1.3	2.0	4.9
Indonesia	0.1	0.1	0.1	0.3	0.5
Other Africa	−0.2	−0.2	−0.3	−0.5	−0.4
Nigeria	−0.1	−0.1	−0.1	0.1	−0.1
South Africa	−0.2	−0.4	−0.4	−0.4	−0.9
Maghreb	0.0	−0.1	−0.3	−0.9	−0.4
Mediterranean	−0.1	−0.1	−0.2	−0.3	0.3
Gulf Region	0.2	0.0	−0.2	0.3	0.1
Other Latin America	−0.3	−0.3	0.0	0.4	0.2
Brazil	0.3	0.4	0.3	0.4	−0.1
Mexico	−0.1	−0.4	−0.5	−0.6	−0.5
United States	0.0	0.0	0.1	0.2	0.1
Canada	−0.2	−0.2	0.0	0.4	0.2
Australia, New Zealand	−0.1	0.0	0.1	0.6	0.4
Japan	0.2	0.4	0.4	0.9	1.6
EEC	0.1	0.3	0.6	0.9	1.9
EFTA	0.3	1.0	1.2	1.6	2.8
European economies in transition	0.1	0.1	0.0	−0.2	0.1
Former Soviet Union	0.0	0.1	0.1	0.7	0.4
In billions of 1992 US dollars					
Africa	−1.3	−1.8	−2.5	−3.1	−3.3
Low-income	2.0	1.3	0.9	3.4	−2.4
Latin America	0.6	0.3	0.6	3.1	−1.7
Other developing	9.7	14.9	13.2	24.2	59.8
OECD	14.2	32.4	54.7	103.6	178.6
Other	0.1	0.8	1.5	5.5	4.1
Total	25.4	48.0	68.4	136.6	235.1

Source: RUNS model.

significant. Given that the changes will be phased in, their impact would be felt gradually during the 1995–2002 implementation period. Simulation 1 suggests that the Uruguay Round is unlikely to have any discernible impact on world prices. To the extent that the simulation predicts changes, they may be understood as reductions in protection, especially in the major OECD producers, which would in turn reduce supply and thus increase prices. The small negative price changes can be attributed to the cross-elasticities among crops, as sugar, rice, and cotton, which receive comparatively greater protection than other crops, would occupy land previously devoted to comparatively less protected crops, such as other cereals.[4]

The modest liberalization depicted in simulation 1 translates into lower welfare gains than have previously been estimated (table 6.5). The total welfare gain in the year 2002 is estimated to be US $25.4 billion. Almost all regions would gain, although small losses are recorded for China, Sub-Saharan Africa, Canada, Australia, Mexico, and other Latin America. The 0.1 percent decline in China's income reflects the decline in the world price of rice. Declines in Mexico and Sub-Saharan Africa are due primarily to the impact of higher cereal prices on these food-importing regions. Latin America would suffer from a decline in tropical beverage and sugar prices, and Australia from lower wool and sugar prices. The modest gains are associated primarily with countries that would benefit from manufacturing liberalization, although in India the gains from lowering its manufacturing protection would be offset to some extent by the decline in the world price of rice, which, as with China, would have a negative impact on rural income. However, liberalization in China is not assumed, since it is not a GATT member and must accede before the offers it made in the Uruguay Round can be ensured as an effective gain.

Simulation 2

In simulation 2, the benchmark is the most recent level of protection, rather than the historical average. The difference between situations 1 and 2 is evident from the different price effects and higher level of gains depicted in simulation 2. The relatively higher level of protection in the more recent period means that the application of the Uruguay Round submissions implies a deeper liberalization, generating a sharply higher total gain of US $48 billion in the year 2002. The contrast between the first two simulations is particularly evident in OECD countries, whose gains from trade reform would more than double over their gains in simulation 1. The two-thirds share of the global gains accounted for by OECD countries in simulation 2 compares with an approximately 55 percent share in simulation 1; the difference reflects the fact that many developing countries have engaged in fundamental trade reforms (often in the context of structural adjustment programs), so that their recent (1989–93) levels of protection are generally below their longer-run (1982–93) average level. Not surprisingly, a comparison of simulations 1 and 2 shows that developing countries would record lower gains with a recent benchmark, since the countries have already achieved most of the gains that in simulation 1 are attributed to the Uruguay Round. This finding is particularly true of Latin America and the low-income countries, which in recent years have made the most comprehensive trade reforms. Because the Uruguay Round under simulation 2 would generate more modest reforms in these developing countries, the supply response that accounts for declines in coffee, cocoa, tea, rice, sugar, and other prices is more muted. In contrast, a deeper reform effort in OECD countries would lead to a sharper supply response, which is the primary determinant of higher price increases for cereals. Deeper reform in OECD countries and more modest reform in developing countries would buttress virtually all prices, and would lead to price increases for sugar and dairy (although modest), rather than to price reductions.

A comparison of simulations 1 and 2 highlights the importance of the base year chosen for analysis. Not surprisingly, the base year was a source of much negotiation in the Uruguay Round, as the more protectionist OECD countries pushed for using the 1986–88 reference period, when protection levels were at a peak. Although protection levels generally declined after 1990, our analysis indicates that the gains from using the 1989–93 reference period nevertheless produce virtually double the benefits of those derived from a longer-run average of protection levels.

Simulation 3

Simulation 3 captures a formula reduction in the input subsidies – 36 percent for OECD countries and 24 percent for other countries. Simulation 3 differs from simulation 2 primarily by the effects of input subsidies on OECD regions in which subsidies are prevalent. The 36 percent reduction in input subsidies would lower OECD production and exports further, reinforcing the effect indicated in simulation 2. The associated increase in world prices, particularly for wheat (6.3 percent) and food (3.9 percent) reflects the importance of input subsidies for these two commodities in the OECD regions. The higher wheat and oil prices, together with higher prices for coarse grains, rice, and sugar, have a negative impact on food-importing regions (see table 6.5); Africa, in particular, would suffer an income loss of US $2.5 billion in the year 2002. Since these regions are net importers of temperate products, their terms of trade would suffer. The losses are cause for concern, because they are concentrated in the most vulnerable regions where food security is a life-threatening issue.

We have emphasized elsewhere that the losses should not be ignored. That they are small compared with the overall gains generated by the Uruguay Round indicates that mechanisms should be found to compensate vulnerable losers. The net gains in this simulation of the Uruguay Round would amount to US $68.4 billion in the year 2002. Deeper liberalization in OECD countries would generate greater gains in the manufacturing and agricultural sectors; in contrast, because part of the reform among all developing countries would be the product of unilateral rather than Uruguay Round action, developing countries would capture a modest (20 percent) share of the global gains.

A comparison of simulation 3 and simulation 2 indicates that the results are sensitive to assumptions about the reduction in domestic distortions. Although these domestic distortions were a major focus of the Uruguay Round at its outset, the final agreement focused on border measures. The broad covenants on domestic support are largely expected to be ineffective at reducing input subsidies. A wide range of subsidy programs are exempt, and, in contrast with border protection, minimum reductions have not been set for commodities, enabling countries to combine high protection on key commodities with lower protection on less significant commodities. Our results suggest that these weaknesses with the Uruguay Round have significant consequences, and that the effective application of a 36/24 percent formula cut in input subsidies could have raised the income gains associated with the Uruguay Round by approximately 40 percent.

Simulation 4

Simulation 4 represents the promise rather than the practice of the Uruguay Round, in that it estimates the effect of applying the formula for tariff reforms and input subsidies that was part of the 1992 Draft Final Act of the Uruguay Round. The Act called for a standard reduction of 36 percent in tariff equivalents for OECD countries and 24 percent for developing countries, phased in over a longer period for developing countries. The introduction of these reductions into the model generates much greater gains than do the simulations that reflect the actual submissions. The benchmark applied in this simulation is the same as in the previous simulation, thus yielding comparable results. The formula reductions more than double the gains. The differences may be interpreted as the cost of compromise, whereby the countries negotiated more modest reforms than intended by the formulas, thus diminishing the potential welfare gains of the Uruguay Round. Simulation 4 yields larger price changes than do the previous simulations – particularly for sugar (11.4 percent), meats (6 percent), and dairy (12.1 percent), which are the three sectors where "dirty tariffication" has been especially evident in key OECD countries and where tariffs have remained relatively untouched by the Uruguay Round. These commodities for which "dirty tariffication" was most evident are also among the most protected commodities, particularly in OECD countries, and they have important implications for the simulation results.

In simulation 4 virtually all prices rise. While this result provides a fair reflection of the impact of formula cuts as initially promised in the Uruguay Round, it conflicts with results derived in our earlier modeling efforts, given that we examined both unilateral and multilateral trade reforms. This chapter has a narrower focus and does not examine the implications of trade policy adjustments that are beyond the domain of the Uruguay Round. For this reason, the reductions in the taxation of agriculture (negative PSEs) that are associated with structural adjustment programs in developing countries are omitted. Their omission heightens the positive price changes evident in our current simulations; production changes reflect reductions in subsidies but not lower taxes on producers.

A comparison of simulation 4 results with simulation 1, 2, and 3 results indicates the extent to which across-the-board liberalization is associated with greater welfare improvements than the analysis based on the final offers (see table 6.5). The total global welfare gain in simulation 4 amounts to US $137 billion in the year 2002. This gain is double the estimate derived with simulation 3, highlighting the difference between the submissions and previous assumptions about the extent of liberalization under the Uruguay Round. OECD countries with high rates of protection benefit most from deeper liberalization, in both relative and absolute terms. They benefit, in part, because their formula commitments were based on a 36 percent reduction in protectionism, compared with 24 percent in developing countries. Whereas the world as a whole would have reaped larger gains from the application of the formula cuts, the agricultural and manufacturing liberalization included in our analysis would have made food-importing countries worse off, given the sharp increases in cereal and other food prices.

Thus, although most countries would be rewarded by the across-the-board reforms modeled in simulation 4, and although the countries that liberalize to the greatest extent would generally gain the most, the rise in world prices would be detrimental to a small number of countries, particularly the food-importing countries of Africa and the Middle East. Goldin, Knudsen, and van der Mensbrugghe (1993) have emphasized that, while these potential losses are cause for concern, they in part reflect the inadequacies of our modeling effort, because we are capturing only part of the benefits of the Uruguay Round. Simulation 4 highlights the extent to which the gains would overwhelm any potential losses from the application of the Draft Dunkel Act of the Uruguay Round. Developing and OECD food exporters would reap the benefits of the significant increases in agricultural prices, and upper-income Asia and the former Soviet Union would benefit from improved manufacturing trade.

Simulation 5

Simulation 5 introduces unemployment. In all other respects, it is comparable to simulation 3. Unemployment exists in all countries, and in many it has reached high levels. The unemployed pose a significant loss to any economy, and their absorption into the labor force offers considerable scope for economywide improvements. But modeling labor markets and including unemployment in general equilibrium analysis remains a controversial issue. To facilitate comparisons with the different modeling results of analysts and in view of the theoretical difficulties of modeling unemployment, simulations 1 to 4 incorporate the orthodox modeling assumptions of flexible labor markets and full employment. Simulation 5 introduces rigidities in wage behavior, calibrated to reflect observed unemployment trends in urban labor markets. These rigidities and the potential for employment expansion alter the effects of trade reform. To the extent that trade reform lowers domestic prices, the pressure on real wages is reduced, leading to higher employment and greater urban and overall welfare. The relationship between trade reforms and the labor market depends on the rigidity of the real wage and the level of unemployment, as well as rural–urban migration. The nature of the transmission of world to domestic prices and vice versa is also important.

In simulation 5, trade reform in OECD countries would generally reduce consumer prices and increase both urban employment and rural–urban migration. Rising demand would increase urban income in OECD countries, which, along with the reduction in the rural labor force, explains why agricultural prices in simulation 5 would rise higher than the estimates in simulation 3, given that labor markets modeling is the only difference between the two simulations. The introduction of wage rigidity into the benchmark simulation would raise global gains by 350 percent, with an increase of US $235 billion in the year 2002.

The distributional results indicate that these gains are concentrated in OECD countries and upper-income (primarily Asian) developing countries. These countries have strong levels of protectionism, so that trade reform would make consumers better off (the domestic price of food would fall despite the rise in commodity prices worldwide). But in Africa, Latin America, and other low-income regions (including China and India), higher world prices would be transmitted into domestic markets, increasing consumer prices. Under assumptions of wage rigidity and unemployment, as in simulation 5, upward pressure on wages would reduce domestic competitiveness and employment. Trade reform would increase food prices, increasing domestic prices and thus making low-income regions comparatively worse off. But this result is derived from a simulation that involves trade reform, not labor market reform. In practice, trade reforms in developing countries have yielded broader economic adjustments, including labor market reform.

Unemployment is a fact of economic life, but the unemployed do represent an immense unused resource. The difficulty of modeling unemployment and uncertainty about the relationship between trade reform and labor market reform mean that these illustrative numbers must be viewed with more than the usual caveats. But they do highlight the fact that, by failing to account for unemployment or other important characteristics of economic activity, such as scale economies, our modeling results capture only one aspect of the implications of trade reform in agricultural and manufacturing trade, which itself is only one dimension of the Uruguay Round.

Conclusion

Our quantitative analysis of the Uruguay Round highlights the extent to which the results differ according to how it is interpreted. The results are highly sensitive to the underlying data and assumptions. The submissions suggest that many countries have not offered significant commitments to liberalize. For some, this reticence reflects their belief that reductions in protection in the 1990–93 period went further than their commitments in the Uruguay Round. For others, it simply reflects the failure of the Round to overcome a mercantilist approach to trade in which countries offered little and demanded a lot. Many developing countries have placed offers well above observed levels, for three primary reasons – to insure against the risk of a collapse in world prices, which might prompt them to raise tariffs to protect domestic farmers; to retain a bargaining chip for future negotiations; and to give governments flexibility to continue to rely on tariff revenue as a significant source of public finance. These factors notwithstanding, it is unlikely that developing countries will increase tariffs. On the contrary, the structural adjustment efforts of developing countries in the past decade indicate that, with a few notable exceptions, many have reduced their tariffs independently of the GATT negotiation process. Our analysis highlights the benefits associated with continued unilateral liberalization. The simulations point to both the downside risks associated with the Uruguay Round agreement and the potentially significant gains for countries that go beyond their offers and apply the spirit rather than the letter of the agreement.

A comparison of the export subsidy commitments agreed to in the Uruguay Round with the levels of exports suggested by our modeling results indicates that export subsidies could become a binding factor in OECD countries. In particular, our modeling results suggest that the United States and the European Union might have to adopt reforms that go beyond our representation of their actual submissions or even the formula reductions in tariffs and input subsidies modeled in simulation 4 if they are to meet their export subsidy commitments. These measures would likely reinforce the effects of the Uruguay Round identified earlier.

We have emphasized from the outset that our quantitative assessment captures only a small part of the welfare gains to be derived from the Uruguay Round. By establishing a comprehensive rule-based system the Uruguay Round has placed world trade on a growth trajectory (see chapter 14). The process of tariffication is now in place, and, through unilateral reforms and future trade negotiations, tariffs will be adopted below the ceilings established in the Uruguay Round.

The inclusion of previously neglected sectors, the reinforcement of dispute settlement mechanisms, and the improved administrative capacity of the new WTO Secretariat provide a solid underpinning for world trade, which, up until the time that the Uruguay Round was signed, was being threatened by growing trade frictions. World trade is displaying remarkable dynamism, with new players and new practices challenging the established system. Developing and formerly centrally planned economies have a particularly large stake in ensuring that newcomers and smaller and more vulnerable countries are not discriminated against. Our quantitative assessment of the Uruguay Round agreement suggests more modest gains than those that had been anticipated. Our simulation results demonstrate forcefully that the extent of the gains will depend on how far the reforms of countries go beyond their offers in the Uruguay Round. They also show that unilateral liberalization, especially by the more protectionist OECD countries, will enhance the welfare of both the liberalizing countries and the global economy.

The overall gains estimated by the model should not mask the losses – particularly those that are concentrated in the vulnerable least-developed countries, where the consequences of higher food prices could be particularly severe. These countries require the vigilance and support of the international community, so that the overwhelming gains of the Uruguay Round are not tarnished by the unacceptable suffering of those that must endure the marginal negative consequences. Greater stability in world prices and other benefits that we have been unable to quantify suggest that overall improvements in welfare should go well beyond those indicated in our assessment, also touching the countries that we identify as net losers. The reform of the MFA, enhanced technological and other transfers, improved market access, more rapid global growth, and a more transparent and egalitarian trade environment will benefit all countries. For developing countries, these factors – which we could not incorporate into our modeling analysis – should offset any possible negative effects associated with higher world food prices. We also emphasize that the price changes expected under the Uruguay Round are well below those associated with normal instability in world markets, and that they are to be phased in during a five- to ten-year period. During this time, prices for primary commodities and food should continue their secular decline, so that the higher prices induced by trade reform will not necessarily imply a structural increase in the cost of food imports to deficit countries.

For food-importing countries and others, the effect of the Uruguay Round will depend ultimately on the actions of the individual countries themselves. Our analysis isolated trade reforms from other economic reforms. The extent to which the potential benefits from trade reforms are passed on to domestic producers and consumers and the agility and flexibility of economies in responding to the opportunities offered by trade reforms will determine the level and distribution of the gains in any country and globally. The message of our analysis is that, although the Uruguay Round established a solid foundation for reform, liberalization has been hesitant at best, particularly in agriculture, where reforms were not as widespread as had initially been intended. Further trade liberalization, undertaken unilaterally by countries and reinforced by subsequent multilateral trade negotiations, will enhance the welfare of reform-minded countries and enrich the global economy. Trade liberalization should remain a top priority, particularly in OECD countries, where protectionist policies continue to undermine welfare and crowd out the exports and economic progress of developing and formerly centrally planned economies.

Appendix A   Regional composition of RUNS

South Asia

> *Afghanistan, Bangladesh, Bhutan, Kampuchea, Democratic Republic of Korea, Laos, Maldives, Mongolia, Myanmar, Nepal, Pakistan, Sri Lanka, Viet Nam*

China

India

East Asia and the Pacific
> *Brunei, Fiji, French Polynesia, Hong Kong, Republic of Korea, Macao, Malaysia, New Caledonia, New Hebrides, Papua New Guinea, Philippines, Singapore, Taiwan, Thailand, Tonga*

Indonesia

Sub-Saharan Africa
> *Angola, Benin, Botswana, Burkina Faso, Burundi, Cameroon, Cape Verde, Central African Republic, Chad, Comoros, People's Republic of the Congo, Côte d'Ivoire, Equatorial Guinea, Ethiopia, Gabon, The Gambia, Ghana, Guinea, Kenya, Lesotho, Liberia, Madagascar, Malawi, Mali, Mauritania, Mauritius, Mozambique, Namibia, Niger, Reunion, Rwanda, Sao Tome and Principe, Senegal, Seychelles, Sierra Leone, Somalia, Sudan, Swaziland, Tanzania, Togo, Uganda, Zaïre, Zambia, Zimbabwe*

Nigeria

South Africa

Maghreb
> *Algeria, Morocco, Tunisia*

Mediterranean
> *Cyprus, Arab Republic of Egypt, Israel, Jordan, Lebanon, Libya, Malta, Syrian Arab Republic, Turkey*

Gulf region
> *Bahrain, Iraq, Islamic Republic of Iran, Kuwait, Oman, Qatar, Saudi Arabia, United Arab Emirates, Yemen Arab Republic, People's Democratic Republic of Yemen*

Other Latin America
> *Anguilla, Antigua and Barbuda, Argentina, the Bahamas, Barbados, Belize, Bermuda, Bolivia, Chile, Columbia, Costa Rica, Cuba, Dominican Republic, Ecuador, El Salvador, French Guiana, Grenada, Guadeloupe, Guatemala, Guyana, Haiti, Honduras, Jamaica, Martinique, Netherlands Antilles, Nicaragua, Panama, Paraguay, Peru, Puerto Rico, Saint Kitts and Nevis, Saint Lucia, Saint Vincent and the Grenadines, Suriname, Trinidad and Tobago, Uruguay, Venezuela, Virgin Islands*

Brazil

Mexico

United States

Canada

Australia/New Zealand

Japan

European Union
> *Belgium, Denmark, France, Federal Republic of Germany (including the former German Democratic Republic), Greece, Ireland, Italy, Luxembourg, Netherlands, Portugal, Spain, United Kingdom*

European Free Trade Association
> *Austria, Finland, Iceland, Norway, Sweden, Switzerland*

European economies in transition
  Albania, Bulgaria, Czechoslovakia, Hungary, Poland, Romania, Yugoslavia
Former Soviet Union
  Armenia, Azerbaijan, Belarus, Estonia, Georgia, Kazakstan, Kyrgyz
  Republic, Latvia, Lithuania, Moldova, Russia, Tajikistan, Turkmenistan,
  Ukraine, Uzbekistan

Appendix B   Specifications for the RUNS model

The RUNS model uses a system of separable multi-input/multi-output production functions to characterize agricultural production. Agricultural production is characterized by two distinct types of farming: crop production and livestock production. The crop production sector produces eleven of the fifteen agricultural commodities (wheat, rice, coarse grains, sugar, coffee, cocoa, tea, vegetable oils, other food, cotton, and other nonfood). The livestock production sector produces the other four (beef, veal, and sheep; other meats; dairy; and wool). Urban production is modeled along the classical lines of many CGE models. A Leontief-fixed coefficients structure models intermediate inputs. Substitution is possible between imports and domestic intermediates. The model incorporates two households, rural and urban. It assumes that all rural income is derived from rural production. Each rural and urban household has its own specific consumption function, although the extended linear expenditure system is used to model both.

The government plays its usual role as tax collector, spender on goods and services, and manager over a wide variety of economic instruments. The main tax is a direct tax on household income. Expenditures on goods and services are modeled as fixed shares of a real aggregate expenditure level. The economic instruments include agricultural input subsidies, agricultural price wedges (described later), import tariffs/subsidies, export taxes/subsidies, agricultural stocks, and income transfers. All these instruments generate additional revenue or expenditures that are allocated as fixed shares between the two households and the government. In the base scenario, the government's budget surplus/deficit is endogenous. In the liberalization scenarios, the real budget surplus/deficit is assumed to be fixed (at the base simulation level), and the direct household tax rates are endogenous.

The model also uses the extended linear expenditure system to determine household savings; they can also be derived as a residual from income minus expenditures. Government savings are the residual between government revenue and expenditures. The final component of savings is foreign savings, which are fixed for each region (the sum over all regions is obviously zero).

Agricultural trade is simply the difference between domestic production and domestic demand (including changes in stocks). Each agricultural commodity is modeled as a perfect substitute globally, and thus requiring no agricultural trade matrix.

Because agricultural commodities are homogeneous across the world, world price generally determines the domestic price. In the RUNS model, the government (and parastatal institutions) may intervene, in which case a wedge is generated between the domestic agricultural price and world price. In all cases, international trade occurs at the world price. In the most general form, the domestic agricultural price is set according to the following formula:

$$pp=(\phi pw+(1-\phi)p)(1+\tau)$$

where pw is the world agricultural price, p is a domestic price index, and τ is a scale variable that may be thought of as a tariff equivalent. The parameter ϕ is a critical parameter; it is a pass-through coefficient.

Each region, thus, has four equilibrating variables: two in the urban sector – wages and capital rental rate (urban capital is assumed to be fully utilized at all times) – and two in the rural sector. The only other equilibrium prices in the model are world agricultural prices. World agricultural prices are determined by the equilibrium between world supply and demand. World supply and demand are calculated as the sum of supply and demand in all regions (this is the same as setting the sum of all regions' net trade to zero). The model uses a tâtonnement procedure to determine all equilibrium prices, the four domestic factor prices, and the fifteen world agricultural prices. The model contains three key macro relations – fiscal closure, investment–savings closure, and trade closure. The fiscal balance in the base model is endogenous, and investment is savings driven. The RUNS model has a fixed trade balance closure rule. In any given period, and in all regions, the net trade balance (in value) must sum to the capital flow.

Notes

The findings, interpretations, and conclusions expressed in this chapter are entirely those of the authors and should not be attributed in any manner to the World Bank, to its affiliated organizations, or to members of its Board of Executive Directors or the countries they represent, or to the European Bank for Reconstruction and Development or OECD or their member countries.

The authors wish to thank Sébastien Dessus for his assistance on the RUNS model, the GATT for providing its Integrated Data Base, Merlinda Ingco for organizing and interpreting the data, Mylène Kherallah for providing research assistance, and Will Martin, Dale Hathaway, Dean DeRosa, and anonymous referees for providing helpful comments.

1. The most frequently cited analyses are Goldin, Knudsen, and van der Mensbrugghe (1993), OECD (1993), and GATT (1993).
2. This chapter relies on the work of Merlinda Ingco in interpreting and transforming the data to meet our modeling requirements, see *inter alia*, chapter 2 above.
3. We define protection as the percentage excess of internal prices over border prices. It is determined by import restrictions for commodities that are imported and by export subsidies for those that are exported. In the real world some regions display two-way trade in some commodities. So far as possible, in our

data we represent protection on a commodity by its tariff equivalent for net importers and by its export subsidy for net exporters. In representing the effects of the Round we generally use the changes implied on the import side, because the export subsidy cannot generally exceed the import tariff equivalent (or reimportation occurs) and because it is difficult to quantify precisely the *ad valorem* effects of the cuts in subsidies.

4. Note that table 6.4 reflects the negative change in world prices in relationship to the numeraire, which is the price of OECD manufacturing exports. Thus, for example, a 1 percent decline in coffee prices will have a negative impact, if inputs are primarily manufactured goods.

References

GATT 1993. "An Analysis of the Proposed Uruguay Round Agreement, with Particular Emphasis on Aspects of Interest to Developing Economies." Geneva: GATT Secretariat, Trade Negotiations Committee Group of Negotiations on Goods.

Goldin, I., O. Knudsen, and D. van der Mensbrugghe 1993. *Trade Liberalization: Global Economic Implications*. Paris: OECD.

OECD 1993. "Assessing the Effects of the Uruguay Round." Trade Policy Issues Paper 2. Paris: OECD.

7 Liberalizing manufactures trade in a changing world economy

Thomas Hertel, Will Martin, Koji Yanagishima and Betina Dimaranan

Production and trade in the developing world have grown more rapidly than in the currently industrial countries, and the share of developing countries in world production and trade is expected to increase substantially (World Bank 1994). These differential growth rates will change both the structure of the world economy and the composition of the groups of industrial and developing countries. Given the large differences in the rates of protection that apply to different industries and commodities, these differential growth rates will in turn have a substantial impact on the costs of protection worldwide.

The emergence of developing countries in world production and trade will substantially change world trading patterns – particularly in textiles and clothing, whose importance in industrial countries will continue to decline as the more dynamic areas of the developing world continue to capture larger shares of these markets. But even within the entire group of developing countries, these industries will likely shift from the current leaders, the so-called newly industrial economies of East Asia, to a range of emerging suppliers. Because protection under the current MFA consists of bilateral quotas that do not respond to shifts in comparative advantage, these shifts can be expected to lead to changes in the protection rates the MFA generates, and hence to changes in the size and distribution of the benefits from liberalization.

The Uruguay Round agreement involves a complex, inter-related package of reforms in each major sector (agriculture, manufacturing, and services), and in the rules governing world trade. Surprisingly, industrial countries are supporting reforms in agriculture, in which developing countries are frequently thought to be the main suppliers of primary commodities. Similarly, developing countries are supporting the removal of the MFA whose quotas transfer rents to developing country exporters. But both of these stances are more understandable in a dynamic world where exports of agricultural products from developing countries are expected to

183

grow rapidly and where the MFA would likely frustrate the attempts of developing countries to seize upon their emerging comparative advantage in textiles and clothing.

The purpose of this chapter is to simulate the impacts on real incomes, output, and trade, of the tariff reductions to be phased in during the ten-year implementation period of the Uruguay Round, the expansions in MFA quotas during the same period, and the eventual abolition of the MFA at the end of the period. Our analysis accounts explicitly for the fact that, during this period, the structure of developing economies is expected to change substantially in response to rapid changes in the size of the labor force, the accumulation of physical capital, and increases in human capital. It thus captures the impact of changes in the structure of the world economy on the gains from trade liberalization.

The extent of protection under Uruguay Round liberalization

Estimates of the pattern and extent of liberalization under the Uruguay Round are provided in other chapters of this volume. Our purpose here is to summarize the reductions in protection actually used in our model simulations – weighted averages for the pre-Round and post-Round tariffs for manufactures and food imports by region, and trade-weighted average price cuts (table 7.1).

Tariff reductions for manufactures

Pre-Round tariffs on nonfood manufactures were quite low among OECD countries, ranging from an average of 4.3 percent in the United States and Canada to 6.5 percent in the European Union. However, they were considerably higher in several East Asian countries. Korea's average pre-Round manufacturing tariff was 16.1 percent; the comparable figures in the Philippines and Thailand were 23.9 percent and 36.2 percent, respectively. The South Asia region had the highest pre-Round rate of manufacturing protection, at 51.9 percent. (Note that Taiwan [China], Hong Kong, and China are not covered by the GATT's IDB. In our quantitative analysis, we set tariffs for Taiwan [China], Hong Kong, and China on the basis of the applied rates used in the GTAP data base [Chyc *et al.* forthcoming], and we use these rates throughout our simulations.)

The largest absolute reductions in manufactures tariffs from the pre- to post-Round rates are in the Republic of Korea, Thailand, and South Asia. The *proportional* reduction is large in OECD countries; for example, Japan's post-Round average tariff on manufactures is less than half of its pre-Round average. But because the initial level of protection was lower in the OECD countries, the effective average cuts in import prices are not significantly larger than the import price cuts in other regions. The largest average cuts in import prices are in Korea (6.8 percent), Thailand (5.9 percent), and South Asia (9.4 percent). The average import price cut in Latin America is only 1.6 percent, despite the region's huge unilateral reductions in applied rates of protection.[1] The reduction in import prices in Sub-Saharan Africa is even smaller, at 0.1 percent, implying that the region's Uruguay Round commitments will impose little discipline on protection in this region.

Reductions in protection for food and agriculture

While not the focus of this chapter, we also consider agricultural liberalization measures under the Uruguay Round because they affect our economy-wide simulations. To the extent that cuts in food and agricultural protection in a given region are relatively deeper than the manufacturing cuts, resources will tend to flow into manufacturing, thus leading to an expansion in manufacturing output. The pre-Uruguay Round tariff equivalents of agricultural protection are based on estimates of the average rate applying during the 1982–92 period to capture the wide year-to-year variability of these tariff equivalents (Ingco forthcoming).

In contrast to the reductions in manufacturing protection, the reductions in food and agriculture protection are much more varied (see table 7.1). Average cuts in the price of agricultural imports are small in North America, Europe, and much of the developing world. Yet they are deeper than the cuts in manufacturing import prices in much of East Asia, where the initial levels of protection were quite high. The pre-Round food tariff for South Asia indicates that the region subsidizes food imports on average, and the extent of this subsidy increases slightly under the Round because the protection on some commodities is reduced.

Reductions in protection from import quotas

The import quotas imposed under the MFA are another important form of industrial sector protection that affects exports from developing countries. Since exporters from developing countries must either purchase a scarce export quota before making an export shipment or pass up the opportunity to sell (or otherwise transfer) a valuable quota received from the government, the effect of these quotas is analogous to an export tax levied by the government in the country of origin; the quota generates rents that accrue to the firms to which the government allocates quotas. The protective effects of these bilateral quotas can thus be estimated on the basis of export-tax equivalents, which differ by country of destination.[2]

Table 7.1 *Average pre- and post-Uruguay Round protection levels, by importing region*

Importing region	Manufactures			Food		
	Pre-Round tariff (percent)	Post-Round tariff (percent)	Average change in import prices (percent)[a]	Pre-Round tariff (percent)	Post-Round tariff (percent)	Average change in import prices (percent)[a]
United States & Canada	4.3	2.8	−1.4	11.7	11.0	−0.6
European Union	6.5	3.9	−2.4	26.5	26.0	−0.3
Japan	4.9	2.1	−2.7	87.8	56.1	−8.1
Korea	16.1	8.2	−6.8	99.5	41.1	−17.9
Taiwan (China)	0.0	0.0	0.0	0.0	0.0	0.0
Hong Kong	0.0	0.0	0.0	0.0	0.0	0.0
China	0.0	0.0	0.0	0.0	0.0	0.0
Indonesia	14.2	13.5	−0.6	21.9	15.5	−4.2
Malaysia	11.0	7.7	−2.9	87.9	34.3	−14.9
Philippines	23.9	21.5	−1.8	86.9	33.4	−15.3
Thailand	36.2	27.6	−5.9	59.8	34.5	−10.8
Latin America	17.1	14.9	−1.6	2.3	1.5	−0.5
Sub-Saharan Africa	9.5	9.4	−0.1	15.6	12.4	−1.7
South Asia	51.9	37.1	−9.4	−3.5	−4.4	−0.7
Rest of world	10.6	9.1	−1.3	15.7	14.1	−1.2

[a]Change in tariff rate divided by the power of the initial tariff rate. This is the average of the disaggregate price cuts, and thus may differ from the price cuts computed from the average tariffs.

Notes: the integrated database does not cover Taiwan (China), Hong Kong, and China. The values in the table were calculated as follows:

1. The trade-weighted average protection rates for manufactures were calculated using disaggregated tariff and trade data obtained from the WTO's IDB files. The pre-Round estimates used are the lower of the Uruguay Round base rate in the IDB and the applied tariff rate reported by the country, generally for 1988, 1989, or 1990. The Uruguay Round base rate is the bound tariff rate if the tariff was bound at the beginning of the Uruguay Round, or the tariff rate applied in September 1986 if the tariff rate was not previously bound. In most industrial countries, the pre-Round bound tariff rate was the same as the applied rate for the vast majority of commodities, and so the rate reported is *both* the bound and the applied rate. In developing countries, only about one fifth of industrial products were subject to bound tariffs prior to the Uruguay Round (see chapter 5), and so the average pre-Round tariffs are more typically the applied rates. The approach means that the Uruguay Round agreement creates a measured tariff reduction only when the final binding is lower than the applied rate in mid-Round.

2. The estimates of post-Round tariffs are calculated with the rule that the rate of protection is reduced when the final, bound tariff is less than the pre-Round tariff rate. Thus, the estimates neglect the liberalizing effects of tariff bindings introduced without any reduction in the applied tariff rates. Since bindings without tariff reductions covered only 3 percent of imports of industrial goods into industrial countries (GATT 1994), this omission is unlikely to be important for these countries. In developing countries, bindings without tariff reductions covered 28 percent of total imports of industrial goods, and this omission may be somewhat more serious. Where these bindings have been set well above currently applied rates, and their liberalizing effects are therefore limited, this omission will not be serious.

3. The figures reported for food import barriers are aggregated from estimates prepared by Ingco (forthcoming), based on average historical protection rates derived from OECD and United States Department of Agriculture to represent the trade distortions that would have prevailed in the absence of the Round, and on country schedule data to represent post-Uruguay Round rates of protection. In this data set, the rate of protection is reduced only when the post-Uruguay Round rate of protection is below the historical average rate of protection. This approach overlooks reductions in average protection rates induced by the introduction of bindings above current rates, but overstates the marginal reduction in protection induced by a binding that reduces protection below its historical average levels (Martin and Francois 1994). This simple approach also rules out estimating the welfare gains obtained from reducing the variability of protection (Francois and Martin 1995).

Source: IDB, WTO.

Our estimates of the effective export-tax equivalents of MFA quotas imposed by the major importing regions against textile and clothing imports from each of the exporting regions or countries (table 7.2, "1992" columns) are based on publicly available data on the value of quotas transferred in Hong Kong, and on detailed country studies in other major exporting countries (see Hertel forthcoming). Our analysis indicates that these bilateral quotas are generally more severely binding for wearing apparel than for textiles, generating larger export-tax equivalents, and that the share of exports from these exporters to the restricted markets is also much larger for wearing apparel. Of the countries and regions in our analysis, Indonesia faces the highest export taxes, with rates of 46 percent on wearing apparel exports to the United States and Canada, and 48 percent to the European Union. China and South Asia face the next highest export taxes in wearing apparel to these markets at an identical 40 percent and 36 percent respectively. Korea, Taiwan (China), and Hong Kong face comparatively low export taxes on wearing apparel, reflecting the fact that they are losing their comparative advantage in this sector.

Table 7.2 also reports the share of textile and wearing apparel exports shipped to the MFA-restricted markets. This share could be an important indicator of the extent to which exports are being diverted from the restricted markets into the generally much less lucrative unrestricted markets. Countries with a small quota allocation relative to their production potential are forced to divert a large share of their exports into unrestricted markets. Yang, Martin, and Yanagishima (forthcoming) show that this share is an important determinant of whether an exporter will gain or lose from the eventual abolition of the MFA.

Quota growth rates

The ATC calls for liberalizing the MFA by increasing quota growth rates during the ten-year transitional period, and by integrating textile and clothing items progressively into the GATT system. The tariff ceilings to be integrated under GATT have been selected by the importing countries, and it appears that few commodities that are currently subject to binding quotas will be integrated into GATT until near the end of the transition period.[3] Our analysis thus deals with these two components separately – acceleration of quota growth rates, and the (re)introduction of the GATT disciplines for textiles and clothing. Specifically, in our simulations, the export-tax equivalents respond to changes in demand and supply relative to the exogenous quota growth rates. The resulting tax equivalents are given in the 2005 columns of table 7.2. A subsequent simulation eliminates the quotas to assess them completely under GATT disciplines.

Table 7.2 *Share of total exports of textiles or wearing apparel sent to restricted markets and export tax equivalents for MFA quotas: percentage of market prices in exporting region, 1992 and 2005*

	Textiles									Wearing apparel								
	Share to restricted markets			Export-tax equivalents						Share to restricted markets			Export-tax equivalents					
				United States & Canada			European Union						United States & Canada			European Union		
MFA exporter	1992	2005	NR	1992	2005	NR	1992	2005	NR	1992	2005	NR	1992	2005	NR	1992	2005	NR
Korea	15	10	14	10	21	14	10	25	16	58	36	54	23	38	35	19	37	33
Taiwan (China)	12	7	7	8	21	25	12	27	28	83	69	76	19	29	33	22	37	39
Hong Kong	7	4	4	7	12	17	8	20	22	81	69	70	17	26	29	16	29	32
China	19	14	12	19	31	36	27	40	44	33	19	20	40	58	62	36	60	63
Indonesia	25	24	22	13	15	18	17	27	26	58	56	58	46	56	56	48	66	64
Malaysia	21	18	17	10	13	16	12	23	22	47	55	32	37	46	52	32	50	54
Philippines	50	42	47	9	11	12	10	29	24	84	74	80	33	42	43	28	50	48
Thailand	40	28	32	9	17	16	13	31	25	44	24	33	35	51	48	36	58	53
Latin America	50	66	58	10	0	5	13	9	12	89	95	93	20	15	19	18	19	21
South Asia	45	44	42	19	18	24	27	36	36	83	79	80	40	47	51	36	53	53
Rest of world	59	71	66	5	0	0	6	3	6	87	95	94	16	12	15	10	14	15

Sources: 1992 shares and export taxes from GTAP data base (Chyc *et al.* forthcoming). 2005 shares and export taxes are from the updated data base in simulation 4. The column headed NR reports 2005 tax equivalents in the absence of Uruguay Round reforms – under the base case scenario simulated later in the chapter.

The growth rates of MFA quotas have been negotiated bilaterally. Although the original objective of the MFA was to allow a quota growth rate of at least 6 percent annually for textiles and clothing (GATT 1973, Annex B, para. 2), subsequent negotiations have allowed the growth rates for some exports to be reduced to zero. The base growth rates applying under the final MFA are reported here on a cumulative basis for our 1992–2005 simulation (table 7.3). These rates are generally higher for the United States and Canada than they are for the European Union. Taiwan (China)'s MFA cumulative growth rate is the lowest of all countries and regions, at only 6 percent for wearing apparel exports into the United States and Canada. This is followed by Korea and the rest of the world. The Southeast Asian suppliers show the highest growth rates during the period. For example, Indonesia's cumulative MFA quota growth rate in exports of both textiles and clothing to the United States and Canada is 114 percent.

These pre-Round quota growth rates are to be increased by 16 percent in the first three years of the ATC. In the next four years, the growth rates are to rise by another 25 percent. In the final three years of the ATC, they will be increased by another 27 percent. For a quota currently growing at the MFA's standard growth rate of 6 percent annually, the growth rate in the last three years of the MFA will be more than 11 percent. The difference between MFA and the ATC quota growth rates (see table 7.3) indicates that the accelerated growth rates increase the cumulative growth rates significantly for all countries and regions except China and Taiwan (China), which were not members of the GATT and will not benefit from the quota growth acceleration or the abolition of quotas until after becoming members.

The projected impact of Uruguay Round liberalization: simulation results

Our simulations project what the rates of protection will be for aggregate groups of commodities under various MFA and ATC quota growth rates and tariff reductions at the end of the 1992–2005 transitional period. We begin with a base-case scenario that projects what quota growth rates would have been between 1992 and 2005 in the absence of the Uruguay Round, building up to the abolition of the quotas in 2005 (table 7.4). We use several exogenous growth projections in each region or country to account for changes in the world economy that must be factored into our simulations (appendix A). The simulation model identifies ten industry groups aggregated from data on the original GTAP industries; textiles and wearing apparel are included as separate categories (appendix B).

Table 7.3 Cumulative quota growth rates under the MFA and the Agreement on Textiles and Clothing: 1992–2005 (percent)

	Textiles				Wearing apparel			
	United States/Canada		European Union		United States/Canada		European Union	
Exporters	MFA quota growth rates	ATC quota growth rates	MFA quota growth rates	ATC quota growth rates	MFA quota growth rates	ATC quota growth rates	MFA quota growth rates	ATC quota growth rates
Korea	70	122	60	96	10	14	33	50
Taiwan (China)	34	34	46	46	6	6	33	33
Hong Kong	48	77	14	21	15	22	19	28
China	50	50	69	69	60	60	53	53
Indonesia	113	191	71	114	114	191	100	166
Malaysia	113	191	65	105	110	186	66	105
Philippines	116	193	0	0	103	171	101[a]	157[a]
Thailand	108	182	51	80	106	177	99	165
Latin America	111	198	62	102	100	180	67	106
South Asia	118	202	89	85	121	208	89	85
Rest of the world	115	195	54	84	87	149	39	61

[a]These growth rates were inadvertently set to zero in the simulations.

Source: S. Bagchi, International Textiles and Clothing Bureau, Geneva, personal communication.

Table 7.4   *Description of the simulations*

Simulation

1. Base case
Real GDP exogenous
Economywide TFP growth rates endogenous
Exogenous MFA quota growth

2. Acceleration of MFA quota growth rates under the ATC
TFP growth exogenous at base case rates
Exogenous quota growth at ATC rates

3. Uruguay Round tariff cuts
TFP and MFA quota growth exogenous at base case rates
Reductions in import tariffs for all merchandise trade
   including agriculture

4. Elimination of MFA from updated 2005 data base, following simulations 2 and 3.

Changes in the world economy: 1992–2005

As background for our analysis we now briefly consider how the world economy is expected to change during the 1992–2005 transitional period. Between 1992 and 2005, more rapid rates of factor accumulation and of productivity growth in developing countries will spur higher rates of income growth in these countries; developing countries will also have proportionately higher rates of population and labor force growth than industrial countries by 2005. Furthermore, given high rates of savings and investment in East Asia in particular, the capital–labor ratios of these economies should increase, exerting supply-side pressures on these countries to change the composition of their output (Krueger 1977; and Leamer 1987). The relatively high rates of human capital accumulation in developing economies (Nehru, Swanson, and Dubey 1995) are also likely to exert pressures for structural change as developing countries upgrade the skill-intensity of their product mix.

Changes in the patterns of economic activity will also be determined by differences in the income responsiveness of demand for particular goods. In general, raw agricultural products, such as grains, are likely to respond little to increases in per capita income, especially in the wealthier economies.[4] Meanwhile, the demand for many services is likely to increase sharply. Changes in the demand for such basic consumer goods as wearing apparel are likely to fall in between, with increases in income having a modest effect on demand.

Particularly important for our purposes are the likely changes in the structure of the clothing sector. It is clear that the more advanced of the MFA exporters (Hong Kong, Taiwan [China], and Korea) are losing competitiveness in these sectors, while the competitiveness of some of the newer exporters in Southeast Asia and South Asia is growing rapidly. If this trend continues, the limited ability of the MFA quota system to allow production to transfer among suppliers will lead to increased costs. Both changes in the pattern of trade in textiles and apparel and changes in the export-tax equivalents of MFA quotas will be crucial determinants of the impacts of liberalization on welfare (Yang, Martin, and Yanagishima forthcoming).

To project what the world economy might look like in the year 2005, we simulate the GTAP model by shocking a relatively small number of fundamental determinants of output. The GTAP model is a standard, multiregion, applied general equilibrium model that assumes perfectly competitive markets and constant returns to scale technology (Hertel and Tsigas forthcoming). Unlike most such models, GTAP relies on a sophisticated representation of consumer demands that allows for differences in the income responsiveness of demand in different regions according to both their level of development and their particular consumption patterns observed in that region.[5] We follow Gehlhar (1994) in using human capital to supplement the usual production technology – that is, we treat it as a complementary input to physical capital in the production function.

Base-case projections: simulation 1

Based on the composition of value-added at constant prices under the base case, the importance of the agricultural and food sectors would decline worldwide except in Sub-Saharan Africa (table 7.5). The decline in the relative importance of food production reflects the lower income elasticities of demand for these products, which tend to decline progressively as per capita income increases. This decline is particularly rapid in the high performing Asian economies where high rates of capital accumulation tend to "pull" labor out of the agricultural sector into other sectors (Martin and Warr 1993; Gehlhar, Hertel, and Martin 1994).

The importance of wearing apparel production would decline in the industrial economies, including Hong Kong, Korea, and Taiwan (China) and increase in Southeast Asian exporters. The size of the transportation machinery and equipment sector would expand in the European Union and the United States and Canada, but the expansion of this sector would be even greater in some of the East Asian economies. With only three exceptions, the service sector would expand worldwide.

Table 7.5 Simulation 1: changes in the composition of value-added 1992–2005 (evaluated at 1992 prices), by region and sector

Regions	Sectors									
	Primary agriculture	Processed food	Natural resource-based industries	Textiles	Wearing apparel	Light manufacturing	Transportation, machinery, and equipment	Heavy manufacturing	Utilities, housing & construction services	Other services
United States and Canada	-18	-20	2	-11	-19	-10	19	1	-1	0
European Union	-22	-25	-9	-23	-45	-18	13	-14	-14	13
Japan	-9	-11	21	-16	-31	0	-9	3	7	1
Korea	-63	-35	7	-36	-60	20	-10	14	-12	21
Taiwan (China)	-50	-32	17	48	-52	44	-37	62	11	-5
Hong Kong	-35	91	36	64	-49	95	20	68	11	-12
China	-82	-9	43	47	23	82	34	113	31	4
Indonesia	-46	-6	-37	9	-2	40	30	61	13	35
Malaysia	-64	-10	-47	3	30	49	-34	-12	-14	62
Philippines	-14	-1	4	0	13	-4	-42	4	-7	10
Thailand	-77	-23	-67	0	-4	47	-19	23	0	40
Latin America	-15	-11	18	-6	-6	-7	-36	-8	-22	12
Sub-Saharan Africa	12	17	-21	11	47	-5	-51	-13	-13	7
South Asia	-30	1	22	23	21	38	33	38	44	-4
Rest of world	-23	-13	-18	-13	-20	-5	-9	-9	-3	11

Under the base case, the total volume of trade would increase dramatically (table 7.6). Trade would increase along all routes, with the largest percentage increases (200 to 300 percent) in intra-Asian trade. The world trade volume would increase by almost $2 trillion at 1992 prices. In essence, international trade would grow dramatically by the end of the Uruguay Round even in the absence of the anticipated cuts in protection.

Because the growth of bilateral quotas would be restricted by the MFA in the absence of the Uruguay Round, export-tax equivalents would adjust during the period. (The columns headed NR in table 7.2 report the projected restricted market shares and export-tax equivalents associated with the MFA under simulation 1.) With the exception of the rest of the world and Latin America, the shares of textiles and apparel exports sold to the restricted markets would diminish over the period, due partly to the rapid growth of demand in other markets (particularly in Asia), and partly to inadequate growth of the quotas. Because the quotas would grow less rapidly than the underlying growth of these markets, the associated bilateral tax equivalents would increase significantly in the 1992–2005 period under MFA quota rates. In other words, had the MFA not been replaced by the WTO agreement, the trade distortions that it induces would have increased significantly, increasing the costs of the arrangement. In the past, exports of MFA-constrained goods have frequently been able to grow more rapidly than the quotas, thus alleviating increases in the quota premiums. But in recent years, the administration of the quotas in the major markets has been tightened considerably, with the increased use of more encompassing quota categories. It thus seems unlikely that exports will be able to grow much more rapidly than the quotas in the future.

The net effect of the Uruguay Round on these export-tax equivalents is uncertain. On the one hand, accelerated quota growth rates under the ATC will reduce the severity of these bilateral restrictions and thus reduce the associated quota rents. On the other, tariff cuts on clothing and wearing apparel will have precisely the opposite effect, since cuts in tariffs on quota-restricted products simply amount to a transfer of this revenue from the importing region to the exporting region.

Impact of accelerated quota growth: simulation 2

Simulation 2 projects the impact of introducing accelerated quota growth rates under the ATC (see table 7.3). Recall that the growth rates – and thus the accelerated growth rates – are greatest for the United States and Canada. As such, we expect that simulation 2 would have the greatest impact on textiles and wearing apparel outputs in the United States and Canada and its predominant suppliers of imports.

Table 7.6 Simulation 1: changes in total volume of exports, 1992–2005 (US $millions, 1992) percentage changes (in parentheses)

				Importers							
Exporting regions	United States and Canada	European Union	Japan	Newly industrializing economies of Asia[a]	China	Association of Southeast Asian Nations[b]	Latin America	Sub-Saharan Africa	South Asia	Rest of world	Total exports
United States & Canada	87,382 (47)	43,532 (26)	22,124 (26)	51,611 (102)	24,655 (182)	27,810 (150)	41,082 (48)	2,245 (51)	5,540 (110)	34,096 (37)	340,077
European Union	42,613 (37)	—	14,821 (34)	24,865 (79)	18,980 (190)	23,252 (134)	18,134 (48)	14,411 (59)	13,618 (138)	89,321 (27)	260,015
Japan	3,412 (3)	−285 (−0)	—	39,217 (57)	13,621 (102)	25,804 (86)	1,160 (7)	891 (23)	3,153 (77)	3,622 (6)	90,594
Newly industrializing economies of Asia[a]	54,475 (89)	34,207 (76)	31,349 (100)	33,598 (134)	67,613 (221)	31,601 (217)	10,747 (123)	4,646 (131)	6,532 (198)	33,787 (92)	308,556
China	56,624 (219)	37,849 (226)	37,582 (216)	102,477 (197)	—	12,531 (345)	4,962 (188)	1,562 (140)	2,712 (213)	36,800 (260)	293,106
Association of Southeast Asian Nations[b]	33,963 (129)	28,089 (137)	34,087 (109)	22,077 (163)	6,540 (208)	11,789 (219)	3,537 (228)	3,617 (249)	4,186 (256)	40,339 (149)	188,224
Latin America	42,990 (54)	26,852 (67)	6,832 (57)	6,027 (113)	2,550 (128)	3,099 (140)	18,341 (59)	764 (71)	930 (121)	9,389 (79)	117,774

Sub-Saharan Africa	2,515	15,893	755	463	738	1,528	396	928	822	1,967	26,004
	(21)	(74)	(51)	(100)	(218)	(213)	(22)	(68)	(152)	(70)	
South Asia	5,494	8,023	986	2,750	581	4,060	573	888	1,377	9,427	34,160
	(87)	(76)	(26)	(102)	(202)	(222)	(165)	(109)	(114)	(111)	
Rest of world	17,619	94,526	16,709	26,757	9,936	25,835	4,634	3,067	14,247	34,759	248,088
	(24)	(30)	(21)	(66)	(105)	(90)	(31)	(64)	(117)	(26)	
Total imports	347,087	288,686	165,245	309,841	145,222	167,310	103,566	33,018	53,118	293,507	1,906,599

[a]The newly industrializing economies of Asia group in this table is Hong Kong, Korea, and Taiwan (China).
[b]The Association of Southeast Asian Nations group is Indonesia, Malaysia, the Philippines, and Thailand.

The consequences of quota acceleration for cumulative changes in output and trade of textiles and clothing from 1992 to 2005 are measured in table 7.7 as the difference between the percentage change in output in simulation 2 and the percentage change in output under the base case. A positive number indicates that output in 2005 will be greater under the ATC than under the MFA. For example, quota acceleration would reduce the output of textiles in the United States and Canada by 7 percent; the volume of textile imports into the United States and Canada would increase by 14 percent. The percentage changes in the output and imports of clothing are twice as large. Since the rates of acceleration are comparable for the two products, this difference may be attributed to the larger elasticity of substitution between clothing imports and domestic clothing (roughly double in size).

Further analysis shows that output would also fall in the European Union, particularly for wearing apparel, whose production would decline by 7 percent and whose imports would increase by 13 percent. Exports from Japan and Sub-Saharan Africa, which are not directly affected by the MFA quotas, would decline as competition from MFA suppliers intensifies under accelerated quota growth. In contrast, the export and output of textiles in Taiwan (China) would actually increase, despite the fact that its quotas are not affected by the ATC (table 7.3). This is because it supplies textile products to the East Asian exporters, particularly Malaysia, Indonesia, and the Philippines, whose output of wearing apparel would increase by 20 to 30 percent under the accelerated quotas.

Impact of reductions in tariffs: simulation 3

Simulation 3 projects the impact of the Uruguay Round tariff cuts (as well as reductions in agricultural export subsidies) on changes in the pattern of output during the 1992–2005 period, with bilateral exports of textiles and clothing to the major MFA import markets – the United States and Canada and the European Union – restricted to grow at base case rates (table 7.8). The results represent the difference between simulation 3 and the base case scenario. Overall, the largest changes in output due to these reductions in import protection would occur in agriculture, food, textiles, and wearing apparel. These areas are targeted for the deepest reductions in import protection.

Agriculture in most of the East Asian economies would contract due to substantial reductions in protection for farm produce; the opposite would be the case with processed food, which would expand in Korea, Taiwan (China), Malaysia, and the Philippines due to lower input costs and an expansion in imports in some of their other markets. In the Philippines, for

Table 7.7 *Effects of quota acceleration and of quota abolition on the output and trade of textiles and wearing apparel by region in 2005 (percentage changes)*

| | Quota acceleration | | | | | | Quota abolition | | | | | |
| | Textiles | | | Wearing apparel | | | Textiles | | | Wearing apparel | | |
Regions	Output	Volume of exports	Volume of imports	Output	Volume of exports	Volume of imports	Output	Volume of exports	Volume of imports	Output	Volume of exports	Volume of imports
United States and Canada	-7	-6	14	-14	-7	32	-12	-10	3	-44	-35	76
European Union	-2	1	15	-7	-1	13	-5	3	17	-46	5	62
Japan	-1	-4	-1	0	-31	0	0	0	-1	0	-64	-3
Korea	5	10	3	2	5	0	8	11	8	11	25	-1
Taiwan (China)	3	6	1	0	0	0	9	13	5	6	17	1
Hong Kong	3	3	2	6	7	1	13	16	0	9	10	-15
China	1	4	0	1	1	0	8	14	12	32	59	11
Indonesia	14	15	15	30	40	4	42	3	74	165	210	18
Malaysia	16	16	8	21	29	1	24	10	17	67	88	0
Philippines	13	20	19	28	41	2	31	10	50	70	92	1
Thailand	8	22	7	8	29	2	15	12	21	26	57	6
Latin America	5	33	6	9	68	3	-4	-13	-5	-11	-49	-4
Sub-Saharan Africa	-4	-17	-6	-23	-85	-3	-8	-21	-11	-37	-82	-6
South Asia	3	9	4	12	32	4	12	23	18	51	123	13
Rest of world	6	21	4	7	25	1	-9	-16	-9	-21	-59	-5

Table 7.8 Impact of all Uruguay Round tariff cuts and agricultural export subsidy reductions on the pattern of output, by region and sector (percentage changes)

Regions	Sectors									
	Primary agriculture	Processed food	Natural resource-based industries	Textiles	Wearing apparel	Light manufac-turing	Transportation, machinery, and equipment	Heavy manufac-turing	Utilities, housing & construction services	Other services
United States and Canada	3	0	0	-2	-1	-2	0	-1	0	0
European Union	-6	-3	0	0	-1	-1	1	0	0	1
Japan	-16	-7	2	3	-7	2	0	1	1	1
Korea	-22	19	-5	103	54	22	-15	2	3	0
Taiwan (China)	3	20	-1	-18	5	0	-3	-6	1	0
Hong Kong	-2	-41	23	-3	5	5	6	0	2	-1
China	3	-11	-3	-13	7	9	-5	-7	1	0
Indonesia	-3	2	-1	0	53	3	2	-1	1	1
Malaysia	-33	292	-21	-23	-92	-49	-36	112	8	-12
Philippines	-39	50	-8	-1	21	-11	5	-10	3	-3
Thailand	-14	-2	-10	-8	82	1	32	8	2	1
Latin America	0	-1	1	-5	-4	-1	-1	-1	0	1
Sub-Saharan Africa	-2	-5	1	2	20	2	1	0	0	1
South Asia	3	17	-3	-4	7	7	-31	-23	0	1
Rest of world	0	-5	-1	-9	-11	2	3	0	0	0

example, the projected impact on the production of processed food would be an increase of 50 percent of its 1992 production; one third of this increase would come from domestic sales.

The output of processed food in Malaysia would increase by an astounding 292 percent over the thirteen-year period due to the reductions in agricultural protection, which would reduce input costs in this industry. Virtually all of this increase would come from an increase in exports, supported primarily by a decline in the cost of producing processed food in Malaysia. Half of the increase in exports would go to the rest of the world, primarily Singapore. Of course, one of the major developments in the rest of the world is the reduction of export subsidies from the European Union, opening up markets for competitive suppliers to the rest of the world. But because Malaysia and the European Union compete only in a few export markets, some of the forecast expansion in processed food exports from Malaysia is probably due to the illusion of competition arising from our model's excessive aggregation of both regions (the rest of the world) and commodities (processed food). These particular results should thus be interpreted with more than the usual caution.

In the textiles industry, tariff cuts would benefit producers in Korea, who would expand to meet the increase in demand by the domestic apparel industry (45 percent of the increase in output) and displace some production in other regions. Tariff cuts in apparel would expand production in most of the developing world with the exception of Latin America and Malaysia (where other sectors would expand significantly). Indeed, given the strong expansion in processed food and heavy manufacturing, most of the other sectors in Malaysia would be forced to contract. The expansion of heavy manufacturing in Malaysia would be due primarily to an increase in exports.

Eliminating the quotas in 2005: simulation 4

Simulation 4 assesses the incremental consequences of eliminating the MFA in the year 2005 after allowing for quota growth and tariff changes. Recall that, relative to 1992, the 2005 equilibrium projected by the model embodies some very important changes to the world economy as a whole. In particular, the comparative size of developing countries will have increased significantly. China, for example, will have grown at a cumulative rate five times higher than the United States and Canada. As a result, it will be almost three times as large in the year 2005 as it was in the 1992 base year. In contrast, the European Union will be only one third larger, meaning that more of the world's market for textiles, apparel, and other products will be in regions other than the United States and Canada and the European Union. The shift is reflected in the generally smaller export shares to these restricted markets in the year 2005.

Equally important is the changing pattern of comparative advantage (see table 7.5). By the year 2005, the developing East Asian economies (with the exception of the Philippines) will have significantly increased their comparative advantage at producing physical and human capital-intensive commodities. In contrast, Latin America and Sub-Saharan Africa, will have actually experienced declines in their capital–labor ratios.

The reduction in output with the abolition of the MFA quotas in the year 2005 will be most significant on apparel – 44 percent in the United States and Canada, and 46 percent in the European Union (table 7.7) – since the elasticity of substitution among products from different sources is relatively larger than for textiles. The reduction in textile output in the European Union due to the elimination of the MFA would be only 5 percent, due in part to an increase in textile exports. The same phenomenon is also evident in the apparel industry of the European Union, simply reflecting the increase in intraindustry trade stimulated by the elimination of the MFA. Intermediate inputs, including designs and specialized inputs, must be supplied to the manufacturers in these regions that export finished clothing to the European Union and the United States and Canada.

The Southeast Asian exporters would show the strongest increase in textile and apparel output (again see table 7.7). Without the reforms, Indonesia would have faced the highest tax equivalents in the European Union and would also have continued to supply a relatively large share of its wearing apparel output to restricted markets in the year 2005. It would thus show the largest increase in clothing output with the elimination of the MFA at 165 percent. It is followed by the Philippines at 70 percent and Malaysia at 67 percent. In Latin America, Sub-Saharan Africa, and the rest of the world, the output of textiles and wearing apparel actually fall with the elimination of the MFA, because these regions would have been relatively unconstrained producers in the year 2005, and face increased competition after abolition of the MFA.

Distribution of welfare gains from the Round

The aggregate welfare effects of the Uruguay Round (that is, increases in real income as a percentage of GDP) are reported here as both percentage changes and as equivalent variations based on expenditure levels in the year 2005 (table 7.9). The global welfare gain from the Uruguay Round would be $258 billion, or 0.89 percent of projected 2005 expenditure levels (last row, second column of table 7.9). The largest aggregate gains would accrue to the European Union, Japan, the newly industrializing economies of

Table 7.9 *Welfare gains (increases in real income) under the Uruguay Round: total by component, by region*

Regions	Percentage change in welfare	US $million	Quota growth acceleration	Tariff cuts	MFA abolition
	Percentage change in welfare		Gains in US $million from individual components (percentage change in parentheses)		
United States and Canada	0.40	32,130	5,829 (18)	2,797 (9)	23,505 (73)
European Union	0.72	56,530	2,674 (5)	28,934 (51)	24,922 (44)
Japan	1.04	43,009	327 (1)	41,923 (97)	759 (2)
Newly industrialized economies of Asia	3.82	39,022	111 (0)	45,221 (116)	−6,310 (−16)
China	1.46	19,993	−522 (−3)	14,644 (73)	5,872 (29)
Indonesia	2.94	7,101	1,019 (14)	3,595 (51)	2,487 (35)
Malaysia	21.38	34,187	242 (1)	34,827 (102)	−881 (−3)
Philippines	6.63	5,497	321 (6)	5,343 (97)	−167 (−3)
Thailand	4.54	10,531	873 (8)	8,947 (85)	711 (7)
Latin America	−0.08	−1,258	585 (−46)	2,453 (−195)	−4,296 (341)
Sub-Saharan Africa	−0.51	−1,233	−78 (6)	−558 (45)	−597 (48)
South Asia	1.93	11,101	1,056 (10)	8,084 (73)	1,960 (18)
Rest of world	0.03	1,147	402 (35)	11,452 (998)	−10,707 (−933)
Total	0.89	257,758	12,838 (5)	207,661 (81)	37,259 (14)

Note: because the underlying model is a relatively standard, constant-returns-to-scale version, these measures reflect only the static gains from trade liberalization for which we have relatively well-developed measurement techniques. Therefore, the numbers should be viewed as conservative estimates of the potential gains under the Round.

Asia, and Malaysia, followed by the United States and Canada. In total, the United States and Canada, the European Union, and Japan would account for almost half of the total gains, the newly industrializing economies of Asia for 15 percent, and developing countries for the remaining 34 percent, or about $87 billion.

Malaysia would stand to reap the largest proportionate gains from the Uruguay Round, with a 21 percent increase. Virtually all of this gain would come from the tariff cuts, which would stimulate large increases in the production of processed food products and heavy manufactures in Malaysia. Combining the effects of the ATC and elimination of the MFA, Malaysia would actually lose from the MFA reform. A similar situation would apply in Thailand, where the Uruguay Round-induced percentage changes in welfare would amount to 6.6 percent; of these gains, 97 percent would come from nonMFA-related cuts.

In contrast to the other countries in the ASEAN, Indonesia would reap half of its total welfare gain (about 3 percent of GDP) from MFA reforms. China and South Asia would reap 27 percent of their respective welfare increases from trade reform in textiles and apparel. The gains to China and to the newly industrial economies of Asia would be much larger if China and Taiwan (China) were members of GATT and thus able to commit to tariff reductions under the Uruguay Round.

The elimination of the MFA is an extremely important source of gains for the restricted importers. The United States and Canada would reap 90 percent of their total gains from the acceleration of the MFA quotas between 1992 and 2005, followed by the elimination of the MFA in 2005. The gains to the European Union from MFA reform are comparable to those for the United States and Canada, but the tariff cuts, combined with reductions in expensive agricultural export subsidies, would benefit the European Union much more, and thus its gain from MFA reform would be smaller.

Two regions would lose from the Uruguay Round package as presented in this chapter: Latin America and Sub-Saharan Africa. Both regions were relatively timid participants in the Uruguay Round, as shown by the depth of cuts in table 7.1. They are also largely on the MFA sideline. Latin America would benefit from the acceleration of quotas under the ATC and the tariff cuts, but would lose from the elimination of the MFA, since it would be displaced from the North American and European markets by Asian suppliers. In the end, the two effects would be offsetting, and Latin America's total loss would be a negligible proportion of GDP.[6]

The only region that would lose significantly under the Uruguay Round would be Sub-Saharan Africa, with losses of around half a percent of GDP. This region would be hurt by all three components of the agreement analyzed here. Its losses from the global tariff reduction package would be due to deteriorations in the terms of trade that would not be offset by sizable efficiency gains from the liberalization of the region's own trade policies. In other regions where more substantial liberalization is undertaken, these efficiency gains would be sufficient to outweigh any losses in terms of trade. Further liberalization seems the most promising approach for overcoming the adverse consequences of the current outcome.

Conclusion: an assessment of the Uruguay Round in a changing world economy

This chapter has assessed the impact of the Uruguay Round in the context of a changing world economy. With the exception of the RUNS model, which focuses on agriculture (see Goldin, Knudsen, and van der Mensbrugghe 1993; and chapter 6 of this volume), most applied general equilibrium analyses of the Uruguay Round have asked the question: "What would be the effect on the world economy in the base year (for example, 1992) had the Uruguay Round been introduced and had its full effect in that year?" This study, however, began with projections of changes in the world economy in the period in which the final agreement will actually be phased in. These projections portray a world economy in which the center of economic gravity is shifting markedly towards the south and towards Asia. In addition, the pattern of comparative advantage is expected to change during the period, as East Asian economies gain a comparative advantage in the production of physical and human capital-intensive products. These changes make a significant difference in our analysis of the Uruguay Round reforms for manufactures in at least two important respects: the textile and clothing quotas become more severely binding over the period leading up to 2005, despite quota acceleration provisions in the ATC; and the global distribution of production and consumption shifts towards the developing countries, with the result that developing countries would be some of the big gainers from the Uruguay Round.

Our analysis also helps put the Uruguay Round reforms in an appropriate perspective by assessing the percentage changes in sectoral and regional output, between 1992 and 2005 under two alternative scenarios (table 7.10). Regardless of the Uruguay Round, strong growth should continue in Asia across a wide range of sectors. The composition of regional output is also expected to change markedly. Even without MFA reform, the output of textiles and wearing apparel – as well as other manufactures – in the low- to middle-income countries of Asia will continue to increase, with much of the incremental output going to other developing countries. In contrast, the

Table 7.10 *Percentage change in sectoral and regional output: base case (upper entries), and full Uruguay Round (lower entries)*

Regions	Primary agriculture	Processed food	Natural resource-based industries	Textiles	Wearing apparel	Light manufacturing	Transportation, machinery, and equipment	Heavy manufacturing	Utilities, housing & construction services	Other services
United States and Canada	23	21	42	30	22	31	60	42	40	41
	27	21	43	7	-41	30	62	41	40	41
European Union	12	8	24	11	-12	15	46	19	19	46
	5	5	24	3	-60	15	48	19	20	47
Japan	30	28	60	23	8	38	30	42	46	40
	13	21	62	25	1	40	29	43	47	40
Korea	65	92	134	91	67	147	117	141	115	148
	43	109	128	221	146	167	98	143	120	148
Taiwan (China)	76	94	143	174	74	170	89	188	137	121
	79	114	142	181	89	168	83	182	139	120
Hong Kong	55	181	126	154	41	185	110	158	101	78
	62	155	164	185	63	198	124	164	98	73
China	121	194	246	250	225	285	237	315	234	207
	125	180	238	262	327	278	220	301	235	207
Indonesia	71	111	79	126	114	157	146	177	130	151
	66	110	73	227	639	142	130	163	133	152
Malaysia	102	156	119	169	196	215	132	154	153	228
	69	441	98	217	262	166	92	262	161	214

Philippines	60	73	79	74	88	71	33	78	68	85
	19	118	67	136	285	53	30	64	71	81
Thailand	95	149	104	171	168	218	152	194	171	212
	77	140	91	205	338	208	168	195	174	210
Latin America	44	48	76	53	53	51	23	50	37	70
	44	47	78	46	42	51	22	50	37	71
Sub-Saharan Africa	76	81	43	75	111	59	13	51	51	71
	75	78	46	58	30	63	16	52	51	73
South Asia	63	94	115	116	114	130	126	131	137	89
	67	108	103	138	241	129	86	102	138	89
Rest of world	14	24	18	24	17	31	27	28	34	47
	15	19	18	9	−11	34	31	29	34	47

Note: the upper row entries refer to the 'base-case' projections, in which the MFA remains in place and none of the Uruguay Round provisions are implemented. The lower entries refer to the outcome when *all* of the Uruguay Round provisions explored in this chapter are implemented – the combined effects of implementing the ATC, tariff cuts, and reductions in agricultural export subsidies in the period 1992–2005, *as well as* the effects of eliminating the MFA in the year 2005.

clothing industry in the industrial economies will be relatively stagnant over the period, with apparel output actually falling in the European Union, despite continuation of the MFA.

For the majority of sectors in the world economy, the impact of the Uruguay Round will be relatively modest. For example, the increase in transportation, machinery, and equipment output in the United States and Canada would be 60 percent in the absence of the Uruguay Round and 62 percent with the Uruguay Round. In China, the Uruguay Round would temper a 237 percent increase in this sector slightly to an increase of 220 percent. Similarly small shifts are evident for most other countries. While not unimportant, these modest changes should be easily absorbed over a period of a decade. Even in agriculture, where Uruguay Round reforms have been particularly contentious, output would continue to increase in all regions (although in many cases the projected rates of technical change mean that the primary factors necessary to attain this rate of increase will diminish).

Yet the impact of the Uruguay Round on some sectors would be quite large – even dominant. Most striking perhaps is trade reform in the textiles and wearing apparel industries, which would turn an increase in output in the clothing sectors of the United States and Canada and the rest of the world into an absolute decline over the period. The reverse is that the strong increase in wearing apparel output in East Asia would become even greater – particularly in Indonesia and the Philippines, where the rate of output growth under the Uruguay Round would be several times larger than in its absence. The overall Uruguay Round package increases the competition faced by exporters from Sub-Saharan Africa to the MFA importing markets. In the model, output of apparel falls from 111 percent to 30 percent. However, this scenario omits the hard-to-quantify benefits to this sector of removing the threat of MFA quota imposition that has hung over any efficient new export-oriented industry.

In conclusion, the Uruguay Round package is a complex and finely balanced package involving progressive liberalization over a ten-year period. The total estimated annual gains in the year 2005 are equal to 0.89 percent of global GDP in that year, or about US $258 billion at 1992 prices. Of this total, about 80 percent would come from tariff and export subsidy reductions, and 20 percent from the elimination of the MFA. For industrial countries, the share of welfare gains from the elimination of the MFA would be much larger – more than 90 percent for the United States and Canada. Outside of Indonesia, the most important gains for developing countries would come from the reduction in the burden imposed by their own tariffs and those of their trading partners. Owing to the rapid rate of increase in south–south trade projected in the next few decades, a growing share of these gains will be realized in trade among developing countries. Finally, we should note that our estimates of welfare gains probably err on the conservative side, since they abstract from efficiency gains due to scale economies, as well as potential enhancements to the rate of growth in developing countries. We are also unable to quantify important benefits from improvements in the rule regime (see chapter 14) and the solid base for future liberalization in agriculture, manufacturing, and services. But despite these limitations, our results highlight the substantial and broadly based gains flowing from the Uruguay Round.

Appendix A *Assumptions used in the projections: cumulative growth in the 1992–2005 period (percentage changes)*

Regions	Population[a] (1)	Labor force[a] (2)	Capital stock[a] (3)	Human capital[a] (4)	k/l (3)–(2) (5)	hk/l (4)–(2) (6)	TFP growth[b] (7)	Real GDP[a] (8)
United States and Canada	10	13	43	67	30	54	4	41
European Union	2	2	19	167	17	165	13	33
Japan	4	–2	52	61	54	63	9	39
Korea	12	12	115	258	103	246	40	127
Taiwan (China)	11	18	136	112	118	95	40	126
Hong Kong	10	9	118	112	109	104	10	90
China	18	16	216	78	199	62	81	203
Indonesia	23	30	132	230	101	200	21	117
Malaysia	32	41	131	299	90	258	39	166
Philippines	25	40	51	71	10	31	20	75
Thailand	19	26	178	332	151	305	16	171
Latin America	25	32	17	119	–15	86	29	59
Sub-Saharan Africa	47	48	39	268	–9	220	15	64
South Asia	26	36	144	74	109	39	15	93
Rest of world	18	36	37	103	1	67	–2	37

[a]International Economic Analysis and Prospects Division, World Bank.
[b]GTAP model simulation.
Sources: (appendix C provides computational details)

Appendix B *Commodity aggregation*

Aggregate groups	Original GTAP industries
1. Primary agriculture	Paddy rice
	Wheat
	Grains, other than wheat and rice
	Nongrain crops
	Wool
	Other livestock products
2. Processed food	Fisheries
	Processed rice
	Meat products
	Milk products
	Other food products
	Beverages and tobacco
3. Natural resource-based industries	Forestry
	Coal
	Oil
	Gas
	Other minerals
	Petroleum and coal products
	Nonmetallic minerals
4. Textiles	Textiles
5. Wearing apparel	Wearing apparel
6. Light manufactures	Leather industries
	Lumber and products
	Pulp, paper, and so on
	Fabricated metal products
	Other manufacturing
7. Transportation, machinery, and equipment	Transport industries
	Machinery and equipment
8. Heavy manufactures	Chemicals, rubber, and plastic
	Primary ferrous metals
	Nonferrous metals
9. Utilities, housing, and construction services	Electricity, gas, and water
	Construction
	Ownership of dwellings
10. Other services	Trade and transport
	Other services (private)
	Other services (government)

Appendix C Assumptions used in the simulations

In the simulations presented in this chapter we use exogenous projections of each region's endowment of agricultural land, physical capital, human capital, technological development, population, and labor force. Because our base case simulation considered most trade distortions to be constant *ad valorem* tariffs, no projections for these variables were required for the baseline (no Uruguay Round) simulations. This experiment is denoted as simulation 1 – the base case experiment (table 7.5). However, since it is the export quotas provided under the MFA, rather than their *ad valorem* equivalents, that are exogenously specified, projections for these quotas were also required, and the associated implicit export taxes are permitted to adjust endogenously.

Given projections of these variables, the model can be solved for the level and structure of output at the end of the Uruguay Round implementation period. In the course of this simulation to the year 2005, the model maintains all of the restrictions imposed by economic theory. Thus, the changes in consumer demands are constrained to add up to changes in total spending; each group's income is determined by spending on its output; each region's total exports equal total imports of these goods minus shipping costs. Changes in the commodity composition of output are determined in part by changes in relative factor endowments and in part by differences in the income elasticities of consumer demand for each good in particular regions.

The ability of any model to generate satisfactory projections depends on its ability to capture the key linkages among variables of interest. The ability of the GTAP model to perform projections of this type has been validated through a retrocasting exercise designed to determine whether the model was able to explain the differences in East Asia's trade patterns between the model's base year (1992) and those observed a decade earlier (Gehlhar 1994). Using only information on the differences in factor endowments between 1992 and 1982, Gehlhar was able to provide accurate projections of trade shares in 1982. (The correlation between actual and predicted trade shares was over 0.9 in every region.) Gehlhar found that the introduction of a human capital factor was crucial to explaining changes in trade shares, implying that this factor had to be added to the standard model before it could be used for the projections. In analyzing long-term changes in trade patterns like those considered in this chapter, Gehlhar also found that predictions were more accurate when higher Armington elasticities of substitution were used. Elasticities of substitution twice as high as the standard GTAP elasticities were used in the projections and tariff liberalization simulations (1–4) reported in this chapter, where the time horizon of the simulation allows ample time for adjustments to take place. Only for the one-off abolition of the MFA (simulation 4) were the standard values for these parameters adopted.

The projected values of exogenous variables used to generate the baseline simulations were presented in appendix A (with details of their derivation given in Hertel, Martin, Yanagishima, and Dimaranan 1995, p. 94). These were based on combinations of historical data and projections of the growth in population, in the labor force, in real GDP, and in investment obtained from World Bank sources. Capital stock projections were generated by adding investment in each year and subtracting depreciation using the methodology of Nehru and Dhareshwar (1995). The human capital projections were based simply on the growth in the stock of tertiary education in each country during the 1980–87 period (Nehru, Swanson, and Dubey 1995). The stock of agricultural land was held constant throughout the analysis. Finally, estimates of TFP growth rates for each of the ten regions were obtained by subtracting the growth in total factor inputs from the real GDP projections with growth in agricultural sector TFP set 0.7 percent annually higher than the overall rate of TFP growth following the approach outlined in Gehlhar, Hertel, and Martin 1994. The resulting TFP growth rates were held constant in the subsequent trade liberalization simulations.

Notes

Mark Gehlhar also provided valuable input into this analysis.
1. Dean, Desai, and Riedel (1994) report a reduction in the average applied rate in this region from 44 to 15 percent, implying a reduction in import prices of 20 percent. But because these unilateral reductions are unbound, and fall outside the domain of the Uruguay Round, they are excluded from the analysis.
2. This specification assumes that all of the rents generated by these quotas accrue to the exporter. Much or all of the quota rent may be dissipated through rent seeking under quota allocation schemes, reducing the gains to exporters from these rents (see Trela and Whalley 1995). If the exporter and importer share these rents, as is suggested by Krishna, Erzan, and Tan (1994) and Bannister (1994), then a rent-sharing parameter must be introduced to distribute the rents between the importer and the exporter.
3. Information kindly provided by Sanjoy Bagchi of the International Textiles and Clothing Bureau, Geneva.
4. In fact, the demand for these commodities may even decline as incomes rise.
5. Hertel (1996) provides a detailed documentation of the model and several illustrative applications that demonstrate its properties.
6. If we used Bannister's (1994) estimate that half of the MFA quota rents would accrue to US importers, then the losses to Latin America from the elimination of the MFA would be cut drastically, and Latin America would in fact gain substantially from the Uruguay Round.

References

Bannister, G. 1994. "Rent Sharing in the Multi-Fibre Arrangement: the Case of Mexico." *Weltwirtschaftliches Archiv* 130(4): 800–27.
Chyc, K., M. Gehlhar, D. Gray, T. Hertel, E. Ianchovichina, B. McDonald, R. McDougall, M. Tsigas, and R. Wigle forthcoming. "Overview of the GTAP

Data Base." In T. Hertel, ed., *Global Trade Analysis Using the GTAP Model*. New York: Cambridge University Press.

Dean, J., S. Desai, and J. Riedel 1994. *Trade Policy Reform in Developing Countries since 1985: A Review of the Evidence*. World Bank Discussion Paper 267, Washington, DC: World Bank.

Francois, J., and W. Martin 1995. "Multilateral Trade Rules and the Expected Cost of Protection." CEPR Discussion Paper 1214. London: Centre for Economic Policy Research.

GATT 1973. "Arrangement Regarding International Trade in Textiles." Geneva: GATT.

———. 1994. "News of the Uruguay Round of Multilateral Trade Negotiations." Geneva: GATT, April.

Gehlhar, M. 1994. "Economic Growth and Trade in the Pacific Rim: An Analysis of Trade Patterns." Unpublished PhD dissertation, Purdue University.

Gehlhar, M., T. Hertel, and W. Martin 1994. "Economic Growth and the Changing Structure of Trade and Production in the Pacific Rim." *American Journal of Agricultural Economics* 76: 1101–10.

Goldin, I., O. Knudsen, and D. van der Mensbrugghe 1993. "Trade Liberalization: Global Economic Implications." Paris: OECD and World Bank.

Hertel, T., ed. forthcoming. *Global Trade Analysis Using the GTAP Model*. New York: Cambridge University Press.

Hertel, T. and M. Tsigas forthcoming. "Structure of the Standard GTAP Model." In T. Hertel, ed., *Global Trade Analysis Using the GTAP Model*. New York: Cambridge University Press.

Hertel, T., W. Martin, K. Yanagishima, and B. Dimaranan 1995. "Liberalizing Manufactures Trade in a Changing World Economy." In W. Martin and L. A. Winters, eds., *The Uruguay Round and the Developing Economies*. World Bank Discussion Paper 307. Washington, DC: World Bank.

Ingco, M. forthcoming. "Agricultural Trade Liberalization in the Uruguay Round: One Step Forward, One Step Back?" *The World Economy*.

Krishna, K., R. Erzan, and L. Tan 1994. "Rent Sharing in the Multifibre Arrangement: Theory and Evidence from US Apparel Imports from Hong Kong." *Review of International Economics* 2(1): 26–73.

Krueger, A. 1977. "Growth, Distortions and Patterns of Trade among Many Countries." Princeton: Princeton Studies in International Finance.

Leamer, E. 1987. "Paths of Development in the Three Factor n-Good General Equilbrium Model." *Journal of Political Economy* 95(5): 961–99.

Martin, W., and J. Francois 1994. "Bindings and Rules as Trade Liberalization." Paper presented at the Festschrift Conference, "Quiet Pioneering: Robert M. Stern and his International Economic Legacy." University of Michigan, Ann Arbor, November 18–20.

Martin, W., and P. G. Warr 1993. "Explaining the Relative Decline of Agriculture: A Supply-Side Analysis for Indonesia." *World Bank Economic Review* 7(3): 381–401.

Nehru, V., and A. Dhareshwar 1993. "A New Database on Physical Capital Stock: Sources, Methodology, and Results." *Revista de Analisis Economico* 8(1): 37–59.

Nehru, V., E. Swanson, and A. Dubey 1995. "A New Database on Human Capital Stock." *Journal of Economic Development* 46: 379–401.

Trela, I., and J. Whalley, 1995. "Internal Quota Allocation Schemes and the Costs of the MFA." *Review of International Economics* 3(3): 284–306.

World Bank 1994. *Global Economic Prospects and the Developing Countries.* Washington, DC: World Bank.

Yang, Y., W. Martin, and K. Yanagishima forthcoming. "Evaluating the Benefits of Abolishing the MFA in the Uruguay Round Package." In T. Hertel, ed., *Global Trade Analysis Using the GTAP Model.* New York: Cambridge University Press.

8 Quantifying the Uruguay Round

Glenn W. Harrison, Thomas F. Rutherford, and
David G. Tarr

How large would the welfare benefits of the Uruguay Round be worldwide? What are the most important quantitative aspects of the Uruguay Round, and what is its impact on developing countries? Would some countries or regions lose from the Uruguay Round, and if so why? How robust are the quantitative answers to these questions, and can different quantitative estimates from different models be reconciled?

We use an applied general equilibrium analysis to answer these questions. For simplicity and to facilitate understanding, we begin with a static model that is characterized by CRTS and perfect competition (our "base" model). We use the model to provide a thorough evaluation of the elimination of the MFA, and we provide the only analysis that decomposes and analyzes the separate components of the agricultural reforms under the Uruguay Round. We then present a set of preferred estimates of steady-state impacts, characterized by imperfect competition and IRTS, and perform a systematic sensitivity analysis of the parameters. This analytical sequence provides a coherent statement of mapping from alternative modeling assumptions to quantitative conclusions, including an assessment of comparable mappings for the other principal models of the Uruguay Round. In doing so, our goal is to provide transparent critical understanding and evaluation of the analysis.

Our base model contains twenty-four countries and regions and twenty-two commodities. Unlike previously published estimates of the impact of the Uruguay Round, our counterfactual simulations are based on the actual commitments made by the countries in the negotiations. Our model is more disaggregated than other models that have assessed the global consequences of the full Uruguay Round, especially at the regional level. As such, our estimates of the effects of the Uruguay Round capture many developing countries, which is not possible with other models that assess the full consequences of the Uruguay Round. But we also aggregate our model to twelve countries and regions, indicating that aggregation exerts a downward bias on the welfare gains from the Uruguay Round, and that the aggregation bias can generate quite different results for certain countries.

Our findings indicate that the world as a whole would gain substantially from the Uruguay Round: about US $96 billion annually under our base model and US $171 billion under our steady-state model.[1] But the gains would be concentrated in industrial countries, particularly the United States, the European Union, and Japan. Under the base model, the United States would gain US $13 billion, the European Union would gain US $39 billion, and Japan would gain US $17 billion.

The overall explanation for this pattern is intuitive: the industrial countries, particularly the United States and the European Union, "gave up" the most in the Uruguay Round in the (misleading) mercantilist sense which often dominates trade negotiations. In other words, these countries are forgoing policies that entail the loss of welfare to themselves, most notably MFA protection and agricultural distortions. Conversely, developing countries are reducing agricultural distortions comparatively less and are not restricting imports under the MFA. The only general exception is that developing countries are reducing protection for manufactures by more than OECD countries, since OECD countries have comparatively less protection in this area to begin with.

But, in fact, some developing countries will be net losers from the Uruguay Round in the short run.[2] The comparative losses for developing countries under our base model are due primarily to two effects: the reduction of agricultural subsidies in the United States, the European Union and the EFTA, which leads to terms-of-trade losses for some countries;[3] and the liberalization of the MFA, which creates losses for some developing countries because OECD countries can now capture MFA quota rents, and for the less efficient clothing exporters of least-developed countries which will lose their market share.

What developing countries can do, however, is reduce their self-inflicted costs by reducing their trade barriers and other distortions further. The Uruguay Round has created a more open global trade environment. Unilateral tariff reductions or reductions in other distortions by developing countries will shift their levels of production and exports toward their comparative advantage, and their export expansion is less likely to be impeded by global protectionism. Moreover, estimates from our steady-state model suggest that an increase in income levels in the long run will lift almost all countries that lose in the short run. Thus, all countries have at least the potential to gain from the Uruguay Round.

Overview of the model and data

Our base model is a relatively standard comparative static CRTS model that captures twenty-four separate countries and regions and twenty-two separate production sectors in each region (table 8.1). Countries denoted "IC" in table 8.1 are defined as industrial countries; all others are considered developing countries. To assess the consequences of regional aggregation, we also use a twelve-region aggregation of the base model in some simulations.

Production entails the use of intermediate inputs and primary factors (labor, capital, and land). Primary factors are mobile across sectors within a region, but are internationally immobile. Each region has a single representative consumer, as well as a single government agent. We assume CES production functions for value added,[4] and Leontief production functions for intermediates and the value-added composite.

Demand is characterized by nested CES utility functions for each agent, which allow multistage budgeting (figure 8.1). Demand at the top level for the composite "Armington" aggregate of each of the twenty-two goods in table 8.1 is specified as a Cobb–Douglas function. Import demands are modeled with a traditional Armington formulation. Source-specific imports substitute with each other in a CES utility function, and the import composite and domestic output substitute for each other in a higher-level CES utility function. The import composite is a composite of the import goods from twenty-three regions. Firm varieties enter into the imperfect competition model, where competition is at the level of the firm.

Relying on our *a priori* beliefs about the plausible values of these elasticities,[5] we assume that the lower-level elasticity of substitution σ_{MM} is 4 and that the higher-level elasticity σ_{DM} is 8. These values are perturbed systematically in the sensitivity analysis, but unless otherwise discussed (as in the MFA analysis) they are held at these values throughout the chapter. Exports are not differentiated by country of destination in the base model.

All distortions are represented as *ad valorem* price-wedge distortions. They include factor taxes in production, value-added taxes, import tariffs, export subsidies, VERs (represented as *ad valorem* export tax equivalents), and nontariff barriers (represented as *ad valorem* import-tariff equivalents). Lump-sum replacement taxes or subsidies ensure that government revenue in each region stays constant at real benchmark levels.[6] Further details regarding modeling are available in Harrison, Rutherford, and Tarr (1995).

Table 8.1 *Sectors and regions captured in the model*

Sectors (all models)
Paddy rice
Wheat
Grains (other than rice and wheat)
Nongrain crops
Forestry, fishing, lumber, wood, paper, and wool
Processed rice
Milk products
Textiles
Wearing apparel
Chemicals, rubber, and plastics
Primary iron and steel
Nonferrous metals
Fabricated metals
Transport industry
Trade and transport
Investment goods
Meat products and livestock
Energy and energy products
Minerals and mineral products
Food, beverages, and tobacco
Machinery, equipment, and other manufacturing
Services and utilities

Twenty-four region model
Australia (IC)
New Zealand (IC)
Canada (IC)
United States (IC)
Japan (IC)
South Korea
European Union (12) (IC)
Indonesia
Malaysia
Philippines
Singapore
Thailand
China
Hong Kong
Taiwan
Argentina
Brazil
Mexico
Rest of Latin America
Sub-Saharan Africa
Middle East and North Africa
Eastern Europe and former Soviet Union
South Asia
Other European (EFTA, Switzerland, Turkey, South Africa) (IC)

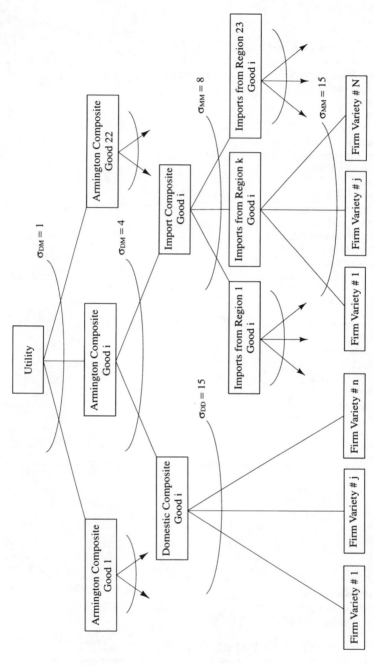

Figure 8.1   Demand structure for representative good i in a representative country, with base elasticity values

The results of the base model

What do we model?

The Uruguay Round is a complex agreement that covers seven broad areas:
- Tariff reductions in manufactured products.
- The tariffication of nontariff barriers in agriculture, as well as binding commitments to reduce the level of agricultural protection.
- The reduction of export and production subsidies in agriculture.
- The elimination of VERs and the MFA.
- Institutional and rule changes, such as the creation of the WTO and safeguards, antidumping, and countervailing duty measures.
- Such new areas as TRIMs, TRIPS, and the GATS.
- Areas receiving greater coverage, such as customs valuation.

Several studies have assessed these areas of the Uruguay Round agreement qualitatively, and so we do not repeat those explanations.[7] Here we quantify the impact of the Uruguay Round in the first four areas listed. To the extent that the Uruguay Round reforms lead to benefits or losses in the other areas, our estimates either underestimate or overestimate the gains from the Uruguay Round.[8]

Our quantitative assessment of pre- and post-Uruguay Round distortions in each area is elaborated in Harrison, Rutherford, and Tarr (1995, appendix A). In agriculture specifically, we assess the impact of the tariffication of nontariff barriers and the reductions in tariffs. In addition to tariff reductions, the Uruguay Round calls for reductions in budgetary outlays for agricultural export subsidies of 36 percent of the tariff-line level in industrial countries and 24 percent for developing countries. We model export subsidies as *ad valorem* export subsidies and model their reduction as a percentage reduction in the *ad valorem* rate of export subsidies.[9] Industrial countries are also to reduce their aggregate measure of support to agriculture, which includes subsidies for domestic production, by 20 percent and developing countries by 13 percent.[10] Some commentators are skeptical about whether the aggregate measure of support will actually bind the contracting parties. In our base simulations we reduce domestic input subsidies by these percentages; later we decompose the impact of the agricultural reforms into their various components so that we may evaluate the quantitative impact of the reforms with and without the reduction in domestic input subsidies.

Our base-model estimates

We report here both the aggregate and region-specific impacts of individual components of the Uruguay Round, and the complete reform package as a whole on welfare gains and losses (table 8.2). We also report the effects

Table 8.2 Base-model impacts on welfare gains and losses annually (1992 US $billions)

Region	Agricultural reform	MFA reform	Manufacturing sector reform	Complete reform package	Complete reform package as percentage of GDP
Australia	0.717	0.024	0.391	1.135	0.4
New Zealand	0.298	0.002	0.083	0.381	1.0
Canada	0.238	0.939	-0.045	1.160	0.2
United States	1.659	10.136	0.772	12.842	0.2
Japan	15.232	-0.531	1.978	16.692	0.5
Korea	4.604	-0.469	0.518	4.574	1.5
European Union (12)	28.539	7.624	2.311	38.845	0.6
Indonesia	0.170	0.617	0.559	1.301	1.1
Malaysia	1.225	0.082	0.696	1.864	3.3
Philippines	0.618	-0.002	0.363	0.890	1.6
Singapore	0.623	-0.149	0.450	0.918	2.1
Thailand	0.747	0.065	1.732	2.435	2.1
China	-0.561	0.876	0.915	1.174	0.3
Hong Kong	0.598	-1.698	-0.188	-1.267	-1.4
Taiwan	0.011	-0.450	0.825	0.404	0.2
Argentina	0.376	0.028	0.236	0.645	0.3
Brazil	0.272	-0.027	1.076	1.310	0.3
Mexico	-0.015	-0.081	0.262	0.145	0.0
Rest of Latin America	1.437	-0.498	0.283	1.198	0.4
Sub-Saharan Africa	-0.292	-0.112	-0.005	-0.418	-0.2

Middle East and North Africa	-0.448	-0.499	0.624	-0.388	-0.1
Eastern Europe & former Soviet Union	-0.246	-0.627	0.526	-0.421	-0.1
South Asia	0.097	0.629	2.730	3.286	1.0
Other European	2.412	0.071	1.663	4.154	0.3
Developing countries (total)	9.213	-2.314	11.602	17.651	0.4
Industrialized countries (total)	49.095	18.264	7.152	75.208	0.4
World	58.309	15.950	18.755	92.859	0.4

of the complete reform package as a percentage of base GDP in each region, to help scale the results for economies of different size.

The world as a whole would gain about $93 billion annually with all reforms implemented under the Uruguay Round, and the dollar gains would be concentrated in industrial countries, especially the United States, Japan, and the European Union, with gains of $13, $17, and $39 billion, respectively. Some smaller countries would gain significantly in percentage terms: Malaysia would gain 3.3 percent of its GDP, Singapore and Thailand about 2.1 percent each, and Korea and the Philippines about 1.6 percent each. Although the Uruguay Round would benefit developing countries as a whole, a few of these countries would lose on balance. We decompose and explain these results in detail later but the explanation for this overall pattern is intuitive: the industrial countries, particularly the United States and the European Union, "gave up" the most under the Uruguay Round in the mercantilist sense. That is, these countries are reducing policies that are very expensive to themselves.

The exception to this pattern is the reduction in manufacturing protection, since industrial countries already have relatively lower protection levels in this area. Thus, as shown under the manufacturing reform scenario, developing countries would tend to gain more from the reduction in manufacturing protection. But developing countries are reducing agricultural distortions comparatively less (although the reduction in production subsidies is important in some cases). Moreover, they do not restrict imports under the MFA. Indeed, the MFA is crucial to understanding the consequences of the Uruguay Round for developing countries.

The impact of the removal of the MFA

The results of the MFA reform simulation show that, although the elimination of the MFA would yield substantial benefits worldwide ($15.9 billion), developing countries as a whole would lose. The large gains to the United States, the European Union, and other quota-constrained countries from MFA reform are simple enough to explain: they should capture quota rents, as well as gains in efficiency from a reduction in excessive domestic production and increased consumption at lower prices, the benefits of which will be larger as elasticity of demand is larger. For households in the United States, for example, the aggregate price of domestic and imported wearing apparel products would decline by 9 percent, implying a substantial reduction in the cost of living.[11] Textile and wearing apparel importers that were previously unconstrained (Japan is the most prominent example) would lose from the removal of the MFA. Exporters would divert sales to the previously constrained markets, worsening terms of trade in such previously unconstrained markets as Japan.

For quota-constrained exporting countries, the welfare effects are mixed – a loss of quota rents in export markets that were constrained; a potential gain in efficiency to the extent that these countries shift resources into textiles and wearing apparel, assuming they gain a comparative advantage in these industries; and a potential gain in terms of trade on the sales of textile and wearing apparel products to such previously unconstrained markets as Japan. The theoretical literature has tended to emphasize that because lost quota rents are a "rectangle," and efficiency gains only a "triangle," exporting countries will likely lose unless they experience significant gains in terms of trade on sales in unconstrained markets – an element that will be strongly influenced by their share of sales to previously constrained markets (Yang, Martin, and Yanagishima forthcoming; and Tarr 1987).

Table 8.3 provides relevant information for understanding the results. It lists three factors for textiles and wearing apparel: the total value of export quota rents by country (to all their export destinations);[12] quota premium rates that apply to exports to the European Union and the United States (the two most prominent constrained markets);[13] and a share parameter for the share of total exports (of the quota-constrained countries) in quota-constrained markets. (The smaller this share of total exports, the more likely an increase in rents in unconstrained markets will compensate for the loss of rents in constrained markets.)

Table 8.4 illustrates the channels through which the MFA works, by presenting our base-model results in which we vary key demand elasticity parameters. The most important elasticities are the trade elasticities – σ_{DM} and σ_{MM} (discussed above).[14] The column "MFA" shows the results of our base-model simulation, where $\sigma_{MM} = 8$ and $\sigma_{DM} = 4$. The mid-level elasticity σ_{DM} is central to the overall welfare gains possible from MFA reform, while the bottom-level elasticity σ_{MM} is central to how the costs of MFA reform are distributed among developing countries.

Under MFA-1 in table 8.4, we lower the values of these trade elasticities to 2 and 4, respectively, characterizing these results as short run. Losses to developing countries as a whole would increase substantially under this short-run scenario, from a loss of $2.314 billion to a loss of $7.826 billion. The reason is that industrial countries import considerably more in the presence of high elasticities of demand, thus allowing greater resource reallocation in developing countries and greater terms-of-trade gains for developing countries in unconstrained markets.

MFA-2 in table 8.4 shows the impact of greater substitutability among the textile and wearing apparel imports of different regions; σ_{MM} is increased to 10, and σ_{DM} is held at our base value of 4. Aggregate gains to

Table 8.3 Quota rents for textiles and wearing apparel

	Textiles				Wearing apparel			
			Quota premium (percent)				Quota premium (percent)	
Region	Value of quota rent ($ mill.)	Percentage of exports constrained	European Union	United States	Value of quota rent ($ mill.)	Percentage of exports constrained	European Union	United States
Korea	119	16	10	10	555	55	19	23
Indonesia	97	24	17	12	512	52	48	47
Malaysia	65	100	12	10	330	100	32	37
Philippines	7	50	10	9	363	81	28	34
Singapore	7	11	10	8	365	100	28	31
Thailand	53	40	13	9	396	42	36	35
China	378	19	27	18	2,223	31	36	40
Hong Kong	48	13	8	8	1,249	100	16	18
Taiwan	95	13	12	8	515	81	22	19
Brazil	65	100	14	9	43	77	18	20
Mexico	41	60	14	9	181	99	18	20
Rest of Latin America	46	45	14	9	619	86	18	20
Middle East and North Africa	84	78	7	5	390	97	9	10
Eastern Europe and former Soviet Union	87	78	9	6	430	97	12	13
South Asia	566	46	27	18	1,375	85	36	40

Table 8.4 *Decomposing the welfare impacts of MFA reform (1992 US $billion)*

Region	MFA	MFA-1	MFA-2	MFA-3	MFA-4	MFA-5	MFA-6
Australia	0.1	0.0	0.0	0.1	0.0	0.0	0.1
New Zealand	0.0	0.0	0.0	0.0	0.0	0.0	0.0
Canada	0.9	0.7	1.0	1.3	1.0	0.7	1.3
United States	10.1	8.3	10.3	14.7	10.5	8.5	15.4
Japan	−0.5	−0.2	−0.6	−0.2	−0.6	−0.2	−0.2
Korea	−0.5	−0.6	−0.5	0.6	−0.4	−0.5	0.7
European Union	7.6	6.7	8.0	7.1	7.9	6.9	7.4
Indonesia	0.6	−0.2	1.0	0.0	0.7	−0.2	0.1
Malaysia	0.1	−0.3	0.3	−0.3	0.1	−0.2	−0.3
Philippines	0.0	−0.2	0.0	0.1	0.1	−0.2	0.2
Singapore	−0.1	−0.3	−0.1	−0.3	−0.1	−0.3	−0.3
Thailand	0.1	−0.3	0.1	0.0	0.1	−0.2	0.1
China	0.9	−1.2	1.4	0.5	1.3	−1.0	1.0
Hong Kong	−1.7	−1.4	−1.8	−0.7	−1.7	−1.4	−0.7
Taiwan	−0.5	−0.6	−0.5	0.2	−0.4	−0.5	0.3
Argentina	0.0	0.0	0.0	0.1	0.0	0.0	0.1
Brazil	0.0	−0.1	0.0	0.1	0.0	−0.1	0.1
Mexico	−0.1	−0.2	−0.1	0.4	0.0	−0.1	0.5
Rest of Latin America	−0.5	−0.6	−0.6	0.5	−0.4	−0.5	0.6
Sub-Saharan Africa	−0.1	−0.1	−0.1	0.3	−0.1	−0.1	0.2
Middle East and North Africa	−0.5	−0.5	−0.6	1.4	−0.4	−0.4	1.5
Eastern Europe and former Soviet Union	−0.6	−0.6	−0.7	0.1	−0.6	−0.5	0.2
South Asia	0.6	−0.9	1.0	0.1	0.9	−0.7	0.4
Other European	0.1	0.3	−0.1	2.5	0.1	0.3	2.6
Developing countries (total)	−2.3	−7.9	−1.3	2.9	−0.9	−7.0	4.8
Industrialized countries (total)	18.3	16.0	18.7	25.5	18.9	16.2	26.7
World	16.0	8.0	17.4	28.4	18.0	9.2	31.5

Note: removal of the MFA in the base model with the following elasticities:

MFA	$\sigma_{MM} = 8$	and $\sigma_{DM} = 4$ for MFA sectors
MFA-1	$\sigma_{MM} = 4$	and $\sigma_{DM} = 2$ for MFA sectors
MFA-2	$\sigma_{MM} = 10$	and $\sigma_{DM} = 4$ for MFA sectors
MFA-3	$\sigma_{MM} = 0$	and $\sigma_{DM} = 15$ for MFA sectors
MFA-4	$\sigma_{MM} = 8$	and $\sigma_{DM} = 4$ for MFA sectors and
	$\sigma_{DC} = 2$	and $\sigma_{DG} = 2$ for MFA sectors
MFA-5	$\sigma_{MM} = 4$	and $\sigma_{DM} = 2$ for MFA sectors *and* $\sigma_{DC} = 2$ and $\sigma_{DG} = 2$
MFA-6	$\sigma_{MM} = 0$	and $\sigma_{DM} = 15$ for MFA sectors *and* $\sigma_{DC} = 2$ and $\sigma_{DG} = 2$

the world would increase because demand elasticities increase, but China, South Asia, Indonesia, Thailand, and Malaysia would become the dominant gainers among developing countries (see the MFA column for the appropriate comparison). The reason is that these countries or regions are the most efficient suppliers (they have the highest quota premiums, as indicated in table 8.3), and they expand exports at the expense of marginally inefficient developing countries when importing nations substitute more readily among alternative foreign suppliers. This scenario is feared by the marginally inefficient suppliers that have been able to maintain sales and obtain rents due only to the quota. Hence, some relatively inefficient MFA exporters would lose even more under MFA-2 than under the MFA simulation – for example, Korea, Taiwan, the rest of Latin America, Sub-Saharan Africa, the Middle East and North Africa, and Eastern Europe and the former Soviet Union.

What assumptions about trade elasticities would enable the marginally inefficient exporters to gain from the MFA reform? The logic of our analysis and base-model results would suggest that industrial countries would have to experience a large increase in demand due to lower prices (thus setting σ_{DM} equal to 15), and that substitution away from marginally inefficient suppliers would have to be restricted (thus setting σ_{MM} equal to 0) – or simulation MFA-3. As expected from a high value of σ_{DM}, the world would capture considerably greater welfare gains, and developing countries as a group would now gain. Moreover, as expected, the two simulations with a high σ_{DM} and a low σ_{MM} (MFA-3 and MFA-6) are the only ones in which most of the marginally inefficient suppliers would gain – that is, Sub-Saharan Africa, Eastern Europe and the former Soviet Union, Latin America, the Middle East and North Africa, Taiwan, Mexico, Brazil, and Korea.

Interestingly, some suppliers – Malaysia, Singapore, and Hong Kong – still register welfare losses, because these suppliers have 100 percent of their benchmark wearing apparel sales in quota-constrained markets (see table 8.3). Thus, even under scenario MFA-3 (with $\sigma_{MM}=0$), they could not share in the terms-of-trade improvement realized by exporters to previously unconstrained markets. Malaysia, one of the most efficient suppliers based on its quota premium on wearing apparel sales, would gain under our simulations if and only if σ_{MM} is high (as in simulation MFA-2). Singapore and Hong Kong, however, are marginally inefficient suppliers without sales in unconstrained markets, and would thus lose under all simulations.

In our model the representative consumer agent and the government agent in each region consume twenty-two goods (at the top level of figure 8.1). Unless otherwise stated, the elasticities of substitution among these twenty-two aggregate goods are unity: $\sigma_{DC}=\sigma_{DG}=1$ in each region. For higher elasticity values, consumers will shift purchases toward goods whose relative prices decrease; in particular, consumers in import-quota-constrained countries will shift income toward textiles and apparel purchases under the MFA reform simulations.

Simulations MFA-4 and MFA-5 increase the top-level elasticity of substitution to 2, otherwise holding elasticities at the values under simulations MFA and MFA-1, respectively. Since the relative prices of textiles and wearing apparel are declining in the constrained markets, the gains to both developing and industrial countries would increase, but not by an overwhelming magnitude. The reason is that households consume a composite of imported and domestic wearing apparel; in the United States, for example, composite wearing apparel prices would fall only by 7.6 percent. Of course, higher values of σ_{DC} and σ_{DG} will magnify the impact observed under MFA-4 and MFA-5, but the plausibility of values much greater than 3 is questionable.

Simulation MFA-6 combines the logic of our analysis of the effects of trade elasticities (from MFA-1 to MFA-3) with the effects of final consumption elasticities (under MFA-4 and MFA-5). It represents the most optimistic configuration of elasticities for generating beneficial welfare reforms among developing countries under the MFA reforms. Even so, Malaysia, Singapore, and Hong Kong would still lose, owing to a low value of σ_{MM} and without initial sales to unconstrained markets (as discussed earlier). The results of our analysis demonstrate that predicting which exporting countries would gain from the elimination of the MFA is complex. For example, the results for Malaysia show that an efficient supplier can overcome the handicap of a small initial share in previously unconstrained markets and gain from the elimination of the MFA, provided that the substitution possibilities are sufficiently great.[15] This possibility had been overlooked in the theoretical analyses by Yang (1994) and Tarr (1987). These analyses suggested that only such countries as Indonesia, which has substantial initial sales of wearing apparel in unconstrained markets, would gain, owing to rectangles of terms-of-trade gains.[16] Although initial shares in constrained markets are important, the most efficient suppliers capture these markets when substitution possibilities among exporters are great.

In sum, import-quota-constrained countries would gain from the elimination of the MFA because they would reap quota rent gains and efficiency gains; unconstrained importers would lose owing to their terms-of-trade loss. The most efficient suppliers among developing countries would also typically gain, but their gains would vary substantially, increasing in the long run when elasticities are expected to be higher.

Many of the marginally inefficient suppliers among the developing countries would lose, because they would lose quota rents *and* in the long run lose market share to more efficient suppliers among developing countries.

Agricultural reform under the Uruguay Round

We assess the impact of agricultural reform by decomposing it into its three major components (table 8.5). Each simulation is implemented in the twenty-four-region version of our model, given our base-trade elasticities of $\sigma_{DM} = 4$ and $\sigma_{MM} = 8$.

Simulation AGR-1 shows the impact of reducing export subsidies in agriculture; other components of agriculture reform are excluded. The European Union would gain $11.5 billion, the principal food-exporting nations of Argentina, New Zealand, Australia, and Canada would gain slightly, and most other regions would lose.[17] This component of agricultural reform was the one feared by the "net food-importing" countries, who suffer an adverse terms of trade loss.

AGR-2 simulates the impact of reducing agricultural production subsidies. With a few exceptions (Hong Kong, Malaysia, Argentina, and Singapore), our data (based on those of the GTAP project) indicate that all countries in the model have at least some production subsidies (see Gehlhar *et al.* forthcoming). In some cases, such as grains in the Middle East and North Africa and paddy rice in Korea, the subsidy is extremely high, although often on a low volume. Thus, reducing this production distortion would benefit most countries, although several net food importers of wheat and grains other than rice and wheat would lose (Japan, Korea, Singapore, Taiwan, Mexico, and Sub-Saharan Africa). The European Union would again reap substantial welfare benefits, while the United States would have smaller gains.

AGR-3 simulates the impact of reducing import protection for agricultural products. The two dominant effects under this simulation are the gains to Japan, which is not surprising given its extremely high level of agricultural protection,[18] and to Korea. Other regions that would gain are also those with comparatively high levels of agricultural protection.[19] China and the European Union would lose under this simulation, by small but not trivial amounts. The European Union would lose under this simulation because it would maintain its export and production subsidies in agriculture. The additional exports it would obtain from the reduction in import protection in the rest of the world would aggravate its already expensive and inefficient export position. China would suffer an adverse terms-of-trade effect because other countries would be lowering tariffs and attracting imports, thus driving up the price of agricultural products in world markets.

Table 8.5 *Decomposing the welfare effects of agricultural reform (1992 US $billion)*

Region	AGR	AGR-1	AGR-2	AGR-3
Australia	0.7	0.1	0.1	0.4
New Zealand	0.3	0.1	0.1	0.1
Canada	0.2	0.0	0.3	−0.1
United States	1.7	0.0	1.5	−0.1
Japan	15.2	−2.2	−0.5	17.7
Korea	4.6	−0.2	0.0	4.7
European Union (12)	28.5	11.5	17.8	−1.2
Indonesia	0.2	0.0	0.1	0.1
Malaysia	1.2	0.0	0.1	1.2
Philippines	0.6	−0.1	0.0	0.8
Singapore	0.6	0.0	0.0	0.6
Thailand	0.7	0.0	0.2	0.6
China	−0.6	−0.2	−0.1	−0.3
Hong Kong	0.6	0.1	0.0	0.5
Taiwan	0.0	0.0	0.0	0.1
Argentina	0.4	0.1	0.2	0.1
Brazil	0.3	0.0	0.2	0.1
Mexico	0.0	0.0	0.0	0.1
Rest of Latin America	1.4	0.0	1.4	0.1
Sub-Saharan Africa	−0.3	−0.4	−0.1	0.3
Middle East and North Africa	−0.4	−0.8	0.2	0.1
Eastern Europe and former Soviet Union	−0.2	−0.6	0.3	0.0
South Asia	0.1	0.0	0.1	0.0
Other European	2.4	−0.6	2.1	0.5
Developing countries (total)	9.2	−2.3	2.4	8.8
Industrialized countries (total)	49.1	9.0	21.5	17.3
World	58.3	6.7	23.9	26.1

Note: AGR   Reduced import distortions and subsidies on agricultural goods.
      AGR-1   Reduced export subsidies in agriculture.
      AGR-2   Reduced production subsidies in agriculture.
      AGR-3   Reduced import distortions in agriculture.

Since protection levels in China would not change, it would not gain from trade liberalization as would the other countries. For the remaining regions, the benefits of more efficient resource allocation would dominate the adverse terms-of-trade effect.

AGR simulates the combined effects of all three components of agricultural reform. The European Union would gain more than $28 billion from the agriculture reform package, given its reduction in agricultural export and import subsidies. Japan would gain with the reduction in its high import protection. Although China and some of the aggregate developing country regions would lose somewhat small amounts, they represent the surprisingly few losers, thus mitigating concerns about losses among the "net food-importing" countries. In effect, most regions have something to gain by reducing their own production subsidies, since most also export some food despite being net food importers overall.

Increasing returns to scale and steady-state effects

Imperfect competition and increasing returns

Owing to evidence that many sectors experience IRTS at the plant or firm level, we modify our base model to incorporate IRTS.[20] We define two types of IRTS models – a static model that captures simply the switch from a CRTS regime to an IRTS regime, and a steady-state IRTS model that captures dynamic gains from trade liberalization under IRTS and imperfect competition. We apply our imperfectly competitive model only to sectors that are subject to IRTS. As such, we continue to use CRTS and competitive markets to model some sectors as in our base model.

For sectors that are subject to IRTS and imperfect competition, the demand side of the model assumes that consumers have preferences for the products of firms (that is, firm-level product differentiation) and allows for the possibility that consumers have preferences for the products of their home firms. The model thus accommodates situations where domestic firms produce goods that conform to the tastes of the citizens of their country. For example, Japanese consumers would prefer automobiles with the steering column on the right-hand side and, thus, all else equal, would prefer Japanese-made vehicles to US-made vehicles. More important, Japanese vehicles would be better substitutes for each other than US vehicles would be for Japanese vehicles.

We implement this preference structure beginning with our nested CES (Armington) structure (again see figure 8.1), but we add an additional nest for the firms in all countries at the bottom level. In our structure, each of the import sources represents the composite of varieties from the firms in that country where varieties within a country substitute for each other with elasticity σ_{DD}.

The literature on CGE models contains a variety of opinions about the implications of this type of specification. One point that has occasionally been overlooked is that, when elasticities at all levels of a nested CES structure are equal, the structure collapses into a single-level CES. This property of CES functions implies that firm-level product differentiation in which elasticities of substitution are equal for all firms and products is a special feature of our model. The advantage of our general structure is that it allows a pure comparison of the results of a CRTS model with those of the IRTS model; that is, we need not change the assumed market-demand curves for consumers in order to implement the IRTS model. Moreover, if elasticities of substitution differ between the domestic and imported varieties of firm products, we can incorporate that difference in our structure; a single-level CES function cannot. In other words, we can accommodate a more general Slutsky substitution matrix with preferences defined over varieties.

On the supply side, we assume the standard IRTS function that firms produce with constant marginal costs and given fixed costs. If fewer firms produce the same industrial output, a rationalization gain would be realized as firms slide down their average cost curve, producing more output with the same fixed costs (see appendix B). This approach requires that we obtain estimates of the extent of unrealized economies of scale; we derived them from econometric estimates of the cost disadvantage ratio, primarily from Pratten (1987) and Neven (1990).[21]

The most striking feature of results from our static IRTS model is how similar they are to our CRTS results (table 8.6). Global welfare would increase from \$93 billion in the CRTS version to just \$96 billion in the IRTS version, contrary to the folklore in the CGE literature that IRTS always generates much larger welfare gains owing to rationalization gains.[22]

These enhanced benefits are small for two reasons. First, we have assumed smaller cost disadvantage ratios than most studies, thus yielding smaller rationalization gains from liberalization. More important, however, we have studiously avoided incorporating a regime switch other than CRTS to IRTS. Many CGE implementations of IRTS simultaneously change something other than the pure IRTS impact, such as elasticities, and it is the regime switch that is driving the larger numbers.[23]

Dynamic impacts of the Uruguay Round

While the dynamic benefits of trade liberalization and the Uruguay Round are often described, they are rarely estimated. We use a steady-state approach to evaluating trade policy change in a multiregion model first implemented in Harrison, Rutherford, and Tarr (1994); our approach has also been used by Francois, McDonald, and Nordström (1994 and chapter 9 in this volume).

Table 8.6 Static IRTS model impacts on welfare gains and losses (1992 US $billion)

Region	Agricultural reform	MFA reform	Manufacturing sector reform	Complete reform package	Complete reform package as percentage of GDP
Australia	0.7	0.0	0.5	1.2	0.4
New Zealand	0.3	0.0	0.1	0.4	1.0
Canada	0.3	0.9	0.1	1.3	0.2
United States	1.8	10.0	1.2	13.3	0.2
Japan	15.1	-0.6	2.2	16.9	0.5
Korea	4.6	-0.5	0.7	4.8	1.6
European Union (12)	28.3	7.6	3.0	39.3	0.6
Indonesia	0.2	0.6	0.6	1.3	1.1
Malaysia	1.2	0.1	0.7	1.8	3.2
Philippines	0.7	0.0	0.4	0.9	1.7
Singapore	0.6	-0.2	0.5	0.9	2.1
Thailand	0.8	0.1	1.8	2.5	2.2
China	-0.5	1.0	0.9	1.3	0.3
Hong Kong	0.6	-1.7	-0.1	-1.2	-1.3
Taiwan	0.0	-0.4	0.8	0.4	0.2
Argentina	0.4	0.0	0.3	0.7	0.3
Brazil	0.3	0.0	1.2	1.4	0.4
Mexico	0.0	-0.1	0.3	0.2	0.0
Rest of Latin America	1.5	-0.5	0.3	1.3	0.5
Sub-Saharan Africa	-0.2	0.0	0.1	-0.3	-0.2

Middle East and North Africa	−0.3	−0.4	0.8	−0.3	0.0
Eastern Europe and former Soviet Union	−0.1	−0.5	0.8	−0.2	0.0
South Asia	0.3	0.9	3.1	3.7	1.1
Other European	2.2	−0.2	1.7	4.2	0.3
Developing countries (total)	9.9	−1.5	12.9	19.4	0.4
Industrialized countries (total)	48.7	17.9	8.7	76.6	0.4
World	58.6	16.4	21.7	96.0	0.4

Briefly stated, we assume that the capital stock in each country is optimal given the rate of return on capital in the initial equilibrium. That is, increases in the rate of return on capital would increase investment until the marginal productivity of capital is driven down to the initial rate of return. The Uruguay Round will produce a new equilibrium, where for almost all countries the rate of return on capital will increase (relative to a price index of consumption), given a more efficient allocation of resources. This new equilibrium implies that the new capital stock can no longer be optimal in a dynamic sense: investment is forthcoming until the marginal productivity of capital is reduced to the long-run equilibrium rate of return on capital.

In the static IRTS model, we allowed the rental rate of capital to vary within each country, while holding constant the aggregate stock of capital in each country. The steady-state IRTS model essentially reverses this: we allow the capital stock in each country to be determined endogenously, while holding the rental rate of capital in each country constant.[24] This expansion of the capital stock then works through our multiregion trade model like an "endowment effect," generating larger welfare gains, since more resources are available to be used. In addition, as the income of the world increases, the demand for goods and the derived demand for factors increase. In this model, the quantity of capital will increase in response, producing a further endowment effect.

Since our steady-state calculation ignores the forgone consumption necessary to obtain the larger capital stock, we emphasize that this calculation provides an upper bound of the potential welfare gains under a long-run, classical Solow-type growth model. Of course, it could underestimate the long-run gains, since it fails to capture endogenous growth effects, such as those from induced improvements in productivity or innovation (so-called "learning by doing").

When we apply this steady-state variant to our twenty-four-region IRTS model, global welfare gains from the Uruguay Round are magnified, from $96 billion in the comparable static model to $171 billion (table 8.7).

Regional aggregation and systematic sensitivity analysis

Regional aggregation

We use our CRTS base model to assess the welfare gains and losses from the Uruguay Round for an aggregate of twelve regions: the United States, Japan, the European Union, China, Sub-Saharan Africa, the Middle East and North Africa, Eastern Europe and the former Soviet Union, South Asia, other OECD countries, Latin America, East Asia, and the other

Table 8.7 *IRTS steady-state model impacts on welfare (1992 US $billion)*

Region	Agricultural reform	MFA reform	Manufacturing sector reform	Complete reform package	Complete reform package as percentage of GDP
Australia	0.9	0.1	2.3	3.3	1.0
New Zealand	0.5	0.0	0.9	1.4	3.5
Canada	0.3	1.0	1.3	2.6	0.4
United States	3.2	9.2	13.7	26.7	0.4
Japan	16.8	−0.5	6.2	22.7	0.6
Korea	5.2	−0.4	2.7	7.5	2.4
European Union (12)	26.4	7.8	14.9	49.9	0.7
Indonesia	0.3	0.9	1.4	2.6	2.0
Malaysia	2.1	0.3	2.6	5.0	8.8
Philippines	1.1	0.2	1.1	2.4	4.2
Singapore	0.5	−0.2	0.4	0.7	1.7
Thailand	1.4	0.8	10.3	12.6	10.7
China	−0.8	1.7	1.2	2.0	0.4
Hong Kong	0.6	−1.5	−0.2	−1.1	−1.2
Taiwan	0.0	−0.3	1.3	1.1	0.5
Argentina	0.7	0.1	1.6	2.3	1.0
Brazil	0.1	0.1	4.0	4.3	1.0
Mexico	0.7	0.2	1.4	2.3	0.6
Rest of Latin America	2.0	−0.3	3.2	4.7	1.6
Sub-Saharan Africa	−0.5	−0.1	0.0	−0.7	−0.5
Middle East and North Africa	0.1	0.2	1.9	1.5	0.2

Table 8.7 (cont.)

Region	Agricultural reform	MFA reform	Manufacturing sector reform	Complete reform package	Complete reform package as percentage of GDP
Eastern Europe and former Soviet Union	0.0	−0.3	2.3	1.2	0.1
South Asia	0.2	1.9	5.3	6.7	1.8
Other European	1.6	−0.8	7.0	8.8	0.7
Developing countries (total)	13.9	3.4	40.5	55.2	1.1
Industrialized countries (total)	49.8	16.9	46.3	115.4	0.6
World	63.7	20.3	86.8	170.6	0.7

European from the twenty-four-region model. The primary result of the regional aggregation is a 5 to 10 percent reduction in the gains from the Uruguay Round, because the aggregation reduces the dispersion of distortions. Since resource misallocation costs increase roughly with the square of the distortion, a model with less dispersion will exert a downward bias on estimates of the welfare impacts of protection. More important, the aggregation sometimes magnifies the effects for individual countries. For example, China would gain much more from elimination of the MFA in the twelve-region model, because Malaysia and Indonesia, which are the most effective competitors in the region, are aggregated into "East Asia," thereby producing a region of only average efficiency. These findings suggest that the greater level of geographic detail in our model is an important extension to the other aggregate models of the Uruguay Round.[25]

Systematic sensitivity analysis

We also conducted a systematic sensitivity analysis of our major results for plausible bounds on elasticities, given that elasticity estimates are subject to a margin of error. To the extent that our major conclusions are robust to perturbations of these bounds, we do not believe that our uncertainty about specific values of these elasticities is a weakness of the model.[26]

Our sensitivity analysis uses the procedures developed by Harrison and Vinod (1992). In essence, these procedures amount to a Monte Carlo simulation exercise in which a wide range of elasticities are independently and simultaneously perturbed from their benchmark values. These perturbations follow prescribed probability distributions, typically uniform, where we specify the relevant parameters of the distributions.[27] For each Monte Carlo run, we solved the counterfactual policy with the selected set of elasticities. We repeated this process 1,000 times and then tabulated the results as a distribution, giving equal weight (by construction) to each Monte Carlo run. The upshot is a probability distribution defined over the endogenous variables of interest. In our case, we focus solely on the welfare impacts of the complete Uruguay Round reform package.

The welfare results, which are for the CRTS static model, are relatively robust with respect to the range of elasticity perturbations considered here (table 8.8). To illustrate the results, consider the welfare results for the world. Of the 1,000 estimates, the smallest was $91.9 billion and the largest was $110.6 billion. The mean of the distribution of the estimates is $100.6 billion and the standard deviation is $3.0 billion. Given the sample size, the distribution should be approximately normal, so that the range $91.5

Table 8.8 *Sensitivity analysis of welfare impacts in the CRTS static version of the base model (1992 US $billion)*

Region	Mean	Standard deviation	Skewness	Kurtosis	Minimum	Maximum
Australia	1.19	0.05	−0.10	2.96	1.02	1.36
New Zealand	0.38	0.02	0.06	2.77	0.33	0.44
Canada	1.17	0.09	0.02	2.71	0.92	1.45
United States	13.13	0.61	0.01	2.50	11.54	14.70
Japan	19.26	1.73	−0.01	2.46	14.36	23.73
Korea	5.67	0.68	0.21	2.60	4.13	7.65
European Union (12)	40.39	1.77	0.04	2.23	35.97	44.38
Indonesia	1.33	0.17	0.18	2.64	0.90	1.85
Malaysia	2.05	0.19	0.15	2.44	1.56	2.60
Philippines	0.98	0.14	0.16	2.33	0.60	1.35
Singapore	0.92	0.11	0.32	2.72	0.63	1.23
Thailand	2.67	0.15	0.01	2.77	2.24	3.15
China	1.31	0.28	0.05	2.79	0.57	2.22
Hong Kong	−1.21	0.08	0.08	2.86	−1.40	−0.99
Taiwan	0.43	0.06	−0.01	2.57	0.25	0.58
Argentina	0.64	0.03	0.04	2.76	0.57	0.72
Brazil	1.39	0.07	−0.04	2.54	1.18	1.60
Mexico	0.17	0.04	−0.02	2.71	0.05	0.29
Rest of Latin America	1.34	0.13	−0.01	2.84	0.91	1.78
Sub-Saharan Africa	−0.37	0.03	−0.03	2.99	−0.48	−0.24
Middle East and North Africa	−0.29	0.13	0.02	2.74	−0.65	0.11
Eastern Europe and former Soviet Union	−0.28	0.13	−0.19	2.52	−0.67	0.02
South Asia	3.71	0.28	0.05	2.80	2.87	4.49
Other European	4.65	0.27	0.08	2.66	3.92	5.55
Developing countries (total)	20.46	1.07	0.15	2.77	16.67	23.59
Industrialized countries (total)	80.17	2.55	0.03	2.75	72.42	88.17
World	100.63	3.03	0.06	2.80	91.92	110.60

billion to $109.7 billion constitutes a 99 percent confidence interval of the estimates. This compares with the point estimate from table 8.2 of $92.9 billion, which is in the low end of the confidence interval, in part for reasons discussed in the above note.

Comparisons with other estimates

Several other studies have measured the quantitative impact of the Uruguay Round, and can usefully be compared with our results. The most important issues here are the size of the welfare gains, the distribution of the welfare gains, and the sensitivity of the results to alternative specifications of the underlying model or policy reform. We evaluate points of agreement and disagreement issue by issue, and then for the Uruguay Round as a whole.

Agricultural reform

Although our estimates are the first to decompose the consequences of agricultural liberalization into its three major components, two comparable CGE studies have been undertaken to simulate the impacts of the reduction in agricultural distortions on total welfare benefits; both use the same underlying "RUNS" model: Goldin, Knudsen, and van der Mensbrugghe (1993) and Goldin and van der Mensbrugghe (1994) used a projected cut of 36 percent in all distortions, which is a much larger cut in a greater amount of distortions than we have used and is the primary reason for the larger aggregate gains they found in their studies.[28] What is useful to examine, however, is their estimate that the agricultural liberalization component of the Uruguay Round would generate 89 percent of the total gains, whereas our static CRTS model estimated that the liberalization component would generate only 63 percent of total welfare gains.

To reconcile these differences, we implemented a RUNS-type elasticity structure in the twelve-region version of our model. The implementation introduced two RUNS-type differences: agricultural goods are homogeneous in RUNS (that is, no Armington or CES assumption is attributed to these goods); and a constant elasticity of transformation between domestic output destined for domestic markets and for export markets is assumed. After altering elasticities in our twelve-region CRTS base model and steady-state IRTS model to approximate the RUNS formulation, we found that agriculture reform was responsible for 87 percent of the gains in the static (short-run) version (close to the RUNS results), although only 60 percent in the long-run version. Clearly, using the Armington and CES formulations for nonagriculture sectors but the homogeneous assumption for agricultural sectors substantially increases the relative importance of agriculture.[29] The key issue, then, is the plausibility of the parameter values chosen.

MFA reform

Other CGE assessments of the impact of eliminating the MFA have been undertaken by Yang, Martin, and Yanagishima (forthcoming), Francois, McDonald, and Nordström (1994 and chapter 9 in this volume), Hertel, Martin, Yanagishima, and Dimaranan (chapter 7), and Trela and Whalley (1990a).

Our results are closest to those of Hertel, Martin, Yanagishima, and Dimaranan (chapter 7). Yang, Martin, and Yanagishima (forthcoming) and Francois, McDonald, and Nordström (1994 and chapter 9 in this volume) report that MFA liberalization accounts for a much larger share of the gains under the Uruguay Round. For example, the Francois study reports that MFA liberalization is responsible for about 50 percent of the gains in many of their simulations, whereas we obtain about 15 percent. The reason is straightforward: our study, as well as that of Hertel, Martin, Yanagishima, and Dimaranan (chapter 7), use updated estimates of the tariff equivalents of MFA quotas from the GTAP data base. The updated values, which are significantly scaled down from the original values, correct an earlier error so that the GTAP data base is consistent with its background documentation.

The model of Hertel, Martin, Yanagishima, and Dimaranan (chapter 7) is a thirteen-sector aggregation of the GTAP data and estimates that the MFA is responsible for about 20 percent of the gains under the Uruguay Round, not far from our estimate of 17 percent. Their estimate is predicated on the removal of quotas in a projected economy of the year 2005; because the world economy would grow more quickly than the quotas under the MFA until that time, the quotas would become more binding, and the MFA would increase in relative importance. But the pattern of gainers and losers among developing countries in their model is similar to the pattern found in our model.

The most important finding from the Trela and Whalley (1990a) analysis is that the vast majority of exporting countries under the MFA would actually gain from MFA reform, notwithstanding losses in quota rents. In their base model, the only countries that would be welfare losers are the Dominican Republic, Haiti, Hong Kong, Macau, and Singapore; the aggregate welfare gain to exporters would have been $8.078 billion in 1986, with aggregate losses for the above five countries totalling only $0.569 billion. In simulation MFA-6 of table 8.4 we show that our model contains parameter values that produce results for developing countries that are almost as positive as those in Trela and Whalley (1990a). Still higher values for the highest-level demand elasticities would generate results even closer to those of Trela and Whalley (1990a), but these are not supported by econometric evidence or our *a priori* beliefs.

Overall evaluations

Francois, McDonald, and Nordström (1994) found that the steady-state impact of the Uruguay Round on global welfare would be $510 billion annually in 1990 dollars.[30] Their estimate of $510 billion is larger than our estimate of $171 billion, primarily because it is based on a simple extrapolation of estimates from 1990 to 2005, using region-specific scalar growth projections that come from "outside the model." To be specific, they obtain the 2005 estimates for each region in their study by multiplying the corresponding 1990 estimates for that region by a scalar based on OECD and World Bank growth projections for that region.[31] Their intention was to provide numbers that are more directly comparable to the estimate of $511 billion obtained by Goldin, Knudsen, and van der Mensbrugghe (1993), based on a projected economy of 2002.[32] But the estimates that would be comparable to ours would exclude the extrapolation to 2005: that estimate is "only" $291 billion. In addition, the updated estimates of Francois, McDonald, and Nordström (chapter 9) reduce the $291 billion estimate to $193 billion. The $193 billion estimate is for their steady-state IRTS scenario, and is thus comparable to our $171 billion estimate.

Hertel *et al.* have estimated the global gains to the world from the Uruguay Round at about $258 billion. Since they do not incorporate dynamic, steady-state or IRTS effects, the appropriate comparison to their model is our static CRTS model (we obtain $93 billion of gains in this version of our model). But their estimates are based on the world in the year 2005, and the projection of the world forward from 1992 roughly doubles the dollar estimates. Even after adjusting for the forward projection, the Hertel *et al.* estimates remain somewhat larger than ours. This is due to two factors: they project that the MFA quotas will grow somewhat less fast than the world economy, so the gains from removing the MFA are slightly larger than in our model; and they employ slightly larger (but plausible) elasticities. Model variants with lower elasticities produce lower estimated gains.

Based on our own systematic sensitivity analysis with respect to parameter specification, we do not regard the remaining differences between our estimates and the WTO and GTAP teams as significant. The broad themes that we have emphasized elsewhere in this chapter are quite similar across the models. In particular, all the models indicate that those countries that liberalized the most, gained the most; and this was the European Union, the United States, and Japan. And the gains may be expected to be larger in the long run when the capital stock can adjust and the responsiveness of firms and consumers to price changes (elasticities) will be higher.

Conclusion

Our evaluation of the Uruguay Round indicates that the static welfare gains would be $96 billion annually in 1992 dollars, with an upper-bound steady-state estimate of $171 billion annually. Although our estimates and others vary according to the assumptions that are made about trade elasticities, and the distortion data and modeling choices used, we have emphasized an approach that should make the results transparent, and allow the reader to draw judgments about their credibility for different time horizons.

We estimate that the European Union, United States, and Japan would gain the most from the Uruguay Round, since these are the regions that are reducing their distortions to the greatest extent. Although there are likely to be some losers from the Uruguay Round, especially in the short run, we are optimistic that unilateral liberalization of both tariffs and production distortions can be implemented to ensure that all regions can gain.

Appendix A   The data

Except for tariff data, the data for calibrating the model come primarily from the GTAP data base for 1992 (version 2), documented in Gehlhar et al. (forthcoming). The twenty-four-region version of the model retains all regions in the GTAP data base. The sectors were selected whereby those in which significant reduction in distortions occurred are retained as individual sectors, thus minimizing the aggregation bias.

The primary source of the data on import tariffs in our base model is the data base assembled by the International Economics Division of the World Bank based on the IDB of the WTO Secretariat. The IDB is based, in turn, on submissions from the contracting parties (the GATT IDB is documented in GATT 1994).

For manufacturing sectors, the data base is a trade-weighted aggregation of the integrated data base of the GATT Secretariat (to the regions and sectors of the GTAP data base). For the agricultural sectors it was necessary to estimate the *ad valorem* tariff equivalents of the specific tariff offers incorporated in the commitments of the GATT contracting parties. These adjustments are documented in Ingco (1994) and chapter 2, and are incorporated in our basic data set on tariffs.[33] These data consist of a matrix of import tariffs before and after the Uruguay Round, showing the *ad valorem* tariff applying on imports of each good from each other region.[34] Thus, our study is distinguished from earlier published estimates of the impact of the Uruguay Round in that our estimates are based on the actual agreed-upon offers, rather than projections of what might be agreed. Further details regarding data are provided in Harrison, Rutherford, and Tarr (1995).

Appendix B   Competition in the IRTS models

We assume that firms are symmetric and determine price and quantities in an oligopoly model in which there is entry and exit, and hence zero profit in equilibrium. Firms compete in a quantity-adjusting oligopoly framework where the quantity conjectures are calibrated to be identical for all firms in each sector and each country, and do not change in the counterfactual. Harrison, Rutherford, and Tarr (1995, Appendix C) show that our formulation yields an equation for the percentage markup of price over marginal costs in each sector which is equal to:

$$
\frac{\tilde{m}_{rr'}}{\Omega_{rr'}} =
\begin{cases}
\dfrac{1}{\sigma_{DD}} + \left\{ \dfrac{1}{\sigma_{DM}} - \dfrac{1}{\sigma_{DD}} \right\} \dfrac{1}{N_r} + \left\{ 1 - \dfrac{1}{\sigma_{DM}} \right\} \dfrac{\theta_{rr}}{N_r} & r = r' \\[4mm]
\dfrac{1}{\sigma_{MM}} + \left\{ \dfrac{1}{\sigma_{DM}} - \dfrac{1}{\sigma_{MM}} \right\} \dfrac{\theta_{rr'}}{N_r \theta_{r'}^M} + \left\{ 1 - \dfrac{1}{\sigma_{DM}} \right\} \dfrac{\theta_{rr'}}{N_r} & r \neq r'
\end{cases}
\tag{1}
$$

where $\theta_{rr'}$ is the market share of firms from region r in country r', θ_r^M is the market share of imports in region r, and $\Omega_{rr'}$ is the conjectural variation for firms from region r selling into region r'.

When tariffs are lowered, firms lose domestic market share but gain market share on export markets. The top part of the above equation refers to the home market. Since σ_{DM} exceeds unity, with a lower domestic share $\theta_{rr'}$ firms lower their markup on domestic sales. But since firms are subject to a zero profit constraint in our model, lower markups induce losses and firm exit. Firm exit allows the remaining firms to increase their output and achieve rationalization gains by sliding down their average cost curves. Exit continues until rationalization gains are sufficient to restore zero profit with the lower markups. Elasticities affect markups both directly and indirectly. There is a direct effect on price. With a larger direct effect on price from higher elasticities, the market share effect will be larger. Then the indirect effect through the markup equation will be larger. Equation (1) illustrates a key point: the induced reduction in firms and rationalization benefits can only be derived from changes in the shares, which typically are not large.

Notes

The views expressed are those of the authors alone and should not be interpreted as the opinion of the World Bank. We are grateful to Will Martin and Joseph Francois for comments.

1. All welfare estimates are in 1992 US dollars.
2. This finding contrasts with the results of Nguyen, Perroni, and Wigle (1991 and 1993) and Francois, McDonald, and Nordström (1994 and chapter 9 in this volume).
3. Goldin, Knudsen, and van der Mensbrugghe (1993) found a similar result.

4. The elasticities of substitution for these value-added production functions were listed in Harrison, Rutherford, and Wooton (1991: table 1, p. 101), and were based on procedures discussed in Harrison, Jones, Kimbell, and Wigle (1993) from time-series data for the United States between 1947 and 1982. Contrary to many of the estimates used in the literature on CGE models, the econometric specification used in this case corresponds to the functional form assumed in the model.

5. The available econometric evidence suggests much lower values than these (Reinert and Roland-Holst 1992 and Shiells and Reinert 1993). But elasticities would be expected to increase over time, and this model assesses an adjustment of about ten years, a rather long period in the context of these estimates.

6. Hence, we do not capture the marginal efficiency cost of governments, having to raise extra revenues with a distortionary domestic tax system. For least-developed countries, these costs could be quite significant, since the revenue losses from trade reform could be sizable.

7. See, for example, Francois, McDonald, and Nordström (1994), GATT (1994), US General Accounting Office (1994), Schott and Buurman (1994), and Baldwin (1994). Virtually all of the major components of the Uruguay Round have a significant temporal dimension, so that most of the liberalization is backloaded in time. We ignore this temporal dimension and focus on the final end-point position of the negotiated agreements. A potentially valuable extension would be an analysis that assessed whether the final results could be affected by the time path.

8. Many of the features of the Uruguay Round require more careful model specifications before one can be confident that their effects are captured properly. The most important, in our judgment, is the "tariffication" that has occurred in least-developed countries, as many countries have agreed to bind tariffs in line with GATT disciplines. Although the short-run impact of these bindings may be protectionist as countries choose to bind at a higher level of protection than applied on average, the longer-run gains may be substantial as GATT-style tariff-cutting formulas can be applied more easily to such distortions. Martin and Francois (1994) discuss these possibilities. In addition, even if the bound rate exceeds the average *ad valorem* equivalent protection level, it will probably truncate extremely high equivalent protection levels; since these higher rates are likely to generate disproportionately greater welfare losses, the net gains may be substantial even before the newly bound rates are liberalized.

9. The agreement on export subsidy reductions also includes a 21 percent reduction in the volume of exports subject to export subsidies. It is possible that this provision will impose an additional constraint on export subsidies, thus increasing the impact we estimate.

10. The European Union is to reduce its aggregate measure of support to agriculture by 16.8 percent.

11. Textiles is the other sector subject to MFA reform. The United States would experience a small (0.8 percent) reduction in textile prices; although this price decline would also help reduce the cost of living in the United States, the

welfare impact would be mitigated by losses to US producers on exports. The price reductions in the European Union would be 1.9 percent for textiles and 7.2 percent for wearing apparel.

12. This is likely an overestimate of developing countries' quota rent losses from MFA elimination to the extent that it ignores rent dissipation costs in developing countries associated with these quota rents. Hamilton (1986) and Trela and Whalley (1990b) review the internal quota allocation schemes underlying the MFA, suggesting substantial dissipated rents. Tarr (1994) estimates that these additional losses could be as high as ten times the standard distortion losses. We do not attempt to incorporate rent-seeking issues into our model since we have doubts as to the appropriate way to do so in an explicit general equilibrium setting (see Brooks and Heijdra 1988 and Tullock 1988).

13. Canada is also a constrained region, and for the EFTA region we take the MFA tariff equivalents at one third the level that exists in the European Union. GATT (1994) took the rates at one half, rather than one third of the European Union, since Austria, Norway, and Finland constrained these imports in the benchmark period, even though Sweden did not. But we also include Turkey in this region, which is a major exporter of textiles and apparel, so we adjusted the quota premium rate downward from the GATT study assumption for the EFTA.

14. Each elasticity applies to imports of all twenty-two goods in all regions. Reinert and Roland-Holst (1992) and Shiells and Reinert (1993) provide detailed estimates.

15. And even if substitution possibilities are great, a marginally inefficient supplier, such as Korea, would typically lose, despite having a comparatively large share in previously constrained markets.

16. Thus, Indonesia would gain under all simulations in which demand in the constrained markets expands significantly (that is, when σ_{DM} is at our base value of 4 or greater).

17. Because the United States also imports a considerable quantity of food products, including imports of processed food, it would lose from the terms-of-trade effects of AGR-1. Reduction of its production subsidies results in gains under AGR-2.

18. Japan's benchmark protection rate on grains is 329 percent. See Appendix A in Harrison, Rutherford, and Tarr (1995).

19. These regions are largely the high-income economies of East Asia. The data on protection rates for these countries come from Ingco (1994), who used the RUNS data base for these countries. The RUNS data yield comparatively high levels of benchmark agricultural protection for these countries.

20. Appendix C of Harrison, Rutherford and Tarr (1995) presents a more formal algebraic description of the IRTS model. We incorporate IRTS and monopolistically competitive pricing rules in essentially the same manner as in Harrison, Rutherford, and Tarr (1994). The primary difference from our earlier formulation is that our counterfactual here does not contain a regime switch that directly affects the perceived elasticity of demand for firms. That complication was appropriate for the policy scenario in Harrison, Rutherford, and Tarr

(1994), which was a closer integration of EU markets from improved internal standardization and fewer internal barriers to trade.

21. Full details of our estimates are provided in Harrison, Rutherford, and Tarr (1995, Appendix B). The cost disadvantage ratios we use are: 13 percent for processed rice; 10 percent for meat products and livestock; 5 percent for forestry, fishing, lumber, wood, paper, and wool; 3 percent for energy and energy products; 8 percent for minerals and mineral products; 3 percent for food, beverages, and tobacco; 6 percent for textiles; 5 percent for primary iron and steel; 11 percent for the transport industry; 5 percent for fabricated metals; 4 percent for chemicals, rubber, and plastics; 5 percent for nonferrous metals; and 6 percent for machinery, equipment, and other manufacturing. We apply these sector-specific ratios to each region in the absence of any data that convince us that they vary across regions in any known manner. Other sectors are modeled as CRTS.

22. Exceptions to the folklore include Nguyen and Wigle (1992) and de Melo and Tarr (1992).

23. For example, Francois, McDonald, and Nordström (1994 and chapter 9 in this volume) increase their elasticities of demand when they introduce IRTS – the impact of the elasticities is what drives the larger estimated welfare gains in their IRTS scenarios. (See Harrison, Rutherford and Tarr [1995] for details.) Harris (1986) used a weighted pricing rule for IRTS sectors which sets prices midway between the prices generated by two pricing rules. One was a simple monopolistically competitive mark-up rule, but the other was a collusive rule whereby all domestic producers would coordinate on a price epsilon below the tariff-inclusive price of imports. Using his model, Harrison, Jones, Kimbell, and Wigle (1993) demonstrate that the weight assigned to the latter pricing rule drives the "big numbers" from trade liberalization, rather than the assumed values of scale elasticities.

24. This approach is in the spirit of the equilibrium concept proposed by Hansen and Koopmans (1972) and Dantzig and Manne (1974) for multisectoral planning models that solve for a time-invariant capital stock. An invariant capital stock equilibrium is a set of price, production, and investment levels for which the economy is able to grow at a steady rate with constant relative prices. In our model the optimal capital stock is defined whereby the cost of investment, including depreciation and interest, is exactly equal to the capital rental rate. This can be viewed as a multisectoral version of the "golden rule" equilibrium from older growth theories. The most important difference between our steady-state calculation and the Hansen and Koopmans (1972) methodology is that we do not explicitly measure the commodity composition of investment. Hence, some uncertainty surrounds the determination of the steady-state capital price. We simply assume that, within each region, the price of capital is identical to the price of a basket of consumption goods. When we further assume that the benchmark capital stock is optimal, it reduces the steady-state calculation to fixing the capital price and permitting the capital stock to find an endogenous level.

25. Harrison, Rutherford, and Tarr (1995) provide the detailed results and interpretation of the twelve-region model.

26. These remarks should not be interpreted as denying the value of any new empirical work on generating such elasticities. On the contrary, any effort that could generate better bounds on these point estimates will generate even more credible policy conclusions, even if those conclusions are still probabilistic in nature. Moreover, we do not consider sensitivity analysis on more general functional forms, although we do share concerns about the restrictiveness of some of the popular forms we use (see Winters [1984], for example, on the separability of trade preferences).

27. In particular, we assume that primary factors have a univariate normal distribution truncated at zero at the bottom, and the following parameters have a uniform distribution that range between 3 and 5 for σ_{DM}; between 6 and 10 for σ_{MM}; between 0.5 and 1.5 for σ_{DC} and σ_{DG} and between 0 and 0.5 for σ_I, the elasticity of substitution between intermediates and primary inputs. Except for σ_I, in all cases of a uniform distribution we take the mean of the distribution to be the point estimate we employed above. This is not possible for σ_I since negative values are not admissible. As a result, the distribution of the estimates may be expected to have a mean larger than the point estimate.

28. For example, the authors cut agricultural export taxes, such as those existing in Sub-Saharan Africa, and their 36 percent reduction in agriculture import taxes is considerably larger than the cuts estimated by Ingco (1994). See Brandão and Martin (1993) for details.

29. Another reason that agriculture is responsible for such a high proportion of the benefits in the Goldin studies is that, given the aggregate characterization of the manufacturing sector, these studies did not model the impact of the elimination of the MFA. Harrison, Rutherford, and Tarr (1995) provide details and a discussion of some other assumptions we modified to approximate the RUNS model.

30. We focus on the aggregate dollar estimate of gains to the world. The aggregate gain is obtained by simply summing over the dollar gains to each country. This is an implicit weighting in a planetary social welfare function. Although other weights of gains across countries may be more appropriate in some contexts, to facilitate comparison of results we use the same implicit weighting.

31. Projections do not account for the Uruguay Round, as stressed correctly by GATT (1994). They estimate annual growth rates in the 1990–2005 period of 3.3 percent for OECD countries, of 8.5 percent for China, of 5.7 percent for Taiwan, and of 4.8 percent for developing and transitional economies, yielding scalar adjustments of 63 percent, 340 percent, 230 percent, and 202 percent.

32. The Goldin (1993 and 1994) studies obtained their estimates by applying the 36 percent cut in all distortions to their projected economy in 2002. Since the economy is larger in 2002 than in 1992, their dollar gains are larger.

33. The GTAP data base had to be rebalanced with the new data on tariff and subsidies. We impose consistency in the benchmark data by making adjustments to the vector of stock change. The data of Ingco (1994) have been revised since the publication of her paper, and we use the revised data.

34. The GATT data base reflects only MFN tariffs. Although the World Bank data base shows some geographically discriminatory tariffs, the discrimination is due only to different aggregations based on different trade weighting of MFN tariff lines. In particular, preferences under the Generalized System of Preferences and the Lomé Convention are ignored. Thus, the possible losses to developing countries from an erosion of these preferences in the Uruguay Round are ignored in the World Bank and GATT data bases.

References

Baldwin, Robert 1994. "An Economic Evaluation of the Uruguay Round Agreements." Unpublished manuscript, Department of Economics, University of Michigan.

Brandão, Antonio Salazar P., and Will J. Martin 1993. "Implications of Agricultural Trade Liberalization for the Developing Countries." *Agricultural Economics* 8: 313–43.

Brooks, Michael A., and Ben J. Heijdra 1988. "In Search of Rent-Seeking." In C. K. Rowley, R. D. Tollison, and G. Tullock, eds., *The Political Economy of Rent-Seeking*. Boston: Kluwer Academic Publishing.

Dantzig, George, and Alan S. Manne 1974. "A Complementarity Algorithm for an Optimal Capital Path with Invariant Proportions." *Journal of Economic Theory* 9: 312–23.

de Melo, Jaime, and David Tarr 1992. *General Equilibrium Analysis of U.S. Foreign Trade Policy*. Cambridge, Mass: MIT Press.

Francois, Joseph F., Bradley McDonald, and Håkan Nordström 1994. "The Uruguay Round: A Global General Equilibrium Assessment." Unpublished Manuscript, GATT Secretariat, Geneva, September.

GATT 1994. *The Results of the Uruguay Round of Multilateral Trade Negotiations*. Geneva: GATT Secretariat, November.

Gehlhar, Mark, Denice Gray, Thomas W. Hertel, Karen Huff, Elena Ianchovichina, Bradley J. McDonald, Robert McDougall, Marinos E. Tsigas, and Randall Wigle forthcoming. "Overview of the GTAP Data Base." in T. W. Hertel, ed., *Global Trade Analysis: Modeling and Applications*. New York: Cambridge University Press.

Goldin, Ian, and Dominique van der Mensbrugghe 1994. "The Uruguay Round: An Initial Assessment." Unpublished draft manuscript. Washington, DC: World Bank, December 9.

Goldin, Ian, Odin Knudsen, and Dominique van der Mensbrugghe 1993. *Trade Liberalization: Global Economic Implications*. Washington, DC: OECD and World Bank.

Hamilton, Carl 1986. "ASEAN Systems for Allocation of Export Licenses Under VERs." In C. Findlay and R. Garnaut, eds., *The Political Economy of Manufacturing Protection: Experiences of ASEAN and Australia*. Sydney: George Allen & Unwin.

Hansen, Terje, and Tjalling Koopmans 1972. "On the Definition and Computation of a Capital Stock Invariant under Optimization." *Journal of Economic Theory* 5: 487–523.

Harris, Richard G. 1986. "Market Structure and Trade Liberalization: A General Equilibrium Assessment." In T. N. Srinivasan and J. Whalley, eds., *General Equilibrium Trade Policy Modelling*. Cambridge, Mass.: MIT Press.

Harrison, Glenn W., and H. D. Vinod 1992. "The Sensitivity Analysis of Applied General Equilibrium Models: Completely Randomized Factorial Sampling Designs." *The Review of Economics & Statistics* 74: 357–62.

Harrison, Glenn W., Thomas F. Rutherford, and David G. Tarr 1994. "Product Standards, Imperfect Competition, and the Completion of the Market in the European Community." Policy Research Working Paper 1293. Washington, DC: International Trade Division, International Economics Department, World Bank, April.

———. 1995. "Quantifying the Uruguay Round." In W. Martin and L. A. Winters, eds., *The Uruguay Round and the Developing Economies*. World Bank Discussion Paper 307. Washington, DC: World Bank.

Harrison, Glenn W., Thomas F. Rutherford, and Ian Wooton 1991. "An Empirical Database for a General Equilibrium Model of the European Communities," *Empirical Economics* 16: 95–120.

Harrison, Glenn W., Richard Jones, Larry J. Kimbell, and Randall Wigle 1993. "How Robust Is Applied General Equilibrium Analysis?" *Journal of Policy Modelling* 15(1): 99–115.

Ingco, Merlinda 1994. "Agricultural Trade Liberalization in the Uruguay Round: One Step Forward, One Step Back?" Unpublished manuscript. Washington, DC: International Trade Division, International Economics Department, World Bank, November.

Martin, Will, and Joseph Francois 1994. "Bindings and Rules as Trade Liberalization." Unpublished manuscript. Washington, DC: International Trade Division, International Economics Department, World Bank, November.

Neven, Damien J. 1990. "Gains and Losses from 1992." *Economic Policy* April: 13–61.

Nguyen, Trien, and Randall Wigle 1992. "Trade Liberalization with Imperfect Competition: The Large and the Small of It." *European Economic Review* 36: 17–35.

Nguyen, Trien, Carlo Perroni, and Randall Wigle 1991. "The Value of a Uruguay Round Success." *The World Economy* 14: 359–74.

———. 1993. "An Evaluation of the Draft Final Act of the Uruguay Round." *Economic Journal* 103: 1540–49.

Pratten, C. 1987. "A Survey of Economies of Scale." Report prepared for the EC Commission, Brussels.

Reinert, Kenneth A., and David W. Roland-Holst 1992. "Armington Elasticities for United States Manufacturing Sectors." *Journal of Policy Modelling* 14(5): 631–39.

Schott, Jeffrey, and Johanna Buurman 1994. *The Uruguay Round: An Assessment.* Washington, DC: Institute for International Economics.

Shiells, C. R., and K. A. Reinert 1993. "Armington Models and Terms-of-Trade Effects: Some Econometric Evidence for North America." *Canadian Journal of Economics* 26(2): 299–316.

Tarr, David G. 1987. "Effects of Restraining Steel Exports from the Republic of Korea and Other Countries to the United States and the European Economic Community." *The World Bank Economic Review* 1(3): 397–418.

1994. "The Welfare Costs of Price Controls for Cars and Color Televisions in Poland: Contrasting Estimates of Rent-Seeking from Recent Experience." *The World Bank Economic Review* 8(3): 415–43.

Trela, Irene, and John Whalley 1990a. "Global Effects of Developed Country Trade Restrictions on Trade and Apparel." *Economic Journal* 100: 1190–205.

1990b. "Internal Quota Allocation Schemes and the Costs of the MFA." Unpublished manuscript, Department of Economics, University of Western Ontario, September.

Tullock, Gordon 1988. "Rents and Rent-Seeking." In C. K. Rowley, R. D. Tollison, and G. Tullock, eds., *The Political Economy of Rent-Seeking.* Boston: Kluwer Academic Publishing.

US General Accounting Office 1994. *The General Agreement on Tariffs and Trade: Uruguay Round Final Act Should Produce Overall U.S. Economic Gains.* Washington, DC: General Accounting Office (GAO/GGD–94–83b), July.

Winters, L. Alan 1984. "Separability and the Specification of Foreign Trade Functions." *Journal of International Economics* 17: 239–63.

Yang, Yongzheng 1994. "The Impact of MFA Phasing Out on World Clothing and Textiles Markets." *Journal of Development Studies* 30(3): 892–915.

Yang, Yongzheng, Will Martin, and Koji Yangishima forthcoming. "Evaluating the Benefits of Abolishing the MFA in the Uruguay Round Package." In T. W. Hertel, ed., *Global Trade Analysis: Modeling and Applications.* New York: Cambridge University Press.

9 The Uruguay Round: a numerically based qualitative assessment

Joseph F. Francois, Bradley McDonald, and
Håkan Nordström

The Uruguay Round agreement and the inauguration of the WTO mark an important milestone for the world trade system. The scope of the system is being broadened to such new areas as services and the trade-related aspects of intellectual property rights, and the Prodigal Sons of agriculture, textiles, and wearing apparel are returning to the trade fold after a long and dubious absence.

In this study, we use variations of a computable general equilibrium model to identify a set of numerically robust qualitative estimates of the impact of the Uruguay Round. In particular, we examine the quantifiable aspects of the Round under a variety of modeling assumptions. While individual estimates are sensitive to theoretical assumptions and the value of parameters, we believe that the overall pattern of results provides useful insights into the implications of the Uruguay Round for different regions of the world economy. Compared with earlier studies, which are surveyed in a technical companion paper (Francois, McDonald, and Nordström 1995), this study benefits from more up-to-date information on the extent of liberalization under various agreements reached in the Uruguay Round. Foremost, the growing consensus is that agricultural liberalization is more modest than previously assumed.

In line with these more cautious expectations, we study a minimal liberalization scenario in agriculture, with only minimum market access commitments and commitments to reduce export subsidies. If this scenario is correct, the expected increase in world market prices will be slight. Net food importers would continue to benefit from artificially low world market prices, sustained by taxpayers and consumers in industrial countries who provide heavy protection or support for agriculture.

Discounting the impact of agricultural liberalization, our results suggest that the greatest benefits of the Uruguay Round are likely to come from the phaseout of industrial nontariff barriers, particularly quotas under the MFA. The importance of the phaseout suggests that, in the end, the

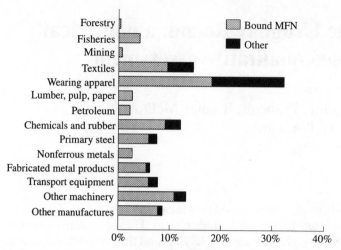

Figure 9.1   Protection by sector: tariff equivalents in OECD countries (excluding primary agriculture)

implications of the Uruguay Round for both industrial and developing countries will hinge crucially on the readiness of WTO members to implement the agreement faithfully and fend off renewed requests for protection from industries now protected by nontariff barriers. They will also depend on the ability of the WTO itself to muster confidence in the system, as the new dispute settlement process comes to play a key role.

The Uruguay Round and market access

In contrast with previous GATT rounds, Uruguay Round negotiations over market access focused on nontariff barriers to trade. The first seven negotiating rounds succeeded in making tariff protection a relatively minor obstacle to trade in industrial countries.[1] But as progress in tariff reductions was made, gains were partially eroded by the emergence of less transparent, nontariff trade barriers. In many sectors of industrial countries, large shares of protection come today not from MFN tariffs bound under GATT, but from nontariff barriers such as textile and clothing quotas under the MFA and antidumping duties (figure 9.1).[2]

Other important aspects of the Uruguay Round were the overhaul of GATT rules, including: procedures for settling trade disputes and providing contingent protection; sector-specific exemptions from general GATT disciplines (such sectors as textiles, clothing, and agriculture); TRIMs and TRIPS; and the incorporation of services through the GATS.

Our numerically based qualitative assessments cover four reforms under the Uruguay Round agreement: improved market access for goods from the reductions in tariffs; the phaseout of MFA quotas on textiles and clothing; the phaseout of other quantitative restrictions on industrial goods as part of the new safeguard agreement; and an agreement to liberalize trade in agricultural products.

Tariffs

The Uruguay Round addressed five aspects of tariff barriers: tariff peaks, nuisance tariffs (whose main protectionist effect stems from the paper work involved in customs clearance), differences in tariff bindings, credits for autonomous liberalization, and tariff escalation. The overall trade-weighted target for tariff reductions was set at 36 percent for industrial countries and two-thirds of that amount (24 percent) for developing countries.

Estimates of the outcomes of the tariff negotiations on an aggregate, trade-weighted basis indicate noteworthy differences between the tariff regimes of industrial countries and those of developing countries (table 9.1). The new tariffs in most of the sectors of industrial countries are less than 5 percent (but are higher in Australia and New Zealand). Tariffs on textiles and clothing, which average from 10 to 30 percent, are an important exception. These tariffs are imposed in conjunction with MFA quotas. The tariffs of developing countries are generally higher and vary substantially by region and by sector within region. Developing countries in East Asia impose tariffs that range from 5 to 15 percent; those in Latin America, Africa, and the Middle East impose tariffs that range from 10 to 25 percent; and those in South Asia impose tariffs that range from 10 to 60 percent. Developing countries tend to protect manufactures more heavily than they do primary goods; industrial countries do just the opposite (with the exception of textiles and clothing). Looming behind all of these tariffs and associated peak rates in manufactures are the "Himalayas" of agricultural protection.

The greatest absolute reductions in tariffs are generally being made by countries that started with the highest tariffs, with the notable exception of African countries.[3] The absolute size of a country's own tariff reductions can be a useful, if crude, indicator of the gains that it can expect from the Uruguay Round. The modest liberalization by countries in Africa explains in part why they would tend to gain less than countries in Asia. By fostering inefficiencies and resource misallocation, protection can be a self-inflicted drag on development.

The largest sectoral tariff reductions were not necessarily made in the sectors with the highest tariffs. Although the absolute size of the reductions

Table 9.1 *Average pre- and post-Uruguay Round tariff rates for nonagricultural products*

Products	Australia and New Zealand			Japan			Canada			United States			European Union			EFTA		
	Old tariff	New tariff	Change	Old tariff	New tariff	Change	Old tariff	New tariff	Change	Old tariff	New tariff	Change	Old tariff	New tariff	Change	Old tariff	New tariff	Change
Forestry	0.2	0.2	0.0	0.0	0.0	0.0	0.0	0.0	0.0	0.3	0.0	-0.3	0.0	0.0	0.0	0.2	0.1	-0.1
Fishery	0.7	0.5	-0.2	5.7	4.1	-1.6	3.2	2.1	-1.1	1.2	0.9	-0.2	12.9	10.7	-2.2	1.7	1.4	-0.3
Mining	1.6	1.1	-0.5	1.1	0.5	-0.6	2.7	1.4	-1.3	1.3	0.8	-0.5	1.1	0.8	-0.3	1.0	0.8	-0.2
Coal	0.0	0.0	0.0	0.0	0.0	0.0	0.0	0.0	0.0	0.0	0.0	0.0	0.5	0.0	-0.5	0.1	0.0	0.0
Crude petroleum	0.2	0.2	0.0	0.2	0.2	0.0	0.3	0.3	0.0	0.6	0.6	0.0	0.0	0.0	0.0	0.6	0.5	-0.1
Gas	4.7	1.9	-2.8	1.3	0.0	-1.3	2.7	2.7	0.0	0.0	0.0	0.0	0.1	0.1	-0.1	1.6	0.9	-0.7
Other minerals	2.3	1.6	-0.7	1.5	0.8	-0.7	4.6	2.3	-2.3	2.4	1.3	-1.2	2.3	1.8	-0.6	1.1	0.9	-0.3
Textiles	24.6	14.5	-10.1	7.4	6.0	-1.4	18.6	11.7	-6.8	10.5	7.5	-3.0	9.0	6.8	-2.3	12.2	8.0	-4.2
Clothing	50.5	34.8	-15.7	13.0	10.2	-2.9	22.9	16.6	-6.3	16.7	15.2	-1.5	12.6	10.9	-1.7	17.0	11.4	-5.6
Lumber, pulp & paper	8.8	4.3	-4.5	2.2	1.2	-1.0	4.8	0.4	-4.4	0.9	0.3	-0.6	4.7	0.5	-4.2	3.8	1.2	-2.6
Lumber & wood prods	8.6	4.2	-4.4	3.6	2.4	-1.1	3.2	1.9	-1.3	1.7	1.0	-0.7	2.9	1.5	-1.4	3.7	2.1	-1.6
Pulp, paper and printing	8.8	4.3	-4.5	0.9	0.0	-0.9	5.3	0.0	-5.3	0.6	0.0	-0.6	5.6	0.0	-5.6	3.8	0.9	-2.9
Petroleum	1.6	0.9	-0.7	1.8	0.2	-1.6	4.1	2.8	-1.4	0.7	0.5	-0.2	0.8	0.5	-0.2	1.4	1.0	-0.4
Chemicals	11.9	7.5	-4.4	4.1	1.6	-2.5	10.3	5.3	-5.0	5.0	3.0	-2.0	7.7	4.2	-3.4	5.8	3.0	-2.8
Primary steel	9.7	1.6	-8.1	3.9	0.6	-3.3	7.4	0.4	-7.1	4.5	0.2	-4.3	5.3	0.5	-4.8	4.1	0.6	-3.5
Primary nonferrous metals	11.2	6.4	-4.8	4.1	2.4	-1.7	4.9	2.7	-2.2	2.8	2.6	-0.2	7.2	5.9	-1.3	4.0	2.9	-1.1
Fabricated metals	16.6	12.8	-3.8	3.4	0.9	-2.6	9.7	6.0	-3.7	4.7	2.8	-1.9	5.7	3.1	-2.6	5.5	3.2	-2.3

	Latin America			South Asia			East Asia			Africa			Economies in transition			Rest of the World		
	Old tariff	New tariff	Change	Old tariff	New tariff	Change	Old tariff	New tariff	Change	Old tariff	New tariff	Change	Old tariff	New tariff	Change	Old tariff	New tariff	Change
Transport equipment	26.0	19.5	-6.5	1.4	0.0	-1.4	8.1	5.4	-2.8	4.8	4.6	-0.2	6.9	6.0	-0.9	8.1	6.7	-1.4
Other machinery	13.1	8.9	-4.2	0.9	0.1	-0.9	6.4	3.1	-3.3	3.4	1.5	-1.9	5.9	2.9	-3.0	4.2	2.4	-1.8
Other manufactures	9.8	6.7	-3.1	2.8	1.7	-1.1	6.5	3.0	-3.5	4.6	2.0	-2.6	5.5	3.1	-2.4	4.8	2.5	-2.3
Leather, fur and wool	13.5	12.1	-1.4	14.3	12.8	-1.5	13.4	8.5	-4.8	5.5	4.8	-0.8	5.4	3.8	-1.6	5.6	4.1	-1.5
Nonmetallic mining	10.2	7.1	-3.1	1.9	1.2	-0.7	5.8	2.2	-3.6	5.1	3.4	-1.6	3.9	2.8	-1.1	3.9	2.6	-1.3
Other manufacturing	9.6	6.4	-3.2	2.1	0.8	-1.3	6.3	2.9	-3.4	4.4	1.4	-3.0	5.9	3.1	-2.8	5.0	2.4	-2.7

	Latin America			South Asia			East Asia			Africa			Economies in transition			Rest of the World		
Products	Old tariff	New tariff	Change	Old tariff	New tariff	Change	Old tariff	New tariff	Change	Old tariff	New tariff	Change	Old tariff	New tariff	Change	Old tariff	New tariff	Change
Forestry	22.0	12.6	-9.4	10.0	9.9	-0.1	3.9	3.4	-0.5	16.0	16.0	0.0	1.0	0.9	-0.1	17.4	13.5	-3.9
Fishery	31.4	20.8	-10.6	4.0	4.0	0.0	30.2	6.9	-23.3	20.8	20.8	0.0	5.7	5.5	-0.2	21.8	20.5	-1.3
Mining	13.9	11.1	-2.8	27.2	19.3	-7.9	7.3	5.2	-2.0	11.6	11.6	0.0	1.8	1.6	-0.2	11.9	10.1	-1.8
Coal	5.6	5.6	0.0	22.5	22.5	0.0	3.0	2.9	-0.1	11.4	11.4	0.0	1.2	1.1	0.0	59.2	59.2	0.0
Crude petroleum	17.8	14.5	-3.3	48.1	48.1	0.0	4.8	4.8	0.0	9.5	9.5	0.0	1.0	1.0	0.0	2.5	0.6	-1.9
Gas	9.9	9.9	0.0	11.0	11.0	0.0	7.1	7.1	0.0	0.9	0.9	0.0	1.2	1.2	0.0	15.0	15.0	0.0
Other minerals	14.6	11.3	-3.3	25.3	16.2	-9.1	9.6	5.7	-3.9	15.8	15.8	0.0	3.0	2.5	-0.5	12.6	10.5	-2.0
Textiles	31.3	22.1	-9.2	63.2	56.4	-6.8	23.7	15.8	-7.9	35.1	35.0	-0.1	11.2	7.9	-3.2	70.6	35.4	-35.2
Clothing	37.0	29.2	-7.8	64.1	64.1	0.0	10.1	8.1	-2.0	40.7	40.7	0.0	13.2	10.9	-2.2	53.5	36.9	-16.6
Lumber, pulp & paper	12.0	9.5	-2.5	38.5	19.2	-19.4	9.7	6.4	-3.3	20.7	20.7	0.0	5.4	4.2	-1.2	16.2	13.1	-3.1
Lumber & wood prods	26.4	17.3	-9.1	18.5	17.0	-1.5	11.7	9.1	-2.6	21.8	21.8	0.0	4.5	3.5	-1.0	8.1	6.3	-1.7

Table 9.1 (*cont.*)

Products	Latin America Old tariff	New tariff	Change	South Asia Old tariff	New tariff	Change	East Asia Old tariff	New tariff	Change	Africa Old tariff	New tariff	Change	Economies in transition Old tariff	New tariff	Change	Rest of the World Old tariff	New tariff	Change
Pulp, paper and printing	10.6	8.8	-1.9	39.8	19.3	-20.5	9.3	5.7	-3.5	20.2	20.2	0.0	5.6	4.3	-1.3	17.5	14.2	-3.4
Petroleum	25.9	19.9	-6.0	47.2	33.8	-13.5	12.2	8.1	-4.1	12.6	12.6	0.0	6.9	4.9	-2.1	9.6	8.7	-0.9
Chemicals	22.1	15.0	-7.1	54.9	34.1	-20.8	13.8	9.9	-3.9	14.8	14.8	0.0	8.4	6.1	-2.3	26.7	18.1	-8.6
Primary steel	15.9	14.8	-1.2	66.8	35.4	-31.4	10.3	5.5	-4.8	15.2	15.2	0.0	6.8	6.2	-0.6	20.2	19.7	-0.5
Primary nonferrous metals	17.8	14.1	-3.7	62.1	59.4	-2.7	12.5	9.3	-3.3	21.9	21.6	-0.4	5.3	4.2	-1.1	27.9	17.4	-10.5
Fabricated metals	29.9	21.3	-8.6	71.4	59.9	-11.6	14.9	12.0	-3.0	26.3	26.3	0.0	7.9	6.4	-1.5	27.7	26.0	-1.7
Transport equipment	30.5	21.8	-8.7	36.3	25.0	-11.3	17.5	14.8	-2.7	20.2	20.2	0.0	12.5	11.7	-0.8	43.8	31.5	-12.3
Other machinery	22.9	16.9	-5.9	44.7	30.0	-14.7	14.5	10.9	-3.6	12.8	12.8	0.0	8.2	6.8	-1.4	10.6	8.8	-1.8
Other manufactures	25.2	18.4	-6.8	45.7	34.7	-11.0	14.0	9.7	-4.3	20.9	20.9	-0.1	7.1	5.6	-1.5	24.4	16.2	-8.1
Leather, fur and wool	36.2	27.1	-9.0	34.1	33.8	-0.2	19.6	12.1	-7.5	27.6	27.6	0.0	7.0	5.3	-1.7	58.2	56.8	-1.4
Nonmetallic mining	14.8	12.4	-2.4	36.0	29.5	-6.4	13.0	10.8	-2.2	19.8	19.8	0.0	6.2	4.8	-1.4	39.0	16.2	-22.8
Other manufacturing	28.6	20.1	-8.4	51.9	37.9	-14.0	13.8	9.3	-4.6	20.6	20.5	-0.1	7.4	5.9	-1.5	16.7	13.4	-3.2

Note: tariffs are weighted-averages, based on MFN trade as reported in the IDB. The base (old) rate for each sector and region is calculated as the average over the tariff lines in the sector, and over the countries in the region with trade shares as weights. The base years center on 1988, and range from 1986 to 1992, depending on the availability of data. The new rate is calculated with the same type of averaging, based on the offered rates for each tariff line as input, except when a country has offered to bind the tariff above the applied base. For such tariff lines, we conclude that no actual reductions will be made.

Source: GATT IDB, concorded to GTAP model sectors. Numbers in the table have been rounded to one decimal point.

in the high-tariff textiles and wearing apparel sectors was large in such countries as Canada, Australia and New Zealand, the absolute size of the reductions in such sectors as primary steel, other (nontransport) machinery, and other manufacturing were similar and, in percentage terms, far exceeded the reductions in textiles and clothing.

The trade-weighted average tariff rates in table 9.1 understate both the extent of tariff protection and the benefit of the Uruguay Round tariff reductions, for several reasons. First, the reported tariff rates do not include customs surcharges and other fees that are common in developing countries. Customs surcharges and fees are tariffs under another name (but sometimes with a different justification) and can increase protection substantially. Indeed, surcharges equivalent to half or more of the average tariff are not uncommon in developing countries.[4] Second, the high level of sectoral and regional aggregation hides the tariff peaks in the real world. Comparing two sectors (regions) that are identical in all respects except for the intra-sectoral (intra-regional) variance in tariffs, we would expect that a uniform tariff reduction would generate a greater welfare gain in the sector (region) with the higher tariff variance (Magee 1972; and Bach and Martin 1995). Our tariff data do not capture this variance, since in effect they treat reductions as if all products in a sector (region) faced identical rates. Third, although the introduction of new tariff bindings has mitigated the uncertainty inherent in unbound tariffs, our model results do not reflect the value of new tariff bindings.[5] As part of the Uruguay Round agreements, tariff bindings for industrial products in developing countries increased from 21 percent of tariff lines to 73 percent; in economies in transition, they increased from 73 to 98 percent, and in industrial countries from 78 to 99 percent (table 9.2). The progress in tariff bindings for agricultural products has been even more dramatic. Nearly all agricultural trade is now covered by bound tariffs.[6]

Textiles and wearing apparel

The ministerial declaration at Punta Del Este stated that the "negotiations in the area of textiles and clothing shall aim to formulate modalities that would permit the eventual integration of this sector into GATT on the basis of strengthened GATT rules and disciplines." The sector has received special treatment with its own regulatory framework, first institutionalized in the early 1960s with the Short-Term Arrangement for international trade in cotton textiles. The arrangement aimed at an "orderly" opening of restricted markets to avoid market disruptions that would be detrimental (to importing countries). The definition of "market disruption" adopted by the contracting parties in 1960 allowed the imports of particular products

Table 9.2 *Tariff bindings on industrial and agricultural products*

	Industrial products				Agricultural products			
	Percentage of tariff lines that are bound		Percentage of imports under bound rates		Percentage of tariff lines that are bound		Percentage of imports under bound rates	
	Pre-	Post-	Pre-	Post-	Pre-	Post-	Pre-	Post-
Total	43	83	68	87	35	100	63	100
By type of country								
Industrial	78	99	94	99	58	100[a]	81	100[a]
Developing	21	73	13	61	17	100[a]	22	100[a]
Economies in transition	73	98	74	96	57	100	59	100
By region								
North America	99	100	99	100	92	100	94	100
Latin America	38	100	57	100	36	100	74	100
Western Europe	79	82	98	98	45	100	87	100
Eastern Europe	63	98	68	97	49	100	54	100
Africa	13	69	26	90	12	100	8	100
Asia	16	68	32	70	15	100[a]	36	100[a]

[a]Under the provision of annex 5 to the agriculture agreement, Japan, Korea, and the Philippines have not yet bound their tariffs on rice, and Israel has not bound its tariff on sheep meat, whole milk powder, and certain cheeses.

Note: figures for developing countries and economies in transition, as well as for Latin America, Eastern Europe, Africa, and Asia, are affected by the fact that comparable data are available only for the twenty-seven of the ninety-three developing economy participants that currently report to the IDB of the GATT.

from particular countries to be singled out as the disruptive source. This provision opened the door for the series of bilaterally negotiated quota restrictions that became the rule under the Long-Term Arrangement of 1963–73, which grew into the first MFA in 1974 when product coverage was extended to noncotton textiles and clothing.

The MFA provides rules that govern the imposition of quotas, either through bilateral agreements or unilateral actions, when surges of imports cause or threaten to cause market disruption in importing countries. In recent years, six industrial economies have applied quotas under the MFA – the European Union, the United States, Canada, Norway, Finland, and Austria – almost exclusively on imports from developing countries.[7] The

Table 9.3 *Integration scheme for textiles and clothing*

	Integration (base: 1990 import volume of the products listed in appendix A)	Growth rate of residual quotas (base: previously agreed-upon growth rates of quotas under the MFA)
Stage 1 (January 1, 1995)	16%	16% higher growth rate than initially (example: 3% to 3.48%)
Stage 2 (January 1, 1998)	Another 17% (total, 33%)	Increase by 25% (example: 3.48% to 4.35%)
Stage 3 (January 1, 2002)	Another 18% (total, 51%)	Increase by 27% (example: 4.35% to 5.52%)
End of the ten-year transition period (January 1, 2005)	Remaining 49% (total, 100%)	

restrictiveness of the applied quotas varies by product and supplier, and aggregate measures are inherently uncertain.

The Uruguay Round agreement on textiles and clothing requires that quota restrictions carried over from the MFA regime be reduced gradually over a ten-year transitional period. Integration of the products covered by the agreement is to be achieved in three stages (table 9.3). In the first stage, effective January 1, 1995, products comprising at least 16 percent of the total volume of each member's 1990 imports of all products listed in the annex to the Agreement were to be integrated. In the second stage, another 17 percent of the products are to be integrated on January 1, 1998; in the third stage, another 18 percent (reaching a cumulative integration of 51 percent) of imports are to be brought under normal GATT rules by January 1, 2002. At the end of the ten-year transitional period, all remaining quantitative restrictions on textiles and clothing (carried over from the MFA regime) are to be eliminated.

Products that remain restricted during the transitional period will benefit from a progressively increasing quota. The previously applied annual growth rates of quotas under the MFA, which had been arranged bilaterally between importing and exporting countries, are to be scaled up by a factor of 16 percent in the first stage – for instance, from 3 percent to (3 × 1.16=) 3.48 percent – by an additional 25 percent in the second stage, and by another 27 percent in the third stage. This progressive scaling will turn a 3 percent initial annual growth rate into a 5.52 percent rate by the third stage. The accelerated growth of quotas could render some of the quotas nonbinding even before they are eliminated formally. It is unclear, however, whether this process will be sufficient to offset the "backloading" of the elimination of the MFA, since 49 percent of product integration may be left to the very end of the transition period.

Other industrial quantitative restrictions

Although Article XI of GATT prohibits quantitative restrictions in principle, some exceptions to this general principle exist and will continue to be allowed under the new Uruguay Round agreement, at least in the short term (Finger 1995). For example, developing countries may impose (temporary) quantitative restrictions under certain conditions in order to safeguard their external financial positions and balance of payments, and they may continue to impose them until the provisions of the new agreement on safeguards go into effect. That is, the agreement stipulates that safeguard measures carried over from the GATT 1947 regime under Article XIX be phased out not later than eight years after the date on which they were first applied or within five years after the WTO agreement goes into effect (by January 1, 2000). The safeguard agreement timetable also applies to "gray area" measures with dubious legal status under GATT 1947. Article XI of the agreement stipulates that members not adopt or maintain any VERs, orderly marketing arrangements, or any other restrictive measures on the export or import side.

The inclusion of nontariff restrictions in numerical analysis is rife with problems, one of which is the absence of data on the protective effect of these measures (Laird forthcoming). We also face a "concordance problem," in that estimates of the protective effect of various measures generally apply only to a subset of sectors or regions in our model. For instance, only some member countries of the European Union restrict the imports of Japanese cars, while only some countries from the EFTA impose MFA constraints. For purposes of modeling, we must "aggregate" the restrictive effect of these measures to an overall effect. But aggregating an inherently uncertain estimate that applies to a subset of products in a subset of markets to an overall protective effect for a sector and region in the model is not an exact science. In cases where such restrictions are prohibitive, low import weights may mask the impact of nontariff barriers in aggregated trade data. The limited data base on quantitative restrictions is reported in table 9.4.

Agriculture

The old GATT framework gave governments relatively generous scope for intervening in the agricultural sector to achieve domestic objectives. These

Table 9.4 *Data on quantitative restrictions*
Price wedges of industrial nontariff barriers

Importer:	European Union			United States		Japan
Exporter:	Japan	East Asia	All sources	Japan	East Asia	All sources
Chemicals	—	—	—	—	—	5.0[a]
Primary steel	—	—	5.0[a]	—	—	—
Fabricated metal products	—	—	—	9.1[ab]	—	—
Transport equipment	7.6[cd]	—	—	8.5[a]	—	—
Other machinery	10.0[a]	10.0[a]	—	0.3[b]	0.3[b]	—
Other manufactures	5.0[a]	5.0[a]	—	—	—	—

Sources: [a]Haaland and Tollefsen 1994, [b]United States International Trade Commission 1993. [c]GATT TPRM reports, [d]Flam and Nordström 1994. For a discussion of the various restrictions, see GATT TPRM reports for respective country.

Price wedges of the MFA

Importers	Eastern Europe	China	East Asia	South Asia	Latin America	Africa	Rest of the world
			Textiles exporters				
Canada	7.4	18.8	9.7	18.8	10.3	5.7	4.5
United States	6.0	15.5	8.5	15.5	8.6	4.4	3.6
European Union	8.6	21.5	11.5	21.5	12.4	6.0	5.2
EFTA	4.7	13.7	6.5	13.7	7.1	3.2	2.8
			Wearing apparel exporters				
Canada	12.3	29.6	17.2	29.6	17.3	6.3	7.8
United States	11.9	28.7	19.8	28.7	16.8	7.7	11.9
European Union	10.8	26.5	19.9	26.5	15.0	7.2	6.7
EFTA	6.0	18.1	12.4	18.1	8.8	3.9	3.6

Sources: Chyc *et al.* forthcoming and United States International Trade Commission 1993. For a discussion of the various restrictions, see GATT TPRM reports for the respective countries.

objectives have not always been mutually consistent, and agricultural trade has occasionally led to trade frictions between contracting parties.[8] One such special agricultural treatment was the exemption of primary products from the ban on export subsidies under Article XVI of the 1947 GATT regime, provided that the subsidy did not give the user more than an "equitable share" of the world market in a particular product. Agricultural trade has also been exempt from the general ban on quantitative import restrictions under Article XI, provided that governments require such restrictions to enforce measures for controlling the domestic production or marketing of similar products. The contracting parties could also seek waivers under Article XXV for otherwise inconsistent measures. These waivers tended to undermine the general discipline. For instance, the so-called "section 22 waiver" granted to the United States – entitling it to impose import quotas on sugar, peanuts, tobacco, and manufactured dairy products – was often referred to by other parties as a justification for their own restrictions.[9] Moreover, recourse to variable levies has tended to exacerbate price fluctuations in the world market, pushing the burden of adjustments on to parties that did not use these instruments to the same extent (Nordström 1995). Governments have also often used marketing boards and state trading enterprises to intervene directly in the agricultural sector. As noted in Article XVII of GATT the operation of these entities may distort trade because public entities are often required to make decisions based on criteria other than profitability.

Reflecting on the shortcomings of the old system, the ministerial declaration at Punta Del Este stated the urgency of bringing "more discipline and predictability to world agricultural trade by correcting and preventing restrictions and distortions, including those related to structural surpluses, so as to reduce the uncertainty, imbalance, and instability in world agricultural markets." The negotiation mandate aimed at three objectives: to improve market access by reducing import barriers; to improve the competitive environment by strengthening disciplines for the use of all direct and indirect subsidies and other measures affecting agricultural trade; and to minimize the trade-distorting effects of sanitary and phytosanitary regulations.

The Uruguay Round agreement on agriculture encompasses several key features (table 9.5). First, as of January 1, 1995, nontariff barriers are to be converted into equivalent tariffs immediately after a country signs the WTO agreement. The converted nontariff barriers and previously bound or applied tariffs are to be reduced by a simple unweighted average of 36 percent by industrial countries and 24 percent by developing countries, with minimums of 15 and 10 percent, respectively, for each tariff line (least-developed countries are generally exempt). Each participant in the

Table 9.5 *Summary of the agreement on agriculture*

	Market access (base: 1986–88)	Export subsidies (base: 1986–90)	Domestic support (base: 1986–88)
Value	Tariffication of nontariff barriers 36% (24%) average tariff cut including converted nontariff barriers 15% (10%) minimum tariff cut per tariff line	36% (24%) cut in budget outlay	Reduction in aggregate measure of support by 20%[a] (13.3%); "Green Box" measures exempt
Volume	Minimum market access of 3%, rising to 5%	21% (14%) reduction in subsidized export quantity	

[a]The European Union is allowed a (special) 16.8 percent reduction in its aggregate measure of support.
Note: provisions for developing countries are in parenthesis. Least-developed countries are exempted.

Uruguay Round was able to determine its own agricultural tariff reductions, as long as it met the minimum average cut and the applicable minimum cut for each tariff line. Second, the agreement includes new minimum market access opportunities at reduced tariff rates for products where trade was minimal at the outset. Minimum market access will be set at 3 percent of domestic consumption at the outset, rising to 5 percent at the end of the implementation period. Third, the budgetary outlay on export subsidies is to be reduced by 36 percent for industrial countries and 24 percent for developing countries, and the volume of subsidized exports is to be reduced by 21 and 14 percent, respectively. This requirement applies on a product-by-product basis. Fourth, the aggregate measure of support is to be reduced by 20 and 13.3 percent, respectively. Exempt are "green box" measures with "no, or at most minimal, trade distortion effects or effects on production." These measures are also nonactionable under the agreement on subsidies and countervailing measures. The reduction in the aggregate measure of support applies on a sector-specific basis.

The agreed-upon reductions in tariffs, domestic support, and export subsidies are to be implemented during transitional periods of six years for industrial countries and ten years for developing countries.

In our previous assessments of the Uruguay Round (Francois,

McDonald, and Nordström 1993 and 1994), we modeled the reductions in agricultural tariffs according to the percentages set forth in the agreement on agriculture. This strategy appears to have been optimistic. As the details of implementation were promulgated at the national level, it became clear that the estimates of Uruguay Round participants of the tariff equivalents of their own nontariff measures exceeded estimates of individual researchers in many cases.[10] This excessive, or "dirty," tariffication was noted in International Agricultural Trade Research Consortium (1994) and later examined by Ingco (forthcoming). It is limited to the share of agricultural trade (less than 15 percent of the total) that went through tariffication. For modeling purposes, we would wish to compare the true tariff equivalents of the nontariff measures with the tariffs that will actually apply at the close of the implementation period, although data problems make doing so difficult.

The problems associated with establishing correct tariff equivalents pertain directly to the problems associated with establishing representative world market prices. The base period for the conversion was 1986–88. Measured agricultural protection was very high during the base period, in part because many agricultural commodity prices were low at that time. Price increases, combined with some actual policy liberalization, have since led to substantial reductions in measured protection, and Uruguay Round participants implicitly receive "credit" for these reductions in measured protection, even if their Uruguay Round commitments do not require actual policy reform by them. In this case, the appropriate comparison is not as clear. Should one assume that prices at the end of the implementation period will resemble the base-period prices of the late 1980s, which might imply substantial effects from the agreement? Or should one assume that the prices of the mid-1990s still apply at the end of the implementation period?

Similar problems are associated with interpreting the liberalization content of the reductions in domestic support. Recall that the agreement mandates a reduction in domestic support of 20 percent for industrial countries and two-thirds of that – or 13.3 percent – for developing countries. The calculation of the base aggregate measure of support, to which these reductions apply, is based on outlays during the 1986–88 period. Comparatively low world market prices during the base period meant that domestic support was relatively high. Given a combination of higher world market prices and domestic reforms, the new commitments, at least in the short to medium term, may not require any additional reductions in domestic support.[11] We calculated base outlays for aggregate measures of support from the schedules and compared them with estimated actual outlays based on OECD and United States Department of Agriculture producer subsidy-equivalent estimates for 1990–92 (table 9.6). The results indicate that, at least for Japan, Canada, and the EFTA, no further real reductions in

Table 9.6 *Domestic agricultural support (US $million)*

	Base outlay (aggregate measures of support) 1986–88	Base outlay in relationship to 1988–90 data on producer subsidy equivalents
Japan	34,299	1.57
Canada	4,608	2.28
United States	23,879	1.00
European Union	93,604	0.98
EFTA	16,461	2.69

Source: data on aggregate measures of support are from schedules. The 1992 data are taken from the GTAP data base (Chyc *et al.* forthcoming), which in turn build on OECD and United States Department of Agriculture estimates of producer subsidy-equivalents.

domestic support are necessary (due largely to recent domestic reforms or to higher world market prices).

These complications make the "true" policy experiment impossible to define. Because we have considered the liberal "face value" scenario in earlier research, we focus here on a minimalist agricultural scenario. We assume no reductions in border protection, beyond the minimum market access commitments, and no reductions in domestic support. We do retain the assumption that export subsides will be reduced as prescribed in the agreement.[12]

A numerical assessment

The numerical analysis is based on a nineteen-sector, thirteen-region CGE model of the world economy (appendix A). A central feature of CGE models is the input–output structure, which explicitly links industries together. The links between sectors are both direct, such as steel input for the production of transport equipment, and indirect, via various economy-wide constraints, such as the scarcity of factors of production at a given time. We assume full employment in factor markets, implying that all sectors cannot expand simultaneously unless the expansion involves technological progress or factor accumulation.

Our data come from several sources. Sectoral and aggregate data are organized as a set of social accounting matrixes, which are linked through trade flows. Most such matrixes are drawn directly from the 1992 GTAP data set (Chyc *et al.* forthcoming). The GTAP social accounting data have been supplemented with additional data, which include production and trade data for the EFTA and the rest of the world.[13] Trade policy data come from several sources, and include data on tariffs, nontariff barriers, and antidumping duties. Tariff data are from the GATT's IDB; the tariff equivalents for nontariff barriers come from estimates in the literature. Data on antidumping duties are drawn from national sources and actions reported to the GATT Secretariat (McDonald 1994).

Versions of the model

We consider results from two versions of the model and with three alternative macroeconomic closure rules. The first version of the model assumes perfect competition, with constant returns to scale technologies in all sectors. To produce output, firms use domestic production factors (capital, labor, and land) and intermediate inputs from domestic and foreign sources. They select inputs so as to minimize costs subject to given input prices and available technology. A single representative, composite household in each region allocates expenditures to personal consumption and savings (future consumption). The actual allocation depends on the capital market closure that is assumed (fixed or endogenous regional savings rates). The composite household of each region owns the factors of production (whose supply is fixed at any point in time) and receives income by selling them to firms. It also receives both income from the receipt of tariff revenue and rents from the sale of import/export quota licenses, where applicable. Part of the income of the composite household is distributed as subsidy payments, primarily to agriculture.

Products from different regions are assumed to be imperfect substitutes in accordance with the so-called "Armington" assumption. We use a single-nest CES structure, with the implication that elasticities of substitution between any pair of import sources and between the domestic product and any import source are equal.

Factor markets are perfectly competitive, and factors are full employed. Labor and capital are assumed to be mobile among sectors but not among countries. We do not model changes in international capital flows induced by the Uruguay Round; rather, we assume that net capital inflows and outflows are constant at their initial levels. We use a third factor, land, only in agricultural production. Prices on goods and factors adjust until all markets are simultaneously in (general) equilibrium.

The second version of the model incorporates scale economies that depend on a firm's own production level, which each firm thus *internalizes*. Firms are monopolisitcally competitive, with firms specialized in particular product varieties (Ethier 1982; and Krugman 1980). An important property of this monopolistic competition model is that increased specialization in the production of intermediates yields greater returns. Sectors using these intermediates become more productive because they have access to a broader range of specialized inputs. These gains spill over between countries into two-way trade in specialized intermediate goods. With these spillovers, trade liberalization can lead to globalwide effects related to specialization. With international scale economies, regional welfare effects depend on a mix of efficiency effects, global scale effects, and terms-of-trade effects (Francois 1994).

Both versions of the model incorporate a simple dynamic link, whereby the static, or direct income, effects of trade liberalization induce shifts in the pattern of savings and investment. These effects have been explored extensively in the theoretical trade literature (Baldwin 1992; Smith 1976 and 1977; and Srinivasan and Bhagwati 1980).[14] The application to empirical trade modeling is discussed in Francois, McDonald, and Nordström (forthcoming). Variations on this mechanism have been incorporated in earlier studies of the Uruguay Round (Francois, McDonald, and Nordström 1993 and 1994; Goldin, Knudsen, and van der Mensbrugghe 1993; Harrison, Rutherford, and Tarr, 1995; and Haaland and Tollefsen, 1994). These capital accumulation effects compound initial output and welfare effects in the medium run, and can magnify income gains or losses. How much they will supplement static effects depends on several factors, including the marginal product of capital and underlying savings behavior.

The policy scenario

The policy scenario presented here is based on the commitments listed in the earlier tables in this chapter and captures the following package of policy changes: tariff reductions for industrial products, the liberalization of industrial nontariff barriers, and reductions in agricultural export subsidies.[15] Liberalization of nontariff barriers includes the elimination of the MFA and a small number of gray-area measures that restrict trade in other industrial products. For agriculture, we model reductions in export subsidies and the imposition of the minimum market access commitments.[16] Antidumping duties are included in our benchmark protection data in order to represent the initial equilibrium more accurately or, in the jargon of one of the authors, to reduce the degree of "dirty calibration."[17] Note also that we keep these antidumping duties constant in all simulations.[18] In the simulations, we compare the impacts of the Uruguay Round on changes in production output and in real wages. We also compare the actual equilibrium in the benchmark year (1992) with a counterfactual ("what if") equilibrium, so as to assess the effect of replacing actual 1992 trade policy with the counterfactual Uruguay Round liberalizations. We report the impact in (1992) dollars and as a percentage of base GDP (the "welfare" effect). The latter can be compared with the percentage effects reported in other studies benchmarked and reported to different years. We did not attempt to project the results to 2005.[19]

Impacts on production under the models

We generate estimates of the effects of the Uruguay Round reform package on production effects both under CRTS and under IRTS (tables 9.7 and 9.8). The largest output changes are concentrated in the textiles and wearing apparel industries, because the elimination of the MFA is the single largest policy shock of the Uruguay Round. While the magnitude of the effects varies considerably by model, the basic pattern remains unchanged. Elimination of the MFA would induce a significant contraction in textile and clothing production in industrial countries, mirrored by an expansion in the developing countries. Among developing countries, the East Asia region would have the largest percentage growth in textile production, followed by the South Asia region. The developing regions of Asia – East Asia, South Asia, and China – would also show large growth in clothing production. Textile and clothing production in Latin America would also expand substantially, particularly under the model versions with IRTS. In contrast, African firms may face a contraction in production, since their quotas have tended to be the least restrictive under the MFA regime. As those quotas are phased out, African producers will lose their (implicit) preferential access to the restricted markets of Europe and the United States. However, African textile producers, who did not enjoy the same degree of preferential access, should be able to expand their production by between 1.6 to 8.5 percent as the MFA quotas are phased out.

Another pattern that holds under all model specifications is a relatively broad-based contraction of other manufacturing sectors in the developing regions of Asia, as resources shift into textiles and clothing, agriculture, and services. This contraction would be strongest in the transport equipment, steel, nonferrous metals, and other machinery sectors, and would create an opportunity for a corresponding expansion of these sectors in industrial countries and other developing countries. Among industrial countries, growth in transport equipment production would be concentrated in Canada and the United States, and growth in nonferrous metals would be concentrated in Australia and New Zealand, the United States, and Europe; growth in other machinery and other manufactures would be concentrated in Europe, the United States, and Canada. These results suggest that US and European protection of textiles and clothing has been

Table 9.7 Estimated effects of the Uruguay Round on production: CRTS and perfect competition (percentage change in output)

	Australia and New Zealand	Japan	Canada	United States	European Union	EFTA	Africa	China	East Asia	South Asia	Latin America	Eastern Europe	Rest of the world
Fixed capital stock													
Grains	1.24	0.21	4.37	0.43	-2.32	-2.37	1.04	-0.11	0.01	-0.52	1.03	3.07	-1.61
Nongrain crops	-0.01	0.21	1.23	-0.13	-0.83	-0.93	0.46	0.16	1.32	0.46	-0.04	0.37	-0.47
Livestock	3.70	0.20	3.80	-0.48	-1.85	-1.78	0.86	1.96	0.51	0.96	1.00	3.81	2.45
Forestry	0.74	0.06	0.52	0.41	0.15	0.40	-0.21	-1.02	-1.29	-1.33	-0.27	-0.74	0.13
Fishery	5.93	0.01	2.92	7.41	0.61	1.19	0.88	-2.14	-4.63	-0.83	1.65	2.00	-1.13
Mining	2.17	0.17	0.85	0.66	1.29	0.64	-0.86	-2.90	-4.25	-7.67	0.70	-0.79	-0.77
Processed food	1.10	0.10	1.43	-0.10	-0.49	0.09	1.46	-0.04	-0.13	-0.61	0.65	-0.79	-1.31
Textiles	-1.39	1.55	-7.36	-4.99	-1.26	-4.37	1.56	5.31	14.82	12.28	1.84	0.79	1.55
Wearing apparel	-1.63	-1.33	-17.09	-20.88	-17.45	-6.09	0.38	31.46	31.46	53.26	5.56	3.88	10.20
Lumber, pulp, and paper	-0.99	-0.09	0.49	0.24	0.22	0.31	-0.16	-1.34	-0.41	-2.09	0.21	0.08	-1.32
Petroleum	0.31	0.16	0.14	0.02	0.02	-0.07	0.22	-1.36	-1.08	-4.07	-0.29	-0.10	0.03
Chemicals	-1.14	0.05	0.08	0.78	0.24	0.32	1.52	-1.36	0.38	-3.72	-0.61	0.33	-0.43
Iron and steel	-1.77	0.23	0.02	0.06	1.04	0.80	-0.15	-2.92	-2.52	-13.01	1.56	2.11	0.68
Nonferrous metals	0.97	-0.01	0.49	1.80	2.57	0.88	-0.65	-5.58	-2.34	-3.80	0.82	-1.42	-4.53
Fabricated metals	-0.52	0.05	0.10	0.85	0.51	0.57	-0.06	-3.32	-0.64	-1.82	-1.55	-0.29	0.54
Transport equip.	-2.45	-1.16	1.71	2.27	0.53	0.89	2.66	-6.07	-3.86	-7.99	-4.47	-0.67	-0.27
Other machinery	-2.71	0.33	1.84	0.58	1.37	0.93	-0.12	-4.35	2.23	-4.62	-0.75	-0.89	1.26
Other manufactures	-2.31	0.37	-2.53	-0.04	0.53	-0.48	0.59	-4.13	1.25	-0.66	0.02	-0.62	3.06
Services	-0.14	-0.04	-0.12	-0.02	0.05	-0.04	-0.09	0.00	-0.70	0.07	-0.22	-0.14	-0.04

Table 9.7 (cont.)

Endogenous capital stock, fixed savings rate

	Australia and New Zealand	Japan	Canada	United States	European Union	EFTA	Africa	China	East Asia	South Asia	Latin America	Eastern Europe	Rest of the world
Grains	1.27	0.25	4.41	0.52	-2.21	-2.34	1.24	0.23	0.27	-0.41	1.06	3.08	-0.98
Nongrain crops	0.03	0.24	1.31	-0.04	-0.70	-0.89	0.61	0.48	1.51	0.56	-0.03	0.35	0.06
Livestock	3.75	0.23	3.86	-0.38	-1.75	-1.75	1.04	2.28	0.75	1.08	1.02	3.80	3.15
Forestry	0.81	0.03	0.60	0.51	0.29	0.43	0.05	-0.48	-0.86	-1.15	-0.27	-0.87	0.87
Fishery	5.99	0.00	2.92	7.54	0.78	1.15	1.12	-1.89	-4.23	-0.74	1.66	1.94	-0.28
Mining	2.17	0.03	0.93	0.76	1.38	0.62	-0.51	-2.15	-3.79	-7.47	0.63	-0.89	-0.01
Processed food	1.14	0.13	1.49	0.00	-0.38	0.12	1.69	0.46	0.09	-0.44	0.68	0.77	-0.69
Textiles	-1.33	1.59	-7.26	-4.92	-1.16	-4.35	1.78	5.73	15.15	12.49	1.86	0.95	2.28
Wearing apparel	-1.60	-1.32	-17.04	-20.86	-17.41	-6.09	0.56	31.76	31.76	53.52	5.57	3.83	11.02
Lumber, pulp, and paper	-0.93	-0.06	0.58	0.33	0.37	0.35	0.11	-0.72	-0.03	-1.85	0.23	0.08	-0.57
Petroleum	0.38	0.17	0.24	0.12	0.17	-0.05	0.49	-0.66	-0.69	-3.83	-0.28	-0.13	0.70
Chemicals	-1.07	0.08	0.18	0.89	0.35	0.35	1.78	-0.74	0.73	-3.50	-0.59	0.33	0.25
Iron and steel	-1.71	0.26	0.13	0.14	1.15	0.84	0.17	-2.09	-2.07	-12.71	1.58	2.10	1.42
Nonferrous metals	1.09	0.02	0.64	1.89	2.71	0.92	-0.31	-4.72	-1.88	-3.48	0.86	-1.44	-3.77
Fabricated metals	-0.46	0.08	0.19	0.94	0.61	0.59	0.21	-2.62	-0.27	-1.56	-1.53	-0.31	1.23
Transport equip.	-2.40	-1.16	1.84	2.33	0.61	0.91	2.92	-5.00	-3.40	-7.61	-4.46	-0.68	0.49
Other machinery	-2.62	0.38	1.96	0.66	1.47	0.98	0.17	-3.54	2.58	-4.31	-0.72	-0.89	1.96
Other manufactures	-2.27	0.38	-2.40	0.03	0.63	-0.47	0.87	-3.66	1.59	-0.44	0.02	-0.65	3.77
Services	-0.08	-0.01	-0.02	0.08	0.17	-0.01	0.16	0.67	-0.36	0.30	-0.20	-0.16	0.63

Endogenous capital stock, endogenous savings rate

Grains	2.03	0.41	6.78	1.05	-2.12	-2.05	1.39	0.42	1.25	-0.20	2.14	3.24	0.62
Nongrain crops	0.32	0.34	1.63	0.07	-0.22	-0.54	0.63	0.87	2.26	0.89	0.79	0.21	1.41
Livestock	4.36	0.34	4.26	-0.17	-1.62	-1.44	1.15	2.79	1.63	1.48	2.01	3.90	4.97
Forestry	1.39	-0.08	1.05	0.67	0.43	0.58	0.09	-0.08	0.76	-0.53	0.97	-0.99	2.77
Fishery	6.43	-0.05	2.93	7.57	0.95	1.23	1.18	-1.69	-2.69	-0.41	2.78	2.00	1.99
Mining	3.05	-0.12	1.66	0.94	1.55	0.81	-0.98	-1.56	-1.51	-6.28	1.93	-0.83	1.97
Processed food	1.59	0.24	1.98	0.18	-0.24	0.45	1.85	1.59	0.92	0.03	1.75	0.77	0.89
Textiles	-0.89	1.65	-6.73	-4.82	-1.10	-4.20	1.63	6.37	16.23	13.28	3.02	1.09	4.03
Wearing apparel	-1.20	-1.32	-16.77	-20.97	-17.44	-5.90	0.37	32.49	32.96	54.65	6.78	3.77	12.84
Lumber, pulp, and paper	-0.33	0.04	1.03	0.49	0.54	0.49	0.17	-0.16	1.39	-1.06	1.37	0.30	1.36
Petroleum	1.05	0.25	0.87	0.30	0.26	0.25	0.49	-0.07	0.80	-3.01	0.89	0.08	2.42
Chemicals	-0.46	0.20	0.85	1.12	0.48	0.54	1.75	-0.10	2.02	-2.70	0.55	0.51	1.95
Iron and steel	-1.14	0.36	0.71	0.27	1.32	0.98	0.01	-1.33	-0.33	-11.67	2.69	2.22	3.28
Nonferrous metals	1.89	0.11	1.44	2.00	2.90	1.00	-0.46	-3.96	-0.23	-2.36	1.94	-1.51	-1.84
Fabricated metals	0.09	0.19	0.74	1.08	0.69	0.72	0.17	-2.00	1.15	-0.65	-0.43	-0.13	2.99
Transport equip.	-1.98	-1.16	2.49	2.45	0.69	1.02	2.68	-3.95	-1.63	-6.25	-3.37	-0.57	2.40
Other machinery	-2.02	0.53	2.59	0.83	1.62	1.14	0.17	-2.78	3.83	-3.28	0.29	-0.69	3.71
Other manufactures	-1.48	0.48	-1.46	0.27	0.75	-0.18	0.87	-2.79	2.09	0.30	1.13	-0.47	5.31
Services	0.53	0.11	0.52	0.24	0.22	0.25	0.26	1.22	0.94	1.05	0.90	0.11	2.34

Table 9.8 Estimated effects of the Uruguay Round on production: IRTS and imperfect competition (percent of change in output)

	Australia and New Zealand	Japan	Canada	United States	European Union	EFTA	Africa	China	East Asia	South Asia	Latin America	Eastern Europe	Rest of the world
Fixed capital stock													
Grains	1.94	0.34	6.16	0.83	-2.90	-2.31	1.34	1.59	-0.62	1.05	1.20	2.99	-2.03
Nongrain crops	-1.28	-1.24	0.53	-0.96	-1.08	-2.70	1.15	-0.62	14.73	3.72	0.17	0.48	-4.76
Livestock	3.33	-0.86	3.20	-0.44	-2.28	-2.03	1.24	4.25	3.52	4.48	1.19	3.99	-6.95
Forestry	0.90	0.42	3.14	-0.07	-0.07	0.75	0.02	0.23	-6.87	-4.38	0.39	-0.77	0.81
Fishery	8.36	0.35	2.95	7.31	0.15	0.85	1.17	0.53	-4.18	0.77	1.85	2.02	-0.72
Mining	4.44	1.15	1.54	1.10	2.51	0.98	-1.52	-2.85	-8.82	-12.45	1.02	-0.90	-0.16
Processed food	1.25	0.21	1.46	0.04	-0.32	0.26	1.79	2.43	-1.91	1.08	0.81	0.60	-0.73
Textiles	-34.16	-16.61	-46.41	-36.40	-17.96	-14.29	7.92	-13.62	133.10	34.45	4.26	10.20	-24.97
Wearing apparel	-43.64	-31.29	-51.17	-87.32	-75.78	-14.60	-8.01	78.49	181.83	101.59	17.80	12.98	1.89
Lumber, pulp, and paper	-1.00	0.23	3.58	1.01	0.66	0.78	-0.69	3.05	-12.58	-9.85	1.32	0.16	-3.06
Petroleum	0.72	0.00	0.36	-0.61	0.20	-0.17	0.29	-1.31	-2.44	-5.94	-0.43	0.01	0.14
Chemicals	0.02	0.27	1.16	2.71	1.39	-2.22	6.49	-1.27	-3.71	-20.90	-3.48	0.82	-1.37
Iron and steel	3.61	3.11	2.99	0.67	6.68	2.61	-4.64	-5.47	-41.60	-48.57	5.70	4.71	5.74
Nonferrous metals	8.32	1.45	3.35	6.94	8.54	3.94	-6.16	-16.45	-46.23	-20.25	-0.32	-8.04	-10.49
Fabricated metals	3.57	1.12	2.08	3.76	2.40	2.24	-1.66	-7.63	-25.85	-8.70	-6.61	-1.59	3.37
Transport equip.	-0.53	-1.03	3.97	4.58	1.78	1.41	1.22	-18.85	-27.14	-21.45	-7.11	-1.36	2.77
Other machinery	-3.51	1.56	7.74	5.04	6.64	3.70	-6.99	-16.75	-34.70	-22.54	-7.65	-4.62	7.53
Other manufactures	-0.44	3.03	-6.97	5.07	3.10	-2.31	1.40	-9.33	-20.98	-5.03	-0.37	-3.01	11.93
Services	0.02	0.02	0.05	0.03	0.09	-0.10	0.17	0.92	0.04	1.12	-0.03	-0.03	0.40

Endogenous capital stock, fixed savings rate

Grains	2.47	0.49	7.24	1.13	-2.76	-2.29	1.95	2.88	0.91	1.86	1.61	3.35	-0.30
Nongrain crops	-1.25	-1.15	0.64	-0.72	-0.90	-2.50	1.65	-0.08	16.25	4.38	0.49	0.62	-3.32
Livestock	3.64	-0.77	3.24	-0.24	-2.12	-1.98	1.76	5.09	5.02	5.28	1.55	4.13	-4.94
Forestry	1.08	0.34	3.11	0.11	0.16	0.59	0.78	2.27	-4.09	-3.03	0.94	-0.16	1.52
Fishery	8.82	0.68	3.19	8.14	0.88	0.97	1.90	1.26	-2.21	1.31	2.33	2.41	-0.04
Mining	4.60	1.03	1.68	1.28	2.90	0.97	-0.42	0.07	-6.54	-10.99	1.42	-0.59	0.98
Processed food	1.27	0.31	1.54	0.22	-0.16	0.28	2.45	4.32	-0.67	2.36	1.19	0.71	1.10
Textiles	-34.79	-16.68	-46.31	-36.22	-17.96	-13.36	8.49	-17.51	138.03	35.47	5.49	11.16	-24.04
Wearing apparel	-43.56	-31.52	-51.02	-87.92	-76.37	-14.06	-7.51	76.33	185.57	102.88	19.66	14.15	4.18
Lumber, pulp, and paper	-1.22	0.23	3.52	1.10	0.84	0.59	-0.15	5.05	-9.61	-8.22	1.79	0.27	0.58
Petroleum	0.81	0.07	0.48	-0.42	0.40	-0.14	1.05	1.51	-0.14	-4.09	-0.03	0.16	2.34
Chemicals	-0.40	0.23	0.71	2.95	1.32	-2.24	7.55	1.01	-0.91	-19.63	-3.28	0.85	0.23
Iron and steel	3.52	3.14	3.11	0.67	6.76	2.57	-3.79	-0.01	-40.01	-47.38	6.49	5.21	8.62
Nonferrous metals	9.10	1.61	3.29	7.22	9.87	3.68	-6.09	-10.02	-45.14	-16.22	-0.02	-8.49	-9.14
Fabricated metals	3.59	1.22	2.02	3.91	2.48	2.17	-1.05	-3.71	-24.24	-6.13	-6.34	-1.53	5.56
Transport equip.	-0.74	-1.23	4.54	4.83	1.45	1.36	1.90	-9.65	-25.28	-17.05	-7.44	-1.34	9.17
Other machinery	-4.27	1.76	8.15	5.03	6.76	3.60	-6.94	-10.49	-33.39	-19.29	-7.85	-5.01	12.15
Other manufactures	-0.95	3.22	-7.57	4.92	3.14	-2.64	2.35	-8.17	-18.44	-2.89	0.13	-3.05	14.24
Services	0.08	0.15	0.15	0.20	0.25	-0.05	0.92	3.66	2.18	2.97	0.37	0.10	3.01

Table 9.8 (*cont.*)

	Australia and New Zealand	Japan	Canada	United States	European Union	EFTA	Africa	China	East Asia	South Asia	Latin America	Eastern Europe	Rest of the world
Endogenous capital stock, endogenous savings rate													
Grains	2.06	0.76	6.23	1.16	-2.68	-2.14	1.75	1.67	-0.49	0.65	2.52	3.69	3.72
Nongrain crops	-0.98	-1.09	1.11	-0.61	-0.80	-2.18	1.45	-0.83	15.27	3.53	1.26	0.73	-0.29
Livestock	3.52	-0.66	3.66	-0.03	-2.04	-1.80	1.56	4.26	3.73	4.20	2.40	4.23	-1.65
Forestry	1.62	0.67	3.24	0.33	0.40	0.75	0.53	0.33	-6.53	-5.29	2.17	-0.20	5.79
Fishery	8.98	0.91	2.77	8.23	1.32	0.95	1.59	0.66	-3.97	0.58	3.08	2.35	4.57
Mining	5.57	1.72	2.18	1.72	3.35	1.17	-1.01	-2.69	-8.72	-13.76	2.45	-0.45	5.50
Processed food	1.68	0.49	2.02	0.43	-0.08	0.43	2.20	2.52	-1.87	0.45	2.11	0.82	5.51
Textiles	-35.25	-17.89	-45.88	-36.53	-18.10	-12.50	8.08	-15.96	137.16	34.87	7.25	11.69	-22.45
Wearing apparel	-44.80	-33.01	-50.41	-88.48	-77.00	-13.41	-7.82	79.29	185.19	101.72	22.16	14.65	5.77
Lumber, pulp, and paper	-0.31	0.50	3.66	1.36	1.19	0.75	-0.26	3.33	-12.33	-10.69	2.99	0.45	6.58
Petroleum	1.49	0.30	0.96	-0.20	0.55	0.02	0.72	-1.21	-2.31	-7.04	1.06	0.29	6.94
Chemicals	0.99	0.58	1.03	3.56	1.41	-1.78	7.97	-1.22	-3.46	-22.99	-2.03	1.27	4.89
Iron and steel	5.00	3.67	3.62	0.84	7.10	2.91	-4.30	-4.99	-44.14	-53.58	8.20	5.78	14.97
Nonferrous metals	11.41	2.02	4.18	7.58	11.22	3.78	-7.52	-16.55	-48.99	-21.63	1.40	-9.07	-4.73
Fabricated metals	4.70	1.48	2.36	4.22	2.59	2.34	-1.24	-7.49	-26.96	-9.94	-5.29	-1.41	10.29
Transport equip.	-0.23	-1.18	5.41	4.98	0.99	1.37	1.59	-17.87	-28.56	-23.37	-7.02	-1.29	17.00
Other machinery	-3.75	2.00	9.27	5.16	6.87	3.66	-7.99	-17.07	-35.94	-24.98	-7.23	-5.25	18.76
Other manufactures	-0.15	3.49	-6.89	5.12	3.12	-2.65	2.09	-8.79	-20.85	-5.27	1.48	-2.99	18.77
Services	0.68	0.36	0.66	0.42	0.36	0.10	0.65	0.98	0.24	0.24	1.39	0.22	7.71

at the expense of transport equipment, machinery, and other manufactures.

In response to agricultural liberalization, grain production would expand by roughly 1.0 to 2.0 percent in Africa and by 1.0 to 2.5 percent in Latin America. Under all specifications of the model, agricultural production would expand throughout all developing countries. The picture for industrial countries is, as expected, mixed. Agriculture production in land-abundant OECD countries – the United States, Canada, Australia, and New Zealand – would expand somewhat. For instance, grain production in the United States would increase by between 0.4 and 1.2 percent. Production in the European Union and the EFTA would fall under all model specifications.

The production results show clearly that, regardless of the model specification, the dominant effects pertain to the elimination of the MFA. If it is phased out as planned, the resulting shift in resources in importing and exporting countries would dominate the other market access components of the Uruguay Round. With the exception of chemicals, petroleum, transport equipment, and other manufactures in Africa and of steel in Latin America, resources would shift away from all other industrial sectors in the developing world into textiles and clothing. The opposite pattern would dominate in the OECD countries, where other industrial sectors would expand.

This finding is consistent with our basic observation earlier – that the MFA is the single largest set of trade restraints scheduled to be dismantled under the Uruguay Round. Although agricultural protection is greater in tariff equivalent terms, the gains from agricultural liberalization will not be as great, for three reasons: because the liberalization assumed under our *de minimus* scenario is limited, because the share of agriculture of GDP is relatively small in the subsidizing industrial countries, and because agricultural production is assumed to operate under CRTS (under all scenarios). But the potential for significant gains exists, if the liberalization is ultimately greater than expected.

Impacts on real wages under the models

We report changes in wage rates in relationship to changes in the cost of the composite consumption good (table 9.9). Under both competition scenarios (CRTS and IRTS) and under all capital market closures, the impacts of the Uruguay Round on wages are positive, although often slight. The largest wage gains would be realized in Asia, in which the production of relatively labor-intensive textiles and clothing would expand to the greatest extent in response to the elimination of the MFA.

Table 9.9 *Estimated effects of the Uruguay Round on real wages with alternative market structures and investment behavior (percentage change)*

	CRTS and perfect competition			IRTS and imperfect competition		
	Fixed capital	Endogenous capital Fixed savings rate	Endogenous capital Endogenous savings rate	Fixed capital	Endogenous capital Fixed savings rate	Endogenous capital Endogenous savings rate
Australia and New Zealand	0.71	0.76	1.22	0.40	0.42	0.89
Japan	0.13	0.16	0.26	0.13	0.23	0.39
Canada	0.67	0.75	1.16	0.61	0.69	1.12
United States	0.30	0.38	0.51	0.32	0.45	0.62
European Union	0.29	0.38	0.44	0.33	0.45	0.53
EFTA	0.33	0.36	0.56	0.29	0.31	0.44
Sub-Saharan and North Africa	0.41	0.60	0.72	0.71	1.29	1.09
China	1.89	2.36	3.18	1.69	4.01	1.68
East Asia	1.93	2.16	2.93	1.49	3.27	1.61
South Asia	2.13	2.32	2.91	2.84	4.65	2.02
Latin America	0.65	0.66	1.48	0.63	0.96	1.86
Economies in transition	0.17	0.16	0.38	0.25	0.34	0.43
Rest of the world	3.10	3.53	4.54	3.39	9.22	13.63

Impacts on national welfare under the models

The effects of the Uruguay Round on national welfare show a similar pattern (tables 9.10 and 9.11). The estimated annual income gain for the world under the 1992 counterfactual simulations would range from $40 billion in the CRTS specification to $214 billion in the IRTS specification with an endogenous savings rate.[20] The income gain to the world would range from 0.17 to 0.94 percent annually. While all regions would come out ahead, with the exception of the economies in transition under the constant returns specification, the results vary considerably by region.

Worldwide, the welfare benefits of textile and clothing reforms exceed those of agricultural liberalization. The opposite is true for individual regions. In Australia and New Zealand, agricultural liberalization would dominate as a source of gains under most of the model specifications, while the primary products and other industry sectors would be a major source of gains in Latin America and Africa under several specifications.

As with the production and wage figures, estimates of the regional welfare or income effects of the Uruguay Round agreement are sensitive to the model specifications. One striking region-specific result, especially when compared with our earlier assessments, is the relatively small impact on the EFTA countries under all specifications. In Francois, McDonald, and Nordström (1994), we estimated relatively large gains for these countries. Most of those gains came from agricultural liberalization. Under the more modest agricultural scenario considered here, the impact on the national welfare of the EFTA countries is correspondingly much smaller. Essentially, the minimal liberalization scenario considered here would induce these countries to maintain the self-inflicted costs of their highly distortionary agricultural policies. Similarly, the less ambitious agricultural reform would have less of an impact on the European Union. The largest relative welfare impacts would be concentrated in developing countries, particularly in Asia and Latin America. Under the CRTS and IRTS specifications, the income effects would range from 0.8 percent to 5.7 percent of GDP for China, from 0.4 to 4.3 percent for East Asia, and from 0.4 to 4.5 percent for South Asia. While agricultural liberalization would have adverse impacts on Africa (because it contains countries that are net food importers), these effects would be outweighed by other aspects of the Uruguay Round. On net, the welfare effects for Africa would range from 0.3 percent to 1.6 percent of GDP.

The distribution of income effects by region also depends on the model specifications. Under the increasing returns specification, the income effects for the United States would range from $16.6 billion to $37 billion in 1992; those for the European Union would range from $17.1 billion to $31.9

Table 9.10 *Estimated effects of the Uruguay Round on national welfare, 1992 counterfactual: CRTS and perfect competition (1992 US $billions)*

	Textiles and clothing	Other industrial goods	Non-agriculture primary products	Agriculture	Total	Total as percentage of GDP
Fixed capital stock						
Australia and New Zealand	0.04	−0.42	0.08	0.59	0.29	0.09
Japan	−0.57	2.41	−0.09	−0.50	1.26	0.04
Canada	0.33	−0.42	0.07	0.74	0.72	0.13
United States	7.12	2.66	0.19	0.10	10.07	0.17
European Union	5.89	3.50	0.38	4.79	14.56	0.22
EFTA	0.65	0.29	−0.04	−0.64	0.27	0.03
Africa	−0.11	1.82	0.51	−0.40	1.81	0.24
China	3.31	0.22	0.04	0.14	3.72	0.84
East Asia	−0.12	3.61	−0.05	0.03	3.47	0.35
South Asia	1.48	−0.02	−0.01	−0.22	1.23	0.37
Latin America	−0.17	−0.04	0.03	0.24	0.06	0.01
Economies in transition	−0.40	0.79	0.05	−0.75	−0.31	−0.04
Rest of the world	0.91	1.31	−0.25	0.52	2.49	0.98
Total	18.38	15.71	0.91	4.65	39.65	0.17
Endogenous capital stock fixed savings rate						
Australia and New Zealand	0.08	−0.62	0.12	0.92	0.51	0.15
Japan	−0.84	4.27	−0.13	−0.84	2.46	0.07
Canada	0.68	−0.71	0.11	1.23	1.31	0.23
United States	10.83	4.26	0.30	0.22	15.62	0.26
European Union	8.60	5.69	0.58	7.25	22.13	0.34
EFTA	1.05	0.53	−0.05	−0.96	0.57	0.06

Africa	-0.11	3.51	0.96	-0.73	3.63	0.48
China	5.44	0.51	0.06	0.41	6.42	1.44
East Asia	-0.01	6.47	-0.08	0.16	6.54	0.66
South Asia	2.09	0.13	0.00	-0.35	1.88	0.56
Latin America	-0.29	-0.11	0.05	0.64	0.29	0.02
Economies in transition	-0.60	1.27	0.08	-1.17	-0.42	-0.05
Rest of the world	1.47	2.06	-0.37	0.77	3.93	1.54
Total	28.41	27.26	1.64	7.55	64.85	0.29
Endogenous capital stock, endogenous savings rate						
Australia and New Zealand	0.23	0.61	0.16	0.77	1.77	0.53
Japan	-0.62	5.89	0.03	-0.26	5.04	0.14
Canada	0.96	1.44	0.10	0.75	3.24	0.57
United States	11.87	10.24	0.46	0.19	22.76	0.38
European Union	9.36	8.89	0.81	1.39	20.45	0.31
EFTA	1.21	1.42	-0.05	0.34	2.93	0.32
Africa	0.24	2.69	1.24	1.78	5.96	0.78
China	5.90	1.28	0.09	0.43	7.70	1.73
East Asia	1.51	8.82	0.31	0.48	11.12	1.13
South Asia	2.38	0.66	0.09	-0.18	2.95	0.88
Latin America	1.03	7.37	0.36	2.33	11.08	0.92
Economies in transition	-0.36	1.74	0.13	0.43	1.93	0.24
Rest of the world	2.00	3.25	-0.17	0.89	5.98	2.34
Total	35.71	54.31	3.54	9.34	102.90	0.45

Note: the income metric is based on equivalent-variation calculations, and reflects base-period expenditure patterns and prices. It measures the national income transfer necessary to achieve the simulated welfare gains in table 9.11, assuming base-period prices and an allocation between consumption and investment based on base-period shares. The equivalent-variations are derived from changes in welfare indices for steady-state temporal consumption.

Table 9.11 Estimated effects of the Uruguay Round on national welfare, 1992 counterfactual: IRTS and imperfect competition (1992 US $billions)

	Textiles and clothing	Other industrial goods	Non-agriculture primary products	Agriculture	Total	Total as percentage of GDP
Fixed capital stock						
Australia and New Zealand	−0.46	−0.09	0.04	0.61	0.09	0.03
Japan	1.98	3.91	−0.01	−0.22	5.67	0.16
Canada	−0.15	0.37	0.09	0.40	0.71	0.12
United States	11.71	5.18	0.08	−0.42	16.55	0.28
European Union	10.28	5.93	0.44	0.47	17.12	0.26
EFTA	−0.63	0.93	−0.01	0.04	0.33	0.04
Africa	0.42	3.48	1.03	1.25	6.17	0.81
China	9.43	2.55	0.15	0.27	12.40	2.79
East Asia	15.23	4.07	0.03	0.40	19.72	2.00
South Asia	8.54	1.10	−0.19	−0.21	9.24	2.77
Latin America	0.07	2.89	−0.06	1.03	3.92	0.33
Economies in transition	−0.25	1.60	0.08	0.28	1.70	0.21
Rest of the world	2.54	3.57	−0.37	0.06	5.82	2.28
Total	58.69	35.48	1.31	3.96	99.44	0.44
Endogenous capital stock, fixed savings rate						
Australia and New Zealand	−0.69	−0.13	0.09	0.92	0.19	0.06
Japan	3.32	6.70	0.38	−0.27	10.14	0.28
Canada	−0.09	0.54	0.18	0.66	1.29	0.23
United States	19.17	7.59	0.40	−0.58	26.57	0.45
European Union	17.34	8.68	1.54	0.19	27.74	0.42
EFTA	−0.91	1.47	0.08	−0.04	0.60	0.07

Africa	2.11	6.37	1.81	1.52	11.80	1.55
China	19.02	5.24	0.50	0.43	25.19	5.66
East Asia	32.91	8.20	0.60	0.55	42.26	4.28
South Asia	13.68	1.95	−0.18	−0.32	15.14	4.53
Latin America	0.77	6.31	0.27	1.58	8.92	0.74
Economies in transition	−0.58	2.60	0.24	0.44	2.70	0.33
Rest of the world	12.10	3.14	5.01	−0.13	20.12	7.89
Total	118.14	58.66	10.91	4.95	192.66	0.85
Endogenous capital stock, endogenous savings rate						
Australia and New Zealand	−0.68	1.23	0.04	0.87	1.46	0.43
Japan	4.21	9.13	1.19	−0.30	14.23	0.40
Canada	0.40	2.50	0.22	0.67	3.79	0.67
United States	22.63	13.44	0.36	0.19	36.62	0.62
European Union	18.48	11.71	0.76	0.91	31.85	0.48
EFTA	−0.90	2.24	0.28	0.06	1.69	0.18
Africa	1.55	4.95	2.82	1.40	10.72	1.41
China	11.24	4.88	0.70	0.82	17.64	3.97
East Asia	22.18	7.00	1.21	0.63	31.02	3.15
South Asia	9.18	2.09	−0.74	−0.25	10.27	3.07
Latin America	1.70	14.06	2.63	1.88	20.26	1.68
Economies in transition	−0.31	3.05	0.19	0.48	3.41	0.42
Rest of the world	18.00	8.29	5.47	−0.28	31.49	12.34
Total	107.68	84.57	15.14	7.08	214.46	0.94

Note: the income metric is based on equivalent-variation calculations, and reflects base-period expenditure patterns and prices. It measures the national income transfer necessary to achieve the simulated gains, assuming base-period prices and an allocation between consumption and investment based on base-period shares. The equivalent-variations are derived from changes in welfare indices for steady-state temporal consumption.

billion. Among developing countries, the range is much wider. Under the increasing returns specification, the largest absolute income gains would be realized by China ($12.4 billion to $25.2 billion), East Asia ($19.7 billion to $42.3 billion), and Latin America ($3.9 billion to $20.3 billion).

A major difference between the constant and increasing returns versions of the model pertains to the impact of the elimination of MFA quotas for clothing and textiles on developing countries – particularly in East Asia, Latin America, and Africa. While the constant returns specification generally predicts a slight loss in these regions, the increasing returns version predicts a substantial gain. Why? Recall that the MFA quotas are administrated through export licenses that allow exporting countries to capture the "quota rents" or scarcity premiums. These quota rents will disappear with the quotas, and the question is whether improved market access will compensate for lower prices. This is where the models disagree. According to the constant returns version of the model, with its inherent regional bias in consumer preferences (the Armington assumption) and thus low demand response to lower import prices, the answer is no; according to the increasing returns version, the answer is yes. That is, whether they will lose or gain from the phaseout of the quotas will depend critically on whether the volume increase compensates for the price reduction (the loss of quota rents).

Conclusion

This chapter has assessed the possible trade and income effects of key market access provisions of the Uruguay Round. This assessment is based on numerical estimates made under a variety of assumptions about market structure, scale economies, and linkages among trade, income, and capital accumulation. In working with these results, our objective has not been to provide a particular estimate, or set of estimates, for the likely impact of the Uruguay Round. The results are sensitive to the structures of the models we used, and, in our view, we cannot say which specification is the most appropriate. On a qualitative level, however, we have identified a set of results that emerge consistently under a broad range of assumptions. These results do lend some useful insight into the implications of the Uruguay Round. They are also open to varying interpretations.

We would like to suggest two alternative methods for interpreting the results presented herein. At one level, they simply indicate possible shifts in production and trade as the Uruguay Round is implemented. On this basis, we have identified a basic pressure for resources to shift into textiles and clothing in developing countries (particularly Asia) away from other industrial sectors. This effect of the market access provisions of the Uruguay

Round dominates, at least in developing countries. The shift away from other industrial production also gives industrial countries, Latin America, and Africa opportunities for expanding industrial production outside of textiles and clothing. Particularly strong pressure would exist in industrial countries for a contraction in textile and apparel production. This leads to our second method for interpreting the results.

In our policy simulations, we held measures of contingent protection constant throughout. While we are not alone in making this assumption, it is probably unrealistic. Moreover, our assumption of a phaseout of gray-area measures (particularly VERs) may also prove unrealistic, since the new agreement on safeguards seems to open up a window for import quotas administered by the exporting member.[21] Given some inertia in the overall level of protection for certain sectors, our results indicate the sectors in which the pressure for offsetting safeguard measures (or contingent protection) will be particularly pertinent.

In general, the Uruguay Round should have a positive impact on the primary metals industries in industrial countries. In particular, the potential shift of developing country producers into other sectors would appear to ease competitive pressures on steel. The opposite is true of textiles and clothing. In those sectors, our results point to very strong adjustment pressure in the textile and clothing sectors of industrial countries. Because the elimination of the MFA is backloaded, with as much as half of the required liberalization saved for the last day of the ten-year transitional period, both industrial and developing countries would be well advised to anticipate future problems in this area and take the actions necessary to head off the possibility of future trade frictions now, rather than later.

Appendix A   Sectors and regions of the CGE model

SECTORS

Paddy rice, wheat, other grains
Nongrain crops
Livestock and livestock products
Forestry and logging
Ocean fishing, coastal fishing, and fishing not elsewhere classified
Coal, crude petroleum and natural gas, other minerals
Processed rice, meat products, milk products, other food products, beverages, and tobacco
Textiles
Wearing apparel
Lumber and wood products, pulp, paper, and printing
Petroleum refineries and miscellaneous coal and petroleum products

Chemicals, rubber, and plastics
Iron and steel basic industries
Non ferrous metal basic indistries
Fabricated metal products
Transport equipment
Other machinery and equipment
Other manufactures
Services

REGIONS

Australia and New Zealand
Japan
Canada
United States
European Union
EFTA
China
East Asia: Korea, Indonesia, Malaysia, Phillipines, Singapore, Thailand, Hong Kong, Taiwan
South Asia: Bangladesh, Bhutan, India, Maldives, Nepal, Pakistan, Sri Lanka
Latin America: all of the Americas, excluding Canada and the United States
Africa: all of Africa (excluding South Africa) and the Middle East
Eastern Europe: Armenia, Azerbaijan, Belarus, Bulgaria, Czech Republic, Estonia, Georgia, Hungary, Kazakhstan, Kyrgyzstan, Latvia, Lithuania, Moldova, Poland, Romania, Russian Federation, Slovakia, Tajikistan, Turkmenistan, Ukraine, Uzbekistan
Rest of world: South Africa, Turkey, and regions not elsewhere classified

Notes

The views expressed here are strictly those of the authors and should not be attributed to any institution with which they may have ever been affiliated. We would like to extend our thanks to Thomas Hertel, Kala Krishna, Will Martin, Thomas Rutherford, and David Tarr for helpful comments and suggestions.
1. Simple average MFN tariffs for the four largest GATT trading entities, as reported in the respective GATT trade policy reviews, were 8.6 percent for Canada (1994); 7.3 percent for the European Union (1992); 6.9 percent for Japan (1992); and 6.7 percent for the United States (1993) (GATT 1995a, GATT 1994a, GATT 1993, and GATT 1992).
2. Although the model data base records tariff protection fully, it does not capture all nontariff barriers. Both total protection and the share of protection from nontariff barriers are thus higher than shown in figure 9.1.

3. This exception reflects, in part, the long-standing tradition of GATT to grant developing countries "special and differential treatment" commensurate with their perceived developmental needs. Somewhat oddly, when acting through the World Bank or International Monetary Fund, many industrial countries push for trade liberalization as a condition for granting developmental assistance to the developing world; yet, when acting through GATT, the very same countries may agree to derogations from obligations to undertake or maintain trade liberalization. Trade ministries and finance ministries, which in many national governments have responsibility for World Bank and International Monetary Fund relations, seem to have conflicting views about trade liberalization. Interestingly, trade ministers seem to be more skeptical about the virtue of trade liberalization.

4. The trade policy reviews published by the GATT Secretariat provide details on the specific countries.

5. The General Agreement limits tariff rates only to the extent that they have been "bound" in the schedules. The applied rate may of course be lower. Tariff bindings reduce the risk of investing in distribution channels that support trade or FDI projects that depend on imported intermediate goods. They also limit the upside of protection. Given the stochastic nature of unbound protection, bindings may have an important liberalizing effect, even when placed above current applied rates (Francois and Martin 1995).

6. Rice in Japan and Korea is a notable exception. Rice tariffication in Japan will be reconsidered in 2000. As a start, these countries have made somewhat larger minimum market access committed than have other countries (4 percent of domestic consumption, rising to 8 percent at the end of the six-year implementation period).

7. In 1991, Sweden liberalized its textile and clothing regime and withdrew from the MFA. Two other industrial countries – Japan and Switzerland – have not imposed any MFA quotas. But they have "signaled" their willingness to do so merely by signing the MFA agreement and by stepping up import surveillance. Import surveillance, at least in concentrated industries, can reduce import levels as producers try to forestall explicit quotas (Winters 1994).

8. These disputes sometimes spill over into other areas of trade. The most recent episode centered on disputes between the United States and the European Union over agricultural subsidies at the end of the Uruguay Round, when the list of products threatened with retaliation by the United States covered a broad range of processed food and industrial products. Agricultural disputes have sometimes evolved in a very bizarre manner. One relic of an earlier episode is the high US tariff on light trucks, which was imposed in the 1960s to punish Germany (particularly Volkswagen) for unfair European trading in broiler chickens. The United States has since used these punitive tariffs to threaten Japanese trade in minivans and sport utility vehicles, supporting the arguments of the US auto industry that it is unfair that Japanese firms do not pay punitive duties on its minivans. But these discussions have not yet been linked formally to Japan's trade practices in broiler chickens.

9. As of March 30, 1994, 113 waivers had been granted under GATT Article XXV:5; forty-five remained in force (GATT 1994b).
10. Participants seem to have made only a few challenges to the tariff equivalents proposed by other participants, despite the fact that this "verification" process took several weeks before the Marrakesh ministerial meeting closed the Uruguay Round. The widespread use of specific, rather than *ad valorem*, tariffs may have complicated the verification process.
11. Some countries hoped for larger reductions in the aggregate measure of support early in the Uruguay Round. As the Uruguay Round progressed, however, many participants came to believe that the main purpose of the reduction requirement was to close off a likely avenue for redirecting import protection and export subsidies into another form of support.
12. Admittedly, our minimalist scenario may be too extreme. Domestic support commitments have been made in nominal terms which may force gradual real cuts in domestic support over time. And inflation on specific tariffs that arose from the conversion of nontariff barriers may, over time, reduce the *ad valorem* equivalents of these measures. (A review of the schedules indicates that high-inflation countries tended to avoid the use of specific tariffs.) The agriculture agreement may offer one of the first microeconomic arguments for rapid expansion of the global monetary base. But it is unlikely that this is the sort of International Monetary Fund–WTO cooperation envisioned in the "Declaration on the Contribution of the World Trade Organization to Achieving Greater Coherence in Global Economic Policymaking" adopted at the Marrakesh meeting in December 1993.
13. More information on data sources for the underlying social accounting and protection data is provided in the technical annex to Francois and Martin (1995). The breakout for EFTA countries was needed because the "rest of world" category in the GTAP data base combines data for these countries with data from South Africa, Turkey, and a number of small developing economies. We have reconstructed the "rest of world" category – without the EFTA – using production and trade data for South Africa and Turkey, which make up 90% of the "rest of world" GDP.
14. These effects relate to classical models of capital accumulation and growth. A separate, though related, set of issues is raised by the more recent literature on trade policy and endogenous growth; see Francois and Shiells (1992) and Grossman and Helpman (1995), for a survey.
15. We assume that China will not modify its own tariff regime as a result of the Uruguay Round, but will continue to receive MFN treatment (and hence will benefit from the liberalizations undertaken by other countries).
16. The scenario we model for agriculture matches, in many ways, the first step of Sampson's (1986) proposal to phase out the MFA by first introducing tariff quotas.
17. This term was coined by Hertel, Ianchovichina, and McDonald (forthcoming) to point out that the misrepresentation of underlying distortions leads to the

use of incorrect reference prices when parameters are calibrated for use in computable general equilibrium models.

18. This is probably an unrealistic assumption. We revisit the issue in the final section of the chapter.

19. Although we have made such projections in previous work to facilitate comparison with other studies, we now doubt the utility of this exercise. Still, such efforts facilitated public discussion on commonly based estimates because policy makers and the press have focused on nominal measures instead of percentage-based income effects. These issues are discussed in Francois and Martin (1995). Note that the global welfare estimates in this chapter, in percentage terms, are comparable to our estimates in Francois, McDonald, and Nordström (1994). Hence, had we translated our results into 2005 "equivalents," they would have been in the same range – about $200 billion under constant returns and $500 billion under increasing returns (measured in 1992 dollars in 2005).

20. While this reflects consumption changes in the steady state, it may not reflect consumption (welfare) effects during the transition to a new steady state. This is because of the cost of accumulating capital to reach the new steady-state level. With variable savings rates, consumption may rise or fall during the transition to a new steady state. Under the fixed savings rate specification, however, investment and consumption increase in tandem, and the above concern does not apply because new capital is paid for from income gains.

21. See Agreement on Safeguards, Article 11, footnote 3.

References

Bach, C. F., and W. Martin 1995. "Would the Right Tariff Aggregation Procedure Please Stand Up?" Manuscript. Washington, DC: World Bank.

Baldwin, R. E. 1992. "Measurable Dynamic Gains from Trade." *Journal of Political Economy* 100: 162–74.

Chyc, K., M. Gehlhar, D. Gray, T. W. Hertel, E. Ianchovichina, B. McDonald, R. McDougall, and M. Tsigas forthcoming. "GTAP Data Base." In T. W. Hertel, ed., *Global Trade Analysis Using the GTAP Model*. New York: Cambridge University Press.

Ethier, W. 1982. "National and International Returns to Scale in the Modern Theory of International Trade." *American Economic Review* 72: 950–59.

Finger, J. M. 1995. "Legalized Backsliding: Safeguard Provisions in the GATT." In W. Martin and L. A. Winters, eds., *The Uruguay Round and the Developing Economies*. Washington, DC: World Bank.

Flam H., and H. Nordström 1994. "Why Do Pre-Tax Car Prices Differ So Much Across European Countries?" CEPR Discussion Paper 1181. London: Centre for Economic Policy Research.

Francois, J. 1994. "Global Production and Trade: Factor Migration and Commercial Policy with International Scale Economies." *International Economics Review* 35: 565–81.

Francois, J. F., and C. R. Shiells 1992. "The Dynamic Effects of Trade Liberalization: A Survey." US International Trade Commission Publication 2608. Washington, DC: US International Trade Commission.

Francois, J., B. McDonald, and H. Nordström 1993. "Economywide Effects of the Uruguay Round." Uruguay Round background paper. Geneva: GATT.

1994. "The Uruguay Round: A Global General Equilibrium Assessment." CEPR Discussion Paper 1067. London: Centre for Economic Policy Research.

1995. "Assessing the Uruguay Round." In W. Martin and L. A. Winters, eds., *The Uruguay Round and the Developing Economies*. World Bank Discussion Paper 307. Washington, DC: World Bank.

forthcoming. "Capital Accumulation in Applied Trade Models." In J. Francois and K. Reinert, eds., *Applied Methods for Trade Policy Analysis*. New York: Cambridge University Press.

GATT 1992. *Trade Policy Review: Japan*, vol. I. Geneva: GATT.

1993. *Trade Policy Review: European Communities*, vol. I. Geneva: GATT.

1994a. *Trade Policy Review: United States*, vol. I. Geneva: GATT.

1994b. *Analytical Index: Guide to GATT Law and Practice*. Geneva: GATT.

1995. *Trade Policy Review: Canada*, vol. I. Geneva: GATT.

Goldin, I., O. Knudsen, and D. van der Mensbrugghe 1993. *Trade Liberalisation: Global Economic Implications*. Paris: OECD and the World Bank.

Grossman, G. M., and E. Helpman 1995. "Technology and Trade." NBER Working Paper 4926. Boston: National Bureau of Economic Research.

Haaland, J., and T. C. Tollefsen 1994. "The Uruguay Round and Trade in Manufactures and Services. General Equilibrium Simulations of Production, Trade and Welfare Effects of Liberalization." CEPR Discussion Paper 1008. London: Centre for Economic Policy Research.

Harrison, G. W., T. F., Rutherford, and D. G. Tarr 1995. "Quantifying the Uruguay Round." In W. Martin and L. A. Winters, eds., *The Uruguay Round and the Developing Economies*. World Bank Discussion Paper 307. Washington, DC: World Bank.

Hertel, T., E. Ianchovichina, and B. McDonald forthcoming. "Multi-Region General Equilibrium Modelling." In J. Francois and K. Reinert, eds., *Applied Methods for Trade Policy and Analysis*. New York: Cambridge University Press.

Ingco, M. forthcoming. "Agricultural Trade Liberalization in the Uruguay Round: One Step Forward, One Step Back?" *World Economy*.

International Agricultural Trade Research Consortium 1994. "The Uruguay Round Agreement on Agriculture: An Evaluation." Commissioned Paper No. 9. University of Minnesota: International Agricultural Consortium.

Krugman, P. R. 1980. "Scale Economies, Product Differentiation, and the Pattern of Trade." *American Economic Review* 70: 950–59.

Laird, S. forthcoming. "Quantifying Commercial Policies." In Francois, J. and K. Reinert, eds. *Applied Methods for Trade Policy Analysis*. Cambridge: Cambridge University Press.

McDonald, B. 1994. "Anti-Dumping Duties for Canada, the European Union and the United States in the Global Trade Analysis Project (GTAP) Database." Mimeo.

Magee, S. P. 1972. "Welfare Effects of Restriction on US Restrictions of Trade." *Brooking Papers on Economic Activity* 3: 645–701.

Nordström, H. 1995. "Tariffication, Price Stability, and Stockpiling." Manuscript. Geneva: World Trade Organisation.

Sampson, G. P. 1986. "Pseudo-Economics of the MFA–A Proposal for Reform." *The World Economy* 10(4): 455–68.

Smith, M. A. M. 1976. "Trade, Growth, and Consumption in Alternative Models of Capital Accumulation." *Journal of International Economics* 6: 385–88.

1977. "Capital Accumulation in the Open Two-Sector Economy." *The Economic Journal* 87: 273–82.

United States International Trade Commission 1993. "The Economic Effects of Significant U.S. Import Restraints, an Update." Washington, DC: USITC (November).

Winters, L. A. 1994. "Import Surveillance as a Strategic Trade Policy." In Paul Krugman and Alisdair Smith, eds., *Empirical Studies of Strategic Trade Policy*. Chicago: University of Chicago Press.

10 The liberalization of services trade: potential impacts in the aftermath of the Uruguay Round

Drusilla K. Brown, Alan V. Deardorff, Alan K. Fox, and Robert M. Stern

This study was designed originally to examine the effects of the liberalization in services trade to be achieved under the Uruguay Round. But the general consensus is that little or no actual liberalization was achieved, and that the services-trade negotiations merely established the institutional structure for negotiating liberalization in the future. The focus of this study thus shifted to the more hypothetical one of examining what the effects of services liberalization might be when it finally occurs. For this purpose, we used Hoekman's (1995) "guesstimates" of the size of trade barriers in services and calculated the effects of an assumed 25 percent reduction in these barriers, which is a reduction that we believe represents a plausible order of magnitude that may eventually be achieved. To provide a benchmark for comparison, we have also calculated the effects of the liberalization in tariffs for industrial products that actually was negotiated. Our focus is on the world's major trading countries/regions which account for the largest part of trade in services and merchandise. Several results emerge from our analysis.

First, the effects of liberalization in services trade are of the same order of magnitude as for liberalization in industrial products. Despite the fact that trade in services is smaller than trade in industrial products, the size of the services sectors, and thus the size of their trade barriers, is large. Because liberalization in services trade is just starting on a process that in the goods sectors began fifty years ago and is now almost complete, it has substantial scope for expanding trade and welfare in the world's economies. The decision to include services in the Uruguay Round negotiations was thus not misplaced.

Second, by including services trade in our model simulations, we were able for the first time to examine the effects of goods-market trade liberalization on trade in services. This relationship yielded a mix of effects; services trade would expand in some countries and sectors and contract in others. We also found that these effects on services trade did not change the results of our analysis that trade liberalization in goods, because it acts as a tax cut in these sectors, would tend to reduce employment in services.

Third, we found that the sectoral effects of services trade liberalization would be substantial in the service sectors themselves. This result holds true despite the fact that services trade is small compared with its outputs, which is again due to the size of the barriers that are assumed to be reduced. Services liberalization also has some notable effects on trade in goods, although whether the two are substitutable or complementary varies across countries.

A description of the analytical model

To estimate the potential economic impacts of the tariff reductions for industrial products negotiated in the Uruguay Round and the gains that might be realized from service sector liberalization in the post-Round period, we use a specially constructed version of the Michigan Brown–Deardorff–Stern CGE model of world production and trade. The model simulates the effects of three liberalization (tariff-reduction scenarios) on trade, economic welfare, and real returns to labor and capital for individual countries and regions.

The model is an extension of the CGE model first constructed by Brown and Stern (1989) to analyze the economic impacts of the Canada–US Trade Agreement, and later for analyses of NAFTA, the extension of NAFTA to some major trading countries in South America, and the formation of an East Asian trading bloc (Brown, Deardorff, and Stern 1992a and b and 1996; Brown, Deardoff, Hummels, and Stern 1994). For the analysis in this chapter, we grouped the thirty-four countries in our data base into eight major countries/regions: the United States, Canada, Mexico, Europe, Japan, the newly industrial economies of Asia, Australia/New Zealand, and a group of other major trading nations.[1] We closed the model by assigning remaining countries to a residual rest-of-world. In each country or region, the model covers twenty-nine sectors; twenty-three are "tradable" (import–export) product categories covering agriculture and manufacturing, and six are "tradable" categories covering services and government.[2]

Assumptions underlying the model

The model assumes that the agricultural sector is perfectly competitive, and that the manufacturing and services sectors are monopolistically competitive, with free entry.[3] Agricultural products are differentiated by country of production. Manufacturing and service-sector products are differentiated by firm to correspond to an imperfectly competitive market structure.[4] The reference year for the data base of the model is 1990. The input–output relationships used in the model refer to various years, depending on the availability of national input–output tables.[5] The data base and documentation, as well as a full statement and description of the equations and parameters of the model, are available from the authors on request.[6]

The model is also built on five assumptions that are important to interpreting our simulation results.

Full employment

The aggregate, or economywide, level of employment is held constant in each country. The simulated effects of the Uruguay Round thus do not change any country's overall rates of employment or unemployment. This assumption is made because overall employment is determined by macroeconomic forces and policies that are not included in a negotiated agreement and thus not contained in the model. The model captures the composition of employment across sectors as determined by the microeconomic interactions between supply and demand due to the Uruguay Round and the liberalization of goods and services trade in the future.

Balanced trade

The model assumes that each country maintains balanced trade (or, more accurately, that any initial trade imbalance remains constant) as trade barriers change. This assumption reflects the prevalence of flexible exchange rates among the countries involved. And as with the full employment assumption, it is an appropriate way to abstract from the macroeconomic forces and policies that are the main determinants of trade balances.

Rents and revenues

Revenue from tariffs is assumed to be redistributed to consumers in the tariff-levying country and spent like any other income. Similarly, the rents from nontariff barriers (and the tariff equivalents of the services barriers discussed in this chapter) are also assumed to remain within the importing country and to be spent like other income. When tariffs and tariff equivalents are reduced, the income available for purchasing imports falls along with the prices of those imports, without exerting any overall bias on expansion or contraction in demand.

Fixed relative wages

While the model adjusts the economywide wage in each country so as to maintain the assumption of full employment, it keeps wages across sectors constant. This feature allows the analysis to focus on the labor-market adjustments that might be required, independently of any wage changes that may induce those adjustments.[7]

Fixed labor supply
The model assumes that total labor supply in each country is fixed, and that cross-border movement of labor does not exist. This assumption does not imply that labor supply will not change as the Uruguay Round liberalization is phased in, but only that the Round will not induce such changes.

Our model also does not account for changes in FDI and the cross-border movement of workers that might occur as the rate of return on capital and real wages change. Nor does the model make any allowance for dynamic efficiency changes and economic growth. We are aware that the Uruguay Round involved much more than negotiated reductions and/or the removal of tariffs and nontariff barriers. It involved numerous changes and clarifications of existing agreements covering antidumping and subsidy/countervailing duty procedures; new agreements covering TRIPS and TRIMs; and the creation of the WTO, in part to strengthen dispute settlement procedures. While these various features of the Uruguay Round may be important, quantifying the roles they will play is difficult. Thus, by assessing only the liberalization of trade in industrial products and services and by abstracting from dynamic changes in efficiency and economic growth, we have provided "incomplete" calculations of the consequences of the Uruguay Round.

Policy input data: comments on reductions in tariffs and tariff equivalents

The policy inputs into the model are the pre- and post-Uruguay Round tariffs for industrial and agricultural products and "guesstimated" tariff equivalents for services (table 10.1). In the analyses, we apply each to the bilateral trade of the countries or regions being modeled.[8] Because our model is static, we assume that the reduction or removal of tariffs and tariff equivalents takes place at one time, rather than in stages. When the policy changes are introduced into the model, the method of solution yields percentage changes in the variables of interest for each country/region. Multiplying the percentage changes by the actual (1990) levels given in the data base yields the absolute changes, positive or negative, that might be the result of liberalization.

Before proceeding with the simulations and analyses, we provide some remarks on these various rates.

Table 10.1 *Weighted average tariffs on industrial and agricultural products and "guesstimated" tariff equivalents on services in the major trading countries/regions (percent)*

Country/region	Industrial products			Agricultural products			Services
	Pre-UR	Post-UR	Percentage reduction	Pre-UR	Post-UR	Percentage reduction	Post-UR
United States	4.9	3.4	30.0	14.9	14.0	6.0	67.5
Canada	7.7	4.5	42.2	2.6	2.3	14.9	57.2
Mexico	11.9	11.9	0.1	35.3	35.3	0.0	76.9
Europe	6.9	4.8	30.4	13.2	11.7	11.1	79.2
Japan	6.0	3.9	36.2	60.9	35.1	42.4	61.2
Newly industrial economies of Asia	0.9	0.7	17.2	12.7	7.9	37.3	46.0
Australia–New Zealand	13.8	9.1	34.3	0.8	0.4	44.8	105.9
Other trading nations	28.9	21.0	27.2	18.6	17.6	5.3	107.4

Sources: industrial products: World Bank Uruguay Round data base; agricultural products: Ingco 1995; and services: Hoekman 1995.

Tariff rates on industrial products

As noted in Martin (1994a), estimates of tariff reductions for industrial products should be based on differences between the Uruguay Round base rate and the Uruguay Round final offer rate as contained in the GATT IDB, which is the primary source of tariff data used in the Uruguay Round negotiations.[9] For industrial countries, the base rate is generally the rate that has been notified officially to the GATT as being legally bound as of 1986; the measure of liberalization to be used is thus the difference between the offer rate and the base rate as long as this difference is negative. If the difference is zero or positive, the tariff liberalization measure is set at zero. This procedure, in effect, excludes any changes in applied rates that industrial countries may have implemented after 1986.

The calculation is more complicated for many developing countries, insofar as they may have been using applied rates that were not previously bound. As noted in Martin (1994b) and Martin and Francois (1994), developing countries participated much more actively in the Uruguay Round than in previous rounds, with the result that the percentage of their industrial tariff lines that became bound increased from 22 to 72 percent. It can be argued that these bound tariffs represent trade liberalization – even if the applied rates have not changed or the rates are bound above the applied rate, since the binding will obviate any future increase in tariffs beyond the bound rate.

As a practical matter, however, the choice for developing countries is to define liberalization as either the difference between the newly bound and the applied rates or, alternatively, the difference between these rates only when the bound rates is below the initial applied rate, and nonexistent (or zero) otherwise. The first measure is misleading, since it would imply an increase in protection if the bound rate were above the applied rate. The second measure avoids this problem of misrepresenting restrictiveness and is thus the one that has been used for our purposes.

Tariff rates on agricultural products

One of the accomplishments of the Uruguay Round was to convert all existing forms of agricultural protection into tariffs. The GATT IDB, however, does not calculate these agricultural tariffs; rather, they were constructed by Ingco (1995) based on information in the country schedules for agricultural and related products. We aggregated these tariffs to correspond to our sectors for agriculture (ISIC 1) and food and related products (ISIC 310). Following Martin (1994a), we used the average pre-Uruguay Round tariff rate for a particular agricultural product category as the base rate, and measured agricultural liberalization as the difference between the base rate and the lower final offer rate. If the final offer tariff rate exceeded the base rate, we set the liberalization measure at zero.[10]

Services-trade barriers

Compared with trade barriers in goods, it is difficult to obtain systematic information on services-trade barriers (appendix A describes how we developed data on "tradable" services). We followed Hoekman (1995) by constructing "guesstimates" of comparative trade restrictiveness across countries, on the assumption that each country "revealed" its policy stance with its commitments in the Uruguay Round GATS.

Hoekman's procedure classifies each country's GATS commitments for each of 155 possible services sectors and each of four modes of supply in terms of the extent to which they indicated restrictions on market access.[11] Values are assigned to each of these 620 (4 × 155) cells for each of ninety-seven countries: 1.0 for the absence of restrictions under the commitments; 0.5 for the presence of restrictions under the commitments; and 0.0 for "unbound," or the absence of commitments. The major two-digit ISIC services sectors are then assigned an index of trade coverage restrictiveness equal to $1 - x/y$, where x is the sum of these values in the cells corresponding to the two-digit sector and y is the number of such cells. The resulting numbers range from "0" to "1" – or from "free access" (no restrictions), to "no access," in the sense that each supply mode in each subsector is "unbound."

Tariff-equivalent benchmarks are then assigned to each two-digit sector under assumptions about the restrictiveness of market access for each country. A benchmark of 200 percent is assigned to sectors in which market access tends to be prohibitive in most countries and which do not appear in most offers (for example, maritime, cabotage, air transport, postal services, voice telecommunications, and life insurance). The remaining sectors are assigned tariff-equivalent benchmarks that range from 20 to 50 percent. Each coverage index (the $1 - x/y$ measure) is then multiplied by the tariff-equivalent benchmark guesstimate to obtain a country/sector-specific tariff equivalent. (For example, in Australia construction services (ISIC 5) have a coverage rate of 0.3, and the tariff equivalent for this sector is set at 40 percent. In this case, then, Australia is assigned a tariff equivalent of 12 percent: 0.3×.40×100=12 percent.) Values for the two-digit ISIC sectors are then aggregated to obtain the one-digit guesstimates in table 10.1. Hoekman's tariff-equivalent guesstimates for ISIC 5 and 6 (construction and wholesale and retail trade) tend to be relatively low; those for ISIC sector 7 (transportation) tend to be relatively high; and those for ISIC sectors 8 and 9 (financial services and personal services) tend to fall in between. The detailed two-digit ISIC guesstimates are available in annex 2 of Hoekman (1995).

Hoekman is aware of the limitations of these judgmental estimates, since it is not clear what the benchmark tariff vector for the "most restrictive" sector(s) should be, and the assumption that the coverage ratios of country offers are correlated with actual policy stances is quite heroic. More research in this area is urgently required. It is unfortunate that efforts in this domain were not initiated during the negotiations. As it stands, the GATS schedules are thus the only source of cross-country information on services-trade policy regimes. Given the arbitrariness of Hoekman's procedure, we emphasize that our main objective here is to get a sense of the comparative importance of trade barriers in services, and the types of interactions that may emerge between the goods and services sectors under the assumption that services are tradable, and that countries open their services markets to foreign competition. In this light, the results we report in this chapter are indicative at best.

How do we use these guesstimates, arbitrary as they may appear? Hoekman has concluded that trade was not liberalized in the Uruguay Round, so that any benefits from liberalization will come in the post-Uruguay Round period. We thus compare the effects of the liberalization associated with the reductions in tariff rates on industrial products under the Uruguay Round with comparable reductions in tariff equivalents for services to be undertaken in the future. This is the strategy that we have followed in implementing our liberalization simulations.

Model simulations

How should we simulate the reduction or elimination of nontariff barriers on industrial products negotiated during the Uruguay Round? Consonant with the spirit of the Uruguay Round negotiations, the most desirable way to handle nontariff barriers would be to convert them into tariff equivalents and then assume that they would be reduced to zero.[12] Unfortunately, we have been unable to obtain sufficient data for measuring nontariff barriers as tariff equivalents. Also at issue is whether or not many of the existing nontariff barriers will in fact be eliminated over whatever period may have been specified in the negotiations. That is, it is conceivable that countries may find ways to continue to impose their nontariff barrier restrictions either in their present form or in some alternative form yet to be determined. In this case, the tariff equivalents of nontariff barriers would be only partially reduced and the quantitative restrictions would remain in place, thus diminishing the effects of the reduction or elimination of tariffs in these sectors. Moreover, as already mentioned in our discussion of services, services barriers were not liberalized in the Uruguay Round, and they thus remain a post-Uruguay Round negotiating option.

Trade coverage ratios are used to represent pre-Uruguay Round nontariff barriers in the data base of our model. If tariffs are reduced or removed and nontariff barriers are assumed to stay in place, the effects of tariff liberalization would be dampened. Alternatively, we could set our nontariff barrier coverage ratios at zero, thus assuming that tariff liberalization would not be dampened. Taking the Uruguay Round commitment to eliminate nontariff barriers at face value, it is this strategy that we have followed in our various computational scenarios:

Simulation 1

Reductions in Uruguay Round tariff rates on industrial products only, with nontariff barrier trade coverage ratios set at zero. (This simulation excludes the effects of the elimination of the MFA.)

Simulation 2

Assumed 25 percent reduction in post-Uruguay Round services-sector *ad valorem* tariff equivalents, with nontariff barrier coverage ratios in the agricultural and manufacturing sectors set at zero.

Simulation 3

Reductions in Uruguay Round tariff rates on industrial products combined with a 25 percent reduction in post-Uruguay Round services-sector *ad valorem* tariff equivalents, with nontariff barrier trade coverage ratios set at zero.

We use our CGE model to analyze both the aggregate impacts of the Uruguay Round under the three liberalization scenarios and the sector-specific impacts of the Round under the three scenarios for the United States and Europe individually as well as in combination. As discussed in the preceding section, we have data on pre- and post-Uruguay Round nominal tariff rates for industrial and agricultural sectors as well as guesstimates of post-Uruguay Round *ad valorem* tariff equivalents of services barriers.

Aggregate impacts of the three liberalization scenarios

The aggregate results measure the impacts of liberalization on the terms of trade, welfare, and factor payments for our eight countries/regions (table 10.2). Of greatest interest is the impact on economic welfare – that is, the "equivalent variation" measure of the change in real GDP.

Table 10.2 *Summary results of the Uruguay Round: changes in terms of trade, welfare, and real return to labor and capital (percentage change)*

Country	Terms of trade (1)	Equivalent variation (2)	Real wage rate (3)	Real return to capital (4)
Simulation 1: industrial products trade liberalization				
United States	−0.1	0.3	0.1	0.3
Canada	−0.2	0.4	0.2	0.3
Mexico	0.1	0.1	0.0	0.2
Europe	−0.1	0.3	0.1	0.3
Japan	0.1	0.6	0.3	−0.1
Asian newly industrial countries	0.9	2.4	1.3	−0.9
Australia–New Zealand	−1.0	1.2	0.3	1.0
Other trading nations	−1.6	0.0	0.2	1.7
Simulation 2: services trade liberalization				
United States	0.2	0.7	0.2	−0.1
Canada	−0.1	1.6	0.5	0.1
Mexico	−0.2	2.7	0.4	0.3
Europe	0.1	0.6	0.1	0.0
Japan	−0.5	0.8	0.2	0.4
Asian newly industrial countries	0.1	1.1	0.7	0.3
Australia–New Zealand	−0.4	2.8	0.3	0.5
Other trading nations	−0.3	1.0	0.3	0.4
Simulation 3: industrial products and services liberalization				
United States	0.2	0.9	0.3	0.2
Canada	−0.3	2.0	0.7	0.4
Mexico	−0.1	2.8	0.4	0.5
Europe	0.0	0.9	0.3	0.3
Japan	−0.4	1.4	0.5	0.3
Asian newly industrial countries	1.0	3.6	2.1	−0.6
Australia–New Zealand	−1.4	3.9	0.6	1.6
Other trading nations	−1.9	1.0	0.5	2.1

Economic welfare

Under simulation 1, economic welfare in all the countries and regions would rise. The largest welfare gains would accrue to Europe (US $20.7 billion, or 0.3 percent of GDP); Japan (US $16.6 billion, or 0.6 percent of GDP); the United States (US $14.5 billion, or 0.3 percent of GDP); and the newly industrial economies of Asia (US $12.2 billion, or 2.4 percent of GDP).[13] Under simulation 2, which assesses what the effects might be in post-Uruguay Round negotiations if services barriers were reduced, economic welfare in Europe would rise by 0.6 percent of GDP (US $39.3 billion), in the United States by 0.7 percent of GDP (US $36.1 billion), and in Japan by 0.8 percent of GDP (US $23.7 billion). Welfare would also increase in all other countries and regions shown.[14]

Under simulation 3, which combines simulations 1 and 2, the welfare gains from a reduction in industrial tariffs and services-trade barriers would reach 0.9 percent of GDP (US $60.1 billion) in Europe, 0.9 percent of GDP (US $50.6 billion) in the United States, 1.4 percent of GDP (US $40.4 billion) in Japan, 3.6 percent of GDP in the newly industrializing economies of Asia, and 2.0 percent GDP (US $11.5 billion) in Canada. To the extent that Hoekman's guesstimates of *ad valorem* tariff equivalents for services provide an indication of services barriers, our results suggest that reducing these barriers in post-Uruguay Round negotiations offers considerable scope for welfare gains.

In interpreting these results, one should note that positive welfare gains are not inevitable when trade is liberalized. Consumers will of course gain as the removal of tariffs will lower prices and as countries begin to specialize in the range of goods in which they have a comparative advantage. But trade liberalization could either increase or worsen a country's terms of trade; if import prices rose and export prices fell, welfare gains from specialization and exchange could be reversed. Each of our simulations shows several instances of negative terms-of-trade effects (see table 10.2). But these effects tend to be relatively small.

Our models also include the effects of economies of scale, which can either raise or lower welfare (results not shown). In industries that exhibit significant economies of scale and thus declining average costs, firms that charge a lower price may also have to increase output in order to break even. As firms lower their average total cost curve, the inputs they require to produce a unit of output will decline on average. If competition pressures force many of the firms in a country to economize on inputs in this way, then the country will be able to produce more under liberalization using the same inputs and technology. The gains from the realization of economies of scale will enhance the more traditional gains from specialization and exchange. It is also possible that scale effects could be negative, which we discuss in more detail later.[15]

Real wages and return to capital

Having established the welfare effects of the three liberalization simulations, we are now interested in which factors of production are likely to gain or lose – specifically the percentage changes in wages and the return to capital that are common to all sectors due to intersectoral labor and capital mobility. Under simulation 1, the real returns to both factors rise by relatively small percentages in the United States, Canada, Mexico, Europe, Australia/New Zealand, and the other trading nations (see table 10.2). In Japan and the newly industrial economies of Asia, real wages rise and the return to capital falls.

Increases in returns to both labor and capital may seem inconsistent with the Stolper–Samuelson theorem, which suggests that trade liberalization will increase the return to the more abundant factor in each country while making the other factor worse off. But in the context of a differentiated products model with IRTS, such as the one we are using, other forces at work may be undermining Stolper–Samuelson-type mechanics (Brown, Deardorff, and Stern 1993). That is, scale effects work much like the relative price effects articulated in the Stolper–Samuelson theorem to determine the implications of trade liberalization for factor prices. Scale effects, as with price effects, tend to accrue only to one factor. For example, an increase in output per firm in an industry will increase the real return to the factor used intensively in that industry and will lower the return to the other factor. But price and scale effects differ in one important respect. If scale effects emerge across the board in nearly all industries, then both factors may gain – a result that emerged several times in our model. But this result is by no means universal, since, as noted, the models yielded several cases in which the changes in factor returns have the opposite sign.

Sector-specific impacts of the three liberalization scenarios

Table 10.3 reports sector-specific results for employment in all countries/regions in simulation 1, reflecting trade liberalization in industrial products only. For simulation 2, reflecting the results of hypothetical liberalization in services, we report more detailed results for the United States, Europe, and Japan (tables 10.4 to 10.6).

Simulation 1

Considering first the sectoral employment results for industrial products trade liberalization, it can be seen in table 10.3 that the Uruguay Round will cause relatively small percentage shifts of employment among sectors, with some sectors gaining employment and others losing, as indicated.[16] In the United States, for example, the largest percentage reductions in employment are reported for clothing and iron and steel and the largest percentage increases are in footwear and leather products. The declines are never

Table 10.3 Simulation 1: industrial products; sectoral employment effects of the Uruguay Round (percentage change)

Sector	United States (1)	Canada (2)	Mexico (3)	European Union (4)	Japan (5)	Newly industrial economies of Asia (6)	Australia and New Zealand (7)	Other major trading nations (8)
1 Agriculture	0.3	0.6	0.0	0.1	-0.2	-1.5	0.9	0.2
310 Food	0.2	0.2	-0.0	0.0	-0.4	-3.0	0.9	0.0
321 Textiles	-0.3	-1.8	0.2	0.2	-0.1	2.0	-3.9	1.6
322 Clothing	-0.9	-2.9	0.1	-0.3	-2.2	5.2	-2.7	3.5
323 Leather products	1.0	-4.2	-0.3	0.1	-0.2	-3.7	0.9	1.5
324 Footwear	2.1	-4.2	0.0	0.4	0.0	-5.6	-3.2	0.5
331 Wood products	0.0	1.3	-0.1	-0.0	-0.3	1.6	-0.2	0.2
332 Furniture, fixtures	-0.4	-1.0	0.0	0.2	-0.4	8.7	-1.4	-0.5
341 Paper products	-0.1	2.9	-0.1	-0.1	-0.1	-0.3	-1.7	-0.1
342 Printing, publishing	0.0	-0.2	-0.2	0.0	0.0	-0.4	0.0	-0.3
35A Chemicals	0.3	0.6	-0.0	0.3	-0.1	-0.0	-2.7	-1.1
35B Petroleum products	0.0	0.0	0.1	0.1	-0.3	-0.5	0.6	-0.2
355 Rubber products	0.1	0.0	-0.1	0.1	-0.1	-1.5	0.2	-0.5
36A Nonmetal min. prod.	-0.1	-1.2	0.0	0.2	-0.1	0.0	-0.3	-0.6
362 Glass products	-0.1	-0.1	-0.1	0.2	0.1	1.8	-0.2	-0.8
371 Iron, steel	-0.8	-1.5	0.1	0.5	0.4	0.8	-1.2	-1.8
372 Nonferrous metals	0.0	3.1	-0.3	-0.0	-0.6	2.4	1.8	-0.1
381 Metal products	-0.0	-0.4	-0.1	0.0	0.0	0.8	-0.5	-0.5
382 Nonelec. machinery	-0.0	-0.6	-0.7	0.6	0.3	-1.7	-2.7	-3.4
383 Electrical machinery	0.3	-1.6	-0.9	-0.7	0.8	6.9	-3.8	-3.2
384 Transport equipment	0.2	-0.4	-0.4	0.1	-0.3	-2.7	-1.3	-1.2

38A Misc. mfrs.	−0.1	2.6	−0.1	−0.2	0.4	1.1	6.7	−2.2
2 Mining, quarrying	−0.3	0.8	0.7	−0.1	−2.2	−9.0	2.0	4.6
4 Utilities	0.0	0.3	0.0	0.0	0.0	0.4	0.1	−0.2
5 Construction	−0.1	−0.1	−0.0	−0.1	−0.0	−0.2	−0.2	−0.6
6 Wholesale trade	0.0	−0.0	−0.0	−0.0	0.0	0.1	0.1	−0.3
7 Transportation	0.1	0.2	0.0	0.0	0.0	−2.7	0.8	0.4
8 Financial services	−0.0	0.1	−0.0	0.0	0.1	0.5	0.2	−0.4
9 Personal services	−0.0	−0.1	0.0	−0.0	−0.0	−0.4	−0.2	−0.5
Total	0.0	0.0	0.0	0.0	0.0	0.0	0.0	0.0

Note: Europe includes the fifteen members of the European Union plus Norway and Switzerland; the newly industrial economies of Asia include Hong Kong, South Korea, Singapore, and Taiwan (China); and the other major trading nations include Argentina, Brazil, Chile, Colombia, India, Israel, Turkey, and Venezuela. Sector 35A comprises industrial chemicals (351) and other chemical products (352); Sector 35B comprises petroleum refineries (353) and miscellaneous products of petroleum and coal (354); Sector 36A comprises pottery, china, and earthenware (361) and other nonmetallic mineral products (369); Sector 38A comprises plastic products not elsewhere classified (356), professional photographic goods, etc. (385), and other manufacturing industries (390).

Table 10.4 *Simulation 2: services; sectoral effects on the United States of the Uruguay Round (percentage change)*

					Change in employment	
Sector	Exports (1)	Imports (2)	Output (3)	No. firms (4)	Percent (5)	1,000s (6)
1 Agriculture	−0.3	0.4	−0.1	0.0	−0.1	−2.7
310 Food	−0.4	0.5	0.0	−0.1	−0.1	−2.3
321 Textiles	−0.4	0.3	0.0	−0.1	−0.1	−1.2
322 Clothing	−0.3	−1.0	0.2	0.1	0.1	0.7
323 Leather products	−0.3	0.6	0.0	−0.2	−0.2	−0.1
324 Footwear	−0.1	−0.7	0.2	0.1	0.2	0.1
331 Wood products	−0.6	0.0	0.0	−0.2	−0.1	−0.9
332 Furniture, fixtures	−0.2	−0.1	0.0	−0.2	−0.1	−0.7
341 Paper products	−0.3	0.1	0.0	−0.2	−0.2	−1.2
342 Printing, publishing	−0.2	0.5	0.1	−0.1	−0.1	−1.3
35A Chemicals	−0.6	0.7	−0.1	−0.3	−0.3	−2.8
35B Petroleum products	−0.3	0.6	0.1	−0.1	0.0	0.0
355 Rubber products	−0.4	1.1	−0.1	−0.2	−0.2	−0.5
36A Nonmetal min. prod.	−0.2	0.5	0.0	−0.2	−0.1	−0.7
362 Glass products	−0.4	0.6	−0.1	−0.3	−0.2	−0.3
371 Iron, steel	−0.6	0.9	−0.2	−0.4	−0.4	−1.8
372 Nonferrous metals	−0.6	0.4	−0.2	−0.4	−0.3	−1.0
381 Metal products	−0.5	0.6	−0.1	−0.2	−0.2	−2.7
382 Nonelec. machinery	−0.7	1.1	−0.2	−0.3	−0.3	−7.1
383 Electrical machinery	−1.0	1.0	−0.5	−0.6	−0.5	−10.0
384 Transport equipment	−0.8	1.7	−0.3	−0.4	−0.4	−9.2
38A Misc. mfrs.	−0.8	0.7	−0.2	−0.3	−0.3	−6.7
2 Mining, quarrying	−0.5	0.8	−0.1	−0.2	−0.2	−1.3
4 Utilities	0.5	−0.4	0.0	−0.1	−0.1	−1.2
5 Construction	4.5	4.3	0.1	−0.1	−0.0	3.2
6 Wholesale trade	6.1	3.6	0.0	−0.1	−0.0	−2.7
7 Transportation	40.4	34.9	1.0	0.7	0.8	53.9
8 Financial services	14.2	13.5	0.1	0.0	0.1	7.3
9 Personal services	16.9	18.5	0.0	0.0	−0.0	−0.4
Total	4.2	3.9	0.0	−0.2	0.0	0.0

Note: see Table 10.3.

Table 10.5. *Simulation 2: services; sectoral effects on Europe of the Uruguay Round (percentage change)*

Sector	Exports (1)	Imports (2)	Output (3)	No. firms (4)	Change in employment Percent (5)	1,000s (6)
1 Agriculture	−0.1	0.3	0.0	0.0	−0.0	−1.2
310 Food	−0.1	0.3	0.0	−0.1	−0.1	−2.9
321 Textiles	−0.2	0.3	0.0	−0.1	−0.1	−1.5
322 Clothing	0.0	−0.6	0.1	0.0	0.0	0.0
323 Leather products	0.0	0.6	0.0	−0.1	−0.1	−0.1
324 Footwear	0.1	−0.7	0.1	0.0	0.0	0.0
331 Wood products	−0.1	0.0	0.1	−0.1	−0.1	−0.4
332 Furniture, fixtures	0.0	−0.1	0.0	−0.1	−0.1	−0.5
341 Paper products	−0.1	0.1	0.0	−0.1	−0.1	−0.9
342 Printing, publishing	−0.2	0.1	0.1	−0.1	−0.0	−0.6
35A Chemicals	−0.2	0.3	0.0	−0.1	−0.1	−3.3
35B Petroleum products	0.1	0.2	0.1	0.0	0.0	0.0
355 Rubber products	−0.1	0.7	0.0	−0.1	−0.1	−0.3
36A Nonmetal min. prod.	−0.1	0.4	0.1	−0.1	−0.1	−0.9
362 Glass products	−0.2	0.4	0.0	−0.1	−0.1	−0.2
371 Iron, steel	−0.1	0.4	0.0	−0.1	−0.1	−1.7
372 Nonferrous metals	−0.2	0.5	0.0	−0.2	−0.1	−0.7
381 Metal products	−0.1	0.2	0.0	−0.1	−0.1	−1.7
382 Nonelec. machinery	−0.2	0.5	0.0	−0.1	−0.1	−4.4
383 Electrical machinery	−0.2	0.3	0.0	−0.1	−0.1	−3.7
384 Transport equipment	−0.2	0.6	0.0	−0.1	−0.1	−4.6
38A Misc. mfrs.	−0.2	0.2	−0.1	−0.1	−0.1	−2.3
2 Mining, quarrying	−0.2	0.3	−0.1	−0.1	−0.1	−1.0
4 Utilities	0.6	0.4	0.0	−0.1	−0.1	−0.7
5 Construction	3.3	7.6	0.1	−0.1	−0.0	−4.4
6 Wholesale trade	6.1	6.7	0.0	0.0	−0.0	−2.7
7 Transportation	36.8	38.5	0.4	0.2	0.3	24.4
8 Financial services	7.9	15.8	0.0	0.0	−0.0	−0.5
9 Personal services	17.2	14.7	0.1	0.0	0.0	16.9
Total	3.2	3.3	0.0	−0.1	0.0	0.0

Note: see Table 10.3.

Table 10.6 *Simulation 2: services; sectoral effects on Japan of the Uruguay Round (percentage change)*

Sector	Exports (1)	Imports (2)	Output (3)	No. firms (4)	Change in employment Percent (5)	Change in employment 1,000s (6)
1 Agriculture	1.1	−0.8	0.1	0.0	0.2	7.3
310 Food	1.2	−1.1	0.0	−0.1	−0.0	−0.4
321 Textiles	1.2	−1.6	0.4	0.2	0.2	1.8
322 Clothing	2.5	−2.7	0.7	0.4	0.5	3.1
323 Leather products	1.6	−1.3	0.4	0.2	0.3	0.2
324 Footwear	2.5	−2.5	0.6	0.4	0.4	0.2
331 Wood products	1.4	−1.1	0.4	0.2	0.3	1.1
332 Furniture, fixtures	1.6	−1.7	0.4	0.2	0.2	0.5
341 Paper products	1.4	−1.2	0.4	0.2	0.2	0.8
342 Printing, publishing	1.2	−1.2	0.1	−0.1	−0.0	−0.1
35A Chemicals	1.2	−1.4	0.4	0.2	0.3	1.4
35B Petroleum products	1.1	−0.5	0.2	0.2	0.2	0.1
355 Rubber products	1.3	−1.4	0.5	0.2	0.3	0.6
36A Nonmetal min. prod.	1.2	−0.9	0.2	0.0	0.0	0.1
362 Glass products	1.3	−1.4	0.4	0.2	0.3	0.3
371 Iron, steel	1.2	−1.4	0.5	0.3	0.4	1.7
372 Nonferrous metals	1.8	−0.6	0.8	0.6	0.7	1.1
381 Metal products	1.3	−1.5	0.2	0.0	0.1	1.0
382 Nonelec. machinery	1.6	−1.8	0.6	0.3	0.3	6.0
383 Electrical machinery	2.3	−2.6	0.9	0.7	0.7	17.5
384 Transport equipment	1.7	−2.0	0.6	0.3	0.3	3.5
38A Misc. mfrs.	2.1	−1.7	0.8	0.5	0.6	7.1
2 Mining, quarrying	2.3	−0.4	1.5	1.3	1.4	0.8
4 Utilities	0.7	−0.5	0.2	0.1	0.1	0.4
5 Construction	4.7	2.5	0.1	−0.2	−0.1	−5.7
6 Wholesale trade	6.2	2.1	0.1	−0.1	0.0	2.4
7 Transportation	33.8	34.5	−0.7	−1.0	−0.9	−33.2
8 Financial services	10.3	15.5	−0.1	−0.2	−0.1	−4.8
9 Personal services	15.0	17.0	−0.1	−0.2	−0.1	−14.6
Total	4.2	4.2	0.2	0.2	0.0	0.0

Note: see Table 10.3.

more than 1 percent, however. The largest absolute reductions in US sectoral employment (not reported in the table) are in personal, community and social services ($-12,500$), clothing ($-8,500$), iron and steel products ($-3,800$), and textiles ($-3,500$), while the absolute largest increases are in agriculture (9,600), transportation services (8,100), transportation equipment (5,700), electrical machinery (4,700), and food and related products (3,900).

Because of the size of the United States and its relatively low initial tariffs, these percentage changes are as small as those reported for any of the other countries/regions, but similar results appear especially for Europe and Japan. Somewhat larger changes are reported for the small industrialized countries/regions of Canada, where employment in leather and footwear both decline by more than 4 percent, and Australia/New Zealand, where employment levels in textiles and electrical machinery both decline by almost 4 percent and employment in miscellaneous manufactures increases by almost 4 percent. The largest percentage employment changes are found in the Asian newly industrial economies and the group of developing other trading nations, but even here the percentage changes in sectoral employment remain in the single digits. Recalling that the results of the Uruguay Round are to be phased in over a period of up to ten years, these employment changes suggest only minimal disruption to domestic labor markets.

One pattern that emerges in the results for simulation 1 is that employment would decline in most of the services sectors in most countries. This result arises naturally in the simulation, since it holds services-trade barriers constant while reducing tariffs throughout most of the rest of the economy. We have observed this result in previous models that did not include "tradable" services. The presence of tariffs on industrial goods in most countries of the world acts much as a tax would in a closed economy, and the reduction in these tariffs is thus similar to a cut in production taxes. Not surprisingly, resources are drawn into these sectors – in this case, industrial products – and away from the sectors in which liberalization has not occurred. Exceptions do of course emerge, but it is interesting that this phenomenon appears in our results even in the presence of trade in services.

Simulation 2

Turning now to the results of hypothetical liberalization of trade in services in simulation 2, sectoral results are reported for the United States, Europe, and Japan in tables 10.4 to 10.6. For each country/region, the percentage changes in total exports and imports are reported in columns 1 and 2. The percentage changes in sectoral output and number of firms are listed in columns 3 and 4. One can determine the change in output per firm, and thus the extent to which economies of scale have been realized, by subtracting column 4 from column 3. The percent and absolute changes in employment are listed in columns 5 and 6. The sectoral results for the remaining countries/regions and for simulation 3 are available from the authors on request.[17]

This simulation assumes a 25 percent reduction in the "guesstimated" *ad valorem* tariff equivalents for the services sectors, ISIC 5–9. Recall that the transportation sector (ISIC 7) had the greatest level of protection, that construction (ISIC 5) and wholesale and retail trade (ISIC 6) had the lowest levels of protection, and that financial services (ISIC 8) and personal, community, and social services (ISIC 9) had levels of protection that fell in between. In the United States, total exports would decline in the goods sectors by relatively small percentages, but would increase significantly in the services sectors (table 10.4). [18] Total imports would rise in almost all sectors. Employment would increase in the transportation services sector (53,900) and in financial services (7,300); it would fall in almost all other sectors.

Very similar results are shown for Europe in table 10.5. Again it is the transportation sector, with its high assumed level of protection, that experiences by far the greatest expansion of both trade and employment. Trade again expands substantially in both financial services and personal services, but in Europe it is the personal services sector that expands substantially in absolute terms rather than financial services. As in the United States, services liberalization causes the industrial sectors to experience small percentage declines in both exports and employment, while imports in these sectors expand slightly.

The story is somewhat different in Japan (table 10.6). Here too both exports and imports expand significantly in all of the services sectors, but in industrial products Japan's exports also expand and imports contract. The reason for this may be inferred from the changes in output and employment, both of which contract in most of Japan's services sectors. Evidently Japan's comparative advantage is not in services.

The results for the United States (and the other countries and regions) suggest that services-trade liberalization would expand output and trade in the services sectors. What is more surprising, however, is that employment in many of these sectors would contract. The reason is that increases in output per firm would accompany the expansion in trade, and thus that fewer workers would be able to produce greater output.

Services trade and goods trade also show relationships, although not consistent, across countries. In the United States, Europe, and the newly industrial economies of Asia, the expansion in services trade would reduce the export of goods, but would expand the export of goods in all of the other countries and regions. Services trade can thus substitute for goods trade or it can complement it, depending, presumably, on the roles that services play as inputs into the production of goods. (Input variables for the model come from the various national input–output tables.)

Simulation 3

This simulation combines the results of the liberalization of industrial products and services that were derived under simulations 1 and 2. Their joint effects can be determined by simple addition. Tables for the results of simulation 3 are available from the authors on request.

Appendix A   Developing data on "tradable" services

As already mentioned, we are applying our Michigan CGE model to tradable services for the first time, having previously treated services as nontradable. To do so, we sought to develop a set of 35×35 matrixes of bilateral trade in the services sectors, ISIC 5–9, for the thirty-four model countries (plus rest of world) with a 1990 base year.[19] This was a problem because of the unavailability of sufficiently disaggregated data. That is, while there is published information for 1990 for the global services trade for all the countries of the model, the data available bilaterally and by sector are seriously deficient.

In order to construct the five bilateral services trade matrixes that we needed for modeling purposes, we first assembled a set of thirty-five-element vectors of total exports and imports for each of the five services sectors. We used these vectors as row and column totals of our target bilateral vectors and applied the rAs method to scale an underlying reference matrix to match.[20] For this purpose, we used our 35×35 data for 1990 bilateral merchandise trade as the underlying matrix that serves as the initial estimate of bilateral flows.[21] This yielded a set of 35×35 matrixes of bilateral trade flows for each of the five services sectors.

The next step was to take advantage of more detailed bilateral services-trade data where available. Here, we had data assembled by the European Community's Statistical Office for intra-EC services trade and EC trade with the EFTA countries, the United States, and Japan. The EC merchandise trade data gave us total exports and imports for each EC member with one another. This allowed us to apply the rAs method to the smaller EC matrix separately and then to overlay the larger matrix with the result.[22] Likewise, EC merchandise trade with the EFTA countries, the United States, and Japan allowed us to scale those trade flows properly. We also included in the final matrix some bilateral services-trade data for the United States that were published in the *U.S. Survey of Current Business*. The five ISIC sectoral 35×35 bilateral services-trade matrixes, as well as additional technical details on their construction, are available from the authors on request.

Notes

1. Europe includes the fifteen members of the European Union plus Norway and Switzerland; the newly industrial economies of Asia include Hong Kong, South Korea, Singapore, and Taiwan (China); and the other major trading nations include Argentina, Brazil, Chile, Colombia, India, Israel, Turkey, and Venezuela.

2. This is the first time that we have treated all twenty-nine model sectors as tradable; doing so enables us to analyze the effects and interaction of the liberalization of both merchandise trade and trade in services.

3. Brown and Stern (1989) discuss issues pertaining to modeling market structure, in using different imperfectly competitive market structures to analyze the economic effects of the Canada–United States Trade Agreement. The model in this chapter uses a structure of monopolistic competition for all manufacturing and service sectors, based on Helpman and Krugman (1985). Firms do not face entry barriers, and each produces a different variety of a good/service at a fixed cost and constant marginal cost for primary and intermediate inputs. In his conference commentary, Sherman Robinson pointed out that our treatment of monopolistic competition may not be appropriate for all sectors and may thus exaggerate the importance of the effects of scale and variety. In principle, we could allow for different market structures in the sectors for our model countries/regions. But doing so would require considerable empirical detail that is not readily available.

4. We use a Dixit–Stiglitz (1977) aggregation function to enter varieties into both utility and production functions, with the implication that greater variety reduces cost and increases utility. As discussed in Brown, Deardorff, and Stern (1996), this structure introduces potential market instability, since the expansion of an industry with the entry of a firm adds varieties and thus makes the product of the industry more desirable as a whole. To avoid this instability, we have introduced a damping parameter that reduces the beneficial effects of variety by 50 percent from the original Dixit–Stiglitz formulation.

5. Using completely up-to-date input–output tables is problematic, given ongoing changes in technology and productivity that would alter the input–output coefficients for particular sectors. Our CGE model, however, relies primarily on the intermediate input-value shares and the shares of primary factors as data. These shares tend to be more stable over time than physical input requirements. For more discussion of this point, see Deardorff and Stern (1990).

6. The sectoral data for merchandise trade, production, and employment come primarily from United Nations sources and to a lesser extent from national sources. The model parameters are constructed from the trade and input–output data for the countries included in the model and from published studies of trade and capital/labor substitution elasticities. More details on the data on agricultural and industrial tariffs and trade and trade barriers for services are provided in the following section. (See also Deardorff and Stern 1990.)

7. In effect, then, we do not distinguish among workers according to their skill characteristics, and, as such, we do not assess how Uruguay Round liberalization will affect the wages and employment of different skill groups.

8. In the absence of tariff equivalents, we model nontariff barriers as percentage of trade subject to those barriers, based primarily on the nontariff barrier inventory data assembled by the UNCTAD. The model uses the nontariff barrier coverage ratios to dampen the effects of tariff reductions undertaken when the nontariff barriers are assumed to remain in place. It is important to emphasize that these measures of nontariff barrier trade coverage are *not* the same as the tariff equivalents of the nontariff barriers. Deardorff and Stern (1990, pp. 23–25) provide a more detailed discussion of this issue.

9. The GATT IDB provides detailed, line-item information for the pre- and post-Uruguay Round tariff rates based on the HS tariff classification. Since we have twenty-three tradable-goods sectors for each country and region in our model, we aggregated the detailed tariff lines using own-country imports as weights, based on a concordance between the HS and our sectoral classification derived from the ISIC codes. We recognize that own-country import weights introduce a downward bias into the aggregate measures since higher tariffs will induce less trade, but we have not corrected for this bias. (The sectoral tariff rates used in our computational analysis are available upon request.)

10. In addition to the tariffication of agricultural protection, the Uruguay Round calls for a 36 percent reduction in export subsidies by industrial countries and a 24 percent reduction by developing countries, as well as a 20 percent reduction in input subsidies by industrial countries and a 13 percent reduction by developing countries.

11. The four modes of supply are cross-border delivery; consumption abroad; commercial presence (FDI); and the temporary entry of persons (professional, technical, sales personnel, and so on).

12. When nontariff barriers remain in place during other trade liberalization, their presence is felt as a quantitative restriction that reduces the response of trade to price changes. When nontariff barriers are removed, this can best be modeled as the elimination of a tariff of equivalent size, capturing the restrictiveness of the nontariff barrier, but in the absence of any restraint on quantitative responses. That is, elimination of the nontariff barriers mimics what is actually being attempted in agriculture: the conversion of import quotas and of the restrictions into tariff equivalents, which are then removed.

13. Details on the absolute dollar changes in welfare for the individual scenarios are available on request.

14. We also ran a simulation for agricultural liberalization. We had expected that reductions in agricultural tariff equivalents would increase the economic welfare of agricultural exporting countries. But the simulation indicated that welfare would decline in the United States and Australia/New Zealand; although output and employment in the agricultural sector would increase significantly in these countries, output and employment in practically all the manufacturing and services sectors would decline. Because the contraction in

output in manufacturing and services would exceed the decline in the number of firms, negative scale effects would occur, thus reducing economic welfare. In Japan and the newly industrial economies of Asia, where an apparently sizable reduction in agricultural tariff rates occurred, output and employment in agriculture would decline, but would increase in all other sectors. Our model is thus rather sensitive to specialization and scale effects when large changes in protection occur in such important sectors as agriculture. This issue will be addressed in our future research. (The results of our agriculture simulation, not reported in this chapter, are available from the authors on request.)

15. Our agricultural liberalization simulation suggested this result for the United States and Australia/New Zealand.
16. Recall that total employment is assumed constant in each country in these simulations.
17. As are the results for variables other than employment for simulation 1.
18. Due to space limitations, we do not report the results for the other countries and regions. They are available on request.
19. We thus have services data for 1990 for these ISIC sectors covering both gross output and employment as well as exports and imports. The ratios of services trade to gross output are relatively small, reflecting the fact that most services sector output is confined to domestic markets.
20. Technical details relating to the rAs method can be found in Bacharach (1970).
21. It should be pointed out that bilateral goods and services flows may not correspond well in cases in which countries are relatively more specialized in one or the other.
22. We overlaid the larger matrix with these figures, rather than scaling them to better match the results of the larger rAs procedure, for two reasons. First, we had much more confidence in the quality of the selective bilateral trade data from the European Union and other sources than we had in the total overall trade flows that came primarily from balance-of-payments sources. Therefore we were unwilling to scale the bilateral flows to make them consistent with the total flows. In addition, we understood that the bilateral trade measurements in many cases included types of services trade that are relatively new and that are likely to be absent from the balance-of-payments-based data. Because we believe that these new types of trade are likely to be concentrated among the industrial countries, we also chose not to scale the other bilateral flows (up) to include them. Instead, therefore, we simply used the bilateral flows directly whenever they were available and used the (partial) results of applying the rAs procedure to the total flows whenever they were not.

References

Bacharach, Michael 1970. *Biproportional Matrices and Input–Output Change.* Cambridge: Cambridge University Press.

Brown, Drusilla K., and Robert M. Stern 1989. "Computable General Equilibrium Estimates of the Gains from U.S.–Canadian Trade Liberalization." In Thomas Hyclak, and Robert J. Thornton, eds., *Economic Aspects of Regional Trading Arrangements*. London: Harvester Wheatsheaf.

Brown, Drusilla K., Alan V. Deardorff, and Robert M. Stern. 1992a. "A North American Free Trade Agreement: Analytical Issues and a Computational Assessment." *The World Economy* 15: 15–29.

1992b. "North American Economic Integration." *Economic Journal* 102: 1507–18.

1993. "Protection and Real Wages: Old and New Trade Theories and their Empirical Counterparts." Discussion Paper 331, Research Forum on International Economics, University of Michigan, May.

1996. "Computational Analysis of the Economic Effects of an East Asian Preferential Trading Bloc," *Journal of the Japanese and International Economies* 10.

Brown, Drusilla K., Alan V. Deardorff, David L. Hummels, and Robert M. Stern 1994. "An Assessment of Extending NAFTA to Other Major Trading Countries in South America." Ann Arbor: University of Michigan, mimeo.

Deardorff, Alan V., and Robert M. Stern 1990. *Computational Analysis of Global Trading Arrangements*. Ann Arbor: University of Michigan Press.

Dixit, Avinash K., and Joseph E. Stiglitz 1977. "Monopolistic Competition and Optimum Product Diversity." *American Economic Review* 67: 297–308.

Helpman, Elhanan, and Paul R. Krugman 1985. *Market Structure and Foreign Trade: Increasing Returns, Imperfect Competition, and the International Economy*. Cambridge, Mass.: MIT Press.

Hoekman, Bernard 1995. "Tentative First Steps: An Assessment of the Uruguay Round Agreement on Services." In W. Martin and L. A. Winters, eds., *The Uruguay Round and the Developing Economies*. World Bank Discussion Paper 307. Washington, DC: World Bank.

Ingco, Merlinda 1995. "Agricultural Trade Liberalization in the Uruguay Round: One Step Forward, One Step Back?" Supplemental Paper to the World Bank Uruguay Round Conference, January 26–27.

Martin, Will 1994a. "Draft Notes on Tariff Bindings as Trade Liberalization." Mimeo (May).

1994b. "Methodology for Evaluating Tariff Reductions in the Round." Mimeo (August).

Martin, Will, and Joseph Francois 1994. "Bindings and Rules as Trade Liberalization." Presented at the Festschrift Conference, "Quiet Pioneering: Robert M. Stern and his International Economic Legacy," University of Michigan, Ann Arbor, November 18–20.

11 Legalized backsliding: safeguard provisions in GATT

J. Michael Finger

GATT is one of the principal instruments with which the international community has constructed and maintained an open international trading system. Yet GATT includes many provisions that allow member countries to maintain old trade restrictions and impose new ones (table 11.1). Article XX (General Exceptions) alone includes ten different subcategories of allowed restrictions. Member countries to GATT frequently use these provisions. To date, developing countries have notified some 3,500 restrictions "to protect the balance of payments" as set out in Article XVIIIB. In industrial countries antidumping has become the most popular mode of GATT-legal protection: there have been some 160 antidumping actions a year since the early 1980s. And, VERs have been regularly accepted because exporters prefer the negotiated "voluntary" restraint to the GATT restraint just around the administrative corner.

Obviously, its framers did not intend that provisions allowing trade restrictions would be the dominant part of GATT. The agreement was drawn up to promote the removal of trade restrictions, not their imposition. How then does GATT attempt to discipline the creation of such restrictions, and to what extent has that discipline been strengthened by the Uruguay Round agreements?

GATT's approach to allowed restrictions

What is the rationale for providing new trade restrictions in GATT? One possible reason is that they make economic sense: the rules separate "good" import restrictions from "bad" ones. An import restriction that overcomes a market imperfection, for example, could have a positive net impact on the economy of the country that imposes it, and/or on the global economy.

A second and perhaps more familiar reason is that, had such provisions not been included, protectionist interests would have prevented realization of the tariff reductions that were the *raison d'être* of GATT from the

316

Table 11.1 *Frequency of use of GATT provisions that allow trade restrictions*

Instrument	Frequency of use
Restrictions requiring specific GATT approval	
Waivers (Article XXV)	Through March 1994, 113 waivers granted, 44 still in force
Retaliation authorized under dispute settlement (Article XXIII)	Once
Exceptions specified in accession agreement (Article XXXIII)	Not tabulated[a]
Releases from bindings for infant-industry protection (Article XVIIIC)	Nine countries in forty-seven years[b]
Releases from bindings by a "more-developed" country to pursue infant-industry protection (Article XVIIID)	Never
Provisions for renegotiating previous concessions and commitments	
Periodic three-year renegotiations at the initiative of the country wanting to increase a bound rate (Articles XXVII.1 and XXVIII.5)	January 1955–March 1994: 206 renegotiation procedures, 128 of these under Article XXVIII.5
Special circumstance renegotiations requiring GATT authorization (Article XXVIII.4)	Sixty-four renegotiations since 1948
Increase of a duty with regard to formation of a customs union (Article XXIV.6)	Follows procedures of Article XXVIII, hence included in figures above
Withdrawal of a concession to provide infant-industry protection (Article XVIIIA)	Nine withdrawals, through March 1994[c]
Restrictions that can be imposed unilaterally	
General exceptions (Article XX)	Notification not required; between 1974 and 1987, six developing countries notified quantitative restrictions under Article XX, covering 131 products[d]
Restrictions to apply standards, to classify (Article XI.2b)	Notification not required; between 1974 and 1987, six developing countries notified quantitative restrictions under Article XX, covering 131 products[e]
Restrictions on agricultural or fisheries products (Article XI.2c)	Notification not required; no information available
National security exception (Article XXI)	One developing country, Thailand, notified under Article XXI between 1974 and 1987; further information not available

Table 11.1 (*cont.*)

Instrument	Frequency of use
Withdrawal of a concession initially negotiated with a government that fails to join GATT or withdraws (Article XXVII)	As of 1994, Article XXVII has been used by fifteen countries with regard to withdrawals by China, Syria, Lebanon, and Liberia; Colombia, which participated in the Annecy Round (1949) but did not accede then; and Korea and the Philippines, which participated in the Torquay Round (1951) but did not accede then
Nonapplication at the time of accession (Article XXXV)	As of 1994, this article had been invoked against Japan by fifty-three countries – invocations since withdrawn by fifty; by sixteen other countries against twenty-one countries; only ten Article XXXV invocations are presently operative.
Countervailing duties (Article VI)	Between July 1985 and June 1992, 187 investigations (27 a year), 106 by the United States, 38 by Australia
Restrictions to safeguard the balance of payments, general (Article VII)	Three countries had such restrictions in place at least one time during the period 1974–86
Restrictions to safeguard the balance of payments, developing countries (Article XVIIIB)	Twenty-four countries had such restrictions in place at least one time during the period 1974–86
Emergency actions (Article XIX)	Between 1950 and 1984, 124 actions (3.6 a year). Between 1985 and 1994, 26 actions (3.25 a year)
Antidumping duties (Article VI)	Between July 1985 and June 1992, 1,148 investigations (164 a year, 300 by the United States, 282 by Australia, 242 by the European Union, 124 by Canada, 84 by Mexico

[a]GATT 1994, p. 948, lists five countries whose protocols of accession included provisions allowing specific measures, otherwise GATT-illegal, to remain in place for a limited time.
[b]Anjaria 1987, p. 670. These countries are Côte d'Ivoire, Indonesia, Malaysia, Thailand, Zimbabwe, Cuba, Haiti, India, and Sri Lanka.
[c]GATT 1994, p. 465. These were made by Benelux on behalf of Suriname (1958), Greece (1956, 1965), Indonesia (1983), Korea (1958), and Sri Lanka (1955, 1956, 1957).
[d]OECD 1992, p. 100. Information relating to Articles XX, XI, and XXI is generally not available since notification is not required. The OECD source cited provides information on developing country *notification* of these articles for the period noted.
[e]*Ibid.*

beginning. Allowing for a step backward was part of the price of achieving two steps forward.

A third reason for new trade restrictions is that any government with a liberal trade policy must have ways to deal with pressure for protectionist exceptions coming from particular domestic sectors.

Discipline over safeguard measures

GATT contains a frequently used subset of provisions referred to here for convenience as the safeguard provisions. They consist of emergency actions to protect industries seriously injured by import competition (Article XIX); import restrictions by developing countries to protect the balance of payments (Article XVIIIB); and antidumping (Article VI). While Article XIX is sometimes called the safeguard provision of GATT, here the term is used generally to mean any provision that permits product-specific restrictions.

Each GATT member reserves the right to take safeguard actions, which do not require explicit permission of the CONTRACTING PARTIES,[1] say, through a formal waiver. Safeguards are, however, subject to other discipline, its form and degree varying from one type of action to another. Action under Article XIX, for example, has a conditions limit – it may be taken only when imports injure competing domestic producers. Such action requires notification to the CONTRACTING PARTIES and consultation with the principal exporting countries affected. Moreover, the country that takes an Article XIX action is obliged to "maintain the balance of concessions" previously negotiated. Exporters have a right to demand compensation and, if the CONTRACTING PARTIES agree that adequate compensation has not been provided, they can authorize retaliation. For antidumping actions, the conditions of which are dumping and injury, the country proposing action must consult with exporting countries, and CONTRACTING PARTIES must be notified of all antidumping investigations as well as actions. But GATT does not require antidumping actions to be compensated, nor does it give exporting countries the right to retaliate.[2]

GATT, then, attempts to discipline safeguard measures in two ways: through conditionality (a preexisting statement of conditions for a trade-restricting action) and reciprocity (giving trading partners the right to retaliate if appropriate compensation is not provided). In some instances, the application of these disciplines is buttressed by notification and consultation requirements.

While conditionality might appear to separate good trade restrictions from bad, GATT conditions do not identify import restrictions that augment the national economic interest of the country imposing them – in economists' jargon, that have a positive net welfare effect. Like reciprocity, the conditions are intended simply to discourage restrictions: less versus more is the metric, not good versus bad.

Emergency actions

Article XIX begins as follows:

If as a result of unforeseen developments and of the effect of the obligations incurred . . . under this Agreement, including tariff concessions, any product is being imported . . . as to cause or threaten serious injury to domestic producers . . . of like or directly competitive products . . . the contracting party shall be free . . . to suspend the obligation . . . or to withdraw or modify the concession.

This obviously authorizes import restrictions. What prevents the authorization to restrict from allowing as many steps back as GATT tariff negotiations manage to take forward? There are two possible sources of constraint: the article's statement of conditions under which safeguard actions can be taken, and the relation between this article and the notion of reciprocity that underlies GATT's tariff-cutting process.

Conditions

According to Article XIX, then, emergency action is conditional on injury both from imports that result from a concession (liberalization) and from "unforeseen developments." The intent of conditioning import relief on unforeseen developments seems obvious: without this qualification, relief would be available each time liberalization had its probable effect – to increase imports – and the emergency action provision would undo all the liberalization negotiated.

Early in GATT's history, a GATT working party interpreted unforeseen developments in a way that eliminated it as a constraint on emergency actions. As Gary Sampson concludes (1987, p. 143), "What this [interpretation] meant in practical terms was that any increase in imports, even if through normal changes in international competitiveness, could therefore be considered actionable under Article XIX." Other interpretations further weakened Article XIX as discipline against emergency actions. The hatters' fur working party also concluded that the country taking emergency action was entitled to the benefit of the doubt in determining injury: to overturn an action, the exporting country had to actively disprove injury (to importing country producers). Around the time of the hatters' fur case, another working party concluded that serious injury from imports did not even require that imports be *increasing* before injury could be determined (Sampson 1987).

As a consequence of these decisions, Article XIX conditions have not been a constraint on Article XIX actions to restrict imports.

Reciprocity

While conditions have not restrained Article XIX actions, the other constraint, reciprocity, has provided discipline. Article XIX explicitly calls for consultations with exporters and explicitly provides for retaliation – suspension of "substantially equivalent concessions or other obligations." Compensation (to buy off retaliation) is implicit in these provisions.

In the early years of its application, most invocations of Article XIX were accompanied by either mutually agreed compensation or retaliation. Of the twenty-five actions taken under the escape clause between 1948 and 1962, compensation was offered in fourteen cases and retaliation took place four times (in three of the latter cases, compensation had been offered).

With reciprocity being the only functional constraint on its actions, Article XIX became interchangeable with GATT's provisions for renegotiation and even with GATT's regular tariff negotiations. All three were subject to the same constraint, reciprocity, and all three involved the same basic international procedures. Article XIX required consultation with exporting countries, and until the Kennedy Round, tariff talks were simply a cluster of bilateral negotiations.[3] Thus many situations that might have led to Article XIX actions were treated instead as renegotiations under Article XXVIII. The renegotiation procedure was frequently used (see table 11.1). Furthermore, nine of the fifteen pre-1962 Article XIX actions of such magnitude that the exporter insisted on compensation (or threatened retaliation) were eventually resolved as Article XXVIII renegotiations. The renegotiations, in turn, were often folded into regular tariff negotiations.

During its first decade and a half, then, GATT provided for safeguard actions, but these derived in considerable part from ongoing negotiations rather than being formally laid out in Article XIX. Meanwhile, the mercantilist ethic of reciprocity was the effective control on safeguard actions: if domestic politics prevented a government from delivering the market access it had contracted to deliver, then that government had either to make it up elsewhere or accept equivalent withdrawals from others. The impact of this ethic was reinforced by treating safeguard problems not as issues in which government actions would be judged against relevant GATT stipulations of conditions, but as issues for negotiation or renegotiation – simply put, as something to be bargained for, not adjudicated.

VERs

By the 1960s, formal use of Article XIX and the renegotiation process began to wane. Action taken under the escape clause tended to involve a negligible amount of world trade in relatively minor product categories.[4] Big problems such as textile and apparel imports were handled another way, through the negotiation of "voluntary" export restraint agreements. These agreements were clearly illegal under GATT.[5] In 1968 a working party focused on both the discriminatory and on the ostensibly voluntary nature of such export restraints and concluded that there "was no provision in the General Agreement that provided a legal basis for discriminatory restraints, even when they were supported by an agreement of a voluntary nature" (GATT 1994, p. 494). While inconsistent with GATT legalisms – conditions for what type of restriction may be imposed and when – VERs harmonize with GATT's mercantilist ethic for several reasons. First, they buy back previously sold market access. A VER being essentially price fixing, the *quid pro quo* is the extra profit that price fixing allows. Second, both the exporting- and the importing-country government avoid the redistribution issue that compensation or retaliation would require. For example, if the United States compensated for higher tariffs on textile imports with lower tariffs on imports of television receivers, the mercantilist benefits would accrue to textile producers, the costs to producers of receivers. The exporting country has the mirror-image redistribution problem. And third, in many instances the troublesome increase of imports came from countries that had not been the "principal suppliers" in initial negotiated concessions. New exporters were displacing not only domestic production in importing countries but the exports of traditional suppliers as well. The mercantilist ethic thus views a VER with the new, troublesome supplier as a defense of the rights of exporters who had paid for the initial concession.

Power politics is another factor. Even though one of GATT's objectives was to neutralize the influence of economic power on the determination of trade policy, large countries frequently use VERs to control imports from smaller countries.

Though the GATT community recognized the danger of VERs to the open trading system even before the 1973–79 Tokyo Round, negotiations over VERs were delayed until the Uruguay Round. During that round victim countries insisted that, as such restraints were illegal under GATT, their removal must be unilateral.

The Uruguay Round safeguard agreement

The contents of the Uruguay Round safeguard agreement suggest that the negotiators could not agree whether their objective was to reduce the number of trade-restricting actions or to make them legal under GATT. The attempt to ban VERs and to constrain safeguard actions reflect the former objective, while the changes that make Article XIX easier to use reflect the latter. From the elaborate procedural requirements that were added negotiators seem to have confused the two objectives.

Ban and phaseout of VERs

The agreement states that a member "shall not seek, take or maintain any voluntary export restraints, orderly marketing arrangements or any similar measures on the export or the import side . . . Any such measures in effect at the time of entry into force of the Agreement establishing the WTO shall be brought into conformity with this Agreement or phased out" (GATT 1994, p. 321). All but one restraint must be phased out within four years. Each member may retain the last restraint until December 31, 1999.[6] As of June 1995, only the European Union had notified an exception, its restraint on Japanese cars and trucks.

The ban on VERs is not however as certain as these statements alone suggest. The following footnote is attached to the ban of VERs: "An import quota applied as a safeguard measure in conformity with the relevant provisions of GATT 1994 and this Agreement may, by mutual agreement, be administered by the exporting Member."

Making Article XIX more attractive

Two changes that make Article XIX more useful to interests seeking protection are the allowance of discriminatory quantitative restrictions and the removal of the exporting country's right to retaliate against a safeguard measure for the first three years it is in place.

The agreement specifies that, in general, quantitative restrictions should not reduce imports from any country below the average level in "the last three representative years." But if "clear justification is given that a different level is necessary to prevent or remedy serious injury," imports may be reduced below those levels (GATT 1994, p. 317). And the importing country can disproportionally restrict certain suppliers provided that consultations are conducted, and that three things are clearly demonstrated to the GATT–WTO Committee on Safeguards: imports from those suppliers have increased disproportionally, the reasons not to allocate shares proportionally are justifiable, and the allocation is "equitable to all suppliers." Such discriminatory safeguard measures have a maximum length of four years and cannot be extended.

The clear-demonstration requirement is a relatively soft control on discriminatory application of quantitative restrictions. Retaliation, for example, requires that the member proposing to retaliate provide prior notice to the Council for Trade in Goods, and that the member take only action "which the Council for Trade and Goods does not disapprove." There is no proviso for the Committee on Safeguards to disapprove discriminatory application of quantitative restrictions.

The stipulation that allocation be equitable to all suppliers reaffirms part of the mercantilist ethic of VERs: it acknowledges the interests of displaced exporters in having more dynamic suppliers disproportionally restrained.

Another feature of the safeguard agreement that will make Article XIX more useful is paragraph 18, which limits supplier countries' right to retaliate: "The right of [retaliation] shall not be exercised for the first three years that a safeguard measure is in effect, provided that the safeguard measure has been taken as a result of an absolute increase in imports" (GATT 1994, p. 320).

Constraints on allowed actions, and procedural requirements

Actions under Article XIX are subject to several limits. The key ones are progressive liberalization of all measures exceeding one year (extension may not tighten, but must continue liberalization); and limits on the duration of safeguard measures. There is a four-year limit on the initial safeguard measure, with only one extension allowed, that limited to four years. Discriminatory quantitative restrictions cannot be extended, and there can be no reapplication within two years or the length of the previous measure, whichever is longer.[7]

Many explicit procedural requirements for transparency and openness that were not in the original Article XIX are contained in the 1994 agreement. First, a member may apply a safeguard measure only after an investigation and determination of injury.[8] The investigation must be carried out according to established procedures established and made public, and it must include public notices to all interested parties and public hearings for the presentation of evidence, views, and comments from all sides.[9] The determination must demonstrate a causal link between imports and injury.[10] The agency that conducts the investigation and makes the determination must publish a detailed analysis setting out its findings and conclusions and clarifying their relationship to the facts of the case and to the applicable law.[11]

More discipline, or a legalization of past practice?

The Uruguay Round agreements' limits on the duration of measures and the requirement that measures be progressively liberalized are substantive constraints. Other than that, the new agreement is a legalization of past practice. It adds only procedural details that do not narrow the circumstances in which an import restraint may be imposed.[12] Moreover, to any country that gears up to meet procedural requirements, footnote 3 to the agreement quoted above explicitly provides the option of an import quota administered by the exporting country – functionally speaking, a VER.

Are the procedural requirements themselves likely to be obstructive? Specifically, is it likely that in the past, restrictive actions were frequently taken in circumstances other than those required by Article XIX? And are the procedural requirements themselves onerous enough to discourage industries from petitioning for protection, or governments from going through the process of granting it?

To the question of whether past actions cheated on the criteria (rather than on the procedure) – if applying to past cases would demonstrate that in those cases there were no injury to domestic producers – the answer is, most likely not. Unless domestic producers had been displaced by imports, there would have been no pressure on government to act against imports. It is thus hardly surprising that the legality of VERs under GATT has been questioned on grounds of their being discriminatory, and not on grounds that they restrict imports when there is no injury to domestic producers.

As for procedural requirements, though they might appear imposing to governments accustomed to acting in a more preemptive manner, the success of the United States, the European Union, Canada, Australia, and recently Mexico in following antidumping regulations with similar procedural requirements suggests that they are not effective in constraining restrictive action.

Restrictions to protect the balance of payments

Quantitative restrictions were widely used when GATT was originally negotiated. GATT's first order of business in promoting a more liberal trading environment was to prohibit quantitative restrictions (Article XI), but not without exception: they were allowed for economic development and to restore equilibrium in the balance of payments as well as for several other purposes.

Industrial country balance-of-payments restrictions

When they acceded to GATT, European governments invoked the balance-of-payments provisions (Article XII) to justify extensive trade controls already in place. But as European economies recovered from World War II disruptions and the balance-of-payments justification for these restrictions waned, many governments were reluctant to remove them. Their industries, they feared, would not be able to survive international competition. Though GATT still justified the restrictions on the grounds of balance-of-payments protection, the motive for restrictions shifted toward ordinary protection (Davey 1994, p. 5).

By the mid-1960s, however, industrialized countries had practically eliminated trade restrictions for balance-of-payments purposes. The venues for the process of negotiating away restrictions included not only GATT consultations under Article XII but also International Monetary Fund reviews and the negotiation of OEEC "liberalization codes."[13] In the 1970s most industrial countries moved to a system of floating exchange rates, which considerably reduced interest in the use of trade restrictions to deal with balance-of-payments disequilibrium.

Developing country balance-of-payments restrictions

Article XII, intended for use by both developed and developing countries, is the original article providing for quantitative restrictions to ease balance-of-payments problems. Not until 1955 was Article XVIII, which deals with government assistance to economic development, revised to include a balance-of-payments provision specifically for developing countries.

Article XVIII contains two exceptions to the ban on quantitative restrictions that are relevant to our discussion here. Provisions under Article XVIIIB allow developing countries to impose quantitative restrictions to address balance-of-payments disequilibrium and to maintain reserves adequate for development. Section C of the same article allows protection to infant industries, or in GATT language, measures to promote the establishment of particular industries in the context of a development program. In practice, the balance-of-payments exception has been invoked far more often than the infant-industry exception. Almost 3,500 restrictions have been declared under the balance-of-payments exception, less than 100 under the infant-industry exception (table 11.2).[14]

Why have there been so few actions under the infant-industry provision? Anjaria (1987, p. 671) surmises that procedural requirements may cause developing countries to leave developmental restrictions unapproved, and more important, "that developing countries [may] find it relatively easy to obtain GATT 'cover' for infant industry protection under the guise of 'balance of payments' reasons which are invoked more frequently." Both a comparison of the requirements of sections B and C and the facts of usage bear out the validity of this speculation.

First, infant-industry (Article XVIIIC) conditions are more severe than balance-of-payments conditions (Article XVIIIB). Article XVIIIB requires

Table 11.2 *Number of CCCN items notified under each GATT article by developing countries, 1974–87*

Article cited as justification	Number
VIII (fees and formalities connected with importation and exportation)	316
XI.2 (restrictions to apply standards or classifications, manage short supplies, or complement agricultural or fisheries support programs)	108
XVII (state trading enterprises)	15
XVIIIB (balance-of-payments measures for developing countries)	3,437
XVIIIC (industrial development)	91
XX (general exceptions)	131
XXI (national security)	4

Source: OECD 1992, p. 100.

prior notification to the CONTRACTING PARTIES and compensation for affected exporters. It also says that CONTRACTING PARTIES can disapprove a proposed action and authorize retaliation if a disapproved action is taken. Article XVIIIB actions require no compensation, cannot be disapproved by the CONTRACTING PARTIES, and are subject to no time limit. Parties declaring such actions must however consult biannually with the GATT Balance of Payments Committee. While these consultations do provide opportunity for other contracting parties to apply political pressure, GATT does not legally obligate a party that imposes Article XVIIIB restrictions to change its macroeconomic or monetary policies so as to render trade restrictions unnecessary.

The facts of usage tell the same story. As Anjaria reports (1987, p. 680), in almost three-fourths of the developing countries that declared Article XVIIIB measures, the measures covered less than half of import categories. If restrictions were truly for purposes of balance of payments, they would cover all import categories.

Pressure to integrate developing countries into the trading system

When GATT was adopted, the prevailing view of development economics equated industrialization with development and saw industrialization as possible only behind high walls of import protection. The widely believed Prebisch thesis cautioned that commodity earnings would inexorably decline and industrialization would require vast imports of capital goods. Thus developing countries would have an unyielding tendency to encounter balance-of-payments problems.[15] Reflecting this thinking, GATT soon evolved a tolerance for developing country trade restrictions.[16] As noted above, Article XVIIIB, added to GATT in 1955, eased constraints on developing countries' trade restrictions for the purpose of balance of payments.

By the 1970s a number of developing countries had become important in world trade, both as potential export markets and as suppliers of imports that increasingly prompted developed country industries to call for protection. The intensified commercial presence of developing countries provoked industrial countries to press for market-opening actions by developing countries. Pressure was applied both through the GATT Balance of Payments Committee and the Trade Committee of the OECD. One of the focal points of this pressure was reduced use by developing countries of Article XVIIIB restrictions.[17]

At the same time, the Asian model of export-led development changed developing countries' view of trade policy. Realistic exchange rates had been an important element in this experience, hence developing countries were more willing to give in on use of Article XVIIIB. By the end of 1992 six developing countries had disinvoked use of Article XVIIIB, while twelve others still had balance-of-payments restrictions in place (GATT 1994, p. 361).

The Uruguay Round understanding

During the Uruguay Round, OECD countries – the United States and Canada in particular – were strong proponents of strengthening GATT balance-of-payments provisions to reflect more accurately changes in economic ideas about the inter-relation of trade and development (box 11.1). The Uruguay Round understanding added statements to encourage use of price-based measures rather than quantitative restrictions, and to encourage phasing out of balance-of-payment measures. But these commitments are qualified.

The most extensive changes are detailed documentation requirements. In light of the growing realization that an exchange rate buttressed by trade control is bad development policy, the requirements ask countries to be honest with themselves about their exchange rate policies. These amendments may turn out to be the Uruguay Round's most effective ones with respect to GATT's policing of trade restrictions rationalized as defense of balance of payments.

Antidumping

Though accusations of dumping have been part of the rhetoric of protection for many centuries, formal antidumping action was a minor instrument when GATT was negotiated, and provision for antidumping regulations was included with little controversy. In 1958, when contracting

---

Box 11.1 *Major features of the Uruguay Round understanding on GATT's balance-of-payments provisions*

Constraints on measures
Schedules to remove measures (may be modified if conditions change).
Seek to avoid quantitative restrictions for balance-of-payments purposes (unless, in critical situations, price-based measures will not do).
Restrictive measures for balance of payments may be used only to control the general level of imports (but "essential products" may be excluded from restrictions and discretionary licensing is acceptable when unavoidable).

Consultation procedures
Restrictions in place (mandatory periodic review).
New restrictions or tightening of existing ones (consultations within four months).

Notification and documentation
Changes, new measures, modifications of schedules for removal must be notified (within thirty days for significant changes, yearly for consolidated notification).
Notifications must include full information, as far as possible (tariff line, type of measure, criteria used for administration, product coverage, and trade flow affected).
Committee may review notifications for adequacy (other members may bring a suspected measure to the attention of the committees, in which case the chairman requests information).

Conclusions of balance-of-payments consultations
On each consultation the committee reports the facts and reasons, the plan and schedule for removal or relaxation, and any conclusions and recommendations.

---

parties finally canvassed themselves about antidumping, the tally showed only thirty-seven antidumping decrees in force across all GATT member countries, twenty-one of these in South Africa (GATT 1958, p. 14).

Antidumping becomes the safeguard instrument

Since then, antidumping has become the major safeguard for industrial countries. In a review of US trade policy for the US National Science Foundation in 1981, it was observed that "administered protection has become the leading edge of trade policy, at least since 1975" (Hufbauer 1981, p. 6). From 1983 to 1993 only 30 Article XIX actions were notified to GATT Council, 3 a year compared with 164 antidumping cases a year. As of June 30, 1992, the Director-General of GATT reported 546 antidumping orders in place among GATT members, compared with 15 orders under Article XIX.[18]

Several features explain the popularity of antidumping. First, the practice permits discriminatory action. Second, in national practice, the injury test for antidumping action tends to be softer than the injury test for action under Article XIX. Third, the rhetoric of foreign unfairness is a vehicle for building a political case for protection. Fourth, antidumping and VERs have proved to be effective complements, that is, the threat of formal action under the antidumping law provides leverage to force an exporter to accept such a restraint.[19] And finally, the Uruguay Round agreement and the 1989 Tokyo Round antidumping Code provide for suspension agreements.[20]

The increased popularity of antidumping measures has led to concerns about misuse. Two are particularly troubling and have been supported by considerable research. First, national regulations allow antidumping action in a broad range of circumstances. The point is stated by different authors in different ways, for example, that such regulations are biased toward finding dumping and toward overstating dumping margins (Bierwagen 1991; Litan and Boltuck 1991), or that antidumping is ordinary protection with a good public relations program (Finger 1993). Second, the investigation process itself tends to curb imports. This is because exporters bear significant legal and administrative costs, while importers face the uncertainty of having to pay backdated antidumping duties once an investigation is completed (Finger 1981; Staiger and Wolak 1994).

The capture of international rules

The Uruguay Round Antidumping Agreement takes the same approach as the Tokyo Round Code: it explicitly permits antidumping, then specifies substantive and procedural conditions that such action must meet.

Do these conditions limit or license antidumping? From an international perspective, it is natural to think of rules as constraints, and after all, GATT's overall purpose is liberalization of trade. It should be remembered, however, that antidumping enforcement is based on *national* antidumping laws and regulations. In national politics, the familiar disparity between diffused user-consumer interests and concentrated producer interests means that the conditions under which antidumping action can be taken will function as a statement of the *entitlements* of producer interests to protection. In national politics, protectionist lobbying works to expand the legal specification of conditions.

Though the elaboration of international codes on antidumping camouflages what has happened, it allows the capture of antidumping regulations to be extended to the international level. Lobbyists were as active in Geneva for the negotiation of the Uruguay Round Antidumping Agreement as they normally are during the preparation or amendment of national regulations

– indeed, many were the very lobbyists who had represented protection-seeking industries during national proceedings. As a result, international agreements now give sanction to expansions of coverage that were first won in domestic politics. In the end, international rules on antidumping do not control the power of protection-seeking interests – they are an expression and application of that power.[21]

The capture of the dispute settlement process

The increased use and apparent misuse of antidumping led exporters to complain to their governments so vociferously that since 1989, fifteen national antidumping actions have become the subject of GATT dispute settlement procedures. Five cases that questioned the imposition of anti-dumping duties (along with a sixth that questioned failure of the United States to review a salmon antidumping order) proceeded to the stage of investigation by a panel. In each case the panel found that the antidumping action in question violated GATT or its antidumping code. Nonetheless, as of this writing (July 1995) four of the five antidumping actions are still in place, and in the last two cases, the panel stated explicitly in its recommendations that the antidumping order need not be removed.

The last point is worth repeating. Though a panel found that the US salmon antidumping action was inconsistent with US obligations under the Tokyo Round antidumping code,

it could not be presumed that a methodology of calculating dumping margins consistent with the Panel's findings . . . would necessarily result in a determination that duties were to be imposed at a different rate. The Panel therefore found that in this situation it could not recommend that the Committee request the United States to revoke the antidumping duty order and reimburse any duties paid or deposited under this order.

In short, the US government could fix the methodological problem without lifting the antidumping order – indeed, as antidumping duties are assessed by the US government, without changing the antidumping charges that the exporter would have to pay. The Uruguay Round agreement explicitly provides for such outcomes.

The Uruguay Round agreement

The Uruguay Round negotiations were a pitched battle between victims and antidumpers. The victim countries concentrated on several well-publicized procedural abuses, such as the comparison of prices of individual export sales with the average price of home market sales.[22]

The Uruguay Round agreement requires that all antidumping actions be terminated after no more than five years unless a review deems that termination would lead to continuation or recurrence of dumping and injury. But a restriction under review can be maintained beyond the five-year limit, and there is no hard-and-fast limit on the length of reviews. Furthermore, there is no limit to the number of times an antidumping duty can be reviewed and extended.

On several points, the victims' successes were more apparent than real. On *de minimis* dumping margins and negligible import volumes, for example, the agreement will lower the threshold below which the US International Trade Commission has traditionally considered imports negligible and therefore safe from antidumping action.[23] Likewise, new details about initiation of an investigation add nothing to substantive requirements: paperwork that was once done during an investigation is now done before it formally opens. As the time limit on investigations begins from the date of initiation, the major effect is to increase the period during which imports come under the threat of antidumping action.

User countries may continue to compare individual export prices with average home market prices, but now they must provide an explanation for this practice (box 11.2).[24] And because of the constraints the agreement places on how dispute settlement panels review explanations, panels are not likely to find them inadequate.

As with other provisions examined here, the major import of public-notice changes is that a country taking an antidumping action will have to produce a great deal of information: data on which the determination is based, a general explanation of how the determination was reached, and particularly, an explanation of why at various stages a particular methodological option was chosen.

As for transparency requirements, all interested parties must be provided the opportunity to defend their interests. They must be given access to any information developed by the investigating authorities and to all non-confidential[25] information supplied by other parties, and be allowed to comment on and make presentations based on that information.

Perhaps the greatest victory of the protectionists is how effectively they have extended capture of the dispute settlement process. Dispute settlement of antidumping will be carried out by Dispute Settlement Body. The anti-dumping agreement itself constrains both what the dispute settlement process may review and how it may review it. What is restricted to the issues raised in the request for a panel and to any facts and reasoning taken up during the investigation. New information is excluded. How is restricted to give a national determination the benefit of the doubt. A panel may not ask if national authorities reached the correct conclusion: it must accept

Box 11.2 *Selected provisions of the Uruguay Round antidumping agreement*

Public notice and explanation
There are detailed public notice, public information, and explanation requirements specified for initiation, preliminary and final determinations (whether affirmative or negative), imposition of a preliminary or a definitive duty, acceptance of a price undertaking, and initiation and completion of sunset reviews.

Evidence (transparency)
"Interested parties" must include exporters, foreign producers, importers, the governments of exporting countries, producers of the like product in the importing country, and associations of exporters, producers, or importers. All interested parties must be given full opportunity to defend their interests, for example, given access to evidence, information, and arguments provided by other parties and by the investigating authority. If any party refuses or does not provide information, a determination may be based on the facts available (best information available).

Duration and review of measures – the sunset clause
Antidumping duties must be terminated after no more than five years unless a review determines that termination would lead to continuation or recurrence of dumping and injury. Existing measures must be reviewed no later than five years after the date of entry into force of the WTO agreement. The duty may remain in force pending the outcome of such review, normally concluded within twelve months.

Comparing normal values with export prices
Comparing normal values with export prices involves either weighted averages of both or individual values of both, unless the authorities find that export prices differ meaningfully among purchasers, regions, or periods, and the authorities explain why average-to-average or transaction-to-transaction comparison is not appropriate.

Administrative, selling, and general costs profits in constructed value
The amounts must be based on actual data.

***De minimis* dumping margins and negligible import volumes**
A case against a particular exporter must be terminated if the dumping margin is determined to be less than 2 percent or the volume of dumped imports is negligible. However, there is no hard-and-fast definition of negligible.

Dispute settlement: *what* is to be reviewed
Only issues raised in the request for a panel, and only the evidence presented or developed in the original investigation, are reviewed.

Dispute settlement: how it will be reviewed
In assessing the facts of the matter, the panel determines if the national authorities' establishment of the facts was proper, and evaluation of those facts objective and unbiased. If both, then "even though the panel might have reached a different conclusion, the evaluation shall not be overturned." Furthermore, when the panel finds that a relevant provision of the agreement admits of more than one permissible interpretation, the panel shall find the authorities' measure to be in conformity with the agreement if it rests on one of those interpretations.

national procedures that the agreement does not explicitly rule out. If at each point of the proceedings authorities followed one of the many implicit options consistent with the agreement, then their determination must not be overturned.

Who won: antidumpers or victims?

Apart from the evadable sunset clause, the Uruguay Round antidumping agreement does not control what a government does to restrict imports, nor when it does it. The major thrust of the agreement is its detailed specification of how to restrict imports – the detailed public notice, explanation, and procedural requirements. There are several reasons to conclude that the new procedural requirements will not reduce the use of antidumping. First, administrative costs will be higher, but these are not borne by the protection-seeking industry. Second, antidumping panels have treated inadequate explanation as reason to recommend that an anti-dumping duty be revised, not that it be removed. Third, the requirements internationalize a combination of US, Canadian, and Australian practices, and as these countries are major antidumpers, the new details are hardly a step toward free trade.[26]

In short, the protectionists won the Uruguay Round. The agreement will not interfere with antidumping, which will continue to be the major instrument of ordinary protection.

Conclusions

What can we conclude from the experience of GATT's safeguard measures and the changes agreed at the Uruguay Round? First, let's consider the nature of these mechanisms.

The nature of GATT safeguards

GATT safeguards make no economic sense

The conditions under which GATT allows a country to take emergency or antidumping action or to impose trade restrictions to protect the balance of payments are not the conditions under which such action would serve the national economic interest of that country. In economics, safeguards are nothing but ordinary protection with sufficient political muscle to prevent antiprotection forces from interfering.

The rationale for safeguards remains political. However, their nonsense economics raises the following question: Could there be safeguard processes that serve as a valve for protectionist pressure and at the same time make economic sense? One of the major disappointments of the Uruguay Round is that this question was never addressed.

GATT rules provide little discipline over use of safeguards

This proposition follows from the following two.

Trade restrictions are fungible

GATT provides a long list of apparently special-purpose restrictions, but the type of restriction a country imposes is not determined by the nature of the problem it faces. Rather, it is determined by the relative ease of qualifying for one or another type of GATT coverage for the restriction. In GATT's first decade, Article XIX actions, renegotiations, and negotiations were impossible to distinguish from each other. At present, antidumping is the instrument of choice for protectionist interests. In the 1970s and 1980s, VERs were the favorite form of protection for industrial countries, while Article XVIIIB balance-of-payments actions were the favorite GATT cover for developing countries' import restrictions.

Safeguard action is always possible under the rules

Injury is the economic test that underlies Article XIX actions, antidumping and countervailing duties. Each of these safeguards includes a second test, "dumping" for antidumping and "unforeseen developments" for Article XIX action. But the meaning of dumping is broad, and the unforeseen-developments condition on Article XIX action was rendered ineffective the first time it was challenged. Thus injury is the sole condition that restrains Article XIX or antidumping action. Injury is identical to comparative disadvantage. Any time that imports displace or threaten to displace domestic production, safeguard action is GATT-legal.

Reciprocity, not conditionality, is the effective constraint on GATT safeguards

The most obvious illustration of this point is Article XIX. Early on, GATT working groups consented to allow users to interpret this article as broadly as they wanted. The only constraint on use was the need to provide compensation, which was offset by the fungibility of renegotiations and negotiations over the use of Article XIX.

The popularity of VERs as a means of restricting trade does not diminish the importance of reciprocity as a motive. GATT's negotiating procedure and its compensation-retaliation procedure harness reciprocity to drive an institutional mechanism that removes or constrains trade restrictions. The VER is a different institutional arrangement, one in which reciprocity generates and preserves trade restrictions. The difference between a VER and a tariff negotiation is not what propels them; the difference is the direction in which the institutional mechanism directs the propulsive force.

GATT's safeguard processes make little political sense

Only in the cheap sense of bowing to political reality are GATT's safeguards defensible. They do nothing to empower the good guys – the interests that would be hurt by the imposition of import restrictions. Worse, GATT's safeguards empower the bad guys. Investigation of injury – on which safeguard actions are premised – serves as a tribune for protectionist interests to make their case. Given the pro-protection logic and structure of the safeguard process, reasons to refuse protection are arbitrary.[27] Free trade, not protection, depends on exploiting the loopholes in trade law.

GATT rules as policy guidelines

One of the applause lines in the trade speech of a US presidential candidate a few years ago was the following: "GATT allows such actions, it is time we took them!" He was referring to protectionist actions under GATT's various safeguard provisions.

As developing countries are drawn increasingly into GATT they, like this presidential candidate, can be expected to interpret its rules as guidelines for policy – in the way World Bank or International Monetary Fund guidelines are viewed. But GATT rules are bad economics. They do not distinguish between government interventions that serve the national economic interest and government interventions that do not.

The safeguard agreement

Even though the ban on new VERs can be circumvented by completing an injury investigation before negotiating with exporters, this provision in the safeguards agreement is a major step in the long series of GATT negotiations to eliminate hard-core import restrictions.

The public notice and transparency requirements added to Article XIX procedures, like similar requirements for antidumping procedures, are laudable in themselves, but they do not correct the bad economics of Article XIX. To do the wrong thing the right way is still to do the wrong thing. In an attempt to make Article XIX more useful, the agreement has added leeway for restrictions to discriminate against dynamic suppliers, and has partly revoked the victim country's right to retaliate. The economics of Article XIX is worse for these changes.

The Article XVIIIB agreement

The thrust of this agreement – toward price-based measures with scheduled phaseout – makes economic sense. Because the control mechanism is the politically loaded consultation process, notification and documentation requirements should complement the improved economics of the conditions for taking Article XVIIIB action.

The decade preceding the Uruguay Round witnessed considerably reduced use of Article XVIIIB by developing countries. This can be attributed in part to pressure from industrialized countries, in part to the Asian example, which demonstrates that sensible exchange rate policy is an important part of development policy.

Antidumping

Though protectionist interests lost on MFA phaseout and elimination of VERs, they dug in their heels on antidumping. The new agreement increases the paperwork of taking antidumping action but is not otherwise restrictive. Because the agreement couches market access issues in distracting legalese, it represents a step in the wrong direction, away from agreement on the trade restrictions that are now falsely sanctified by the label antidumping.

Because GATT cover for import restrictions is fungible, *GATT discipline is as strong as its weakest link.* Even if several of the tricks used by antidumpers are exposed, the myriad detail of every antidumping case leaves ample room to conclude that dumping and injury have occurred. So long as any import restriction can be justified under GATT as an antidumping action, reform of Articles XIX and XVIIIB will not hamper protectionists. The fungibility of trade restrictions brings with it Gresham's law of policymaking: bad policy mechanisms drive out good.

Notes

This chapter was prepared with the assistance of Rebecca Hardy.
1. As specified in Article XXV, whenever reference is made in GATT to CONTRACTING PARTIES acting jointly, they are designated as CONTRACTING PARTIES, in caps.
2. Article XXI (National Security Exceptions) and Article XX (General Exceptions) do not even include notification requirements.
3. All tariff cuts so negotiated were applied on an MFN basis.
4. 1980 statistics show that actions taken under Article XIX covered imports valued at $1.6 billion while total world trade was at the same time valued at $2,000 billion. Sampson (1987), p. 145.

5. VERs on textiles and apparel were first brought under the GATT legal umbrella through negotiation in 1961 of the Short-Term Arrangement on Cotton Textiles. This arrangement was superseded first in 1962 by the Long-Term Arrangement on Cotton Textiles, then in 1973 by the MFA.

6. Likewise, existing Article XIX measures (legal under GATT) must be phased out eight years after application or five years after the WTO agreement enters into force, whichever comes later.

7. Measures lasting 180 days or under have less strenuous reapplication limits.

8. The familiar details of Article XIX are retained, for example, "serious" injury, "cause or threaten."

9. Information and views may be presented on the safeguards measure and its relation to the public interest.

10. The "unforeseen circumstances" requirement of Article XIX has been removed.

11. Extension of a safeguard measure is subject to the same requirements as the initial action.

12. The phrases "clear demonstration" and "clear justification" appear many times in the agreement.

13. Anjaria (1987, p. 672) reports that by 1964 only three industrial countries were still invoking Article XII.

14. Article XVIII, sections A and D, also provide in slightly different ways for import restrictions to support industry development. As of March 1994, section A of Article XVIII had been invoked nine times, while section D had not been invoked at all. For details on the use of section A, see GATT (1994), p. 465.

15. Little (1982) is a good source on development thinking of that era. Finger (1991) compares development thinking and the evolution of GATT's development provisions.

16. Hudec (1987) documents and analyzes this evolution.

17. In the 1980s, the phrase "integration of developing countries into the trading system," used by the OECD Trade Committee to describe part of its work program, became a code for efforts to get developing countries to bring their trade restrictions in line with those in industrial countries.

18. GATT (1993), pp. 16 and 26. The tally of antidumping orders is partial.

19. Finger and Murray (1993) report that from, 1980 to 1988, 348 of 774 US anti-dumping cases were superseded by VERs.

20. Stegmann (1992, p. 8) reports that from July 1980 to June 1989, of 384 anti-dumping actions taken by the European Community, 184 were price under-takings. Though the Tokyo Round Code does not explicitly provide for such settlement, both US and EU antidumping regulations allow for suspension through acceptance by the exporter of a quantity limit (Jackson and Vermulst, 1989, pp. 52 and 116).

21. Finger and Dhar (1994) explain that the national politics of antidumping has come to dominate the international.

22. Palmeter (1991) explains this and other abuses.

23. The observation, made by Anne Brunsdale, former chairperson of the US International Trade Commission, is reported by Ferguson (1994).
24. In the salmon case, Norway objected to the United States comparing home-market averages with individual export prices. The GATT panel that reviewed the case did not find US practice on this point to have been in violation of the Tokyo Round Code.
25. There are constraints on what can be supplied confidentially.
26. Public notice and transparency are virtues, but they must stand on their own merits. The economics of antidumping and other trade remedies demonstrates that good process does not assure good policy.
27. Take, for example, antiprotectionists' opposition to "cumulation," the adding up of injuries from many exporters, no one of which is large enough to cause serious injury. But is it reasonable to provide protection to an industry that has been devoured by a shark, while denying protection to an industry nibbled to death by piranhas? Finger (1992) takes up in detail the point that the constraints on safeguard actions are arbitrary.

References

Anjaria, S. J. 1987. "Balance of Payments and Related Issues in the Uruguay Round of Trade Negotiations." *The World Bank Economic Review* 1(4): 669–88.

Bierwagen, R. M. 1991. *GATT Article VI and the Protectionist Bias in Antidumping Law*. Vol. 7, Kluwer Studies in Transnational Law. Deventer and Boston: Kluwer Law and Taxation Publishers.

Davey, W. J. 1994. "Escape Clauses and Exceptions." Paper prepared for presentation at a seminar on the Uruguay Round Agreements from an Asia-Pacific Perspective, August 1–3. Washington, DC.

Deardorff, A. V., and R. M. Stern, eds. 1994. *Analytical and Negotiating Issues in the Global Trading System*. Ann Arbor: University of Michigan Press.

Ferguson, T. W. 1994. "She Changed Customas at a Trade Body." *Wall Street Journal*, March 8, 1994, p. A17.

Finger, J. M. 1981. "The Industry–Country Incidence of 'Less than Fair Value' Cases in U.S. Import Trade." In W. Baer and M. Gillis, eds., *Export Diversification and the New Protectionism*. Boston: National Bureau of Economic Research, and Champaign, Ill.: Bureau of Business and Economic Research, University of Illinois.

1991. "Development Economics and the General Agreement on Tariffs and Trade." In J. de Melo and A. Sapir, eds., *Trade and Economic Reform*. Cambridge, Mass.: Blackwell.

1992. "The Meaning of 'Unfair' in United States Import Policy." *Minnesota Journal of Global Trade* 1(1): 35–56.

1993. *Antidumping: How It Works and Who Gets Hurt*. Ann Arbor: University of Michigan Press.

Finger, J. M., and S. Dhar 1994. "Do Rules Control Power? GATT Articles and Agreements in the Uruguay Round." In Deardorf and Stern 1994.

Finger, J. M., and T. Murray 1993. "Antidumping and Countervailing Duty Enforcement in the United States." In Finger 1993.

Finger, J.M., and A. Olechowski, eds. 1987. *The Uruguay Round: A Handbook for the Multilateral Trade Negotiations*. Washington, DC: World Bank.

GATT 1958. *Antidumping and Countervailing Duties*. Geneva: GATT.

—— 1993. *International Trade and the Trading System: Report by the Director General, 1992–93*. Geneva: GATT.

—— 1994. *Analytical Index: Guide to GATT Law and Practice*. 6th edn. Geneva: GATT.

Hudec, R.E. 1987. *Developing Countries in the GATT Legal System*. London: Gower.

Hufbauer, G. C. 1981. *Analyzing the Effects of U.S. Trade Policy Instruments*. Washington, DC: National Science Foundation.

Jackson, J. H., and E. A. Vermulst 1989. *Antidumping Law and Practice: A Comparative Study*. Ann Arbor, Mich.: University of Michigan Press.

Litan, R. E., and R. Boltuck, eds. 1991. *Down in the Dumps: Administration of the Unfair Trade Laws*. Washington, DC: Brookings.

Little, I. M. D. 1982. *Economic Development: Theory, Policy and International Relations*. New York: Basic Books.

OECD 1992. *Integration of Developing Countries into the International Trading System*. Washington, DC: OECD.

Palmeter, N. D. 1991. "The Antidumping Law: A Legal and Administrative Nontariff Barrier." In Litan and Boltuck 1991.

Sampson, G. 1987. "Safeguards." In Finger and Olechowski 1987.

Staiger, R. W., and F. Wolak 1994. "The Trade Effects of Antiduming Investigations: Theory and Evidence." In Deardorff and Stern 1994.

Stegemann, K. 1992. *Price Undertakings to Settle Antidumping Cases*. Ottawa: The Institute for Research on Public Policy.

12 Trade-related intellectual property issues: the Uruguay Round agreement and its economic implications

Carlos A. Primo Braga

Debate on trade-related aspects of IPRs in GATT can be traced back to the Tokyo Round of multilateral trade negotiations (1973–79). At that time, the discussion focused narrowly on counterfeit trading. In the Uruguay Round, IPRs became a major topic for negotiation. The resulting "Agreement on Trade-Related Aspects of Intellectual Property Rights, including Trade in Counterfeit Goods" (TRIPS), is the most comprehensive international agreement on IPRs ever negotiated.

TRIPS, services, and TRIMs represented the so-called "new issues" negotiated in the Uruguay Round. The growing demand for multilateral disciplines in these areas was driven by the internationalization of economic activities. As such, these themes were particularly crucial to transnational corporations and industrial economies. Most developing economies, in turn, initially opposed these negotiations. The TRIPS negotiations, in particular, became a symbol of the north–south split, even though they were also the source of many disagreements among industrial nations.

This chapter assesses three basic questions that pertain to the effects of the TRIPS agreement on developing countries. First, how will the agreement change the IPR regimes of developing countries? Second, what are the economic implications of the agreement for developing countries? Third, how effective will the TRIPS agreement be in promoting worldwide harmonization of IPR protection?

IPRs: the terms of the debate

Intellectual property can be defined as information with a commercial value (National Consumer Council 1991).[1] IPRs, in turn, have been characterized as a composite of "ideas, inventions and creative expression" plus the "public willingness to bestow the status of property" on them (Sherwood 1990). As in the case of tangible property, IPRs give their

341

owners the right "to exclude others from access to or use of protected subject matter" (Dratler 1991).

The main legal instruments for protecting IPRs are patents, copyright (and neighboring rights), industrial designs, geographical indications, and trademarks (table 12.1). Special *sui generis* forms of protection have also emerged, addressing the specific needs of knowledge-producers – for example, plant breeders' rights and the protection of the design specifications for integrated circuits. Moreover, many countries enforce trade-secret laws to protect undisclosed information that gives a competitive advantage to its owner.

These legal instruments are just one of the pieces that form a national system of intellectual property protection. The institutions in charge of administering the system, as well as the mechanisms available for enforcing these rights, are other crucial elements of the system's overall effectiveness.

IPRs are territorial; they are created by national laws. Accordingly, nations must reach accommodation as their residents seek protection for their works abroad. Attempts to address this problem have generated numerous international treaties on IPRs. The first ones were negotiated more than a century ago: the Paris Convention for the Protection of Industrial Property (1883) and the Berne Convention for the Protection of Literary and Artistic Works (1886). These conventions have since been revised several times, and many additional treaties covering IPRs have been negotiated (see table 12.1). Most of these conventions are currently administered by the WIPO, a United Nations' specialized agency established in 1967.

Despite WIPO efforts to promote international comity toward IPR protection, countries had achieved little harmony by the mid-1980s. In most cases, WIPO conventions simply required that their signatories follow national treatment, and they lacked minimum standards either for levels of protection or for the coverage of subject matter. The prevailing perception was also that WIPO lacked effective powers to discipline signatories for noncompliance (Kastenmeier and Beier 1989).

These regulatory and institutional shortcomings prompted a bloc of US-led industrial countries to push for the inclusion of IPRs in multilateral trade negotiations in the early 1980s. The negotiations required to bring IPRs to the GATT have been reviewed extensively in the literature, and here we focus on the outcome of this process.[2]

The TRIPS agreement

The TRIPS agreement, the GATS, and GATT 1994 form the tripod that will serve as a basis for the WTO. The TRIPS agreement follows the GATT tradition of adopting the multilateral disciplines of nondiscrimination (as

Types of IPRs	Types of instruments	Subject matter	Main fields of application	Major international agreements
Industrial property	Patents	New, nonobvious, indigenous applica-ble inventions	Manufacturing	Paris Convention Patent Cooperation Treaty Budapest Treaty Strasbourg Agreement
	Utility models Industrial designs	Functional designs Ornamental designs	Manufacturing Clothing, automobiles, electronics, etc.	Hague Agreement Nice Agreement
	Trademarks	Signs or symbols to identify goods and services	All industries	Madrid Agreement Nice Agreement
	Geographical indications			Lisbon Agreement
Literary and artistic property	Copyrights and neighboring rights	Original works of authorship	Printing entertainment (audio, video, motion pictures) software broadcasting	Berne Convention Rome Convention Geneva Convention Brussels Convention
Sui generis protection	Breeders' rights	New, stable homogeneous, distinguishable varieties	Agriculture and food industry	UPOV
	Integrated circuits	Original layout designs	Microelectronic industry	Washington Treaty
Trade secrets		Secret business information	All industries	

Note: with the exception of UPOV, all treaties identified above are administered by WIPO. The Washington Treaty, not yet in force, has also been negotiated under WIPO auspices.
Source: adapted by the author from United Nations 1993, Table 2; WIPO 1994.

Box 12.1 *The structure of the Agreement on Trade-Related Aspects of Intellectual Property Rights*

Part I   General Provisions and Basic Principles

Part II   Standards Concerning the Availability, Scope and Use of Intellectual Property Rights
1. Copyright and related rights
2. Trademarks
3. Geographical indications
4. Industrial designs
5. Patents
6. Layout designs (topographies) of integrated circuits
7. Protection of undisclosed information
8. Control of anticompetitive practices in contractual licenses

Part III   Enforcement of Intellectual Property Rights
1. General obligations
2. Civil and administrative procedures and remedies
3. Provisional measures
4. Special requirements related to border measures
5. Criminal procedures

Part IV   Acquisition and Maintenance of Intellectual Property Rights and Related *Inter Parties* Procedures

Part V   Dispute Prevention and Settlement

Part VI   Transititional Arrangements

Part VII   Institutional Arrangements; Final Provisions

Source: GATT 1994a, p. 365.

---

embedded in the MFN and the national treatment principles) and a commitment to transparency. But TRIPS is also an innovation, having established minimum standards of protection and guidelines for enforcement, while giving member countries discretion in how these standards are implemented. The agreement goes beyond the comity approach of most IPR conventions. Moreover, the pursuit of minimum standards of protection requires that governments take positive action on IPRs, in contrast with the discipline-based approach for trade in goods (GATT 1994) or trade in services (GATS), which does not "require governments to pursue specific policies" (Hoekman 1994).

The TRIPS agreement consists of seven parts and seventy-three articles, organized as set out in box 12.1. Each of these parts is discussed in more detail below.

Part I: general provisions and basic principles

Article 3 of the TRIPS agreement stipulates that each "Member shall accord to the nationals of other Members treatment no less favorable than that it accords to its own nationals" for the protection of intellectual property (GATT 1994a). National treatment in the agreement applies to persons (or legal entities), rather than to goods, as in GATT; in this respect, it is similar to existing IPR conventions. Article 4, in turn, brings the concept of MFN treatment to the realm of international agreements on IPRs. It stipulates that "any advantage, favour, privilege or immunity granted by a Member to the nationals of any other country shall be accorded immediately and unconditionally to the nationals of all other Members" (GATT 1994a).

But the agreement also allows exemptions to these obligations. It recognizes the exceptions to national treatment that are identified in international conventions – such as the Paris Convention (the revised version of 1967), the Berne Convention (revised in 1971), the Rome Convention, and the Washington Treaty. These exceptions refer, for example, to judicial and administrative procedures, to the designation of an address for service within the jurisdiction of a member, or to recourse to reciprocity in specific areas. Exceptions for MFN treatment are allowed for copyright protection in certain areas granted on the basis of reciprocity, consistent with the Berne Convention (1971) or the Rome Convention. Deviations from MFN treatment are also allowed if they reflect international agreements on judicial assistance or legal enforcement of a general nature, on the rights of performers, producers of phonograms, and broadcasting organizations not covered by the TRIPS agreement, or international IPR agreements that were in force prior to the WTO agreement – as long as they "do not constitute an arbitrary or unjustifiable discrimination against nationals of other Members" (GATT 1994a).

Article 63, in turn, introduces the principle of transparency, also as a general obligation. Members are required to publish or promulgate laws and regulations, as well as final judicial decisions and administrative rulings, related to the agreement. The intention is to allow governments and right holders to acquaint themselves with measures that can affect their interests in the area of IPRs (GATT 1994a).

Part II: standards

Part II of the TRIPS agreement establishes minimum standards governing the availability, scope, and use of IPRs. It covers copyright and related rights, trademarks, geographical indications, industrial designs, patents, layout designs (topographies) of integrated circuits, undisclosed information (trade secrets), and anticompetitive practices in contractual licenses.[3]

Copyright and related rights

Copyright law protects the work of authors from the time they create it (typically when the material is first produced). It covers the original *expression* of an idea, rather than the idea itself. Related (or "neighboring") rights, in turn, protect the work of performers, phonogram producers, and broadcasters.

The TRIPS agreement stipulates that countries should comply with the disciplines of the Berne Convention (1971) but does not require that Article 6bis of that convention be observed – that is the issue of "moral rights," or an author's inalienable right to protect the integrity of his or her work and to object to changes that would be prejudicial to his or her honor or reputation. As such, Correa (1994a) has argued that the agreement is actually a "Berne-minus" solution.

But by bringing the minimum standards of protection under the Berne Convention (with the exception of moral rights) to the fold of the WTO, the TRIPS agreement will strengthen the monitoring and enforcement of copyright protection worldwide.[4] Among the 123 countries that were GATT contracting parties by April 1994, thirty-three were not party to the Berne Convention (see appendix A for a list of GATT and other convention numbers). Accordingly, the agreement will help foster greater harmony and introduce greater levels of protection in countries that did not apply Berne standards.

The TRIPS agreement also expands and clarifies Berne disciplines in other areas. It states, for example, that the term of protection should not be less than fifty years when "calculated on a basis other than the life of a natural person" (Article 12; GATT 1994a), thus providing clear guidance for the protection of works that belong to corporations. The main innovations of the agreement, however, pertain to computer programs and data compilations (Article 10) and to rental rights (Article 11).

The agreement establishes that both computer programs (software) and data compilations are to be protected as literary works under the Berne Convention. It confirms copyright law as the basic instrument of protection despite the still ongoing debate about the appropriateness of this solution.[5] And stipulating that these products be protected as literary works, it requires that the term of protection be extended in many countries (discussed later).

The TRIPS agreement also introduces multilateral disciplines for rental rights. Article 11 stipulates that titleholders of computer programs and cinematographic works be entitled "to authorize or prohibit the commercial rental to the public of originals or copies of their copyright works" (GATT 1994a). This obligation, however, applies only to cinematographic works whose widespread copying and then rental is impairing the economic rights of the titleholder (which, it is argued, is occurring in some developing countries).

Article 14 endorses the relevant Berne and Rome Convention disciplines for neighboring rights. As already mentioned, the broader membership of the WTO will ensure a greater degree of harmony than previously.[6] The TRIPS agreement should, for example, inhibit the distribution of "bootleg" copies of the works of foreign performers in countries with weak protection of broadcasts or performances. Moreover, the adoption of a fifty-year minimum term of protection for performers and producers of phonograms expands the duration of protection (twenty years) required under the Rome Convention.[7] And the agreement extends rental rights to the producers of phonograms (and other rights holders in sound recordings), with the proviso that if a "system of equitable remuneration" were in place by April 15, 1994, the member country could maintain this regime in lieu of exclusive rental rights. This exception was tailor-made to grandfathering the "hybrid" Japanese rental system that provides for exclusive rental rights for just one year.

Trademarks

Trademarks are commercial symbols used to identify goods and services or their producers. The TRIPS agreement confirms and clarifies the disciplines of the Paris Convention (1967). Procedures for registration should be transparent and not related to the nature of the goods or services to which the trademark is applied for. Article 16 clarifies the scope of the rights conferred and strengthens the protection of well-known trademarks. It determines that owners of well-known trademarks should be allowed to challenge confusingly similar marks (including those used for goods and services that are not similar to those covered by the well-known trademark). This provision is expected to deter "speculative" registration, a common practice in many developing countries.

The term of protection between registration and its renewal is to be not less than seven years, and indefinite renewal is to be allowed. A registered trademark may be canceled if it is not used for a continuous period of at least three years. But circumstances that may impede compliance with eventual use requirements that are beyond the owner's control (for example, import restrictions) "shall be recognized as valid reasons for non-use" (Article 19; GATT 1994a). The agreement also does not require that domestic marks be displayed in combination with foreign marks. Article 21, in turn, permits members to regulate the licensing and assignment of trademarks, but prohibits the use of compulsory licensing.

Geographical indications

Geographical indications "identify a good as originating in the territory of a Member, or a region or a locality in that territory, where a given quality, reputation or other characteristic of the good is essentially attributable to its geographical origin" (Article 22; GATT 1994a). Beyond establishing the right to take action against the misleading use of a geographical indication, the TRIPS agreement stipulates that members not be allowed to register trademarks that can mislead the public about the true place of origin of the good.

The European Union and Switzerland were the main proponents of high levels of protection for geographical indications. During the negotiations, they argued for strict rules even for indications that connote the generic name of a product (such as China for porcelain) or that have become semigeneric (such as California champagne) (Ross and Wasserman 1993). The section on geographical indications of the agreement reflects these demands to a certain extent. Article 23, in particular, provides additional protection for wines and spirits, restricting the use of geographical indications even when followed by such appropriate qualifications as "kind," "type," or "imitation". In practice, the immediate impact of the agreement is limited, given the exceptions allowed by Article 24. Terms that have become customary for certain goods or that have been used continuously for at least ten years before April 15, 1994, or used in good faith before this date may be exempt from protection. Article 24, however, also requires that members negotiate additional protection for geographical indications for wines and spirits.

Industrial designs

Industrial designs protect the ornamental features of a useful product (the shape of the article, and lines, designs, and colors). The requirements for protection are "weak" in the sense that designs need be only novel or original to qualify for protection.[8] The agreement stipulates that the term of protection be at least ten years. Owners of protected designs can impede the "making, selling, or importing" of articles that infringe on their rights (GATT 1994a). The agreement will foster harmonization in this area by expanding the number of countries with industrial design protection.

Patents

Patents protect novel, nonobvious, and useful inventions. A patentee has the right to exclude others from using, making, or selling the patented invention for a limited period of time.

Those that favored stronger IPR protection cited several problem areas with patents: limited coverage of products and processes, short terms of protection, broad scope for compulsory licensing, and ineffective enforcement (US Chamber of Commerce 1987). The agreement addresses all of these areas, advancing harmonization and introducing higher standards of patent protection than those available under the Paris Convention (basically national treatment).

Article 27 defines patentable subject matter broadly – that patents "shall be available for any inventions, whether products or processes, in all fields of technology" (GATT 1994a). This definition will require that many developing countries revise their patent laws to cover, for example, food, pharmaceutical and chemical products or processes (discussed later). Exclusions from patentability are allowed for the protection of public order or morality, the prevention of environmental degradation, and the protection of human, animal, or plant life. These broad exceptions, however, are constrained by the requirement that the nonpatentable invention also be barred from commercial exploitation in the member country.

Exemptions from patentability are also allowed for "diagnostic, therapeutic and surgical methods" (Article 27.3(a)), an approach consistent with the patent laws of most countries. The exemption established in Article 27.3(b), however, is more controversial, reflecting the challenges posed to the patent system by developments in biotechnology. The agreement adopts a conservative approach by allowing nonpatentability of plants and animals, in contrast with the US position, which favored broad patent coverage. The exclusion does not apply to micro-organisms, microbiological processes, and plant varieties.

TRIPS standards imply that countries are required to provide protection for biotechnological inventions – both "frontier" innovations (for example, cell and gene manipulations) and more conventional ones (fermentation processes) – but may exclude traditional breeding methods and higher life organisms from patentability. But members are required to provide protection for plant varieties "either by patents or by an effective sui generis system or by any combination thereof" (GATT 1994a). Accordingly, many developing countries will have to expand coverage of their patent systems or introduce *sui generis* protection (for example, plant breeders' rights) for plant varieties.[9]

Article 27.3(b) contains a clause that calls for reviewing the provisions of the article four years after the WTO agreement goes into force. This clause suggests that, even among industrial countries, little consensus has been reached on how protection should be provided in a field characterized by rapid technological change and pervasive environmental, philosophical, and ethical concerns.

In identifying the rights of the patentee, the TRIPS agreement explicitly mentions an exclusive right of importation (Article 28), which the laws of many countries do not yet recognize. The agreement, however, does not stipulate the conditions for the "exhaustion" of IPRs at the international level.[10] Actually, Article 6 stipulates against using the TRIPS dispute settlement procedures to address the issue of exhaustion. In this context, conflicts associated with parallel imports will continue to depend on domestic law for their resolution.

TRIPS agreement provisions on compulsory licenses are also quite relevant. Article 31 specifies the conditions under which the subject matter of a patent can be used without the authorization of the titleholder (the term "compulsory licensing" is not used in this respect). It does not challenge the grant of compulsory licensing. Actually, the agreement lists most of the circumstances that typically provide grounds for compulsory licensing under domestic law: for public health, nutrition or other reasons of public interest (Article 8), national emergency, anticompetitive practices, public noncommercial use, and the exploitation of dependent patents. Article 31 actually imposes strict conditions on the granting of compulsory licenses (GATT 1994a); they call for prior negotiations with the titleholder and are limited to nonexclusive, temporary licenses "predominantly for the supply of the domestic market." Licenses to permit the exploitation of dependent patents require that the "second" patent cover an "important technical advance of considerable economic significance" vis-à-vis the original invention. Moreover, the titleholder is entitled to "adequate remuneration" and to an appropriate review of decisions leading to compulsory licensing.

It can be argued that Article 27.1 introduces the main new discipline for compulsory licensing. It establishes that "patents shall be available and patent rights enjoyable without discrimination as to the place of invention, the field of technology and whether products are imported or locally produced" (GATT 1994a). In other words, importation should be accepted as meeting the obligation to work a patent. Accordingly, working obligations which require that an invention be produced domestically – a common practice in developing countries – will no longer provide grounds for granting compulsory licenses.

The TRIPS agreement will have a strong harmonizing impact on the protection of patents by requiring that they be granted for a period of not less than twenty years "counted from the filing date" (GATT 1994a). Numerous countries will have to change their laws to extend the existing term of protection (discussed later).

The section on patents ends with Article 34, which introduces enforcement issues. Specifically, it establishes that in civil litigations the reversal of the burden of proof should be available under certain circumstances. In other words, the defendant will have to "prove that the process to obtain an identical product is different from the patented process" (GATT 1994a). This discipline and Article 28.1(b) – which extends the patentee's rights to the products obtained directly under the protected process – are expected to strengthen the protection granted by process patents.

Layout designs of integrated circuits

The semiconductor chip is the basic building block of the modern electronics industry. Invented in 1959, chips are "integrated circuits containing transistors, resistors, capacitors and their interconnections, fabricated into a tiny, single piece of semiconductor material" (Besen and Raskind 1991). Mask works are the masks that bear the design of the circuitry used to produce the chip. Since the mid-1980s, several industrial countries have adopted *sui generis* legislation to protect the intellectual property rights of chip producers.[11] Attempts to internationalize protection in this area led to the negotiation of the Treaty on Intellectual Property in Respect of Integrated Circuits (the Washington Treaty, 1989).

Many industrial countries believe that the Washington Treaty lacks adequate standards of protection. As such, none of the major producers of semiconductor chips has ratified the treaty. The TRIPS agreement adopts several of the provisions of the Washington Treaty, but it introduces changes that strengthen the protection for layout designs. The scope of protection extends not only to the layout design or to an integrated circuit based on it, but also to articles that incorporate the unlawfully reproduced design. Innocent infringers are liable to pay "a sum equivalent to a reasonable royalty" after receiving an appropriate communication of infringement, but cannot be prohibited from using existing or on-order stock of the infringing product (Article 37; GATT 1994a). The term of protection is a minimum of ten years from filing (in countries that require registration) or the first commercial exploitation – in contrast to the eight-year term of protection under the Washington Treaty. The TRIPS agreement also introduces stricter rules on compulsory licensing for semiconductor technology. In short, the agreement can be characterized as a "Washington-plus" solution.

Protection of undisclosed information

Article 39 of the agreement refers explicitly to the protection of undisclosed information (trade secrets).[12] In broad terms, a trade secret (a term not used in the agreement) is any technological or business information that is controlled as a secret and that provides a competitive advantage to its owner. Countries protect trade secrets in different ways: as legal property (the United States), under contract law (Switzerland) or in the context of ethical business practices (Germany) (Sherwood 1990). Most developing countries, however, do not have specific laws protecting trade secrets. Criminal prosecution is often an alternative for parties interested in fighting breaches of secrecy, although most analysts deny its effectiveness.

North–south debate on the protection of undisclosed information was heated; developing countries strongly opposed treating trade secrets as an IPR. This opposition relied in part on the argument that disclosure is a necessary counterpart of the "social bargain" associated with the granting of IPRs (discussed later); since trade secrets are at odds with the idea of disclosure, they should not be characterized as IPRs.

The strategy adopted in the TRIPS agreement was to identify undisclosed information as a category of IPRs, but to link its protection to practices against unfair competition as identified in Article 10bis of the Paris Convention (1967). The agreement does not grant exclusive rights to the holder of the trade secret. As pointed out by Reichman (1993), trade secrets "that are voluntarily revealed, insufficiently guarded or reverse-engineered lose all protection." Only the acquisition of undisclosed information "in a manner contrary to honest commercial practices" can lead to action against the infringer (GATT 1994a). The agreement also requires that test data submitted to governments as procedures for "approving the marketing of pharmaceutical or of agricultural chemical products" be protected against unfair commercial use and unnecessary disclosure (GATT 1994a).

Control of anti-competitive practices in contractual licenses

The last section of part II addresses one of the main concerns of developing countries: the use of IPRs to impose abusive contract terms that might inhibit the transfer and diffusion of technology. Article 40 recognizes that licensing practices and the exercise of IPRs may have anticompetitive effects. But it gives member countries discretion over implementing measures to counter such practices, on the condition that they should not conflict with other provisions of the agreement. It also calls for a system of bilateral consultations between member countries to provide access to information necessary for evaluating anticompetitive practices and to avoid the arbitrary enforcement of remedies against anticompetitive practices.

Article 40 establishes a link between the multilateral trade regime and national laws on competition. It can be argued that it reflects the long-standing efforts of developing countries to negotiate an "International Code of Conduct on Transfer of Technology" under UNCTAD auspices (UNCTAD 1994). But the language of Article 40 is essentially prescriptive without providing a precise definition of anticompetitive practices.[13] These vague prescriptions are more likely to generate friction among trading partners than to deter anticompetitive practices effectively.

Part III: the enforcement of IPRs

Part III of the TRIPS agreement introduces detailed provisions for IPR enforcement. These disciplines were a major negotiating objective of industrial countries, since the standards of protection introduced in part II are relevant only if enforceable.

Under the general obligations for enforcement, members are required to provide "expeditious remedies to prevent infringements and remedies which constitute a deterrent to further infringements" (GATT 1994a). These measures should be fair and equitable, not overly complex or expensive, available to both foreign and national rights holders, not susceptible to barriers to legitimate trade, and open to judicial review. It is important to note, however, that countries are not obligated to establish a dedicated judicial system for IPRs.

The TRIPS agreement requires that rights holders have access to civil and administrative procedures, including provisions on evidence of proof, injunctive relief, payments for damages, and indemnification of parties wrongfully enjoined or restrained. Provisional measures for expeditious action – when, for example, evidence is at risk of being destroyed – should also be available, as should border measures that allow customs authorities to suspend the release of suspect counterfeit trademark goods or pirated copyright goods. Moreover, members should provide for criminal procedures "at least in cases of wilful trademark.counterfeiting or copyright piracy on a commercial scale" (GATT 1994a).

Overall, these disciplines will require that most developing countries overhaul their enforcement practices. As discussed later below, this area will inevitably be the source of many disputes about compliance, given the limited administrative resources and capabilities of the judicial systems in many developing countries.

Part IV: acquisition and maintenance of IPRs

Article 62 of the TRIPS agreement establishes disciplines for imposing conditions on the acquisition or maintenance of IPRs. It basically requires that these procedures and formalities be consistent with the overall provisions of the agreement, and that they be expeditious enough "to avoid unwarranted curtailment of the period of protection" (GATT 1994a).

Part V: dispute prevention and settlement

One important outcome of the Uruguay Round is the integrated dispute settlement mechanism that provides automatic procedures and strict

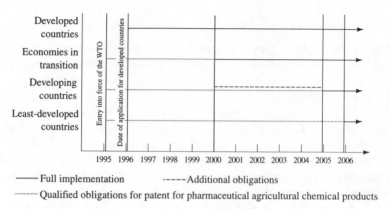

—— Full implementation   -----Additional obligations
········ Qualified obligations for patent for pharmaceutical agricultural chemical products

Figure 12.1   Transitional periods for TRIPS implementation

timetables (Jackson 1994). Disputes over TRIPS matters will be handled by a dispute settlement body established in Article 2 of the "Understanding of Rules and Procedures Governing the Settlement of Disputes" of the Marrakesh Agreement. The possibility of cross-sectoral retaliation is expected to help strengthen the protection of IPRs worldwide.

But a "five-year moratorium" (equal to the Part VI standard transitional period for developing countries) has been placed on the use of the integrated dispute settlement procedures for indirect violations of the agreement.[14] In other words, measures that may nullify or impair the benefits of the agreement without being a direct violation of its obligations (for example, the application of an unusually high creativity threshold for acquiring copyright protection) cannot be brought to the attention of a panel in the next five years. According to Article 64.3, WTO members will use the "moratorium" period to examine decisions on how complaints of this modality should be treated.

Part VI: transitional arrangements

The TRIPS agreement gives all countries a one-year transitional period after the entry into force of the WTO agreement to begin applying the TRIPS provisions (figure 12.1).[15] Developing countries and economies in transition (former centrally planned economies) are entitled to an additional four-year transitional period except for obligations pertaining to national and MFN treatment.[16] But developing countries are also entitled to an additional five-year transitional period for product patents in fields of technology that are not protected by the time they apply the agreement (Article 65.4).[17]

The least-developed countries are entitled to a ten-year transitional period from the date of application of the TRIPS provisions – that is, eleven years after entry into force of the WTO agreement – to enable them to comply with the obligations of the agreement (again, except for national and MFN treatment). They are also allowed to request an extension of this period (Article 66.1).

Although the long transitional periods for developing countries are tantamount to special and differential treatment, they do not involve permanent derogations of the TRIPS obligations (a solution preferred by some developing countries during the negotiations). It can be argued that obtaining "universal" coverage rather than a codified solution for TRIPS was a necessary compromise.[18]

Part VI of the TRIPS agreement also obligates industrial countries to provide "technical and financial cooperation in favour of developing and least-developed country Members" on request (GATT 1994a). Such cooperation includes legal assistance, support for enforcement and institutional strengthening, and personnel training. But Article 67 emphasizes that the technical cooperation should be provided on "mutually agreed terms and conditions." As such, it is inherently biased toward countries that are willing to converge toward the IPR protection standards of industrial countries.

Part VII: institutional arrangements

The agreement concludes with a series of articles addressing the creation of a TRIPS council for monitoring the agreement and helping members implement it, an exhortation for international cooperation, measures to address obligations for protecting preexisting subject matter, and conditions for review, amendment, reservations, and security exceptions.

Particularly relevant to developing countries is Article 70, dealing with the protection of existing subject matter. The agreement does not obligate member countries for acts that were implemented before its date of application, nor does it require that they restore the protection of subject matter that has fallen into public domain. In essence, the article confirms that members are not obliged to provide "pipeline" protection to subject matter already patented in another country and not yet marketed in the country that will be assuming the new obligations under TRIPS. Article 70.4 does allow members to limit the remedies available to right holders for acts which become infringements when the agreement is applied.

Paragraphs 8 and 9 of Article 70 qualify the long transitional periods available for the protection of pharmaceutical and agricultural chemical product patents. Developing countries that do not protect these products and avail themselves of the transitional arrangements must accept applications for patents in these fields as of the date of entry into force of the WTO agreement. Although patents filed during the transitional period will be examined only at the end of the period, their novelty (a criterion of patentability) will be judged on the basis of the state of the art at the time of filing.

Moreover, if the product for which the patent application has been filed is approved for market distribution, then (under certain conditions) an exclusive marketing right should be provided. This right should extend for a period of five years or until the patent is either granted or denied, "whichever period is shorter."[19] In short, in these critical fields of technology the long transitional period comes together with a series of additional obligations for developing countries.

How will the TRIPS agreement affect the IPRs regimes of countries?

The agreement will require significant reforms in developing countries' legal regimes. This outcome should be no surprise, given that the negotiating objective was to promote effective and adequate protection of IPRs with the introduction of higher standards of protection. But industrial countries will also have to adapt their IPR regimes in many cases. As such the TRIPS agreement provisions are arguably the most significant ones coming from the Uruguay Round negotiations on new issues, including GATS and TRIMs. Although the broad scope of the agreement and its level of detail preclude a complete description of its legal implications here, some basic indicators can be used to illustrate the types of legal reform that will be required.

For patents, several developing countries will have to extend protection to pharmaceutical and chemical products, subject matters often excluded from protection in national law. Among the ninety-eight developing countries that are members of the WTO[20] twenty-five had not provided patents for pharmaceutical products and thirteen had not provided patents for chemical products as of April 1994 (figure 12.2). Moreover, a large number of these countries provide terms of protection that are shorter than the twenty-year term from filing mandated by the agreement, allow exceptions to the twenty-year term, or use another date (for example the date of the grant or date of publication) to mark the beginning of the term. In all these instances, changes will be required.

For copyrights, arguably the main implication of the agreement is the requirement that software be protected as literary works. Fifty-seven developing countries (and two industrial countries) had not provided any type of protection for computer software as of April 1994, and a few countries had provided forms of legal protection for software other than copyright

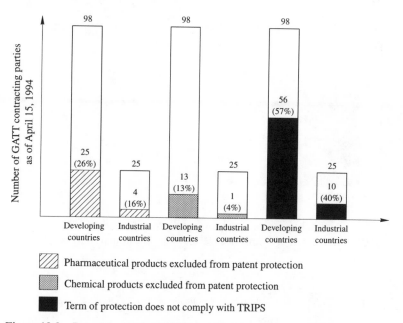

Pharmaceutical products excluded from patent protection

Chemical products excluded from patent protection

Term of protection does not comply with TRIPS

Figure 12.2   Patent protection, 1994
Sources: WIPO 1990a and 1990b; World Intellectual Property Report (several issues); United States Trade Representative (several years); and national sources.

law (figure 12.3). It is also worth noting that among the thirty-six developing countries that already protected software with copyright law approximately half had implemented specific provisions, rather than covering them generally as literary works. In short, significant legal reform will be required in this area as the agreement is implemented.

Another relevant issue for developing countries is the protection of plant varieties. The agreement requires that protection be provided either by patents or by a *sui generis* system, or a combination of both. Thirty-one developing and six industrial countries provide no protection for plant varieties (figure 12.4). Plant breeders' rights are often available in industrial countries, since most of these countries are members of the UPOV Convention. Only a few developing countries are UPOV members, and only a few provide for their own *sui generis* protection (Argentina, Chile, Kenya, Korea, Uruguay, and Zimbabwe).[21] In short the TRIPS obligations will also require reform in this field of technology in a significant number of developing countries.

These three indicators provide at best a limited picture of the types of changes in IPR regimes required by the agreement. Effective enforcement

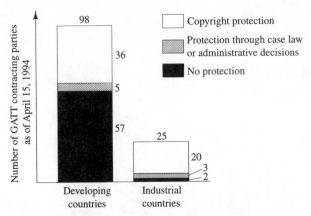

Figure 12.3   Copyright protection for computer programs, 1994
Sources: US Department of Commerce (several years); national sources.

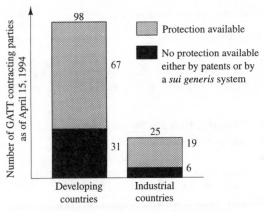

Figure 12.4   Protection for plant varieties, 1994
Sources: UPOV 1993; Wijk, Cohen, and Komen 1993; and national sources.

and compulsory licensing practices will also demand numerous changes in national legislation and procedures, particularly in developing countries. The overextended judicial systems of most developing countries will be challenged to provide effective and appropriate means of enforcement. Weak coordination between customs and judicial authorities, for example, can undermine the effectiveness of available remedies independently of the efficiency of the courts and the adequacy of the regulatory environment.

In an analysis of compulsory licensing practices in developing countries, Sherwood (1995) found that eight of the twelve Latin American countries

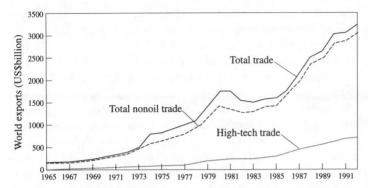

Figure 12.5   Total trade, nonoil trade, and high-tech trade, 1965–92
Source: United Nations Statistical Office Comtrade Data Base.

analyzed will have to alter their compulsory licensing provisions to comply with the agreement. His basic conclusion is that virtually "every country that has a compulsory licensing provision written prior to 1993 will need to make adjustments to respond to the TRIPS Agreement." These necessary adjustments reflect the introduction of concepts in Article 31 that were not traditionally used in patent laws around the world (for example, the obligation that compulsory licenses be provided predominantly for the supply of the domestic market and the specific reference to semiconductor technology).

The economic implications of TRIPS

Some aspects of the economic debate on IPRs are not controversial (appendix B discusses the economic rationale for IPR protection). First, the broad consensus is that the economic interests involved are significant. As pointed out by Maskus (1994), "at some level nearly all legitimately traded goods and services operate under patent, copyright, or trademark protection." For example, the evolution of international trade in high-tech, R&D-intensive products during the 1965–92 period shows that their share in global trade increased from 11 percent in 1965 to 23 percent by 1992, amounting to approximately US $740 billion (figure 12.5) (Primo Braga and Yeats 1994). It is also worth noting that trade in goods and services from the entertainment industry and in luxury trademark products has also been expanding rapidly. IPRs protection is of special interest to all these industries, and their dynamism in international trade has paved the way for the multilateral negotiations on TRIPS.

Second, as economies become increasingly integrated in the world economy, the potential for conflicts over IPRs will increase. The growing integration of the world economy and the dynamism of industries that rely on IPR protection confirm the importance of multilateral disciplines in this area. TRIPS is required not only to address the economics of IPRs protection at the international level, but also to provide a political forum for diffusing trade frictions.

Third, the importance of IPRs for decisions about investment, technological transfers, and innovation differ significantly across industries. Patents, for example, are much more important in such industries as pharmaceuticals and chemicals than they are in others. This finding is consistent with research showing that patents have a greater impact on imitation costs in these industries than in such industries as electronics and machinery (Mansfield, Schwartz, and Wagner 1981).

The other economic implications of a global push toward higher standards of IPR protection are more controversial. In what follows, I adopt a utilitarian approach to assess the potential economic costs and benefits of the TRIPS agreement. This approach, of course, is at odds with the idea that intellectual property encompasses "natural" rights, and that respect for these rights should guide policy as a matter of principle. This chapter does not discuss this issue or its normative implications. But it is worth noting that both developing and industrial countries have adopted IPR regimes pragmatically over time in response to technological developments and changes in perceptions of "national interests."[22]

TRIPS and trade flows

IPR regimes may influence trade flows. Stern (1987), for example, points out that discrepancies among national IPR regimes generate effects analogous to nontariff barriers. Exporters in the north face additional costs when they export to the south (rather than to other countries in the north), because they must engage in activities to inhibit local imitation. It can also be argued that the international harmonization of IPR regimes will diminish the transaction costs of operating in different regulatory environments.

The net impact of stronger IPR protection on trade flows in the south is, however, ambiguous. As pointed out by Maskus and Penubarti (1994), the higher level of protection fosters two conflicting effects. First, it will enhance the market power of the titleholder, reducing the elasticity of demand for his or her products. Second, it will expand the net demand for the protected products as imitators are displaced. The net trade effect will depend on which effect dominates. If the market-power effect is larger than the market-expansion effect (as would likely be the case in countries with limited productive capacity), then trade flows may decline in the aftermath of the reform. If the opposite is true, then strengthening IPR protection will lead to trade expansion. In other words, the net trade effect of the TRIPS agreement is in essence an empirical question.

Using data from the early 1980s, Ferrantino (1993) investigated the role of IPR regimes in influencing US arm's-length trade, intra-firm trade, and "establishment-trade" (the sales of US overseas affiliates in the local market). The overall results suggest at best a weak association between IPRs and arm's-length US exports (only the length of patent protection shows a significant positive impact), no influence of IPRs on establishment trade, but significant effects on intra-firm trade. His main conclusion is that intra-firm exports tend to be higher in countries with weaker IPR protection – an indication that US transnational corporations prefer to keep production within US borders and engage in intra-firm trade, rather than risk the loss of proprietary information by adopting a more integrated system of production in partner countries that have weaker IPR regimes.

Using data from the US 1989 Benchmark Survey covering forty-two countries, I estimated gravity models for the same dependent variables analyzed in Ferrantino: arm's length trade, intra-firm trade, and "establishment trade" for US companies. The explanatory variables included GDP, population, geographical distance from the United States, an estimate of trade barriers, dummies for Europe and landlocked countries, and an index in which patent protection is used to proxy the strength of an IPR regime (Rapp and Rozek 1990).[23] All equations fielded positive coefficients for the IPRs, but the coefficient was significant only for arm's-length trade, in contrast to Ferrantino's results. Taking this result at its face value, it seems that market-expansion dominates market-power effects – that is, stronger IPR protection promotes greater trade.

This result is in fact confirmed by Maskus and Penubarti (1994), who use an augmented version of the Helpman–Krugman model of monopolistic competition to examine bilateral trade flows. Their results suggest that firms are influenced by the strength of the patent regimes of importing countries when they engage in export activities. Countries with stronger patent regimes import more than what is predicted by the Helpman–Krugman model. Moreover, the impact of patent protection on trade flows is larger in the larger developing countries, a result that is consistent with the proposition that the market-expansion effect is more likely to predominate in these economies.

Maskus and Penubarti (1994) also analyzed sectoral exports by clustering industries in three different categories of expected sensitivity to patent laws: high-sensitivity industries (R&D-intensive industries and industries that have reported significant damage from "piracy"), low-sensitivity industries, and least-sensitive industries. They found more significant and larger coefficients for the patent index in low-sensitivity industries than in the least-sensitive industries. They interpret this result as a function of either larger market-power effects or the interplay between trade and FDI decisions in highly sensitive industries (as FDI replaces trade as a mode of delivery in countries with weaker patent regimes). They also argue that the Rapp and Rozek patent index may be capturing other dimensions of the IPR regime (for example, copyright and trademark protection) that are relevant for the low-sensitivity group.

In sum, Maskus and Penubarti (1994) provide mounting evidence "that IPRs are indeed "trade-related." Their results are, of course, model specific and should be interpreted with care. But they do indicate that the implementation of TRIPS will have a net trade creating impact. Although no precise welfare predictions can be derived from them, they suggest that TRIPS may have a positive allocative impact at the global level, and that market expansion will dominate the market-power effect in developing countries.

TRIPS and FDI

It is often argued that foreign firms avoid investing in countries with weak IPR regimes (OECD 1989). But the magnitude of the impact of weak protection on FDI decisions is debatable. First, evidence based on surveys of foreign investors that identify IPRs as a relevant variable for FDI decisions tend also to point out that other considerations – in essence, the overall investment climate of the country – are more important (Frischtak 1989). Second, as already pointed out, FDI may replace trade flows as firms try to maintain control of proprietary information in countries with weak IPR protection. In this case, the impact of TRIPS would be to diminish the incentives of R&D-intensive industries for FDI at the margin (Maskus and Konan 1994).

Mansfield (1994) provided some new insight into the IPR–FDI link. His analysis, based on survey data collected from patent attorneys and executives of major US manufacturing firms, indicates clearly that IPR regimes are relevant for some but not all types of FDI decisions. Not surprisingly, he found that IPR protection is much more relevant for decisions about investment in R&D facilities than for FDI in sales and distribution outlets. He also found sharp differences in the perceptions of industries about the importance of IPR regimes in their decisions about FDI. While the chemical and pharmaceutical industries reported that IPRs played a major role in their decisions about investment in joint ventures abroad, the metals and food industries believed that IPR protection had marginal significance.

Mansfield (1994) also reported ongoing econometric work that tries to explain US foreign direct investment flows to the sixteen countries encompassed by his survey, using the host-country GDP and his own index of protection as independent variables (a dummy for Mexico is also included in the model). The overall results are not particularly robust, but the exclusion of Japan and Spain from the sample made both aggregate manufacturing FDI flows and FDI flows to certain industries (particularly machinery and food) sensitive to weaknesses in IPR regimes – that is, US FDI flows increase with the perceived strength of the IPR regime.

I implemented a similar exercise with a larger set of (fifty-two) countries and the Rapp–Rozek index, using the total assets of US firms abroad in 1992 as the dependent variable (US Department of Commerce 1994). I tested several explanatory variables, including GDP, growth rates, the IPR index, a proxy for trade barriers, and a dummy for Canada and Mexico. The results for manufacturing as a whole show consistently that IPRs have a positive impact on the level of US investment abroad. The sectoral results are less robust, although the IPR index showed positive coefficients for electrical equipment.

These results on the IPR–FDI link are tentative, and additional work must be done in this area. But it can be argued that in a world of growing competition for FDI flows, future compliance with the minimum standards of the TRIPS agreement will be perceived as a threshold indicator, since it will influence the perceptions of foreign investors about the relative attractiveness of competing investment locations.

TRIPS and the transfer of technology

Probably the most traditional argument for protecting IPRs in developing countries is that the risk of piracy makes technology owners less willing to transfer proprietary knowledge to countries with weak IPR regimes. Support for this argument typically comes from surveys of firms in the north. Mansfield (1994), for example, found that US firms "tend to regard intellectual property protection as being more important in decisions regarding the transfer of advanced technology than in investment decisions."

Some analysts, however, remain skeptical about the relevance of this effect. Subramanian (1990) points out that north–south conflict occurs primarily in fields in which imitation is possible independently of technological transfer (for example, pharmaceutical and chemical products, and software). Accordingly, the potential benefits of greater IPR protection are disputed to the extent that imitation is a sound alternative for the formal transfer of technology. Nogues (1993), in turn, argues "that the decision to license and transfer technology depends much more on the legal strength of the licensing agreement and the adaptable capacity of the buyer to absorb technology" than on the strength of the IPR regime.

Note, however, that firms in the north react to imitation by investing in "masking" technologies (for example, the encryption of software codes) that increase the costs of imitation (Taylor 1993). Moreover, the lack of protection in sectors that are imitation-prone influences the overall perception of the IPR regime in the developing country. To the extent that the country is not perceived to be "playing by the rules," it will have greater difficulty in obtaining the transfer of technology in fields in which the cooperation of the inventor is fundamental. On balance, the TRIPS agreement should promote north–south technological transfers.

TRIPS and rent transfer

One of the main concerns of developing countries about the TRIPS agreement is the potential increase in domestic prices and rent transfers abroad (Rodrik 1994). Potential rent transfers are significant, given that non-residents account for most of the patents granted in developing countries.

The introduction of patents for pharmaceutical inventions has attracted considerable attention.[24] Many developing countries do not offer IPR protection in this area and closely monitor price levels according to health policies and other social objectives.

The literature provides estimates of price increases, domestic welfare losses (from consumer and domestic producer surpluses), and potential rent transfers (as measured by the rise in foreign profits). As expected, the static effects of the introduction of patents for pharmaceutical inventions in developing countries imply domestic economic losses for the south that are larger than the benefits accruing to innovators in the north. The estimates, however, are quite sensitive to assumptions about market structure and firm behavior.

A worst-case scenario of economic losses and rent transfers can be developed if one assumes that the introduction of patents turns a domestic competitive industry into a foreign-owned monopoly (Nogues 1993). The domestic economic loss is demonstrated by the significant price increase that occurs under the scenario. If the original market structure is characterized by a domestic and foreign firm duopoly that evolves into a foreign-controlled monopoly, then the scope for a price increase is limited, but a significant economic loss still ensues, due primarily to the loss of domestic producer surplus.

As Maskus and Konan (1994) point out, however, these scenarios do not realistically capture the market for pharmaceutical products in most developing countries. The results change when one assumes that, under prereform circumstances, the dominant foreign firm faces a competitive fringe of imitators and, eventually, of producers of generic drugs that are close substitutes for the patented drugs. First, the price impact and consumer surplus losses are significantly reduced. They will be larger in countries in which the competitive fringe of imitators is relatively larger (for example, India and Argentina) than in others where imitators have a more limited market share to start with (for example, Brazil).[25] Second, the potential for rent transfers also decreases dramatically.

The basic message of these exercises is that, although the TRIPS agreement will generate rent transfers from the south to the north, the magnitude of these transfers is unlikely to be as large as in the worst-case scenarios discussed above. Moreover, as discussed in Subramanian (1994), the transitional provisions of the agreement further dilute these static losses. It takes an average of ten years after a patent is filed for a drug to receive marketing approval. Accordingly, the direct impact of the agreement will begin to be felt in developing countries only by 2005. And the full impact – that is, the complete displacement of "pirates" – will materialize only by 2015, assuming a linear rate of introduction of new drugs in the world pharmaceutical market and effective enforcement of the law.[26]

TRIPS and the displacement of "pirates"

Estimates of revenue foregone by innovators in the north due to weak IPR protection in the south vary widely, but that is no doubt that the values involved are significant (US International Trade Commission 1988, and IIPA 1994). In the same vein, "pirates" (those who ride freely on the intellectual property of others, independent of the legality of their actions) have substantial economic interests in the south, particularly in industries in which imitation is relatively easy (for example, trademarked goods and software).

The displacement of "pirates" *per se* does not necessarily entail a social welfare loss, since these producers may be replaced by others operating under licenses from foreign titleholders. Some countries that have reformed their IPR regimes (for example, Singapore) provide evidence that "pirates" are often well positioned to switch to legitimate activities when the legal environment changes, particularly in industries characterized by low entry barriers (for example, the production of video and audio cassettes).[27]

The issue for trademarked goods is essentially one of enforcement. As mentioned earlier, institutional weaknesses and the lack of resources are expected to continue to constrain developing countries despite their TRIPS obligations. Technical and financial assistance from the north can play an important role in this area, assuming that the political will to curb "piracy" is mustered.

TRIPS and investments in R&D

The analysis thus far has concentrated primarily on the allocative implications of the TRIPS agreement. This is a partial approach, to the extent that it does not account for the dynamic benefits associated with strengthening IPR regimes. The impact of TRIPS on R&D investments in both industrial and developing countries is the main issue in this context.[28]

Evidence on the response of R&D investments in developing countries to changes in IPR protection remains scarce. Still, there is growing appreciation for the role played by innovation in economic development. Gould and Gruben (1994), for example, found that IPR protection has a marginally significant positive effect on economic growth, which they attribute to the role of IPRs in fostering R&D investments. They also found that the contribution of IPRs to economic growth increases with the openness of the economy. Based on these results, an argument can be made that the trade liberalization fostered by the Uruguay Round will enhance the potential dynamic benefits of the TRIPS agreement. But more research is required to confirm this proposition.

Another aspect of the TRIPS–R&D link pertains to the impact of greater IPR protection in the south on R&D investments in the north. The small-country assumption adopted in the analysis of the pharmaceutical industry, for example, may not be appropriate on aggregate terms or for products that are particularly relevant to developing countries (for example, drugs to fight tropical diseases). The relevance of this proposition remains an empirical question, but in theory it opens the door for "Pareto-efficient" bargains between industrial and developing countries (Subramanian 1994).

The agreement may also affect the composition of R&D investments in the south. Agricultural research in developing countries, for example, has traditionally been implemented by the public sector. The introduction of protection for plant varieties is expected to foster the privatization of agricultural research. The reaction of national or international governmental research centers to this trend is likely to have important economic implications. As innovators claim IPRs over plant varieties, the policy of free germplasm exchange among research centers will have to be adapted (Barton and Siebeck 1994). A possible danger in this context is the adoption of cumbersome bureaucratic procedures for germplasm exchanges in response to the introduction of property rights.

Conclusion and policy implications

The TRIPS agreement will require that developing countries significantly reform their IPR regime. As countries introduce the required minimum standards of protection, IPRs will gradually be strengthened worldwide. As such, the agreement will deliver a much greater level of "harmonization" for IPR protection than was thought feasible at the start of the Uruguay Round negotiations.

From a static perspective, the agreement is an exercise in rent transfer from the south to the north. But its negative economic implications for developing countries are significantly diluted by the long transitional periods adopted. Moreover, both industrial and developing countries can explore positive-sum games in trade, foreign direct investment, and technological transfers as IPR protection is strengthened.

For developing countries, the main task ahead is to transform their IPR regimes into effective instruments to promote innovation. This challenge is of course significant, given the institutional and financial constraints facing these countries. Technical assistance from industrial countries and multilateral institutions may play a positive role in this process.

It is important to recognize, however, that the achievements of the agreement fall short of the expectations of knowledge-intensive industries in industrial countries.[29] Unilateral actions as a lever to promote change will continue to be supported by these industries. The question of enforcement, for example, is likely to become a major area of contention in the years to come. A more definitive evaluation of the TRIPS agreement will have to include an analysis of its effectiveness – together with the integrated dispute settlement mechanism of the WTO – at diffusing trade-related IPR frictions and preventing unilateral actions by major trading nations.

Appendix A Membership in GATT and in major WIPO conventions

GATT membership:	Paris Convention	Berne Convention
Developing countries and economies in Transition[a]		
Angola	•	
Antigua and Barbuda		
Argentina	•	•
Bahrain		
Bangladesh [b]	•	
Barbados	•	•
Belize		
Benin[b]	•	•
Bolivia	•	•
Botswana[b]		
Brazil	•	•
Brunei		
Burkina Faso[b]	•	•
Burundi[b]	•	

GATT membership:	Paris Convention	Berne Convention
Cameroon	•	•
Central African Rep.[b]	•	•
Chad[b]	•	•
Chile	•	•
Colombia		•
Congo	•	•
Costa Rica		•
Côte d'Ivoire	•	•
Cuba	•	
Cyprus	•	•
Czech Republic	•	•
Dominica		
Dominican Republic	•	
Egypt	•	•
El Salvador	•	•
Fiji		•
Gabon	•	•
Gambia[b]	•	•
Ghana	•	•
Grenada		
Guatemala		
Guinea Bissau[b]	•	•
Guyana		
Haiti[b]	•	
Honduras	•	•
Hong Kong		
Hungary	•	•
India		•
Indonesia		
Israel	•	•
Jamaica		•
Kenya	•	•
Korea, Rep. of	•	
Kuwait		
Lesotho[b]	•	•
Macau		
Madagascar[b]	•	•
Malawi[b]	•	•
Malaysia	•	•
Maldives[b]		
Mali[b]	•	•
Malta	•	•
Mauritania[b]	•	•
Mauritius	•	•

GATT membership:	Paris Convention	Berne Convention
Mexico	•	•
Morocco	•	•
Mozambique[b]		
Myanmar[b]		
Namibia		•
Nicaragua		
Niger[b]	•	•
Nigeria	•	•
Pakistan		•
Paraguay		•
Peru		•
Philippines	•	•
Poland	•	•
Qatar		
Romania	•	•
Rwanda[b]	•	•
Saint Kitts and Nevis		
Saint Lucia		•
St Vincent & Grenadines		
Senegal	•	•
Sierra Leone[b]		
Singapore		
Slovak Republic	•	•
Sri Lanka	•	•
Suriname	•	•
Swaziland	•	
Tanzania		
Thailand		•
Togo[b]	•	•
Trinidad and Tobago	•	•
Tunisia	•	•
Turkey	•	•
Uganda[b]	•	
United Arab Emirates		
Uruguay	•	•
Venezuela		•
Yugoslavia	•	•
Zaire[b]	•	•
Zambia[b]	•	•
Zimbabwe	•	•
Developed countries		
Australia	•	•
Austria	•	•
Belgium	•	•

GATT membership:	Paris Convention	Berne Convention
Canada	•	•
Denmark	•	•
Finland	•	•
France	•	•
Germany	•	•
Greece	•	•
Iceland	•	•
Ireland	•	•
Italy	•	•
Japan	•	•
Liechtenstein	•	•
Luxembourg	•	•
Netherlands	•	•
New Zealand	•	•
Norway	•	•
Portugal	•	•
South Africa	•	•
Spain	•	•
Sweden	•	•
Switzerland	•	•
United Kingdom	•	•
United States	•	•

[a]According to GATT, developing countries include Latin America, Europe (Romania, Turkey, and Yugoslavia), Africa (excluding South Africa), the Middle East, and Asia (including Oceanic) less the OECD members therein. Economies in transition encompass the Czech Republic, Hungary, Poland, and the Slovak Republic.
[b]Least-developed countries according to the United Nations.
Note: this list is as of April 15, 1994.
Sources: GATT 1994b; WIPO 1994; and UNCTAD 1993.

Appendix B The economics of IPRs

The conventional economic rationale for the protection of IPRs is often framed in terms of Arrow's (1962) seminal work on the incomplete appropriability of knowledge (Primo Braga 1990a and Besen and Raskind 1991 discuss the relevant literature). IPRs can be understood as second-best solutions to the problems created by the "public good" nature of knowledge. To the extent that they enhance "appropriability," they are expected to foster investment in R&D and knowledge creation. But they create a static distortion, because they constrain the current consumption of knowledge by enhancing the market power of titleholders. In short, IPRs involve a "bargain" between the producers of knowledge and society, which is mediated by the government.[30]

This rationale is typically used to explain the economics of patent and copyright laws. With respect to trademarks and industrial designs, the basis for protection is frequently framed in terms of incentives for investments in reputation (quality) rather than innovation *per se*. Trade secrets, in turn, are rationalized as a necessary supplement to the patent system. Their main positive role is to foster innovations that do not comply with the strict requirements for the patentability of products and processes.

The long-term trend for IPR protection in industrial economies has clearly been in the direction of stronger rights. As pointed out by Winter (1989), however, there is no clear theoretical presumption that a movement towards stronger standards of protection will be always welfare enhancing. Patent races may lead to overinvestment in R&D. Private returns may exceed social returns as protection increases and as inventors appropriate additional gains in assets that are complementary to the innovation. And the increase in static distortions in the consumption of knowledge (due to monopolistic practices) may overcome the dynamic benefits of additional R&D.

The caveats that apply to the desirability of increasingly stronger IPR protection at the national level gain an important additional dimension when the analysis moves to the international level. If the existing (or potential) titleholders are predominantly foreigners, the strengthening of protection raises the possibility of an international rent transfer.[31] The net welfare impact of the reform on a country will depend on how local consumers and producers are affected, as well as on its implications for the levels (and composition) of R&D worldwide.

Many different scenarios can be modeled to capture these effects.[32] If a country is small (that is, its IPR regime does not affect R&D worldwide) and if it has limited production and innovation capabilities, higher standards of protection are likely to be welfare improving as long as they permit access to products that would not be available otherwise. If, however, the country has some production capabilities (a proxy for its capacity to imitate) but limited innovative capacity (as measured by its R&D activities, for example), higher standards of protection are likely to have a negative welfare impact, as local producers are displaced, prices increase, and a rent transfer from local consumers and producers to foreign titleholders ensues. Finally, if the small country has both well-developed production and innovative capabilities (as with the newly industrial economies of East Asia), the result will be indeterminate, depending on the elasticity of the supply of domestic innovations for IPR protection.

If the developing country is large enough to affect innovation in the north, then one must also account for the possibility of an increase (or reorganization) of R&D investments worldwide. Under this scenario, higher levels of protection in the south may be a better solution for the world as a whole in a dynamic sense, even if the immediate losses for the south are larger than the benefits for innovators in the north.

This brief review underscores the limitations of normative recommendations about changes in IPR rules at the world level. For the south, the strengthening of IPR protection will have different welfare implications, depending on the characteristics of each country. Generalizations can be made only if strong assumptions are adopted. For example, if one assumes that the supply of innovations in the south is rather inelastic and that IPR regimes are of limited relevance in influencing trade, FDI, and technological transfer, then it follows that the agreement is in essence an exercise in rent transfer (Subramanian 1990). A much more optimistic view of its welfare implications for developing countries, however, can be put together if the opposite assumptions are made (Sherwood 1993).

Notes

Comments and assistance from M. Geuze, D. Gisselquist, K. Maskus, R. Sherwood, and the GATT and WIPO Secretariats are gratefully acknowledged. Pietro Croccioni and Carsten Fink provided research assistance. The views expressed here are the author's own, and they should not be attributed to the World Bank.

1. This section is based on Primo Braga (1989 and 1990a) and UNCTAD and the World Bank (1994).
2. Ross and Wasserman (1993) provide a detailed analysis of the history of the GATT negotiations on IPRs. See also Bradley (1987), Gadbaw and Gwynn (1988), Maskus (1990a) and Primo Braga (1995).
3. Utility models (sometimes called "petty patents") and plant breeders' rights are other instruments of intellectual property protection that are not mentioned explicitly in the agreement. Siebeck (1990) provides details on these instruments.
4. The Berne minimum standards (under Article 2[1])include a broad definition of the works of authorship (including "every production in the literary, scientific and artistic domain, whatever may be the mode or form of expression"), as well as economic and moral rights, and they define the term of protection as the lifetime of the author plus fifty years.
5. Reichman (1989) and US Congress (1992) provide arguments in favor of a *sui generis* approach to protection in these areas.
6. Only forty-five countries were members of the Rome Convention as of January 27, 1994. WIPO (1994) provides details.
7. The agreement, however, has maintained a term of protection of twenty years for the rights of broadcasting organizations.
8. For textile designs, the TRIPS agreement allows protection under either copyright law or industrial design law. Reichman (1993) argues "that countries that currently subject industrial designs to the full patent protection model of protection, including the test of non-obviousness, may have to enact less stringent, sui generis regimes" to comply with the agreement.
9. As Correa (1994b) points out, it is not clear why an agreement that pursues global standards for IPR protection did not specify the plant breeders' rights regime promoted by the 1991 Act of the UPOV Convention as the appropriate *sui generis* model.
10. The exhaustion of IPRs means that "after the first distribution of a product (for which a patent, trade mark, or copyright protection is available), a title-holder

will no longer be entitled to make use of his/her exclusive rights to prevent further distribution of the protected product in the domestic market" (Yusuf and Von Hase 1992). The concept, however, is typically applied on an exclusive territorial basis (or a regional basis by the European Union), rather than in an international context.

11. In the United States, for example, the Semiconductor Chip Protection Act of 1984 provides a ten-year term of protection for mask works, codifies the practice of reverse engineering, and introduces remedies similar to those available under copyright law (Goldberg 1993).

12. NAFTA was the first trade agreement to refer explicitly to trade secrets. Primo Braga (1993a) and Hufbauer and Schott (1993) provide additional details on the NAFTA provisions on IPRs.

13. Article 40.2 mentions only three examples of anticompetitive practices explicitly: "exclusive grantback conditions, conditions preventing challenges to validity and coercive package licensing" (GATT 1994a). It is worth noting that the draft UNCTAD's Code of Conduct covers a much broader list of measures, including patent pool and cross-licensing agreements.

14. Article 64 determines that subparagraphs "1(b) and 1(c) of Article XXIII of GATT 1994 shall not apply to the settlement of disputes under this Agreement for a period of five years from the date of entry into force of the WTO Agreement" (GATT 1994a).

15. As illustrated in figure 12.1, the WTO agreement entered into force on January 1, 1995. The date of application for the TRIPS provisions is January 1, 1996.

16. An economy in transition can take this longer transitional period only if it is in the process of reforming of its intellectual property regime and is "facing special problems in the preparation and implementation of intellectual property laws and regulations" (GATT 1994a).

17. Note that Article 65.5 bars changes that would lead to a "lesser degree of consistency with the provisions" during the transitional periods (GATT 1994a). In other words, countries that have recently reformed their IPR regimes cannot reverse this process in order to qualify for the transitional period under TRIPS (Correa 1994b).

18. During the negotiations, many analysts speculated that a "code" approach – with limited participation – would be the most likely outcome of the TRIPS negotiations. On this topic see Maskus (1990b) and Primo Braga (1991).

19. All of this, however, is contingent to a patent being filed and granted and marketing approval obtained in another member country after the entry into force of the WTO. See Article 70.9 in GATT (1994a, p. 402).

20. Appendix A lists the GATT membership as of April 15, 1994. After the conclusion of the Uruguay Round, Slovenia acceded in October 1994, and by the end of 1994 accession working parties for twenty-one countries (including the Russian Federation) were active. Another working party was also analyzing the status of China's membership.

21. The Czech Republic, Israel, Poland, and the Slovak Republic were UPOV members as of April 1994. Mexico is expected to introduce plant breeders'

rights and comply with UPOV obligations not later than two years after the signature of NAFTA (NAFTA 1992, Annex 1701.3).

22. The fact that patents are provided for a limited term, for example, suggests the limits of the "natural rights" approach. David (1993) provides a detailed discussion of the evolution of IPR regimes around the world. See also Primo Braga (1990b, 1991, 1993b).

23. Rather than using membership in IPR conventions as an indicator of the overall strength of an IPR regime, Rapp and Rozek compiled an index of the IPR strength based on the strength of patent protection at the country level. A zero value is assigned to countries without patent protection and a maximum value of five is assigned to those that meet or exceed minimum standards described in US Chamber of Commerce (1987). Following Maskus and Penubarti (1994), the analysis described here adopted instruments-variable approach to correct for potential measurement errors and endogeneity problems in the Rapp and Rozek index. Estimates based on the "corrected" index do not differ, however, from those based on the "raw" index. Econometric results are available on request.

24. See, for example, Nogues (1993), Subramanian (1994), and Maskus and Konan (1994).

25. In all these exercises, information on market size and the relative importance of patented, copied, and nonpatented drugs relies on Gadbaw and Richards (1988).

26. Note that the least-developed countries can postpone the adjustment even further, as discussed earlier.

27. The net economic impact of combating counterfeiting of trademarked goods is ambiguous. But most analysts agree that deceptive counterfeiting can be particularly harmful to consumer interests. See Grossman and Shapiro (1988a and 1988b).

28. It is implicitly assumed that there is underinvestment in R&D at the global level and that stronger protection of IPRs fosters investment in R&D. This assumption does not necessarily imply that stronger IPR protection will enhance economic welfare, as pointed out by Helpman (1993).

29. See, for example, IFAC-3 (1994) for a summary of the perceptions of US knowledge-intensive industries about the TRIPS agreement.

30. Machlup (1958) provides an early discussion of the terms of this bargain – specifically, see the "monopoly profit incentive" and the "exchange for secrets" theses.

31. Available statistics suggest that this description in the situation of developing countries is valid. By 1982, for example, 175,000 (87.5 percent) of the 200,000 patents awarded by developing countries were awarded to foreign patentees. For the major developing countries, the share was around 79 percent. See WIPO (1983) and Subramanian (1994).

32. For formal models, see Berkowitz and Kotowitz (1982), Chin and Grossman (1988), Diwan and Rodrik (1990), and Deardorff (1992). For a discussion of the optimal level of protection in the south, see Frischtak (1993).

References

Barton, J. H., and W. E. Siebeck 1994. *Material Transfer Agreements in Genetic Resources Exchange – the Case of the International Agricultural Research Centres.* Issues in Genetic Resources (1). Rome: IPGRI.

Berkowitz, M. K., and Y. Kotowitz 1982. "Patents Policy in an Open Economy." *Canadian Journal of Economics* 15(1): 1–17.

Besen, S. M., and L. J. Raskind 1991. "An Introduction to the Law and Economics of Intellectual Property." *Journal of Economic Perspectives* 5(1): 3–27.

Bradley, A. J. 1987. "Intellectual Property Rights, Investment, and Trade in Services in the Uruguay Round: Laying the Foundations." *Standard Journal of International Law* 23: 57–87.

Chin, J. C., and G. M. Grossman 1988. "Intellectual Property Rights and North–South Trade." Research Working Paper Series (2769). Cambridge, Mass.: National Bureau of Economic Research.

Correa, C. M. 1994a. "TRIPs Agreement: Copyright and Related Rights." *International Review of Industrial Property and Copyright Law* (4): 543–52.

1994b. The GATT Agreement on Trade-Related Aspects of Intellectual Property Rights: New Standards for Patent Protection." *EIPR* 8: 327–35.

David, P. 1993. "Intellectual Property Institutions and the Panda's Thumb: Patents, Copyrights, and Trade Secrets in Economic Theory and History." In M. Wallerstein, M. E. Mogee, and R. A. Schoen, eds., *Global Dimensions of Intellectual Property Rights in Science and Technology.* Washington, DC: National Academy Press.

Deardorff, A. V. 1992. "Welfare Effects of Global Patent Protection." *Economica* 59: 35–51.

Diwan, I., and D. Rodrik 1990. "Patents, Appropriate Technology and North–South Trade." *Journal of International Economics* 30: 27–47.

Dratler, J. 1991. *Intellectual Property Law: Commercial, Creative and Industrial Property.* New York: Law Journal and Seminars Press.

Ferrantino, M. J. 1993. "The Effect of Intellectual Property Rights on International Trade and Investment." *Weltwirtschaftliches Archiv* 129: 300–31.

Frischtak, C. R. 1989. "The Protection of Intellectual Property Rights and Industrial Technological Development in Brazil." World Bank Industry Series Paper 13. Washington, DC: World Bank.

1993. "Harmonization Versus Differentiation in Intellectual Property Right Regimes." In M. Wallerstein, M. E. Mogee, and R. A. Schoen, eds., *Global Dimensions of Intellectual Property Rights in Science and Technology.* Washington, DC: National Academy Press.

Gadbaw, R. M., and R. E. Gwynn 1988. "Intellectual Property Rights in the New GATT Round." In Gadbaw and Richards 1988.

Gadbaw, R. M. and T. Richards 1988. *Intellectual Property Rights: Global Consensus, Global Conflict?* Boulder, Colo.: Westview Press.

GATT 1994a. *Final Act Embodying the Results of the Uruguay Round of Multilateral Negotiations.* Geneva: GATT Secretariat.

1994b. *The Results of the Uruguay Round of Multilateral Trade Negotiations.* Geneva: GATT Secretariat.

Goldberg, M. D. 1993. "Semiconductor Chip Protection as a Case Study." In M. Wallerstein, M. E. Mogee, and R. A. Schoen, eds., *Global Dimensions of Intellectual Property Rights in Science and Technology.* Washington, DC: National Academy Press.

Gould, D. and W. Bruben 1994. "The Role of Intellectual Property Rights in Economic Growth." Research Department Working Paper 94–09. Dallas, Tex.: Federal Reserve Bank of Dallas.

Grossman, G. M., and C. Shapiro 1988a. "Counterfeit-Product Trade." *American Economic Review* 78: 59–75.

1988b. "Foreign Counterfeiting of Status Goods." *Quarterly Journal of Economics* 103: 79–100.

Helpman, E. 1993. "Innovation, Imitation, and Intellectual Property Rights." *Econometrica* 61: 1247–80.

Hoekman, B. 1994. "Services and Intellectual Property Rights." In S. Collins and B. Bosworth, eds., *The New GATT Implications for the United States.* Washington, DC: Brookings Institution.

Hufbauer, G. C., and J. Schott 1993. *NAFTA: An Assessment*, Washington, DC: Institute for International Economics.

IFAC-3 1994. "Committee Report on Trade-Related Aspects of Intellectual Property Rights Including Trade in Counterfeit Goods (TRIPs)." Washington, DC: Industry Functional Advisory Committee.

IIPA 1994. *1994 Special 310 Recommendations and Estimated Trade Losses.* Washington, DC: International Intellectual Property Alliance.

Jackson, J. 1994. "The World Trade Organization, Dispute Settlement, and Codes of Conduct." In S. Collins and B. Bosworth, eds., *The New GATT Implications for the United States.* Washington, DC: Brookings Institution.

Kastenmeier, R. W., and D. Beier 1989. "International Trade and Intellectual Property: Promise, Risks, and Reality." *Vanderbilt Journal of Transnational Law* 22(2): 285–307.

Machlup, F. 1958. "An Economic Review of the Patent System." Subcommittee on Patents, Trademarks and Copyrights, Committee on the Judiciary, US Senate Study 15. Washington, DC: US Government Printing Office.

Mansfield, E. 1994. "Intellectual Property Protection, Foreign Direct Investment, and Technology Transfer." IFC Discussion Paper 19. Washington, DC: World Bank.

Mansfield, E., M. Schwarz, and S. Wagner 1981. "Imitation Costs and Patents: An Empirical Study." *The Economic Journal* December: 907–18.

Maskus, K. E. 1990a. "Normative Concerns in the International Protection of Intellectual Property Rights." *The World Economy* 13: 387–409.

1990b. "Intellectual Property." In J. Schott, ed., *Completing the Uruguay Round: A Results-Oriented Approach to the GATT Trade Negotiations.* Washington, DC: Institute for International Economics.

1994. "Uruguay Round Agreement on Intellectual Property Rights." Paper presented at the seminar "Uruguay Round Agreements from an Asia-Pacific Perspective," George Washington University, Washington, DC.

Maskus, K. E., and D. Eby Konan 1994. "Trade-Related Intellectual Property Rights: Issues and Exploratory Results." In A. Deardorff and R. Stern, eds., *Analytical and Negotiating Issues in the Global Trading System*. Ann Arbor: University of Michigan Press.

Maskus, K. E., and M. Penubarti 1994. "How Trade-Related Are Intellectual Property Rights?" Manuscript, University of Colorado.

NAFTA 1992. Vols. I and II. Washington, DC: US Government Printing Office.

Nogues, J. J. 1993. "Social Costs and Benefits of Introducing Patent Protection for Pharmaceutical Drugs in Developing Countries." *The Developing Economies* 31(1): 24–53.

OECD 1989. "Economic Arguments for Protecting Intellectual Property Rights Effectively." TC/WP(88) 70. Paris: OECD.

Primo Braga, C. A. 1989. "The Economics of Intellectual Property Rights and the GATT: A View from the South." *Vanderbilt Journal of Transnational Law* 20: 243–64.

1990a. "Guidance from Economic Theory." In Siebeck 1990.

1990b. "The Developing Country Case for and against Intellectual Property Protection." In Siebeck 1990.

1991. "The North–South Debate on Intellectual Property Rights." In M. G. Smith, ed., *Global Rivalry & Intellectual Property*. Halifax, N. S., Institute for Research on Public Policy.

1993a. "Intellectual Property Rights in NAFTA: Implications for International Trade." In A. R. Riggs and T. Velk, eds., *Beyond NAFTA*. Vancouver: Fraser Institute.

1993b. "The Newly Industrializing Economies." In M. Wallerstein, M. E. Mogee, and R. A. Schoen, eds., *Global Dimensions of Intellectual Property Rights in Science and Technology*. Washington, DC: National Academy Press.

1995. "Trade-Related Intellectual Property Issues: The Uruguay Round Agreement and its Economic Implications." In W. Martin and L. A. Winters, eds., *The Uruguay Round and the Developing Economies*. World Bank Discussion Paper 307. Washington, DC: World Bank.

Primo Braga, C. A., and A. Yeats 1994. "Minilateral and Managed Trade in the Post-Uruguay Round World." *Minnesota Journal of Global Trade* 3(2): 231–58.

Rapp, R., and R. Rozek 1990. "Benefits and Costs of Intellectual Property Protection in Developing Countries." Working Paper 3. Washington, DC: National Economic Research Associates, Inc.

Reichman, J. H. 1989. "Computer Programs as Applied Scientific Know-How: Implications of Copyright protection for Commercialized University Research." *Vanderbilt Law Review* 42(3): 639–723.

1993. *Implications of the Draft Trips Agreement for Developing Countries as Competitors in an Integrated World Market*. Discussion Paper 73. Geneva: UNCTAD.

Rodrik, D. 1994. "Comments." In A. Deardoff and R. Stern, eds., *Analytical and Negotiating Issues in the Uruguay Round*. Ann Arbor: University of Michigan Press.

Ross, J. C., and J. A. Wasserman 1993. *Trade-Related Aspects of Intellectual Property Rights*. Deventer: Kluwer Law and Taxation Publishers.

Sherwood, R. M. 1990. *Intellectual Property and Economic Development*. Boulder, Colo.: Westview Press.

_____ 1993. "Why a Uniform Intellectual Property System Makes Sense for the World." In M. Wallerstein, M. E., Mogee, and R. A. Schoen, eds., *Global Dimensions of Intellectual Property Rights in Science and Technology*. Washington, DC: National Academy Press.

_____ 1995. "Compulsory Licensing under the TRIPs Agreement." *Latin American Law & Business Report* 3(1): 25–29.

Siebeck, W. E., ed. 1990. *Strengthening Protection of Intellectual Property in Developing Countries: A Survey of the Literature*. Washington, DC: World Bank.

Stern, R. 1987. "Intellectual Property." In M. Finger and J. Olechowski, eds., *The Uruguay Round: A Handbook on the Multilateral Trade Negotiations*. Washington, DC: World Bank.

Subramanian, A. 1990. "TRIPs and the Paradigm of the GATT: A Tropical, Temperate View." *The World Economy* 13(4): 509–21.

_____ 1994. "Putting Some Numbers on the TRIPs Pharmaceutical Debate." *International Journal of Technology Management* 10: 1–17.

Taylor, M. S. 1993. "Trips, Trade, and Technology Transfer." *Canadian Journal of Economics* 16(2): 625–37.

UNCTAD 1994. *The Outcome of the Uruguay Round: An Initial Assessment Supporting*. Geneva: UNCTAD.

_____ 1993. *Handbook of International Trade and Development Statistics*. New York: United Nations.

UNCTAD and the World Bank 1994. *Liberalizing International Transactions in Services: A Handbook*. Geneva: United Nations.

United Nations 1993. *Intellectual Property Rights and Foreign Direct Investment*. New York: United Nations Transnational Corporations and Management Division.

UPOV 1993. "Overview of Plant Variety Protection in the World." Presented at the seminar "Regional Seminar on the Nature of and the Nationale for the Protection of Plant Varieties under the UPOV Convention." Geneva: UPOV.

US Chamber of Commerce 1987. *Guidelines for Standards for the Protection and Enforcement of Intellectual Property Rights*. Washington, DC: US Chamber of Commerce.

US Congress 1992. Office of Technology Assessment. *Finding a Balance: Computer Software, Intellectual Property, and the Challenge of Technological Change*. OTA-TCA-527. Washington, DC: US Government Printing Office.

US Department of Commerce 1994. *U.S. Direct Investment Abroad Operations of*

U.S. Parent Companies and their Foreign Affiliates Preliminary 1992 Estimates.
Washington, DC: US Department of Commerce.
US International Trade Commission 1988. *Foreign Protection of Intellectual Property Rights and the Effect on U.S. Industry and Trade.* Washington, DC: US International Trade Commission.
Wijk, Jeroen van, Joel I. Cohen, and John Komen 1993. "Intellectual Property Rights for Agricultural Biotechnology: Options and Implications for Developing Countries." *International Service for National Agricultural Research (ISNAR)* report no. 3. The Hague.
Winter, S. 1989. "Patents in Complex Contexts: Incentives and Effectiveness." In V. Weil and J. Snapper, eds., *Owning Scientific and Technical Information.* New Brunswick, N.J.: Rutgers University Press.
WIPO 1983. *100 Years of Industrial Property Statistics.* Geneva: WIPO.
   1990a. *Consultative Meeting of Developing Countries on the Harmonization of Patent Laws.* HL/CM/INF/1 Rev. Geneva: WIPO.
   1990b. *Consultative Meeting of Developing Countries on the Harmonization of Patent Laws.* HL/CM/INF/2. Geneva: WIPO.
   1994. *World Intellectual Property Organization General Information.* Geneva: WIPO.
Yusuf, A. A., and A. M. Von Hase 1992. "Intellectual Property Protection and International Trade." *World Competition Law and Economics Review* 16(1): 115–31.

13 Beyond TRIMs: a case for multilateral action on investment rules and competition policy?

Patrick Low and Arvind Subramanian

Article 9 of the Uruguay Round agreement on TRIMs calls for a review of the agreement not later than five years after its entry into force. In addition to assessing its operation, the review will consider whether the agreement "should be complemented with provisions on investment policy and competition policy." What did the TRIMs agreement achieve? Can a case be made for extending WTO rules into the domains of investment policy and competition policy?

TRIMs are measures employed usually, but not exclusively, by developing countries to compel or induce multinational enterprises to meet certain yardsticks of performance (box 13.1). They tend to be concentrated in specific industries: automotive, chemical and petrochemical, and computer/informatics. At the time of the Punta del Este Declaration, TRIMs was seen as one of the new issues. Along with services and TRIPS, TRIMs was to be part of a trinity of issues underpinning a revised GATT that would respond to the changing conditions of international competition in the world. The United States, the most insistent *demandeur*, wanted a broad remit for the TRIMs negotiations, including "pure" investment issues such as rights of establishment, national treatment, and investment incentives. The original negotiating agenda as proposed by the United States would have created a "GATT for investment." In the face of opposition from developing countries, which sought to preserve their sovereignty over investment policy, the United States conceded, for the sake of keeping TRIPS and services on the agenda, to a narrow mandate for the TRIMs negotiations. Thus from the outset it was clear that pure investment issues would not be addressed in the Uruguay Round.

The TRIMs negotiations produced a modest outcome, more modest than interested governments had hoped.[1] Despite the limited result, TRIMs discussions raised broad questions concerning multilateral disciplines on investment and competition, questions that WTO members have committed themselves to examining further. The possibility of establishing a "GATT for investment" has been debated for many years,[2] but not until TRIMs negotiations did the notion of multilateral disciplines on investment gain significant momentum. Several factors appear to have provoked a reappraisal of the question. Foreign "direct" investment flows have increased dramatically over the last decade or so, contributing to the widely observed though not entirely new phenomenon of globalization (tables 13.1 and 13.2).[3] The intensification of economic links among countries has many causes, including technological advances and changes in corporate strategy. At the same time, new policies involving deregulation, privatization, and liberalization have created an atmosphere more favorable to globalized economic activity. The Uruguay Round negotiations are significant not so much for the results achieved in the TRIMs negotiations but because, following the Uruguay Round, it was no longer anathema to contemplate multilateral disciplines in the investment area.

The effect of the TRIMs discussion on competition policy is less definite. This is in part because competition policy encompasses a vast range of economic activity. In principle, any government or private sector action that undermines market contestability could be the subject of pro-competition policies. Such policies can be shaped to alter economic structures (demonopolization) or asset ownership (privatization) in an effort to foster freer markets. However, in the TRIMs negotiations, the main consideration with respect to competition was the monopolistic behavior of multinational enterprises. Developing countries in particular argued that if they liberalized their investment regimes by accepting constraints on TRIMs, they would be left with no policy to curtail multinationals' abuse of market power. The proponents of controls on TRIMs argued that TRIMs constitute government interference that impedes competition.

The Uruguay Round results

The Uruguay Round TRIMs agreement essentially reaffirms existing GATT disciplines relating to national treatment (Article III) and the prohibition of quantitative restrictions (Article XI). Two TRIMs – local-content and trade-balancing requirements – are identified as being inconsistent with Article III, while three TRIMs – trade-balancing restrictions, foreign-exchange-balancing restrictions, and domestic-sales requirements – are identified as quantitative restrictions.[4] The agreement requires the notification to the WTO, within ninety days of the WTO's entry into force, of any TRIMs that are inconsistent with its rules.

A timetable is included for phasing out inconsistent TRIMs. Industrial, developing, and least-developed countries are required to phase out such TRIMs within two, five, and seven years, respectively. Transition periods

Table 13.1 *Inflows and outflows of FDI, 1981–93*

Country	Billions of dollars					Share in total (percentage)				
	Annual average					Annual average				
	1981–85	1986–90	1991	1992	1993[a]	1981–85	1986–90	1991	1992	1993[a]
Developed countries										
Inflows	37	130	121	102	109	74	84	74	65	56
Outflows	47	163	185	162	181	98	96	96	95	—
Developing countries										
Inflows	13	25	39	51	80	26	16	24	32	41
Outflows	1	6	7	9	14	2	4	4	5	—
Central and Eastern Europe[b]										
Inflows	0.02	0.1	2	4	5	0.04	0.1	1	3	3
Outflows	0.004	0.02	0.01	0.03	—	0.01	0.01	0.005	0.02	—
All countries										
Inflows	50	155	162	158	194	100	100	100	100	100
Outflows	48	168	192	171	195	100	100	100	100	—

[a]Based on preliminary estimates.

[b]Former Yugoslavia is included in developing countries.

Note: The levels of worldwide inward and outward FDI flows and stocks should balance; however, in practice, they do not. The causes of the discrepancy include differences between countries in the definition and valuation of the FDI; the treatment of unremitted branch profits in inward and outward direct investment; treatment of unrealized capital gains and losses; the recording of transactions of "offshore" enterprises; the recording of reinvested earnings in inward and outward direct investment; the treatment of real estate and construction investment; and the share-in-equity threshold in inward and outward direct investment.
Source: World Investment Report, UNCTAD 1994.

Table 13.2 *Macroeconomic indicators and FDI inflows in developing countries, 1986–93 (percent)*

Item	Total	Africa[a]	Latin America and the Caribbean	Western Asia[b]	South, East and South-east Asia	World
Growth rate of FDI inflows						
1986–90	21.0	7.4	15.7	21.4	35.9	32.6
(average)						
1991	24.3	18.3	73.6	−1.9	4.9	−21.3
1992	18.7	12.5	−2.6	−50.0	36.5	−6.0
1993	57.0	—	—	—	—	23.0
Growth rate of GDP[c]						
1986–90	4.7	2.5	2.0	3.4	7.1	3.6
(average)						
1991	4.5	1.6	3.3	2.4	6.1	0.6
1992	5.8	0.4	2.5	7.8	7.8	1.7
1993[d]	6.1	1.6	3.4	3.4	8.7	2.2
Export growth rate[e]						
1986–90	11.4	3.7	5.0	7.6	13.1	6.1
(average)						
1991	8.1	1.9	4.7	3.1	11.9	2.4
1992	9.5	2.1	8.5	8.4	11.2	4.6
1993	9.4	0.1	4.1	6.9	12.7	3.0

[a]Egypt and Libyan Arab Jamahiriya are included in Western Asia except for the item on FDI.
[b]Includes Cyprus, Malta, and Turkey, except for the item on FDI.
[c]Data in this block are not weighted averages.
[d]Projection by the International Monetary Fund.
[e]Volume of merchandise exports.
Source: World Investment Report, UNCTAD 1994.

will be extended for developing and least-developed countries if they encounter difficulty. In accordance with a standstill clause, existing TRIMs are not to be intensified during the transition period. A special provision permits the imposition of TRIMs on new enterprises during the transition period if that is deemed necessary in order not to disadvantage established enterprises already subject to TRIMs. A TRIMs committee will be established to monitor the implementation of the TRIMs agreement.

Box 13.1 *A list of TRIMs*

- *Local-content requirements* mandate that a certain amount of local input be used in production.
- *Trade-balancing requirements* mandate that imports be a certain proportion of exports.
- *Foreign-exchange balancing requirements* mandate that the availability of foreign exchange for imports be a certain proportion of exports and other foreign exchange brought in by a firm.
- *Manufacturing requirements* mandate that certain products be manufactured locally.
- *Export-performance requirements* mandate that a certain share of output be exported.
- *Product-mandating requirements* mandate that an investor supply certain markets with a designated product manufactured from a specified facility or operation. Alternatively, the measures can be implemented by requiring a commitment to assign to the affiliated company the exclusive right to export specified products worldwide or to certain regional markets. This condition has the effect of preempting exports from other countries.
- *Exchange restrictions* limit access to foreign exchange and hence restrict imports.
- *Domestic-sales requirements* mandate that a company sell a certain proportion of output locally, which amounts to a restriction against exportation.
- *Manufacturing limitations* prevent companies from manufacturing certain products or product lines in the host country.
- *Technology-transfer requirements* mandate that specified technologies be transferred on noncommercial terms and/or that specific levels and types of research and development be conducted locally.
- *Licensing requirements* mandate that the investor license technologies similiar or unrelated to those being used in the host country by the foreign firm to host country firms.
- *Remittance restrictions* limit the right of a foreign investor to repatriate returns from an investment.
- *Local-equity requirements* specify that no more than a certain percentage of a firm's equity may be held by local investors.

The economics of TRIMs

In some second-best situations, a local-content requirement can be welfare enhancing for a country. But under standard assumptions of perfect competition in the final- and intermediate-goods markets, and in the absence of other government intervention, such a requirement is unambiguously welfare deteriorating (Grossman 1981). It acts like a tariff on the intermediate good and raises the effective price paid by the final good producer.[5] The effective price is the weighted average of the price of imported and domestically produced components, where weights are those shares of the component that must be of foreign or local origin. Local-content requirements have been used by developing countries to promote local-component industries (table 13.3). As for trade-balancing and foreign-exchange-balancing requirements, they have the effect of restraining imports and act like quantitative restrictions.

TRIMs have traditionally been seen as a tool for promoting development objectives such as technology transfer, industrialization, and export expansion (Maskus and Eby 1990). Another justification for their deployment has been to curtail the monopolistic power of multinational enterprises. In either guise, a TRIM is the *quid pro quo* extracted for the right to invest or for some other advantage, such as a subsidy. As noted above, a formal case can be made, under specified conditions, that a TRIM is welfare enhancing,[6] and some policy commentators have recommended TRIMs on these grounds (Balasubramanyam 1991). Others have argued that using TRIMs for this purpose may be detrimental in the long run – the outcome is fraught with uncertainty – and is liable to encourage wasteful rent-seeking behavior.

A global measure of the welfare gains from the Uruguay Round elimination of local-content requirements would be difficult to calculate. One would need disaggregated firm-specific data on the exact specification of the TRIM, data on the relevant sector and its technological characteristics, and world prices of appropriate inputs and outputs.[7] Nonetheless, it is generally clear that several developing countries will be affected by the elimination of local-content requirements, for between 1991 and 1994 nineteen developing countries (out of twenty-seven for which the GATT's TPRM reports were analyzed) maintained such requirements in various sectors of their economies.[8]

Moreover, studies show that the actual effect of TRIMs (in the sense of foreign firms perceiving themselves to be constrained by them) is less than the hypothetical or nominal amount of investment covered by TRIMs. Surveys undertaken by the US Department of Commerce in 1977 and 1982 indicated that only 6 percent of all overseas affiliates of US corporations considered themselves to be affected by TRIMs, although a far greater percentage (45 to 60 percent) is nominally affected by TRIMs (Evans and Walsh 1994). In most cases, because they are discretionary and negotiable, TRIMs do not bite. Furthermore, many TRIMs require a course of action that firms would pursue even in their absence.

Table 13.3 *Local-content requirements in developing countries*

	Local-content requirement
Argentina	Automobiles: for passenger cars and small pickups, foreign content allowed in 1991 was 21 percent, increased to 24 percent in 1994; for large pickups and trucks and large transportation vehicles, foreign content allowed in 1991 was 30 percent, increased to 42 percent in 1994.
Bangladesh	Incentives to use locally produced inputs include duty drawback scheme at flat rates and system of back-to-back letters of credit for exporters in garment industry, restricting foreign-exchange entitlements to 70 percent of export revenue. Value-added in Bangladesh shall not be less than 30 percent for eligibility for this facility.
Bolivia	None.
Brazil	Official credit and government procurement contain 60 percent requirement.
Chile	Requirements for motor vehicles (e.g., completely knocked-down kits have a 13 percent requirement).
Colombia	None.
Egypt	According to negative list valid to end of 1993, unless requirement of 40 percent was met, investment in audio/video appliances for domestic use, passenger cars, and pharmaceuticals was banned. Unless local content was at least 60 percent, investment in specific household appliances, trucks and buses, certain agricultural machinery, motorcycles, bicycles, diesel engines, and electric motors was banned. Assembling industries aided by customs-duty reductions on imported inputs are tied to local content.
Ghana	In certain investment areas, enterprises utilizing domestic raw materials and labor over imported machinery are granted an income tax rebate that varies by sector. Mining companies required to give preference to locally made products.
Hong Kong	None.
Hungary	None.
India	Phased manufacturing program aimed at replacing inputs with domestic substitutes through industrial licensing and concessional tariff-rate incentives was abolished for new projects in 1991. Import-duty concessions for automobile manufactures meeting program requirements were terminated in 1993. Several duty-exemption schemes, including for firms in export-processing zones, have domestic value-added requirements.
Indonesia	Numerous, detailed, and discretionary local-content schemes exist, especially in machinery, engineering, metal, and transport equipment.
Kenya	No formal requirements, though the government considers job creation and local-sourcing targets in deciding whether to approve foreign investments.

Table 13.3 (*cont.*)

	Local-content requirement
Korea	A localization program to encourage substitution of domestic for imported goods has existed since 1986.
Malaysia	Local content is a factor in determining investment incentives under Pioneer Status and Investment Tax Allowance Program. There is also a local-content program for motor vehicles.
Mexico	There is a 36 percent requirement for small cars and a 40 percent requirement for larger cars, trucks, and buses.
Nigeria	Certain food and drink industries have requirements ranging from 70 to 80 percent. Chemicals have a 60 percent requirement and petrochemicals and machine tools have a 50 percent requirement.
Peru	Requirements apply to use of milk powder and anhydrous milk fat in dairy processing. Condensed-milk producers had to purchase 70 percent of fresh milk domestically until end of 1993, after which it increased to 80 percent. By 1994 it was 90 percent, by 1995, 100 percent.
Philippines	No requirements. However, participants in the Car Development Program must reach local content of at least 40 percent.
Poland	None.
Romania	None.
Senegal	Certain fiscal exemptions require 65 percent domestic intermediate inputs or that the value of imported components not exceed 35 percent of total cost.
Singapore	None.
South Africa	Local content encouraged by levying excise taxes in inverse proportion to the amount of domestic value added. Local input is one to which at least 25 percent of value has been added locally.
Thailand	Requirements exist for tea leaf and dust, silk and silk yarn, pasteurized and skim milk, automobiles, motorcycles, and various manufactured goods. These may change from time to time, and they may at times be revoked if specified standards in an export market would not be met as a result.
Turkey	None.
Uruguay	A requirement of 30 percent for passenger cars existed until at least 1992. Nature of subsequent regime unclear. There were other requirements for diesel engines and boats. An indirect tax on nonalcoholic fruit beverages differs according to local content.

Source: GATT TPRM reports, various years.

The TRIMs result

It is telling that toward the end of the Uruguay Round, TRIMs were grouped with antidumping, subsidies, and safeguards. The negotiating effort had become part of the drive to strengthen GATT's existing rules and did not venture into new areas. From a strictly legal perspective the TRIMs agreement was retrograde, recognizing that countries were in violation of their GATT obligations and giving them time, perhaps negotiable, to conform. Local-content requirements could presumably have been eliminated more expeditiously if countries using them had been challenged through the regular GATT dispute settlement process, as indeed Canada was, successfully, by the United States.

Nonetheless, several developing countries have been employing TRIMs, confident that they will go unchallenged because the measures involved were inconsequential, or at least not consequential enough to justify the effort by affected countries of going through the GATT dispute settlement procedure. Without the TRIMs agreement, then, many TRIMs may well have been maintained, with affected countries turning a blind eye.[9] The multilateral trading system would probably not have been significantly affected by TRIMs-related derogations. But the fact remains that the TRIMs agreement represents a commitment by GATT members to better observance of the rules.[10] In domestic policy terms, the TRIMs agreement also locks in unilateral liberalization with some guarantee against future reversal. Overall, given that local-content requirements were used predominantly by developing countries, the impact of the TRIMs agreement will be greatest on their trade and industrial policies.[11]

The most serious failure of the TRIMs agreement lies in not addressing export-performance requirements. During negotiations, the attitude of developing countries to such requirements varied. Larger nations such as India resisted attempts to prohibit them because of a continuing desire to extract export performance from foreign enterprises in return for the carrot of entry into their large, protected markets. Smaller, more open developing countries, cognizant of the ability of large countries to divert investment away from them, were correspondingly more willing to eliminate export-performance requirements. Under certain conditions, such requirements can be shown to be welfare-enhancing, but as with local-content requirements this is not the preferred situation (Rodrik 1987). Allowing export-performance requirements, while prohibiting their close cousins, export subsidies (in manufacturing), is an unjustifiable anomaly in GATT's legal framework.

From TRIMs to multilateral investment rules

Nearly ten years have passed since developing countries energetically resisted proposals by the United States for a comprehensive multilateral investment regime. But in the intervening years, significant growth of FDI has accompanied economic liberalization in many countries.[12] The attitude shift underlying widespread liberalization means that for the most part countries now make more effort to attract foreign investment than to constrain investors. As a practical matter, most developing countries have shed much of the suspicion with which they once viewed multinational enterprises. One of the most visible signs of this was the abandonment in 1992 of the long-standing effort, under the auspices of the United Nations, to establish a code of conduct for transnational corporations. The regional agreement on investment disciplines currently being discussed by the APEC nations reflects new thinking among some developing countries about FDI (Low 1994). Policy related to this area, including restrictions on entry and establishment and on ownership and control, performance requirements, and principles of nondiscrimination and national treatment, has grown progressively more liberal during the 1980s and 1990s (UNCTAD 1994).[13]

If it is true that new attitudes prevail about the positive contribution made by foreign investment to the process of development, it may be legitimately asked why this was not reflected in a more far-reaching TRIMs agreement. Positions on TRIMs were largely fixed only in the mid-1980s, and as is often the case, it takes time for new realities to be incorporated in negotiating positions. Moreover, the change in attitude should not be exaggerated. A more market-oriented and positive view of the role of FDI is by no means universally shared. Doubts linger about just how monopolistic the behavior of multinationals might be in some circumstances, and worries about the degree of sovereign control of resources continue to cut political ice. Such concerns are likely to be encountered in all host countries, including industrial ones.[14]

Finally, for reasons that this chapter will not attempt to explain, many countries were unwilling in the Uruguay Round to bank the liberalization that they had undertaken unilaterally in previous years. For example, most developing countries have established tariff bindings on a wide array of products far in excess of applied tariff rates (Harmsen and Subramanian 1994). To the extent that this behavior reflects a considered policy position, a preference for maintaining policy flexibility at home seems to have outweighed any perceived advantage of locking in policy reforms and fortifying them against future erosion by special interest groups.[15] The same attitude may be assumed to inform areas other than tariffs, for instance, investment policy.

The case for multilateral rules on investment

Putting aside speculation about the strength of government support for multilateral disciplines on investment, the case for establishing rules in this area rests first on grounds similar to those invoked for rules on trade.[16] Freer trade and more open investment are both worthy welfare objectives. However, in a world economy where trade policy induces tariff-jumping investment, and investment and trade are treated as substitute means of accessing a market, a second-best argument can be made for restrictive investment policy.

But the relevance of this argument is diminishing if, as some authors assert, it is true that tariff-jumping investments are being superseded by FDI as a complement to rather than a substitute for trade (Julius 1990; Oman 1994). Certainly this would seem consistent with the reductions in tariffs taking place in many countries.[17] That investment complements trade is attributed to the increasing tendency of enterprises producing goods and services to spread their operations around the world.[18] Enterprises both trade and invest as part of coordinated international production and marketing strategies. This situation has led Julius (1994) to make a plea for "modal neutrality,"[19] that is equality of policy treatment regardless of the means by which producers choose to supply a given market – whether through imports, foreign direct investment, temporary presence, or the licensing of domestic producers.

There is a difference between saying that liberal investment and trade are desirable, and saying that a case exists for trying to establish international rules in either or both of these spheres. The fact that much liberalization of investment has occurred without an international legal framework does raise the question of whether one is necessary. Negotiation over rules might open up opportunities for interest groups to demand exceptions, which might actually have the effect of impeding liberalization.

However, there are at least six reasons why international rules might help. First, governments that have liberalized their investment regimes could use a multilateral framework of commitments to make the reversal of such liberalization more difficult. Second, in a world economy so often dominated by mercantilist sentiment, common ground rules and a common purpose may provide a fillip to liberalization. Third, a framework of international commitments with dispute settlement provisions would provide policy continuity and therefore more secure investment opportunities. Fourth, with regionally based agreements among countries continually springing up, an international framework might ensure that agreements do not operate in ways that would fragment the international economy.

The fifth reason relates to the incentive side of investment regimes. While it may be true that TRIMs are losing favor as governments seek to attract investment, governments will likely be more tempted to compete with each other in the incentives they offer investors, a costly game that they may feel forced to play even if basic macroeconomic polices are sound and the political climate is conducive to investment. As with trade subsidies, investment incentives tend to distort the allocation of FDI without necessarily augmenting the total supply of investment or doing so in an economically efficient manner (Dunning 1993). The possibility of controlling this kind of destructive competition among national finance ministries is perhaps one of the strongest arguments for international investment rules.[20] Moreover, poorer countries are likely to be at a disadvantage if investment location is determined primarily by the relative attractiveness of various nations' fiscal incentive packages.

Finally, an obvious imbalance exists in the WTO's legal framework. The organization establishes rules on trade in goods and services and on investment in services, but not on investment in the goods sector. An overarching agreement on investment might well be a natural complement to existing WTO rules. This approach would raise the question of how to treat investment in services, which is already covered in the GATS. For reasons discussed below, the GATS' framework is not the most conducive to liberalization, and the adoption of a broad-based horizontal structure of investment rules within the WTO could provide an opportunity to improve on existing arrangements.[21]

The ingredients of a multilateral investment agreement

The analogy with trade is also relevant when considering the kind of rules that an investment agreement might contain. A good investment agreement would give pride of place to the nondiscrimination (MFN) principle and the national treatment principle.[22] The nondiscrimination principle serves a similar function in both trade and investment regimes, but national treatment is somewhat different. The national treatment principle is the single most important determinant of market access in the investment field. National treatment in an investment regime is the conceptual equivalent of free trade in the cross-border exchange of goods and services.[23] National treatment guarantees the right of foreign investors to establish a presence in the domestic market and to operate under conditions at least as favorable as those facing their domestic counterparts.

Because of the complete openness implied by unrestricted national treatment in an investment regime, investment agreements frequently contain exceptions, reservations, and derogations. These are plentiful in NAFTA, OECD investment agreements, and the Asia Pacific Investment Code. In these instances, however, commitments apply unless a specific stipulation is made to the contrary. This is the so-called negative-list approach to rule making, requiring the establishment of exception lists. The alternative positive-list approach identifies areas or sectors where commitments apply rather than where they do not.

GATS employed the positive-list approach. National treatment, transformed from a principle into negotiating currency, is only a requirement for sectors inscribed in the schedules (positive lists) of the members.[24] Liberalization is likely to be more partial and slower in coming under the positive-list approach, and the entire arrangement is less transparent than those that use negative lists. But a negative list can be disadvantageous if too many exceptions are inscribed, as is often the case.

One reason negative-list exceptions are common is the all-or-nothing nature of unqualified national treatment. If it is granted, the equivalent of free-trade conditions are established, while if it is denied, market access commitments are non-existent. Instruments that could be used to qualify national treatment include procurement, subsidies, and taxes. A precedent for this exists in GATT, where subsidies and procurement practices are explicitly exempted from the national treatment provisions of Article III. If a price-based wedge of this sort were to be introduced, the size of the underlying tax, subsidy, or procurement price advantage could be bound and subject to reduction and eventual elimination in future negotiations. The fundamental question, however, is whether this approach would produce more or less liberalization at the end of the day.

A comprehensive investment regime, like a trade regime, would need to contain a range of supplementary provisions relating to such matters as transparency, investment incentives, taxation of multinational enterprises, performance requirements, investment guarantees, enforcement, and dispute settlement. Given the potential for rules of origin to distort investment decisions, the investment regime would also need to contain clear disciplines on how origin could be determined by national authorities.[25] As in the trade sphere, informal barriers threaten to undermine formal market access commitments. At least one study (Industry Canada 1994) argues that putative liberalization of investment regimes has been significantly curtailed by such barriers.

Informal barriers may be quite specific (and surreptitious), relying on discretionary policymaking authority, or they may emanate from the private sector being shaped by corporate structures and governance. Whether barriers to access are government sponsored or government sanctioned, they are perceived as denying investors the level of reciprocity

---

Box 13.2 *Typical practices and market structures regulated by competition policy*

Horizontal arrangements are those between firms selling the same product or group of products; arrangements include price fixing, output restrictions, and other forms of cartelization.

Vertical arrangements are agreements or relationships between manufacturers and suppliers, and manufacturers and distributors. Regulated vertical arrangements include tying (where a seller requires that, as a condition for buying one product, the purchaser must buy another product as well); exclusive dealing (a seller requires that the buyer restrict purchases only to items sold by the seller); territorial restraints (a seller requires that, as a condition for buying a product for resale, that is, acting as a distributor, the buyer resell the product within specified geographic areas); and resale price maintenance (a seller requires that, as a condition of buying a product for resale, the purchaser agrees to resell the product only at a specified price).

Technology licensing arrangements may include such restrictive practices as patent pooling (three or more parties each grant an interest in an intellectual property right); grantback (the licensee is required to assign inventions made in the course of working the transferred technology back to the licensor); and challenges to validity (the licensee is prevented from contesting the validity of the intellectual property rights or other rights of the licensor).

Mergers and acquisition policies are designed to ensure the contestability of markets by guarding against strong monopolies through the establishment of concentrated ownership.

---

usually demanded under international commitments as well as the true value of commitments undertaken. Informal barriers pose significant obstacles to full liberalization in the investment field (not to mention hampering market access via trade). One approach to dealing with them is through competition policy.

Competition policy

Competition policy is difficult to define precisely because it encompasses a wide range of government policies. Any policy that promotes the contestability of markets – for instance, trade liberalization, more open government-procurement arrangements, control of the protectionist abuse of technical standards, and the reduction of subsidies – can be called a competition policy. Complicating matters, there is competition policy *per se*, a body of economywide laws and regulations governing private producer behavior and the market structure within which producers interact (box 13.2). The central question to consider here is what

Table 13.4 *Competition law in a few developing and emerging market economies*

Region/country	Year passed
Africa	
Côte d'Ivoire	1993
Kenya	1988
South Africa	1979
Ghana, Morocco, Senegal, Zambia, Zimbabwe	(legislative initiatives)
Asia	
India	1969
South Korea	1980
Pakistan	1970
Philippines	(legislative initiatives)
Sri Lanka	1987
Thailand	1979
Latin America/Caribbean	
Argentina	1919, 1946, 1980 (revisions under way)
Brazil	1962 (revisions under way)
Chile	1959, 1973
Colombia	1959, 1992
Ecuador	(legislative initiatives)
Jamaica	1993
Mexico	1993
Venezuela	1991
Post-communist countries	
Belarus	1992
Czech and Slovak Republics	1992
Russia	1991
Other	1990–93

Source: Khemani and Dutz 1995.

kind of competition policies, if any, should be the subject of international rule-making. Almost all industrial countries have competition laws and bureaucracies, and many developing countries are building them (table 13.4). Should international commitments be built on these structures in some way so that competition policy disciplines would stand alongside trade and, perhaps, investment rules?

Three approaches to international rule-making about competition suggest themselves. The most ambitious is to seek international norms encompassing competition policy standards and their national enforcement.[26] These could be established as minimum norms permitting some international diversity or they could be harmonized norms. This course of action has been advocated by some, including the European Union's trade commissioner, Sir Leon Brittan (Brittan 1992). A group of eminent lawyers gave flesh to Sir Leon's proposal by publishing the Draft International Antitrust Code (International Antitrust Code Working Group 1994). Another approach would be to focus exclusively on enforcement. National competition policy standards would not be subject to negotiation, but governments would accept international obligations on the enforcement of existing national laws and regulations (as in NAFTA's side agreement on labor standards) or of newly negotiated minimum or harmonized standards relating to the national enforcement of competition policies. Finally, international competition policy commitments could be more modest and, like services and TRIPS under the WTO (see below), go no further than providing for an exchange of information. In all these scenarios, provisions for consultation and dispute settlement would underpin basic commitments.

Five reasons are commonly cited for favoring the establishment of international rules on competition (Hoekman and Mavroidis 1994a; Subramanian 1994). First, the absence of national antitrust rules or their inadequate enforcement may create trade distortions, for example, restrictions in distribution arrangements that hampered import sales. Second, deficiencies in national antitrust regimes such as the antitrust exemption commonly granted for export cartels may similarly distort trade. Third, multinational enterprises may wield market power across national boundaries and outside the reach of any national jurisdiction. Fourth, antidumping rules, conceptually at odds with national competition policy, amount to an anticompetitive intervention that should be replaced by international competition policy.[27] Finally, government-mandated monopolies such as IPRs may have the effect of conferring excessive market power on firms that might need to be tempered by competition policy.[28] The latter three reasons are of particular relevance to developing countries' perspective on international competition policy.

The case for international competition policy

The notion that international action is required to remedy deficiencies in national competition policies or laws has been most apparent in discussions of the "Japan problem," that is, the perception that private barriers in the form of informal relationships between Japanese companies substitute for government barriers in keeping markets closed to outsiders. The charge that foreign sources of supply (imports and investment) are kept out of the Japanese market by ineffective enforcement can be supported in some instances, for example, bid rigging by domestic firms in the construction sector. In other cases, such as those that raise the vexing issue of whether restrictive practices are merely exclusionary or represent efficient business practice, the arguments are far from conclusive (McMillan 1994). It is noteworthy, however, that many demands on Japan, such as those made by the United States in the Economic Framework talks, relate almost entirely to enforcement rather than standards. This weakens the case for attempting to establish substantive standards for international competition policy, although there may still be a case for international commitments on the national enforcement of competition policy.

Another more general argument about the adverse trade effects of deficient competition policy relates to the actual standards of national laws. National competition policy can create trade conflict and encourage beggar-thy-neighbor practices. Consider exemptions from competition policies that are found in the laws of all industrial countries. Weak or nonexistent competition standards serve as *de facto* industrial policy by giving an advantage to domestic firms in domestic and foreign markets. The economic effect of export-cartel exemptions, for example, is to raise export prices, thereby securing a terms of trade gain for the exporting country and a corresponding loss for the importing country.[29]

Another example is exemptions of cooperative research and development ventures granted, despite their anticompetitive effect, on the grounds that they increase research and development incentives that might otherwise be blunted. Such lenient treatment, analogous to subsidization, can confer benefits on domestic firms relative to foreign rivals.[30] Clearly, such exemptions have the potential to complicate international competition policy. When used to promote the competitiveness of domestic firms exemptions can improve the welfare of individual countries, but this gain occurs at the expense of other countries. When competition policy creates a terms of trade advantage for one country, another inevitably loses.

This is the familiar "prisoner's dilemma" rationale for cooperation: each country may be better off if it employs competition policies to secure a national advantage, but the pursuit of such a strategy by all countries renders them collectively worse off. International cooperation on competition policy would have to involve the prohibition or circumscription of exemptions for export and research and development cartels.[31] How important such an agreement would be in terms of removing trade distortions and increasing welfare is unclear and must be judged empirically, for little information is available on the incidence and effects of such cartels. At least as far as export cartels are concerned – one of the most egregious trade-related anticompetitive phenomena – there is little evidence that they are widespread or cause significant economic harm. In many sectors, the existence of alternative supply sources will likely constrain the power of export cartels to raise prices in international markets. It is incumbent upon those who believe there are significant problems in this area to document them and make the case for an international initiative.

Another argument in favor of developing norms for international competition policy is that trade policy is powerless to assail certain obstacles to market contestibility – for example, where there are international monopolies. Developing countries have been the most active in articulating concerns about the market power of multinational enterprises. In addition to the Code of Conduct for Transnational Corporations, developing countries were instrumental in drawing up the UNCTAD-sponsored Set of Multilaterally Agreed Principles and Rules for the Control of Restrictive Business Practices (1980) and Code of Conduct on the Transfer of Technology (1981).

The concern underlying these efforts also found expression in the TRIMs and TRIPS negotiations. During those discussions it was alleged that the market power of foreign suppliers is wielded to drive down the prices of local-input suppliers. A variant of this argument was that multinationals obtain inputs from home-country suppliers rather than from local producers; local content requirements were advocated as a means of offsetting this restrictive practice.[32] Similarly, export-performance requirements were seen as a way of offsetting export restrictions imposed on subsidiaries of foreign enterprises. In TRIPS, the concern was the effect that government-mandated proprietary rights would have on the price of and access to foreign technology. Once again, the seriousness of this problem has to be judged empirically. A persuasive argument can be made that at least some restrictive multinational-enterprise practices were only sustainable because of protectionist policies in host countries.

An exploration of the TRIPS agreement may be warranted to establish whether the international regime for the generation and diffusion of technology is best from a global as well as from a developing country perspective.[33] While too little intellectual-property protection can retard the incentive to innovate, too much can make markets monopolistic and impede the diffusion of technology. Some research also shows that dominant firms might also create too little technology (Graham 1994). An assessment of the technology regime would need to take into account the joint operation of intellectual-property and competition-policy laws. A more active use of the latter might mitigate an overpowering intellectual-property regime. A better policy would be to secure appropriate adjustments to underlying intellectual-property arrangements, which after all, are also the product of international negotiations.

Another reason trade liberalization may not result in market contestability is the presence of nontradables. This argument only holds up, however, in the presence of barriers to investment. If investment is treated like trade, that is, as an alternative means of accessing a market, the case for international competition policy disappears. Liberalizing investment would be a better way of addressing the problem of nontradables, and if governments are unwilling to do that it is far from certain that they would be willing to sign on to competition policies instead.

Perhaps the strongest reason for supporting international competition policy is that the protectionism inherent in antidumping could be directly addressed through the substitution of this policy with competition rules. With predation the only economically rational grounds for taking antidumping action, the standards domestic firms apply to predation should be extended to foreign firms (Leidy 1994). In view of the growing role that antidumping plays in an increasing number of countries (Low and Yeats 1994), and the difficulty of controlling this tendency through multilateral negotiation, the substitution of antitrust for antidumping would be highly beneficial. There would be expanded export opportunity for developing countries if industrial country antidumping – increasingly directed at developing country exports – were curbed. Furthermore, significant welfare benefits would curb the ominously rising tendency of developing countries to use antidumping measures.

But if conditions are not propitious for controlling antidumping, why would governments agree to such a change? In the European Union, the European Economic Area Agreement, and the Australia–New Zealand Closer Economic Relations Trade Agreement, antidumping provisions have been superseded by antitrust provisions. This did not prove possible in NAFTA, nor in the association agreements between the European Union and certain Eastern European countries. As Hoekman and Mavroidis (1994b) argue, bringing internationalized competition policy to bear in the field of antidumping appears to require a prior commitment to close economic integration. Even then, there is no guarantee that the transformation will be achieved.

Even if it is accepted that substituting antitrust for antidumping is a long-run goal, an important role can still be played now by national competition law. The relationship Mexico established between its antidumping law and its new competition law is an example. Authorities in Mexico are required to examine antidumping petitions and analyze the likely effects of antidumping actions on the competitive conditions in relevant product markets. Similar arrangements appear to be in place in a number of Eastern European countries (Hoekman and Mavroidis 1994c).[34]

The case against international competition policy

The basic case against international competition policy relates to its role as an indirect way of attacking obstacles to market contestability when such obstacles are better addressed at source. This argument would apply with the same force to both the more ambitious (standards and enforcement) and less ambitious (enforcement only) approaches to international competition policy. Trade liberalization is the most obvious example of a pro-competitive policy that would render *per se* competition policy redundant to a large extent (and indeed wide-ranging measures of trade liberalization are the subject of international commitments in the GATT/WTO framework).[35] Internal regulations or government-bestowed privileges may often support anticompetitive outcomes that exert an influence on trade. If such obstacles to competition are to be removed, governments must decide to address the underlying malaise, rather applying the balm of competition policy to attack its effects.[36]

An integral part of the concern to address market contestability problems at source relates to dangers of political capture (Neven, Nuttal, and Seabright 1993). The adoption of *per se* competition policies, whether domestically or internationally, involves bureaucracy-building and the introduction of new regulations. The relationship between regulators and regulated is always a complicated one, at the levels of both design and implementation.[37] The most desirable policy of liberalization entails the withdrawal and dismantling of policy interventions. Competition policy moves in the opposite direction. Before adopting competition policy in the name of promoting market-friendly outcomes, therefore, governments should be sure that less risky alternatives are unavailable.

Apart from the standard case made against international rules on competition policy, the question of whether there is a constituency in the private sector seeking such rules is not clear. Except for the so-called Japan problem, which can be addressed directly, there does not seem to be the same commercial imperative for new rules as there was for rules on services or TRIPS; at least, existing arrangements such as the principle of limited cooperation embodied in bilateral agreements between the United States and the European Union and between the United States and Canada appear adequate to dealing with commercial friction arising from competition policy.

GATT/WTO and international competition policies

In addition to TRIMs, the new GATT contains provisions on competition policy in two agreements: TRIPS and the GATS. TRIPS calls for the control of anticompetitive practices or conditions in contractual licenses relating to the transfer of technology or of other proprietary information. The agreement recognizes the right of countries to regulate such practices through domestic laws. It also provides for consultations and the exchange of information between governments where there is reason to believe that licensing practices or conditions constitute an abuse and have an adverse effect on competition in the relevant market. The GATS agreement contains provisions on consultation and exchange of information similar to those in TRIPS. In addition, it requires countries to ensure that monopoly service providers do not abuse their position in activities outside the scope of their monopoly.

What GATT in its present guise cannot regulate directly or indirectly is anticompetitive behavior emanating exclusively from the private sector, with no government support of any kind. Multilateral rules cannot easily regulate export behavior other than by quantitative limitations.[38] Moreover, the international trading system has never directly tried to influence market structure or concentrated ownership and control within sectors, merely targeting certain kinds of anticompetitive behavior that may result.[39] As far as remedies are concerned, or legal recourse via the multilateral dispute settlement system, a direct challenge to anticompetitive behavior is only possible through an allegation of infringement of a GATT rule. Hoekman and Mavroidis (1994a) construct a case for the invocation of nonviolation complaints where an expected GATT-derived benefit has been allegedly nullified or impaired by another party's actions, even though no GATT provisions have been breached.[40]

Do the shortcomings in the existing GATT/WTO legal framework lead to the conclusion that a new initiative is required to incorporate competition policy rules into the multilateral trading system? If the earlier argument is correct that *per se* competition policy would, in a liberal trade and investment regime, only address a modest set of residually intractable problems, then the case for negotiations is weak, regardless of whether they address substantive norms or only enforcement. At the very least, it is incumbent upon those arguing for international competition policy to demonstrate the empirical strength of their case.[41]

Conclusion

The TRIMs negotiations in the Uruguay Round produced a modest result, largely reaffirming certain preexisting disciplines. The agreement disappointed some countries, which had proposed the establishment of more far-reaching international rules on investment. But TRIMs did raise questions about the desirability of seeking international disciplines in the fields of investment and competition policy. The chapter argues there is a case for a more comprehensive multilateral effort to make rules on investment, but concludes with a faintly qualified "no" on the question of international competition policy rules.

The fundamental case for international investment rules is the same as that for trade rules – they would strengthen opportunity to benefit from the welfare gains of international economic specialization. Increasing internationalization of production and stronger links between investment and trade are boosting the desirability of "modal neutrality," for it would allow investors to make their own choice on how to gain access to a particular market. There may be some merit in the proposition that autonomous investment liberalization and an ever more widespread repudiation of TRIMs is occurring without the interference of international negotiators and bureaucrats, and that therefore governments should leave well enough alone.[42] How does this proposition hold up against the case for international action? There are six main arguments in favor. First, international commitments support national commitments and make them harder to reverse. Second, concerted international action may further encourage liberalization. Third, international rules impart the economic benefit of greater certainty and policy predictability. Fourth, international investment agreements may lower the risk of divergence among regional initiatives that could lead to fragmented and exclusive arrangements. Fifth, international cooperation could control the wasteful practice of governments competing to attract foreign investment through fiscal and other incentives. Sixth, a broad-based investment agreement would fill an illogical gap in existing multilateral rules, while at the same time presenting the opportunity to reconsider the positive-list approach to investment liberalization adopted in GATS. For all of these reasons, a comprehensive multilateral effort to draft rules on investment would seem beneficial.

Trade and investment liberalization – together with domestic deregulation – offers a more convincing and efficient avenue for addressing the great majority of obstacles to market contestability than does *per se* international competition policy. Moreover, because the latter approach would introduce requirements and regulations rather than remove them, it would also carry with it the risks of political capture. Problematic areas of economic behavior that are not reached directly through liberalization would appear at first sight to be of limited empirical significance.

It is clear, however, that international competition policy would improve welfare if it were to replace antidumping policy, which is protectionist in both intent and effect. While the case for this substitution is theoretically persuasive, its political feasibility is uncertain. Experience suggests that a precondition for replacing antidumping with antitrust is economic integration of a high order, which has only been achieved so far among relatively few countries on a regional basis. Pending progress in this regard, national competition policy can still make a worthwhile contribution if it is brought to bear on decisions about whether antidumping duties should be applied. This would be especially useful in small countries, where antidumping duties are most likely to confer a monopolistic advantage on domestic industry.

In sum, the case for negotiations to establish multilateral competition policy norms, whether through harmonization or enforcement only, has yet to be made by its proponents. Bearing in mind the cost in efficiency of an indirect approach to facilitating market contestability, and the risks of political capture implicit in the establishment of new rules, proponents need to establish a convincing case.

Notes

The views expressed here are the authors' own and should not be attributed to the institutions with which they are associated.

1. The United States was the strongest advocate of the negotiations, but a number of other industrial countries supported them. For reasons discussed later, enthusiasm for a strong agreement waned as the negotiations proceeded.
2. The first explicit proposal to incorporate investment rules in a GATT-like framework was made by Goldberg and Kindleberger (1970).
3. One partial indication of growing globalization is that growth rates for FDI have consistently exceeded those for GDP and trade. The difference is more pronounced for developing countries than for industrial countries. UNCTAD (1994) also presents indicators demonstrating growing global interdependence in banking and financial markets. See Julius (1990), Graham and Krugman (1993), Dunning (1993) and Oman (1994) for analyses of various aspects of globalization and the role of international investment.
4. Trade- and foreign-exchange-balancing restrictions are quota restrictions on imports, and domestic sales requirements are a quota restriction on exports.
5. However, the government does not collect any revenue from a local-content requirement. In fact, if domestic and imported goods are differentiated, the government could even lose revenue.
6. For example, McCulloch (1990) cites the case where a tariff, which is welfare reducing, attracts FDI and then a TRIM is used to extract some of the rents for the local market that result from the investment.
7. Roughly, a 50 percent local-content requirement on inputs that comprise 25 percent of the cost of production of a good is akin to a tariff of 6.3 percent, if the local cost of inputs is 50 percent greater than that of imported inputs. An illustrative calculation of the welfare cost of a local-content requirement is presented in Krugman and Obstfeld (1987), who report that the US oil import

quota in the 1960s and 1970s cost consumers about US $5 billion per year. Most of this represented a transfer to domestic oil producers, resulting in a net welfare loss of about US $1–2 billion.

8. Several countries – Mexico, Argentina, India, and Brazil – decided to eliminate local-content requirements before the conclusion of the Uruguay Round. It is doubtful in these cases that the action was directly attributable to the Uruguay Round TRIM agreement.

9. Interestingly, the political economy of TRIMs was such as not to generate overwhelming pressure in favor of reform. Existing enterprises affected by TRIMs soft-pedaled reform because stronger disciplines could have disadvantaged them relative to new investors. Moreover, often the bitter pill of TRIMs was sugar coated through subsidies or other advantages granted by regulating governments.

10. For Japan, the reaffirmation of the prohibition of local-content requirements was seen as valuable in restraining US pressure on Japanese companies to use US-produced components; such pressure was tantamount, in spirit if not letter, to local-content requirements.

11. In both developing and industrial countries, local-content requirements are pervasive in the area of government procurement but the TRIMs agreement does not address these requirements. Most developing countries are not signatories to the Uruguay Round agreement on government procurement and hence face no restraints on the use of local-content requirements in the context of government procurement. This is because of the exception in Article III of GATT permitting the grant of preferences to local producers in government procurement. Restraints on the use of local-content requirements by industrial countries, which are signatories to the Uruguay Round agreement on government procurement, are limited by the incomplete coverage of this agreement.

12. Data on growth in FDI show that developing countries are attracting an increasingly large share of the flow, accounting for an estimated 41 percent. Significantly, the inflow of FDI fell between 1990 and 1993 for industrial countries but increased sharply for developing countries. The flow to the developing world is concentrated in a few countries in Asia and Latin America. Julius (1994) points out that the expansion of FDI occurring over the last decade or so has been spread across sectors.

13. Graham (1994) summarizes this shift in thinking as follows: "Much of the old, antagonistic thinking about multinational enterprises was in fact based on the fear of market power by large firms. This fear was not without foundation because, indeed, the most accepted theories of multinational enterprise specify that in order to be a multinational, a firm must possess some sort of firm-specific asset, e.g., technology, that would give it market power. Current realization, however, is that these assets, in combination with what is in the literature termed 'internalization advantages,' also make the firm efficient. Notions of contestability have also crept into thinking about multinationals, notably that in a dynamic world a firm that becomes complacent about constantly upgrading its technologies and other firm-specific assets will likely be

beset by aggressive rivals . . . Old fears of dependence upon multinationals have thus become throughout the developing world leavened with an appreciation that these firms can help . . . by means of better utilization of resources."

14. The debate on trade in autos between the United States and Japan, where some US interests have been pressing for local-content requirements, and the Exxon-Florio amendments to investment rules are both examples of this.

15. This discussion assumes that developing countries are price takers in world markets and therefore can gain no terms-of-trade advantage from retaining taxes on imports.

16. Similar arguments for strategic intervention built around market imperfections apply in both cases, as do counterarguments based on public choice and other factors.

17. The move toward more open markets may have been partially offset in some sectors by increasing recourse to nontariff barriers, notably voluntary export restraints and antidumping actions.

18. In the case of most services, FDI is a prerequisite for delivery. The East Asian model of investment in export-oriented rather than import-substituting production illustrates the complementarity of trade and investment.

19. In DeAnne Julius's draft paper from which this reference comes, the author offers a prize to anyone who can come up with a term that better captures the meaning behind the phrase modal neutrality.

20. Multilateral rules that curb the use of incentives to attract investment would prevent a potential negative externality and the attendant welfare loss at the international level.

21. Such a structure was adopted in the NAFTA. The services chapter in NAFTA deals with cross-border trade, while a separate investment chapter covers all investment in goods and services.

22. A right of establishment, or the right to a commercial presence, could be either an integral part of the national treatment commitment or separately formulated. It is assumed here that the right of establishment is part of a national treatment commitment.

23. In cross-border trade, national treatment underwrites the market access commitment made at the frontier (a tariff binding and the absence of quantitative restrictions), but it does not define the *degree* of market access being guaranteed.

24. Inscribing a sector or service activity in a schedule is not a sufficient condition for guaranteeing national treatment. The right to specify conditions and qualifications to national treatment is also recognized.

25. Suppose the European Union imposed an antidumping duty on imports from Japan, which induced a shift in investment away from the latter either to the European Union itself or to a third entity. If the European Union then extended the antidumping duty – through rules of origin for antidumping action – to encompass the newly diverted operation (either in the European Union or the third entity), it would have redefined origin with respect to investment, with a crucial impact on the location of investment.

26. This approach would be the same as that adopted in TRIPS under the WTO. The question of supranational enforcement is largely a matter of how binding multilateral dispute settlement procedures can be made. Arguably the new WTO procedures, with more automatic adoption and implementation of panel reports, move in the direction of supranational enforcement.

27. Antidumping is in effect the only trade policy through which private rights of action are created under GATT. The Uruguay Round agreements on services and intellectual property are more cognizant of action, but the relative scarcity of private rights of action in existing institutional arrangements is cited as a deficiency that could be addressed through international competition policies (Lloyd and Sampson 1994).

28. The extraterritorial application of competition policies by countries such as the United States is another issue that would need to be addressed.

29. The converse is the use of import cartels to improve terms of trade by reducing import prices. In the past, state trading monopolies were often created to improve terms of trade on the import and export side.

30. In a 1990 decision, the European Commission granted an exemption from competition laws for a cooperative research and development production and marketing venture between two European Community companies; the commission argued that "Community companies ... find it difficult to compete with other larger non-European competitors," and the success of the latter in winning international contracts was adduced to support its case (Sapir, Buiges, and Jacquemin 1993).

31. Some discipline on research and development cartels would also be consistent in spirit with the Uruguay Round agreement on subsidies, which limits the scope of research and development subsidies that enjoy "green box" (non-actionable) treatment: only if subsidies amount to less than 75 percent of the cost of research or 50 percent of the cost of precompetitive development activity can they be deemed nonactionable. Further, disciplining the research and development exemption would parallel attempts to discipline investment incentives guaranteeing that investment location was a comparative advantage rather than policy driven.

32. This argument is reminiscent of claims by US auto suppliers that Japanese transplant factories in the United States imported their inputs because of *keiretsu* relationships with Japanese firms at home. The same remedy was also advocated in this case.

33. At a theoretical level, the effect of the TRIPS agreement on FDI (and on technology transfer) is positive because of the security offered to foreign investors. However, it should be remembered that in the key areas of TRIPS negotiations – pharmaceuticals and chemicals – inadequate foreign investment or foreign technology was never viewed as a cost to developing countries arising from low-level intellectual property protection.

34. In Hoekman and Mavroidis (1994b), the authors make a proposal that would involve authorities in the countries of both the petitioner and the respondent in antidumping cases. This is an interesting idea, especially because it advocates the internationalization of competition policy without any attempt at policy

harmonization. But it is unclear how readily competition policy authorities in the exporting country would cooperate in such arrangements.

35. Even in one of the most contentious areas – Japan's alleged lack of enforcement of competition policy in bidding procedures in the construction sector – the best solution is to seek international rules on government procurement; international rules on enforcement of competition policy would be a less direct way of addressing the problem.

36. Securing optimal remedies in the face of impaired market contestability is equally important in the national and the international context.

37. The argument here is not that competition policy is intrinsically more susceptible to capture, but merely that this risk should be fully recognized when considering whether to promote international competition policy.

38. Quantitative export restrictions violate Article XI of GATT. GATT does not pronounce on export taxes, nor have successive rounds of trade negotiations seriously sought to bind export taxes in the same way as import taxes. Persistent disregard for this illogical state of affairs can be attributed to the mercantilist underpinning of GATT.

39. GATT's traditional hands-off approach to market structure and ownership is being modified somewhat in GATT/WTO accession negotiations involving former centrally planned economies, but it is unclear where this will lead.

40. This approach has not been tested, and it is unclear how successful dispute settlement procedures would be in this context. Governments may fear that such a use of dispute settlement would err too much on the side of implicitly creating new rules rather than interpreting existing ones. Moreover, the standards for bringing a nonviolation complaint are quite high – there must be a preexisting tariff binding and a negation of reasonable expectation about the value of the latter commitment.

41. An additional question, of course, is whether governments would embrace the idea and be willing to invest resources and political capital in such a venture. It appears unlikely that, in the foreseeable future, governments would be willing to do anything requiring the effort expended on the TRIPS and services negotiations in the Uruguay Round (Hindley 1994).

42. In popular US idiom, the argument goes "if it ain't broke, why fix it?"

References

Balasubramanyam, V. N. 1991. "Putting TRIMs to Good Use." *World Development* 19(9): 1215–24.

Brittan, L. 1992. *European Competition Policy: Keeping the Playing Field Level.* Brussels: Centre for European Policy Studies.

Dunning, J. 1993. *Multinational Enterprises and the Global Economy.* Wokingham: Addison Wesley.

Evans, P., and T. Walsh 1994. "The EIU Guide to the new GATT." Economist Intelligence Unit Research Report. London: Economist Intelligence Unit.

Goldberg, P. M., and C. P. Kindleberger 1970. "Toward a GATT for Foreign Investment: A Proposal for Supervision of the International Corporation." *Law and Public Policy in International Business* Summer: 295–323.

Graham, E., and P. Krugman 1993. "The Surge in Foreign Direct Investment in the 1980s." In Kenneth A. Foot, ed., *Foreign Direct Investment*. Chicago: Chicago University Press.

Graham, E. M. 1994. "Competition Policy and the New Trade Agenda." Address Prepared for the OECD Roundtable on New Dimensions of Market Access in a Globalizing World Economy, Paris.

Grossman, G. 1981. "The Theory of Domestic Content Protection and Content Preference." *Quarterly Journal of Economics* 96(4): 583–603.

Harmsen, R. and A. Subramanian 1994. "Economic Implications of the Uruguay Round." In N. Kirmani *et al.*, eds., *International Trade Policies: The Uruguay Round and Beyond*. Vol. II, *Background Papers*. Washington, DC: International Monetary Fund.

Hindley, B. 1994. "Contingent Protection after the Uruguay Round: Safeguards, VERs, and Anti-Dumping Actions." Paper presented at OECD Workshop on the New World Trading System. Paris, April 25–26.

Hoekman, B., and P. C. Mavroidis 1994a. "Competition, Competition Policy and the GATT." *The World Economy*, 17(2): 121–50.

1994b. "Antitrust-Based Remedies and Dumping in International Trade." Policy Research Paper 1347. Washington, DC: World Bank.

1994c. "Linking Competition and Trade Policies in Central and Eastern European Countries." Policy Research Working Paper 1346. Washington, DC: World Bank.

Industry Canada 1994. "Formal and Informal Investment Barriers in the G-7 Countries." Occasional Paper 1, vols. 1 and 2. Government of Canada, Ottawa.

International Antitrust Code Working Group 1994. "Draft International Antitrust Code as a GATT–MTO–Plurilateral Trade Agreement." *Aussenwirtschaft* 49 (2–3): 310–25.

Julius, D. 1990. *Global Companies and Public Policy: The Growing Challenge of Direct Investment*. London: Pinter.

1994. "International Direct Investment: Strengthening the Policy Regime." Paper prepared for IIE Conference on Managing the World Economy of the Future: Lessons from the First Fifty Years after Bretton Woods. Washington, DC, May.

Khemani, R. S., and M. A. Dutz 1995. "The Instruments of Competition Policy and their Relevance for Economic Development." In C. Frischtak, ed., *Regulatory Policies and Reform in Industrializing Countries*. Washington, DC: World Bank.

Krugman, P., and M. Obstfeld 1987. *International Economics: Theory and Practice*. Glenview, Ill.: Scott, Foresman.

Leidy, M. 1994. "Antidumping: Solution or Problem in the 1990s?" In N. Kirmani *et al.*, eds., *International Trade Policies: The Uruguay Round and Beyond*. Vol. II, *Background Papers*. Washington, DC: International Monetary Fund.

Lloyd, P., and G. Sampson 1994. "Competition and Trade Policy: Identifying the Issues after the Uruguay Round." Mimeograph. GATT: Geneva, October.

Low, P. 1994. "Market Access through Market Presence." Paper prepared for the OECD Roundtable on the New Dimensions of Market Access in a Globalizing World Economy, Paris, July.

Low, P., and A. Yeats 1994. "Nontariff Measures and Developing Countries: Has the Uruguay Round Leveled the Playing Field?" Policy Research Working Paper 1353. Washington DC: World Bank.

McCulloch, R. 1990. "Investment Policy in the GATT." *The World Economy* 13(4): 541–53.

McMillan, J. 1994. "Why Does Japan Resist Foreign Market-Opening Pressure?" Paper presented for the Ford Foundation/American Society of International Law Project on Fairness and Harmonization, Washington DC, June.

Maskus, K. E., and D. R. Eby 1990. "Developing New Rules and Disciplines on Trade-Related Investment Measures." *The World Economy* 13(4): 523–53.

Neven, D., R. Nuttal, and P. Seabright 1993. *Merger in Daylight: The Economics and Politics of European Merger Control.* London: Centre for Economic Policy Research.

Oman, C. 1994. *Globalization and Regionalization: The Challenge for Developing Countries.* Paris: OECD.

Rodrik, D. 1987. "The Economics of Export-Performance Requirements." *Quarterly Journal of Economics* 102(3): 633–50.

Sapir, A., P. Buigues, and A. Jacquemin 1993. "European Competition Policy in Manufacturing and Services: A Two-Speed Approach." *Oxford Review of Economic Policy* 9(2): 113–32.

Subramanian, A. 1994. "The International Dimension of Competition Policies." In N. Kirmani *et al.*, eds., *International Trade Policies: The Uruguay Round and Beyond.* Vol. II, *Background Papers.* Washington, DC: International Monetary Fund.

UNCTAD 1994. *World Investment Report: Transnational Corporations, Employment and the Workplace.* New York and Geneva: United Nations.

14 Developing countries and system strengthening in the Uruguay Round

John Whalley

During seven years of negotiations, *system strengthening* almost came to symbolize the Uruguay Round for developing countries. Although not articulated when the Uruguay Round was launched, this key objective became the focal point for developing countries as negotiations progressed, and as some of these countries perceived that they might be excluded from the growing regional trade blocs. And according to the instant analysts at the conclusion of the Uruguay Round, the negotiations did indeed generate a strong multilateral trade system.

Yet, fears about their exclusion from the trade blocs also drove developing countries to a position of compromise at the end of the Uruguay Round. They had entered the negotiations with the belief that a rules-based, enforceable multilateral trading system was a strong and overriding interest. In fact, the declaration that launched the Uruguay Round included the broad outlines of an eventual agreement for strengthening the rule regime and enforcement in such areas as agriculture, textiles, dispute settlement, VERs, and others. But as the arduous negotiations wore on, the notion of strengthening the quantity and quality of access that drove developing countries to participate in the Uruguay Round was progressively replaced with a more defensive concept of preserving what already existed in the system, rather than achieving something further in the way of new disciplines. In the end, the forward-looking "access" strategy that had brought so many of them actively into the Uruguay Round early on had instead become a slogan for preventing a deterioration of global trade arrangements.[1]

The meaning of system and system strengthening

In 1947, the framers of GATT clearly sought to achieve a well-ordered trading system. Their introduction of all-encompassing trade rules and principles was intended to limit the use of trade-restricting measures by national governments. New nontariff barriers in the form of quotas were to be prevented; only existing quotas were to be allowed to remain in place. Border measures (tariffs) were to be made more transparent so as to support subsequent multilateral negotiations at reducing trade barriers. But as the post-War era unfolded, the coexistence of so many arrangements beyond the GATT framework and inconsistent with its principles has broadened the concept of "system" to the mere accumulation of trade arrangements that we see today.

The erosion of the GATT system from 1947 on prompted many developing countries in the Uruguay Round to stress repeatedly their interest in a "strengthened" trading system, even if it meant ceding preferential status and treatment. In fact, when the Uruguay Round was launched in Punta del Este in 1986, a coalition of small to medium-size developing countries, along with a coalition of industrial countries of similar size (the Swiss–Columbia bloc), emphasized the desire for a more enforceable, rule-based, nondiscriminatory multilateral trading system, and their commitment to make this system functional. Indeed displaying a zeal for negotiations not evident in earlier rounds of GATT, these blocs sharply reversed their strategy of pursuing preferential treatment, made proposals, participated actively in meetings, unilaterally liberalized their trade regimes before the Uruguay Round concluded, and then partially bound their liberalization at the end.[2] But in the end, the active cooperation of developing countries in the liberalization process was driven more by the fear that the nondiscriminatory multilateral trade system would collapse if the Round failed, and, in turn, that they would be excluded from trading blocs under any "system" that would emerge. They essentially softened their calls for a "stronger system" in recognition that the potential loss to them from a major breakdown in negotiations outweighed whatever benefits might accrue to them from more direct, incremental enhancements to system structure.

Thus, the concepts of "system" and "system strengthening" have been defined dynamically as world trade arrangements have evolved in the post-War era. How they are currently defined is a prelude to our assessment of system strengthening under the Uruguay Round.

Defining the system

When applied to global trade arrangements, the term *system* implies a coordinated and well-organized set of rules and institutions that oversee and regulate world trade.[3]

In reality, the global trade system consists of four distinct, interacting subsystems which form a patchwork of overlapping and, at times, highly inconsistent arrangements. The first covers the multilateral trade rules originally delineated by GATT in 1947 and now embodied in the charter of the new WTO. It also includes multilateral tariff reductions and additional arrangements negotiated in the various GATT rounds preceding the Uruguay Round. The second subsystem is a series of derogations from GATT rules and principles prior to the completion of the Uruguay Round – arrangements in some way accommodated by the multilateral system, but either formally or apparently incompatible with GATT. This subsystem includes special arrangements covering trade in textiles, agriculture, and other products, as well as the application of special instruments such as VERs, that are inconsistent with GATT rules. The third subsystem includes bilateral and multilateral regional arrangements beyond the GATT rules and principles, established under various regional free-trade area and customs union agreements. This subsystem conflicts openly with the non-discriminatory principles of GATT and has grown sharply in recent years with NAFTA, the Canada–US Agreement, European integration arrangements, and various Latin American and Asian trade arrangements.[4] The fourth subsystem comprises a variety of nontraditional trade arrangements, covering several interacting trade and other policy subsystems not covered by the original GATT disciplines – domestic distribution systems, competition and antitrust policies, investment, environmental policy, and others.

Behind these four subsystems lie the domestic legal and administrative structures that prevail in the respective countries. These structures govern how trade measures (tariffs, antidumping, and countervailing duties) are administered, how product and safety standards are set, how trade in toxic and other waste products is controlled, and how many other trade-related laws and regulations are implemented. Together, these constitute the global trading system, rather than only the multilateral rules and disciplines represented by GATT (and now the WTO). The post-War years have seen efforts to harmonize some of these in GATT and elsewhere: common customs nomenclatures, limits on lengthy or overly complex border procedures, and codes on the use of antidumping duties and subsidies. But despite these efforts, even greater diversity has been introduced into other functional systems, exacerbating the inconsistency of the system.

Defining system strengthening

The literature gives little guidance about how the term *system strengthening* should be defined as it pertains to the trade system that has emerged.[5] Notions of "strength" applied to a system of trade (or any other rules) are not unidimensional, making it difficult to measure strength.

Generally speaking, all international legal arrangements are thought to be weak compared to domestic law. International policing and prosecution are difficult; the penalties that can be invoked are relatively minor; and the coverage of international laws is usually limited. Thus, a starting point in evaluating whether the Uruguay Round has strengthened the trading system is the recognition that the system of rules was comparatively weak to begin with.

Three distinct sets of characteristics can be associated with the strength of the system; each has its own subcharacteristics (table 14.1). Because these subcharacteristics do not substitute perfectly for each other,[6] developing clear metrics for system strengthening along any of these dimensions is difficult. Thus, the overall strength of a multilateral trade system can be gauged by the strength of its weakest subcharacteristics. Strengthening one or more essential elements of a set of characteristics may do little to improve the overall strength of the system if another key component of strength within the set remains unchanged or is even weakened. Put another way, systems of trade rules are only as strong as their weakest links.

Thus, in dispute settlement, tightening procedures for forming panels and treating panel reports may have little impact if penalties are relatively minor. Similarly, if antidumping, countervailing mechanisms, and safeguards are treated as a single effective system of contingent protection, and antidumping is more accessible for those seeking protection than GATT safeguard measures, agreements that strengthen only safeguards may be ineffective measures for system strengthening. And if new contingencies are added to the qualifying list for trade remedy measures, such as environmental or labor standard justifications for protection, the net effect may be to weaken the system further, despite the fact that subsystem components (for example, formal safeguards under GATT Article XIX) appear to be strengthened.

But despite such conceptual issues, the question that arises in developing countries is whether they got something of value from the Uruguay Round in the sense of a stronger system. And if so, what was it? Was it less discrimination and firmer guarantees of market access, new institutions, and stronger dispute settlement? Or was it the consolation that the system would have been much worse had the Uruguay Round not been concluded successfully?

System strengthening in the Uruguay Round

All of the different characteristics of system strengthening identified in table 14.1 factored into the negotiations in the Uruguay Round, and each in its own way is reflected in the final decisions. Table 14.2 uses the characteristics

Table 14.1 *Key measures of the strength of systems of trade rules*

Key measures of strength	Essential elements
Strength of rules (under the assumption that the rules are enforced)	Force – the extent of restraint on trade-restricting policy. (For example, a system that binds tariffs at, say, 20 percent implies less restraint and is thus less forceful than one that binds tariffs at 10 percent.)
	Consistency and transparency – the comparability between the rules and the basic principles of the system, and the extent to which the rules apply equally and fairly to all parties.
	Effectiveness – the extent to which measures of restraint on trade-restricting policy (force) actually keep markets open – that is, whether countries are prevented from using substitute instruments to circumvent the restraints. (For example, forceful tariff bindings with few or no restrictions on the use of quotas, voluntary export restraints, antidumping, and other measures would not characterize a strong system.)
	Coverage – the comparative proportion of the trade regime (agriculture, manufacturing, and services) covered by the rules.
Degree of enforcement	Clarity – the extent to which the interpretation of the rule is unambiguous.
	Ease of grievance procedures – the extent to which complaints will be heard and acted upon.
	The rigor of penalties – the extent to which the threat of sanctions are an incentive for following system rules.[a]
	Credibility – the extent to which sanctions are enforced.
Sustainability of rule regime	Ability to withstand internal erosion – the extent to which the rule regime can avoid outcomes contrary to the system principles – for example, nontransparent voluntary export restraints in a regime dedicated to transparency.
	Ability to withstand external erosion – the extent to which the rule regime can avoid, say, the emergence of regional trade blocs or movement toward large trade blocs in a multilateral system.
	Ability to withstand rapid implosion – the extent to which the rule regime is at risk of experiencing

Table 14.1 (*cont.*)

Key measures of strength	Essential elements
	rapid dynamic instability that might escalate trade conflicts and create a major contraction in world trade (and thus an implosion of global income comparable to what happened in the 1930s).[b] Participation in and support for the system – the extent to which the system has broad political support by smaller and lower-income countries, and the extent to which these countries participate in discussions about the system and its rules.

[a]A key issue here, especially in the context of GATT and the WTO, is whether the penalties are informal or formal. Formal penalties (say, the withdrawal of equivalent concessions) may be small, but informal penalties in the form of community pressure (the general expectation that rulings will be upheld, and that noncompliance will be subject to diplomatic consequences) may be a more significant penalty mechanism. (This observation comes from Bob Hudec.)
[b]Kindleberger 1973 provides a detailed discussion of the implosion of the 1930s.

of system strengthening (and weakening) identified in Table 14.1. In some cases, the Uruguay Round strengthened the system; in others, it weakened it (table 14.2).[7] Narrowly construed, decisions in the Uruguay Round to change trade disciplines and procedures strengthened the system significantly; more broadly, the system may have been weakened while the Uruguay Round was in progress by developments within the system but outside the Round (for example, increased regionalism), which may have fragmented the system and harmed the interests of developing countries. As mentioned, the broader need of developing countries to strengthen the system in order to preserve multilateral cooperation at the end of the Uruguay Round came to dominate their narrower interest in strengthening disciplines.

The strength of rules

Force and consistency

The additional tariff cuts implemented in the Uruguay Round will likely improve the access of developing countries to markets; but, at the same time, the impacts will likely be small because tariffs in industrial countries were already low (except in the apparel area), and the tariff cuts are also concentrated in areas of least importance to the developing countries (table 14.3). The Uruguay Round met its aggregate percentage cut targets

Table 14.2 *The effects of the Uruguay Round on system strengthening*

Strength of rules	Force and consistency: moderate to significant strengthening
	  Extension of tariff bindings (substantial for developing
	  countries)
	  Elimination of voluntary export restraints in four years
	  Tariffication and new bindings in agriculture (border
	  measures, internal supports, and export subsidies)
	  Termination of the MFA in ten years; strengthened
	  safeguard for domestic textile and wearing apparel
	  industries
	  Further tariff cuts beyond Tokyo Round agreements
	  New institutional framework of WTO
	Effectiveness: little change
	  Little substantive change in antidumping and safeguards
	  Antidumping as a potential replacement regime for the
	  MFA
	Coverage: significant strengthening
	  New agreements on services, investment, and trade-related
	  aspects of intellectual property

Degree of
enforcement
	Clarity/interpretation: potential weakening
	  Lengthy text and new schedules create potential for new
	  trade conflicts
	Ease of proceeding with a complaint: significant
	strengthening with new WTO procedures
	  Virtually automatic rights to a panel
	  Consensus needed to reject a panel report
	  Time limits on procedures
	Penalties: no change in level of penalties; but new rules make
	penalties automatic

Sustainability of
rule regime
	Internal erosion: major strengthening
	  Termination of voluntary export restraints
	  Agriculture subject to discipline
	  Textiles/apparel sector to return fully to the GATT/WTO
	  system
	External erosion: major strengthening
	  Incentives for both small and large countries to participate
	  in new regional agreements were reduced sharply with the
	  conclusion of the Uruguay Round
	Risk of rapid implosion: major strengthening
	  Cooperative outcome preserves accommodation, provides
	  momentum for further eventual negotiation
	  Creation of the WTO

Note: Schott 1994 and UNCTAD 1994 provide a comprehensive review of the decisions reached in the Uruguay Round.

Table 14.3 *Tariff cuts and bindings in the Uruguay Round*

					Regions				
	United States		European Union		Canada		Developing and transitional economies	
Products	Pre-Round	Post-Round	Pre-Round	Post-Round	Pre-Round	Post-Round	Pre-Round	Post-Round
Pre- and post-Round tariff rates								
Nongrain crops, wool, and livestock	3.9	3.1	5.8	3.6	4.0	3.7	18.1	13.9
Coal, oil, gas, and other minerals	1.3	0.8	1.2	0.8	2.6	1.3	11.5	9.4
Processed food, beverages, and other manufactured items	3.6	1.6	5.6	2.6	6.3	2.9	18.0	13.3
Trade and transport services	0.0	0.0	0.0	0.0	0.0	0.0	0.0	0.0
Utilities, construction, and other private and government services	0.0	0.0	0.0	0.0	0.0	0.0	0.0	0.0
Forestry products	0.0	0.0	0.0	0.0	0.0	0.0	0.1	0.1
Fishery products	1.2	0.9	12.9	10.1	3.2	2.1	35.2	8.1
Paddy rice, wheat, and other grains	1.6	1.0	4.2	0.2	1.0	0.7	17.3	13.4
Textiles	10.5	1.5	9.0	6.8	18.6.	11.7	30.3	20.3
Clothing	16.7	15.2	12.6	10.9	22.9	16.6	14.6	10.8
Chemicals and rubber	5.0	3.0	1.1	4.2	10.3	5.3	19.1	13.2

Primary iron and steel	4.5	0.2	5.3	4.9	7.4	3.6	8.7	6.1
Primary nonferrous metals	2.9	2.6	7.2	5.9	4.9	2.7	2.7	2.1
Fabricated metal products	4.7	2.8	5.8	3.1	9.7	6.0	8.5	6.9
Transport equipment	4.8	4.6	6.9	6.0	8.1	5.4	27.2	17.3
All merchandise trade	4.6	3.2	5.4	5.2	7.4	4.2	13.5	9.8

Tariff bindings on industrial products (percentage of tariff line items bound)

	Pre-Round	Post-Round
United States, North America	99	100
Western Europe	79	82
Industrial countries	78	99
Developing countries	22	72
Economies in transition	73	98

Source: Francois, McDonald, and Nordström 1994, table 13 and figure 2. (See also chapter 9 of this volume.) Pre-Round refers to 1986 base data; post-Round refers to the end of the Uruguay Round implementation period.

by committing the largest percentage cuts to the smallest tariffs, and then averaging the percentage reductions.[8] In the area of textiles and apparel, for instance, tariff cuts are smaller than average cuts. Concerns were expressed by other developing countries, particularly those in Africa, about the erosion of margins of tariff preference that would be caused by the Uruguay Round under such regional agreements as Lomé, although eliminating preferences is a move toward greater consistency within the system.

Because many of the reduced tariffs have been bound at lower levels (particularly by the developed countries), the Uruguay Round strengthened the system by preventing a return to higher barriers. The new bindings by the developing countries represent an especially important component of system strengthening, extending tariff bindings from only 22 percent of tariff line items previously to 72 percent when the Uruguay Round is fully implemented.

The termination of the "gray area" measures under the Uruguay Round is another source of system strengthening that should benefit developing countries. VERs are to end four years after the Uruguay Round agreement goes into effect, and they will not be used in the future.[9] Assuming that the termination of VERs is fully implemented, the system will be strengthened because it will be more consistent with GATT principles and contain new restraints on protection. But the credibility of this commitment is an issue, since most VERs are negotiated bilaterally under the threat of some more severe sanction. Not all are notified to GATT, and the contracting parties made several standstill and rollback commitments on VERs prior to the completion of the Uruguay Round, as well as in the declaration that launched the Round (see appendix A). Yet, none of this has prevented the introduction of new VERs, many of which are price or other undertakings agreed to in return for the withdrawal of antidumping petitions by firms in industrial countries. Only one VER has ever been taken to a GATT panel, and that was by the European Union over the United States–Japan computer chip agreement.

In agriculture, substantial debate has also emerged about the implications of the Uruguay Round decisions. Tangermann (1994) and Hathaway and Ingco (chapter 2), for example, have argued that "dirty" tariffication (the conversion of existing nontariff barriers into ad valorem equivalent trade restrictions at higher levels than represented by the initial barriers) has already offset some of the original intent of the liberalization in agriculture. In addition, the introduction of minimum-access commitments (effectively tariff quotas) not only further constrains the liberalization that has occurred, but also potentially introduces new and discriminatory instruments in the form of country-specific minimum-access commitments. Both features have caused Tangermann to argue that liberalization in agriculture has probably not been substantial, although important bindings have been introduced on the use of trade-restricting measures in the agricultural area. These bindings eliminate the unbound right of the United States to use trade restrictions under its 1955 Waiver, and restrain the claimed rights of the European Union to use variable levies to protect its domestic agricultural market.[10] Tangermann has gone so far as to argue that these bindings are by far the greater achievement in agriculture under the Uruguay Round, with the implication that system strengthening in agriculture in the sense of preventing a reversion to higher barriers may be much more important than system strengthening in the sense of consistency – that is, returning agriculture to traditional GATT disciplines.

In textiles and apparel, doubts have also been raised about the eventual depth of liberalization. Industrial countries are committed to returning textiles and apparel to normal GATT disciplines, with the abolition of the MFA over a ten-year period. The integration of textiles and apparel into GATT will occur in three stages, in each of which the growth rates of the MFA quotas will be increased progressively and some products initially covered by MFA quota restrictions will be returned to the normal GATT system.[11] At the same time, a new system of temporary selective safeguards is to be implemented. These safeguards can be used to protect domestic industries harmed by the quota changes, but they can be maintained only for three years, and can be applied only against products not yet integrated into GATT/WTO disciplines and those not subject to an MFA quota.

Some have argued both that the proportional increase in quota growth rates will have little effect when initial quota growth rates are low, and that the early stages of the abolition of the MFA will entail eliminating non-binding quotas first, thus leaving most of the adjustment until the end of the ten-year period.[12] The postponement of much of the adjustment has raised some questions about the commitment of industrial countries to eliminating the MFA.

Effectiveness
The effectiveness of the rule regime has seemingly changed little, given the extent of instrument substitution that may occur. For example, some commentators have argued that the elimination of the MFA could be accompanied by a series of antidumping petitions filed by producers in industrial countries as liberalization in this area leads to a decline in domestic market prices – thus the danger of having one protective regime replaced by another. In contrast with agriculture, where the issue is the extent of liberalization actually implied by the negotiated agreements, the negotiated agreements in textiles could be far-reaching if fully executed. Debate focuses instead on the credibility of the commitment, and whether

accompanying changes elsewhere will negate the effect of the change. The extent of system strengthening in this area is thus unclear.

The decisions of the Uruguay Round also changed the effectiveness of trade rules, although probably to a less significant degree. The Safeguards agreement eliminates VERs, and places time limits on the use of safeguard measures, but allows the use of discriminatory quantitative restrictions.[13] The antidumping decisions pertain largely to procedural matters associated with implementing antidumping duties, and do not address the economic consequences of antidumping actions. Some commentators have suggested that the decisions worsen the pre-Uruguay Round regime by codifying what were previously only informal practices for determining dumping and margins (Hindley 1994). In subsidies and countervailing duties important clarifications to the definition of subsidy appear, and a classification between actionable, nonactionable, and prohibited subsidies is now included.

Coverage

Uruguay Round agreements in three new areas – services, investment, and intellectual property – strengthened the system by broadening the coverage of areas and trade-restricting measures within the trading system, and bringing them into the framework of WTO/GATT disciplines. One of the central arguments made in the initial discussions on services liberalization was that the new protective trade measures for services would be unrestrained in the absence of any agreement from the Uruguay Round, which, in turn, could erode wider performance from the global economy. The argument was that new disciplines were necessary.

But the broader coverage has also weakened the system in some senses. For example, retaliation in intellectual property is now possible, with the application of higher trade barriers on goods trade allowed where violations of intellectual property protection norms occur, possibly compromising the trade system for nontrade objectives. In this sense, the trading system might be weakened in the name of achieving a better performing, global policy system. Similar issues will arise after the Uruguay Round in such areas as trade and the environment, and trade and the rights of workers and citizens.

In the areas covered by the new issues, the view is that negotiations over liberalization have been initiated, and have significantly broadened system coverage, especially for services. While the substantive provisions of the services agreement are comparatively limited owing to restricted sectoral coverage, and while many of the specific commitments that have been made are seemingly symbolic at this stage, many believe that the opportunity exists for deeper liberalization in the future. Combined with more substantive decisions in intellectual property that many developing countries initially resisted but implicitly agreed to later under bilateral pressure, the new issues have provided a clear direction for the liberalization process, and thus system strengthening, in the future.

Degree of enforcement

The change in the dispute settlement procedures of the WTO/GATT under the Uruguay Round has strengthened the system by creating stronger enforcement of trade disciplines. The level of penalties for rules violations remain the same, and no special efforts have been made beyond dispute settlement to address the clarity and interpretation of rules. But rights to retaliate now accrue automatically, removing the previous defendant's right to block authorization of retaliation.

The enforcement system was seen as weak to begin with; prior to the Uruguay Round existing trade rules were not applied vigorously, for one of three reasons: trade rules violations had gone unchallenged, ambiguities in the interpretation of GATT rules slowed or diluted their translation into operational force, or the penalties for violations of the rule regime were not strong enough to ensure compliance.[14] More broadly, small and developing countries did not use the dispute settlement procedures, and cases involving large countries were occasionally delayed or blocked.[15]

One example of these weaknesses is how GATT treated regional trade agreements. Although many regional trade agreements had been notified to GATT and been assigned GATT working parties prior to the Uruguay Round, in no case was any clear determination made about GATT incompatibility under Article 24 (Hart 1987). These arrangements included both the original European Community and the Common Agricultural Policy.

In resolutions of typical trade disputes under the pre-Uruguay Round procedures, protagonists had several opportunities to block the dispute settlement procedures at various stages – when panels were formed, panel reports were adopted, and final agreements were reached about rights to retaliate.[16] Indeed, only once in the post-War era have rights to retaliate been granted in a dispute – to the Netherlands in a celebrated agricultural case with the United States in 1951, which, in part, led to a US request for an open-ended waiver for agricultural protection (Hudec 1991).

The Uruguay Round has significantly strengthened dispute settlement procedures. A unified dispute settlement process now covers goods, services, and investment. Rights to a panel are virtually automatic; panel reports now must be rejected (rather than accepted) by consensus, strict time limits apply to each stage of the procedures, thus all but eliminating blocking and delay tactics; and the contracting parties have made an explicit commitment to conform to panel reports. Many also believe that smaller countries (including developing countries) will now be able to raise disputes more effectively and have them settled in their favor. But a new WTO appellate body has also been established, causing some to suggest that governments will appeal panel decisions routinely so that they can demonstrate their earnestness to domestic industries. The one source of disquiet is the US judicial review process, better known as "three strikes and you're out," under which three negative reviews of WTO decisions by the United States could trigger US withdrawal from the WTO.

But these changes are also accompanied by new elements that might weaken the system. One is whether these disciplines will be strong enough to restrain countries from taking actions that fall outside system rules, and hence whether the net effect will simply be to create more conflict. For example, the United States may continue to use section 301 measures under this new regime, creating more open conflict within the system than previously. The caseload of dispute settlements may also be unmanageable given the 26,000 pages of text in the Uruguay Round Final Act, which could overwhelm the ability of the GATT/WTO Secretariat to deal adequately with disputes and undermine the credibility of the process (Jackson 1994).

It may also be naive to believe that developing countries, having previously refrained from using dispute settlement procedures merely because the process was difficult, will now come forward with multiple complaints. Mexico, for example, soft-pedaled in its tuna-dolphin dispute with the United States in part because the resulting GATT panel report might have adversely affected its trilateral NAFTA negotiations.

Penalties

Some also claim that without a change in formal penalties, the other changes in dispute settlement procedures may not be as significant as they appear on paper. Yet, although penalty levels were adjusted only slightly, the right to impose penalties now accrues automatically, which is a major change. In addition, prior to the conclusion of the Uruguay Round, the penalty regime was actually stronger than often claimed; although large countries could usually impose formal panel decisions on small countries, decisions in favor of smaller countries against the larger were typically imposed by community pressure.[17] But as the Uruguay Round drew to its conclusion, the force of community pressure was being eroded, as resistance to rulings grew more frequent.

Sustainability of the rule regime

The sustainability of the rule regime under the Uruguay Round is perhaps the most difficult element of system strengthening to assess, but it is also one of the most critical determinants of system performance in the long run, and one of the most important elements to developing countries. Here, too, the Uruguay Round decisions may have strengthened the system significantly, but some changes could also create a weaker system.

Political support

The concern about the political sustainability of the new regime is that the Uruguay Round embodies many changes in the legal regime governing international trade for which the larger countries do not have either the political support domestically or the political will to enforce.[18] Thus, each contracting party may have felt compelled to agree to changes in trade rules and procedures for the sake of preserving multilateral accommodation, despite recognizing their limited ability to implement fully. As such, the Uruguay Round could prove to be a gamble, whose risks include less than wholehearted implementation, deflated expectations, and eventually even further erosion in a system that the Uruguay Round sought to strengthen.

Implosion and external erosion

The Uruguay Round did not address the ability of the system to resist the introduction of new elements of protection effectively or to avoid the fragmentation of the system into trade blocs that would weaken the economies of individual countries and undermine the whole. Concerns about inter-country trade conflict have emerged, especially of the type that occurred in the 1930s, as have concerns about growing pressure for new regionalism and thus elevated trade blocs.

GATT still does not codify how countries are to behave toward each other if a trade conflict emerges outside of GATT disciplines, nor how frequently they may retaliate and on what grounds and how nonprotagonists are to be treated.

Toward the conclusion of the Uruguay Round, this notion of system strengthening – the sustainability of the system in the face of large power conflict – was what preoccupied developing countries. They believed that a positive conclusion to the Uruguay Round would reinforce the cooperation that had been achieved under seven previous GATT rounds, and would both strengthen future cooperation and help prevent trade conflicts in the future.[19] This belief reflects the so-called "bicycle" theory of multilateralism – that to preserve what you have, you have to keep moving forward on the GATT bicycle or else risk falling off the bicycle when it stops (Bergsten 1975).

The argument that the Uruguay Round has strengthened the system by improving measures of sustainability is based on the fact that the Round has been concluded. It has reinforced cooperation from previous rounds, and multilateralism can now move forward to strengthening forms of cooperation in the future. The conclusion of the Uruguay Round has removed several pressures for new regional arrangements – including the rush of small countries toward regional arrangements in fear that the Uruguay Round would fail, so as to be inside at least one bloc before conflict started. But the conclusion has also prevented large countries from using the threat of regional negotiations to pressure other, larger multilateral partners, as well as smaller countries from offering larger countries regional negotiations for this purpose in an effort to improve their own regional terms.

The counterargument is that it is a false analogy to appeal to GATT-based multilateral cooperation for preserving trade peace, given the many other ways to achieve cooperation in trade policy matters. In the 1980s, for example, three instances of bilateral trade retaliation between the United States and the European Community – all pertaining to the Common Agricultural Policy, the United States, and European Community enlargement – were subdued by mutual agreement to place implicit limits on the size of each step in the process of retaliation, the time between retaliatory measures, and the value of trade affected. Each outbreak of trade conflict was eventually mediated bilaterally outside of the GATT process.

Thus, while the possibility of retaliation outside of formal GATT/WTO channels weakens the system, the fact that such cases have been resolved with seemingly more efficient non-GATT/WTO mechanisms might mitigate this weakness. Although a weakening of the multilateral system may increase the risk of trade conflicts that would swallow up smaller countries, particularly the developing countries, it might also be the case that mediation among the parties may be expedient and effective outside the formal multilateral system.

Internal erosion

The ability to resist domestic protectionist pressures also applies to the sustainability of the system. While little in the formal Uruguay Round decisions may be directly relevant to this sense of system strengthening, the Uruguay Round has clear implications for the application of these pressures in the future. Bindings in agriculture or on the tariffs of developing countries, for example, represent a clear restraint on domestic protectionist pressures. But to achieve tariffication and other liberalization in agriculture, the Uruguay Round created new safeguard arrangements within agriculture that introduce the potential for trade-restricting measures that did not previously exist. One may also argue that pressures will grow, say, for the substitution of antidumping duties for MFA quotas or even reduced tariffs. Yet, the termination of VERs, the imposition of discipline on agriculture, and the return of textiles and apparel to the GATT/WTO system are signs that the Uruguay Round has strengthened the ability of the system to withstand internal erosion.

The WTO and system strengthening

One of the more prominent system-strengthening decisions in the Uruguay Round has been the creation of a new WTO to supersede the GATT.[20] Although not envisaged when the Round was launched, and indeed only emerging as a possibility later in the negotiations, the decision to create the WTO has attracted much fanfare, but has also generated much controversy – from concerns about national sovereignty in the United States, India, and elsewhere to concerns about whether the WTO can integrate disciplines on goods, services, and intellectual property, given the possibility of cross-retaliation with the new dispute settlement procedures agreed to under the Uruguay Round.

The all or nothing approach that has been adopted to implement the decisions of the Uruguay Round – in which countries must accept the results of the Round without exception – is stronger than the menu-driven approach that characterized the Tokyo Round, in which countries could accede to some codes but not others. But the fact that the WTO is largely a framework into which previous GATT agreements are placed along with the decisions of the Uruguay Round has been criticized on the grounds that opportunities have been lost for defining clear principles governing such areas as trade and environment.

The benefits of a WTO: a more permanent rules-based system

More than any other facet of the WTO, the permanence of the new WTO has been the subject of greatest debate – that is, the move from a provisionally applied *protocol* of application under GATT to an enduring world trade institution represented by the WTO, or to a stronger global trade arrangement. One of the strongest proponents of the institutional redesign of global trade has been Jackson; in particular, Jackson (1989) delineated his ideas on how GATT should be restructured, which proved remarkably close to the WTO structure agreed to under the Uruguay Round. He proposed a new draft charter for a global trade institution that imposed few substantive obligations but would apply them on a definitive, rather than provisional basis.

Jackson believed that the major benefit from pursuing such an arrangement was the coherence that would be embodied by the organization under its constitution, clear mandate, and orderly rules for its Secretariat – that is, not so much the substantive content of new institutional arrangements but more its organizational structure. Moving from the provisionally applied GATT to the permanent WTO will give trade arrangements greater legal bite and greater transparency.

Key features of the WTO

The new trade organization embodies a single institutional framework, encompassing GATT (as modified by the Uruguay Round), all of its agreements and arrangements, and the results of the Uruguay Round itself. The organization is to be headed by a ministerial conference that will meet every two years and a general council has been established to oversee operations and to serve as a dispute settlement body. The general council is to establish three subsidiary bodies: a goods council, a services council, and a trade-related aspects of intellectual property rights (TRIPS) council. Reviews of country trade policies will continue under the TPRM process initiated in GATT at the Uruguay Round Mid-Term Review in 1988.

The WTO's dispute settlement body will be permitted to consider imposing cross-retaliation, involving disputes in one area and possibly the withdrawal of concessions in others. The core of its structure embodies the major changes in dispute settlement procedures that had largely been agreed to earlier in the Uruguay Round (prior to the commitment to form the WTO). These changes include automatic rights to a panel, clear time limits on each stage of the dispute settlement process, and, perhaps most important, the requirement that a dispute panel report be rejected – not accepted – by consensus. The major change in dispute procedures is the right to appeal and the requirement that countries follow through with WTO procedures without resorting to unilateral measures outside of the dispute settlement process. It is thus clear that dispute settlement procedures within this new set of WTO rules have been strengthened.

What does creation of the WTO mean for the trade system in the future?

The central issue is the extent to which the WTO is a major change from the previous organizational structure of GATT. For some, the WTO is a major step toward trade institution building that substantially strengthens the global trading system beyond GATT arrangements. Some argued at the end of the Uruguay Round that GATT was already becoming cumbersome, complex, and increasingly inconsistent; where new decisions should be located in the General Agreement was becoming an emerging issue. The WTO is considered a new, permanent organization comparable in status to the World Bank and the International Monetary Fund. Its creation has given recognition to linkage between trade and finance, and has provided some hope that cooperation among the three institutions will improve. The consolidation of all the agreements and arrangements under a single umbrella thus represents a major simplification in the structure of global institutions. But the resource commitment to the WTO in no way matches that to the World Bank or International Monetary Fund; nor is it clear that the current GATT contracting parties actually seek an institution with as much policy independence as these two bodies currently enjoy.

One potentially important feature of the WTO is the ministerial conference meeting at two-year intervals, since one of the challenges after the Uruguay Round will be to monitor whether agreements are being implemented fully. Some also believe that the biennial ministerial conferences represent the first step toward permanent negotiations[21] and a move toward stronger global trade policy management.

But whether the ministerial conference will actually come to embody permanent negotiations is unclear. In my view, the ministerial conferences are unlikely to be the forum for substantive major reciprocity negotiations of the type that have occurred under GATT in the post-War era. Such conferences can help mediate conflicts and reduce tensions in the system, as well as facilitate monitoring the implementation of previous agreements, but clear agendas for major negotiations must be agreed to with timetables in advance.

Most post-War GATT negotiations have sought to address unresolved business from immediately preceding negotiating rounds by combining it with an agenda of newer issues. This process also seems likely in the period after the Uruguay Round, and perhaps during the ten-year implementation period for the Uruguay Round agreements on agriculture and textiles. The Uruguay Round process of GATT is slow and incremental, and this is likely to continue under the WTO. Ministerial conferences are likely to contribute to this process, but are unlikely to replace it.

Time will tell whether the WTO provides a basis for a revived world trade order. The fact that it emerged at the end of the Round rather than centrally at its launch, and that its public profile of major change seems so different from its *de facto* form of continuity, indicates that the WTO must be viewed with a mixture of cautious realism and optimistic hope.

How have developing countries benefited from system strengthening?

Estimates of gains from the Uruguay Round generated by computer models before the conclusion of the Round estimated that annual real income gains globally would range from US $200 to $500 billion from newly created market access and increased trade – corresponding to around 4 to 7 percent of world trade, and about one half to one and a half percent of global product (OECD 1993; Nguyen, Perroni, and Wigle 1993; and Francois, McDonald, and Nordström 1994). In these model results, the majority of gains occur in agriculture and textiles, but more so in agriculture. Most of the gains also accrue to industrial rather than developing countries (even after allowing for differences in the size of countries), and on the demand side and in textiles and agriculture as restrictions are weakened.[22] Subsequent runs with the Nguyen, Perroni, and Wigle (forthcoming) model, which more accurately capture the barrier changes agreed to, suggest gains of approximately $70 billion globally, down from their earlier estimate of $210 billion. The model-based analyses presented in this volume also provide estimates that are smaller than those generated before the Round outcome, but still substantial.

Perhaps the more important point associated with quantifying the system strengthening benefits to developing countries under the Uruguay Round is that, at the end of the day, the developing countries as a group believed that their paramount concern was to maintain forward momentum within the trading system by achieving any concrete outcome. While still driven by a desire to "strengthen" the system, their objective was also to prevent a breakdown in the trading system and a substantial weakening of GATT. By that stage, developing countries appeared to be willing to accept almost any agreement by the end of the Uruguay Round, as long as it was a firm agreement that preserved multilateral accommodation. As such, evaluating whether developing countries gained or lost from the various elements of system strengthening under the Uruguay Round may be of secondary importance to assessing the consequences of further conflict and erosion in the multilateral system.

A recent article that sheds light on the orders of magnitude involved with this notion of strengthening is a numerical global general equilibrium trade modeling piece by Perroni and Whalley (1994). With the model, they trace the consequences of a full sequence of retaliatory trade measures in a global tit-for-tat scenario as part of an evaluation of the incentives for smaller countries to seek regional trade agreements with large neighboring countries with whom they have a large proportion of their trade. In their view of the world, much of the new regionalism under the trading system – such as the US–Canada agreement, NAFTA, and the European accession agreements – are insurance-driven arrangements.

Their model, which uses a seven-regional structure calibrated to 1986 data, suggests that developing countries could suffer major consequences from a wide-ranging global trade conflict that was pursued in its full form to a Nash equilibrium. In the Nash equilibrium, they compute a real income loss of around 6 percent to the global economy as compared with the 1986 status quo, while the loss to smaller European and North American countries would be around 30 percent of income. Losses to developing countries (treated here as a single bloc) would be around 10 percent of income. Extremely high tariffs would exist in both the United States and the European Union. The interest of developing countries in preserving system cooperation, especially among the large industrial countries, emerges strongly in these results. And thus the precise system strengthening benefits they would derive from relatively small changes in system rules are perhaps less consequential than the preservation of cooperation.

Conclusion

Both when it was launched and during the long protracted negotiations that eventually concluded the Uruguay Round, developing countries repeatedly stressed their overriding interest in system strengthening. System strengthening is usually equated with an interest in firm, nondiscriminatory, multilateral-based trade rules that protect developing countries from bilateral pressure and that both restore and preserve openness in the trading system. But by the end of the Uruguay Round, developing countries were willing to accept almost any agreement that maintained cooperation in the trading system among large industrial countries, for fear that failed negotiations would further weaken multilateral order and force a reversion to conflict-ridden regional trade arrangements.

The strengthening of the system in market access areas under the Uruguay Round is, in all likelihood, less than what was desired by developing countries, since there are questions about the extent and durability of Round-based liberalization in agriculture and textiles. But the Uruguay Round provides potential for new liberalization built on bindings, particularly in agriculture, which may be a major long-run benefit to them. Combined with stronger dispute settlement procedures, and an expansion in the coverage of the system to such new areas as services, the benefits of incremental system strengthening in the conventional sense seem clearly to be of longer-run consequence to developing countries. Their overriding interest in avoiding a system breakdown determined their late-stage responses in the Uruguay Round, and the quantitative dimensions of that interest seemingly outweighed that in further incremental changes in their more traditional sense.

Appendix A   Standstill and rollback commitments in the Punta del Este declaration

In the Punta del Este declaration, contracting parties agreed that, "commencing immediately and continuing until the formal completion of the negotiations, each participant apply the following commitments:

(1) *Standstill*
(a) not to take any trade restrictive or distorting measure inconsistent with the provisions of the General Agreement of the Instruments negotiated within the framework of GATT or under its auspices;
(b) not to take any trade restrictive or distorting measure in the legitimate exercise of its GATT rights, that would go beyond that which is necessary to remedy specific situations, as provided for in the General Agreement and the Instruments referred to in (a) above;
(2) *Rollback*
(a) that all trade restrictive or distorting measures inconsistent with the provisions of the General Agreement or Instruments negotiated within the framework of GATT or under its auspices shall be phased out or brought into conformity within an agreed time frame not later than by the date of the formal completion of negotiations, taking into account multilateral agreements, undertakings and understandings, including strengthened rules and disciplines, reached in pursuance of the Objectives of the Negotiations;
(b) there shall be progressive implementation of this commitment on an equitable basis in consultations among participants concerned, including all affected participants. This commitment shall take account of the concerns expressed by any participant about measures directly affecting its trade interests;
(c) there shall be no GATT concessions requested for the elimination of these measures;
(3) *Surveillance of Standstill and Rollback*
    Each participant agrees that the implementation of these commitments on standstill and rollback shall be subject to multilateral surveillance so as to ensure that these commitments are being met. The Trade Negotiations Committee will decide on the appropriate mechanisms to carry out the surveillance, including periodic reviews and evaluations. Any participant may bring to the attention of the appropriate surveillance mechanism any actions or omissions it believes to be relevant to the fulfillment of these commitments. These notifications should be addressed to the GATT Secretariat which may also provide further relevant information."

Notes

I am grateful to Colleen Hamilton and Carlo Perroni for helpful discussions, and to Kym Anderson, Bob Hudec, Will Martin, Wendy Takacs, and Alan Winters for comments on earlier drafts of this chapter.

1. This more defensive posture is clearly reflected in newspaper headlines about the Uruguay Round toward its conclusion: "Third World Countries Fear GATT Sellout," *Globe and Mail*, December 20, 1993; "Countries Ponder the Fruits of Trade Accord," *Financial Times*, December 16, 1993; and "Trade Talks Spark Fears of New Colonialism," *Globe and Mail*, July 5, 1993.

2. From the launch of the Uruguay Round up to January 1989, approximately 170 of 400 proposals made in the Uruguay Round were tabled by developing countries singly, jointly, or with industrial countries (Whalley 1989). Moreover, based on information available to the GATT Secretariat, developing countries as a group increased their coverage of bindings from 22 percent of tariff ceilings to 78 percent (Francois, McDonald, and Nordström 1994). Rodrik (1993) also discusses the trade policy reform of developing countries.

3. Hamilton and Whalley (1994) provide a more in-depth discussion of the term "system" when applied to global trade arrangements.

4. In the period January 1992 to April 1993, eighteen new regional trade agreements were notified to GATT.

5. For example, the widely cited book on the global trading system by Jackson (1989) does not define the term.

6. Thus, table 14.1 can be thought of as implicitly characterizing a tree structure of system characteristics and subcharacteristics with varying degrees of substitution between each, and separability between the elements in each of the key characteristics. System strength (S) can thus be defined by the nested function:

$$S = S(E_1 [E_{11}...E_{1N}], E_2 [E_{21},...E_{2N}],...E_N[.])$$

over the characteristics E_i and the subcharacteristics E_{ij}

Thus, the extent to which changes in E_1 can be offset by changes in E_2 depends on the ease of substitution between them. It also follows that the strength of the rules (E_1 in table 14.1) can be increased and enforcement (E_2 in table 14.1) can be weakened so as to leave the overall system strength, S, unchanged. And, equally, E can be left unchanged by offsetting changes between, say, E_{11} and E_{12}. Overall, S is defined only by a strict minimum function if there is perfect substitutability between E_1, E_2 ... and E_N, and E_{11}, E_{12} ... E_{1N} and in other subcharacteristic functions.

7. Another key issue is what exactly was being strengthened in the Uruguay Round, and why. Thus, one of the objectives of the Punta del Este declaration that launched the Uruguay Round was to "strengthen the role of GATT, improve the multilateral trading system based on the principles and rules of the GATT, and bring about a wider coverage of world trade under agreed, effective, and enforceable multilateral disciplines." The Chairman of the contracting parties at the end of the Round referred to Uruguay Round results that "must serve as a vehicle for strong economic growth" (GATT 1994); others referred to strengthened *disciplines* (dispute settlement, antidumping, subsidies, and countervailing mechanisms), rather than a strengthened system.

8. Overall, tariffs were to be reduced by approximately 35 percent in the Uruguay Round. As noted in table 14.3, a large number of tariffs were also bound, especially by developing countries.

9. Low and Yeats (forthcoming) attach special significance to this Uruguay Round commitment as a source of gains for developing countries. Using data on 1992 trade flows, they calculate that the import coverage of nontariff measures for nonoil imports to industrial countries will drop from more than 18 percent 1992 to less than 4 percent when the Uruguay Round is fully implemented. But much of this reduction is accounted for by agricultural tariffication and the abolition of the MFA, rather than by the formal elimination of VERs.

10. But speculation continues about whether the EU bindings are high enough to permit the continued *de facto* use of a variable levy system, even if nominally restrained by bindings. Alan Winters and Kym Anderson provided this observation.

11. Textiles and clothing are to be integrated into the GATT according to the following timetable (GATT 1993). In stage 1 (January 1, 1995 to December 31, 1997), each country would integrate products from a list that represents 16 percent of the total volume of 1990 imports; annual quota growth rates are also to be 16 percent higher. In stage 2 (January 1, 1998 to December 31, 2001), 17 percent of products are to be integrated; growth rates are to increase by 25 percent. In stage 3 (January 1, 2002 to December 31, 2004), all remaining products are to be integrated; annual growth rates should be 27 percent higher than in stage 2.

12. Low and Yeats (forthcoming) estimate that 49 percent of all MFA quotas in place in 1990 could still be in place by the end of the transitional period in 2005. Given that quotas taken out of operation early in this process will typically be nonbinding, the proportion of originally binding quotas still in place will be considerably higher.

13. Quota modulation is the adjustment of safeguard actions over time by subproduct category and by exporter within set levels for more aggregate restrictions.

14. Hudec (1993) provides a detailed discussion and quantitative analysis of post-War GATT dispute settlement cases.

15. Egypt, for example, had not brought any dispute nor had any dispute been brought against it by the time of its GATT trade policy review mechanism (in 1991). It simply had had no involvement whatsoever in any GATT dispute settlement cases.

16. Jackson (1994) interprets both these weaknesses and the improvements initiated by the Uruguay Round.

17. Bob Hudec provided this observation.

18. Bob Hudec also provided this observation.

19. Modern game theory does not address adequately how cooperation in small-group situations either emerges or works. Some basic notions of cooperation preserving mechanisms have been forwarded – such as Rubinstein's (1982) Folk theorem, which calls for making penalty systems strong enough to enforce any outcome – none can easily be applied directly to the GATT process.

20. This section draws on the argument in Whalley (1994), in a piece prepared for a UNDP/ESCAP/KDI conference held at the Korean Development Institute, November 1994.
21. According to Director-General Sutherland, the institutional change will mean an end to *ad hoc* negotiation rounds, implying that multilateral trade negotiations "will become a permanent event" (GATT 1994).
22. The OECD (1993) model suggests that only 11 percent of gains will accrue to developing countries.

References

Bergsten, C. F. 1975. *Toward a New International Economic Order: Selected Papers of C. Fred Bergsten, 1972–74*. Lexington, Mass: Lexington Books.

Francois, J., B. McDonald, and H. Nordström 1994. "The Uruguay Round: A Global General Equilibrium Assessment." Paper presented at a conference on "Challenges and Opportunities for East-Asian Trade," Canberra, Australia, July.

GATT 1993. *Uruguay Round of Multilateral Trade Negotiations, Final Act.* MTN/FA, UR–93–0246. Geneva: GATT, December 15.

1994. "GATT Members Urged to Build on Uruguay Round Success." *Focus: GATT Newsletter* no. 105 January–February.

Hamilton, C., and J. Whalley 1994. *The Trading System after The Uruguay Round.* Washington, D.C.: Institute of International Economics.

Hart, M. 1987. "GATT Article XXIV and Canada–United States Trade Negotiations." *Review of International Business Law* December: 547–62.

Hindley, B. 1994. "Contingent Protection after the Uruguay Round: Safeguards, VERs, and Antidumping Actions." Paper presented at OECD Workshop on the New World Trading System. Paris, April 25–26.

Hudec, R. E. 1991. "Dispute Settlement." In J. S. Schott, ed., *Completing the Uruguay Round*. Washington, DC: Institute for International Economies.

1993. *Enforcing International Trade Law: The Evolution of the Modern GATT Legal System*. Salem, N. H.: Butterworth Legal Publishers.

Jackson, J. H. 1989. *The World Trading System*. Cambridge, Mass.: MIT Press.

1994. "Dispute Settlement." Paper presented at OECD Workshop on New World Trading System. Paris, April 25–26.

Kindleberger, C. P. 1973. *The World in Depression 1929–1939*. London: Allen Lane/Penguin Press.

Low, P., and A. Yeats forthcoming. "Non-Tariff Measures and Developing Countries: Has the Uruguay Round Leveled the Playing Field." *The World Economy*.

Nguyen, T. C. Perroni. and R. Wigle 1993. "An Evaluation of the Draft Final Act of the Uruguay Round." *Economic Journal* 103: 1540–49.

"A Uruguay Round Success?" *The World Economy*.

OECD 1993. *Assessing the Effects of the Uruguay Round*. Paris: OECD.

Perroni, C., and J. Whalley 1994. "The New Regionalism: Trade Liberalization or

Insurance?" Working Paper 4626. Cambridge, Mass.: National Bureau of Economic Research.

Rodrik, D. 1993. "Trade and Industrial Policy Reform in Developing Countries: A Review of Recent Theory and Evidence." In J. Behrman and T. N. Srinivasan, eds., *Handbook of Development Economics*. Amsterdam: North-Holland.

Rubinstein, A. 1982. "Perfect Equilibrium in a Bargaining Model." *Econometrica* 50(1): 97–109.

Schott, Jeffrey 1994. *The Uruguay Round: An Assessment*. Washington, DC: Institute for International Economics.

Tangermann, S. 1994. "An Assessment of the Uruguay Round Agreements on Agriculture and on Sanitary and Phytosanitary Measures." Draft paper prepared for the Directorate for Food Agriculture and Fisheries, and the Trade Directorate of OECD. Institute of Agricultural Economics, University of Gottingen.

UNCTAD 1994. *The Outcome of the Uruguay Round: An Initial Assessment – Supporting Papers to the Trade and Development Report, 1994*. New York: United Nations.

Whalley, J., ed. 1989. *The Uruguay Round and Beyond: The Final Report*. London: Macmillan Press Ltd.

1994. "The WTO and the Future of the Trading System." Paper presented at ESCAP/UNDP/KDI Regional Symposium on the Uruguay Round Agreements, Seoul, Korea, December 1–3.

15 The intrusion of environmental and labor standards into trade policy

Kym Anderson

Environmental standards, and possibly labor standards, promise to be considered for the agenda of the next multilateral trade negotiations. The two issues rose to prominence in the early 1990s, with the US Congress expressing its unwillingness to ratify the NAFTA unless it was accompanied by supplemental agreements on environmental and labor standards. Labor standards were an issue also during heated debate over a social charter among EU governments at Maastricht in 1992. In its closing stages the Uruguay Round included specific mention of a work program on trade and environment issues to be carried out by the WTO, and labor standards were discussed as well (albeit informally) among some GATT contracting parties.

One reason for the increasing prominence of labor and environmental issues stems from a substantial relaxation in recent decades of governmental border policies that inhibit the flow of goods, services, and capital.[1] The exposure of national economies to more competition from abroad – in part due to the success of GATT in reducing trade barriers – has focused attention on domestic policies, including cost-raising environmental and labor standards, that reduce the international competitiveness of some firms and industries (Bhagwati 1995). Producers are especially likely to protest when significant players with lower standards enter global markets, as has happened increasingly over the past quarter century. First there was the growth of Asia's newly industrializing economies, then the opening up of China and some other transition and developing countries. The phenomenon has also occurred at the regional level, with poorer members being admitted to free-trade blocs (Mediterranean nations to the European Community and Mexico to NAFTA). Within such blocs, advocates for higher standards seek to impose their policy preferences.

With respect to trade outside the main blocs, advocates for higher standards tend to support discriminatory import restrictions on like products from lower-standard countries. This is because restrictions reduce opposition by local firms to higher standards at home and at the same time increase the incentive for foreign firms and their governments to adopt higher standards abroad. However, such trade policy practices are discriminatory and protectionist. Advocates are brought into direct conflict with supporters of liberal world trade, and into coalition with traditional protectionist interests. Fear of attaching superficial respectability to traditional protectionism has led to charges that "social correctness" is the new protectionism (Steil 1994).

Why environmental issues are becoming more entwined with trade policy

In recent years the list of environmental concerns of global dimension has grown rapidly. People are not just worried about air, water, and soil pollution at the local, national, and regional levels; [2] some pollution is believed to be damaging the global environment, for example through ozone depletion and climate change. Some people in industrial countries are concerned that environmental problems will be exacerbated by economic growth in developing countries with laxer standards. And more and more people are anxious about resource depletion, species extinction, and animal rights at the global level. Integration of the world economy, along with rising consumption of imported products, brings with it new health and safety concerns. Needless to say, personal values play an important role in debates on these issues. Hence there is considerable scope for friction between countries with different priorities, resource endowments, incomes, and knowledge about how different activities and policies affect the environment.

Fluctuate though they might with the business cycle, such concerns are likely to keep growing. One reason is that environment-related science is perceived to be more solid now than twenty years ago. Another reason is that both the world's population and its real per capita income are increasing at rapid rates, while supplies of most natural resources are limited, and markets for environmental services are incomplete or absent.[3] Markets are underdeveloped because of disputed or nonexistent property rights, or because of the high cost of enforcing those rights.

The advanced industrial economies have established institutional structures to help achieve social consensus on appropriate environmental or sustainable development policies and their enforcement. Some traditional societies – before they begin to "modernize" and subject their resources to the pressure of overpopulation – have structures that serve a similar function. But such structures are lacking in the newly developing economies where the world's population and consumption growth are expected to be concentrated in the foreseeable future. And at the multilateral level, cooperative inter-governmental mechanisms have only recently begun to be formed in the environmental area, and it will take some time before many of them become effective.

With forums for multilateral environmental dialogue yet to be developed, and with the latest scientific evidence giving new urgency to environmental questions, environmental groups, especially in the more industrial economies, are increasingly turning to one of the few policy instruments available to their governments for influencing environmental outcomes both at home and abroad: trade restrictions. Environmentalists perceive trade policy as a means both of raising standards at home and abroad and of inducing countries to become signatories to international agreements. These groups are aware that, unless compensated, firms will oppose the raising of domestic standards if competitors abroad are not subjected to similar costly regulations. But the loss of competitiveness can be offset by import restrictions on products from lower-standard countries, removing opposition by domestic firms to higher standards while increasing the incentive for foreign firms and their governments to adopt higher standards. With respect to international environmental agreements, trade measures look attractive because they are relatively easy to enforce and immediate in their impact – they make effective sticks and carrots. Even the threat of trade sanctions can rapidly persuade a country to join an international environmental agreement and abide by its rules.

Discriminatory trade restrictions have already been shown to affect particular targeted products. The Montreal Protocol on phasing out CFCs, which deplete the ozone layer, is one example. There have also been proposals to use trade sanctions against products not directly related to environmental issues in an effort to persuade developing countries to adopt stricter environmental standards. Threats have been made, for example, to provide less open access to textile and other markets in industrial countries unless logging is managed on a more sustainable basis in developing countries.[4]

Economic growth, trade, and the environment

The standard theory of changing comparative advantages in a growing world economy can readily be modified to incorporate at least some environmental concerns. As espoused by Krueger (1977) and Leamer (1987), the theory suggests that when a developing country opens up to international trade, its exports will initially be specialized in primary products because stocks of produced capital relative to natural resources are comparatively low. Should capital stocks per worker expand more for the country than for the global economy, the country's comparative advantage will gradually shift from the extraction of raw materials to more capital-

and skill-intensive activities, particularly manufactures and services. This is the case except in countries relatively well endowed with land per capita, where produced capital and new capital-intensive technologies tend to be employed more to extract minerals or farm the land. The more natural resource-poor or densely populated the country, the greater the tendency, initially, for nonprimary exports to be intensive in the use of unskilled labor. In the case of manufactures, the process of upgrading to capital-intensive production over time leaves room in international markets for later-industrializing countries to begin with labor-intensive, export-oriented manufacturing.

This theory need be complicated only slightly by considering nonmarketed environmental services and pollution byproducts. One must allow for the fact that as a country's per capita income and industrial output grow, the value its citizens place on the environment increases and with it their demands for proper valuation of environmental resources, for the assigning and better policing of property rights, and for the implementation of costly domestic pollution abatement policies.[5] The severity of abatement policies is often positively correlated with per capita income, population density, and the degree of urbanization.

If all economies were growing equally rapidly, the progressive introduction of national environmental taxes and regulations would tend to cause pollution-intensive production processes[6] to relocate gradually from wealthier and/or more densely populated countries to developing and/or more sparsely populated countries.[7] They would also slow or reverse growth in the demand for products whose consumption is pollutive, and more so in wealthier and/or more densely populated countries where taxes on such products tend to be higher. If more advanced economies are net importers (net exporters) of products whose production (consumption) is pollutive, their optimal environmental policies would worsen their terms of trade to the benefit of poorer economies, and the converse (Siebert, Eichberger, Gronych, and Pethig 1980; Anderson 1992a). Thus even countries without (or with unchanged) environmental policies will be affected through trade and investment by the development of environmental policies that accompany growth in other economies.[8]

The story becomes more complicated when account is taken of policy reactions to international environmental problems such as the global commons, species depletion, and animal rights. The ban on ivory trade under the CITES is an extreme example: the strong comparative advantage that Southern African nations had in elephant products evaporated when the ban was introduced in 1989. Another is the recent ban, adopted under the Basel Convention relating to hazardous waste, on exports of so-called hazardous recyclables from industrial to developing countries; the ban threatens the growth prospects for recycling industries in developing countries. A third example is the proposed limitation on imports into some high-income countries of tropical hardwoods, the aim of which is to discourage deforestation. An import ban of this kind would reduce export growth in logs and perhaps sawn timber in those developing countries still well endowed with hardwood forests, while improving the terms of trade of net importers of hardwood such as Japan, Korea, and Taiwan. The Montreal Protocol on phasing out the use of ozone-depleting CFCs incorporates discriminatory trade provisions designed to limit the relocation from signatory to nonsignatory countries of industries producing or using CFCs, as well as encouraging nonsignatories to accede to the protocol.[9] And there is the infamous example of the US ban on the importation of Mexican tuna, which US authorities deemed to have been caught in dolphin-unfriendly nets. Domestic US regulations affecting the use of dolphin-unfriendly nets on US registered fishing vessels, if implemented alone, would have boosted Mexican competitiveness in tuna fishing, but the subsequent ban on tuna imports instead reduced it. As is clear in the latter two examples, the motive for trade policy action is often a mixed bag of concerns for national competitiveness, the global commons, and animal welfare.

Two facts therefore need to be recognized. First, there are significant international environmental issues that transcend simpler transborder matters of the sort that can be handled through negotiations between neighboring governments. These relate not just to the physical damage human activity, regardless of its location, can do to the global environment. There are as well – for want of a better term – psychological spillovers. For example, I may grieve if your country's activities threaten a particular animal or plant species. Or I may grieve if I believe your desire for higher national environmental standards is not sufficiently recognized by your national government (a political market failure). In these circumstances there is a perceived need for multilateral action to reduce global problems, and that is where trade policy measures come in.

The other fact is that one country's environmental policy is not independent of the policy choices of other countries. Why? Because the imposition of higher standards or pollution charges at home alters the international competitiveness of industries, in particular by harming more pollution-intensive ones. Unless their competitors abroad are subjected to similar cost-raising policies, such industries lobby against the imposition of higher standards at home. And while it is true that less-pollutive industries at home benefit from stricter environmental policy, being more diffuse they are not likely to add much support to environmental lobbying.

Trade policy became implicated in environmental politics in the late 1960s, when the first wave of widespread environmental concern was expressed in industrial countries. Environmental groups perceived that the loss of competitiveness of pollution-intensive industries could be offset by restrictions on imports from lower-standard countries, at once reducing opposition by industry to higher standards at home and increasing the incentive for foreign firms and their governments to adopt higher standards abroad to avoid being subjected to anti- "eco-dumping" duties.

Over time, the demand for unilateral use of trade policy for environmental purposes has grown in two ways. First, with the decline in traditional trade barriers (tariffs, transport and communication costs, etc.), any given environmental charge is becoming relatively more important as a determinant of international competitiveness, ceteris paribus. Second, with the deregulation of financial markets and markets for direct foreign investment in the 1980s, opportunities for firms to disinvest in high-standard countries and relocate their factories in lower-standard countries ("pollution havens") have expanded. Environmental groups fear this will result in governments delaying the introduction or enforcement of environmental policies – and possibly even lowering standards, a "race to the bottom" – in the attempt to attract or retain investments and hence jobs.

Both the use of trade policy unilaterally for environmental purpose and increasing its use in multilateral environmental agreements raise the likelihood of conflict between rich and poorer countries. And the fact that discriminatory trade measures are being more frequently applied to achieve the environmental objectives of rich countries, without regard to poorer countries' legitimate concern for economic development, increases the likelihood of environment-related trade disputes. There is even dispute over what constitutes the global commons. Some would argue that a country or region should not have to bow to international pressure to preserve endangered species in their territory (or at least not without adequate compensation), while others would argue that such countries are merely the custodians of those resources for the benefit of humankind generally.

The rising popularity of using discriminatory trade measures to address environmental issues should concern the world at large, and developing countries in particular, for at least four reasons. First, trade policy measures typically are not the best instruments for achieving environmental objectives. This is because trade sanctions or the threat of sanctions do not directly affect the root causes of environmental problems. Their use in place of more efficient instruments unnecessarily reduces the level and growth of global economic welfare as conventionally measured – and may even encourage rather than reduce global environmental degradation and resource depletion.[10]

The second reason for concern is that producer interest groups and some environmental groups are nevertheless finding it mutually advantageous to use environmental arguments in support of their claims for unilateral import restrictions, particularly following the costly imposition of stricter environmental standards on domestic producers.[11] In this sense, the environment serves as a convenient additional excuse for raising trade barriers, one that is socially respectable. Unfortunately, such protectionist action reduces real income not just at home but elsewhere too, especially in developing and natural resource-abundant countries.

Third, protectionist measures threaten to be followed by retaliatory and counterretaliatory action, ultimately undermining the rules-based open global trading system on which the dynamism of developing economies continues to depend.

Fourth, in addition to proposing the use of trade restrictions, some environmentalists oppose trade and investment liberalization. They oppose GATT's attempts to reduce barriers on at least two grounds: freer trade means more output and income, which they presume would mean more consumption and hence resource depletion and degradation of the natural environment; and freer trade and investment encourage the relocation of environmentally degrading industries to countries with lower environmental protection standards and/or more fragile natural environments. This, the argument goes, would both give polluters freer rein and expand transportation activity, further contributing to environmental damage.

Neither of these assertions is unambiguously supported by empirical evidence. The notion that increased output and income mean greater damage to the environment may be true initially for some poorer countries, but once middle-income status is reached people tend to alter their behavior in ways that reduce pressure on the environment. A key factor here is family size: higher average income leads in time to a lower rate of population growth (Baldwin 1994). This, along with expanded employment opportunities and hence higher wages resulting from trade liberalization, is likely to reduce the rate of environmental degradation due to population pressure in developing countries. In rural areas it means fewer people denuding hillsides to eke out a subsistence income, while in urban areas it means fewer unemployed or underemployed squatters in shanty towns with poor sanitation and water.

Another common behavioral change as economies open up and incomes rise is increased demand for education. With more income and education comes more skillful management of resources and more forceful demands on governments to pass and enforce stringent environmental policies (Radetski 1992; Grossman 1994). As well, the political cost of implementing such policy reforms tends to fall because of increased opportunities for businesses to acquire more and cheaper environmentally benign production processes and products from abroad.

The other major assertion by environmentalists, that the global environment is harmed by the relocation of production following trade and investment liberalization, is also questionable. We know from the law of comparative advantage that not all industries will be relocated from rich to poor countries when the former's trade barriers are lowered: some industries in the north will expand at the expense of industries in the south, and vice versa. In any case, it should not be assumed that relocating some production to the south necessarily worsens the environment. Recent preliminary examinations of the likely environmental effects of reducing government assistance to two of the north's most protected industries, coal and food, reveal that in both cases the global environment may well be improved by trade liberalization, especially if complementary environmental policies are in place (Anderson 1992b; Steenblik and Coroyannakis 1995). Nor does the risk of environmental damage from transport activity necessarily increase with trade reform. The lowering of import barriers to processed primary products, for example, would allow more raw materials to be processed in resource-rich countries, thereby reducing shipped cargo. But it will take many more empirical studies before the more extreme environmental groups alter their perception of and publicity against multilateral trade reform as an environmentally unfriendly activity.

GATT and the environment prior to the Uruguay Round

How "green" are the GATT rules, and how have they been adapted over time?[12] From the outset GATT has been a conservationist institution, since one of its purposes has been to reduce trade barriers and thereby the inefficiency in the use of the world's resources. The heart of GATT, signed by 23 contracting parties in 1947 and since then by another 100 or so, is the nondiscrimination requirements of Articles I and III. These obligate parties to treat imports from any GATT-contracting party no less favorably than other imports (the "MFN" requirement) and no less favorably, after border taxes are paid, than similar domestic products (the national treatment requirement).

Article XX provides exceptions to these general rules, however, including provisions for some environmental regulations. Specifically, parts (b) and (g) of Article XX allow trade restrictions "necessary to protect human, animal, or plant life or health" and "relating to the conservation of exhaustible natural resources if such measures are made effective in conjunction with restrictions on domestic production or consumption," as long as such restrictions "are not applied in a manner which would constitute a means of arbitrary or unjustifiable discrimination between countries where the same conditions prevail, or a disguised restriction on international trade." The latter has been interpreted to mean that the measure must be primarily for a conservation purpose (rather than for mixed motives) and must be necessary in the sense of being the least GATT-inconsistent measure available. These provisos have resulted in rather narrow interpretations of Article XX, which is partly why some environmental groups have called for further greening of the GATT (Charnovitz 1991; Esty 1994). But there is nothing in the GATT that prevents a country from adopting production or consumption measures to offset environmental externalities associated with either. And because trade itself is almost never claimed to be the root cause of an environmental problem, supporters of the institution see little need to consider trade measures as part of the solutions to those problems.

When widespread public interest in trade and environmental issues surfaced in rich countries in the late 1960s to early 1970s, concern focused mainly on industrial pollution within and between neighboring advanced economies. Foreign trade and investment issues centered on how the imposition of stricter pollution standards at home might damage a country's international competitiveness, and how to avoid such damage through border protection measures. Where environmental damage caused by production is purely local, calls by disadvantaged firms for trade restrictions or subsidies to offset the effect of raised standards have no economic logic: such assistance encourages domestic production which tends to offset the desired effect of limiting pollution.[13] Nor is it reasonable to conclude that other countries are engaging in eco-dumping if their imports are produced with laxer environmental standards, for those lower standards may be consistent with their priorities and natural resource endowments. Even so, claims for protection against eco-dumping have political appeal and may result in higher import barriers or export subsidies in advanced economies.[14]

Trade policy actions are more likely to occur, and to be more difficult to dismiss as inappropriate, when environmentalists view damage to the environment as unacceptable regardless of the nation in which the damage occurs. This case is more problematic if the damage is not just psychological (as with animal welfare) but also physical, for then the relocation of production to a country with laxer environmental standards may worsen the environment at home, in addition to reducing the profitability of home firms. The US–Mexico dispute over the use of dolphin-unfriendly nets by tuna fishermen again comes to mind. In that case GATT ruled against the US ban on imports of tuna from Mexico, partly because the ban did not distinguish which type of net was used, but mainly because to do otherwise would have created a huge loophole in the GATT for any country unilaterally to apply trade restrictions as a means of imposing its environmental standards on other countries. Such a loophole would work against the main objective of the multilateral trading system, which is to provide stable and predictable nondiscriminatory market access through agreed rules and disciplines and bound tariffs on imports.

Environmental ramifications of the Uruguay Round agreements

The wave of public concern for the natural environment leading up to and following UNCED held in Brazil in June 1992, is much more intense, widespread, and likely to be sustained than the environmental movement of the 1960s and early 1970s. The Uruguay Round agenda was set by 1986, before the current wave had built up, so the trade/environment issue was not a separate item for negotiation. Nor did the Uruguay Round produce an environmental impact assessment. However, the GATT's Working Group on Environmental Measures and International Trade, formed in 1971, was activated for the first time in 1991 and has met frequently since then. As well, several of the Uruguay Round agreements contain provisions that relate to the environment and build on articles in the original GATT.

The most fundamental provision in the Uruguay Round act is expressed in the preamble to the agreement to establish the WTO. The WTO's objective is to enable all contracting parties maximum opportunity for: "expanding the production and trade in goods and services, while allowing for the optimal use of the world's resources in accordance with the objective of sustainable development, seeking both to protect and preserve the environment and enhance the means for doing so in a manner consistent with their respective needs and concerns at different levels of economic development." In Marrakesh in April 1994, when ministers signed the Final Act of the Uruguay Round, they agreed to establish a Committee on Trade and Environment to report to the first biennial meeting of ministers (in late 1996). A subcommittee of the Preparatory Committee began work immediately pending the establishment of the WTO. The new GATS and agreements on trade in goods are to be considered by the committee, which among other things will examine:[15]

- the relationship between trade measures and environmental measures in promoting sustainable development, and the need for rules to enhance that positive interaction;
- the relationship between the multilateral trading system and trade measures used for environmental purposes, including in multilateral environmental agreements;
- the relationship between the multilateral trading system and environmental measures with significant effects on trade;
- the environmental effects of trade liberalization; and
- the relationship between the WTO's dispute settlement mechanisms and those in multilateral environmental agreements.

The Uruguay Round agreement contains five other major environmental provisions, as set out in the following sections.

Technical barriers to trade

The 1994 agreement on such barriers is an amplification of an agreement that arose out of the Tokyo Round in 1979. Its main purpose is to ensure that mandatory technical regulations, voluntary product standards, and conformity-assessment procedures do not create unnecessary barriers to trade. It recognizes that countries should not be prevented from taking measures necessary to protect all forms of life, health, and the environment, and that each country has the right to set the level of (preferably international) standards it deems appropriate. The agreement requires governments to apply regulations in a manner that is nondiscriminatory (satisfying MFN and national treatment disciplines) and no more trade restrictive than necessary to meet environmental objectives. It is noteworthy that of the 400 technical barriers brought to the GATT Secretariat's attention since 1980, none has ever been challenged as being unnecessarily trade restrictive. This can be attributed in part to the high degree of transparency required under the technical barrier agreement, which facilitates consultations and amendments. The agreement will continue to provide governments ample room to address environmental problems without facing challenges from their trading partners. Where disputes do arise, either party can call on technical experts to help resolve them.

Sanitary and phytosanitary measures

This agreement elaborates what was part of the 1979 technical barrier agreement. It covers measures that protect animal and plant health and guarantee human and animal food safety. As with the technical barrier agreement, measures should not exceed what is necessary for health protection, where possible using international, nondiscriminatory standards that are the least trade restrictive. One aim of the agreement has been to tighten provisions to lessen abuse in the name of traditional protection. Again, technical experts can be called in to settle disputes.

The agreement on agriculture

This is an agreement to reduce agricultural-support policies. One potential environmental benefit will be the reduction in incentives for intensive farming in ill-suited areas (Anderson 1992c). But there are exemptions from commitments to reduce domestic support. One is for direct payments under environmental programs, up to the full cost of loss of income involved in complying with the program – a violation of the polluter-pays principle. Another exemption is for price supports under production-limiting programs. Because one effect of acreage set-aside policies and the like is to raise the value of land, this will offset somewhat the environmental advantage of other parts of the agreement relating to the intensity of production on remaining acreage (since land to be set aside is not necessarily the most ecologically fragile).

The agreement on subsidies and countervailing duties

This revision of the subsidies agreement that came out of the Tokyo Round identifies nonactionable subsidies on which countervailing duties cannot be applied. It includes assistance to adapt existing facilities to new environmental laws, whereby up to one fifth of the cost of adaptation is considered a nonactionable subsidy – another violation of the polluter-pays principle. However, a WTO member cannot legitimately countervail nonexistence of an environmental regulation, that is, the new agreement does not consider the absence or weakness of an environmental regulation or charge as an implicit subsidy.

The agreement on TRIPS

This agreement provides more enforceable patent protection for trade-related intellectual property, which will encourage research and provide better access to new technologies. There is, however, the possibility for excluding inventions from patent if preventing their commercial exploitation is considered necessary to protect the environment.

Overall, then, the trade liberalization resulting from the Uruguay Round is likely to conserve resources and reduce environmental degradation. Ironically, some of the clauses included at the behest of environmental groups may violate the polluter-pays principle.

GATT/WTO and multilateral environmental agreements

As mentioned earlier, there is yet another, somewhat more valid, way in which trade policy is being called on to help achieve environmental objectives: as a carrot or stick to entice countries to sign and abide by multilateral environmental agreements. The free-rider problem is inherent in combating global environmental problems such as ozone depletion or climate change. One of the more obvious and possibly cost-effective ways to inhibit free riding is to write trade provisions into agreements, as was done in the 1987

Montreal Protocol on reducing the use of CFCs and halons to slow ozone depletion. To date, no GATT contracting party has formally objected to that use of trade policy. Nor has any objection been made to the ban on trade in ivory, rhino horn, and tiger products that are part of CITES or to the trade provisions in the Basel Convention on trade in hazardous waste. Conflicts may well arise, however, if trade provisions are drafted into more contentious multilateral environmental agreements such as one imposing a global carbon tax. The matter is a priority on the agenda of the new WTO Committee on Trade and Environment. So far, discussions in the WTO have centered on the idea of providing waivers on a case-by-case basis, or alternatively of providing an "environmental window" for multilateral environmental agreements within the GATT exceptions clause (Article XX).

In assessing the appropriate role for trade policy in multilateral environmental agreements, it is helpful to recall that supporters of trade liberalization and of environmental protection share a common goal: improving social welfare. They also share a common problem: the need to foster multilateral cooperation to achieve that objective, because in each sphere (the economy and the environment) there is considerable and increasing interdependence among nations. But the two groups differ in one important respect: supporters of liberal world trade have understood its virtues for two centuries and have been active for more than fifty years in building institutions such as the WTO to help achieve their goal, whereas supporters of environmental protection, a relatively new concept, entered only recently as significant players in international policy arenas.

Understandably, supporters of liberal trade and the GATT/WTO resent these "new kids on the block." They are not jealously protecting their hard-won territory; they genuinely believe that reducing trade barriers is likely to be environmentally friendly and consistent with sustainable development in the long run because it allows the world to use its resources more efficiently.[16] Equally, advocates for greater environmental protection are frustrated that international agreements as important as those resulting from the recent Uruguay Round can be implemented without mandatory environmental impact assessments or environmental safeguards.

Clearly there is scope for greater understanding and altered strategies on both sides. More important, there is the distinct possibility that, by working together, both groups will further their objectives – a "win–win" outcome. If this is to happen, it will require much more than just greening the GATT/WTO. In particular, as Esty (1994) suggests, it may ultimately require a world environment organization to set rules, negotiate multilateral agreements, and settle disputes over environmental policies in the same way that GATT has presided over trade policies for the past five decades. For liberal traders, the advantage of a world environment organization is that it would direct environmentalists' attention toward more appropriate instruments than trade policy for achieving environmental objectives. As a result, both sets of policies would more effectively contribute to the common goals of sustainable development and social welfare. Even so, the issue of which would have precedence, the WTO or the environmental organization, would need to be resolved. It is noteworthy that the side agreement to NAFTA gives a degree of precedence to environmental concerns. A more appropriate approach, when environmental and trade issues conflict, would be to strike a compromise in the interests of optimizing social welfare.

Without doubt, the trade policy community needs to be involved in the negotiating of multilateral environmental agreements that are likely to include trade provisions, and to develop criteria by which WTO members could assess in advance the extent to which trade restrictions are acceptable. Some of the relevant criteria were enunciated at UNCED. Trade provisions must be strictly necessary and effective in achieving stated environmental objectives. For the reasons outlined earlier, there will often be a more effective instrument than trade restrictions. In the absence of superior instruments, trade instruments should be minimally restrictive and used only in proportion to the size of the environmental problem. In addition, they ought to be transparent and not protectionist, and where possible consistent with GATT principles of nondiscrimination and key environmental principles such as the polluter pays.

GATT/WTO and labor standards

An even more inappropriate part of the WTO's potential agenda, and one that has an even clearer north–south dimension, is the issue of labor standards (Bhagwati and Dahejia 1994). Government and/or labor union action in setting minimum labor standards is often considered necessary to reduce the risk of exploitation of (particularly low-skilled) workers by capitalists. As with environmental standards, labor standards differ from country to country and tend to be less stringent in developing ones. The direct effect of such factors as shorter working weeks, higher overtime pay, longer annual leave, and safer working conditions may be to raise worker welfare, but they also raise the cost of employing labor – otherwise they would have been adopted voluntarily and there would be no need for government or union action.[17] Labor standards are therefore similar to taxes on production that differ across industries: their indirect effects need to be considered as well (Ehrenberg 1994). Specifically, they tend to hurt (particularly low-skilled) labor-intensive industries most in high-standard countries, reducing the capacity of those industries to compete with producers in low-standard countries while enhancing the capacity of the latter to compete (Rybczynski 1959).

Harmed industries can respond to demands for higher labor standards by lobbying against their imposition and/or by demanding protection from imports from lower-standard countries until their standards are raised. Thus one country's choice of standards is not independent of the choices in other countries, nor are the country's trade policies independent. The decline in traditional trade barriers that has accompanied the internationalization of the global economy means that any given cost-raising standard is relatively more important as a determinant of international competitiveness. Meanwhile, the deregulation of direct foreign investment abroad has increased opportunities for firms to relocate their factories from higher- to lower-standard countries.

Is there a claim for placing labor standards on the WTO's agenda because of international spillovers? Many economists would say no, because they perceive no physical spillovers of the sort that push environmental issues on to that agenda (global warming, ozone depletion). There may, however, be some validity to the claim when one considers the effect of high standards for low-skilled workers in attracting unwanted migrants from less-developed economies across borders that may be difficult to police.[18] Furthermore, there is the possibility of psychological spillover. People may grieve because of the abuse of what they perceive as worker rights or poor working conditions abroad, just as they may grieve for low environmental standards or abuse of human rights generally. But, while that may justify action of some sort at the international level, only under very limited circumstances are multilateral trade measures worthy of consideration as sticks or carrots for encouraging other countries to raise their standards. One case is when, as happened in the NAFTA negotiations, significant negotiating parties refuse to enter further multilateral trade negotiations unless labor standards are on the agenda. Then, a judgment has to be made by the other negotiating parties as to whether it is worth continuing under such a condition. Another is when aggrieved high-standard countries can find no lower-cost way to influence the policies of lower-standard countries. Even then, the psychological benefits to the north may be insufficient to warrant the costs to consumers and exporters in high-standard countries. A third possible circumstance is when a country might be reluctant to raise its own standards because of the fear of eroding the international competitiveness of its domestic industries.

Ostensibly, the concern in high-standard countries is not so much the average-wage difference but such factors as occupational health and safety standards, worker rights to form unions and seek a minimum wage, child or forced labor, and the derogation of national labor laws in export-processing zones. The United States and France, for example, were at pains to make clear at Marrakesh that their push for the WTO to consider trade/labor issues focused on differences in labor standards other than wages. Human rights activists and nongovernmental organizations often add support to union calls for higher standards in developing countries, even though the formal raising of labor standards is more likely to drive employment into the informal sector (where labor standards are even lower), or to expand the ranks of unemployed people seeking high-standard, formal-sector jobs.[19]

Like environmental groups, traditional protectionist forces in high-income countries are quick to support calls for import restraint against goods from lower-standard countries. Sometimes they quote simple trade theory (the Factor-Price Equalization and Stolper–Samuelson theorems) in support of their argument that liberal trade leads to factor-price convergence and in particular to a drop in low-skill wages in high-wage countries. Such theorems are not very robust when more than two countries' goods and factors are involved (Falvey 1995); nor are they supported by empirical-simulation results of trade-liberalization agreements such as the Uruguay Round.[20] There is also the risk, in a low-standard country, that support for openness will be challenged by those who lose from the forced raising of standards; they might be driven to lobby against their country's exposure to other cultures.

Why has the issue of labor standards suddenly become more entangled with GATT/WTO and trade policy issues? The entwining of trade and labor issues, a century-old practice,[21] tends to recur when the trading system is in the news and particularly if labor markets are in trouble. It became an issue when the International Trade Organization was being conceived in 1947,[22] again at the end of the Tokyo Round, and now as the WTO establishes itself and implementation of the Uruguay Round gets underway. It is no coincidence that this is happening when industrial countries are currently experiencing poor labor market performance, with unemployment above 10 percent in Europe and the relative earnings of unskilled labor in the United States deteriorating.

The issue is gradually becoming more prominent, not just because of the declining trade and investment barriers mentioned earlier that have meant cost-raising standards are more important determinants of international competitiveness. Cheaper communications also have meant that citizens of high-standard countries have more access to information on labor standards in other countries. That, together with the growing sense of a global village, allows concern for human rights to spread beyond national boundaries, a tendency that can be expected to continue indefinitely as global economic growth and integration proceed. Around that upward trend in concern will be fluctuations in the opposite direction to the business cycle: the worse the labor market is performing in high-wage countries, the more likely it is that imports from low-wage countries will be blamed,[23] notwithstanding clear evidence that such imports are at most only a minor contributor (Lawrence 1994; McDougall and Tyers 1995). That likelihood is exacerbated by the information revolution, which together with other forces is increasing the demand for skilled relative to unskilled workers (Wood 1994).

Another reason labor standards have become more prominent in the multilateral trade arena is that they have recently penetrated regional integration agreements. One example is the Protocol on Social Policy which was annexed to the Treaty of Maastricht signed by EU member governments in February 1992 (Sapir 1996). Another is that labor was the subject of a side agreement to NAFTA in 1993 – a price American president Clinton paid to buy off opposition from labor groups to NAFTA's passage through the US Congress. Encouraged by their success in those regional agreements, and earlier in some minor trade and investment agreements (Lawrence 1994), labor advocates – like environmental lobby groups – are now seeking influence at the multilateral trade level. Both lobby groups were taking advantage of the desire of GATT's contracting parties to bring the Uruguay Round agreements to a conclusion. Their impact is in large part attributable to the superficial popular appeal of their cause, while the downside in terms of potential risk to the global trading system is far from obvious to the layperson. Despite such risk, at the conclusion of the Uruguay Round the only mention made of labor was in the final remarks of the chairman of the Trade Negotiations Committee. Without actually naming the United States and France, he noted that some participants requested examination by the WTO of the relationships between trade and various domestic policies, including labor standards.

Developing countries and "social imperialism"

The Uruguay Round agreement is good news for developing countries. However, demand for greater harmonization of domestic policies in the quest for "fair" trade coupled with the greening of world politics and growing interest in international human rights is likely to pressure the WTO into performing tasks for which it is not designed. The WTO needs to consolidate its role in the world and ensure implementation of the Uruguay Round before moving into thornier issues that are only peripherally connected with trade.[24]

Such pressure on the WTO is of concern to developing countries, not so much because the imposition of higher standards would be costly to them. In fact, middle-income, mid-standard countries could be net beneficiaries if low-income, low-standard countries were required to raise their standards to minimum acceptable levels. And even the negative direct effect for low-income economies of having to raise their standards might be offset somewhat, at least for the most labor-abundant poor countries, by a terms-of-trade improvement if many countries were to raise their labor standards multilaterally and if that reduced the global supply of low-skilled labor time.

What kindles the suspicion of many developing countries is a perception of social imperialism on the part of OECD countries. Developing countries feel that they are being denied their national sovereignty. While they are not being targeted *per se*, the fact that developing countries are poorer, and that their comparative advantages tend to be in labor-, natural-resource-, and pollution-intensive industries, means they are particularly vulnerable to pressure for stricter standards and to the prospect of less market access in stricter-standard countries. Furthermore, should the use of trade policy to harmonize standards upward lead to trade retaliation and counterretaliation, it could weaken the multilateral trading system on which developing countries are becoming more dependent as they liberalize their economies. It could also encourage developing countries to seek refuge from anti-eco or -social dumping duties by association with or accession to the European Union or NAFTA, where they might expect to receive greater compensation for raising their social standards. Were that to happen, though, the net gain they might enjoy could well be at the expense of excluded developing countries.

With the entwining of social issues and trade policy more likely to tighten in the foreseeable future, developing countries must decide how to respond. One way would be to disseminate more widely the sound arguments for not using trade-restrictive measures to achieve environmental or labor objectives. These arguments include the following:

- differences in standards are a legitimate source of comparative advantage insofar as they reflect differences in resource endowment, social preference, and ability to afford the good things in life;
- standards rise with per capita income, and liberal trade promotes income growth; theory and empirical evidence provide little reason to expect that differences in standards contribute significantly to differences in costs of production and hence to trade and investment patterns, or that downward harmonization of standards is occurring; [25]
- if freer trade were to worsen the welfare of, say, low-skilled workers, adjustment-assistance programs would be much cheaper solutions than trade restrictions, as would nontrade measures such as labeling ("dolphin-friendly tuna", "made with unionized labor") that allow consumers to exercise their preferences in the market;

- even advanced economies such as the United States employ children for such things as babysitting, housework, and delivering newspapers, and they had lower standards at earlier stages of their development;
- because developing countries have contributed a disproportionately small amount per capita to global environmental problems such as the greenhouse effect, they should be compensated accordingly for contributing to their solution rather than have a contribution demanded of them under the threat of trade sanctions; and
- the GATT multilateral trading system is threatened by environmental and labor groups being captured by traditional protectionist groups in high-standard countries, and by resulting trade restrictions and pressure to raise standards being used by protectionist groups in lower-standard countries to argue against export-oriented development strategies.

Helpful though such arguments are, more dialogue and compromise between high-income and developing countries is needed. If developing countries were to commit themselves to enforcing minimum standards and to gradually raising those standards on a specified schedule, in return for gradual improvements in OECD market access, high-income countries would be less able to deny that improvements in social standards are positively related to income and trade growth. Likewise, if developing countries were seen to be enforcing reasonable standards on their foreign investors, concern about capital outflow to pollution or cheap labor havens and the consequent loss of jobs in high-standard countries would be less justifiable.[26] Similarly, anxiety over deforestation would wane if developing countries demonstrated that they were able and willing to police restrictions on felling in return for adequate compensation.

A more controversial suggestion (Rodrik 1994) is for high-standard countries to take action against a trading partner if trade with that country violates a widely held social standard (one that is accepted by export and consumer interests in those countries and by aggrieved import-competing producers and environmental/labor groups). An erosion of confidence in the fairness of the trading system, the reasoning goes, may ultimately be more costly to the world economy than the action against the offending trading partner, suggesting the Safeguards Agreement of the Uruguay Round be broadened to allow a "social safeguards" clause that would allow a country to restrict the offending imports and compensate the trading partner. Its proponent recognizes this could do more harm than good (not least because it would formalize a link between trade policy and social standards). Even so, Rodrik argues, its merits need to be weighed against other options available to developing countries to minimize damage from the encroachment of

---

Box 15.1 *Guiding principles on trade and environmental and labor standards*

1. Trade, environmental, and labor policies should promote efficient resource use, in which case trade liberalization and economic development will be consistent with conserving natural resources and enhancing both the natural and the work environment.

2. Governments should implement and enforce appropriate domestic environmental and labor policies that deal with the root causes of environmental problems and unemployment/slow wage growth. They should do this particularly through internalizing environmental costs, investing appropriately in education and training, and removing labor-market distortions wherever possible.

3. Governments should refrain from unnecessary use of trade measures for environmental and labor-market purposes, trade measures not generally being the most effective way of meeting specific environmental and labor-market objectives. Ideally, when trade measures are deemed necessary for environmental purposes, they should be transparent, not protectionist in impact, nondiscriminatory, proportional to benefits, and least trade restrictive.

4. Governments should establish appropriate mechanisms for inter-governmental cooperation in the environmental and labor arenas. Consistent with the principle of subsidiarity, international environmental agreements should be sought in cases of transboundary and global environmental problems where cooperative action is more appropriate or more effective than, or a necessary addition to, policy action at the national level. As with national policies, such international agreements should refrain from unnecessary use of trade measures but if trade measures are necessary as sticks or carrots, they should pass the tests listed in number 3.

5. Governments should work together toward mutual recognition of environmental and labor goals, of standards, and/or of standard setting criteria, bearing in mind that while minimum standards and upward harmonization may be desirable and likely to accompany economic growth and trade liberalization, the scope for harmonization is constrained by current economic circumstances, ecological diversity, and developmental differences between countries.

Source: adapted from Anderson and Drake-Brockman 1995.

---

social issues into trade policy. The sobering history of abuse of GATT's other safeguards clauses (see chapter 11), however, leaves little room for enthusiasm for this proposal.

Perhaps the most productive step that can be taken at this stage is for developing countries to consider with higher-standard countries the principles that ought to govern the design of trade policies and trade-related environmental and labor policies. A summary of those already mentioned is provided in box 15.1 as a check list.

Finally, it is instructive to examine the progress of social policy in the regional arena of the European Union. In Europe there have always been optimists who believe economic integration breeds economic growth and equitable social policy (International Labor Office 1956), and pessimists who believe upward harmonization needs to be imposed on lower-standard countries to improve their social conditions and avoid "social dumping" through trade (Sapir 1996). In practice, relatively little has been imposed on the poorer members of the European Union; the most that has been achieved is the adoption of some minimum standards and mutual recognition. Yet standards have risen rapidly with the acceleration of income growth in poorer EU countries. If this message can get through to those in high-standard countries who have been advocating that trade policy be linked with environmental and labor standards, perhaps there will be less need for other use of the GATT acronym (the general agreement to talk and talk) to be carried into the WTO.

Notes

Thanks are due to Jane Drake-Brockman, Bernard Hoekman, Will Martin, David Richardson, Dani Rodrik, and other conference participants for helpful comments, and to the World Bank and the Australian Research Council for financial support.
  1. Reductions are reflected in the volume of merchandise trade, which has been growing nearly twice as fast as the volume of merchandise output globally (3.9 compared with 2.1 percent annually during 1980 to 1992). Trade in commercial services has grown even faster, rising from 17 percent of global exports of goods and commercial services to 21 percent during 1980–92 (GATT 1994). DFI, meanwhile, has grown nearly twice as fast as international trade over the past decade or so, following the deregulation of financial markets and the revolution in communications and data transmission.
  2. Transborder pollution issues affecting adjoining countries are not discussed here because they are usually resolved by intergovernmental agreement without trade policy involvement. The free-rider problem is not significant in such situations because they typically involve only a small number of countries.
  3. This does not apply equally to all natural resources and environmental services. The doomsdayers such as Meadows et al. (1972) have been proven wrong in predicting the exhaustion of minerals and energy raw materials, for example, because they have failed to take into account economic feedback mechanisms. Beckerman (1992) notes that the world consumption of many minerals over the past quarter century exceeded known reserves at the beginning of that period, yet today's revised known reserves nevertheless exceed those of twenty-five years ago! The same cannot be said for tropical hardwoods and some fish species. However, in these cases there is still scope to move further away from the current "hunter/gatherer" technology and, as with agriculture, to use land or water more intensively to plant trees or breed fish.

4. This is not unlike the United States using the threat of withdrawal of the MFN trade privileges for Chinese goods unless China improves its human rights situation.

5. Three recent papers reporting evidence in support of the claim that the demand for implementing and enforcing pollution-abatement policy is income-elastic are Grossman and Krueger (1993), Radetzki (1992), and Grossman (1994). See also Deacon and Shapiro (1975) on the correlation between income levels and voter attitudes toward environmental priorities.

6. The term pollution-intensive production processes should be broadly interpreted to include activities such as mining in pristine areas or leisure services that may attract undesired tourism. The presumption is that industries are not affected equally by the progressive raising of environmental standards and charges, for otherwise there would be little change in the pattern of a country's trade.

7. The extent of international relocation of productive activities due to the enforcement of environmental standards should not be exaggerated. Recent studies suggest that the effect of such policies on comparative costs may be minor. See, for example, Leonard (1988), Low (1992), and Jaffe, Peterson, Portney, and Stavins (1995). As well, Tobey (1990) finds little evidence of actual changes in patterns of trade specialization in response to the imposition of environmental regulations since the 1960s. However, as noted by Hoekman and Leidy (1992), the absence of change may be due to the raising of import barriers to offset decline in the competitiveness of affected industries.

8. Similarly, if during their growth economies were institutionally to shorten working hours, raise wages for overtime, or otherwise increase the cost of labor time in attempting to raise standards, that would speed the transformation of their comparative advantages away from labor-intensive activities. If such institutional changes affected mainly unskilled labor, the competitiveness of less-developed economies in unskilled labor-intensive products would grow even faster.

9. For details of the Montreal Protocol see, for example, Benedick (1991) and Enders and Porges (1992). A list of the other major international environmental agreements with trade provisions is provided in GATT (1992, appendix 1) and Esty (1994, appendix D).

10. The ban on ivory trade is another case in point. By lowering the value of elephant products, the ban reduces the incentive for rural Africans to tolerate elephants trampling their crops and so ultimately could result in more rather than less culling of elephants in some areas. In other areas, the ivory trade ban has reduced the value of the animal so much that it is no longer profitable to cull the herd. An unfortunate consequence is that bushland in national parks is being destroyed by the increased number of elephants, which is of course endangering other species (Barbier, Burgess, Swanson, and Pearce 1990).

    Even the *threat* of trade restrictions can be environmentally counter-productive. The talk of European import bans on tropical hardwood logs (together with tariff escalation on timber-product imports) has encouraged

Indonesia to ban log exports. But since felling has been allowed to continue, this policy has lowered the domestic price of logs and thereby greatly assisted Indonesia's furniture and other timber-using industries (GATT 1991). With lower log prices and possibly lower-quality saw-milling techniques, less of each tree is now used. It is possible that almost as many trees are being felled now as before the log-export ban.

11. See the discussion in Hillman and Ursprung (1992) and Hoekman and Leidy (1992), as well as the empirical evidence analyzed by Van Grasstek (1992) of the voting behavior of US senators.

12. For a detailed legal assessment see, for example, Hudec (1996).

13. See, for example, Baumol (1971), Siebert (1974), and Walter (1975, 1976). Such protection from import competition cannot be justified on the grounds of economic efficiency (nor, for that matter, on environmental grounds), because the environmental policy aims to eliminate an unjustifiable (implicit) subsidy arising through undervaluation of environmental resources, rather than to add an unjustifiable tax (Snape, 1992).

14. Prior to the United Nations Conference on the Human Environment held in Stockholm in June 1972, the GATT Secretariat produced a background paper on these issues (GATT 1971), and a Working Group on Environmental Measures and International Trade was established. But no significant changes to the GATT occurred as a result of these concerns being expressed, and it was two decades before the working group met for the first time.

15. Meanwhile, the GATT Secretariat/WTO has become active in contributing to trade/environment discussions in other international forums. For example, following the transformation of UNCED into the Commission on Sustainable Development, the GATT Secretariat began participating in its meetings, providing for the second meeting in May 1994 a detailed assessment of the Uruguay Round outcome. The GATT Secretariat also organized a large conference on trade, environment, and sustainable development, held in Geneva in June 1994, where major nongovernmental organizations presented a wide range of papers for discussion.

16. See the literature review in, for example, Ulph (1994). Liberal traders should acknowledge, however, that in the absence of adequate policing, opening up trade can lead to the depletion of common-property resources (for example, tropical forests, in which case there may be a second-best case for restricting trade until that enforcement is addressed (Chichilnisky 1994).

17. So-called neo-institutionalists argue that higher labor standards would raise worker productivity (see, for example, Hanson 1983), but it is reasonable to assume that firms will have already recognized any such possibilities and incorporated them in their work practices. If not, the best role for government is to subsidize the provision of information about such opportunities.

18. My thanks to David Richardson for offering this suggestion. The best solution to such a problem is likely to involve measures to reduce illegal immigration.

19. This could easily be shown using a Harris–Todaro type of model as modified, for example, by Corden and Findlay (1975). The consequences of raising labor

standards in a multigood, multicountry world can be complex and counterintuitive, depending on the assumptions adopted. See the excellent theoretical analysis of several possibilities by Brown, Deardorff, and Stern (1996).

20. In their recent simulation work, Francois, McDonald, and Nordström (chapter 9) found real wages in all country groups to increase as a result of the Uruguay Round's implementation.

21. The history is patchy but goes back more than a hundred years (Hanson 1983; and Charnovitz 1987). The text of the GATT itself mentions labor only briefly, in Article XX(e), which allows contracting parties to exclude imports of goods produced with prison labor.

22. Article 7 of chapter 2 of the 1948 (Havana) Charter of the International Trade Organization addresses the issue as follows: "The members recognize that unfair labor conditions, particularly in the production for export, create difficulties in international trade, and accordingly, each member shall take whatever action may be appropriate and feasible to eliminate such conditions within its territory." See Charnovitz (1987).

23. It is the opposite case with the environment, concerns for which tend to fluctuate procyclically.

24. It has been suggested, for example, that the WTO become active in monitoring and enforcing agreed minimum social standards. Presumably that would involve the review of environmental and labor standards as part of the GATT/WTO regular trade policy reviews. Given that the GATT Secretariat's review mechanism is already stretched to the limit, such an addition to its workload would require substantially more resources – not to mention the extra burden on those employed in national capitals when reviews are under way. An even greater potential increase in workload would result for the WTO's dispute settlement mechanism.

25. Surveys of the relevant theory can be found in Bhagwati and Srinivasan (1996), Wilson (1996), and Brown, Deardorff, and Stern (1996). For empirical evidence see, for example, Tobey (1990), Low (1992), and Levinson (1996) on environmental standards and Krugman and Lawrence (1993) and Bhagwati (1996) on labor standards.

26. Alternatively, developing countries could transfer the burden back to high-standard countries, insisting that their firms adhere to the same high standards when investing in developing countries.

References

Anderson, K. 1992a. "The Standard Welfare Economics of Policies Affecting Trade and the Environment." In K. Anderson and R. Blackhurst, eds., *The Greening of World Trade Issues*. Ann Arbor: University of Michigan Press, and London: Harvester Wheatsheaf.

1992b. "Effects on the Environment and Welfare of Liberalizing World Trade: The Cases of Coal and Food." In K. Anderson and R. Blackhurst, eds., *The*

Greening of World Trade Issues. Ann Arbor: University of Michigan Press, and London: Harvester Wheatsheaf.

1992c. "Agricultural Trade Liberalization and the Environment: A Global Perspective." *The World Economy* 15(1): 153–71.

Anderson, K., and J. Drake-Brockman 1995. "Trade and Environment Policy Issues: Implications for the Asia-Pacific Region." Canberra: Australian Pacific Economic Cooperation Committee.

Baldwin, R. 1994. "Does Sustainability Require Growth?" In I. Goldin and L. A. Winters, eds., *The Economics of Sustainable Development*. Cambridge: Cambridge University Press.

Barbier, E. B., J. C. Burgess, T. M., Swanson, and D. W. Pearce 1990. *Elephants, Economics and Ivory*. London: Earthscan.

Baumol, W. 1971. *Environmental Protection, International Spillovers and Trade*. Stockholm: Almqvist and Wiksell.

Beckerman, W. 1992. "Economic Growth and the Environment: Whose Growth? Whose Environment?" *World Development* 20(4): 481–96.

Benedick, R. E. 1991. *Ozone Diplomacy*. Cambridge, Mass.: Harvard University Press.

Bhagwati, J. N. 1995. "Trade and Wages: Choosing Among Alternative Explanations." *Federal Reserve Bank of New York Economic Policy Review* January.

1996. "The Demand to Reduce Domestic Diversity among Trading Nations." In J. N. Bhagwati and R. E. Hudec, eds., *Fair Trade and Harmonization: Prerequisites for Free Trade?* Cambridge, Mass.: MIT Press.

Bhagwati, J. N., and V. Dahejia 1994. "Freer Trade and Wages of the Unskilled: Is Marx Striking Again?" In J. N. Bhagwati and M. Kasters, eds., *Trade and Wages: Leveling Wages Down?* Washington, DC: American Enterprise Institute.

Bhagwati, J. N., and T. N. Srinivasan 1996. "Trade and the Environment: Does Environmental Diversity Detract from the Case for Free Trade?" Paper prepared for Ford Foundation-financed project on Fair Trade and Harmonization, July.

Brown, D. K., A. V. Deardorff, and R. M. Stern 1996. "International Labor Standards and Trade: A Theoretical Analysis." In J. N. Bhagwati and R. E. Hudec, eds., *Fair Trade and Harmonization: Prerequisites for Free Trade?* Cambridge, Mass: MIT Press.

Charnovitz, S. 1987. "The Influence of International Labor Standards on the World Trading Regime: A Historical Review." *International Labor Review* 126(5): 565–84.

1991. "Exploring the Environmental Exceptions in GATT Article XX." *Journal of World Trade* 25(5): 37–55.

Chichilnisky, G. 1994. "North–South Trade and the Global Environment." *American Economic Review* 84(4): 851–74.

Corden, W. M., and R. Findlay 1975. "Urban Unemployment, Intersectoral Capital Mobility and Development Policy." *Economica* 42: 59–78.

Deacon, R., and P. Shapiro 1975. "Private Preference for Collective Goods

Revealed through Voting on Referenda." *American Economic Review* 65: 943–55.

Ehrenberg, R. 1994. *Labor Markets and Integrating National Economies.* Washington, DC: Brookings Institution.

Enders, A., and A. Porges 1992. "Successful Conventions and Conventional Success: Saving the Ozone Layer." In K. Anderson and R. Blackhurst, eds., *The Greening of World Trade Issues.* Ann Arbor: University of Michigan Press, and London: Harvester Wheatsheaf.

Esty, D. C. 1994. *Greening the GATT: Trade, Environment, and the Future.* Washington, DC: Institute for International Economics.

Falvey, R. 1995. "Factor Price Convergence." Mimeograph. Australian National University, Canberra, January.

GATT 1971. "Industrial Pollution Control and International Trade." *GATT Studies in International Trade.* Geneva: GATT Secretariat.

1991. *Trade Policy Review: Indonesia.* Geneva: GATT Secretariat.

1992. *International Trade, 1990–91,* vol. I. Geneva: GATT Secretariat.

1994. *International Trade Statistics, 1994.* Geneva: GATT Secretariat.

Grossman, G. M. 1994. "Pollution and Growth: What Do We Know?" In I. Goldin and L. A. Winters, eds., *The Economics of Sustainable Development.* Cambridge: Cambridge University Press.

Grossman, G. M., and A. B. Krueger 1993. "Environmental Impacts of a North American Free Trade Agreement." In P. M. Garber, eds., *The Mexico–U.S. Free Trade Agreement.* Cambridge, Mass: MIT Press.

Hanson, G. 1983. *Social Clauses and International Trade: An Economic Analysis of Labor Standards in Trade Policy.* New York: St. Martin's Press.

Hillman, A. L., and H. N. Ursprung 1992. "The Influence of Environmental Concerns on the Political Determination of Trade Policy." In K. Anderson and R. Blackhurst, eds., *The Greening of World Trade Issues.* Ann Arbor: University of Michigan Press, and London: Harvester Wheatsheaf.

Hoekman, B., and M. Leidy 1992. "Environmental Policy Formation in a Trading Economy: A Public Choice Perspective." In K. Anderson and R. Blackhurst, eds., *The Greening of World Trade Issues.* Ann Arbor: University of Michigan Press, and London: Harvester Wheatsheaf.

Hudec, R. E. 1996. "GATT Legal Restraints on the Use of Trade Measures against Foreign Environmental Practices." In J. N. Bhagwati and R. E. Hudec, eds., *Fair Trade ad Harmonization: Prerequisites for Free Trade?* Cambridge, Mass: MIT Press.

International Labor Office 1956. "Social Aspects of European Economic Cooperation." The Ohlin Report. Geneva: International Labor Office.

Jaffe, A. B., S. R. Peterson, P. R. Portney, and R. N. Stavins 1995. "Environmental Regulation and the Competitiveness of U.S. Manufacturing: What Does the Evidence Tell Us?" *Journal of Economic Literature* 33(1): 132–63.

Kruger, A. 1977. *Growth, Distortions and Patterns of Trade Among Many Countries.* Princeton, N.J.: International Finance Section.

Krugman, P., and R. Z. Lawrence 1993. "Trade, Jobs, and Wages." National Bureau of Economic Research Working Paper 4478. Cambridge, Mass.: National Bureau of Economic Research.

Lawrence, R. Z. 1994. "Trade, Multinationals, and Labor." In P. Low and J. Dwyer, eds., *International Integration of the Australian Economy*. Sydney: Reserve Bank of Australia.

Leamer, E. E. 1987. "Paths of Development in the Three Factor, n-Good General Equilibrium Model." *Journal of Political Economy* 95(5): 961–99.

Leonard, N. J. 1988. *Pollution and the Struggle for World Product: Multinational Corporations, Environment and International Comparative Advantage*. Cambridge: Cambridge University Press.

Levinson, A. 1996. "Environmental Regulation and Industry Location: International and Domestic Evidence." In J. N. Bhagwati and R. E. Hudec, eds., *Fair Trade and Harmonization: Prerequisites for Free Trade?* Cambridge, Mass.: MIT Press.

Low, P. 1992. "Trade Measures and Environmental Quality: The Implications for Mexico's Exports." In P. Low, ed., *International Trade and the Environment*. World Bank Discussion Paper 159. Washington, DC: World Bank.

McDougall, R., and R. Tyers 1995. "Developed Country Factor Market Effects of Asian Trade and Growth: Preliminary GTAP Results." CIES Seminar Paper 95–08. University of Adelaide, May.

Meadows, D. H., *et al.* 1972. *The Limits to Growth*. New York: Universe Books.

Radetzki, M. 1992. "Economic Growth and Environment. In P. Low, ed., *International Trade and the Environment*. World Bank Discussion Papr 159. Washington, DC: World Bank.

Rodrik, D. 1994. "Developing Countries after the Uruguay Round." CEPR Discussion Paper 1084. London: Centre for Economic Policy Research.

Rybczynski, T. M. 1959. "Factor Endowment and Relative Commodity Prices. *Economica* 22(84): 336–41.

Sapir, A. 1996. "Trade Liberalization and the Harmonization of Social Policies: Lessons from European Integration." In J. N. Bhagwati and R. E. Hudec, eds., *Fair Trade and Harmonization: Prerequisites for Free Trade?* Cambridge, Mass.: MIT Press.

Siebert, H. 1974. "Environmental Protection and International Specialization." *Welwirtschaftliches Archiv* 110: 494–508.

Siebert, H., J. Eichberger, R. Gronych, and R. Pethig 1980. *Trade and Environment: A Theoretical Enquiry*. Amsterdam: Elsevier.

Snape, R. H. 1992. "The Environment, International Trade and Competitiveness." In K. Anderson and R. Blackhurst, eds., *The Greening of World Trade Issues*. Ann Arbor: University of Michigan Press, and London: Harvester Wheatsheaf.

Steenblik, R. P., and P. Coroyannakis 1995. "Reform of Coal Policies in Western and Central Europe: Implications for the Environment." *Energy Policy* 23(6): 537–54.

Steil, B. 1994. "Social Correctness is the New Protectionism." *Foreign Affairs* 73(1): 14–20.

Tobey, J. A. 1990. "The Effects of Domestic Environmental Policies on Patterns of World Trade: An Empirical Test." *Kyklos* 43(2): 191–209.

Ulph, A. 1994. "Environmental Policy and International Trade: A Survey of Recent Economic Analysis." Paper presented to the Workshop on Designing Economic Policy for the Management of Natural Resources and the Environment, Crete, September 7–9.

Van Grasstek, C. 1992. "The Political Economy of Trade and the Environment in the United States." In P. Low, ed., *International Trade and the Environment.* World Bank Discussion Paper 159, Washington, DC: World Bank.

Walter, I. 1975. *The International Economics of Pollution.* London: Macmillan.

Walter, I., ed. 1976. *Studies in International Environmental Economics.* New York: Wiley.

Wilson, J. D. 1996. "Capital Mobility and Environmental Standards: Is There a Theoretical Basis for a Race to the Bottom?" In J. N. Bhagwati and R. E. Hudec, eds., *Fair Trade and Harmonization: Prerequisites for Free Trade?* Cambridge, Mass.: MIT Press.

Wood, A. 1994. *North–South Trade, Employment and Inequality: Changing Fortunes in a Skill-Driven World.* Oxford: Clarendon Press.

Index